Sport and Exercise Psychology

Although sport is played with the body, it is won in the mind. Inspired by this idea, the second edition of this successful textbook provides a comprehensive critical introduction to sport and exercise psychology – a discipline that is concerned with the theory and practice of helping athletes to do their best when it matters the most.

The book is organized into four parts: Part one investigates the nature, foundations and current status of the discipline. Part two reviews the latest research findings on motivation, anxiety, concentration, mental imagery and expertise in athletes. Part three examines group processes and team dynamics. Part four explores exercise behaviour and the psychology of injury rehabilitation. Each chapter contains specially designed critical thinking exercises to encourage students to explore the deeper issues, and also features an invaluable list of suggestions for independent research projects by students. The text has been extensively rewritten and updated with new material to take account of hot topics such as neuroscience and motor imagery, as well as issues such as "grunting" in tennis, the psychology of penalty shootouts, mindfulness training as a concentration technique, the effects of music on physical activity, and "exergaming" – the use of computer games to increase physical activity/exercise.

Written in a lively, accessible style, the book is brimful of vivid contemporary examples and insights from the world's leading athletes, to provide a compelling bridge between theory and practice for undergraduate and postgraduate students of sport psychology, health psychology, sport science, physical education, kinesiology and leisure management.

Aidan P. Moran is a Professor of Cognitive Psychology and Director of the Psychology Research Laboratory in University College Dublin. A Fulbright Scholar, he has written fifteen books and many scientific articles on cognitive processes such as mental imagery and attention (including eye-tracking) in athletes. He is the inaugural editor-in-chief of the *International Review of Sport and Exercise Psychology* (IRSEP: Taylor & Francis, Abingdon).

Sport and Exercise Psychology

A Critical Introduction

Second Edition

Aidan P. Moran

Routledge
Taylor & Francis Group

LONDON AND NEW YORK

First edition published 2004
This edition published 2012
by Routledge
27 Church Road, Hove, East Sussex BN3 2FA

Simultaneously published in the USA and Canada
by Routledge
711 Third Avenue, New York, NY 10017

www.psypress.com

Routledge is an imprint of the Taylor & Francis Group, an Informa business

British Library Cataloguing in Publication Data
A catalogue record for this book is available from the British Library

Library of Congress Cataloging in Publication Data
Moran, Aidan P.
    Sport and exercise psychology : a critical introduction / Aidan P. Moran.
       p. cm.
    Includes bibliographical references and index.
    ISBN 978-0-415-43430-0 (hb : alk. paper) - - ISBN 978-0-415-43431-7 (soft cover : alk. paper)
    1. Sports- -Psychological aspects. 2. Exercise- -Psychological aspects. I. Title.
    GV706.4.M67 2012
    796.01- -dc23
                                                              2011034081

ISBN: 978-0-415-43430-0 (hbk)
ISBN: 978-0-415-43431-7 (pbk)
ISBN: 978-0-203-12765-0 (ebk)

Typeset in Century
by Integra Software Services Pvt. Ltd, Pondicherry, India

Cover design by Anú Design

MIX
Paper from
responsible sources
FSC www.fsc.org FSC® C004839

Printed and bound in Great Britain by
TJ International Ltd, Padstow, Cornwall

To my wife, Angela, and my son, Kevin, with all my love

Contents

CONTENTS

Foreword

I have had a lifelong love affair with books and it is always a special thrill to open the pages of a new one. The pleasure is all the greater when the book is one I have been eagerly awaiting, the second edition of Aidan Moran's excellent textbook, *Sport and Exercise Psychology: A Critical Introduction*. And the delight is beyond compare when I know that I am one of the very first to read the words within. It has been a special thrill to preview this book and write this Foreword.

I teach sport psychology at Western Connecticut State University and it is a popular class, filling up weeks in advance. I like to think that the students are keen to receive my words of wisdom every year but I know that a lot of the credit for the good reputation of the course goes to Aidan Moran. I have been using this book as my course textbook since the first edition appeared and it is well liked by all the students, many of whom are competitive athletes at the college or local level. The book appeals to students because it is a pleasure to read – written in clear, straightforward language and organized with the needs of student learners in mind. Perhaps because his own special area of expertise is attention, Aidan Moran captures your attention immediately in each chapter with the fascinating quotes he finds from the world of sports. Hearing about psychological issues from the star athletes and coaches themselves gets students engaged in sport psychology from the get-go, and that attention is sustained with numerous interesting real-life examples throughout each chapter. What could be more relevant to student readers than watching the heart-stopping penalty shootouts in the 2011 Women's World Cup games between the United States and Brazil and Japan and then reading the compelling analysis *Why do top players miss penalty kicks?* in Box 3.5? Or, after watching a grunt-filled grand slam final between Maria Sharapova and Petra Kvitova, reading and discussing Box 3.3 on *Thinking critically about … grunting in tennis: what a racket!* I love using these creative examples as the basis for informed debates in our classes, and the students learn much more when they can relate to examples they have seen and experienced.

Student learning is front and centre in the organization and presentation of each chapter. Even the subheadings within chapters get students thinking, asking

"What is?", "How do?", and "Why?" questions throughout. Each chapter contains *Thinking critically about* exercises that provide descriptions of relevant research and theory for the learner and then ask a series of questions that compel thoughtful analysis – perfect for in-class discussions or take-home writing assignments! My personal favourites are the ideas for research projects at the end of every chapter. They are detailed yet explained very simply and in my experience students can use them for their own research projects, helping them learn the basics of the scientific approach to sport psychology, including hypothesis generation, experimental design and analysis. All these features combine to create a peerless learning experience and they make this textbook perfect for undergraduate courses in sport and exercise psychology.

The content of the textbook is thoughtfully chosen, with nine chapters comprising a comprehensive overview of our fascinating field. I am glad that the chapter topics have remained constant, as the topic coverage of this text is a major strength. Professor Moran covers all the main areas of sport and performance psychology, from motivation and concentration, to teamwork, health, exercise and injury. I find that the chapter topics fit comfortably into a one semester format and still allow me to add one or two topics of my own choosing to my course. Because he is a true expert in sport psychology himself, he is not content to merely rehash the ideas of others, but he critically presents and assesses the theories and research he discusses. This sets the tone for the reader and encourages us to critically analyse the research. I have never read more thoughtful presentations of the complicated neuroscientific research on concentration and imagery that can be found in Chapters 4 and 5. Student learners are lucky to have such a competent and engaging guide to the mysteries of the interactions between brain and body that lie at the heart of sport psychology.

There is so much that is new in this second edition, I will leave it to you to discover its many delights for yourself. But I must mention the inclusion of a couple of updated sections that especially enchanted me. My daily exercise routine contains an aerobic walk while listening to my trusty iPod (a beloved gift from my children on my fiftieth birthday), so I was delighted to read Box 8.4 on *The effects of music on physical activity: exercise for the iPod generation* and I am sure students will enjoy it, too. In the same chapter is the provocative Box 8.7 on *Thinking critically about … exergaming: is it even better than the real thing?*, which as a sport psychology researcher who happens to study video games and their effects I found especially interesting. Just two examples, of many, that indicate how contemporary and in tune with today's students this textbook is.

I anticipated a special treat when I received the advance copy of this second edition and I was not disappointed. This book is hands-on, down-to-earth, contemporary, engaging, provocative, thoughtful, informative and accessible. I suspect that you are as eager as I was to open its pages and commence the journey of discovery. Let me facilitate the start of that adventure by ending the Foreword and handing you over to Aidan Moran. Enjoy – I know you will.

Shane Murphy, PhD
Department of Psychology
Western Connecticut State University
Danbury, Connecticut, USA

Preface to the second edition: what's new?

Sport and exercise psychology is flourishing both as an academic discipline and as a profession. For example, since 2007, at least five new scholarly journals have been published, and many new graduate training courses developed, in this field. To keep you abreast of such exciting developments, I have made a lot of changes to the second edition of *Sport and Exercise Psychology: A Critical Introduction*. These changes can be summarized as follows. First, and perhaps most obviously, I have included over 500 new references, thereby updating greatly the topical coverage (especially in the neuroscientific foundations of athletic performance) provided by the book. Second, as a consequence of the inclusion of this new material, I have extensively rewritten the text and lengthened it from about 120,000 words to about 157,000 words. Among the new topics that I have focused on are what sport psychologists do at the Olympic Games (Chapter 1), goal-setting in a team environment (Chapter 2), why players "grunt" in tennis (Chapter 3), attentional control theory (Chapter 3), the psychology of penalty shootouts (Chapter 3), mindfulness training as a concentration technique (Chapter 4), motor imagery (Chapter 5), the neuroscience of expertise (Chapter 6), the question of whether or not team cohesion can ever be harmful (Chapter 7), the effects of music on physical activity (Chapter 8), self-determination theory (Chapter 8), the increasingly popular activity of exergaming (or the use of computer games like Wii Fit to increase physical activity/exercise: see Chapter 8), and some rather unusual causes of sports injuries (Chapter 9). Third, building on some of the unique features of the first edition, I have devised additional critical thinking exercises (increased from 25 to 30) and have also revised, updated and increased (from 41 to 44) my suggestions for independent research projects throughout the book. Fourth, I have tried to enrich the text and bridge the gap between theory and practice by including a wealth of vivid contemporary examples and compelling insights from the world's leading athletes (e.g., Roger Federer,

Michael Phelps) and coaches (e.g., Sir Alex Ferguson, José Mourinho) as well as some new photographs to accompany the text.

As before, the book is divided into four parts. In Part one, I introduce the field of sport and exercise psychology as both an academic discipline and as a profession. In Chapter 1, I've added a new section on confidence, new material on sport psychology at the Olympic Games and revised and updated the coverage of mental toughness, sport psychology as an academic discipline, research methods in sport and exercise psychology, and new journals in the field. In Part two, I investigate the various psychological processes that affect individual athletes in their pursuit of excellence. Included here are chapters on motivation, anxiety, concentration, mental imagery and expertise. In Chapter 2, I've updated the coverage of achievement goal theory, attribution theory and goal-setting (and have developed a new critical thinking box on this topic) and I've also included some new suggestions for research projects on motivation in athletes. In Chapter 3, I've updated my coverage of the topics of anxiety in athletes and the conscious processing hypothesis. I've also devised a new critical thinking box on "grunting" in tennis as well as a new section on attentional control theory. I've added new material on the issue of why top footballers often miss penalty kicks as well as a new critical thinking box on simulation training. I've also developed some new suggestions for research projects on anxiety in athletes. In Chapter 4, I've updated the material on the nature and importance of concentration, on why athletes appear to "lose" their concentration so easily, and also on concentration training exercises and techniques. I've developed a new critical thinking box on mindfulness training as a concentration technique and offered some new suggestions for research on concentration processes in athletes. In Chapter 5, I've updated material on the nature, types and dimensions of mental imagery and also updated the section on mental chronometry in action. I've added new boxes on the PETTLEP model of motor imagery, the Vividness of Movement Imagery Questionnaire (Revised) and on motor imagery. I've also included new suggestions for research on mental imagery in athletes. In Chapter 6, I've updated material on the nature and determinants of expertise in sport and on the research methods used in the study of expertise. I've updated material on research findings on expert–novice differences in athletes as well as on Ericsson's theory of deliberate practice. I've also included new boxes on the neuroscience of fast-ball sports and on what experts tell us about the factors that determined their success and also some new suggestions for research on expertise in athletes. In Part three, I address the role of team cohesion in athletic performance. In Chapter 7, I've updated material on team dynamics, team cohesion and team-building in sport. I've added new boxes on whether or not team cohesion can ever be harmful, on building a successful team, and on team-building exercises in rugby. I've also included some new suggestions for research on team cohesion in athletes. In Part four, I explore exercise psychology and the psychology of physical injury. In Chapter 8, I've updated material on the nature of exercise psychology, the benefits of physical activity and on some possible adverse effects of exercise on health. I've added new boxes on the assessment of physical activity, the effects of music on physical activity, and the emerging phenomenon of "exergaming". I've also included new material on self-determination theory as well as some new suggestions for research on exercise psychology. In Chapter 9, I've updated material on the nature of injuries in sport, the causes of injury among athletes, how athletes react psychologically to injury, and on the rehabilitation of injured athletes. I've added a new box on injury rehabilitation in rugby and included some new suggestions for research on injuries in sport. In conclusion, I hope that this book manages to convey the scope and excitement of contemporary sport and exercise psychology in an accurate and accessible manner.

Acknowledgements

This book would not have been possible without the help that I received from a large number of friends and colleagues. To begin with, I would like to acknowledge the wonderful editorial support and encouragement that I received from Lucy Kennedy, Sharla Plant, Erasmis Kidd, Tara Stebnicky and Rebekah Waldron of Routledge and Psychology Press. Next, I wish to thank my friend and colleague Shane Murphy (Western Connecticut State University) for agreeing to write the Foreword to the second edition of this book and also for sharing with me his many novel insights into mental imagery processes in athletes. I'm extremely grateful to Aymeric Guillot (Université Claude Bernard Lyon 1, France) and Rich Masters (University of Hong Kong) for their generous endorsements of this book. I also wish to thank three former PhD students and now research collaborators – James Matthews, Peter Slattery and John Toner – for their enthusiasm, meticulous research assistance and reference suggestions. In addition, I'm very grateful to James Matthews and Tadhg MacIntyre for their contributions to Chapter 8. Next, I wish to acknowledge the help that I received from Suzanne Bailey and Georgina Dwyer (University College Dublin, Sport), Norman McCloskey (Inpho Photography), Seán O'Dómhnaill (University College Dublin, Media Services), Mark McDermott (Irish Rugby Football Union) and Colin Burke and Andrew Flood (both of University College Dublin, School of Psychology) with regard to the photographs and other illustrations used in the book. I would like to acknowledge the generous assistance of Martha Gullo (Human Kinetics, Inc., USA) in relation to copyright clearance for certain figures in the book. Furthermore, I wish to express my gratitude to a number of academic colleagues who influenced the content and structure of this book. In particular, I am extremely grateful to John Kremer (Queen's University of Belfast) for his friendship, encouragement and insights over the many fruitful years of our colla-boration. Similarly, the advice and support of David Lavallee (University of Stirling) and Mark Williams (Liverpool John Moores University and University of Sydney) are deeply appreciated. Two key reviewers whose constructive comments and suggestions contributed greatly to the book are Simon Hartley (Be World Class) and Arnold LeUnes (Texas A&M University). Other research colleagues in psychology whose ideas encouraged me at various stages in writing this book are Raj Aggarwal (Imperial College, London), Sonal Arora (Imperial College, London), Jamie Barker (Staffordshire University), Mark Campbell (University of Limerick), Christian Collet (Université Claude Bernard Lyon 1, France), Derek Dorris (University College Cork), Anders Ericsson (Florida State University), Mary Flaherty (Edith Cowan University, Perth), Iain Greenlees (University of Chichester), Olivia Hurley (Institute of Art, Design and Technology, Dublin), Chris Janelle (University of Florida), Marc Jones (Staffordshire University), Kate Kirby (University College Dublin), Chris Lonsdale (University of Western Sydney), Tadhg MacIntyre (University of Ulster) and Paul McCarthy (Glasgow Caledonian University). Within University College Dublin, special gratitude is extended to my colleagues and friends in the School of Psychology – Mary Boyle, Nuala Brady, Jessica Bramham, Adrian Brock, Teresa Burke, Alan Carr, Betty Cody, Margaret Daly, Barbara Dooley, Suzanne Guerin, Eilis Hennessy, Tina Hickey, Mary Ivers, Helena McCann, Geraldine Moane, Mick O'Connell and Joan Tiernan. Also, I would like to thank Lorna Dodd and Ursula Byrne (Library), Philip Harvey (Campus Bookshop) and Brian Mullins and his staff (UCD Sports Centre) for their help and also Bridget Laffan, the outgoing Principal of the College of Human Sciences, for her constant encouragement for my research. I'm also deeply indebted to Julitta Clancy for her painstaking work in compiling the indexes for this book. In addition, I would like to acknowledge that my research for this book was facilitated greatly by a research grant from the Irish Research Council for the Humanities and Social Sciences (IRCHSS) and by a President's Research Fellowship from University College Dublin. Finally, I wish to acknowledge the love, support and understanding that I have received from my wife, Angela, my son, Kevin, my brothers, Ciaran and Dermot (and Dermot's family), my sister, Patricia, and her husband, Tom, and my friends, especially, Brendan Burgess, Michael Griffin, Neil Hogan, Dermot O'Halloran, Brendan O'Neill, and all my tennis partners in Lansdowne Lawn Tennis Club.

Figures

FIGURES

INTRODUCING SPORT AND EXERCISE PSYCHOLOGY

Overview

Many prominent athletes and coaches believe that although sport is played with the body, it is won in the mind. If so, sport offers psychologists an exciting opportunity to develop academic theories (e.g., about how expert athletes differ from novices in a variety of mental skills) and practical strategies (e.g., teaching athletes how to cope with pressure situations) about mental aspects of skilled performance. Part one of this book introduces **sport and exercise psychology** as both an academic discipline and as a profession.

Introducing sport and exercise psychology: discipline and profession

The bottom line is that this is a very mental game. Everybody is strong, everybody is pushing hard. But the difference between the top players is the mental ability to cope with the pressure and hit the right shots at the right time and stay calm in the moments when you need to stay calm.

(Novak Djokovic, current world number 1 tennis player; cited in Harman, 2009, p. 5)

chapter 1

Introduction

Many prominent athletes and coaches believe that although sport is played with the body, it is won in the mind (see Figure 1.1). This idea applies both to individual and to **team** sports. To illustrate, consider what Tiger Woods, one of the greatest golfers in the history of the game, said about the importance of the mental side of the game:

> You have to keep pushing yourself from within. It's not about what other people think and what other people say. It's about what you want to accomplish and do you want to go out there and be prepared to beat everyone you play or face?
>
> (cited in Gola, 2008, p. 5)

Similarly, the celebrated footballer Xavi Hernández (a World Cup winner with Spain in 2010) revealed that when he joined Barcelona, "the first thing they teach is: Think, think, think" (cited in Lowe, 2011, pp. 6–7). If mental processes are crucial for athletic success, psychologists should be able to help sports competitors to enhance their athletic performance by providing them with practical advice on how to do their best when it matters most. Influenced by this possibility, increasing numbers of athletes,

Figure 1.1 Sport is played with the body but won in the mind
Source: Courtesy of University College Dublin, Sport

coaches and teams have turned to sport psychologists in an effort to gain a winning edge over their rivals. For example, when Tiger Woods was only 6 years old, his late father, Earl Woods, gave him an audiocassette containing inspirational affirmation phrases (e.g., "I focus and give it my all") which he would dutifully write out and pin to his bedroom wall (Shannon, 2008). Although such an early exposure to mental aspects of sport is unusual, the quest to increase psychological strength is apparent in virtually all competitive games, it is especially evident in mentally demanding individual sports such as golf. Not surprisingly, therefore, major championship winning golfers such as Ernie Els (Aitken, 2008) and Pádraig Harrington (P. Dixon, 2008) have acknowledged the contribution of sport psychologists to their success in recent years. Interestingly, Phil Mickelson, one of the best players in the world, has a degree in psychology. Also, according to D. Davies (2003), Davis Love III, whose twenty wins on the PGA tour have earned him a lifetime exemption from pre-qualification, has consulted up to *three* sport psychologists on a regular basis! It would be wrong, however, to assume that athlete–psychologist consultations are always about performance enhancement. Thus Keefe (2003, p. 73) suggested that one reason why so many professional golfers hire psychologists is simply that they "need to tell their story to someone" who has little direct involvement in their lives. Until recently, this idea that athletes have a story to tell in order to make sense of their existence has attracted little research attention. However, with the emergence of a new field of research called **narrative inquiry** in sport psychology (see review by B. Smith and Sparkes, 2009), a set of conceptual and methodological tools is now available to explore the "stories" of athletes' lives.

Regardless of whether its origins are pragmatic or therapeutic, athletes' interest in consulting psychologists is particularly noticeable at the elite grade of sport performance where minimal differences exist between competitors in technical ability and/or **physical fitness** (G. Jones et al., 2002). This observation is endorsed by the former English tennis player Tim Henman, who proposed that "the mental side is the difference between the top guys and the rest" (cited in Pitt, 1998a). Perhaps more importantly, mental resilience can be developed through appropriate practice and training. Thus Pádraig Harrington, a three times major championship winner, said: "I know I can't swing it well every day but there's no reason why I can't think well every day" (cited in K. Morris, 2006, p. 24). Although anecdotal, these insights into the importance of psychological factors in sport are supported by scientific evidence. For example, research on the "peak performance" experiences of athletes (S. Jackson et al., 2008; see also Chapter 4) as well as in-depth interviews with Olympic champions (Gould et al., 2002b) indicate that **mental toughness** (to be considered later in the chapter) and the ability to concentrate effectively are among the factors which distinguish top athletes from less successful counterparts. But apart from having some vague awareness of its importance to athletic success, what do we really know about the "mental side" of sport? More generally, how did the discipline of sport and exercise psychology originate? What type of work do sport psychologists engage in with their clients and do their interventions actually work? How can one qualify as a professional in this field? The purpose of this chapter is to provide some answers to these and other relevant questions, thereby introducing you to sport and exercise psychology both as a scientific discipline and as a profession. Please note, however, that the emphasis in this book is primarily on the *sport* rather than the **exercise** components of this field (although the latter is considered in Chapters 8 and 9).

This chapter is organized as follows. First, in this section, I introduce the field of sport and exercise psychology. In the second section, I explore the mental side of sport – paying special attention to two related terms that are widely associated with athletic success: **confidence** and mental toughness. Interestingly, some researchers (e.g., Vealey, 2009) believe that the key to mental toughness is a level of self-belief "that is robust and resilient in the face of obstacles and setbacks" (p. 43). In this section, I also discuss the factors that influence the mental demands of a given sport. In the third section, I briefly review the nature and history of, and research methods used in, the academic discipline of sport and exercise psychology. The fourth section of the chapter focuses on professional aspects of this field. Included here will be a discussion of four key questions: What type of work do sport psychologists actually do? What is the best way to deliver sport psychology services to athletes and coaches? How can I qualify professionally as a sport psychologist? Where can I learn more about sport and exercise psychology? In the fifth section, I provide a brief evaluation of the current status of sport and exercise psychology. This section considers not only the scientific standing of this discipline but also people's views of it. Finally, I suggest an idea for a possible research project on the mental side of sport.

At the outset, however, some words of caution are necessary. From the initial paragraphs, you may have assumed that sport and exercise psychology has a single objective (namely, performance enhancement), a coherent identity (i.e., as an accepted subdiscipline of psychology), clearly agreed academic pathways to profes-sional qualifications, and an established role within the sporting community. Unfortunately, each of these four assumptions is questionable. First, as we indicated earlier, performance enhancement is not the only goal of sport and exercise psychol-ogy. Since the late 1990s, this discipline has been concerned increasingly with the promotion of health and exercise among people of all ages – whether they are athletic or not (see Chapter 8). Also, sport psychologists have begun to apply their theories and techniques to business (Ievleva and Terry, 2008) and to everyday work settings (Gordon, 2008) as part of the burgeoning field of coaching psychology. Second, the assumption that sport and exercise psychology is an applied field within the discipline of psychology is only partly true – simply because not all *sport* psychologists are professional psychologists. To explain, consider the case of sport psychologists in the United States and United Kingdom. Although some of them belong to Division 47 (Exercise and Sport Psychology – note the prominence of "exercise" in the title; see also Chapter 8) of the American Psychological Association (APA) and/or to the Division of Sport and Exercise Psychology (DSEP) of the British Psychological Society (BPS), others have an academic background in sport science and are members of interdisciplinary organizations such as the North American Society for Psychology of Sport and Physical Activity (NASPSPA) and/or the British Association of Sport and Exercise Sciences (BASES) (these organizations are listed later in the chapter in Box 1.3). Third, in view of this "twin-track" identity of sport psychologists, there are several ways of qualifying professionally in this field (see details of professional training routes in Eubank et al. 2009). For students of psychology, there are four steps to becoming a chartered sport and exercise psychologist. First, one has to obtain a BPS-accredited undergraduate qualification in psychology (i.e., by having a recognized undergraduate degree or a recognized graduate conversion course in this subject). Second, one has to obtain a BPS-accredited master's degree in sport and exercise Psychology (or pass the BPS's Stage 1 qualification. Third, one must obtain either the BPS's own Stage 2 Qualification in Sport and Exercise Psychology or a BPS-accredited Stage 2 Qualification in Sport and Exercise Psychology. Fourth, one can apply for registration as a chartered sport and exercise psychologist. Finally, and perhaps most controversially, it is important to point out that sport psychology has not always been welcomed or appreciated by athletes. In this regard, a number of examples spring to mind from a variety of team and individual sports. For instance, Pelé, arguably the greatest footballer of all time, was almost excluded from the Brazilian soccer team that won the 1958 World Cup on the advice of the team psychologist, Dr Joao Carvalho. Apparently, Carvalho considered Pelé to be "infantile" and lacking in the fighting spirit that was required for the team's success. Fortunately, Vicente Feola, the manager of the team, ignored this advice and stated that "If Pelé's knee is ready, he plays" (Pelé, 2006, p. 8). More recently, Magnus Hedman, the former Celtic goalkeeper, related a story about his first encounter with a sport psychologist during his playing career:

> The first thing he asked me was what I would do if I found an intruder trying to break into my apartment – I told him that I would attack the guy and kick him down the stairs. So he says to me "I want you to I imagine the penalty area is your apartment and you have to kick out like that to protect your goal". I knew then that he had never thought about referees and me getting sent off in every game I played for violent conduct. So, I decided to handle my own problems after that.
>
> (cited in Hannigan, 2003)

Also consider what Gary Player the golfer had to say about sport psychology:

> When you need to out a two iron on the back of the green to win the Open, how is a psychologist going to help you? If he hasn't got the experience, what can he tell you? I'm not totally against psychologists but you have to do a certain amount yourself.
>
> (cited in Buckley, 2005, p. 12)

Similar views were expressed by Butch Harmon, the golf coach who worked with Tiger Woods for over a decade, who remarked of sport psychologists:

> They may not be doing any harm but I fail to see what good they are doing. When a player is facing a crucial shot and the red dot (camera) is trained on him, alone, … where is the mental coach then?
>
> (cited in Browne, 2008, p. 182)

Another pot-shot at sport psychology was taken by Andy Murray, one of the world's best tennis players, who said that a sport psychologist had approached him during Wimbledon in 2006 and offered to help him with a book that the psychologist had written on the mental side of tennis. His response was somewhat jaundiced: "I had the last laugh – I chucked it in the bin!" (cited in Harman, 2006, p. 67). Similarly, consider the lukewarm views about sport psychology offered by Ronnie "The Rocket" O'Sullivan, a three-time world champion in **snooker**, and arguably the most gifted ball-potter in the game (e.g., he holds the record for the fastest maximum score in snooker – 147 – achieved in five minutes and twenty seconds). Specifically, he said "I tried a sports [*sic*] psychologist once and I never really got much out of it … if you're on, you're on; if you're off, you're off and there's not a lot you can do about it" (cited in White, 2002c, p. 10). Unfortunately, this fatalistic view of his sporting performance appears to reflect a deeper struggle that O'Sullivan has experienced throughout his remarkable career – a volatility spawned by recurrent bouts of depression (Everton, 2011). Thus he has revealed paradoxically that "I love the game but I don't really care whether I play or not" (cited in Everton, 2009, p. 12). I hope that this book will convince you that O'Sullivan is wrong to believe that there is nothing one can do to increase one's chance of success in sport. Nevertheless, the preceding quotations suggest that some athletes are indifferent to, if not openly sceptical of, sport psychology. But how typical are these attitudes? One way of answering this question is to examine what sport performers think of this field. In this regard, Lavallee et al. (2005) investigated the attitudes of a large sample of elite Irish athletes (n=240) to seeking a consultation with a sport psychologist. Using the Sport Psychology Attitudes – Revised (SPA-R) questionnaire (S. Martin et al., 2002), these authors discovered a generally positive attitude to sport psychology among the athletes in the sample. In addition, contrary to previous studies (e.g., Leffingwell et al., 2001) indicating that some US athletes perceived a stigma associated with consulting a sport psychologist, Irish athletes showed an openness to this form of help. Interestingly, some years ago, Hoberman (1992) compared the discipline of sport psychology to the "human potential" movement of the 1960s because it appeared to propagate "romantic theories of untapped energy and mind-body unity [that] recall the naïve **psychophysiology** of the *fin de siècle* and its speculations about human limits". Overall, his critique led him to conclude that sport psychology was not an established discipline but merely "an eclectic group of theories and therapies in search of scientific respectability" (Hoberman, 1992, pp. 187–188). Although this latter criticism is now outdated because sport psychology *is* now regarded as an established field of psychology (see Box 1.3 later in the chapter), Hoberman's criticism challenges us to adopt an evidence-based approach in evaluating any claims made about this discipline. For this reason, Hoberman's (1992) critique should be welcomed not dismissed. I shall return to this issue of scepticism towards sport psychology in the fourth section of this chapter. To summarize, having examined four mistaken assumptions about sport and exercise psychology, let us return from our preamble to explore the first topic in the chapter – namely, an analysis of the mental side of sport.

The mental side of sport

Sport scientists typically distinguish between four hypothetical aspects of athletic performance: physical, technical, tactical and psychological (see Figure 1.2). First, within this quadrant, physical aspects of sport performance refer to phenomena such as fitness, strength and stamina which can be measured objectively. Second, technical aspects of performance refer mainly to the proficiency with which athletes can execute fundamental skills required by their specialist sport. For example, a competitive swimmer in freestyle events must be able to perform a turn. This skill involves approaching the wall, dropping one's leading arm, lowering one's chin to one's chest, tucking in one's knees and then flipping over one's feet when they hit the wall. Third, the tactical part of the quadrant in Figure 1.2 concerns strategic aspects of athletic performance. Included here are such skills as planning and decision making. For example, a shrewd tactical performer can devise and adhere to a specific game plan in competitive situations. Fourth, we come to the familiar yet mysterious domain called the psychological (or mental) side of performance in sport. At this stage, you should note the paradox of psychology in sport. How can something be familiar yet mysterious? To explain, this domain is *familiar* because, almost every week, we hear about or see athletes who make uncharacteristic mistakes (e.g., missing a penalty kick in football or a short putt in golf) due to the temporary influence of psychological factors like **anxiety** (see also Chapter 3). In a sense, therefore, lapses in performance allow us to catch a glimpse of the psychological side of athletes' minds. Unfortunately, despite their ubiquity, mental influences on athletic performance are not well understood in mainstream psychology. This regrettable situation owes its origins to an historical reluctance by psychologists to regard sport as a suitable domain in which to explore how the mind works (Moran, 1996). Given such reluctance to investigate the sporting mind, how do we go about exploring the mental side of athletes' competitive experiences?

Perhaps the most obvious way to investigate the mental side of sport is to ask athletes what they have learned from their personal experience about the mental factors that seem to affect their performance. Using this strategy, we can gain useful insights into the psychological challenges of team and individual sports. For example, Nick Faldo, who has won six major tournaments, highlighted the importance of maintaining momentum and **concentration** when he observed that "golf is

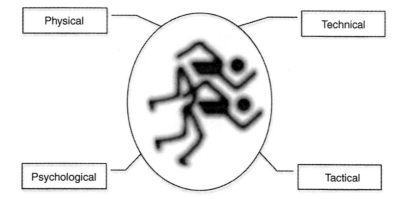

Figure 1.2 Four aspects of athletic performance
Source: Courtesy of Colin Burke, University College Dublin, School of Psychology

unusual in that you have to pick up where you left off the day before. Four days of mental intensity take it out of you" (cited in Nicholas, 2002). Unfortunately, despite its superficial plausibility, the practice of asking athletes about mental aspects of sport performance has at least three major limitations as a research strategy. First, when interviewing athletes, it is difficult to avoid asking them "leading" questions or putting words into their mouths. Second, it is hard to be unbiased when editing or analysing interview data. After all, most people (including scientists) tend to see what they *believe* – rather than believe what they see! Third, as athletes' insights are invariably sport-specific, they are rather limited in their generality of application. For example, the world of sailing is full of unknown variables (e.g., variability of wind speed and direction) whereas that of snooker is very predictable. Given these environmental constraints, it would be naive to expect identical mental preparation strategies to be as effective among competitive sailors as among snooker players.

In view of the preceding difficulties, a systematic and objective research strategy is required to explore mental aspects of athletic performance. An obvious technique in this regard is the research questionnaire. Using a specially designed survey instrument, Scully and Hume (1995) elicited the views of a sample of elite athletes and coaches about mental aspects of sport. In particular, they asked these participants what the term "sport psychology" meant to them and also inquired about the psychological attributes that they believed to be most influential in determining athletic success. Results revealed that sport psychology was defined mainly in terms of mental preparation for competition (a point to which we shall return later in the chapter). In addition, these researchers found that mental toughness was perceived to be the most important determinant of success in sport. Interestingly, this latter **construct** was also identified by the golfer Nick Faldo (Nicholas, 2002) and by a sample of Olympic gold medallists as a crucial prerequisite of athletic success (Gould et al., 2002b). Before we analyse this term, however, let us consider briefly a key characteristic of mentally tough athletes – self-confidence.

What is confidence?

Confidence, or "the belief that one has the internal resources, particularly abilities, to achieve success" (Vealey, 2009, p. 43), is usually correlated positively with peak athletic performance (Zinsser et al., 2010). Not surprisingly, many elite athletes regard self-belief as the cornerstone of mental toughness (Connaughton et al., 2008). Conversely, at a practical level, an apparent *lack* of confidence is one of the problems most commonly reported by athletes to sport psychologists (Kremer and Moran, 2008a). At first glance, the fragility of confidence, even in successful athletes, may seem surprising. But when we discover from Bandura's (1997) theory of **self-efficacy** that confidence is essentially a belief, then we can understand why it may vary significantly from one context to another. According to Bandura (1997, p. 3), self-efficacy is the belief that one has the capacity to "execute the courses of action required to produce given attainments" – or, put simply, to achieve a specific goal. This "I can do it" belief, however, is not all pervasive but actually situation-specific. Thus a golfer may be more confident in driving the ball from the teebox than in chipping it from the rough. Similarly, a tennis player may be more confident in playing ground-strokes from the baseline than in volleying at the net. And because confidence is largely belief-based rather than fact-based, it requires constant replenishment. For example, Mia Hamm, the former US soccer player who has scored more international goals than any other player in history, revealed that confidence "takes constant nurturing. It's not something you go in and turn on the light switch and say 'I'm confident' and it stays on until the light bulb burns out" (cited in Vealey and Chase, 2008, p. 66). In summary, self-confidence is a vital yet fragile ingredient of athletic success.

Although a considerable amount of research has been conducted on the origins of self-confidence in sport (e.g., see Vealey et al., 1998) and on ways of building confidence in athletes (e.g., see Vealey and Chase, 2008; Vealey and Vernau, 2010; Zinsser et al., 2010), few investigators have attempted to measure the "robustness" of self-confidence or the capacity to maintain one's belief in one's ability in the face of adversity. Filling this gap in the research literature, Beattie et al., (2011) developed the Trait Robustness of Self-Confidence Inventory (TROSCI) to measure "the ability to maintain confidence beliefs in the face of adversity" (Beattie et al., 2011, p. 184). This eight-item inventory contains items such as "A bad result in competition has a very negative effect on my self-confidence" (item 1) and "My self-confidence is stable; it does not vary much at all" (item 5). Initial psychometric analysis suggests that this scale shows satisfactory **internal consistency**, good test-retest reliability and reasonable predictive validity.

What is mental toughness? Meaning and measurement

"Mental toughness" is one of the most widely used terms in everyday sporting discourse. Garside (2008, p. 15) claimed that "a common trait in all the champions … including Prost, Senna, Michael Schumacher and Mika Hakkinen has been an immense mental toughness … the difference between winning and losing". Typically, the term mental toughness is used as a synonym for determination, resilience and/or an exceptional immunity to pressure situations. Ronald Smith (2006) described it as a characteristic that enables athletes to react well to adversity and to persist in the face of setbacks. Despite its popularity, the term mental toughness is a relatively recent addition to the vernacular of academic psychology. Nevertheless, mental toughness has attracted a great deal of attention from sport psychologists in recent years (for an account of research in this field, see Sheard, 2010). Not surprisingly, there is now a profusion of definitions of this term and theories about how to develop it. Unfortunately, as Connaughton and Hanton (2009) pointed out in their valuable critique of research on this topic, most of the definitions of mental toughness are atheoretical in nature, owing more to *anecdotal* plausibility than to empirical research. Therefore, considerable caution is required when attempting to draw conclusions about the nature, characteristics, determinants and development of mental toughness in sport.

Since 2001, a number of researchers (e.g., Clough et al., 2002; Connaughton et al., 2008; Crust, 2008; Earle et al. 2008; Gucciardi and Mallett, 2010; G. Jones et al.,

2002) have explored theoretical and practical aspects of this construct in detail (for a popular book on this topic, see also Hemmings et al., 2007). Two key themes emerge from empirical studies of this construct. First, mental toughness is widely regarded as the key to sporting success. Second, little agreement exists about what the construct itself actually means – or about what theoretical mechanisms underlie it. Before we consider these themes, however, let us examine some athletes' views on mental toughness.

Athletes' views on mental toughness can be gauged from anecdotal sources and also from formal interviews with top performers. With regard to the former, according to Tim Henman, the former English tennis star who was once ranked number 4 in the world, mental toughness can be defined simply as the ability "to perform under pressure" (Coaching Excellence, 1996). This opinion was echoed by Selvey (1998), who described the former England cricketer Mike Atherton as "the most mentally tough batsman of his generation" because of his extraordinary ability to raise his game under pressure. In an effort to complement these anecdotal insights, Connaughton et al. (2008) interviewed a sample (n=7) of elite international athletes about the development and maintenance of mental toughness. Results indicated that these athletes believed that mental toughness develops as a long-term outcome of a complex range of interacting factors. Among these factors was a **motivational climate** (see also Chapter 2 for further discussion of this term) surrounding the athlete's training that was challenging yet enjoyable. Although they provide interesting **anecdotal evidence**, athletes' insights into psychological constructs should be treated with caution because their reports are vulnerable to biases of perception and recollection. Clearly, a more rigorous conceptual analysis of mental toughness is required if this construct is to gain scientific credibility.

Historically, one of the earliest references to mental toughness is found in Loehr's (1982) popular self-help book on athletic excellence. Loehr (1982) proposed that mental toughness involved the possession of a positive attitude to stressful and/ or challenging situations in sport. Unfortunately, Loehr's intuitive but atheoretical approach appears somewhat simplistic and is hampered by a lack of empirical evidence. Since the early 1990s, however, the construct of mental toughness has attracted interest from a number of research groups in the UK and Australia. The studies that have emerged in these countries have developed in three main waves – first, intuitive accounts of mental toughness (Loehr, 1982), second, descriptive studies of mental toughness in samples of elite athletes (e.g., Clough et al., 2002; G. Jones et al., 2002), and third, theoretical syntheses of the field (Crust, 2008; Sheard, 2010). What is clear from these publications is that mental toughness is a complex multidimensional construct. Let us now review some key studies in this field.

Clough et al. (2002), influenced by Kobasa's (1979) research on **hardiness**, used a specially devised questionnaire to measure mental toughness. By way of background, Kobasa (1979) proposed that hardiness is a constellation of personality characteristics that enables people to mitigate the adverse effects of stressful situations. Building on this idea, Clough et al. (2002) postulated four key components of mental toughness in their 4Cs model of this construct. The first of these four components is *control* or the capacity to feel and act as if one could exert an influence in the situation in question. The second component of the construct is *challenge*, which refers to the habit of perceiving potentially stressful situations as positive opportunities rather than as threats. For example, a challenge-oriented golfer may see a par-five hole as an opportunity to make a birdie than as a potential bogey situation (Earle et al., 2008). The third component of mental toughness is *commitment* or stickability (Earle et al., 2008). Fourth, and differentiating this model from the hardiness approach, *confidence* was defined as a component of mental toughness that designates a strong belief in one's ability to complete a task successfully. Combining these four elements, Clough et al. (2002) defined mentally tough athletes as people who have "a high sense of self-belief and an unshakeable faith that they can control their own destiny" and who can "remain relatively unaffected by competition or adversity" (Clough et al., 2002, p. 38). In addition, these researchers devised an eighteen-item measure called the Mental Toughness Questionnaire, which requires respondents to use a five-point **Likert scale** to indicate their level of agreement with such items as "Even when under considerable pressure, I usually remain calm" (item 1) or "I generally feel in control" (item 10) or "I usually find it difficult to make a mental effort when I am tired" (item 17). These authors reported a **reliability coefficient** for this scale of $r=0.90$ and **construct validity** data based on predicted relationships with such constructs as self-efficacy or a belief on one's ability to achieve certain outcomes regardless of the situation ($r=0.56$, $p<0.05$). Although such **psychometric data** are encouraging, a great deal of additional validation evidence is required before this scale can be accepted as a worthwhile tool for the measurement of the rather nebulous construct of mental toughness.

Another study of mental toughness was carried out by G. Jones et al. (2002) using **qualitative research** methodology (described later in the chapter in Box 1.4; for a practical guide, see also Forrester, 2010). G. Jones et al. (2002, p. 209) postulated that it involves having a psychological edge that enables an athlete to cope better than opponents with the demands of competitive sport – thereby remaining focused and in control under pressure. G. Jones et al. (2002) believed that mental toughness denoted a range of psychological processes such as the ability to cope with pressure, the ability to rebound from failure, a determination to persist in the face of adversity, and mental resilience. They adopted the theoretical framework of personal construct psychology (G. Kelly, 1955) – an approach that emphasizes the unique ways in which people perceive and strive to make sense of their experience. Using a combination of a **focus group** (i.e., a data collection technique based on group discussion that is led by a trained facilitator) and individual interviews with a sample (n = 10) of international sport performers, G. Jones et al. (2002) tried to elicit the meaning of mental toughness as well as the characteristics associated with it. Results showed that mental toughness was perceived to comprise both general and specific components. The general component of this construct was a perception of having a "natural or developed psychological edge" that enables an athlete to cope better than his or her opponents with competitive lifestyle and training demands. The specific components of mental toughness were perceived to be the capacity to remain more determined, focused, confident and in control than one's athletic rivals. Although superficially compelling, the theory of mental toughness (G. Jones et al., 2002) has several weaknesses (Gucciardi et al., 2009a). For example, little detail is provided on the precise components of the psychological edge that mentally tough athletes are assumed to possess. Similarly, the idea that mental toughness is apparent only when one surpasses an opponent's performance seems short-sighted as it neglects the possibility that true mental toughness requires the ability to achieve one's goals – irrespective of the performance of one's opponent. Nevertheless, G. Jones et al. (2002) provided some valuable data on twelve perceived characteristics of mental toughness. These characteristics included having an unshakeable belief in one's ability, having an unshakeable belief in one's unique qualities, having an insatiable desire to succeed, having the ability to bounce back from setbacks, being able to thrive on the pressure of competition, being able to cope with competition and performance anxiety, being able to ignore others' performance, being able to switch focus when required, the ability to remain focused on the task at hand, the ability to push oneself through physical and emotional pain, and the ability to regain control after unexpected events. The authors classified these twelve attributes into such categories as **motivation, focus** (or concentration), the ability to deal with pressure and anxiety, and the ability to cope with physical and emotional pain. Unfortunately, the results of this study must be interpreted cautiously due to the small sample size (e.g., the focus group comprised only three participants) and the restricted range of sports represented by the participants. In a later study, G. Jones et al. (2007) interviewed a sample of eight Olympic or world champion athletes, three top coaches and four sport psychologists. From these interviews, a number of features of mental toughness were identified and organized along four key dimensions: the attitudes and beliefs of the performer (mindset) and the three major contexts of athletic performance – namely, training (e.g., using long-term goals as a source of motivation and pushing oneself to the limit), competition (e.g., ability to handle pressure) and post-competition (e.g., ability to handle failure and setbacks). In addition to these generic studies of mental toughness, several sport-specific investigations have been conducted on this construct. Thelwell et al. (2005) interviewed forty-three professional soccer players and asked them to rank the perceived attributes of mental toughness. Results showed that self-belief, wanting the ball at all times (even when playing badly) and having the ability to remain calm under pressure were among the key characteristics of mental toughness in soccer.

One of the more recent theoretically driven accounts of mental toughness was provided by Gucciardi et al. (2009a). Adopting the perspective of personal construct psychology (G. Kelly, 1955), as G. Jones et al. (2002) had done previousy, these researchers postulated that this construct can be understood best by probing how athletes perceive and respond to a range of challenging situations in sport. Gucciardi et al. (2009a) suggested that questions such as "What did you predict would happen?" or "What did you learn from this experience?" could be helpful in eliciting athletes' perceptions of mental toughness. Interestingly, Gucciardi et al. (2009c) developed and evaluated a mental toughness training programme for Australian Rules football players. Their results were encouraging but need to be validated by further research before firm conclusions can be drawn about the best ways to develop mental toughness in athletes. Connaughton et al. (2010) interviewed a sample of world-class performers (including athletes and coaches) about the development and maintenance of mental toughness. Among the factors perceived to influence mental toughness development were skill-mastery, competitiveness, and the use of psychological skills. However, it is notable that these authors concluded their study by highlighting "the overriding need to develop … a conceptually accurate and psychometrically valid and reliable measure of mental toughness" (Connaughton et al., 2010, p. 192).

In summary, we have learned in this section that athletes and researchers regard mental toughness as a key characteristic of successful athletes. But are you really convinced about the validity of this construct? As Box 1.1 shows, there are several unresolved conceptual issues arising from research on mental toughness. As you can see from Box 1.1, the term mental toughness is far from clear.

Box 1.1 Thinking critically about … mental toughness in sport

Although we think all the time, few of us are skilled at *critical* thinking – or the ability and willingness to evaluate claims (whether in science or in everyday life) in an open-minded and careful manner (Bensley, 2010; Lilienfeld et al., 2009). So, in an effort to help you to think more critically about key topics and issues in sport and exercise psychology (e.g., in this case, mental toughness) here are some questions to consider (see also the conceptual critiques offered by Connaughton and Hanton (2009) and Sheard (2010) and a good discussion by Gucciardi and Mallett (2010) of some practical implications of mental toughness for applied sport psychology).

Critical thinking questions
First, do you think that it is valid to define mental toughness without reference to any aspect of behaviour *other* than the end-state of winning? Put differently, has mental toughness become the "default explanation" (Barnes, 2009) for athletic success? Recall that the athletes interviewed by G. Jones et al. (2002) claimed that this construct gives performers a "psychological edge" over their rivals. But how is this edge evident? Is it present only if an athlete defeats someone else? Could mental toughness not also influence athletes to perform better than they have done previously – regardless of the presence of others? Can you think of a way of defining mental toughness in a more objective manner? Is there a danger of circularity defining this construct because of the lack of an independent index of mental toughness? Second, is there a danger that in presenting mental toughness as a complex, multifaceted construct which is difficult to define (e.g., Gucciardi and Mallett, 2010), its explanatory efficiency and scientific utility are diminished? Third, if we adopt the perspective of personal construct psychology (G. Kelly, 1955), one way of exploring people's understanding of a term is to ask them to identify the opposite of it. But what exactly is the *opposite* of mental toughness? If this latter term is "mental weakness", how would we recognize it? Is losing a match a sign of mental weakness? If not, what criteria should we apply to help us to define this latter term precisely? Fourth, do you think that mental toughness is learned or innate? Which view do you favour and why?

In summary, having explored the mental side of sport in general, and having examined the specific construct of mental toughness in athletes, there is one more question to address in this section of the chapter. Specifically, what factors influence the mental demands of a given sport?

What factors influence the mental demands of a given sport?

Although a considerable amount of research has been conducted on mental factors in athletic performance, surprisingly little analysis has been undertaken on the different mental challenges posed by different athletic activities. What follows is a brief analysis of this important issue.

At the outset, it is widely agreed that sports differ significantly in the *physical* demands that they make of performers. For example, sprinting requires a short burst of explosive power whereas marathon running demands not only great stamina but also the ability to maintain a steady pace throughout a race. Interestingly, research on marathon runners indicates that they can lose up to 8 per cent of their body mass during the race (Cooper, 2003) and face the risk of dehydration, muscular damage and possible sudden death. Perhaps not surprisingly, the psychological requirements of different sports also appear to vary widely. To illustrate, whereas some sports like weightlifting require short periods of intense concentration for a limited duration, other athletic activities like cycling demand sustained alertness for longer periods of time. But what causes such differences in the mental demands of these activities?

Among the most important determinants of the psychological demands of any sport are its nature and structure. For example, consider some differences between a field game like soccer and and an indoor game such as snooker. Whereas the former is a timed, physical contact, team game, the latter is an untimed, non-contact, individual sport. These differences are likely to affect the mental challenges posed by these activities. For example, whereas motivation, communication skills, and an ability to anticipate opponents' moves would seem to be vital for soccer players, snooker performers appear to depend more on cognitive skills like concentration, decision making and the ability to recover mentally from errors. Put simply, a footballer can try to win the ball back off an opponent by chasing and tackling him or her, but a snooker player can only sit and watch while his or her opponent is potting balls on the table. In short, the structure of a sport can affect its psychological requirements. To emphasize this point, consider the phenomenon of sitting passively "in the chair" in snooker. Briefly, in this game, the player who is not scoring (or building breaks) at the snooker table has to sit and wait for his or her opponent to miss before returning to the table. Clearly, the challenge of sitting in the chair is to retain one's focus rather than becoming annoyed at oneself for previous mistakes. But what goes through snooker players' minds as they wait for their opponents? Stephen Hendry (seven times world champion snooker star) referred to "hoping you don't have to play a certain shot, dreading that you might" (cited in White, 2001, p. 18) when forced to watch and wait. But not all snooker players feel as helpless as does Hendry in this situation. For example, Peter Ebdon, who won the world championship in 2002, claimed that although "the chair is the toughest place in sport ... Well it is and it isn't. *It depends on what you do with your time there*. There's certain routines that you can be going through mentally which help you for when you get your chance" (cited in White, 2003, p. 20, italics mine). One of the most popular "chair routines" used by former world snooker champions such as Steve Davis or Ken Doherty (cited in BBC, 2003) is to imagine oneself playing the shots that one's opponent is confronted with (see also Chapter 5) so that one will be ready to recommence at the table when the opportunity arises. Another psychological technique that helps players to maintain their concentration is to scrutinize the layout of the balls facing one's opponent – hoping that one can anticipate precisely when the opponent might miss a shot or lose position on the table. To summarize, most top snooker players use psychological strategies to prevent lapses in concentration in situations where passivity is likely (see also Chapter 4 on concentration).

Let us now consider the mental demands of a popular sport – golf. This sport is interesting because, as I mentioned earlier, many of its leading players are enthusiastic advocates of sport psychology. What is so special about golf from a psychological point of view?

Golf is a psychologically demanding game for at least three reasons. First, it is an untimed sport so players have to be prepared to play for as long as it takes (often, up to five hours) to complete a round or match. Sadly, many club-level and leisure players allow themselves to become upset at the apparently slow play of those ahead of them. Naturally, this self-generated annoyance usually hampers their performance. Second, golf is a tough sport mentally because players have to take full responsibility for their own performance on the course. They cannot be substituted if they are playing poorly. Unfortunately, many players try to evade this responsibility by making excuses: blaming course conditions, their clubs, the weather and/or the balls that they are using. In this regard, an old adage in sport psychology is relevant: "Winners are workers – only *losers* make excuses" (but see Box 1.2). Third, the "stop-start" nature of golf means that players spend more time *thinking* about playing than actually hitting the ball. Indeed, some golf analysts believe that less than 20 per cent of the time on a course is devoted to hitting the ball. Usually, the remainder of the time is spent walking, talking, looking for balls, regretting mistakes, losing concentration and, of course, making excuses! Unfortunately, it is during this fallow time that players lose concentration either by thinking too far ahead or by regretting mistakes and/or lost opportunities in the past. Overall, this disjunction in golf between playing time and thinking time may explain why Sam Snead, a former player, once remarked that *thinking* was the biggest problem in the game (Moran, 2000a). In summary, golf is demanding mentally because it is an untimed, individual and discontinuous sport. In the light of these unique features, the mental challenge for golfers is to learn to concentrate on playing one shot at a time (see also Chapter 4). One way in which this challenge can be accomplished is for golfers to learn to *restructure* the game in their minds. For example, instead of perceiving golf as an eighteen-hole competition against others, people can be trained to see it as a *single-shot* contest between themselves and the target at which they are aiming. Using this technique of **cognitive restructuring** (see also Chapter 3), they can learn to shorten their focus so that they are concentrating only on the present shot. Before we conclude this section, let us return briefly to the ubiquitous phenomenon of excuse-making in sport. The worst sporting excuses have been documented by Hodgkinson (2002) and the *Observer* magazine (Observer, 2004) (see Box 1.2).

Box 1.2 Some classic excuses in sport: can they be serious?

Athletes and coaches often make excuses to avoid taking personal responsibility for errors, mistakes or missed opportunities in sport. Sometimes, however, these excuses are presented in an ironic fashion. Consider what Brian Little, the former Wrexham Football Club manager, said after his team was defeated by Wycombe Wanderers in March 2008: "I'm not looking for excuses but another 24 hours would have been nice to have prepared for the game. But that's about the only excuse if I'm looking for an excuse, which I'm not but it was a factor" (cited in BBC Sport, 2008). Among the most famous excuses in sport are such gems as:

- The suggestion that the grey colour of Manchester United's shirts prevented teammates from seeing and passing to each other properly (Alex Ferguson, manager of Manchester United, after his team's 3–1 defeat by Southampton in 1996).
- The claim that "the balls were too bouncy" (Kenny Dalglish, then manager of Newcastle, after his team's 1–1 draw with Stevenage in an FA Cup match in 1998).
- The explanation that England's defeat by South Africa in 1999 in a cricket test match held in Johannesburg was due to "low cloud" conditions.
- The claim by the Sri Lankan cricket team that their loss to Pakistan in the 2001 ICC Champions Trophy was due to the intolerably tight sports clothes that they had been required to wear during the match (Observer, 2004).
- The fact that Mervyn King, the darts player, blamed the hum of the air-conditioning for his defeat by Raymond Barneveld in the 2003 world darts championships semi-final (Observer, 2004).

One interesting point about excuses is that some athletes love to hear competitors using them. Jack Nicklaus, who won eighteen professional major golf tournaments in his career, loved to hear rival players making excuses before a competition: "'The rough is too high. The greens are too fast'. Check him off. You just check guys off as they complain themselves right out of this championship" (cited in Gilleece, 1999a, p. 2). A similar view was expressed by Michael Campbell, the New Zealand golfer and US Open winner in 2005, when he remarked that when players make excuses, "they've added a two-shot penalty before they even tee off" (cited in McGinty, 2006).

Sport and exercise psychology as an academic discipline

Having scratched the surface of the mental dimension of sport, let us now introduce the discipline of sport and exercise psychology. Sport and exercise psychology can be defined as the application of psychological theory and methods to understand the performance, mental processes and well-being of people who are involved in sport and exercise. As the history of this discipline has been well documented (e.g., see Kornspan, 2011; Kremer et al. 2012), it is sufficient to note here that empirical research on mental aspects of athletic performance is at least as old as psychology itself. In the nineteenth century, Triplett (1898) found that racing cyclists tended to perform at least 25 per cent faster when competing against other cyclists (or pacemakers) than when performing alone against the clock. This discovery that individual athletic activity is facilitated by the presence of others became known as **social facilitation** and was attributed to the capacity of rival performers to "liberate latent energy not ordinarily available" (Triplett, 1898, p. 532). Triplett's research led to a robust empirical principle in social psychology. Specifically, the presence of other people tends to enhance the performance of well-learned skills but to impair the performance of poorly learned skills (Cashmore, 2008).

Despite having a research tradition spanning more than a century (for brief historical accounts, see Kornspan, 2007; Kremer and Moran, 2008b) the field of sport psychology is difficult to define precisely. This is due, in part, to the twin-track identity of the discipline. To explain, as we indicated in the previous section, not only is sport and exercise psychology regarded as a subfield of mainstream psychology but also it is seen as one of the sport sciences. Indeed, in 2000, Diane Gill (2000, p. 7) classified sport and exercise psychology as a "branch of exercise and sport science" rather than of psychology.

Despite this semantic difficulty of defining the discipline precisely, three characteristics of sport psychology are noteworthy. First, it is generally regarded as a science. As such, it is committed to the principle that its claims should be falsifiable or capable of being tested through objective and systematic methods of empirical inquiry (see Box 1.4 later in the chapter). Second, sport psychology is not just about sport – it involves the study of *exercise* as well as of competitive athletic behaviour. Thus **physical activity** undertaken for health and leisure is just as important to sport and exercise psychologists as is competitive sport. Early pioneers of **exercise psychology** included Dorothy Harris and William Morgan (Harris, 1973; Morgan and Goldston, 1987). In general, exercise psychology has two main research themes – the study of the initiation and maintenance of physical activity and the study of the psychological *outcomes* of such activity (Williams et al., 2008b). In formal recognition of the increasing importance of physical activity to sport science researchers, the title of the *Journal of Sport Psychology* was changed to the *Journal of Sport and Exercise Psychology* in 1988. We shall explore the psychology of exercise and health in Chapter 8. Third, sport and exercise psychology is a *profession* as well as a science. Therefore, there are *applied* as well as theoretical dimensions to this discipline. So whereas some sport psychologists are engaged in basic research designed to establish how the mind works in a variety of athletic and exercise settings, others provide practical advice and training on performance enhancement and/or on healthy living. Recognizing this distinction, in 1986, the Association for Applied Sport Psychology (AASP) was established in order to cater for the growing interests of applied sport psychologists (see also Box 1.3 later in the chapter). Each of these three key features of sport psychology – the commitment to scientific procedures, the emphasis on the study of exercise as well as sport, and the existence of an applied dimension to the discipline – will be emphasized throughout this book. In passing, it should be noted that the relationship between theorists and applied professionals in sport psychology has not always been harmonious. Kontos and Feltz (2008) observed that some basic researchers in the field believe that professional services should not be provided to athletes and coaches until a solid body of knowledge has been established using empirical methods. However, many applied researchers argue that there is an urgent demand for psychological services within the sporting community and that such work should drive the theory and practice of sport psychology.

In spite of this debate between theorists and practitioners, applied sport psychology has grown rapidly in recent years. To illustrate, this subfield has its own professional organizations (e.g., the AASP), a number of international journals (see Box 1.8 later in the chapter) and over one hundred postgraduate training programmes in the United States, Canada, Australia, Finland, Singapore and the UK (see K. Burke et al., 2008). However, the vast majority of these programmes are located in exercise science departments rather than in departments of psychology – a fact which suggests that applied sport and exercise psychology has not yet been fully integrated into mainstream psychology. We shall deal with this issue of professional qualification and training in more detail in the next section of the chapter. At this point, however, let us outline briefly some key events in the history of the discipline.

A brief history of sport and exercise psychology

In the two decades which followed Triplett's (1898) research, investigators such as Swift (1910) and Lashley (1915) explored the determinants of sport skills such as ball-tossing and archery. Interestingly, such research was complemented by applied work in actual sport settings. In the 1920s, the Chicago Cubs baseball team employed the services of a sport psychologist at the University of Illinois named Coleman Griffith. This researcher and practitioner is widely regarded as the progenitor of this discipline (see Green, 2003). Indeed, it was Griffith who had established the first sport psychology research facility, called the Athletic Research Laboratory, in the United States in 1925 (at the University of Illinois). Unfortunately, this laboratory closed in 1932 and despite Griffith's pioneering fusion of theory and practice in this field, research in sport psychology encountered a barren era between the 1920s and 1960s. It was during the 1960s, however, that sport psychology emerged as an independent discipline. Specifically, in 1965 the International Society of Sport Psychology was established by an Italian named Ferruccio Antonelli (LeUnes, 2008). This development heralded the arrival of sport psychology as a distinct subfield of sport science. Unfortunately, within mainstream academic psychology, formal recognition of the burgeoning subfield of sport psychology was slow to arrive: it was not until 1986 that Division 47 (Exercise and Sport Psychology) was established by the American Psychological Association. A similar pattern of late recognition of sport psychology was apparent in Australia and Britain. For example, it was 1991 before the Board of Sport Psychologists was established within the Australian Psychological Society and 1993 before a sport and exercise psychology section was formed by the British Psychological Society. For a short summary of some key dates in the evolution of this discipline, see Box 1.3.

Box 1.3 Key dates in the history of sport and exercise psychology

Date	Significant event
1897–1898	Triplett's experimental research on psychological factors in cycling
1925	Coleman Roberts Griffith established the Athletic Research Laboratory in the University of Illinois
1965	Establishment of International Society of Sport Psychology (ISSP) / First International Congress of Sport Psychology held in Rome
1967	Establishment of North American Society for the Psychology of Sport and Physical Activity (NASPSPA)
1969	Establishment of Fédération Européenne de Psychologie des Sport et des Activités Corporelles (FEPSAC)
1970	Publication of first issue of *International Journal of Sport Psychology*
1979	Publication of first issue of the *Journal of Sport Psychology* (changed to the *Journal of Sport and Exercise Psychology* in 1988)
1986	Formation of Association for the Advancement of Applied Sport Psychology (AAASP) – later renamed Association for Applied Sport Psychology (AASP)
1986	Publication of first issue of *The Sport Psychologist*
1986	Establishment of Division 47 of American Psychological Association on Exercise and Sport Psychology
1989	Publication of first issue of *Journal of Applied Sport Psychology*
1991	Formation of Board of Sport Psychologists within the Australian Psychological Society
1993	Establishment of Sport and Exercise Psychology Section of the British Psychological Society (later became Division of Sport and Exercise Psychology)
2000	Publication of first issue of *Psychology of Sport and Exercise*
2003	Renaming *International Journal of Sport Psychology* as *International Journal of Sport and Exercise Psychology*
2004	Establishment of Division of Sport and Exercise Psychology (DSEP) within the British Psychological Society
2008	Publication of first issue of *International Review of Sport and Exercise Psychology*
2009	Publication of first issue of *Qualitative Research in Sport and Exercise*
2010	Publication of first issue of *Journal of Sport Psychology in Action* (official journal of Association for Applied Sport Psychology)
2012	Publication of first issue of *Sport, Exercise and Performance Psychology* (official publication of APA Division 47, Exercise and Sport Psychology)

As you can see from Box 1.3, the discipline of sport and exercise psychology has had many landmarks since Norman Triplett conducted his cycling studies in the 1890s. Since the mid-1960s, however, many important developments have occurred in this field, but space restrictions in this chapter prevent a detailed analysis of these developments. For accounts of the history of sport and exercise psychology, see Brewer and Van Raalte (in press), Green and Benjamin (2009) and Kremer and Moran (2008b).

Research methods in sport and exercise psychology

In the previous section, I indicated that sport and exercise psychology is commonly regarded as an applied science. If so, what research techniques does it use? As you might expect, there is a large toolbox of research methods available to sport and exercise psychologists. One way of classifying these techniques is to distinguish between traditional quantitative or numbers-based methods (i.e., where measurement is used to assess the "amount" of something and where statistical analysis is then applied to make sense of the resulting data; see Conroy et al., 2008) and more recently developed qualitative approaches that are concerned more with understanding the meaning of events, situations and actions for people involved in a given study (see Brustad, 2008; Culver et al., 2003). An example of a qualitative study in sport comes from Bishop et al. (2007), who investigated young tennis players' use of music to manipulate their moods and emotional states using an approach called **grounded theory** (whereby a researcher attempts to develop a theory of a phenomenon from the analysis of a set of qualitative data derived from people's experience of that phenomenon). Not surprisingly, in light of their potential richness, qualitative techniques have become increasingly popular in sport and exercise psychology since 2000 and have led to the development of a new journal dedicated to this field – *Qualitative Research in Sport, Exercise and Health* (first published in 2009 – see Gilbourne and Smith, 2009). Another way to classify research methods in sport and exercise psychology is to distinguish between descriptive, correlational and experimental techniques (Passer et al., 2009). Let us now consider each of these three categories briefly.

First, the aim of **descriptive research** is to record and analyse certain aspects of behaviour, especially in natural settings. Included in this category are such methods as **case study** (which is an intensive or in-depth analysis of individuals, **groups** or events), **naturalistic observation** (where researchers observe behaviour as it occurs in its own natural environment), **survey research** (where information is collected about the behaviour, experiences or attitudes of many people using a series of questions about the topic of interest) and **psychometric testing** (where differences between people on some psychological construct are assessed using specially designed, standardized instruments). Second, the purpose of **correlational research** is to measure the relationship or degree of association between two or more variables. For example, what is the relationship between athletes' anxiety levels and their performance in athletic competition? (see Chapter 3). Third, the objective of **experimental research** is to determine cause-and-effect relationships between two or more variables. Using this method, a researcher tries to manipulate an independent variable under controlled conditions in order to study its effects on a dependent variable. For example, what is the relative efficacy of mental versus physical practice in the learning and performance of a motor skill (see Chapter 5)?

Before we conclude this section, it is important to mention a research design that is attracting increasing attention in sport and exercise psychology – namely, the single-case design. **Single-case research designs** are a group of quasi-experimental methods that grew out of attempts in the applied behaviour analysis tradition to understand an individual's behaviour – especially his or her response to an intervention programme (Kratochwill and Levin, 2010). They can be used to study the effect, time course, or variability of an indepenent variable (e.g., an intervention programme or psychological process) on some designated dependent (outcome) variables. Single-case research is typically used both for theoretical reasons (e.g., to test conceptually derived hypotheses) and for practical reasons (e.g., to validate the efficacy of a specific intervention programme in order to establish evidence-based practice). Barker et al. (2011) provided a comprehensive review of the nature and applications of single-case research designs in sport and exercise psychology.

As you have probably encountered these various categories of research methods already in other academic courses (e.g., in your laboratory practicals and methodology courses), I shall provide only a brief outline of their strengths and weaknesses here. Therefore, in Box 1.4, I have summarized the main research methods used in sport and exercise psychology along with appropriate sample studies drawn from different areas of the field.

Sport and exercise psychology as a profession

In the previous section, sport and exercise psychology as an academic discipline was discussed. This section examines its status as a profession. In this regard, three important questions need to be addressed. First, what exactly do sport psychologists do? Second, what is the best model for the provision of sport psychology services to clients such as athletes and coaches? Third, how can one qualify as a sport psychologist? Let us now consider each of these questions in turn (for a discussion of these issues, see also Lavallee et al., 2012).

What type of work do sport psychologists actually do?

For a quick overview of what sport psychologists do, it is worth visiting the web page of the Division of Sport and Exercise Psychology of the British Psychological Society (see www.bps.org.uk/spex/) or that of the Division of Exercise and Sport Psychology (Division 47) of the American Psychological Association (see http://apa47.org/). Typically, the professional activities of sport and exercise psychologists fall into three main categories: applied consultancy work (including advice on performance enhancement as well as the provision of counselling and clinical psychology services); education; and research. Before we explore these functions, however, two cautions should be noted. First, there is considerable overlap between these three categories in practice (a point to which we shall return later in this section). Second, the majority of sport psychologists work only part-time in this field. Usually, the professional work from which they derive most of their income (i.e., their "day job") lies in some other area of psychology or sport science such as lecturing and research.

Applied consultancy work

This category of sport psychology services may be subdivided into two types of work: advice on performance enhancement and the provision of counselling/clinical

Box 1.4 Research methods in sport and exercise psychology

Method	Goal	Data obtained	Advantages	Limitations	Example
Experiments	To study cause–effect relationships by manipulation of certain variables and control of others	Quantitative – usually interval level of measurement	• Random assignment of Ss • Precise control of independent variables • Causal inference possible	• May be somewhat artificial – not always possible to generalize results beyond lab. setting • Vulnerable to certain biases	Castaneda and Gray (2007) examined the effects of different foci of attention (internal – movement of the hands; or external – the ball) on baseball batting performance
Surveys, questionnaires and psychological tests	To measure people's attitudes, beliefs and/or skills and abilities	Quantitative or qualitative	• Easy to administer, score and analyse • Can be tailored to specific populations	• Limited to conscious experiences and processes • Vulnerable to certain biases	Gucciardi et al. (2009b) developed a scale to measure mental toughness in Australian Rules football
Interviews and focus groups (see also "narrative inquiry" (a form of qualitative research focusing on people's stories as they unfold over time – see B. Smith, 2010)	To explore people's knowledge and experiences of a topic "in depth"	Qualitative (main themes) and quantitative (e.g., frequency analysis of key words)	• Richness of data collected • Flexible • Can lead to "grounded theory"	• Very laborious and time-consuming to analyse • Interviewer may contaminate findings	Gustafsson et al. (2008) interviewed a sample of elite Swedish athletes who had quit sport due to burnout
Case studies	To provide an intensive analysis of a single case or example	Qualitative	Can yield detailed information of a phenomenon over time	Difficult to generalize from findings	Hare et al. (2008) investigated an Olympic athlete's use of mental imagery during physical rehabilitation from injury
Naturalistic observation	To observe and analyse naturally occurring behaviour in real-life settings	Qualitative	Can help to understand the nature and context of certain behaviour	• No experimental control over variables • Presence of observer may influence findings	Augé and Augé (1999) studied the use of illegal performance-enhancing drugs by bodybuilders

psychology services. Interestingly, demand for the latter services has increased with the public admission by some top athletes that they have suffered from psychological problems such as depression. Mark Allen (one of the world's top snooker players) and Michael Trescothick (the England cricket star) have revealed their susceptibility to this latter problem (Goulding, 2011; Hopps, 2011). But let us now get back to the main reasons why athletes consult sport psychologists.

The most obvious reason for such consultation is to gain practical advice on ways of improving their mental preparation and/or competitive performance. Such requests may come directly as self-referrals or indirectly through coaches, general practitioners, governing bodies of sports and/or national "carding schemes" whereby elite athletes may be given funded access to medical and sport science advisers. Typically, these consultations are motivated by a desire to realize some unfulfilled athletic potential and/or to gain a competitive edge over rival performers. Indeed, research suggests that a desire to perform better is the reason most frequently cited by athletes for their decision to consult sport psychologists. As well as providing practical strategies to enhance athletic performance, sport psychologists are often asked to help athletes to resolve a heterogeneous array of alleged "psychological problems" (e.g., poor concentration, performance anxiety, low self-confidence) which tend to be self-diagnosed and vaguely expressed. Indeed, Clough et al. (2002, p. 32) captured the frustration engendered by this unreliable referral system when they remarked that "being asked to solve a problem that is ill-conceived, ill-defined and ill-considered is the lifeblood of sport psychology. Coaches and athletes are more prone than most to using cliches, abbreviations, or shorthand phrases". Interestingly, the demand for sport psychology services at the Olympics continues to increase. For example, whereas only one official sport psychologist was part of the US team prior to the 2000 Games in Sydney, the 2008 Games in Beijing was attended by five full-time official psychologists in the US team as well as a number of colleagues hired privately by national governing bodies (J. Bauman, 2008).

Does sport psychology work? According to Thelwell (2008), at least three meta-analyses (meta-analysis is a statistical technique that involves summarizing and reviewing previous quantitative studies) have been conducted in order to evaluate the efficacy of psychological skills training (PST) interventions in sport. First, Greenspan and Feltz (1989) reviewed nineteen studies that assessed the effects of PST in competitive sport situations. The results revealed that such interventions were generally effective in over 80 per cent of these studies. Second, Vealey (1994) reported a figure of over 75 per cent effectiveness of PST following a similar review. Third, Weinberg and Comar (1994) showed that psychological skills training is effective for athletes in competitive settings. Since the mid-1990s, however, there have been no published quantitative reviews of the efficacy of PST in sport psychology.

Let us now consider the second type of applied professional services that sport psychologists tend to provide for their clients – namely, consultations in the fields of counselling and clinical psychology. Since 2000, there has been a growth of research interest in the personal problems (e.g., eating disorders, alcohol abuse, stress and **burnout**) that may afflict those involved in sport and exercise. Torstveit et al. (2008) found that clinical eating disorders were significantly more prevalent in elite female athletes in "leanness" sports (i.e., those in which a specific body shape and weight are important – such as gymnastics, diving, bodybuilding) than in "non-leanness" sports (such as most ball-sport team games). On a different note, a survey of professional soccer players in Britain for the BBC current affairs programme *Real Story* found that 46 per cent of them were aware of colleagues who used illegal recreational and/or performance-enhancing drugs on a regular basis (Jacob, 2003). Not surprisingly, such shocking findings have led to a call for the provision of medical and psychological services for athletes who suffer from drug and/or alcohol dependence problems. In a related vein, Samulski (2008) edited a special issue of the *International Journal of Sport and Exercise Psychology* on counselling Olympic athletes. This special issue examined theoretical and practical aspects of the counselling interventions provided for athletes from different countries at the Olympic Games.

Not surprisingly, appropriate formal postgraduate qualifications and a great deal of sensitivity are required by sport psychologists who offer counselling and/or clinical services because many athletes are afraid or embarrassed to seek professional help for personal problems. Typically, such performers fear the possibility of ridicule from their peers for seeking a consultation with a "shrink". Unfortunately, media coverage of sport psychology may serve only to exaggerate this problem due to the way in which this discipline is portrayed. For example, *The Times* (2002) reported that Graham Taylor (former manager of Aston Villa) called in "the shrinks" to offer psychological services to the players. In view of this caricature of the discipline, it is interesting to note that a scale has been developed by researchers to assess athletes' attitudes to seeking help from sport psychologists (see S. Martin et al., 2002).

Education

Many sport and exercise psychologists are involved in educational aspects of the discipline. This professional role usually involves teaching students, athletes, coaches and perhaps business people about the principles, methods and findings of sport psychology. Such educational services are extremely important. For example, in the absence of accurate and up-to-date information conveyed by sport psychology professionals, myths and false assumptions about the discipline can arise. At a more practical level, coaches and managers are usually eager to obtain advice from psychologists about practical strategies for forging **team spirit** in their players (see also Chapter 7). Finally, there is an increasing demand for the services of sport and exercise psychologists in translating certain mental skills displayed by top athletes (e.g., **goal-setting**, coping with pressure) into practical life skills for business people.

Research

Research in sport psychology is extremely important because it can provide evidence-based answers to a number of practical questions. For example, is there a link between the way in which athletes prepare mentally for a competition and how they perform in it subsequently? What are the greatest mental challenges of a particular sport? Do relaxation CDs really work for athletes? What is the most effective way of promoting the benefits of physical activity among a sample of sedentary young people?

So far, we have seen that the work of sport and exercise psychologists falls into three main categories. Nevertheless, as I explained earlier, these categories overlap considerably in practice. To illustrate, consider the types of professional services which sport psychologists provide at the Olympic Games (see Box 1.5).

Box 1.5 What do sport psychologists do at the Olympics? Insights from the front line

For most athletes, coaches and applied sport psychologists, the opportunity to participate in the Olympic Games is a highly cherished ambition. However, due to its global importance and unique competitive environment, the Olympics can overwhelm even the most experienced international athletes. In an effort to to help people to prepare optimally for such a pressure cauldron, several applied researchers (e.g., Hodge, 2010; Samulski, 2008) have analysed the type of services that sport psychologists are typically required to deliver at the Games. To begin with, Hodge (2010) explained that the most common athletic challenges that he addressed concerned stress management (e.g., arising from athletes living together in close proximity under cramped conditions in the Olympic Village), pre-event mental preparation (e.g., to maintain a focus on one's performance rather than on the possibility of winning a medal), "Games wobbles" (i.e., the tendency to radically change one's routine in response to the perceived pressure of the event), interpersonal conflict (e.g., with teammates, coaches, managers and other officials), psychological aspects of injury and illness, "second-week blues" (i.e., a tendency to become homesick after the first week of the competition), and unintentional distractions posed by family and friends. In dealing with these problems, the most important practical advice offered by Hodge (2010) was "be available, but don't get in the way!" Another fascinating account of psychology at the Olympic Games is available from a special issue of the *International Journal of Sport and Exercise Psychology* on the provision of sport psychology services at this event (Samulski, 2008). In this issue, McCann (2008) reflected on his experience of providing sport psychology services to US athletes at *seven* Olympic Games as part of the US Olympic Committee (USOC) Sport Psychology Department. The scale of this service provision is remarkable because the United States typically sends over 200 athletes to the Winter Olympics and over 500 to the Summer Olympics. Not surprisingly, give the significance of these Games, US Olympic athletes have sought help from McCann and his colleagues for a wide spectrum of difficulties. These problems include clinical issues (e.g., depression arising from a family bereavement), adjustment problems (e.g., financial difficulties, homesickness), interpersonal conflicts (e.g., with coaches, fellow athletes), countless distractions (e.g., dealing with the media) and various types of performance pressure (e.g., those arising from national expectations of success). In such circumstances, McCann (2008, p. 269) claims that "every issue, whether it is difficulty focusing in the starting gate, a conflict between coaches, or mourning a grandmother who died the day before, is a performance issue". Clearly, the ability to deal effectively with these problems involves a mixture of performance-enhancement and educational activities. In 2008, five sport psychologists from the USOC attended the 2008 Olympic Games in Beijing. Apart from this official group, a number of other US psychologists worked privately with teams from sports such as diving, taekwondo and rowing. A flavour of the philosophy underlying the work of these sport psychologists can be gleaned from the following quotations (Schwartz, 2008):

- Dr James Bauman (who worked with US athletes in swimming and track and field): "People now understand we're there to help them with their strengths".
- Dr Chris Carr (who worked with the US diving team): "My role is to help the divers focus on what they can control … their thoughts, their emotions and their preparation to dive at the their best each time".
- Dr Colleen Hacker (who worked with the US field hockey team): "I try to empower athletes to have the skills necessary to produce optimal performance at elite levels, to be at their best more often and to play at their best when it counts most".
- Dr Sean McCann (who worked with the US shooting and weightlifting teams): "It's my job to help them deal with what they can control".
- Dr Margaret Ottley (who worked with the US track and field team): "I support athletes' self-determination and drive to achieve their personal goals".
- Dr Marshall Mintz (who worked with the US men's and women's rowing teams): "My goal is to try to help the athletes to stay intensely focused and committed to the task at hand".

From these quotations, a common theme emerges – namely, the importance of helping athletes to focus only on what they can control. I'll return to this principle later, in Chapter 4.

In summary, this section shows that sport and exercise psychologists have multifaceted professional roles. Unfortunately, these roles cannot be performed adequately until an important question has been explored. Specifically, what model facilitates the optimal delivery of sport psychology services to athletes and coaches?

What is the best way to deliver sport psychology services to athletes and coaches?

Although discussion of the theoretical basis of service delivery may seem somewhat removed from the practical concerns of applied sport psychology, it has profound practical importance for the field. To explain, if sport psychologists work according to a traditional medical model, they will be expected to provide "quick fixes" and instant "cures" for athletes with problems in much the same way as physicians are expected to treat their patients through the prescription of suitable medication. What is wrong with this traditional medical model of service delivery and is there any alternative to it?

Unfortunately, there are at least three problems associated with a medical model of applied sport psychology (Kremer and Scully, 1998; Kremer and Moran, 2008a). First, it places the burden of responsibility on the "expert" psychologist to "cure" whatever problems are presented by the athlete or coach. This situation may encourage clients to depend excessively on their sport psychologist, thereby impeding their growth towards self-reliance. Interestingly, in a discussion of his service delivery philosophies, Gordin (2003) advocated the importance of empowering athletes when he remarked that

> it is my intent to put myself out of a job with a client. That is, a goal of mine is to make the client self-sufficient and independent. Once these athletes have achieved independence, then the relationship is appropriately terminated or altered.
>
> (Gordin, 2003, pp. 64–65)

A second problem with the medical model of intervention is that "expert" sport psychologists are often on shaky ground theoretically because many of the intervention techniques which they recommend have not been validated adequately. Third, the distinction between "expert" and "client" ignores the fact that sportspeople, including athletes and coaches, are naive psychologists in the sense that they have already developed informal theoretical intuitive psychological theories to account for the behaviour of their players (see Chapter 9 for information on the late Bill Shankly's attitude to injured soccer players). In these cases, such intuitive theories need to be deconstructed through discussion with sport psychologists before a client can be helped. Taken together, these three problems highlight the weaknesses of the traditional role of the medically oriented sport psychologist.

Fortunately, an alternative model has been proposed for the delivery of sport psychology services to athletes and coaches (see Kremer and Scully, 1998). This model identifies the *coach* rather than the athlete as the primary target for psychological education. Accordingly, the role of the sport psychologist changes from that of a medical expert to that of a management consultant – somebody who works as part of a team with the coach or manager and his or her support staff. Of course, this new model does not eliminate the need for individual consultation. There will always be situations which warrant "one-to-one" consultations between athletes and sport psychologists. However, the adoption of Kremer and Scully's (1998) model does change one feature of the client–psychologist relationship. Specifically, it challenges the myth that sport psychologists are "shrinks" or "mind benders" who can provide instant solutions for athletes whose problems have baffled their coaches. Evaluating the model that underlies one's services is not the only self-appraisal task faced by sport and exercise psychologists. Increasingly, in this era of accountability and evidence-based practice, there is a need for psychologists to *demonstrate* the efficacy of the professional services that they provide. How can a sport psychologist tackle this question? This issue is examined in Box 1.6.

Box 1.6 Thinking critically about ... evaluating the efficacy of sport psychology consultations

How can sport psychologists assess the efficacy of their professional work? At first glance, the answer to this question is simple. All they have to do is to evaluate their interventions and services empirically from time to time and publish the results accordingly. Unfortunately, for at least three reasons, this strategy has not proved popular in sport and exercise psychology. First, many practitioners are too busy to engage in evaluative activities. Second, until recently, few assessment tools were available for this purpose. Third, given certain inherent biases of the publication system, there is a danger that the only outcomes which sport psychologists might be willing to publish are *successful* ones. To illustrate, have you ever come across an article by a sport psychologist in which he or she revealed the complete *failure* of an intervention? Have you ever read a paper by a sport psychologist in which he or she referred to clients' failure to follow up on his or her advice? Given these problems, how can a sport psychologist evaluate his or her consultancy services? Anderson (2002) developed an instrument called the Assessment of Consultant Effectiveness (ACE) to help practitioners to assess the quality of their professional services. Briefly, this instrument asks clients to evaluate statements concerning "customer service" using a rating scale. Typical items include "The sport psychologist was a good listener" (item 5) or "The sport psychologist presented information in a clear and easy to understand way" (item 22).

Critical thinking questions
Is there any danger that clients may not tell the truth when answering this questionnaire? How can this problem be overcome? How could this instrument be validated? Can you think of any other ways of evaluating the efficacy of a sport psychologist's professional services?

In this section of the chapter, we have explored the type of work that sport psychologists do as well as issues concerning the optimal delivery of psychological services to athletes and coaches. Now it is time to examine the question of how one can qualify as a sport psychologist.

How can I qualify professionally as a sport psychologist?

Earlier in this chapter, I introduced sport and exercise psychology as a hybrid discipline with roots in both psychology and sport science. Given this dual-track disciplinary background, perhaps it is not surprising that there is no simple or universally agreed academic pathway to professional qualification in sport and exercise psychology at present. And so, the crucial question of who is certified to call themselves sport psychologists has been debated vigorously in such countries as Australia, Canada, the UK, and the United States. In most of these countries, there has been a disjunction between psychology associations and sport science organizations with regard to the issue of labelling and/or accrediting people as sport psychologists. For example, in the United States, anyone who receives a recognized doctoral degree in psychology qualifies for licensure (or statutory registration) as a "psychologist". Unfortunately, the American Psychological Association (APA) does not yet accredit programmes in *sport* psychology. Therefore, this organization accepts that a psychologist's decision to claim a professional specialization in sport psychology is a personal one which should be taken only in the light of full awareness of relevant APA ethical guidelines. For example, one of these guidelines stipulates that psychologists should work only within the boundaries of their competence. Working apart from the APA, sport science organizations have made important advances in accrediting sport psychology practitioners. For example, in the United States, the Association for Applied Sport Psychology (AASP) developed a certification procedure for sport psychology in 1989. People who satisfy the criteria stipulated by AASP are entitled to call themselves "Certified Consultant, AASP" – but not "Certified Sport Psychologist". This latter title is precluded because, as explained above, the term psychologist is protected by state licence in the United States. Similar certification processes have been established in Britain where the British Association of Sport and Exercise Sciences (BASES) has a psychology section. So, how can one qualify as a sport psychologist in Britain?

In Britain, at the time of writing, there are two main routes to professional practice as a chartered psychologist practising in sport psychology. The first route is through the British Psychological Society (BPS). Here, one must have a primary degree in psychology from a degree or conversion course that is approved by the BPS (i.e., a course that confers eligibility for "Graduate Basis for Chartered Membership", or GBC, previously known as "Graduate Basis for Registration" or GBR). Having obtained GBC, one needs to have achieved either a BPS accredited masters in sport and exercise psychology or Stage 1 of the BPS's qualification in sport and exercise psychology and then Stage 2 of this qualification (two years of relevant supervised practice). In order to use the title "sport and exercise psychologist", however, one will need to register with the Health Professionals Council (HPC). The second route to professional training in Britain is for people who do not have qualifications leading to GBC in psychology but who have either completed, or are in the process of completing, the accreditation procedure established by the British Association of Sport and Exercise Sciences. At the time of writing, to qualify as an accredited sport and exercise psychologist with BASES, one needs to have a primary degree in sport and exercise science (which includes subjects such as physiology and biomechanics), a master's degree in sport and exercise science/psychology and at least three years' supervision by a BASES accredited sport and exercise psychology practitioner. What is the difference between these routes? As I have indicated, the main difference between Chartered (BPS) and Accredited (BASES) sport psychologists concerns the nature of the undergraduate training received. Whereas psychology degrees provide undergraduates with a rich coverage of psychological fields and topics, they do not normally provide information on coaching techniques or on disciplines such as biomechanics. By contrast, whereas sport and exercise science degrees provide core modules in physiology and biomechanics, they do not normally cover a wide a variety of psychology modules. In the late 1990s, a European Master's Programme in Sport and Exercise Psychology was established as an interdisciplinary mobility course run by a consortium of twelve European universities. This programme is organized by the Fédération Européenne de Psychologie des Sport et des Activités Corporelles (FEPSAC), takes place over a minimum of one year of study and aims to educate highly qualified researchers and practitioners in the field of sport and exercise psychology (see FEPSAC website in Box 1.7 for further details). In summary, the issue of titles and certification in sport psychology is quite complex. But this complexity is not surprising, however, in view of the interdisciplinary foundations of sport and exercise psychology.

Where can I learn more about sport and exercise psychology?

If you would like to find out more about sport and exercise psychology using the internet, there are at least two options. First, you could subscribe to an electronic bulletin board devoted to sport and exercise psychology. At present, there are two such bulletin boards in the field: Division 47 of the American Psychological Association and "SportPsy". Division 47 of the APA has an email list for members (remember that to join APA Division 47, you must be a member or affiliate of the APA and also request affiliation to Division 47). The purpose of this list is to post issues, questions and findings concerning research in sport and exercise psychology as well as related professional practice issues in this field. In order to join this list, you should send an email message to: listserv@lists.apa.org

Leave the subject field blank and type <subscribe div47 your name> in the body of the text. When your application is approved, you may send messages to the list by using the following address: div47@lists.apa.org

The SportPsy list has well over 1,000 members and is maintained at Temple University. To join it, go to http://listserv.temple.edu/archives/sportpsy/html and select 'Join or leave the list' which will take you to a secure page or send a message to listserv@listserv.temple.edu with nothing in the subject heading and only the following in the text: SUB SPORTPSY [your name]

The second option is to consult the websites of some of the professional organizations listed in Box 1.7.

Box 1.7 Learning more about sport psychology: locating websites of professional organizations in the field

American Psychological Association – Division 47 (Exercise and Sport Psychology)
www.psyc.unt.edu/apadiv47/
Provides articles, information on the division, newsletter updates, membership news, book reviews and a conference calendar

Association for Applied Sport Psychology (AASP)
www.aaasponline.org/index2.html
Aims to promote the development of psychological theory, research and intervention strategies in sport and exercise psychology

British Association of Sport and Exercise Sciences (BASES)
www.bases.org.uk
Aims to develop and spread knowledge about the application of science to sport and exercise

British Psychological Society (Division of Sport and Exercise Psychology)
www.bps.org.uk/sub-syst/SPEX/about.cfm
Section aims to promote the development of psychology in sport and exercise through academic study and research

Fédération Européenne de Psychologie des Sports et des Activités Corporelles (FEPSAC; European Federation of Sport Psychology)
www.itp.lu.se/fepsac/
Aims to promote scientific, educational and professional work in sport psychology

International Society of Sport Psychology (ISSP)
www.phyed.duth.gr/sportpsy/international.html
Devoted to promoting research and development in the discipline of sport and exercise psychology

North American Society for Psychology of Sport and Physical Activity (NASPSPA)
www.naspspa.org/info/
An interdisciplinary association which aims to develop and advance the scientific study of human behaviour when individuals are engaged in sport and physical activity

To conclude this section, Martindale and Collins (2011) provide some good practical advice on how to get help in your search for a sport psychologist.

Current status of sport and exercise psychology: respect or scepticism?

Now that we have explored the scientific foundations and professional applications of sport and exercise psychology, let us consider its status as a discipline. At first glance, the field of sport and exercise psychology appears to be an intellectually challenging, vibrant and highly valued interdisciplinary enterprise. This conclusion is based on four strands of evidence.

First, since the 1970s, sport and exercise psychology has expanded its topical coverage as well as the range of populations at which its interventions have been aimed. To explain, whereas this discipline used to be concerned mainly with performance enhancement in sport performers, its scope has now enlarged to accommodate aspects of exercise and health in people of all ages – regardless of their athletic status. Second, the extent and quality of research in sport and exercise are indicated by the number of international peer-reviewed journals in this field: since 2007, five new international journals have been published in sport and exercise psychology. A selection of scholarly journals which contain the words "sport" and/ or "exercise" in their titles is presented in Box 1.8.

Box 1.8 Alphabetical list of selected journals in the field of sport and exercise psychology

International Journal of Sport and Exercise Psychology (the official publication of the International Society of Sport Psychology and published by Fitness Information Technology; first published in 1970 and renamed in 2003)

International Journal of Sport Psychology (published by Edizioni Luigi Pozzi, Italy; first published in 1970 and renamed in 2003)

International Review of Sport and Exercise Psychology (published by Routledge/Taylor & Francis; first published in 2008)

Journal of Applied Sport Psychology (published by the Association for Applied Sport Psychology (AASP); first published in 1989)

Journal of Clinical Sport Psychology (published by Human Kinetics; first published in 2007)

Journal of Sport and Exercise Psychology (published by the North American Society for the Psychology of Sport and Physical Activity (NASPSPA); first published in 1979)

Journal of Sport Behaviour (published by the United States Sports Academy; first published in 1978)

Journal of Sport Psychology in Action (published by Taylor & Francis; first published in 2010)

Journal of Sports Sciences (published by Taylor & Francis; first published in 1982)

Psychology of Sport and Exercise (published by Elsevier; first published in 2000)

Qualitative Research in Sport, Exercise and Health (published by Routledge; first published in 2009)

Research Quarterly for Exercise and Sport (published by American Alliance for Health, Physical Education, Recreation and Dance; first published in 1930)

Sport, Exercise, and Performance Psychology (published by the American Psychological Association; first published in 2012)

The Sport Psychologist (published by the International Society of Sport Psychology; first published in 1987)

The third reason for attributing a healthy status to the field of sport and exercise psychology comes from the formal recognition of this discipline by mainstream psychology. In particular, as indicated earlier in Box 1.3, professional psychological associations in the United States (in 1986), Australia (in 1991) and Britain (in 2004) have established special divisions or sections to cater for the needs of members who are interested in the application of psychology to sport and exercise settings. Fourth, the practical value of sport psychology is evident from the increasing number of performers and coaches around the world who are using its services – mainly for performance enhancement. For example, among the top athletes who have publicly acknowledged the help of sport psychologists are major golf championship winners such as Pádraig Harrington and Trevor Immelman. But it is not just individual athletes who have emerged as enthusiastic advocates of sport psychology. Many countries competing at the Olympic Games employ sport psychologists as advisers (see Box 1.5 above) as do teams in soccer (e.g., Arsenal: King and Ridley, 2006), baseball (Seppa, 1996), cricket (e.g., the Australian squad: see Wilde, 1998) and rugby (e.g., the Irish national team: see Thornley, 1997). In summary, the preceding strands of evidence suggest that sport and exercise psychology is now firmly established as a scientifically respectable and useful discipline. Unfortunately, this conclusion has been challenged by critics both from within and outside the discipline. Let us now consider briefly the nature and validity of their counter-arguments.

Within the discipline, Dishman (1983) argued that sport psychology is deeply flawed due to a combination of shaky theoretical foundations and unreliable intervention strategies. These sentiments were echoed by Morgan (1997) who bemoaned the absence of scientific evidence to support many of the intervention techniques promulgated by practitioners in this field. A similar point was made by Moran (1996) who noted that few concentration skills training programmes in applied sport psychology have been subjected to either conceptual or empirical evaluation. Augmenting these criticisms of theory and research in sport psychology are accounts of practitioners' disenchantment with the professional side of this discipline. For example, consider Meyers' (1997) candid account of his experiences as an "on site" sport psychologist at the US Olympic Festival. Working in this situation, he noted that although there was a clear demand for sport psychological services, "there exists little respect for what we do" (Meyers, 1997, p. 466).

As indicated earlier in our analysis of the work of Hoberman (1992), criticisms have also been levelled at sport psychology from sceptical athletes and journalists. For example, Goran Ivanisevic, the former Wimbledon champion, dismissed the value of sport psychologists by saying that "You lie on a couch, they take your money, and you walk out more bananas than when you walk in" (cited in LeUnes and Nation, 2002, p. 18; see also Figure 1.3). Likewise, Sergio Garcia, the Spanish golfer who has been ranked consistently among the top ten players in the world, claimed that, with reference to sport psychology, "I've never been a big believer in it and you can't try to do something if you don't believe in it" (cited in Corrigan, 2007). For some journalists, golf psychologists are especially irksome. Thus Paul Mahoney (2007) proclaimed that they are "the latest gurus to milk millions of pounds by teaching mantras of the bleeding [sic] obvious to golfers short on confidence and the ability to think for themselves". Similar scepticism of the value of sport psychology

Figure 1.3 It is a myth that sport psychologists are "shrinks"

is evident in professional football in England. For example, in 1997, a survey of forty-four football clubs was conducted by the BBC Radio 5 Live documentary team *On The Line*. Results showed that three-quarters of the clubs questioned either had never used, or would not ever consider using, a sport psychologist (see Bent et al., 2000). These clubs justified this decision by claiming that their own coaching staff, who are usually former professional players, knew best how to deal with the psychological needs of their footballers. Fortunately for psychology, Sven-Göran Eriksson, the former England team manager, did not share this view and emphasized the importance of recruiting sport psychologists to deal with the mental side of football. Thus he suggested that "if we go into the heads of players we need a specialist to do it, but I believe that this is the future of the game" (cited in Every, 2002, p. 1). For a fascinating account of the work of sport psychologists in professional football, see Nesti (2010).

What is the origin of this scepticism of sport psychology among athletes, coaches and journalists? One possibility is that it stems from a popular myth – the misidentification of psychology with psychiatry. Unfortunately, headlines that refer to managers who consult "shrinks" promulgate two potentially damaging ideas about sport psychology. First, by using the word "shrinks" (which is a popular slang abbreviation of the term "head shrinkers"), the headline suggests that sport psychologists are *psychiatrists*. Second, it implies that they are consulted or called in only when there is a problem to be solved. It is worth noting that this view of sport psychology as a branch of psychiatry is based on the medical model that we explored in the previous section of this chapter. Perhaps it is this myth that players are "patients" who need to be "shrunk" by medical specialists that lies at the heart of certain athletes', coaches' and journalists' scepticism of sport psychology (see also an article on this issue by Gee, 2010). Unfortunately, as Box 1.9 shows, this discipline has also been associated in the popular mind with spoon bending and faith healing. In the light of this caricature of sport psychology as portrayed by some media, is it any wonder that Graham Taylor was pilloried in certain quarters for using a psychologist with the England team in the European Championships in 1992 (G. Taylor, 2002)?

Box 1.9 Thinking critically about ... sport psychology, plasticine and faith healing

Advice on sport psychology has not always received a universal welcome from the athletic community – especially in British soccer. To illustrate, Dickinson (2007) and Simon Hartley (7 January 2011, personal communication) described what happened when Howard Wilkinson, who was manager of Sunderland in the 2002–2003 season of the Premier League, hired a management consultancy firm to provide some **team-building** strategies to improve the club's fortunes. In one of the management consultants' first sessions with the squad, they allegedly gave the players some plasticine with which to make a shape that reflected their perceived role in the team. When the "shrink" (Dickinson's term) examined what the players had produced, he found "five pairs of breasts, 14 phalluses and one group who had clubbed together to build a substitutes' bench!" Sadly, but not too surprisingly, Sunderland were relegated that year. A few years earlier, Glenn Hoddle, who was then manager of the England national soccer team, appointed a faith-healer named Eileen Drewery to his backroom staff. One of the reasons which Hoddle gave in justification for this decision was that Drewery "is a bit of a psychologist because she puts your mind at ease when she talks to you" (cited in Thorp, 1998).

Critical thinking questions
Do you think that the public image of sport psychology is affected by incidents such as the ones described above? What are the similarities and differences between faith healing and applied sport psychology? If putting "your mind at ease" is all that footballers require in order to play well, does it matter whether or not a technique that achieves this purpose is accepted as "scientific"? How can sport psychologists change the popular image of their profession? List two or three practical strategies to address this issue.

Fortunately, in spite of the myths surrounding the discipline and the negative publicity engendered by the events described in Box 1.9, sport psychology has begun to make inroads into the world of professional football in Britain since the late 1990s. This upsurge of interest in psychology has been caused by three key changes in the sport.

First, improvements in the standard of coach education programmes have led to increased acceptance of the role that sport science (including psychology) plays in professional football. Put simply, if clubs are willing to accept the principle that regular physiological testing is a good way of maintaining physical fitness among players, then they should also accept the notion that footballers' mental fitness can be facilitated by advice from sport psychologists. Second, there has been an influx of foreign coaches and players into British football since 1990, when Dr Jozef Vengloš was appointed manager of a top-flight club, Aston Villa. These people have introduced indigenous players to the benefits of such sport scientific practices as "warming down" after games, adhering to a balanced diet, and preparing mentally for matches (L. Dixon, 2002). Third, and perhaps most importantly, the fact that successful coaches such as Sven-Göran Eriksson and Alex Ferguson have employed sport psychologists (H. Winter, 2002) has influenced other coaches to copy them. Mindful of these three developments, the Football Association in England launched a campaign to encourage football clubs in Britain to recruit more sport psychologists (H. Winter, 2002). In summary, available evidence suggests that sport psychology in football is expanding not "shrinking" (Moran, 2002b).

To summarize this section, in spite of its struggle against certain persistent criticisms and misconceptions, sport and exercise psychology is making encouraging progress in establishing itself as a respected discipline. Of course, this conclusion must be tempered by awareness of at least two unresolved issues in the field. First, it is essential for the long-term viability of sport and exercise psychology that professional psychological organizations such as the American Psychological Association and the British Psychological Society should develop accreditation criteria for postgraduate training courses in this field. Second, in an effort to safeguard the public against the possibility of malpractice, professional issues concerning titles and certification need to be addressed urgently. For a more extensive discussion of ethical issues in applied sport and exercise psychology, see Hankes (in press), Kremer et al. (2012), Oliver (2010) and Stapleton et al. (2010).

An idea for a research project on sport psychology

Here is an idea for a possible research project on the psychological aspects of sport. Its objectives are:

1   to find out what athletes mean by "mental preparation"
2   to establish how important it is to them
3   to estimate what proportion of their training time they devote to it on average.

To conduct this project, you will need a digital voice recorder and some volunteer athletes. Find three people who play different types of sports (e.g., a team game, an individual game) who have been actively involved in competitive performance for at least five years. Request their permission to record your interview with them on the voice recorder. Then, ask them the following questions:

•   What does the term "mental preparation" mean to you?
•   On a scale of 0 (meaning "not at all important") to 5 (meaning "extremely important"), how important do you think that proper mental preparation is for successful performance in your sport?
•   What sort of things do you do as physical training for your sport?

- What sort of things, if any, do you do as mental preparation for your sport?
- About what percentage of your training time do you devote to physical preparation? Give a rough percentage figure.
- And to mental preparation? Give an approximate percentage figure, please.

Compare and contrast the athletes' answers to your questions. You will probably discover that although these people think that mental preparation is important for optimal performance, they devote relatively little time to it. If this finding emerges, how do you interpret it? If not, what did the athletes say? Did the type of sport make a difference to the athletes' views?

Summary

- Sport and exercise psychology is both a science and a profession in which the principles and methods of psychology are applied in sport and exercise settings.
- The second section investigated the nature and determinants of the mental side of sport as well as the related constructs of confidence and mental toughness in athletes.
- The third section outlined the nature, history and research methods of the discipline of sport and exercise psychology.
- The fourth section explored professional aspects of this field. Included here was a discussion of four key questions:

  1   What type of work do sport psychologists actually do?
  2   What is the best way to deliver sport psychology services to athletes and coaches?
  3   How can I qualify professionally as a sport psychologist?
  4   Where can I learn more about sport and exercise psychology?

- The fifth section provided a brief evaluation of the current status of sport and exercise psychology. This section addressed this question by assessing both the scientific standing of this discipline as well as people's perception of it.
- Finally, the chapter provided a practical suggestion for a research project on the mental side of sport.

EXPLORING ATHLETIC PERFORMANCE: KEY CONSTRUCTS

Overview

Part one of the book examined the nature of the discipline and profession of sport and exercise psychology. Part two investigates the various psychological processes that affect individual athletes in their pursuit of excellence. Chapter 2 explores the psychology of motivation in athletes. Chapter 3 examines anxiety in sport performers. Chapter 4 addresses the topic of concentration. Chapter 5 tackles imagery processes in athletes. Chapter 6 addresses the question of what determines expertise in sport.

Motivation and goal-setting in sport

The biggest difficulty you have in this job is not to motivate the players but to get them relaxed enough to express their talent.

(Arsène Wenger, Arsenal manager, cited in Fanning, 2004a, p. 5)

Introduction

Motivation plays a crucial if somewhat misunderstood role in exercise and sport. For example, a high degree of motivation is required to maintain involvement in physical activity programmes – a fact which explains why so many people drop out of exercise classes (I consider this problem in more detail in Chapter 8). Similarly, in sport, the role of motivation is *crucial* in the sense that athletic success depends significantly on the willingness of sports performers to exert mental as well as physical effort in pursuit of excellence (see also Chapter 6). In this regard, José Mourinho, manager of Real Madrid and one of the most successful coaches in world football, claimed that "motivation is the most important thing. Some of them can and they don't want [to], some of them want and they can't. We want players who can do it and at the same time *want* to do it" (cited in Honigsbaum, 2004, p. 18; italics mine). Delving deeper into this idea, Alex Ferguson (Manchester United), another extraordinarily successful coach, revealed that athletes' motivation can be influenced by managers – once they understand how players differ from each other. Specifically, he said:

> footballers are all different human beings. Some are self-motivators, they need to be left alone … For some, you need causes, your country, them and us, your religion. And those causes can be created by the manager … at Manchester United, we have to be better than everyone else.
>
> (cited in White, 1999)

Despite these valuable insights, the contribution of motivation to optimal performance in sport is widely misunderstood. For example, as Glyn Roberts (2001) pointed out, motivation is often confused with being "psyched up" (see also Chapter 3) – a view that Arsène Wenger shares (see Figure 2.1). In this regard, consider the importance attached by Teddy Sheringham (the former Manchester United and England striker) to a rousing team talk that Alex Ferguson had delivered to Manchester United before their (last-minute) victory over Bayern Munich in the 1999 European Cup final:

> The manager gave us a great speech. He told us that if we lost, "you'll have to go up and get our losers' medals and you will be just six feet away from the European Cup but you won't be able to touch it. And for many of you that will be the closest you will ever get. Don't you dare come back in here without giving your all."
>
> (cited in Thorp, 1999)

Contrary to Sheringham's experience, however, there is little research evidence that "psyching up" athletes by emphasizing the disastrous consequences of failure is an effective ploy. Indeed, if anything, such a strategy may prove counterproductive because high levels of **arousal** are known to impair athletes' performance (Gee, 2010) and concentration skills (see Chapter 4). To illustrate, Webster (1984) reported that due to the effects of excessive anxiety, *not one* member of an Australian Rules

Figure 2.1 Arsène Wenger believes that footballers perform best when they are relaxed
Source: Courtesy of Inpho photography

football team could recall any of the coach's instructions in a vital game just *five minutes* after his rousing pre-match address! Interestingly, as the quote at the beginning of the chapter shows, Arsène Wenger, who is not only the most successful manager in the history of Arsenal football club but also the first person to guide his team through an entire season without defeat, observed that his role was not to motivate players, but to help them to relax on the pitch. And this brings us to the question of motivation through fear. This issue was highlighted sharply by reports that Iraqi footballers were regularly beaten and tortured in the early 1990s for losing matches under the regime of Uday Hussein, son of Saddam Hussein (Goldenberg, 2003) – a brutal practice which did nothing to enhance team morale or performance. But anecdotal reports suggest that some athletes use fear to motivate themselves. For example, Pádraig Harrington, three times a golf major winner, admitted that

> fear has always been a motivating factor in my golf … This is my 12th year on Tour and certainly for eight or nine years, every time I took my winter break, I was very anxious I would come out and it would still be there … Yes, fear is a big part of me.
>
> (Pádraig Harrington, cited in *Irish Times*, 2008)

By contrast, Arsène Wenger claims that the fear is incompatible with peak performance. Specifically, he said that "fear is the best way *not* to achieve what you want to achieve" (cited in J. Jackson, 2010; italics mine). In general, empirical research supports Wenger's position because a strong fear of failure is associated with psychological problems such as anxiety, depression and withdrawal from sport, especially among young athletes (Sagar et al., 2007). Given this background of confusion and inconsistency about the role of motivational factors in sport and exercise, this chapter attempts to answer the following questions. What exactly does the term "motivation" mean? What types of motivation have been identified? What theoretical approaches have been used to explore this construct? How can athletes increase their motivation? Finally, what factors motivate people to participate in dangerous sports? In order to address these issues, the chapter is organized as follows.

The nature and types of motivation in athletes are considered in the next section. The third section of the chapter presents a brief overview of theoretical approaches to this construct in sport psychology. Special consideration will be given here to two influential cognitive models of motivational processes in athletes – **achievement goal theory** and **attribution theory**. The fourth section explores the theory and practice of increasing motivation in athletes through goal-setting techniques. The fifth section examines a motivational question that has attracted popular debate: why do some people take part in risky activities in sport and exercise settings? In the final section of the chapter, I provide some practical suggestions for possible research projects in the psychology of motivation.

Nature and types of motivation

The term motivation refers to "the direction and intensity of one's effort" (Weinberg, 2009, p. 7). It is derived from the Latin word *movere* (meaning "to move": Onions, 1996) and is concerned with those factors that energize, direct and regulate achievement behaviour. Within sport and exercise psychology, motivational issues are implicated whenever "a person undertakes a task at which he or she is evaluated or enters into competition with others, or attempts to attain some standard of excellence" (G. Roberts, 2001, p. 6). Unfortunately, as I have suggested already, the term motivation is plagued by a great deal of conceptual confusion. Box 2.1 presents some persistent myths surrounding this construct.

Box 2.1 Thinking critically about ... popular understanding of "motivation"

According to Roberts and Kristiansen (2010), motivation is widely misunderstood. In particular, three myths about it need to be addressed. First, motivation is often confused with arousal. But athletes cannot be motivated simply by "psyching" them up into a frenzy of adrenaline. If anything, arousal needs to be *channelled* in a specific direction for effective motivation to occur (see also Chapter 3). The second myth about motivation is that it can be enhanced through positive thinking. For example, it may be assumed that if athletes can be encouraged to imagine themselves holding up the winner's trophy, their motivation will be strengthened. Unfortunately, research on goal-setting (see later in this chapter) shows that people's objectives have to be controllable and realistic to be effective. In the third myth, some coaches believe that motivation is a genetically inherited characteristic – something that one either has or has not got. Again, this view is contradicted by research evidence which shows that motivation can be changed through appropriate instruction (see later in chapter). Given these popular misconceptions, is it any wonder that sport psychologists have to be careful when using the term motivation? As Glyn Roberts warned in 2001, "it is defined so broadly by some that it incorporates the whole field of psychology, so narrowly by others that it is almost useless as an organising construct" (G. Roberts, 2001, p. 3).

Critical thinking questions
Do you agree with Roberts and Kistiansen (2010) that motivation is widely misunderstood in sport? Why do you think that many people mistake a heightened state of arousal for motivation? Are there any distinctive behavioural signs or expressions of motivation? How would you design a study to explore athletes' understanding of motivation? Does the myth of motivation extend to people's understanding of the work that sport psychologists engage in with their clients? Why do many people mistakenly believe that sport psychology is mainly about motivating athletes to perform well?

In the light of the confusion surrounding motivational processes in sport, how should we approach this construct scientifically? Traditionally, sport psychologists have distinguished between two different types of motivation – intrinsic and extrinsic (see review by Vallerand and Rousseau, 2001). **Intrinsic motivation** refers to people's impetus to perform an activity for its own sake – "for itself and the pleasure and satisfaction derived from participation" (Vallerand and Rousseau, 2001, p. 390). For example, many people love walking or running simply because it gives them feelings of fun and freedom and also because it enhances their subjective sense of well-being. Anecdotally, it is precisely this sense of intrinsic joy or satisfaction which seems to characterize the motivation of top athletes in sports like swimming, golf and cricket. Thus consider the importance which the Australian Olympic gold medal winning swimmer Kieren Perkins attached to intrinsic influences in his sport when he said: "I always *race against myself to improve my own performances*. The fact that I sometimes set world records in the process is a bonus. My personal best performance is the goal, not necessarily the world record" (Clews and Gross, 1995, pp. 98–99; italics mine). A similar emphasis on intrinsic satisfaction is evident in the approach of Phil Taylor, fifteen times world champion darts player. He said: "I love everything about my job – getting up every morning, practising and dedicating myself;. I always try to better myself … There's always that 1 per cent that I can improve" (cited in P. Newman, 2010, p. 12). Yet another example of intrinsic motivation comes from Derval O'Rourke, a twice European silver medalist in the 100 metre hurdles, who said after her second success in the 2010 European Athletics Championship in Barcelona, "I run for myself … I don't feel any pressure from anyone else" (cited in O'Riordan, 2010, p. 7). Finally, the Indian cricket star Sachin Tendulkar, who inspired India to victory in the 2011 World Cup and who is the world's leading run scorer in test cricket, claimed that "I don't set myself any targets. I just concentrate on trying to bat well … When I was a kid, I played cricket because I loved it and I still love it now" (Funday Times, 2002). An in-depth study of the motivational processes of elite track-and-field athletes (those who had finished in the top ten at either the Olympic Games or the world championships) supported these anecdotal insights. Mallett and Hanrahan (2003) interviewed these athletes in an effort to identify the factors which sustained their motivation to compete at the highest level. Results showed that these athletes were driven mainly by personal goals and achievements rather than by financial incentives. Nevertheless, the ego-oriented goal of defeating others remains a powerful source of motivation for many athletes. For example, former rower Sam Lynch, who successfully defended his lightweight single sculls title at the World Rowing Championships in 2002, said afterwards, "I was aware that the conditions were fast but the title always comes first. You don't go for a world record in a race like this. It may come but *winning the title comes first*" (cited in R. Jones, 2002; italics mine). Interestingly (according to M. Martens and Webber, 2002), intrinsic motivation is associated with increased enjoyment of an activity, stronger sportspersonship (see also Chapter 7) and a reduced likelihood of dropping out from sport.

Extrinsic motivation applies whenever a person is involved in a task largely as a result of external factors or constraints. This term refers to "engaging in an activity as a means to an end and not for its own sake" (Vallerand and Rousseau, 2001, p. 391). Typical extrinsic factors held to motivate athletes include money, trophies, praise and/or other forms of social approval from others. For example, golfers would be regarded as extrinsically motivated if they joined a golf club because they wanted to make new business contacts – not because they actually enjoyed the game of golf. In summary, extrinsic motivators are factors which influence a person to do something either because they provide a reward for such behaviour or because they provide some punishment or sanction for *not* doing it. In general, research shows that extrinsic motivation is associated with increased anxiety in, and increased likelihood of dropping out from, sporting activities (see M. Martens and Webber, 2002). More recently, researchers have explored children's reasons either for taking part in or for dropping out from organized sport. For example, C. Foster et al. (2007) discovered that extrinsic factors such as gender and cultural stereotyping of certain sports, the costs of participation in organized activities and increasing emphasis on technical and performance issues rather than on having fun were cited as facilitating variables for children under 8 years old. By contrast, the "turn ons" for these children were enjoyment of the activities and parental and peer support. Perhaps not surprisingly, feelings of burnout (i.e., a syndrome characterized by withdrawal from one's sport and overriding sense of physical and psychological exhaustion; see Goodger et al., 2010; Gustafsson et al., 2011) in elite athletes are often associated with an extrinsic motivational orientation (Lemyre et al., 2006).

Theoretically, intrinsic and extrinsic motivation can be differentiated on at least three criteria (Vallerand and Fortier, 1998). First, consider the purpose of the activity. As indicated earlier, whereas intrinsically motivated activities are under-taken for their own sake, extrinsically motivated tasks are typically conducted for some perceived instrumental benefit. Second, although people who are intrinsically motivated tend to seek experiential rewards, those who are extrinsically motivated tend to be influenced more by social and/or objective rewards (e.g., money). Third, Vallerand and Fortier (1998) proposed that intrinsically motivated performers tend to experience less pressure than extrinsically motivated counterparts when competing because the former people are largely concerned with the experience of participation itself.

Despite these theoretical distinctions, intrinsic and extrinsic motivation often overlap in real life. Indeed, as Box 2.2 shows, extrinsic rewards can affect intrinsic motivation under certain circumstances.

Box 2.2 Thinking critically about … how rewards can change people's motivation

The National Coaching Foundation (1996) presented an apocryphal tale which has a long history in psychology (e.g., see another version of this story in Myers et al., 2010, p. 172). This story portrays the principle that the withdrawal of rewards can change people's motivation in surprising ways.

An old man was plagued by teenagers playing football and making noise on the street outside his house. No matter what he said to them, they ignored him. In fact, the more he pleaded with them to stop, the more they persisted and the more obnoxiously they behaved. He was at his wits' end. Then one day, following a chat with a psychologist friend, he decided to try a new approach to the problem. Briefly, instead of scolding the boys, he decided to give them a *reward* (two euros each) for playing noisily outside his house. Of course, the boys were delighted with this decision. Imagine getting paid for doing something which they really enjoyed – making the old man's life miserable! When the boys returned the following evening, they received the same reward again – another two euros each. This practice puzzled the boys but they continued to wreak havoc on the old man. After a week, however, the man told them that he could not afford to pay each of them the two euros that they had been given previously. In fact, all he could manage was fifty cents each. This disappointed the boys a little but they continued to torment the man. Another week elapsed and this time, the old man reduced the reward to twenty cents each. Again, this was very frustrating to the boys who had grown used to receiving a larger reward. Eventually, the old man reduced the reward to two cents each – at which time, the leader of the boys grew very angry. Shouting at the old man, he said, "We've had enough of your meanness. If you think that we're going to play football for your entertainment outside your house for two cents, then you've got another think coming! We're off!" Clearly, the moral of this tale is that when the old man removed extrinsic motivation for the football, the boys lost interest in doing what they had done previously for nothing.

Critical thinking questions
Do you think that this story has any relevance for understanding why highly paid sports performers sometimes lose their motivation? From your knowledge

---

of other areas of psychology (e.g., behaviour modification), can you think of any other explanation of the boys' loss of motivation? Can cognitive evaluation theory (see text for description) offer any insights into what happened in this story?

As you can see from Box 2.2, if people who are performing an activity for the sheer fun of it are given external rewards, their level of intrinsic motivation may decrease (Deci, 1971). Interestingly, there is evidence that athletes who engage in sporting activity to receive a trophy tend to show a subsequent decrease in intrinsic motivation as measured by self-report scales (Vallerand and Rousseau, 2001). In an effort to explain this somewhat surprising finding, **cognitive evaluation theory** (Deci and Ryan, 1991) suggested that the way in which rewards are perceived must be considered. Briefly, this theory assumes that rewards can fulfil one of two functions: *controlling* (i.e., those which influence behaviour) or *informational* (i.e., those which provide feedback about the performer's level of performance on a given task). Depending on how athletes perceive rewards, their intrinsic motivation may be either enhanced or reduced. For example, if they believe that their sporting behaviour is controlled by external rewards, their level of intrinsic motivation may decline. However, if rewards are perceived as merely providing feedback, intrinsic motivation will probably increase. According to cognitive evaluation theory, controlling rewards tend to impair intrinsic motivation whereas informational rewards may strengthen it. Before we conclude this section, it is important to consider the relationship between praise (which we can define as communicating a positive evaluation of another person's performance or attributes to him or her) and motivation. It has long been assumed that praise enhances children's motivation. But is this really true? In a critique of this claim, Henderlong and Lepper (2002) argued that when praise is perceived as being sincere, it is beneficial to motivation as long as it conveys attainable standards and expectations and encourages people to make **attributions** (see later in chapter) to controllable causes. Interestingly, praise may inadvertently undermine children's motivation – perhaps because it encourages invidious social comparison processes.

Theories of motivation: from personality to cognition

Having considered the nature and types of motivation, let us now review the main theoretical approaches to this construct in sport and exercise psychology. Historically, two major theoretical approaches have dominated research on motivational processes in sport and exercise since the 1960s – the personality model (epitomized by research on individual differences in people's need for achievement) and two social-cognitive models (including the goal-orientation approach and attribution theory). Perhaps the most important difference between these two approaches is that whereas personality theorists view people as being driven by deep-seated psychological needs, social-cognitive researchers are more concerned with understanding how people's thoughts and perceptions guide their behaviour. Another difference between these approaches is that whereas personality theorists are concerned mainly with the origins of people's achievement strivings (i.e., the past determinants of their needs), cognitive motivational researchers are more interested in people's choice of future actions (G. Roberts, 2001). The theoretical rationale of each of these approaches is reviewed in more detail below.

The personality approach

Initially, sport psychologists tried to account for athletes' motivational processes by referring to two types of variables – innate instincts and learned drives. Superficially, such theories seem plausible. For example, aggressive behaviour on the football field is commonly attributed to the possession of an aggressive nature. But on closer inspection, this approach is flawed by the circularity of the reasoning involved. The difficulty here is that any scientific explanation for a phenomenon must be independent of the phenomenon itself. Otherwise, one unknown variable is used to "explain" another. This problem of proposing circular explanations for people's behaviour has a long history and was satirized by Molière in *La Malade Imaginaire* when he made fun of doctors who had suggested that what gives opium its soporific quality is its *virtus dormitiva* – or soporific quality! In a similar vein, aggressive actions cannot be explained adequately by appealing to hypothetical aggressive instincts, because the existence of these instincts depends on evidence of aggressive behaviour. On logical grounds, therefore, instinct theories of motivation have been discredited significantly in psychology.

Following the demise of instinct theory, sport psychologists turned to *personality traits* in an effort to account for motivational phenomena. One trait of particular interest was a construct called "need for achievement" (see McClelland et al., 1953). Briefly, this trait was believed to be elicited by situations involving approach-avoidance conflicts. In such situations, people face a dilemma in which their natural desire to achieve success (i.e., their "need to achieve") is challenged by their fear of failure. Theoretically, athletes were said to have a relatively high level of **achievement motivation** if their need to achieve was greater than their fear of failure. Conversely, they were alleged to have a relatively low level of achievement motivation when their fear of failure exceeded their desire to succeed. According to McClelland et al. (1953), people with high achievement needs are impelled to seek challenging but realistic objectives for their performance in competitive settings. Applied to sport, this principle suggests that athletes who have a high need to achieve should prefer to compete against opponents of a similar, or slightly higher, level of ability. By contrast, athletes with low achievement motivation tend to avoid challenging situations and should prefer to compete against opponents of lower ability levels. Despite its intuitive appeal, this theory has made little progress in accounting for the motivational behaviour of sport performers. This situation is attributable to two main problems. First, there is a dearth of valid instruments available for the measurement of achievement motivation in athletes (G. Roberts et al., 1999). Second, researchers have criticized the assumption in traditional achievement motivation theory that success and failure may be defined objectively. Thus Maehr and Nicholls (1980) argued that these variables are largely subjective because they are usually defined in relation to people's *perception* of goal achievement. For example, whereas some athletes may regard "success" as being defined by defeating an opponent or winning a competition, others may perceive it in relation to achieving a "personal best" performance or impressing their coach or parents (I shall return to this point in the next section).

Recognition of this subjective influence on people's achievement strivings influenced researchers to switch from a personality-based to a social-cognitive approach in the study of motivation in athletes. This change in emphasis had important theoretical implications for sport psychology. As Kremer et al. (2003, p. 188) observed, it "switched attention from the 'what' or content of motivation to the 'why' or process whereby we are or are not motivated". Within the social-cognitive **paradigm** of motivation research, two conceptual models deserve special mention: achievement goal theory and attribution theory. Let us now examine each of these approaches briefly.

The social-cognitive approach: achievement goal theory

Achievement goal theory (J. Nicholls, 1984) was developed in an effort to understand students' adaptive and maladaptive responses to achievement challenges. Two main types of goals were identified: **mastery goals** (which focus mainly on acquiring competence in a given skill) and **performance goals** (which emphasize instead the importance of demonstrating one's competence by performing better than others). For an excellent critique of the history and current status of this theory, see Senko et al. (2011).

Applied to sport and exercise psychology, this approach is also known as "goal orientation theory" (see reviews by Harwood et al., 2008; G. Roberts et al. 2007) and is concerned mainly with how people perceive and define successful achievement. The cornerstone of this theoretical approach to motivation in sport is the assumption that athletes' behaviour in competitive situations is a consequence of their perception of "success". More precisely, this approach suggests that in order to understand athletes' motivation, we need to explore what success *means* to them. Put differently, whether athletes consider a given outcome as a success or failure depends on how they define "success" and "failure" initially (Weinberg, 2009). Arising from this fundamental assumption, Maehr and Nicholls (1980, p. 228) proposed that success and failure "are not concrete events. They are psychological states consequent on perception of reaching or not reaching goals".

Achievement goal theory postulates that two main types of motivation (or goal orientations) may be identified in athletes depending on how they interpret the goal of their achievements (or success) – task motivation (also known as mastery motivation) and ego motivation (also known as competitive orientation). Task-motivated athletes are interested mainly in subjective indices of success such as skill-learning, tactical development, mastery of challenges and technical self-improvement. For example, task-oriented athletes may perceive themselves to be successful if they can perform a specific sport skill (e.g., serving a tennis ball) better today than they did three weeks ago. By contrast, ego-motivated athletes tend to view "success" normatively, through comparison with the attainments of other people. For example, ego-oriented athletes regard themselves as successful only if they perform better than others, regardless of any personal improvements in performance that they may have achieved. By defeating others, they believe, they have demonstrated superior ability to rival athletes. Therefore, winning and beating others are the main preoccupations of ego-oriented athletes. Originally, these two goal orientations were assumed to be "orthogonal" or independent (J. Nicholls, 1989). In other words, a person may achieve a high or a low score on either goal orientation or on both at the same time. More recently, however, this assumption has been challenged. Harwood et al. (2008) proposed that athletes cannot be task-oriented and ego-oriented at the same time. However, as Kremer et al. (2012) noted, there is evidence that many elite athletes regard an ego-orientation as complementary, rather than inimical, to a **task orientation**. To complicate matters further, Elliott and Conroy (2005) proposed that as well as investigating the distinction between task-orientation and ego-orientation, we need to explore whether athletes are motivated by approach (striving to be competent) or avoidance (fear of being seen to be incompetent) motives. More precisely, they postulated that achievement targets that are motivated by a desire to meet a specific challenge (approach goals) are likely to encourage persistence whereas targets that are motivated by a desire not to fail (avoidance goals) are unlikely to sustain commitment. Based on Elliott and Conroy's (2005) theory, we can distinguish between four different achievement goals:

- *mastery approach* (i.e., striving to learn or improve skills: "I want to learn as much as possible from this group coaching session")
- *mastery avoidance* (i.e., striving to avoid learning failures or a decline in skills: e.g., "I'm concerned that I may not learn what I need to learn in this session")
- *performance approach* (i.e., striving to perform better than others: e.g., "It's important for me to do better than the other students in this session")
- *performance avoidance* (i.e., striving to avoid doing worse than others e.g., "My priority in this session is to avoid performing poorly").

There is increasing evidence (e.g., see C. Wang et al., 2007) that the addition of this new approach–avoidance dimension strengthens achievement goal theory in sport and exercise psychology.

Returning to the original distinction between task-motivation and ego-motivation, what does research reveal about the correlates of these two motives? According to Lemyre et al. (2002), task-oriented athletes perceive achievement in sport in self-referenced terms involving skill improvement/mastery and technical development. As a consequence, they tend to be intrinsically interested in the task, willing to expend effort in persisting with it and, above all, guided by personal standards of achievement rather than by prevailing social norms. Conversely, ego-oriented athletes strive to "demonstrate superior normative ability, or avoid the demonstration of incompetence at the task at hand" (Lemyre et al., 2002, p. 122). In other words, they judge their own success by the degree to which they can perform better than others. Thus winning and defeating others is their primary concern in athletic situations. This description of ego-oriented performers brings to mind a quotation attributed to the writer Gore Vidal: "it's not enough to succeed – others must fail!" (cited in McErlane, 2002).

Having outlined briefly what these two goal orientations involve, let us now consider how they can be measured psychologically before sketching some general findings in this field.

Measuring achievement goal orientations

Task and ego goal orientations may be assessed using questionnaires such as the Task and Ego Orientation in Sport Questionnaire (TEOSQ: Duda and Nicholls, 1992) and/or the Perceptions of Success Questionnaire (POSQ: G. Roberts et al., 1998). The TEOSQ consists of thirteen items – seven of which measure a task orientation and six of which assess an **ego orientation**. Participants are required to respond to the generic stem "I feel most successful in my sport when …" using a five-point Likert scale. Responses range from 1 (strongly disagree) to 5 (strongly agree). Typical items in the task orientation scale are "I learn a new skill by trying hard" or "I do my very best". Similarly, typical items on the ego orientation scale include "The others can't do as well as me" or "I'm the best". Early psychometric research indicates that these scales possess adequate reliability (Duda and Whitehead, 1998). For example, Hanrahan and Cerin (2009) reported that the internal consistency of the task orientation scale was 0.80 and that for the ego orientation scale was 0.83. The POSQ is a twelve-item test of task and ego orientation with six items in each subscale. In this test, the stem item is "When playing my sport, I feel most successful when …". Typical items in the task orientation subscale include: "I work hard" (item 1) or "I master something I couldn't do before". Meanwhile, the ego orientation subscale comprises items such as "I am the best" or "I accomplish something others can't do". As with the TEOSQ, there is evidence of acceptable validity and reliability for the POSQ (Harwood, 2002).

Some research findings on achievement goal theory

At least four predictions from achievement goal theory have been tested by researchers. First, children who hold task-oriented goals (e.g., wanting to learn new skills) should show persistence in sport situations whereas more ego-motivated counter-parts may drop out of sport at an earlier stage. Some support for this prediction has been found (see review by Weiss and Ferrer-Caja, 2002). Second, achievement goal theory predicts that athletes with different goal orientations will have different beliefs about the causes of their success. As in the previous case, this hypothesis has received some empirical support. Thus task-oriented athletes tend to regard athletic success as being determined significantly by the expenditure of effort. By contrast, athletes with an ego orientation typically believe that success is achieved mainly by having high ability (G. Roberts, 2001). Interestingly, the belief that effort rather than ability leads to success may help to explain why task-oriented athletes tend to persist longer in sport than do ego-oriented counterparts. A third trend in research findings in this field is that athletes' goal orientations are related to the way in which they cope with anxiety. For example, Ntoumanis et al. (1999) discovered that when exposed to stressful situations, task-oriented student athletes tended to use problem-solving strategies (e.g., exerting more effort, seeking social support) whereas those with a predominant ego orientation tended to rely on emotion-focused coping strategies (e.g., venting their emotions). Furthermore, a task orientation was found to be negatively associated with thoughts about wanting to escape from a losing situation in sport whereas an ego orientation was positively associated with such thoughts (Hatzigeorgiadis, 2002). Fourth, the relationship between goal orientation and sportspersonship has been investigated with some interesting results. In general, greater levels of ego orientation are associated with lower levels of moral reasoning and a greater likelihood of approval of unsportsmanlike behaviour. By contrast, higher levels of task orientation are associated with good sportspersonship and less tolerance for aggression and cheating (Weiss et al., 2008).

So far, we have examined the predictions of achievement goal theory in sport as if no moderating variables were involved. Unfortunately, the impact of situational factors in this field needs to be considered carefully. Not surprisingly, therefore, researchers in this field have postulated that an intervening variable called "motivational climate" regulates the relationship between goal orientation and athletic performance. According to Ames (1992), motivational climate refers to the perceived structure of the achievement environment as mediated by the coach's attitudes and behaviour. In general, two types of climate may be identified. A "mastery" climate is perceived when the coach places the emphasis on personal effort and skill development. In such an environment, mistakes are regarded as sources of feedback and learning. By contrast, an "ego-oriented" motivational climate is said to prevail when athletes are compared with, and pitted against, each other and when their mistakes are criticized and punished (Duda and Pensgaard, 2002). A scale has been developed by Walling et al. (1993) to measure the Perceived Motivational Climate in Sport.

Several trends are evident from research findings on motivational climates in sport. To begin with, available evidence (over fourteen studies based on about 4,500 participants) suggests that a task-orientation or mastery climate is correlated significantly positively with athletes' satisfaction and intrinsic motivation (r of approximately 0.70). Next, an ego-oriented climate is typically correlated negatively with similar motivational indices (approximate $r = 0.3$) (Harwood and Biddle, 2002). One possible reason for the perceived advantage of the task-oriented climate over the ego-oriented one is that in the former, the athlete is encouraged to focus on factors within his or her control whereas in the latter, athletes tend to use social comparison processes when assessing their own competence (Duda and Hall, 2001). Generally, most achievement goal theorists (e.g., Ames, 1992; J. Nicholls, 1992) advocate the importance of cultivating a task-oriented climate in which athletes are taught to value effort, skill-mastery and intrinsic motivation rather than an ego-oriented climate in which the goal of defeating others is paramount. Theoretically, task-oriented motivational climates can be cultivated by the provision of coaching feedback that focuses on athletes' performance relative to self-referenced criteria of achievement and improvement. The value of an ego-oriented climate should not be dismissed completely, however. Thus L. Hardy et al. (1996) argued that some degree of ego involvement is a necessary prerequisite of success for any elite athlete.

Having sketched the nature, measurement and predictions of achievement goal theory, it is time to evaluate its contribution to motivational research in sport. Box 2.3 presents a brief critical appraisal of this theory.

Box 2.3 Thinking critically about ... achievement goal theory in sport

In 2001, Duda and Hall (2001, p. 417) hailed achievement goal theory as "a major theoretical paradigm in sport psychology". Is this claim still valid? Unfortunately, this theory has been plagued by a number of troublesome issues (for reviews of achievement goal theory, see also Harwood et al., 2008; Senko et al., 2011). First, as Duda and Hall (2001) acknowledged, achievement goal theorists are rather vague about the ways in which athletes' goal orientations interact with situational factors such as perceived motivational climate in order to determine motivational behaviour. Second, a preoccupation with task-oriented and ego-oriented goal orientations has led to the neglect of *other* possible goal perspectives in sport such as affiliative needs. A third problem with achievement goal theory was noted by Kremer and Busby (1998) in relation to understanding participant motivation – the question of why some people persist with physical activity whereas other people drop out of it. In particular, these authors pointed out that it is somewhat naive to expect that task and ego orientations do not overlap considerably in real life. For example, whereas some people may initially involve themselves in physical activity for task-oriented reasons (such as losing weight), they may learn to love such activity for its own sake over time. In other words, people's motivational orientation is neither fixed nor static. A fourth problem with achievement goal theory in sport psychology is that although there have been many studies on athletes' goal orientations, there have been fewer studies on athletes' "goal states" – or the type of achievement goals that athletes pursue in specific sport situations (Harwood and Biddle, 2002). Finally, as Harwood (2002) pointed out, **nomothetic** measures of goal orientation (i.e., ones that seek to establish general laws of human behaviour from data mainly obtained through group comparisons) such as the TEOSQ (Duda and Nicholls, 1992) are often used inappropriately for the purposes of quantitative **idiographic** assessment of individual athletes (i.e., evaluation of the intensive study of individuals over time) even though such tests are poor at identifying the differences between high, moderate and low task-orientation scores. Furthermore, there is some evidence (Harwood, 2002) that athletes' goal orientations may be more context-specific than had previously been realized. For example, an athlete's goal orientation in training may differ significantly from that which the athlete displays in competitive settings. Also, as Glyn Roberts (2001) acknowledged, athletes may shift their goal orientation within a game. To illustrate, a tennis player may begin a match with the ego-related aim of defeating an opponent but may soon realize that this will probably prove impossible. So, gradually, this player may choose instead to disregard the score and use the game as an opportunity to practise some new technical skills that he or she has acquired.

In summary, achievement goal theory has historically been plagued by a variety of conceptual and methodological issues.

Critical thinking questions
Does a typology like task-oriented versus ego-oriented motivation really explain anything – or is it merely a convenient way of classifying behaviour? What specific predictions does goal achievement theory make about the relationship between goal orientation and athletic performance? As there are many anecdotal examples of elite athletes with prominent ego orientations (e.g., John McEnroe), is this type of goal perspective necessarily a bad thing for athletes?

Social-cognitive approach: attribution theory

Having reviewed research on achievement goal theory, let us now turn to the second of the social-cognitive approaches to motivation in sport psychology – namely, attribution theory or the study of how people construct explanations for the successes and failures which they experience. We are all intuitive psychologists because we spend much of our waking life trying to understand not only the world around us but also why people behave as they do. Attribution theory is a field in mainstream psychology that explores people's explanations for the causes of events that occur in their lives as well as of their own and other people's behaviour. In sport psychology, attribution theory was a "hot topic" in the 1980s (see reviews by Biddle and Hanrahan, 1998; Biddle et al., 2001; McAuley and Blissmer, 2002) but declined considerably in popularity since 2000 (although for an appeal for a resurgence of interest in this field, see Rees et al., 2005). Before analysing the relevance of this theory for understanding motivational processes in sport and exercise, some background information is required.

To begin with, the term *attribution* (which is associated with Heider (1958), one of the progenitors of this field) refers to the cause or reason which people propose when they try to explain why something happened to them. For example, a tennis player may attribute her victory over an opponent in a long match to her own "never say die" attitude on court. Conversely, a manager of a football team may ascribe a defeat to some misfortune over which he had no control (e.g., a series of unfair refereeing decisions during the match). There is an important difference between these two examples of attribution, however. In the first case, the tennis player's attribution is made to a *personal* quality – namely, her high motivation – whereas in the second case, the football manager's attribution is made to an external cause (the referee). This distinction highlights the difference between internal or **dispositional attributions** (i.e., explanations that invoke stable individual personality characteristics of the person in question) and external or **situational attributions** (i.e., explanations that refer to environmental causes of a given outcome or event). Attributions may also vary in dimensions other than this one of internal versus external locus of causality. Thus some attribution theorists postulate that people's explanations for events vary in stability (i.e., whether the perceived cause is consistent or variable over time) as well as **controllability** (i.e., the degree to which the person involved – the "actor" – could exert personal influence over the outcome in question). In summary, based on Heider's (1958) ideas, Weiner (1985) proposed that people's attributions may be classified along three causal dimensions as follows: *locus of control* (internal or external), *stability* (stable or unstable) and *personal control* (personally controllable or uncontrollable). A great deal of attribution theory research in sport psychology has been inspired by Weiner's (1985) model.

Some research findings on attribution theory

In sport and exercise psychology, one of the earliest attributional questions addressed was whether or not winners differ from losers in the type of explanation which they provide for their sporting behaviour. As one might expect, research findings have generally supported this hypothesis (see Biddle and Hanrahan, 1998). Specifically, in contrast to their less successful counterparts, winners in sport tend to favour attributions to *internal* and *personally controllable* factors such as degree of preparation or amount of practice conducted. This general finding applies to winners in individual sports (e.g., table tennis: McAuley, 1985) as well as to successful counterparts in team sports (e.g., soccer: Robinson and Howe, 1987). Such attributions for success are important because of their practical implications. To illustrate, they may be predictive of *future* athletic achievement. Thus if a young sprinter attributes a sequence of poor performances to a lack of ability (a relatively stable internal factor) rather than to the high quality of his or her opponents (a variable external factor), then the sprinter may become demoralized and lose motivation. In this way, attribution theory, or the study of how people construct explanations for their successes and failures, has a number of practical implications for everyday life. To illustrate, consider the common finding that people tend to accept personal responsibility for successful outcomes but blame others for significant failures (the so-called "credit for success, blame for failure" tendency). For example, a student who passes an exam is likely to attribute this result to internal factors like hard work or high intelligence but a student who fails an exam may explain it with reference to bad luck or being asked the "wrong" questions. In a similar vein, managers of losing teams tend to make excuses for poor results (see Figure 2.2). Of course, players are not immune from excuse-making either. For example, in the wake of England's poor performance at the 2010 World Cup in South Africa, the players had a rebellious team meeting and blamed their manager, Fabio Capello. Specifically, they claimed that he had picked the wrong team, played the wrong formation and introduced the wrong substitutes (Northcroft and Walsh, 2010)! Commenting on this display of player power, a former England international, Gareth Southgate (2010), remarked that "we are breeding players that look for excuses, that don't want to take responsibility".

Why do managers tend to make excuses for poor results or performances by their teams? One obvious explanation is that managers may use excuses in order to preserve their sense of self-esteem in the fickle world of sporting success. Another

Figure 2.2 Managers of losing teams tend to make excuses

possible explanation is that excuses help people to present a favourable image to others. In order to explore further this tendency for people to *internalize* their successes and to *externalize* their failures, try the research exercise in Box 2.4.

Box 2.4 Exploring the self-serving bias by analysing sports reports in newspapers (based on McIlveen, 1992)

The **self-serving attributional bias** is a tendency for people to make internal attributions for success and external (usually situational) attributions for failures. They do this mainly to protect their self-esteem. But as this tendency has been usually tested using laboratory paradigms in which the participants have little personal interest in the outcomes under consideration, it is difficult to generalize such research to everyday life settings. This problem can be overcome, however, by taking advantage of a naturally occurring situation in which people are asked to give explanations for events which occurred in their lives and which affect them in significant ways (Lau and Russell, 1980). A good example of such a situation is the post match interview with football managers. In this situation, self-serving biases are likely to occur as managers try to explain the apparent causes of match outcomes (see McIlveen, 1992).

Hypothesis
That victories in football matches will be attributed more frequently to internal than to external factors whereas defeats will be attributed more frequently to external than to internal factors.

Instructions

The first step in this exercise is to locate possible attributional content in newspaper coverage of football matches. In particular, you should try to find twenty attributions for team success or failure in matches involving the Premier League and/or Championship in England. Both tabloid and broadsheet daily newspapers should be consulted in this regard. Look out especially for quotations from players or managers that contain a possible explanation for the outcome of the match. The match result could be coded crudely as a success if the attributor's team won the match and a failure if the team lost the match. The perceived cause of the attribution should be deemed internal if the player or manager referred to something personal about the team (e.g., its character or ability) in the explanation provided. Conversely, the locus of causality may be deemed external if the player or manager attributed the result to something *outside* the team or its players (e.g., bad weather).

Analysis

A 2×2 contingency table should be constructed in which outcome (success or failure) and perceived cause (internal or external) are the row and column variables, respectively. Next, enter the number of attributions that fall into each of the four categories in this table. Then, using a chi-square test (check your statistics book or notes to find out how to use this test), work out the statistical relationship between match outcome and type of attribution. If the self-serving bias is present, we would expect a significantly higher proportion of internal than external attributions for successful results and a significantly higher proportion of external than internal attributions for failure outcomes.

Issues for discussion

Are success and failure objective events? How would achievement goal theorists answer this question? In any case, can we be sure that people's attributions expressed in public situations reflect what they really believe? How do you think that the emotional state of the person may affect the self-serving bias? Note that Mezulis et al. (2004) found that depressed people are much less likely than non-depressed peers to display a self-serving bias. Indeed, depressed people tend to take too little credit for success and too much credit for their failures.

A new line of inquiry in attribution research in sport psychology concerns the relationship between athletes' attributions and their emotional responses to poor performances in competition. Investigating this topic, M. Allen et al. (2011) asked a large sample (86) of golfers to report their emotional states before a competition and then asked them to complete measures of attribution and emotion after this competition. Results showed that these golfers' emotions were linked to the attributions that they provided for poor performances. For example, high levels of anger were apparent when poor performances were attributed to internal factors – and this emotion intensified when the causes of their performance were perceived as being relatively stable over time.

Weaknesses of attribution theory

So far, we have presented attribution theory as a powerful theory of people's attempt to make sense of their world. But this theory suffers from several limitations. At least four weaknesses have been identified in the application of attribution theory to sport (Biddle et al., 2001; Rees et al., 2005). First, it seems clear that athletic success and failure are neither objective events nor synonymous with winning and losing, respectively. To illustrate, imagine interviewing an athlete who had won a competitive race – but by a very close margin. Superficially, this performer embodies a winning mentality. But what if this person's opponents were of a low athletic standard? In this case, the athlete may not regard barely winning a race against a poor field as being a successful performance at all. Therefore, Biddle et al. (2001) argued that a win is not always perceived as being a success and a loss is not always seen as an index of failure. The practical implication of this principle is that attribution researchers in sport and exercise psychology now tend to use *subjective* indices of success and failure whenever possible. A second problem for attribution theory in sport is that researchers cannot always be sure about what participants mean when they use certain words or phrases. For example, if a golfer says that his or her opponent "played better" than he or she did in a match-play event, does this signal a stable attribution ("My opponent is likely to defeat me again because they are simply a better player") or an unstable attribution ("My opponent defeated me on the day – but I believe that I can defeat them the next time we play")? Clearly, researchers in this field should adopt a painstaking approach when investigating what participants mean in using certain phrases (Biddle et al., 2001). Third, another complication for attribution research in sport is that individual differences in explanatory tendencies may affect the attributions that athletes make. Indeed, research suggests that there is a link between the way in which athletes tend to explain events (their **attributional style**) and their motivation to compete. Put simply, optimism and pessimism have motivational consequences. For example, when sport performers habitually explain negative outcomes (such as losing a match) by references to personal factors (i.e., to perceived causes which are internal, stable and global, such as "It's down to me; I can't change it and it seems to affect my whole life"), they are said to display a *pessimistic* explanatory style. In this frame of mind, people may behave as if they are powerless to change their situation. Not surprisingly, this despondency often leads to a loss in motivation. By contrast, when athletes attribute negative outcomes to external, unstable and specific causes (e.g., "My defeat was just a freak occurrence and it doesn't affect the most important things in my life"), they are displaying an *optimistic* explanatory style – which helps them to learn from their defeat and to work harder in the future. Clearly, certain athletes can achieve a healthy resilience by thinking optimistically in the face of adversity. Why does optimism make athletes more resilient? One possible explanation (Seligman, 1998) is that an optimistic outlook allows athletes to keep their confidence levels high – encouraging them to believe that they have the ability to overcome any temporary setbacks. Put simply, therefore, athletes with low motivation tend to interpret setbacks as being permanent. Optimists tend to believe that positive outcomes (e.g., winning a football match) are not caused by luck but have causes that are relatively permanent in nature (such as ability). Fourth, attributional researchers in sport have not always acknowledged the role of timing in the explanations offered by athletes and coaches. For example, Schoenemann and Curry (1990) suggested that although the self-serving bias (see Box 2.4) is often evident immediately after an event, it may change over time. Specifically, these authors argued that with the benefit of hindsight, people tend to take personal responsibility for their failures as well as their successes. Clearly, this theory indicates that immediate attributions for a sporting outcome may differ from delayed attributions for the same event.

Attributional style and athletic performance

Earlier, we examined achievement goal orientations which may be regarded as how people perceive and define "success". Now, we turn to a related idea – the notion of attributional style or how people typically seek to explain success and failure in their lives. The terms attributional style or explanatory style refer to people's tendency to offer similar kinds of explanations for different events in their lives. More precisely, they reflect "how people habitually explain the causes of events" (C. Peterson et al., 1995, p. 19). Attributional style can be measured using a general self-report instrument called the Attributional Style Questionnaire (ASQ: C. Peterson et al., 1982), which requires people to identify causes for twelve hypothetical situations (involving six "good" outcomes and six "bad" outcomes) and to rate these causes along three bipolar dimensions: locus of causality, stability and globality. As explained earlier, the first of these dimensions refers to whether the alleged causal event is internal (due to the person involved) or external (due to someone else). The second dimension relates to whether the cause in question is stable (or likely to last for the foreseeable future) or unstable (i.e., short-lived). The third dimension refers to whether it is global (i.e., likely to affect every aspect of one's life) or specific (i.e., highly circumscribed in its effects). Although the ASQ is psychometrically adequate, it is not designed specifically for athletic populations. Therefore, an alternative test called the Sport Attributional Style Scale (SASS: Hanrahan et al., 1989) was devised for use in sport and exercise settings. This sixteen-item scale is also available in a shortened (ten-item) format (Hanrahan and Grove, 1990). In general, psychometric evidence in support of the SASS has been encouraging (Biddle and Hanrahan, 1998). For example, most of its subscales appear to be correlated significantly with those of the criterion instrument, the Attributional Style Questionnaire.

Research on the relationship between explanatory style and athletic performance has generated some interesting findings. First, Seligman et al. (1990) discovered that university swimmers with a pessimistic explanatory style (ES) were more likely to perform below the level of coaches' expectations during the season than were swimmers with a more optimistic outlook. In fact, the pessimists on the Attributional Style Questionnaire had about twice as many unexpectedly poor swims as did their optimistic colleagues. Second, pessimistic swimmers were less likely to "bounce back" from simulated defeats than were optimistic counterparts. Third, the explanatory style scores of the swimmers were significantly predictive of swimming performance even after coaches' judgements of ability to overcome a setback had been controlled for in the data analysis. Interestingly, these findings show that explanatory style is quite separate from athletic ability. Thus pessimistic ES profiles were as prevalent among high-level as among low-level performers. One implication of this finding is that a successful performance by itself will not engender confidence in an athlete. In other words, a sports performer has to *learn* to attribute successful events constructively in order to benefit optimally from them.

In another series of studies, Rettew and Reivich (1995) explored the correlates of explanatory style in a sample of professional athletes drawn from team sports such as basketball and baseball. Briefly, these authors found that basketball teams with relatively optimistic ES scores tended to perform significantly better than did those with a more pessimistic outlook. However, ES did not predict overall win percentage. Likewise, baseball teams with an optimistic ES profile tended to win more games than did their more pessimistic colleagues. Taken together, these studies show that explanatory style can predict certain aspects of team performance in sport – even when athletic ability levels are taken into consideration. A practical implication of these findings concerns attributional retraining. Specifically, Rettew and Reivich (1995, p. 185) suggest that the most helpful ES in terms of future athletic success is one "that motivates the individual to continue doing whatever he or she does when things are going well but galvanises the player when things are not going well".

Hanrahan and Cerin (2009) investigated the relationship between type of sport and attributional style. They found that athletes competing in individual sports (e.g., diving, track-and-field, and golf) made more internal, stable and global, and less externally controllable attributions, for positive events, and more internal attributions for negative events, than did team sport (e.g., field hockey) athletes. Hanrahan and Cerin (2009) suggested that it is logical for athletes competing in individual sports to make more internal attributions than those in team sports because the former do not have teammates to whom they can assign credit or blame.

So far, our discussion of attributional styles has been largely theoretical. But for a practical insight into this topic, try the exercise in Box 2.5.

Box 2.5 What is your typical explanatory style?

When something unpleasant or negative happens to you (e.g., failing an examination), ask yourself the following questions. First, what do you think was the main cause of the event? More precisely, are you responsible for it or is it due to some external circumstances? This question relates to the internal–external attributional dimension. Second, do you think that the cause will persist in the future? This question concerns the permanence of the attribution. Third, there is the pervasiveness issue. How much will this event affect other areas of your life? By the way, if you cannot see the difference between "permanence" and "pervasiveness", try thinking of the former as relating to time and the latter to space.

Overall, if you attributed the event to yourself (Q 1) and to things which will not change in the future (Q 2) and if you believe that it affects all of your life (Q 3), then you probably have a *pessimistic* explanatory style. If so, then you have a tendency to explain misfortune by saying "it's my fault" (personalization), "it will never change" (permanence) and "it's going to ruin my whole life" (pervasiveness). *Optimists* tend to interpret setbacks as being caused by temporary circumstances which may change in the future.

Implications of research on explanatory styles

Before concluding this section of the chapter, I would like to explore the coaching implications of research on explanatory styles. According to Seligman (1998), research on attributional style has several practical implications for sport performance. First, an optimistic explanatory style is not something that is immediately apparent to coaches. As this author put it, the ASQ "measures something you can't. It predicts success beyond experienced coaches' judgements and handicappers' expertise" (Seligman, 1998, p. 166). Second, athletes' or players' levels of optimism have implications for when to use them in team events. Thus, in general, pessimistic players should be used only after they have done well – not when they are in a run of poor form. Third, in talent search programmes, optimists may be better bets than pessimists as they will probably perform better in the long run. Fourth, pessimistic athletes can be trained to become more optimistic. As Seligman put it, "unlike IQ or your waistline, pessimism is one of those characteristics that is entirely changeable" (cited in DeAngelis, 1996, p. 33).

Having learned about the nature of athletes' attributional tendencies, can these thinking patterns be changed through professional intervention? On the basis that this practice has produced some encouraging results in clinical psychology (see Fosterling, 1988), attributional retraining may be worth trying in sport settings. For example, if a coach could change a lazy athlete's tendency to make attributions to unstable/internal dimensions, such a performer may discover that the expenditure of additional effort is helpful. Conversely, performers who are prone to "depressogenic" attributions (e.g., by ascribing unwanted outcomes to stable/internal factors) may be helped by encouraging them to externalize their explanations. In general, coaches can help athletes to become more self-reliant by helping them to decrease their tendency to use external attributions after poor performances and instead to use internal attributions. For example, a golfer may confide in her coach that she had been lucky to get away with a bunker shot that barely skimmed the rim of the bunker before landing on the green. This attribution to an external unstable factor (e.g., luck) may erode a player's confidence over time. But if the golfer could be trained to rephrase this attribution to an internal source (e.g., "If I concentrate on getting more elevation on my sand shots, I will become a much better bunker player"), she will probably be more motivated to practise her bunker play more assiduously.

In a study of this topic, Orbach et al. (1999) investigated the effects of an attributional training programme on the manner in which thirty-five tennis players explained failure on a tennis skills test. Performers were assigned to one of three treatment groups: those involving controllable and unstable attributions (CU group), those involving uncontrollable and stable attributions (US group) and those in a non-attributional control condition. Results showed that not only is it possible to alter people's attributions for their performance, but also such modified attributions remained stable for at least three weeks afterwards. Interestingly, attributional retraining has also been applied successfully to young athletes. Sinnott and Biddle (1998) tested twelve children aged between 11 and 12 years. Half of these children rated their performance on a ball-dribbling task as being poor while the other half rated themselves as performing this skill successfully. Following attributional retraining, the former group showed significant increases not only in their self-ratings but also in their level of intrinsic motivation (see Chapter 2). Although the potential value of attributional retraining is impressive, a great deal of additional research is required to evaluate the nature and scope of this phenomenon in sport and exercise psychology.

Increasing motivation in athletes: goal-setting in sport

Now that we have explored the nature of motivation and some theoretical perspectives on it, let us turn to the question of how it can be increased in athletes. Effective motivation requires a sense of *direction* as well as drive or energy. To understand this idea, consider the following analogy. Imagine a car being driven around in circles in a carpark. Although its engine is in perfect working order, the vehicle is not actually going anywhere. Clearly, what is needed is a signpost that can direct the driver out of the carpark and towards his or her destination. By analogy, athletes require a map or signpost which will channel their motivational energy effectively. One way of providing this signpost is through goal-setting – the process by which people set "goals" or targets (i.e., what they are trying to accomplish: Locke and Latham, 1985). As we shall see, goal-setting can enhance athletic performance significantly, which explains why this technique is perhaps the most frequently used psychological intervention among US Olympic athletes and coaches (Weinberg, 2009) and "arguably the most effective performance enhancement technique on the behavioural sciences" (Burton and Weiss, 2008, p. 344). Reviews of research on goal-setting have been published by Burton and Weiss (2008), Gould (2010) and Kingston and Wilson (2009). Before summarizing the findings of these reviews, some introductory information is necessary.

What is goal-setting?

A goal is a target or objective which people strive to attain. It is "attaining a specific standard of proficiency on a task, usually within a specific time frame" ((Locke et al., 1981, p. 145) or alternatively as "what an individual is trying to accomplish; it is the object or aim of an action" (Locke et al., 1981, p. 126). Typical goals could include winning a match, being selected for a club team or national squad, becoming fitter than one is at present or losing weight. So, goal-setting is the process by which people establish desirable aims or objectives for their actions. It should be noted, however, that goals are not always held consciously (Locke and Latham, 1990). For example, focusing on a goal such as winning a tennis match (a conscious goal) may interfere with a player's performance of habitual skills such as serving or volleying (Burton and Weiss, 2008). Within sport and exercise psychology, research on goal-setting has been influenced by two distinct theoretical traditions: cognitive learning theory and organizational psychology (where it was studied under the heading of "management by objectives": Burton and Weiss, 2008). To illustrate the former source of influence, cognitive researchers such as Tolman (1932) proclaimed that human actions are understood best as the outcome of internally represented conscious goals rather than as the product of environmental forces. The organizational roots of research in this field are more prominent, however, and may be traced back to theorists like F.W. Taylor (1967) and Locke and Latham (1985) who extolled the merits of goal-setting for enhanced productivity in the workplace. In an early review of this topic within organizational psychology, Locke et al. (1981, p. 145) concluded that "the beneficial effect of goal-setting on task performance is one of the most replicable findings in the psychological literature. Ninety per cent of the studies showed positive or partially positive effects". Later Locke and Latham (1990) claimed that of 201 studies on goal-setting, positive effects on performance were shown for 183 of them – resulting in an estimate of 91 per cent success rate for goal-setting. More generally, from over 500 studies on goal-setting (Burton and Weiss, 2008), two key findings have emerged (Kingston and Wilson, 2009). First, "difficult" goals tend to elicit higher levels of performance than do "easy" goals. Second, goals that are phrased more specifically tend to be more effective than vague "do your best" goals or no goals at all. But how well do these findings transfer to the domain of sport? Similar, but more modest, claims about the efficacy of goal-setting have emerged from studies in sport settings. Burton et al. (2001) reported that 44 out of 56 published studies (almost 79 per cent) yielded moderate to strong effects of goal-setting on athletic performance. From a cursory inspection of these figures, it appears that the effects of goal-setting in sport are not quite as impressive as they are in organizational settings. We shall return to this issue later. At this stage, however, we need to explore what psychological research reveals about goal-setting in athletes.

Types of goals

Three main types of goals have been identified in sport and exercise psychology research (Hardy and Nelson, 1988). First, *outcome goals* or **result goals** are based on the outcome of a specific event and usually require some kind of interpersonal comparison. They represent the *why* of motivational processes (Kremer et al., 2012) and are objective targets such as winning a competition, defeating an opponent or achieving a desired finishing position (e.g., making the cut in a golf tournament). What is not often appreciated about such goals, however, is the extent to which their achievement depends on the ability and performance of one's *opponents*. For example, a tennis player could play the best game of his or her life but still lose a match because the opposing player has played better on the day. So, outcome goals usually involve performing better than one's opponents and are largely uncontrollable. The second type of objective encountered in sport is the *performance goal*.

This type of goal, which represents the *what* of sporting motivation (Kremer et al., 2012), is usually self-referenced (i.e., it relates only to one's own performance) and involves a numeric value of some kind (e.g., trying to reduce the total number of putts one takes in a round of golf). Performance goals usually refer to the attainment of a designated personal standard of competence with regard to technique (e.g., learning to hit a top-spin backhand in tennis), effort (e.g., "giving 100 per cent effort at all times in a match"), time (running a marathon in less than four hours) distance and/or height (in certain athletic events) or form (e.g., adopting a certain gymnastics position). Unlike outcome goals, performance goals are largely under the control of the person who sets them. For example, a golfer could set as her performance goal the task of putting to within 30cm of the hole every time she is on the green. Nobody can stop the player from achieving this level of accuracy because putting is a self-paced skill. The third type of goal studied in sport psychology is the **process goal** – a behavioural strategy by which an athlete executes a particular skill or tries to attain a specific performance outcome. For example, in golf, a process goal in putting might be to keep one's head steady while taking a slow backswing. Similarly, for the free throw in basketball, a process goal might involve focusing on a high follow-through after releasing the ball. In general, process goals reflect the *how* of motivation in sport (Kremer et al., 2012).

As they can be controlled directly, performance and process goals are usually regarded as being more motivational for athletes than are result goals. Weinberg (2002, p. 38) exhorted people "to set goals that are based on their own levels of performance rather than on the outcome of winning and losing". Likewise, Orlick (1986) proclaimed that

> day-to-day goals for training and for competition should focus on the means by which you can draw out your own potential. Daily goals should be aimed at the improvement of personal control over your performance, yourself, and the obstacles you face.
>
> (Orlick 1986, p. 10)

In a similar vein, Gould (1998, p. 187) proposed that athletes should "set process and performance goals as opposed to outcome goals" and Hodge and McKenzie (1999, p. 31) advised athletes to "set performance goals rather than outcome goals". Unfortunately, this emphasis on performance goals is not completely supported by research findings. A quantitative literature review by Kyllo and Landers (1995) found that performance goals were no more effective than result goals in enhancing skills. But why exactly do goals motivate athletes and improve their performance?

Why do goals enhance performance?

Goal-setting is believed to affect athletic performance in at least five ways (Locke and Latham, 2002; Weinberg, 2009). First, goals serve to focus and direct **attention** towards relevant actions. For example, if an athlete is told that unless she becomes fitter she will be dropped from a basketball team, she may not know what action to take. But if she is advised to improve her performance on a specific index of fitness such as the "bleep test" by a certain date, she is clearer about what is expected of her. Likewise, a tennis player who tries to achieve at least 70 per cent accuracy on his first serve should be less distractible on court than a player who has no objective for the match. Second, goals help to elicit effort and commitment from athletes. Presumably, that is why coaches give "pep talks" at half-time in football matches (see Chapter 3): to remind players what they are striving for collectively. Third, goals provide incentives that may foster persistence in athletes, especially if they can measure their progress towards the targets in question. For example, a weekly fitness chart could be maintained for all members of a squad in order to encourage them to adhere to prescribed training regimes. According to Burton et al. (2001), the preceding theoretical mechanisms may explain why goals tend to have impressive short-term influences on athletic performance. But how do they enhance the development of new strategies over a longer period of time? This leads us to the fourth putative mechanism of goal-setting effects. Specifically, goals may work simply because they help athletes to break large problems into smaller components and then develop action plans (or jobs that are within one's control) for dealing with these sub-goals. For example, golfers who want to achieve greater accuracy off the tee may go to the driving range to hit buckets of balls at a designated target – not finishing until they hit that target a certain number of times. In so doing, they have begun to practise using a problem-solving approach to the game. Fifth, goals may influence athletic performance indirectly by boosting athletes' self-confidence (e.g., "I'm delighted to have achieved that goal – it restores my faith in my own ability") as well as their sense of satisfaction ("That win felt really great"). This latter possibility that goals may influence performance through the mediation of cognitive factors reminds us of the achievement goal theory that we mentioned earlier in this chapter. As you may recall, this theory proposes that athletes' motivational behaviour is influenced by their goal orientation (whether task-related or ego-related) as well as by their perception of their own athletic ability.

Research on goal-setting in sport and exercise psychology: principles, findings and issues

Goal-setting is not only one of the most widely used performance-enhancement techniques in sport and exercise psychology but also one of the most extensively researched. The typical paradigm for such research involves a comparison between the performance of people who have been instructed to set goals according to certain criteria (e.g., specific goals) with that of counterparts who have been told simply to "do your best". Often, a third sample of participants is used: a control group of people who are given no advice on goal-setting. Using this paradigm, researchers have sought to explore the characteristics of goals that make them most effective in sport settings. This topic is known as "goal attribute" research (Burton and Naylor, 2002).

Based largely on organizational psychology (see Locke and Latham, 1985), five theoretical principles have been postulated in an effort to guide research on goal-setting in sport (Weinberg, 2009). First, the more specific the goal, the more likely it is to be effective. Second, goals are alleged to work best when they are realistic but challenging. Third, goals should be written down to ensure maximum compliance. Fourth, separate goals should be established for practice and competition. Fifth, progress towards goal achievement should be evaluated regularly for optimal benefits to occur. Have these principles been supported? In testing these ideas, the following general findings have emerged (see comprehensive reviews by Burton et al., 2001; Burton and Naylor, 2002; H. Hall and Kerr, 2001; Weinberg, 2002).

First, although goal-setting is one of the most widely used interventions in applied sport psychology, most athletes rate goals as being "only moderately effective" (Burton et al., 2001, p. 497) facilitators of performance. This is largely because sport performers are not entirely clear about how best to maximize the effectiveness of their goals. In the next section, I consider some practical ways of setting effective goals. Second, there is general agreement among researchers that specific goals are more effective than general goals, vague goals or no goals at all (H. Hall and Kerr, 2001). This finding, which is called the "goal specificity" effect, may be attributable to the greater precision of specific goals than general goals. However, an important caveat must be noted here. To explain, research on goal-setting in sport shows that it may not provide any incremental benefits to athletes who are *already* motivated to do their best (a phenomenon called the "ceiling effect"; see also Box 2.6 later in the chapter). This point is illustrated by the fact that not all top athletes set goals for their performance. For example, as we learned earlier in this chapter, the Indian batsman Sachin Tendulkar claimed that he does not set any targets before matches. Another complicating factor here is that the complexity of the skill in question may serve as a mediating variable. Burton (1989) investigated the effects of specific versus general goals on basketball skills of varying degrees of complexity. Results showed that although specific goals *did* enhance performance relative to general goals as predicted, this benefit was mediated by the level of complexity of the task – a fact which had not been predicted. As a third general finding in goal-setting research, Burton et al. (2001) claim that performance goals are more effective than result goals in improving athletic performance – presumably because the former type of goals facilitate improved concentration processes in athletes (for a discussion of goal-setting as a concentration technique, see Chapter 4). It should be noted, however, that goal-setting practice studies show that athletes tend to set both types of goals – performance and result – equally often (Burton et al., 2001). A fourth general finding in the goal-setting research literature is that athletes and coaches are not systematic in writing down their goals (Weinberg, 2002). Fifth, research has accumulated on the "goal proximity" prediction – namely, the suggestion that short-term goals should be more effective motivationally than long-term goals. Surprisingly, this hypothesis has received only modest support in sport and exercise psychology (H. Hall and Kerr, 2001). Sixth, a number of practical barriers appear to hamper goal-setting practices among athletes. These barriers include such factors as a lack of time and distractions arising from social relationships (Weinberg, 2002). Seventh, the relationship between goals and performance is mediated by a host of intervening variables. For example, the level of ability of the performer, the extent to which he or she is committed to the goal, and the quantity and quality of feedback provided are all important factors in moderating the influence of goals on performance (H. Hall and Kerr, 2001). Finally, research evidence is accumulating to suggest that goal-setting skills can be taught to athletes. Thus Swain and Jones (1995) used a single-subject, multiple-baseline research design to examine the effects of a goal-setting intervention programme on the selected basketball skills (e.g., getting rebounds) of four elite university performers over a series of sixteen matches in a competitive season. Results showed that the intervention yielded significant positive effects on the targeted basketball skills for three out of four of the participants in the study.

In addition to the preceding findings, research in sport and exercise psychology has yielded two recurrent themes: "first, goals work well in sport, but not as well as in business; second, goal-setting is a paradox because this simple technique is somewhat more complicated than it looks" (Burton et al., 2001, p. 497). Overall, such research indicates that although goal-setting affects performance, many of its principles derived from organizational contexts do not generalize well to athletic domains. For example, setting specific goals is not always more effective in sport than is the practice of exhorting people to do their best. Having summarized the main principles and findings in this field, let us conclude this section by evaluating some unresolved issues in goal-setting research.

One of the most contentious issues in this field is the fact that goal-setting seems to be more effective in business settings than in sport. In an effort to explain this anomaly, Locke (1991) suggested that methodological factors may be involved. Specifically, he claimed that perhaps participants in the "no goal" and the "do your best" goal conditions actually set goals for themselves spontaneously. Also, there are many important conceptual differences between the fields of work and sport. For example, consider the issue of choice. To explain, H. Hall and Kerr (2001) noted that whereas most athletes have chosen to invest time and effort in pursuit of their sporting goals, the decision about whether or not to work is far less influenced by personal factors. In short, people *choose* to play sport – but they *have* to work, for economic reasons. This is why Weinberg and Weigand (1996) suggested that as they have chosen to participate in their chosen activities, sports performers are usually more motivated than average workers. Another problem with goal-setting studies in sport is that they are rather atheoretical. To explain, few researchers in this field have attempted to find out *why* people set the goals that they do. As H. Hall and Kerr (2001, p. 186) observed, few investigators have studied "the causes underlying the particular goals an individual might adopt".

Practical application: motivational properties of goals

Having outlined relevant theory and research on goal-setting in sport, we should now consider some practical applications. As indicated earlier, goal-attribute research suggests that certain properties of goals should elicit increased effort from or energize the behaviour of athletes. In particular, four characteristics of goals have been deemed to be especially motivational. These properties concern goal difficulty, goal specificity, goal proximity and goal focus (Kingston and Wilson, 2009).

Goal difficulty

According to Locke and Latham (1990), the more challenging or difficult a goal is, at least in organizational settings, the more motivation it elicits. More precisely, these authors suggested that there is a positive linear relationship between goal difficulty and task performance and that difficult goals encourage greater effort and persistence than do simple goals. In general, this prediction has been supported in the general goal-setting research literature (with mean **effect sizes** ranging between 0.52 and 0.82) but it has not been supported consistently in research on goal-setting in sport and exercise psychology. Burton and Naylor (2002) reported that only ten out of nineteen relevant studies in sport settings supported the goal-difficulty hypothesis. Furthermore, surveys of goal-setting practices in athletes (reviewed in Burton and Naylor, 2002) indicated that sports performers are motivated best by *moderately* challenging goals.

Goal specificity

Evidence suggests that goal specificity – or the extent to which goals are stated in clear, specific and attainable terms – tends to elicit more effort and better performance than do goals which are stated in more vague terms. For example, a golfer who is told to "drive the ball straight down the fairway – but don't worry about the distance you achieve" should try harder than someone who is told simply to "do your best". In this regard, Weinberg et al. (1994) found that college lacrosse players who had been given specific tasks to achieve during a season performed significantly better than did counterparts assigned to "do your best" goals.

Goal proximity

The issue of how far into the future goals are projected tends to affect people's motivation. Bandura (1997) claimed that whereas proximal or short-term goals mobilize effort and persistence effectively, "distal goals alone are too far removed in time to provide effective incentives and guides for present action" (Bandura 1997, p. 134).

Goal focus

The term "goal focus" refers to whether a given goal is an outcome (e.g., finishing first in a race), a performance (e.g., self-referenced targets such as the number of putts taken in a round of golf) or a process (e.g., keeping one's head steady as one putts). Munroe-Chandler et al. (2004) found that athletes tended to use performance and process goals in training but focused more on outcome goals in competition.

In addition to these features, goals should be stated positively as much as possible. For example, in soccer, it is better for a striker to set a positive goal, such as "I am going to practise timing my runs into the box", than a negative goal, such as "I must try not to get caught off-side so often". The reason for this advice is that a goal which is stated positively tells the person what to do, whereas a negatively stated goal does not provide such explicit guidance.

Does goal-setting really work?

A classic meta-analytic review on the effects of goal-setting was conducted by Kyllo and Landers (1995) using data from thirty-six studies in this field. To explain this type of review, **meta-analysis** is a quantitative statistical technique which combines the results of a large number of studies in order to determine the overall size of a statistical effect. According to Kyllo and Landers (1995), goal-setting was effective in enhancing performance in sport over baseline measures by about one-third of a standard deviation (mean effect size of 0.34). This effect was increased when goals of a moderate level of difficulty were used. Also, as mentioned earlier, these researchers found that the greatest effects were obtained when the goals were result based (which contradicts the received wisdom that performance goals work best), moderately difficult and agreed by the athletes themselves (i.e., self-set) rather than imposed from outside. Burton and Weiss (2008) reported that of eighty-eight published goal-setting studies in sport and physical activity settings, seventy demonstrated moderate to strong goal-setting effects.

Earlier, we learned that most studies on goal-setting have been based on the theories of Locke and Latham (1985, 2002) in organizational psychology. These authors predicted that relative to either "no goal" or vague "do your best" instructions, athletes' performance should be enhanced when they use goals that are specific, short-term and difficult yet realistic. Unfortunately, research designed to test Locke and Latham's predictions in sport has produced equivocal findings. Several studies have failed to establish the allegedly beneficial effects of specific and realistic goals on people's performance of motor tasks. Weinberg et al. (1990) found that the performance of hand strength and "sit-up" tasks was related neither to goal difficulty nor to goal specificity. In an effort to explain this anomaly, a variety of conceptual and methodological issues in research on goal-setting in sport may be identified (Weinberg, 2002). These issues are discussed in Box 2.6.

Box 2.6 Thinking critically about ... research on goal-setting in sport

Sport psychology is replete with claims about the value of goal-setting as a performance-enhancement strategy in sport. Thus H. Hall and Kerr (2001, p. 183) asserted that "not only is the efficacy of goal setting assumed; it is also claimed that the technique is a fundamental psychological skill that all athletes must develop if they are to maximize athletic potential". But are these claims warranted by available evidence? How well do the goal-setting principles emerging from organizational settings apply to the world of sport? Although Locke (1991) claimed that goal-setting effects in sport are similar to those in business, Weinberg et al. (1985) argued that there are significant differences between these two spheres. Kremer and Scully (1994, p. 145) observed that the extrinsic rewards arising from the world of work "stand in contrast to the intrinsic motivators which have been identified as being so crucial to maintaining an interest in amateur sport". Other problems in this field come from the following methodological flaws in research on goal-setting (see Burton et al., 2001; Burton and Naylor, 2002; Burton and Weiss, 2008).

- *Possible ceiling effects*: There is evidence that the goal effectiveness curve flattens out or reaches a ceiling as people approach the limits of their ability. In other words, ability factors restrict the amount of improvement that can be made through goal-setting.
- *Complexity of task or skill*: Goal-setting effects may not be noticeable when the tasks used to assess them require complex skills. In fact, research indicates that as tasks become more complex, athletes must learn to adopt strategic plans to extract maximum benefit from goal-setting practices (H. Hall and Kerr, 2001).
- *Individual differences*: The relationship between goal-setting and performance may be moderated by strategic factors. Burton et al. (2001) claimed that such factors as self-efficacy can affect the impact of goal-setting practices on skilled performance.
- *Spontaneous goal-setting in control group*: In the typical experimental paradigm used to study goal-setting effects (see earlier in chapter), it is difficult to ensure that participants in control groups do not set goals spontaneously for themselves. Indeed, there is evidence (Weinberg et al., 1985) that over 80 per cent of participants in a "no goal" control group admitted later that they had set goals for themselves.

Critical thinking questions
What are the similarities and differences between goal-setting processes in business and sport? What factors could account for the tendency for goal-setting to be less effective in sport than in business contexts? In sport, is it possible to eliminate the possibility of spontaneous goal-setting among people in control groups? Why do you think so few studies on goal-setting have used athletes studied in field settings?

Future directions in research on goal-setting

According to Burton and Weiss (2008), the following new directions can be sketched for research on goal-setting in athletes. First, more research is required to establish the optimal level of goal difficulty for athletes in specific types of sports. Second, little is known, at present, about the relationship between the frequency with which people monitor their goal-setting behaviour and the efficacy of their goals. Third, additional research needs to be conducted on the role that "action plans" play in goal-setting effectiveness. Fourth, goal-setting researchers need to move on from studying atheoretical questions such as "what types of goals are most effective?" to investigating the psychological mechanisms underlying the motivational effects of goals on specific sport skills. Finally, more longitudinal field studies are required to establish the actual goal-setting practices of athletes and coaches over the course of a competitive season.

Box 2.7 Thinking critically about ... goal-setting in a team environment

Although a lot of research has been conducted on goal-setting in individual athletes, relatively few studies have investigated **team goal-setting** – or the process by which teams plan "the future state of affairs desired by enough members of a group to work towards its achievement" (D. Johnson and F. Johnson, 1987, p. 132). Team goal-setting is believed to enhance team performance by increasing team **cohesion** (U. Schmidt et al., 2005) and/or by improving collective efficacy (Greenlees et al., 2000).

In the early days of goal-setting research, Locke and Latham (1985, p. 212) suggested that the process of setting goals in team sports is similar to that in individual sports because "each individual has a specific job to do that requires particular skills". Over time, however, it became clear that this position is somewhat simplistic. For example, O'Leary-Kelly et al. (1994) suggested that team goal-setting is more complex than individual goal-setting for at least two reasons. First, team planning requires more coordination than individual goal-setting. Second, team goal-setting may take place at several levels (e.g., individual, unit, team) whereas individual goal-setting largely takes place at only one level. The different levels of team goal-setting may not always be mutually compatible. In Formula One motor racing, the Ferrari team was fined $100,000 by the FIA World Motor Sport Council in July 2010 for bringing the sport into disrepute in a controversial "team orders" (whereby a racing team decides which of its team members it wishes to win a race) incident in which one of its drivers, the Brazilian Felipe Massa, was apparently ordered to stand aside and let a teammate, the Spanish Fernando Alonso, win the German Grand Prix (Cary, 2010). A similar incident occurred in the 2002 Austrian Grand Prix when the Brazilian Rubens Barrichello was ordered by Ferrari to pull over on the finishing straight to allow his German teammate Michael Schumacher to win the race (Owen, 2010). In one case study, Thelwell (2009) described how he had developed and evaluated a psychological intervention programme in an effort to improve team goal-setting for a professional soccer team playing in the Championship (second tier of the Football League in England). Following some initial focus group meetings with the coaching staff to plan aspects of the intervention, a *performance profiling* exercise was conducted with the squad. Using this technique (based on Butler, 1996), athletes are typically requested to indicate on a diagram (resembling a dartboard) "where I am now" and "where I would like to be" on a list of attributes deemed essential for success in their field (see example of use in Kremer and Moran, 2008a). Thelwell (2009) used performance profiling to elicit from the players and staff the team characteristics that would be required to secure the team's promotion to the Premier League. Evaluation of the intervention showed an improvement in perceived team qualities such as "being able to keep winning" and "positive responses to goping behind/conceding late".

Critical thinking questions
Is there really such a thing as "team" goal-setting? In other words, is goal-setting not always an *individual* process? Can you think of any psychological theories that may help to explain why an individual athlete's goals could be different from those of a team? Do you think that a coach's communication style could influence how athletes in a team game interpret the goals that they strive to achieve during a competitive season? Give reasons for your answer. Based on Thelwell's (2009) research, what methods could you use – apart from performance profiling – to elicit team goals? What are the strengths and weaknesses of these methods?

Practical goal-setting: the SMART approach

To be effective as a motivational technique, goal-setting should be conducted according to sound psychological principles. These principles have been encapsulated in various acronyms in applied sport psychology. For example, Weinberg (2009) refers to INSPIRED where I stands for "internalized", N for "nurturing", S for "specific", P for "planned", I for "in your control", R for "reviewed regularly", E for "energizing" and D for "documented". Another well-known acronym is the SMART approach to goal-setting (Bull et al., 1996). This approach is illustrated in Box 2.8 with regard to the task of motivating oneself to exercise more regularly (see also Chapter 8).

Box 2.8 The SMART approach to goal-setting (based on Bull et al., 1996)

How can you motivate yourself to take physical exercise more regularly? One way of achieving this goal is to use the SMART approach to goal-setting. This approach is based on the idea that goal-setting works best when it follows certain principles that are captured by the acronym SMART. The SMART approach can be applied to your exercise behaviour as follows.

S = specific
The clearer and more specific your goal is, the more likely you are to achieve it. For example, "I want to visit the gym three times a week for the next three months" is better than saying "I would like to become fitter in the future".

M = measurable
If you cannot measure your progress towards your goal, you will quickly lose interest in it, so it is important to keep a record of your progress towards your

fitness objective. For example, you could measure the length of time it takes you to run a mile and then try to improve on it every three weeks.

A = action-related
Unless you identify a number of stepping stones (i.e., tasks which take you a step nearer to your goal and which involve specific actions that are under your control) for your goals, you may feel confused about what to do next. One action step is to join a gym and a second is to get a weekly assessment of your progress from a qualified fitness instructor.

R = realistic
Your goals should be realistic for your present level of health and fitness. Therefore, it is important that you get a full health check-up before you begin an exercise programme so that your fitness level and exercise aspirations can be assessed. Otherwise, your fitness goals may be unrealistic.

T = timetabled
In order to motivate yourself to exercise regularly, you must build some daily physical activity into your timetable. Planned exercise is the key to better fitness levels (see also Chapter 8).

So far in this chapter, we have explored the nature and types of motivation, various theoretical approaches to the study of this construct and a strategy (goal-setting) that attempts to increase motivation in athletes. The final section will address a rather puzzling question in this field. What motivates people to participate in dangerous sports? This question is perplexing because involvement in risky sports is counter-intuitive. After all, dangerous sports elicit fear – and fear is supposed to dissuade people from danger, not attract them to it (Piet, 1987). So, why do people engage in sporting behaviour that does not seem to make any psychological sense?

What motivates people to take part in high-risk sports?

On 8 August 2010, a Russian man named Vladimir Ladyzhenskiy collapsed and died with severe burns while competing in the Sauna World Championships in Heinola, Finland. Contestants in this extreme endurance event had to sit in a sweltering room and withstand temperatures as high as 230 degrees Fahrenheit (110 degrees Celsius) while water was tossed onto a searing stove. Why did he push his body to its final physiological limit? Similarly, what motivates someone to sky-dive from very tall urban buildings, bridges, cranes and cliffs? This latter activity is known as BASE (Buildings, Aerials, Spans and Earth) jumping and it has a fatality rate of about one in six participants (Wollaston, 2010). According to Dan Witchalls, one of the world's most famous BASE jumpers who has leaped off Wembley Stadium, Nelson's Column and the Millennium Dome, it's a matter of intrinsic thrill-seeking: "I like doing it because it's fun ... only get one chance. You can't make mistakes up there" (cited in Ronay, 2010, p. 8).

A sport is usually defined as being risky or dangerous if the consequences of something going wrong in it are life threatening for the participants involved (Woodman et al., 2010). Based on this definition, sports such as mountain-climbing, ballooning, hang-gliding, parachute-jumping, white-water kayaking, sky-diving and motorcycle racing are highly risky. So, what motivates people to engage in such dangerous activities? At least three psychological theories have been proposed to answer this question.

First, some theorists believe that dangerous activities offer people an escape from a world that the writer Al Alvarez describes as increasingly "constricted by comfort" (cited in Delingpole, 2001, p. 8). According to this theory, many people feel excessively cosseted by the materialistic comforts of our contemporary society and hence seek dangerous experiences in an effort to fill a gap in their lives. As western city life "is now tame and increasingly controlled" (Vidal, 2001, p. 2), some people look for danger in outdoor experiences. Therefore, risk-taking behaviour may represent a conscious backlash against the bland and sterile security of every-day life. Although this theory is speculative, it seems plausible that alienated people may experience a heightened state of awareness when they are faced with the prospect of injury or death. Indeed, Schrader and Wann (1999, p. 427) suggested that one way to achieve the illusion of control over one's mortality is by "cheating death" through involvement in high-risk activities.

A second theory of risk-taking behaviour is the proposition that it stems from a personality trait called **sensation seeking**. According to Zuckerman (1979, 2007), this trait involves the propensity to seek "novel and complex sensations and experiences and the willingness to take physical and social risks for the sake of such experiences" (Zuckerman 1979, p. 10). Originally, Zuckerman speculated that people who participated in risky sports were high sensation seekers who displayed a tendency to underestimate the dangers posed by these sports. Subsequently, how-ever, he revised this view by suggesting instead that sensation seekers are actually accurate in their risk assessment – even though they apparently believe that the rewards of arousal outweigh the degree of risk involved by the activity in question (Zuckerman, 1994). This trait of sensation seeking can be measured using the Sensation Seeking Scale (Zuckerman, 1984) which assesses such dimensions of the construct as "thrill and adventure seeking" (the desire to engage in adventurous activities), "experience seeking" (the tendency to seek arousal through mental and sensory means), "disinhibition" (seeking a release through such activities as drink-ing and gambling) and "boredom susceptibility" (an aversion to monotony). For a critical perspective on this test, see Box 2.9.

Box 2.9 Thinking critically about ... sensation seeking in sport

What factors are associated with people's involvement in risky sporting activities? Schrader and Wann (1999) investigated the role of variables such as gender, "death anxiety" (i.e., the degree to which one feels that one can cheat death by participating in high-risk activities) and sensation seeking

(Zuckerman, 1979, 2007) in people's involvement in dangerous sports. Results showed that only two variables accounted for significant amounts of variance in thrill-seeking behaviour. These variables were gender and sensation seeking. Schrader and Wann (1999) found that a much higher proportion of males (about 62 per cent) than females (approximately 37 per cent) participated in high-risk recreation activities. In addition, sensation seeking, as measured by the Sensation Seeking Scale V (SSSV: Zuckerman 1979, 1994), was significantly associated with involvement in high-risk activities.

Critical thinking questions

Are you satisfied with the defintion above for "risky" sports? Is it too simplistic? Note that Woodman et al. (2010) pointed out that although proportionately more people are injured playing soccer than bungee-jumping, soccer is not regarded as a dangerous sport. In any case, do you think that correlations between risk-taking behaviour and personality variables really explain anything? After all, to say that someone chooses dangerous sports because they enjoy the thrill of danger seems rather circular. Furthermore, how can we be sure that participants regard their chosen athletic behaviour as "risky" unless we assess their perceptions of the actual danger involved in it? What other implicit assumptions do researchers in this field make? Why do you think that proportionately more males than females tend to participate in risky sporting activities? If thrill-seeking behaviour is as addictive as is often claimed (Vidal, 2001), why do people tend to choose *only one* outlet for their risky behaviour? For example, why do rock-climbers rarely become interested in other dangerous sports like motor-racing or bungee-jumping?

The third theoretical approach to risky behaviour in sports comes from the cognitive tradition. To illustrate, consider the idiosyncratic ways in which people estimate the risks associated with certain activities. John Kerr (1997) noted that athletes who participate in dangerous sports often confess to a fear of participating in *other* sports which are equally dangerous. Carl Llewellyn, a British National Hunt jockey who has suffered a catalogue of serious injuries in his sport, confessed to being petrified of activities like bungee-jumping. Presumably, familiarity with the risks of one's sport blinds one to the dangers which they pose. In an effort to explain this phenomenon, Kerr (1997) speculated that athletes who take part in dangerous sports tend to construct subjective "protective frames" which give them a feeling of invincibility, although such frames do not appear to extend to less familiar sports.

Before we conclude this section, it is worth nothing that there may be a neurochemical basis to risk-taking behaviour. Zorpette (1999) claimed that such behaviour is addictive physiologically because dopamine is released by the brain as a chemical reward for experiencing dangerous situations. As yet, however, there have been few systematic attempts to explore the brains of thrill-seekers using **neuroscientific imaging** technology.

Ideas for research projects on motivation in athletes

Here are seven ideas for possible research projects on motivation in athletes.

1   Is there a relationship between the motivation of athletes and the type of sport which they play? To answer this question, you could compare and contrast the motivation of performers from individual and team sports using a questionnaire such as the Sport Motivation Scale (M. Martens and Webber, 2002).
2   What factors sustain the motivation of elite athletes who still compete at a high level? See Mallett and Hanrahan (2003) for a study on this topic.
3   Have you ever wondered about the factors that motivate aspiring marathon runners to put themselves through such arduous training schedules? If so, you could replicate a study by Ogles and Masters (2003) on the motives of people who participate in marathons.
4   Do the coping strategies of task-oriented athletes differ from those used by ego-oriented athletes in stressful situations?
5   Relatively little is known about the actual goal-setting practices of athletes who have been tested in field settings (but see Mellalieu et al., 2006b). Historically, most goal-setting studies have been conducted in laboratory settings on non-athlete samples. In view of this oversight in the research literature, you may wish to investigate the goal-setting practices of athletes in a specific sport over the course of a season. For example, Mellalieu et al. (2006b) explored goal-setting in five collegiate rugby players over a competitive season. This study may give you some ideas on how to proceed with your own research.
6   What factors motivate prolonged engagement in high-risk sports? It would be interesting to extend a study by Woodman et al. (2010) which addressed this question.
7   What is the relationship between the representation of team goals and individual goals in sports teams (see Kingston and Wilson, 2009)?

Summary

- Motivation plays a vital but often misunderstood role in sport and exercise. The role is critical because athletic success depends significantly on people's willingness to exert mental as well as physical effort in pursuit of excellence. Unfortunately, the role of motivation in sport is also potentially confusing because of certain myths that surround this term (e.g., the idea that being "psyched up" is synonymous with being appropriately motivated for competitive action). Therefore, the purpose of this chapter was to examine selected theories and research on motivational processes in athletes.
- The second section considered the nature and types of motivation.
- The third section provided a brief overview of two influential cognitive models of motivational processes in athletes: achievement goal theory and attribution theory.

- The fourth section examined the theory and practice of goal-setting as a motivational strategy in sport. This section concluded with a discussion of some key conceptual and methodological issues affecting research in this field.
- The fifth section considered the motivational factors which impel some people to take part in dangerous athletic pursuits.
- Finally, seven practical suggestions were presented for possible research projects on the psychology of motivation in sport.

"Psyching up" and calming down: anxiety in sport

I was still one shot ahead going into the 10th and then things went all pear-shaped after that ... I can't really put my finger on what went wrong ... I just hit a poor tee shot on 10 and sort of unravelled from there.

> (Golf star, Rory McIlroy, on his disastrous final round on the final day of the 2011 US Masters championship in Augusta; cited in Garrod, 2011, p. 64)

chapter 3

Introduction

Competitive sport can make even the world's most successful athletes feel nervous. For example, consider the anxiety experienced by seasoned performers such as England rugby World-Cup winner Jonny Wilkinson and triple golf major tournament winner Pádraig Harrington. Interestingly, Wilkinson admitted that "I am always nervous before a rugby match. I always have been ... the condition wasn't physical fear ... it was the thought of losing and letting myself down at something which meant so much to me" (Wikinson, 2006, pp. 49–50). Surprisingly, Harrington suggested that athletes' ability to cope with anxiety may not improve with age. For example, although he has represented Europe in six Ryder Cup teams since 1999, he still feels nervous on the first tee of this latter competition. As he pointed out: "it all goes into a blur because you're so nervous and eventually you just have to go hit it ... it's the height of nervousness" (cited in Clerkin, 2010, p. 2) (see Figure 3.1). Extrapolating from these experiences, we can conclude that most athletes have discovered that if they wish to perform consistently well in competition, they must

Figure 3.1 According to Pádraig Harrington, playing in the Ryder Cup can be a nerve-racking experience
Source: Courtesy of Inpho photography

Figure 3.2 Rafael Nadal believes that he plays best when he is calm
Source: Courtesy of Inpho photography

learn to acknowledge and control their arousal levels effectively. And the first step in this process is for athletes to admit that they get anxious from time to time. So, the former world number 1 golfer Nick Faldo claimed that "the player who recognizes that he is nervous is streets ahead of the fellow who is in denial" (cited in Mair, 2004, p. 3). With this realization comes empowerment. Andy Murray, the Scottish tennis star, proclaimed: "I'm happy with nerves. For a sportsperson ... to go into matches being nervous is good. Having that adrenaline gets your mind focused on the match" (cited in Mitchell, 2010a). Clearly, athletes have to be able either to "psych themselves up" (see Chapter 2) or to calm themselves down as required by the situation. In this latter regard, Rafael Nadal (one of the greatest tennis players of all time) revealed that "the important thing is for me to have the calm. It is what is needed to play my best tennis" (cited in Flatman, 2010, p. 14) (see Figure 3.2). Similarly, José Mourinho (current manager of Real Madrid and twice a coach of Champions' League winning teams) observed that in his experience, "without emotional control, you cannot play ... you cannot react. You have to know what you have to do ... You have to be cool (cited in Guardian, 2005) (see Figure 3.3). Nevertheless, some sports challenge the performer to *alternate* regularly between psyching up and calming down within the same competition. For example, gymnasts must be able to energize themselves before attempting a vault exercise but must then switch to relaxation mode when preparing to perform a routine on the beam. Otherwise, they may slip – literally, as happened to Andrea Raducan, the 2000 Olympic gymnastics champion, who fell off the balance beam at the 2002 world championships in Hungary (Sarkar, 2002). Interestingly, the importance of arousal control in sport was highlighted by Mike Atherton, a former captain of England's cricket team, who observed:

there are two sorts of player: those who are quite placid people ... who need an adrenaline flow to get them up for it, and so find nerves a real help. And then there are those who are naturally hyper for whom that additional flow may not be such a good thing. When I look at players now I can see who fits into which category and then *their ability to cope depends on whether they can either bring themselves up or take themselves down.*

(cited in Selvey, 1998; italics mine)

Similar sentiments were expressed by Sam Torrance, the captain of the victorious European golf team before the 2002 Ryder Cup, when he urged his players to use their nervous energy effectively (see O'Sullivan, 2002a, p. 19), and by Christine Ohuruogu, the British 2008 Olympic champion 400 metres athlete, who admitted that "you need some level of pre-race nerves to get the adrenaline going but it is crucial to keep it under control" (cited in Guardian, 2009). Given the importance of anxiety control in sport, how can athletes manage to calm themselves down before or during a competition? More generally, what does "anxiety" mean to athletes and does it help or hinder their performance? What causes it and how can it be measured in sport settings? The purpose of this chapter is to provide answers to these and other questions raised by the study of arousal and anxiety in sport.

The chapter is organized as follows. The next section explores the nature, causes and types of anxiety in sport performers as well as its meaning for the athletes themselves. In the third section, various ways of measuring anxiety in athletes are evaluated briefly. The fourth section reviews research findings on the relationship between anxiety and athletic performance. This section also features a discussion of the nature and causes of "choking" under pressure in sport. In the fifth

Figure 3.3 José Mourinho believes that emotional control is essential for success in sport
Source: Courtesy of Inpho photography

section, the topic of anxiety *control* is addressed. This section provides several practical techniques used by athletes to cope with pressure situations in sport. The sixth section indicates some unresolved issues and new directions in research on anxiety in athletes. Finally, I present a practical suggestion for a research project in this field.

Anxiety in athletes

According to Onions (1996), the term anxiety is derived from the Latin word *angere*, meaning "to choke". This Latin origin is interesting because it shows that anxiety is at the root of "choking" under pressure – a phenomenon in which athletes perform worse than expected in pressure situations that have a degree of perceived importance (Jordet, 2009). We discuss this topic of choking in more detail later in this chapter. For the present, however, anxiety in sport psychology refers to an unpleasant emotion which is characterized by vague but persistent feelings of apprehension and dread (Cashmore, 2008). A similar view of this construct was provided by Buckworth and Dishman (2002, p. 116) who defined anxiety as a state of "worry, apprehension, or tension that often occurs in the absence of real or obvious danger". Typically, the tension felt by anxious people is accompanied by a heightened state of physiological arousal mediated by the **autonomic nervous system (ANS)**.

In order to understand anxiety properly, we need to explore its psychological components and also to distinguish it from similar constructs such as *fear*, a brief emotional reaction to a stimulus that is perceived as threatening, and *arousal*, a diffuse state of bodily alertness or "readiness" (Cashmore, 2008). The latter distinctions are very important because anxiety research in sport has been plagued by conceptual confusion (Gould et al., 2002c; Fletcher et al., 2006; Mellalieu et al., 2006a). For example, the terms anxiety, fear and arousal are sometimes used interchangeably even though these constructs have quite different meanings – as I shall explain shortly.

Components of anxiety: cognitive, somatic and behavioural

Most psychologists regard anxiety as a multidimensional construct with at least three dimensions or components: cognitive (i.e. mental), somatic (i.e. physical) and behavioural (Gould et al., 2002c). Let us now examine each of these components in turn.

First, **cognitive anxiety** involves worrying or having negative expectations about some impending situation or performance and engaging in task-irrelevant thinking as a consequence (see also Chapter 4 on concentration in athletes). More precisely, it refers to "negative expectations and cognitive concerns about oneself, the situation at hand and potential consequences" (L. Morris et al., 1981, p. 541). But what do athletes worry about in sport? Although relatively little research has been conducted on this issue, John Dunn (1999) and Dunn and Syrotuik (2003) discovered four main themes in their analysis of cognitive anxiety in intercollegiate ice-hockey players. These themes were a fear of performance failure, apprehension about negative evaluation by others, concerns about physical injury or danger, and an unspecified fear of the unknown. On average, the players in this study were more concerned about performance failure and negative evaluation by others than about the other two worry domains. A similar concern about poor performance (specifically, the possibility of making mistakes) was evident among a multisport sample of French athletes tested by Martinent and Ferrand (2007). In general, cognitive anxiety has a debilitating effect on athletic performance (Cashmore, 2008). I return to this issue in the fourth section of the chapter when I explore why some athletes "choke" under pressure. By the way, cognitive anxiety about future performance is also widespread among performers other than athletes. For example, performance anxiety or stage fright has blighted the careers of such talented people as the singer Barbra Streisand, who forgot the words of one of her songs during a concert in Central Park, New York, in front of 135,000 people – an event which prompted her to avoid singing "live" for another twenty-seven years (Sutcliffe, 1997). Similar problems of excessive anxiety have been documented in the cases of actors Vanessa Redgrave, Derek Jacobi and Stephen Fry (Harlow, 1999).

The second component of the construct of anxiety involves somatic or bodily processes. **Somatic anxiety** refers to the *physical* (including psychophysiological) manifestation of anxiety and may be defined as "one's perception of the physiological-affective elements of the anxiety experience, that is, indications of autonomic arousal and unpleasant feeling states such as nervousness and tension" (L. Morris et al., 1981, p. 541). In sport, this component of anxiety is apparent when an athlete is afflicted by such physical markers as neuroendocrine responses (e.g., secretion of cortisol – the "stress hormone"), increased perspiration, a pounding heart, rapid shallow breathing, clammy hands and a feeling of butterflies in the stomach. Whereas cognitive anxiety is characterized by negative thoughts and worries, somatic anxiety is associated with signs of autonomic arousal such as the release of hormones such as cortisol. It should be noted, however, that some researchers (e.g., J. Kerr, 1997) have suggested that increases in physiological arousal may accompany emotions other than anxiety. In particular, excitement and anger appear to have physiological substrates similar to those of anxiety.

The third component of the construct of anxiety is **behavioural anxiety**. In this domain, indices of anxiety include tense facial expressions, changes in communication patterns (e.g., unusually rapid speech delivery) and agitation and restlessness (Gould et al., 2002c). Surprisingly, relatively little research has been conducted on the behavioural manifestations of anxiety in athletes – mainly because of the dearth of objective measures and suitable checklists for the assessment of such phenomena. Nevertheless, it is widely believed that anxiety produces jerky and inefficient muscular movements in athletes which can be assessed using kinematic measures. In this regard, a good example of how these three dimensions of anxiety interact comes from a study by Pijpers et al. (2003). Briefly, these researchers conducted an experiment designed to compare the effects of low-anxiety and high-anxiety conditions on novice climbers. They manipulated the level of anxiety among the participants by using a climbing wall with routes defined at different heights (low and high). Results revealed that, as predicted, the effects of anxiety were evident psychologically at three different levels. First, at the experiential level, the novice climbers reported feeling more anxiety when they traversed a higher route on the climbing wall as compared with an identical but lower route. Second, at the physiological level, the climbers on the higher route exhibited significantly greater heart rates, more muscle fatigue and higher blood lactate concentrations than they did when tackling the lower route on the wall. Third, anxiety affected the climbers' bodily movements which was apparent in indices such as a less smooth displacement of the body's centre of gravity in the high-anxiety as compared with the low-anxiety condition. Before concluding this section, two important theoretical issues need to be addressed concerning the tri-dimensional nature of anxiety.

In the first theoretical issue, given the inextricable links between mind and body in sport, is it valid to postulate that cognitive and somatic anxiety are truly separate dimensions of this construct? There are at least two sources of evidence to support this distinction (Burton, 1998). First, factor analyses of self-report state anxiety scales tend to reveal a multidimensional rather than a unidimensional structure. Second, there are grounds for believing that cognitive and somatic anxiety emanate from different types of pre-competitive patterns. For example, research suggests that whereas cognitive anxiety remains relatively high and stable prior to competition for most athletes, somatic anxiety tends to remain low until one or two days before the event – at which point it increases steadily before peaking at the start of a competition. After that, it tends to dissipate rapidly. With regard to this issue, Fenz and Epstein (1967) explored the temporal pattern of physiological arousal responses among expert and novice sky-divers prior to performance. Results showed that in the expert performers, peak arousal levels were reached significantly in advance of the jump. By contrast, the physiological arousal of the novice parachutists started at a relatively low level but increased progressively in the time leading up to the jump. More recently, Strahler et al. (2010), examined the anticipatory anxiety – as manifested in psychological and neuroendocrine stress responses – of athletes one week before an important competition. They were especially interested in the cortisol awakening response (CAR), which is a marker of hypothalamic-pituitary-adrenal activity. Typically obtained from saliva samples, CAR may provide insight into how people react psychophysiologically over time to the anticipated demands of an impending challenge. Obtaining CAR data for the first time in a sport psychology setting, Strahler et al. (2010) were surprised to discover that whereas the athletes in their study reported experiencing a significant rise in somatic anxiety as the day of a competition loomed, there was no significant increase in CAR activity. The authors interpreted this finding as indicating that experienced athletes appear to habituate certain hormonal activity in response to repeated exposure to stressful situations. Interestingly, the results of this study also highlight the fact that self-report and neuroendocrine responses to anxiety may differ significantly from each other. In summary, evidence from psychometric studies of self-report scales and that from studies of changes in the pattern of athletes' affect over time suggests that cognitive and somatic anxiety are in fact independent dimensions of anxiety.

The second theoretical issue that arises from the tri-dimensional model of anxiety concerns the distinction between *intensity* and *directionality* of this construct. To explain, until the early 1990s, most anxiety researchers tended to focus only on the intensity or level (or amount) of symptoms experienced by performers when assessing their cognitive and somatic anxiety (Thomas et al., 2009). However, with the discovery that the experience of anxiety was *not* always detrimental to performance (see subsection below on "Athletes' interpretation of anxiety symptoms"), researchers began to investigate the *directional* interpretation of anxiety. In other words, is it perceived by the performer as being facilitative or debilitative of performance? As we shall see later in the chapter, this emphasis on the importance of perception as a mediating factor in athletes' experience of anxiety has led to useful coping strategies such as "cognitive restructuring" (illustrated in Box 3.7 later in the chapter).

Anxiety, fear and arousal

So far, we have been using the terms anxiety, arousal and fear quite loosely. Let us now distinguish between them more precisely. Anxiety is believed to differ from fear in lasting longer (Buckworth and Dishman, 2002) and in tending to be more undifferentiated than fear – because people can be anxious about something that is not physically present or immediately perceptible. Despite these differences, however, anxiety is similar to a fear in some ways. To explain, anxiety is elicited whenever people interpret a particular person, event or situation as posing a *threat* to them in some way. This perception of threat may be based on realistic or imaginary fears – although the distinction between these two factors is often blurred in everyday life. For example, if you are a tennis player and serving at match point in your local club championship, you will probably feel a little anxious – even though your feelings in this case are completely disproportionate to the physical danger involved in the situation (unless, of course, your opponent has a reputation for being physically violent on court if he or she loses)! But if you are a novice parachutist facing your first jump with no instructor around, you may have every reason to feel nervous because of the potential danger to your life. Let us turn now to the distinction between anxiety and arousal.

In psychology, the term "arousal" refers to a type of bodily energy which primes or prepares us for emergency action. For example, when we are threatened physically, our body's sympathetic nervous system prepares us either to confront the source of danger or to run away from it. This fight or flight response triggers such bodily reactions as a faster heart beat, release of glucose into the bloodstream and heightened levels of arousal. But what does arousal involve? According to Gould et al. (2002c, p. 227), it is a "general physiological and psychological activation of the organism which varies on a continuum from deep sleep to intense excitement". In other words, arousal is an undifferentiated somatic state which prepares people to respond to anticipated demands for action (Whelan et al., 1990). Physiologically, feelings of arousal are mediated by the sympathetic nervous system. Thus when we become aroused, our brain's reticular activating system triggers the release of biochemical substances like **epinephrine** and **norepinephrine** into the blood-stream so that our body is energized appropriately for action. Therefore, anxiety can be distinguished from arousal as follows. Although arousal involves undifferentiated bodily energy, anxiety is an emotional label for a *particular type* of arousal experience (L. Hardy et al., 1996). This view is endorsed in a model of arousal developed by Gould et al. (2002c). In this model, cognitive anxiety is believed to emerge from the interpretation or appraisal of arousal. Therefore, anxiety can be regarded as *negatively interpreted* arousal. This proposition raises the question of individual differences in arousal interpretation.

It has long been known that athletes differ from each other in the labels that they attach to their arousal states. Thus certain bodily symptoms (e.g., rapid heart beat, shortness of breath) may be perceived as "pleasant excitement" by one athlete but regarded as unpleasant anxiety by another performer. To illustrate a *positive* interpretation of an arousal state, note what Sam Torrance, captain of the victorious 2002 European Ryder Cup golf team, said to his players before the competition started:

> If you're not nervous then there is something wrong with you. Nerves create adrenaline and I told them to use that, use it in your own advantageous way, to make you feel better, get pumped up; just get psyched up.
>
> (cited in O'Sullivan, 2002a, p. 19)

A similarly positive attitude to nervousness was shown by the former tennis star Andre Agassi, who described how he had felt about his opening match in the 2002 US Open: "Going out there I was pretty nervous, and excited, and I felt like I controlled everything that I wanted to. That's a good sign" (cited in B. Wood, 2002). Notice that Agassi labelled his nervousness as excitement. In a similar vein, Tiger Woods revealed that "the challenge is hitting good golf shots when you have to ... to do it when the nerves are fluttering, the heart pounding, the palms sweating ... that's the *thrill*" (cited in D. Davies, 2001; italics mine).

These comments by Agassi and Woods highlight the role that perception plays in the emotional experiences of elite athletes. For example, a low level of arousal may be experienced either as a relaxed state of readiness or as an undesirable "flat", lethargic or sluggish feeling. This idea that athletes' arousal levels may be *interpreted* in either positive or negative terms raises the issue of what anxiety means to sport performers.

Athletes' interpretation of anxiety symptoms: help or hindrance?

Traditionally, arousal and anxiety have been regarded as factors to be controlled in case they hampered athletic performance. However, this assumption was challenged by research which showed that, in many athletic situations, it is not the *amount* of arousal that affects performance but the way in which such arousal is interpreted. For example, M. Mahoney and Avener (1977) found that successful gymnasts (i.e., those who qualified for the 1976 US Olympic squad) tended to perceive precompetitive arousal as a form of anticipatory excitement – a view which apparently facilitated their subsequent performance. Conversely, less successful counterparts (i.e., athletes who failed to qualify for the US team) tended to treat their arousal levels negatively, interpreting them as unwelcome signs of impending failure. Influenced by this finding, Jones and his colleagues in the early 1990s began to investigate the directional interpretation of anxiety (i.e., the extent to which athletes perceived anxiety as a help or a hindrance to their performance). Thus G. Jones and Swain (1992, 1995) and Hanton and Jones (1999) showed that somatic symptoms of anxiety can have either a *facilitative* effect or a *debilitative* effect on sport performance depending on how the athlete perceives them. To illustrate, a performer who interprets sweaty palms as a sign of uncertainty is experiencing debilitative anxiety whereas someone who regards similar symptoms as a sign of readiness to do well is experiencing facilitative anxiety (as in the cases of Andre Agassi and Tiger Woods above). Since the early 1990s, a substantial volume of studies has been conducted on the benefits of perceiving anxiety symptoms as facilitative of performance. Thomas et al. (2009) highlighted research showing that athletes with this latter view tend to perform better, have higher levels of self-confidence, use more effective coping strategies and display more resilience than do counterparts who perceive anxiety symptoms as debilitative of performance. Clearly, it is beneficial to see anxiety as a help rather than a hindrance. But although this directional perception theory of anxiety in sport seems plausible, it is marred by conceptual and methodological difficulties. The former stem mainly from the terminology involved. G. Jones and Hanton (2001) acknowledged that the term "facilitative anxiety" seems like an oxymoron. To explain, as the term "anxiety" has negative connotations, and as it is difficult to distinguish between somatic anxiety and other emotions (J. Kerr, 1997), then perhaps athletes who label "anxiety" symptoms as facilitative may not be experiencing anxiety at all, but rather a sense of excitement or challenge (see the preceding quote from Tiger Woods). Compounding this semantic issue is a formidable methodological challenge (Uphill, 2008). Specifically, how can researchers distinguish empirically between athletes' anxiety state, their perception of that state, their perception of the impact of that state on their performance, and the actual impact of that state on their performance? Additional research is required to resolve these conceptual and methodological issues. Despite such problems, it is clear that the way in which athletes *label* their arousal levels (if not their anxiety) seems to play a significant role in whether they feel challenged or overwhelmed by pressure situations.

This idea that a given level of arousal is amenable to different interpretative labels has significant theoretical and practical implications. On the theoretical side, it suggests that attempts to measure anxiety should include indices of *direction* or interpretation as well as of intensity. With regard to practical implications, directionality effects highlight the importance of teaching athletes to reframe their physiological symptoms constructively. Hanton and Jones (1999) reported that elite swimmers benefited from learning to interpret pre-race anxiety symptoms in a positive manner. As these authors put it so memorably, the elite swimmers in their study had learned to make their butterflies "fly in formation"! In an effort to explore the meaning of anxiety to athletes, try the exercise in Box 3.1.

Box 3.1 Exploring the meaning of anxiety to athletes

The purpose of this exercise is to explore what performance anxiety means to athletes and to investigate how they cope with it. In order to complete this exercise, you will need to interview three competitive athletes – preferably from

different sports. Before you begin, however, please ensure that these participants have been informed about the purpose of the study and have consented to
have their views recorded and analysed. Then, using an electronic voice-
recorder, ask them the following questions:

1 What does the word "anxiety" mean to you? Do you think that it is helpful or
   harmful to your performance?
2 On a scale of 0 (meaning "not at all important") to 5 (meaning "extremely
   important"), how important do you think that the ability to control anxiety is
   for successful performance in your sport?
3 Do you prefer to be psyched up or calm before a competitive event in your
   sport? Why? Please explain.
4 What things make you anxious *before* a competition? How do these factors
   affect your performance? Explain.
5 What things make you anxious *during* a competition? How do these factors
   affect your performance? Explain.
6 What techniques do you use, if any, to cope with anxiety in your sport?
   Where did you learn these techniques?

Analysis
Do the athletes differ in their understanding of anxiety? If so, are these
differences related to the sports that they play? From the athletes' experiences,
what factors make them anxious before and/or during competition? Do the
athletes use any specific techniques to cope with anxiety? If so, where did they
learn these techniques?

In summary, we have learned so far that anxiety is a multidimensional
construct with cognitive, somatic and behavioural components. We have also discovered that this construct can be distinguished from fear and arousal experiences.
In addition, we saw how athletes differed in the way in which they interpret their
arousal levels as being either facilitative or debilitative of their sport performance.
At this stage, however, we need to tackle the question of whether or not different
types of anxiety can be identified.

Types of anxiety: state and trait

Since the seminal research of Spielberger (1966), a distinction has been drawn by
psychologists between anxiety as a mood state (state anxiety) and anxiety as a
personality characteristic (trait anxiety). Whereas the former term (also known as
"A-state") describes transient, situation-specific feelings of fear, worry and physiological arousal, the latter one (also called "A-trait") refers to a relatively stable
personality trait (or chronic predisposition) which is characterized by a tendency
to perceive certain situations as anxiety-provoking. Thus as Spielberger (1966, p. 17)
explained, **state anxiety** may be defined as "subjective, consciously perceived
feelings of tension and apprehension", whereas **trait anxiety** refers to a general

disposition among people to feel anxious in certain environmental situations (e.g., when playing an important match). Applied to sport, the concept of state anxiety may be used to describe situations in which an athlete's feelings of tension may change during a match. A footballer may feel nervous in the dressing-room before an important match but may become calmer once the competitive action begins. However, a player who scores highly on trait anxiety may feel pessimistic most of the time. Another way of explaining this distinction is to say that trait anxiety is a predisposition to experience state anxiety under certain circumstances. According to this view, athletes who display a high degree of trait anxiety are more likely to interpret sport situations as threatening than are less anxious counterparts.

What causes anxiety in athletes?

Although it is easy to identify typical *antecedents* of anxiety in athletes, it is very difficult to establish the precise causal nature of these factors because of ethical issues. To explain, researchers are precluded from manipulating any variable that may induce anxiety among the participants in their studies. Accordingly, most research on anxiety in sport is correlational rather than experimental in nature. Overall, the personal and situational antecedents of anxiety may be summarized as follows (see also Uphill, 2008).

Perceived importance of the competition

In general, the more importance that is attached to a forthcoming competition by athletes, the more anxiety they are likely to experience in it (Dowthwaite and Armstrong, 1984).

Predispositions: trait anxiety

Many sport psychologists (e.g., Anshel, 1995) believe that athletes' levels of trait anxiety are important determinants of the amount of state anxiety which they are likely to experience in a given situation. But, as I indicated in Chapter 2, it is not valid to use a personality trait as an "explanation" for a mental state. After all, one cannot explain aggressive behaviour by saying that a person has an "aggressive" personality. Clearly, we must be careful to avoid circular reasoning when seeking to explain why athletes become anxious in certain situations.

Attribution/expectations

As I explained in Chapter 2, a tendency to attribute successful outcomes to external and unstable factors (e.g., luck) and to attribute unsuccessful outcomes to internal and stable factors (e.g., low levels of skill) is likely to induce anxiety in athletes.

Perceptions of audience expectations are also important determinants of performance anxiety. For example, the soprano June Anderson said:

> in the beginning of your career … nobody knows who you are, and they don't have any expectations. There's less to lose. Later on, when you're known, people are coming to see you, and they have certain expectations. You have a lot to lose.
>
> (cited in Blau, 1998, p. 17)

Perfectionism

Research on the question of how **perfectionism** (or the striving for flawlessness and the setting of excessively high standards for one's performance: Stoeber and Stoeber, 2009) is related to anxiety and athletic performance is equivocal. Whereas some investigators (e.g., Gould et al., 2002b) regard perfectionism as a stepping-stone to Olympic excellence, others (e.g., Flett and Hewitt, 2005) view it as an impediment to sport success. To illustrate the latter opinion, Flett and Hewitt (2005, p. 14) argued that perfectionism is "primarily a negative factor that contributes to maladaptive outcomes among athletes and exercisers". One reason for this apparent disagreement is that perfectionism is a *multidimensional* construct with at least two components (Slaney et al., 2002) – adaptive perfectionism (e.g., striving to achieve high standards) and maladaptive perfectionism (e.g., displaying excessive concern about mistakes). In relation to making mistakes, research suggests that athletes who set impossibly high standards for their performances may feel anxious when things go wrong for them. Frost and Henderson (1991) discovered that athletes who displayed a significant concern for their mistakes (a key dimension of perfectionism) tended to experience more anxiety than did less perfectionistic colleagues. A similar problem is apparent in the performing arts. For example, the pianist Louis Lortie attributed stage fright and other forms of anxiety to the fact that "we were brought up with the idea that there shouldn't be mistakes" (cited in Blau, 1998, p. 17). Gotwals and Dunn (2009) developed a test of perfectionism in sport called the Sport Multidimensional Perfectionism Scale-2 (Sport-MPS-2). Support for the validity of this scale was provided by Gotwals et al. (2010).

Fear of failure

Many athletes are indoctrinated to adopt a "win at all costs" attitude, which ultimately makes them vulnerable to performance anxiety. If they believe that their self-esteem is tied inextricably to what they achieve, they are especially likely to become nervous at the prospect of defeat as it constitutes a threat to their self-worth.

Lack of confidence

Some sport psychologists have speculated that athletes who have little confidence in their own abilities are likely to experience high levels of anxiety in competitive situations. This hypothesis is supported by research (e.g., J. Martin and Gill, 1991) which shows that runners who scored highly in self-confidence reported experiencing little cognitive anxiety.

Time to competition

Research suggests that different types of anxiety follow different temporal patterns before competition (Uphill, 2008). Specifically, whereas cognitive anxiety tends to remain high and stable in the days preceding an important competitive event, somatic anxiety remains relatively low until one or two days before this encounter. At this point, it tends to increase until the competition begins.

In summary, at least four conclusions have emerged from studying anxiety in athletes. First, even the world's best athletes get nervous before competition. Second, many athletes and coaches (e.g., José Mourinho, who is widely regarded as one of the top managers in world football) believe that competitive performance is determined significantly by the ability to control and channel one's nervous energy effectively. Third, we have learned that anxiety tends to affect people at different levels – via their thinking, feeling and behaviour. In short, anxiety causes athletes to think pessimistically about the future and to feel tense and agitated. Fourth, we have identified a number of antecedents of anxiety in athletes.

Measuring anxiety in athletes

In the previous section, we learned that the construct of anxiety has three different dimensions: cognitive, somatic and behavioural. Within sport psychology, attempts to measure anxiety have focused largely on the first and second of these dimensions, with few studies available on the behavioural aspect of this construct (but see Pijpers et al. (2003), who measured climbers' rigid posture and jerky muscular movement characteristics as behavioural indices of anxiety). Of the measures developed, the most popular tools for anxiety assessment have been self-report scales – probably as a result of the availability and convenience of these instruments.

Physiological measures

As anxiety is analogous to a fear reaction, it has a strong physiological basis. Thus Spielberger (1966, p. 17) proposed that anxiety states are "accompanied by or associated with activation of the autonomic nervous system". This activation results in such typical symptoms of anxiety as elevated heart rate, increased blood pressure, fast and shallow breathing, sweaty palms and tense musculature. If such indices could be measured conveniently, they would facilitate research in this area as they are relatively unaffected by **response sets** such as people's tendency to guess the purposes of questionnaire items so that they can present themselves in a maximally desirable light (a tendency called **social desirability**). Unfortunately, until the 1990s, physiological measures of anxiety were relatively rare in sport psychology for at least five reasons. First, there is no single, universally agreed physiological index of anxiety. Second, as athletes differ in the way in which they *interpret* autonomic arousal (i.e., as facilitative or debilitative of their performance), physiological measures of anxiety are of limited value. Third, most physiological measures assess *arousal* not anxiety. Fourth, physiological indices of arousal are not highly inter-correlated, a fact which suggests that they are not all measuring the same construct. Fifth, physiological assessment of athletes is time-consuming and inconvenient. For these reasons, researchers in sport psychology have tended to use self-report rather than physiological instruments to measure anxiety states in athletes. Since 2000, however, there has been a surge of interest among psychology researchers in the use of neuroendocrine responses (e.g., the release of hormones such as cortisol) to measure anxiety (recall the study by Strahler et al. (2010), discussed earlier in the section on components of anxiety). Additional research is required to establish the validity and utility of cortisol-based measures of anxiety in athletes.

Self-report instruments

Given their simplicity, brevity and convenience, paper-and-pencil tests of anxiety have proliferated in sport psychology research. Unfortunately, as we shall see, all of these instruments have psychometric limitations which threaten their validity. This problem led Uphill (2008, p. 41) to conclude that we need a "healthy dose of skepticism when interpreting the results" of anxiety tests. With this caveat in mind, let us now briefly consider three popular self-report instruments in this field – namely, the "Sport Competition Anxiety Test" (SCAT: R. Martens, 1977), the "Sport Anxiety Scale" (SAS: R. E. Smith et al., 1990; see also the SAS-2: R. Smith et al., 2006) and the "Competitive State Anxiety Inventory-2" (CSAI-2: R. Martens et al., 1990). (By the way the "Mental Readiness Form" (MRF: Krane, 1994) was devised as a short version of the CSAI-2.) In general, these scales have focused largely on the measurement of anxiety intensity in athletes rather than on how anxiety is interpreted by them.

Sport Competition Anxiety Test

The Sport Competition Anxiety Test (SCAT: R. Martens, 1977) is a ten-item unidimensional inventory which purports to measure trait anxiety in sport performers. Parallel versions of this test are available for children (aged 10–14 years) and for adults (of 15 years and above). Typical items include "When I compete I worry about making mistakes" and "Before I compete I get a queasy feeling in my stomach". Respondents are required to indicate their agreement with each item by selecting their preferred answer from the three categories of "hardly ever", "sometimes" and "often". Reverse scoring is used on certain items (e.g., "Before I compete I feel calm") and overall test scores can range from 10 to 30. Internal consistency coefficients range from 0.8 to 0.9 and test-retest reliability values cluster around 0.77 (R. Smith et al., 1998). Validation studies suggest that the SCAT is mainly a measure of somatic anxiety (R. Smith et al., 1998). Evidence of convergent validity comes from studies which show that the test is correlated moderately with various general anxiety inventories. Unfortunately, as the

SCAT does not distinguish between or measure adequately individual differences in cognitive and somatic anxiety, its utility is limited (R. Smith et al., 2006). A revised version of this instrument entitled the Competitive State Anxiety Inventory-2 (CSAI-2) was published by R. Martens et al. (1990).

Sport Anxiety Scale-2

The Sport Anxiety Scale-2 (SAS-2: R. Smith et al., 2006), which is a revised version of the Sport Anxiety Scale (SAS: R. Smith et al., 1990), is a multidimensional instrument that purports to measure individual differences in somatic anxiety, worry and concentration disruption in children (from the age of 9) and adults. It contains fifteen items that load onto three subscales, each comprising five items: somatic anxiety (e.g., "My body feels tense"), worry (e.g., "I worry that I will not play well") and concentration disruption (e.g., "It is hard to concentrate on the game"). According to R. Smith et al. (2006), the SAS-2 not only correlates highly (r=0.90) with its predecessor, the SAS – a sign of convergent validity – but also has strong reliability. For example, subscale reliabilities were estimated at 0.84 (for somatic anxiety), 0.89 (for worry) and 0.84 (for concentration disruption). In summary, the SAS-2 appears to be a reliable and valid measure of multidimensional anxiety in children and adults. The original version of the SAS contains twenty-one items which are divided into three subscales: somatic anxiety (nine items such as "I feel nervous"), worry (seven items such as "I have self-doubts") and a "concentration disruption" (five items such as "My mind wanders during sport competition") subscale. Reliability data for this scale are encouraging, with internal consistency estimated at between 0.88 (somatic anxiety), 0.87 (worry) and 0.69 (concentration-disruption) (J. Dunn et al., 2000) and test-retest figures at 0.77 for an inter-test interval of eighteen days (R. Smith et al., 1990). Evidence of convergent validity for this scale was reported by R. Smith et al. (1990), who calculated significant correlations (ranging between 0.47 and 0.81) between its subscales and the Sport Competition Anxiety Test (R. Martens, 1977). Discriminant validity for the SAS is supported by evidence of low correlations between it and general mental health measures (see R. Smith et al., 1998). Factor analyses have also confirmed that the SAS assesses three separate dimensions: somatic anxiety, cognitive anxiety/worry, and concentration-disruption (J. Dunn et al., 2000). Unfortunately, the SAS was not suitable for children – a fact that prompted the SAS-2. According to R. Smith et al. (2006), however, the SAS-2 not only correlates highly (r=0.90) with the SAS – a sign of convergent validity – but also has strong reliability. For example, subscale reliabilities were estimated at 0.84 (for somatic anxiety), 0.89 (for worry) and 0.84 (for concentration disruption). In summary, the SAS-2 appears to be a reliable and valid measure of multidimensional anxiety in children and adults.

Competitive State Anxiety Inventory-2

The Competitive State Anxiety Inventory-2 (CSAI-2: R. Martens et al., 1990) is a popular test of cognitive and somatic anxiety. It comprises twenty-seven items which are divided into three subscales (with each containing nine items): cognitive anxiety, somatic anxiety and self-confidence. Typical items in the somatic anxiety subscale include "I feel nervous" and "My body feels tense". A sample item in the cognitive anxiety subscale is "I am concerned about losing". The "self-confidence" subscale is included in the test because a lack of confidence is believed to be a sign of cognitive anxiety (R. Martens et al., 1990). On a four-point scale (with 1 = "not at all" and 4 = "very much so"), respondents are required to rate the intensity of their anxiety experiences prior to competition. Following a review of forty-nine studies using the CSAI-2, Burton (1998) reported that internal consistency estimates for these three subscales ranged from 0.76 to 0.91. Doubts about the factorial validity of the CSAI-2 were raised by Lane et al. (1999). For example, these authors suggested that only one of the items on the cognitive anxiety subscale ("I have self-doubts") validly measures this type of anxiety. In response to some of the early criticisms of this scale (summarized in Uphill, 2008), a revised version of this test, called the Revised Competitive State Anxiety Inventory (CSAI-2R), was developed by Cox et al. (2003). This seventeen-item scale purports to measure the intensity components of cognitive anxiety (five items), somatic anxiety (seven items) and self-confidence (five items).

The previous section of the chapter indicated the importance of athletes' interpretations of their arousal symptoms. In this regard, the CSAI-2 is hampered by a significant methodological deficiency – namely, its neglect of the issue of "direction" or personal meaning of anxiety symptoms for athletes (G. Jones, 1995). To rectify this problem, some researchers advocate the addition of a *directional* measure to all "intensity" indices of anxiety (G. Jones and Swain, 1992). In this case, respondents may be required first to complete the CSAI-2 in order to elicit the intensity with which they experience the twenty-seven symptoms listed in this test. Then, they may be asked to rate the degree to which the experienced intensity of each symptom is facilitative or debilitative of their subsequent athletic performance. A seven-item Likert response scale is used, with values ranging from –3 (indicating "very negative") to +3 (indicating "very positive"). To illustrate, an athlete might respond with a maximum "4" to the statement "I am concerned about losing" but might then rate this concern with a +3 on the interpretation scale. Through these scores, the performer is indicating that he or she feels that this concern about losing is likely to have a facilitative effect on his or her forthcoming performance. With this modification, CSAI-2 **direction of anxiety** scores can vary between –27 and +27. Internal consistency reliability estimates for this facilitative/debilitative measure range from 0.72 (for the somatic anxiety subscale) to 0.83 (for the cognitive anxiety subscale) (Swain and Jones, 1996). When this directional modification scale has been used in conjunction with the CSAI-2, the resulting instrument is called the DM-CSAI-2 (Burton, 1998) or the CSAI-2(d) (M. Jones and Uphill, 2004). But how valid is this procedure? See Box 3.2.

Box 3.2 Thinking critically about … research on direction of anxiety

In sport psychology, the term "direction of anxiety" refers to whether an athlete sees anxiety as facilitative or debilitative of athletic performance. To indicate the value of this variable, G. Jones and Swain (1992) added a Likert scale of directionality to each item of the Competitive State Anxiety Inventory-2 to explore the degree to which athletes viewed anxiety as facilitative of their performance. They also administered a test of competitiveness to each athlete. Results showed that highly competitive athletes believed more significantly in the facilitative effects of anxiety than did less successful counterparts. Another study by G. Jones et al. (1994) found that successful swimmers viewed their anxiety as being more facilitative of performance than did less successful swimmers – even though the groups did not differ significantly on anxiety intensity. Based on such evidence, G. Jones (1995) recommended a "directional modification" of the Competitive State Anxiety Inventory-2. Since the late 1990s, however, at least three conceptual and methodological criticisms of direction of anxiety have been raised, as well as an alternative model of the relationship between arousal and performance.

First, Burton (1998) has queried the rationale underlying G. Jones's approach. In particular, he wondered whether or not anxiety can ever be regarded as "facilitative". Is it possible that researchers have been confusing somatic anxiety with more positive emotional states such as excitement or challenge (see also J. Kerr, 1997)? Burton (1998) argued that **cognitive appraisal** processes determine whether people experience a positive emotion, such as excitement/ challenge, or a negative emotion, such as anxiety, when they are aroused in athletic competition. Clearly, more research is required to distinguish between the different emotional experiences of athletes. The second weakness of G. Jones's approach is that measurement of direction of anxiety relies on self-report data. As indicated in Chapter 1, however, people are not always reliable judges of their own behaviour. Therefore, we should not assume that athletes are always correct when they tell us that anxiety had a *facilitative* effect on their performance. Third, **reversal theory** (a conceptual model of motivation and emotion which suggests that people switch back and forth between different frames of mind: see J. Kerr, 1997) also highlights the importance of individual differences in the interpretation of arousal symptoms. For example, when athletes are in a **telic dominance** state (i.e., highly task oriented), high arousal may be interpreted as unpleasant anxiety whereas low anxiety may be interpreted as pleasant relaxation. By contrast, athletes who are in a **paratelic dominance** state (characterized by a fun-loving, present-centred focus) may regard high arousal as pleasantly exciting whereas they may perceive low arousal as unpleasant boredom. In summary, despite its intuitive plausibility, the concept of direction of anxiety has not been validated adequately in sport psychology.

Critical thinking questions

Can you think of a way of assessing whether anxiety facilitates or hampers athletic performance without using a **quantitative research** design or self-report scales? In particular, would qualitative research methodology (see Chapter 1) offer a viable alternative to the self-report approach? How could you validate athletes' insights into their own emotional experiences? Can reversal theory help to explain why athletes may switch from perceiving anxiety as facilitative to perceiving it as debilitative of their performance (see Hudson and Walker, 2002)?

Despite the issues raised in Box 3.2, several studies have supported the validity of the DM-CSAI-2. For example, G. Jones et al. (1994) discovered that elite swimmers reported that they had interpreted cognitive and somatic anxiety as being more facilitative of their performance than did their less successful counterparts. Not surprisingly, a significant proportion of the non-elite swimmers reported anxiety as being debilitative to their performance. Before we conclude this section, it should be noted that concern has been expressed about the psychometric adequacy of the CSAI-2. Briefly, Craft et al. (2003) conducted a meta-analysis of the association between this test and athletic performance. Unfortunately, relationships between the three subscales (cognitive anxiety, somatic anxiety and self-confidence) and sport performance were generally weak – thereby raising doubts about the construct validity of the CSAI-2. Let us now consider in more detail the issue of how anxiety affects athletic performance.

Arousal, anxiety and athletic performance

At the beginning of this chapter, we suggested that the ability to regulate one's arousal level is a vital determinant of success in sport. Endorsing this principle, many athletes and coaches have developed informal methods of either energizing themselves or lowering their arousal levels before important competitions. For example, athletes who are involved in sports which require strength and power (e.g., wrestling and weightlifting) and/or physical contact (e.g., soccer, rugby) tend to favour "psych up" strategies such as listening to inspirational music in the hours or minutes before the competition begins (for a list of popular music tracks that are used for psych up purposes, see Karageorghis, 2008; see also Box 8.4 in Chapter 8 for a summary of some recent research on the effects of music on endurance performance). Of course, music is not the only psych up strategy used in sport: some coaches believe that if players are taunted or made *angry* before they compete, their perfor-mance will be improved. Laurent Seigne, the French rugby coach, is reported to have punched members of his team, Brive, before a match in order to psych them up appropriately (S. Jones, 1997). As yet, however, this theory has not been tested empirically in sport psychology – and ethical prohibitions make this possibility unlikely if not impossible! Arousal regulation strategies are also used in precision sports such as golf, snooker and archery where performers need to calm down in order to play well. For example, the American archer Darrell Pace, twice an Olympic gold medal winner, extolled the benefits of a controlled breathing technique as a preparation strategy before competitions. In this breathing technique, Pace synchronized the pattern of his inhalations and exhalations with covert repetition of the word "relax" (Vealey and Walter, 1994). Another way of dealing with anxiety in ball-sports is to exhale as one strikes the ball. This idea brings us to the controversial issue of "grunting" in tennis (see Box 3.3).

Box 3.3 Thinking critically about … grunting in tennis: what a racket!

Since 2000, at almost all the leading international tennis tournaments, the distinctive "thwack" of the ball being hit by a racket has been drowned out by a rather more grating sound – the extraordinary grunt, moan, shriek or piercing wail that increasingly accompanies many tennis players' serves and groundstrokes. Although this problem may seem recent, grunting in tennis has been practised since the 1970s, with Jimmy Connors being one of its famous early exponents. Indeed, according to the journalist Clive James, Connors' grunt was faster than the ball he was hitting and his opponent had no option but to return the grunt *before* the ball (Fraser, 2009)!

The controversy raised by grunting in tennis may be presented as an argument between two factions. On one side of the fence, grunting has been complained about by players (who claim that it is a form of intimidation or gamesmanship), spectators (who regard it as an aural abomination that is incompatible with the genteel spirit of the game of tennis) and tennis officials (who have noted that a player's grunt can extend into the hitting preparation time of his or her opponent). Among these objectors is Martina Navratilova, the former world number 1 player, who proclaimed, "I call it cheating and it has to stop" (Navratilova, 2009). On the other side of the fence, the practice of grunting has been defended on the grounds that it is simply a habit resulting from a natural and harmless exhalation of air. In other words, it is simply a way of releasing tension by players. Indeed, Jo Durie, the former British champion, claimed that grunting can benefit a player's timing if it is performed quietly like a gentle exhale (Geoghegan, 2009). Similarly, the veteran tennis coach Nick Bollettieri believes that grunting *relaxes* players by helping them to release tension on court (Geoghegan, 2009). Although these rival arguments have been debated widely, what is not in dispute is the actual decibel level achieved by top tennis grunters. To illustrate, Maria Sharapova's grunts have been recorded at 101 decibels – about 9 decibels below the sound of a lion's roar (Flatman, 2009)! The Williams sisters are also inveterate grunters, with 2009 Wimbledon champion Serena reaching 93.2 decibels and Venus hitting 85 decibels (Morrissey, 2009). Debate about this issue came to a head in the 2009 French Open when a French player, Aravane Rezai, complained that the shrieks of her teenage opponent, the Portuguese player Michelle Larcher de Brito, were distracting her. No action was taken against the "grunter" on this occasion, however.

Moving from speculation to science, does grunting *actually* give tennis players an advantage over their rivals? The first study to address this question empirically was published by Sinnett and Kingstone (2010). Briefly, these researchers created a number of video clips of a professional tennis player hitting the ball either to the left or right of a video camera. These clips were edited to include an accompanying grunt or not. Then, a sample of recreational tennis players was required to indicate, as quickly and as accurately as possible, the direction of the shot in each clip. Results showed that participants' response times and accuracy were significantly adversely affected by the presence of grunting sounds. However, the authors were unable to determine the precise mechanisms underlying this effect – such as auditory masking (the possibility that grunting prevents opponents from hearing the sound of the ball being struck by the racket) or distraction (the possibility that grunting distracts opponents' attention away from the sound of the ball). Clearly, additional research is required on this topic. In conclusion, despite the findings of Sinnett and Kingstone (2010), there are no explicit *rules* against grunting in tennis. An umpire *can* penalize a player for "noise hindrance", but it is up to the official to decide whether such noise is intentional or not.

Critical thinking questions
The professional tennis community is divided on the issue of grunting. What do you make of Michelle Larcher de Brito's claim that "nobody can tell me to stop grunting. Tennis is an individual sport and I'm an individual player" (cited in Fraser, 2009, p. 77). How does this view compare with Martina Navratilova's opinion that grunting is a diversionary tactic that prevents opposing players from using auditory cues to anticipate the type of shot that is being played by the grunter. Can you think of a way of extending Sinnett and Kingstone's (2010) research to arbitrate between "masking" and "attentional" explanations of the adverse effects of grunting?

Theories of arousal–performance and anxiety–performance relationships

Although the preceding discussion has highlighted the importance of arousal control to athletes, it does not really illuminate the relationship between anxiety and performance. Fortunately, there is a considerable empirical research literature on this topic (e.g., see reviews by Gould et al., 2002c; M. Wilson, 2008; Woodman and Hardy, 2003). Let us now evaluate briefly the main theories and findings emerging from this research literature. Since the early 1990s, a considerable amount of psychological research has been conducted on the relationship between people's arousal levels and their subsequent performance on skilled tasks. In general, this research has been influenced by at least five main theories: **drive theory** (based on Hull, 1943), the **inverted-U hypothesis** (based on Yerkes and Dodson, 1908), **catastrophe theory** (e.g., L. Hardy, 1990, 1996; L. Hardy and Parfitt, 1991; L. Hardy et al., 2007), the **conscious processing hypothesis** or **reinvestment hypothesis** (R. Masters, 1992; Masters and Maxwell, 2008) and **attentional control theory** (Eysenck et al., 2007). Although the earlier theories (e.g., drive theory, the inverted-U hypothesis) applied mainly to *arousal*–performance relationships, the more recent ones (e.g., catastrophe theory, conscious processing hypothesis and attentional control theory) deal more with *anxiety*–performance relationships. Other theoretical approaches such as the **individual zone of optimal functioning** hypothesis (Hagtvet and Hanin, 2007; Hanin, 1997) and reversal theory (J. Kerr, 1997) have also been postulated.

Drive theory

In learning theory, a "drive" is regarded as a psychological state of arousal that is created by an imbalance in the homeostatic mechanisms of the body and that impels the organism to take ameliorative action. In general, two types of drives have been identified (Cashmore, 2008). Primary drives arise from the pursuit of basic biological needs such as eating, drinking and restoring homeostasis (or the internal equilibrium of the body). Secondary drives are stimuli (e.g., earning money, winning titles) that acquire the motivational characteristics of primary drives as a result of conditioning or other forms of learning. Applied to sport, drive theory postulates a positive and linear relationship between arousal level and performance. In other words, the more aroused an athlete is, the better his or her performance should be. Initially, support for this theory was claimed by researchers like Oxendine (1984), who argued that in power and/or speed sports such as weightlifting or sprinting, a high level of arousal tends to enhance athletic performance. Although superficially plausible, this theory does not stand up to scientific scrutiny. Consider the problem of false starts in sprinting. Here, athletes may become so aroused physiologically that they anticipate wrongly and end up "jumping the gun". This very problem occurred in the 1996 Olympic Games when the British sprinter Linford Christie made *two* false starts in the 100 metres race and was subsequently disqualified. Since 2010, athletes who make even *one* false start are disqualified from races. In the 100 metres final at the 2011 World Athletics Championships, the world record holder Usain Bolt (see also Chapter 6) was disqualified because he had made a single false start. In an effort to counteract this problem of over-anticipation, official starters in sprint competitions tend to use variable foreperiods before firing their pistols. Similar problems stemming from over-arousal can occur in weightlifting when athletes fail to "chalk up" before lifting the barbell. In team sports, over-arousal may be prompted by rousing pep talks delivered by a coach to his or her players before a game. Such talks may capture the attention of the players, especially if they refer to alleged insults by opponents. Thus Jeremy Guscott, the former England and Lions rugby player, remarked that "nothing is a better motivator than being bad-mouthed by the opposition" (Guscott, 1997, p. 44). However, there is little or no empirical evidence to indicate that pep talks channel players' arousal effectively. Recall from Chapter 2 that motivation requires *direction* as well as intensity. Clearly, the problem with rousing pep talks is that they usually lack this important directional component (Anshel, 1995).

The inverted-U hypothesis

According to the inverted-U hypothesis (Oxendine, 1984), the relationship between arousal and performance is curvilinear rather than linear. In other words, increased arousal is postulated to improve skilled performance up to a certain point, beyond which further increases in arousal may impair it. To illustrate this theory, imagine being required to sit an examination just after you wake up (low arousal) or after you have run a marathon (high arousal). At both of these extreme ends of the arousal continuum, your academic performance would probably be poor, whereas if you had a good night's sleep and felt properly prepared for the exam, you should perform at your best. This proposition that arousal has diminishing returns on task performance is derived from the Yerkes–Dodson law (Yerkes and Dodson, 1908). Briefly, this law proposed that there is an optimal level of arousal for performance on any task. Specifically, performance tends to be poor at low or high levels of arousal but is best at intermediate levels of arousal. A summary of the Yerkes–Dodson law is presented in Box 3.4.

Box 3.4 Of mice and men (and women) ... the Yerkes–Dodson law

Although the Yerkes–Dodson law is widely cited in sport psychology, its origins lie in research on animal learning in the early 1900s. Specifically, in 1908, Robert Yerkes and John Dodson reported experiments on the relationship between arousal level and task difficulty. Briefly, they devised a paradigm in which mice could avoid electrical shocks by entering the brighter of two compartments. Arousal level was varied by changing the intensity of the electrical shocks administered to the mice. Task difficulty was manipulated by varying the contrast in brightness between the two compartments. Results showed that the amount of practice required by the mice to learn the discrimination task increased as the difference in brightness between the compartments decreased. In other words, when the task was easy (i.e., when the brighter compartment was easy to identify), the mice performed best at high levels of arousal (i.e., larger electric shocks). However, when the task was difficult (i.e., when there was little difference between the brightness of the two compartments), the mice performed best at low levels of arousal (i.e., small electrical shocks). These findings led Yerkes and Dodson (1908, pp. 481–482) to conclude that "an easily acquired habit, that is, one which does not demand difficult sense discrimination or complex associations, may readily be formed under strong stimulation, whereas a difficult habit may be acquired readily only under relatively weak stimulation". Thus the Yerkes–Dodson law consists of two parts.

Part one suggests that people's performance on skilled tasks is best when their level of arousal is intermediate and that it deteriorates as their arousal either increases or decreases from that optimal level. In other words, the relationship between arousal and performance looks like an inverted "U". For example, when you are either drowsy (under-aroused) or very excited (over-aroused), it is difficult to do an exam to the best of your ability. Part two of the Yerkes–Dodson law suggests that as the complexity of a skill increases, the amount of arousal required for optimal performance of it *decreases*. In other words, the performance of difficult tasks decreases as arousal increases whereas the performance of easy tasks increases as arousal increases. In summary, the Yerkes–Dodson law suggests that optimal performance occurs when people's arousal levels are intermediate in strength. Further details of this law may be found in Teigen (1994).

If the Yerkes–Dodson theory is correct, athletic performance that occurs under conditions of either high or low arousal should be inferior to that displayed at intermediate levels. This hypothesis has received some empirical support. For example, Klavora (1978) found that within a sample of high-school basketball players, the highest levels of performance were displayed by people who had reported moderate levels of somatic anxiety. Unfortunately, despite its plausibility, the Yerkes–Dodson principle is marred by at least four conceptual and methodological weaknesses. First, as Landers and Arent (2010) pointed out, the inverted-U hypothesis does not provide a satisfactory explanation of arousal–performance relationships because it does not address the putative internal mechanisms underlying it. Second, as we learned earlier, it is not easy to devise or agree on a satisfactory independent measure of the construct of arousal. As a result, researchers find it difficult to decide whether a given arousal level is too low or too high for a performer. Third, there is an inherent flaw at the heart of this law. In particular, as researchers cannot predict in advance the point of diminishing returns for the effects of arousal on skilled performance, the inverted-U hypothesis is "immune to falsification" (Neiss, 1988, p. 353). Fourth, researchers disagree about the best way in which to induce different levels of arousal in participants. For ethical reasons, contemporary investigators cannot use electric shocks or other forms of aversive stimuli for this purpose – unlike their predecessors Yerkes and Dodson (1908). In summary, the inverted-U theory has several flaws as a possible explanation of the link between arousal and performance. Perhaps most significantly, it does not elucidate putative theoretical mechanisms which might account for the link between arousal and performance. Thus the inverted-U is "a general prediction, not a theory that explains how, why, or precisely when arousal affects performance" (Gould et al., 2002c, p. 214). Unfortunately, despite these limitations, this hypothesis has been promulgated as an established fact by some applied sport psychologists. To illustrate, G. Winter and Martin (1991, p. 17) used it to justify their advice to tennis players on "controlling 'psych' levels".

Catastrophe theory

The cusp catastrophe theory of anxiety (e.g., L. Hardy, 1990, 1996; L. Hardy and Parfitt, 1991; L. Hardy et al., 2007) is based on the assumption that anxiety is a multidimensional construct comprising a cognitive component and a physiological arousal component. This theory is different from the two previous arousal–performance models in proposing that physiological arousal *interacts* with certain aspects of anxiety (in this case, cognitive state anxiety or worry) to influence athletic performance. More precisely, this theory postulates that arousal is associated with athletic performance in a manner described by the inverted-U curve – but only when athletes have low cognitive state anxiety (i.e., when they are not worried). When cognitive anxiety is high, however, increases in arousal tend to improve performance up to a certain point beyond which further increases may produce a swift, dramatic and discontinuous (hence the term "catastrophic") decline in performance rather than a slow or gradual deterioration. Therefore, the cornerstone of catastrophe theory is the assumption that arousal may have different effects on athletic performance depending on the prevailing level of cognitive anxiety in the performer.

Based on this assumption, at least two predictions are possible (Gould et al., 2002c). First, the interaction of physiological arousal and cognitive state anxiety will determine athletic performance more than will the absolute value of either variable alone. Thus high cognitive anxiety should enhance performance at low levels of physiological arousal but should hinder performance at relatively higher levels of arousal. This prediction is interesting because it suggests that, contrary to popular opinion, cognitive anxiety does not always hamper performance (L. Hardy, 1997). The second prediction is that when an athlete experiences high cognitive anxiety, the arousal–performance curve should follow a different path under conditions of increasing versus decreasing physiological arousal (a phenomenon known as "hysteresis"). This hypothesis was supported, in part, by Vickers and Williams (2007), who discovered that high level of cognitive anxiety combined with a high level of physiological arousal sometimes led to "choking" (see later in chapter) among biathlon performers – but not when these athletes were able to pay attention to task-relevant information. Put differently, these authors showed that visual attentional processes mediate the relationship between anxiety and performance. Although the cusp catastrophe theory has received some empirical support in sport psychology (e.g., see Edwards et al., 2002), it has also been challenged. A. Cohen et al. (2003) found no support for the hysteresis hypothesis in a dart-throwing task. The complexity of catastrophe theory (stemming from its three-dimensional nature) renders it difficult to test. Nevertheless, this approach remains an intriguing model which deserves additional empirical scrutiny.

Conscious processing (or reinvestment) hypothesis

The conscious processing (or reinvestment) hypothesis (CPH: R. Masters, 1992; R. Masters and Maxwell, 2008) attempts to investigate what happens when people become conscious of the task-related movements that they are performing. It has generated a considerable amount of research in sport and exercise psychology (see review by R. Masters and Maxwell, 2008) – especially with regard to the relationship between conscious (motor) processing and skilled performance under anxiety-provoking conditions. It was spawned, in part, by an attempt to explain the well-known "paralysis-by-analysis" phenomenon whereby skilled performance tends to deteriorate whenever people try to exert conscious control over movements that had previously been under automatic control (see Figure 3.4). Note that once a skill has become automatic, its execution is implemented implicitly and does not require the resources of **working memory** (a cognitive system that regulates the storage and manipulation of currently relevant information).

According to R. Masters (1992), the performance impairment suffered by skilled but highly anxious athletes is caused mainly by the disruption of automatic control processes. To explain in more detail, when athletes experience increases in their anxiety levels, they attempt to ensure task success by reverting to a mode of conscious control that is associated mainly with an *early* stage of motor learning

Figure 3.4 Overanalysis can unravel people's sport skills
Source: Courtesy of Inpho photography

(i.e., one that relies on explicit rules and that typically results in slow and effortful movements). This temporary regression is held to involve a "reinvestment" of **cognitive processes** in perceptual-motor control. So, the conscious processing hypothesis postulates that performance breakdown occurs when performers "reinvest" their verbal knowledge of task components in an effort to consciously control their movements. This reinvestment is most likely to happen, according to R. Masters and Maxwell (2008), in pressure situations. In other words, anxiety is postulated to exert its debilitating influence upon performance by *increasing a participant's self-consciousness* of their movements. This heightened self-consciousness may result in the performer manipulating "conscious, explicit, rule based knowledge, by working memory, to control the mechanics of one's movements during motor output" (R. Masters and Maxwell, 2004, p. 208). If this conscious processing theory is correct, anxiety should have *differential* effects on skilled performance – depending on how the skill had been acquired originally (i.e., whether it had been learned explicitly or implicitly).

In an effort to test this prediction using the skill of golf putting, R. Masters (1992) devised an intriguing experimental paradigm in which participants who acquired the skill of golf putting using explicit knowledge subsequently experienced impaired performance when tested under conditions of high anxiety. To explain this experiment in more detail, participants were initially required to perform putting skills in both training and testing phases. Two conditions were crucial to the experiment. In the explicit condition, participants were instructed to read coaching manuals on golf putting. Conversely, in the implicit condition, participants were given no instructions but had to putt golf balls while performing a secondary task which had been designed to prevent them from thinking about the instructions on putting. There were four training sessions in which participants had to try to hole one hundred golf balls. The number of putts holed was measured in each case. After the fourth training session, a source of stress was introduced. This stress was induced by a combination of evaluation apprehension (e.g., requesting an alleged golfing expert to judge their putting performance) and financial inducement. Results suggested that the implicit learning group showed no deterioration in performance under stress in contrast to the golfers in the explicit learning condition. R. Masters (1992) interpreted this to mean that the skills of athletes with a small pool of explicit knowledge were less likely to fail than were those of performers with relatively larger amounts of explicit knowledge. In other words, the prediction of the conscious processing theory was corroborated. Anxiety appears to have *different* effects on performance depending on how the skill was acquired in the first place (i.e., through *explicit* or *implicit* learning). Subsequently, R. Masters et al. (1993) developed a measure of individual differences in dispositional reinvestment – or people's tendency to attempt to gain conscious control over an automatic skill in pressure situations – called the Reinvestment Scale. This twenty-item scale purports to measure the extent of people's self-consciousness in everyday situations. Typical items include "I'm aware of the way my mind works when I work through a problem" and "I'm concerned about my style of doing things". Evidence to support the predictive validity of this scale was reported by R. Jackson et al. (2006), who found that high "reinvesters" displayed greater susceptibility to skill failure under pressure than did low "reinvester" counterparts. Toner and Moran (2011) investigated the effects of two different types of conscious processing (making technical adjustments to a stroke and simply paying attention to the execution of the stroke) on putting performance by expert golfers. Results showed that although technical adjustments did not affect these experts' putting proficiency (as measured by number of putts holed), they impaired kinematic aspects (e.g., swing consistency) of the putting stroke.

To summarize, the conscious processing hypothesis predicts that athletes whose cognitive anxiety increases will tend to revert to conscious control of normally automatic skills. This theory has received considerable empirical support in sport and exercise psychology (R. Masters and Maxwell, 2008). For example, many experimental studies have shown that people's performance deteriorates when pressure manipulations require them to consciously attend to their movements (e.g., see Pijpers et al., 2003; M. Wilson et al., 2007b).

Attentional control theory

Attentional control theory (ACT: Derakshan and Eysenck, 2009; Eysenck et al., 2007), which is a successor to **processing efficiency theory** (PET: Eysenck and Calvo, 1992), was postulated to investigate theoretical relationships between anxiety, working memory (our mental system for storing and manipulating currently relevant information for a brief period of time) and skilled performance.

ACT and PET make three key assumptions. First, they assume that we can distinguish between performance *effectiveness* (i.e., the quality of task performance) and performance *efficiency* (i.e., the relationship between performance effectiveness and use of processing resources). Second, they assume that anxiety impairs processing efficiency more than performance effectiveness. Third, both theories assume that cognitive anxiety (or worrying) impairs the efficiency of the central executive component of the working memory system and diverts the performer's attention from task-relevant to task-*irrelevant* information. ACT, however, goes beyond PET in addressing the putative theoretical mechanisms by which anxiety impairs cognitive performance.

To explain, a central prediction of ACT is that anxiety hampers performance via "attentional control" – which is a key function of the central executive. According to Corbetta and Shulman (2002), there are two attentional systems – one influenced by a person's current goals and expectations (a top-down, goal-driven system) and the other, a bottom-up, stimulus driven system which is triggered by salient environmental events. According to ACT, anxiety affects attentional control. Specifically, it "disrupts the balance between these two systems by enhancing the influence of the stimulus driven, bottom-up processes over the efficient top-down goal-driven processes" (Derakshan and Eysenck, 2009, p. 170). Furthermore, ACT predicts that anxiety "increases attention to task irrelevant stimuli (especially threat-related)" and "reduces attentional focus on concurrent task demands" (Derakshan and Eysenck, 2009, p. 170). More precisely, ACT predicts that anxiety disrupts performance not only by impairing *attentional inhibition* (the process by which, under normal circumstances, people can restrain themselves from directing their attention at task-irrelevant factors) but also by impairing *attentional shifting* (the process by which people can normally switch their attention in response to changing task requirements).

Research provides some empirical support for the predictions of ACT. M. Wilson et al. (2009) used **eye-tracking technology** to analyse the visual search behaviour of soccer players as they prepared to take penalties in five-a-side matches (where there is a smaller distance between the goal posts than in eleven-a-side matches) under various conditions of anxiety. Results supported a prediction of ACT by indicating that when anxious, the penalty takers displayed an attentional bias towards a salient and threatening stimulus (the goalkeeper) rather than to the ideal target for their kick (just inside the goal post). Extending this research, G. Wood and Wilson (2010) investigated the performance of experienced footballers who took penalties while wearing eye-tracking equipment under counterbalanced conditions of threat (low versus high) and goalkeeper movement (stationary versus arm-waving). Results revealed that under high-threat conditions, the kickers found it difficult to disengage their attention from the moving/distracting goalkeepers – which again corroborates the predictions of ACT. Clearly, further research is required in sport psychology to test the predictions of this emerging theory of the relationship between anxiety and performance.

Conclusions about arousal–performance and anxiety–performance relationship

At least three general conclusions have emerged from the preceeding theories and research (see also Weinberg and Gould, 2007). First, anxiety and arousal are multi-dimensional constructs which do not have simple linear relationships with athletic performance. Second, increases in physiological arousal and cognitive state anxiety do not inevitably lead to a deterioration in athletic performance. Recall that the effects of both of these variables depend crucially on how the performer *interprets* the perceived changes in arousal. For example, increased arousal may be perceived as energizing rather than overwhelming and hence facilitative of performance. Third, the interaction between arousal and cognitive anxiety seems to be more important in determining performance than is the absolute value of either variable on its own. With these general conclusions in mind, let us now consider what happens when anxiety hampers athletic performance.

Performance anxiety in sport: "choking" under pressure

Earlier in the chapter, we learned that the term anxiety is derived from the Latin word *angere*, which means "to choke". Not surprisingly, the phenomenon of **choking under pressure**, whereby athletic performance is suddenly impaired by intense anxiety, has attracted both popular interest (e.g., Beilock, 2010a; Dobson, 1998) and scientific scrutiny (e.g., Gucciardi and Dimmock, 2008; Hill et al., 2010; Otten, 2009). As we shall see in Box 3.5, however, researchers disagree not only about how to define this term but also about the psychological mechanisms that explain its impact on behaviour. Nevertheless, choking is such a ubiquitous experience among competitive athletes that it has a variety of sport-specific synonyms, such as "icing" (in basketball), "dartitis" (in darts) and the "yips" (in golf). Although it affects athletes of all levels of ability and/or experience, choking is especially prevalent among performers of individual precision sports such as golf, tennis, snooker, darts and cricket. To illustrate, successful golfers like Greg Norman, Stewart Cink, Scott Hoch, Jean van de Velde (who led by three strokes at the final hole of 1999 Open Championship at Carnoustie but who triple-bogied it before losing to Paul Lawrie in a play-off: P. Dixon and Kidd, 2006) and more recently, the Irish prodigy Rory McIlroy, who squandered a four-shot lead in the final round of the 2011 US Masters championship in Augusta and ended up shooting an 8 over par score of 80 and finishing ten shots behind the winner, Charl Schwartzel. Despite this setback, McIlroy displayed remarkable mental strength to win the next competition that he played after the US Masters – namely, the 2011 US Open (see Figure 3.5). Of course, choking also happens in team sports. For example, in 2004, the New York Yankees became the first team in baseball history to lose a best-of-seven series, having held a 3–0 lead against the Boston Red Sox (Viner, 2011). Choking is widespread in soccer. For example, consider how some of the world's best footballers appear to crumble under the pressure of penalty-taking (see Box 3.5).

Figure 3.5 Rory McIlroy displayed remarkable mental strength to win the 2011 US Open golf championship
Source: Courtesy of Inpho photography

Box 3.5 Choking under pressure in soccer: why do top players miss penalty kicks?

Ever since the penalty shootout was introduced by the Fédération Internationale de Football Association (FIFA) in 1970 to resolve elimination matches when two teams are tied after extra time, it has attracted praise and controversy in equal measure. But is it really a test of players' nerve and skill – or merely a contest based entirely on chance? At first glance, the penalty kick presents a straightforward technical challenge. It is a self-paced task in which the kicker tries to beat the goalkeeper from a distance of approximately 11 metres. Furthermore, the kicker is allowed to place the static ball on the penalty spot and no interference to his or her "run-up" or kick is allowed from other players. But closer examination of the psychological factors involved in penalty taking raises an obvious question. Specifically, if penalty kicks are so easy to take, why do so many top professional players miss them in important matches (e.g., recall the misses of Italy's Robert Baggio against Brazil in the 1994 World Cup final and of England's Gareth Southgate against Germany in the European Championship semi-final in 1996)?

Some possible answers to this question have emerged from empirical studies on the anxiety mechanisms underlying poor penalty taking in soccer. For example, consider the research of Jordet and his colleagues (e.g., Jordet, 2009; Jordet and Hartman, 2008; Jordet et al., 2006, 2007) on choking in penalty takers in major international soccer tournaments. Jordet et al. (2006) investigated the relationship between players' *perception of control* and penalty outcome. He discovered that players who felt that a penalty shootout was a lottery were more likely to miss their shots than those who believed that they were in control of the outcome of the kick. Furthermore, Jordet and Hartman (2008) found that a key factor associated with penalty misses was the *immediate importance* of the shot. To illustrate, consider the success rate of penalty kicks in situations either where a kicker's shot can ensure that his or her team wins, or alternatively, where *missing* the kick can mean instant defeat for his or her team. Jordet and Hartman (2008) discovered that in the latter situations (i.e., in cases of shots where a miss instantly produces a team loss), players typically respond anxiously (e.g., by speeding up their preparation for the kick) and perform considerably worse than in situations where a successful kick can ensure an immediate team win. According to Keh (2010), whereas the success rate for kickers whose penalties can mean an immediate win for their teams is about 92 per cent, it drops to about 60 per cent for players whose missed penalties would lead to instant defeat for their teams. Jordet (2009) discovered from analysis of video footage taken at major international tournaments that publicly esteemed "superstar" players (i.e., those who had received prestigious awards for their skills) tended to perform worse than less renowned players in penalty shootouts – presumably because of the perceived pressure they experienced.

Unfortunately, choking not only is debilitating but also can affect athletes over a long period of time. For example, the Welsh golfer Ian Woosnam admitted that he had suffered from the "yips" for three years. More precisely, he said:

> it got to the stage where the right hand would suddenly jerk into action and you'd putt to the left ... Then, as it goes on, you don't know where the right path is and you get even more tense. I was suffering so much when I got onto the green I was feeling physically sick.
>
> (cited in White, 2002b, p. 22)

Fortunately, this problem disappeared when he made a technical adjustment to his stroke by switching to a "broom handle" putter. Similarly, Eric Bristow, who won the world darts championship five times, choked so badly at times that he could not release the dart from his fingers. It took him years to overcome this problem (Middleton, 1996). Other athletes have not been so lucky. The former snooker star Patsy Fagan had to abandon the sport because of his failure to overcome anxiety problems which affected his cueing action (Dobson, 1998). Less dramatically, anxiety has prompted remarkable collapses in the performance of such athletes as Jana Novotna and Greg Norman. To illustrate, consider what happened in the 1993 Wimbledon Ladies' Singles final between Jana Novotna (Czech Republic) and Steffi Graf (Germany). Serving at 4–1 in the third set, with a point for 5–1, Novotna began to lose control. She produced a double fault and some wild shots to lose that game. Later, she served *three* consecutive double faults in her anxiety to increase her 4–3 lead over Graf (Thornley, 1993, p. 6). Interestingly, Novotna played in a similar fashion in the third round of the 1995 French Open championship in Paris when she lost a match to the American player Chanda Rubin despite having nine match points when leading 5–0, 40–0 in the third set. The golfer Greg Norman surrendered a six-shot lead in the final round of the 1996 US Masters' championship in Augusta to lose to Nick Faldo. Likewise, the American golfer John Daly admitted that "when the heat was on, I choked" (The Title, 1998) in the 1998 golf World Cup in New Zealand. Interestingly, in the case of Daly, a curious moderating factor was at work – namely, the effects of alcohol. Daly believed that the effects of anxiety on his golf performance had been intensified by the fact that he had given up drinking before the tournament. Ironically, Daly's sobriety had caused him to feel more nervous than he would have been in the past:

> Usually, when I have that situation I don't feel the pressure, I usually just knock them in. But now it's totally different. I guess I used to be so drunk I didn't care. Now it's tough, I feel all the nerves and the pressure more than ever.
>
> (The Title, 1998)

In summary, the preceding examples show clearly that choking is a potentially significant problem for many athletes. But what do we really know about the nature and causes of this problem?

What exactly is choking?

The term choking is used by sport psychologists to refer to a phenomenon in which athletic performance is impaired suddenly by anxiety. Baumeister (1984) offered an early and seminal definition of this term when he claimed that it referred to "the occurrence of suboptimal performance under pressure conditions" (Baumeister and Showers, 1986, p. 362). But there are at least three problems with this definition. First, as Hill et al. (2010) pointed out, for any suboptimal performance to be regarded as a choke in sport, and hence distinguished from a random lapse, we must be sure that the athlete in question was *capable* of performing better, was *motivated* sufficiently to succeed, and perceived the sport situation as *important*. Second, Gucciardi and Dimmock (2008) argued that the deterioration in performance that characterizes choking should be *significant* – not trivial. Third, as Hill et al. (2010) noted, in order to qualify as a choke, the performance impairment should be *acute* rather than gradual. Regardless of these semantic issues, choking is an intriguing mental state because it stems from a motivational paradox. To explain, in the pressure situations that prompt choking, the more effort the athlete puts into his or her performance, the *worse* it becomes. Put simply, choking occurs paradoxically because people try *too* hard to perform well.

The symptoms of choking are similar to those of any arousal state (see earlier in chapter). They include tense muscles, shaky limbs, rapid heart and pulse rates, shortness of breath, butterflies in the stomach, racing thoughts and feelings of panic. In addition, choking may involve the sensation that one cannot complete the stroke or movement that one intends. In this way, choking is similar to another form of performance failure called the yips (a type of focal dystonia). Golfers who suffer from this condition often feel themselves getting tense over the ball and cannot complete a putting stroke due to interference from sudden involuntary movements. Likewise, bowlers in cricket who suffer from anxiety attacks suddenly feel as if they cannot release the ball. Phil Edmonds, the former Middlesex and England bowler, was so badly afflicted with anxiety that he ended up standing in the crease and lobbing the ball at the batter's end (Middleton, 1996). Choking reactions may also be character-ized by a tiny muscular spasm that occurs just as the stroke is about to be executed – even in practice situations. Eric Bristow, a world champion in darts for three consecutive years, revealed: "I had it so bad I was even getting it when I was practising ... It took me six or seven years to sort it out" (cited in Dobson, 1998, p. 16). Before concluding this section, it should be noted that choking seems to occur more frequently in untimed individual sports (e.g., golf, tennis) than in timed team games (e.g., football, rugby). As yet, however, the precise reasons for this phenom-enon remain unknown. Happily, some progress has been made in understanding the aetiology of the "yips" in golf. Briefly, A. Smith et al. (2003) distinguished between two types of yips phenomena on the basis of whether they were caused by neuro-logical or psychological factors. "Type 1" yips was postulated to reflect a neurolo-gical condition called dystonia, in which a deterioration occurs in the motor pathways involving the basal ganglia. "Type 2" yips probably results from severe performance anxiety or choking. These authors speculated that golfers who suffer from the neurologically mediated type 1 yips may have to learn a new stance or else switch to a longer putter as the prognosis for this condition is poor. Research suggests that neurologically based yips conditions appear to be exacerbated by stress (Clark et al., 2005).

What causes choking in sport? Attentional theories

In contemporary sport psychology, choking is regarded as an anxiety-based atten-tional difficulty (see also Chapter 4) rather than as a personality problem. This distinction is important because it suggests that the propensity to choke is not some sort of character flaw but instead, a cognitive problem arising from an interaction between anxiety and attention. If this *attentional* perspective is correct, then any athletes, regardless of their personality, can choke if they concentrate on the "wrong" target – anything which is outside their control or which is irrelevant to the task at hand. But what psychological mechanisms could underlie this choking effect?

According to Gucciardi and Dimmock (2008) and Hill et al. (2010), two types of attentional theories of choking may be identified – *distraction* theories, such as processing efficiency theory (PET: Eysenck and Calvo, 1992) and *self-focus* theories (e.g., Baumeister, 1984; Beilock and Carr, 2001; R. Masters, 1992). In general, distraction theories postulate that pressure (as perceived by the performer) induces anxiety which consumes working memory resources and causes inefficient processing of task-relevant information – thereby shifting attention away from task execution. By contrast, self-focus models of choking propose that anxiety increases athletes' levels of self-consciousness and causes them to focus their attention inwards (see also Chapter 4). This shift to self-focused attention encourages athletes to attempt to consciously monitor and/or control their skill execution which may induce choking through a form of "paralysis by analysis" (see above). In general, PET explains choking by suggesting that anxious athletes may try to maintain their level of performance by investing extra effort in it. Although this increased effort investment may appear to generate immediate benefits, it soon reaches a point of diminishing returns. At this stage, athletes may conclude that too much effort is required and so they give up. At that point, their performance deteriorates rapidly. Unfortunately, this theory is hampered by the difficulty of measuring mental effort objectively. Turning to self-focus theories of choking, two models are especially prominent – the conscious processing (or reinvestment) hypothesis (CPH: R. Masters, 1992, explained on p. 105) and the "explicit monitoring" hypothesis (EMH: Beilock and Carr, 2001). Although these two approaches share many similarities (see R. Masters and Maxwell, 2004), they differ in at least one important issue (Hill et al., 2010). Whereas the EMH suggests that athletic performance is disrupted by performers *monitoring* their step-by-step execution of the skill, CPH postulates that the disruption is cased by athletes consciously *controlling* the skill involved.

Applying the self-focus model to sport, when people experience a great deal of pressure to perform well they tend to think more about themselves and the importance of the event in which they are competing than they would normally. This excessive self-consciousness causes people to attempt to gain conscious control over previously automatic skills – just as a novice would do. As a result of this attempt to invest automatic processes with conscious control, skilled performance tends to unravel. According to some athletes, this unravelling of skill, which is caused by thinking too much about automatic movements, may happen more frequently as one gets older. For example, consider Ian Woosnam's experience of trying to correct his putting stroke in golf. In particular, he said:

> putting shouldn't be hard … but that's where the mind comes in. So much is running through your mind – hold it this way, keep the blade square – whereas when you're young, you just get hold of it and hit it. When you get old too much goes through your mind.
>
> (cited in White, 2002b, p. 22)

This self-consciousness approach is similar to the conscious processing hypothesis (R. Masters, 1992) discussed in the previous section. Indeed, this latter hypothesis suggests that under pressure, "the individual begins thinking about how he or she is executing the skill, and endeavours to operate it with his or her explicit knowledge of its mechanics" (R. Masters, 1992, p. 345).

Overall, according to Gucciardi and Dimmock (2008), empirical support for distraction models of choking is strongest for tasks (e.g., mathematical computation) that load heavily on working memory resources. By contrast, self-focus models of choking appear to be supported best by studies involving tasks that make few demands on working memory (e.g., golf putting). For a brief account of conceptual issues in psychological explanations of choking, see Box 3.6.

Box 3.6 Thinking critically about … explanations of choking behaviour in athletes

At first glance, the phenomenon of choking in sport is simple to define and easy to explain. Is it not just a case of an athlete performing poorly due to nervousness? When we delve a little deeper into this lay "explanation" of this phenomenon, however, we discover a hornet's nest of conceptual problems. As we explained in the subsection on "What exactly is choking?", there is no universal agreement among researchers as to the precise meaning of the term choking. In addition, the idea that we can attribute choking behaviour to nervousness is fraught with diffculty. To explain, as we learned in Chapter 2, trait explanations of behaviour are rather dubious. Logically, traits are inferences from, rather than causes of, behaviour. Therefore, there is always a danger of circularity when "explaining" behaviour using traits (e.g., "she acted nervously because she is an anxious person"). Instead of explaining choking in terms of anxiety-proneness, modern sport psychology researchers tend to consider it as an attentional problem. Specifically, it seems to be caused by focusing on oneself when one should be concentrating on the task at hand. To illustrate this approach, consider the research of Roy Baumeister in this field (see Azar, 1996). Baumeister (1984) began by distinguishing between sports that are dominated primarily by skill (e.g., golf, gymnastics) and those which require sustained effort (e.g., running, weightlifting). According to him, the pressure of a competition can facilitate performance of an "effortful" skill but can impede the performance of a precision skill. This theory was tested using simulated pressure situations in laboratory conditions. Baumeister (1984) devised an effortful task by timing the speed and accuracy with which college students could arrange a deck of cards in numerical order. However, he introduced a pressure component into this task by telling the respondents that if they did better than their previous score, he would pay them $5. In general, results showed an improvement in sport performance in the pressure group. But when Baumeister used a skilful task (e.g., playing a videogame), different findings emerged. Thus Baumeister suggested that although pressure from competition or from public scrutiny makes people try harder on effortful tasks, it does not make them perform better on skill-based tasks. This happens because pressure tends to make people pay attention to automatic (i.e., highly practised) aspects of a given task. But here the picture becomes more complex. To explain, Baumeister (1984) proposes that athletes who are used to focusing on themselves choke less frequently than do counterparts who engage in less self-focused observation. But participants in Baumeister's studies were novices and hence may have maintained their performance level under pressure conditions not because they were trained under high levels of self-consciousness but instead, because skill-focused attention is required for effective performance at their level of ability (J. Wang et al., 2004). In other words, pressure may not alter the chronic self-focus achieved by some people – but it *does* seem to affect the behaviour of people who do not normally concentrate on their own actions.

Critical thinking questions
Can you think of any alternative explanation of Baumeister's (1984) results? Do you agree with him that excessive self-awareness is the main cause of choking in athletes? Why do you think choking is more prevalent in untimed individual sports rather than timed group sports?

In summary, we have learned that choking under pressure is a pervasive problem in sport. Unfortunately, no consensus has been reached as yet about the theoretical mechanisms that cause it. Nevertheless, most theories of this phenomenon agree that anxiety impairs performance by inducing the athlete to think too much, thereby regressing to an earlier stage of skill acquisition. By the way, some helpful practical tips on how to counteract choking are provided by Beilock (2010a). This leads us to the next section of the chapter, which explains how athletes can learn to control anxiety and cope with pressure situations in sport.

Controlling anxiety in sport: how do athletes and coaches cope with pressure situations?

Given the ubiquity of performance anxiety in sport, it is not surprising that psychologists have devised a variety of strategies in an effort to reduce athletes' anxiety levels. In this section, I describe the most popular of these coping strategies and outline some recent research on the coping techniques used by elite athletes and coaches. Before I address these two objectives, however, some important background information is required. First, we must distinguish between pressure *situations* and pressure *reactions* in sport. This distinction is extremely important in applied sport psychology because athletes need to be trained to understand that they do not automatically have to experience "pressure" (i.e., an anxiety response) in pressure situations. Second, we need to understand what effective anxiety control or "coping" actually means. According to Lazarus and Folkman (1984, p. 141), coping involves "cognitive and behavioural efforts to manage specific external and/or internal demands that are appraised as taxing or exceeding the resources of the person". Put simply, it refers to any techniques which a person uses to master, reduce or otherwise tolerate pressure. Commonly, psychologists distinguish between problem-focused and emotion-focused coping (Lazarus and Folkman,

1984; see also review by A. Nicholls and Polman, 2007). To explain, some athletes like to confront the pressure situation directly. This strategy is known as *problem-focused coping* and involves such activities as obtaining as much information as possible about the pressure to be faced, setting specific and relevant goals, and/or forming a plan of action designed to reduce expected pressure. In *emotion-focused coping*, sports performers actively seek to change their interpretation of, and behavioural reaction to, the pressure situation in question. Therefore, they may use one of the many intervention strategies recommended by sport psychologists for anxiety reduction such as physical relaxation (e.g., see J. Williams, 2010). Typically, problem-focused coping techniques are advisable when preparing for *controllable* sources of pressure whereas emotion-focused strategies are usually more appropriate when the pressure situation is *uncontrollable*.

With these two ideas in mind – that pressure lies in the mind of the beholder and that different strategies are available to facilitate active coping – here is a summary of some of the most popular techniques used by athletes to counteract the effects of unwanted anxiety in sport.

Understanding the experience of pressure

According to psychologists, we experience pressure and concomitant anxiety symptoms whenever we believe that a current or impending situation threatens us in some way. For example, a soccer player might be apprehensive about making a mistake in an important match in front of the home supporters. A swimmer may feel tense at the prospect of competing under the watchful eye of a feared coach. More generally, whenever there is a discrepancy between what we *think* we can do (i.e., our assessment of our own abilities) and what we believe we are *expected* to do (i.e., the perceived demands of the situation), we put *ourselves* under pressure. Psychologically, therefore, pressure is a subjective interpretation of certain objective circumstances (the "pressure situation"). Another point to note is that although we cannot change a pressure situation, we *can* change our reaction to it. Specifically, by restructuring the situation in our minds, we can learn to interpret it as a challenge to our abilities rather than as a threat to our well-being. To illustrate, consider what Jack Nicklaus, who is statistically the greatest golfer ever by virtue of winning eighteen major tournaments, revealed about the distinction between feeling nervous and excited. Specifically, he said:

> Sure, you're nervous, but that's the difference between being able to win and not being able to win. And that's the fun of it, to put yourself in the position of being nervous, being excited. I never look on it as pressure. I look on it as fun and excitement. That's why you're doing it.
>
> (cited in Gilleece, 1996)

Unfortunately, this skill of perceiving pressure situations as *challenges* does not normally develop spontaneously in athletes. It can be cultivated through specialist advice and training, however. To learn the rudiments of cognitive restructuring in practical terms, try the exercise in Box 3.7.

Box 3.7 Cognitive restructuring in action: turning a pressure situation into a challenge

The purpose of this exercise is to show you how to use a technique called cognitive restructuring to turn a feared pressure situation into a manageable challenge (based on Moran, 1998). To begin, think of a situation in your sport or daily life that usually makes you feel anxious. Now, describe this situation by finishing the following sentence:

"I hate the pressure of ..."

Fill in the missing words with reference to the pressure situation you have experienced. For example, you might write down "I hate the pressure of serving for the match when playing tennis". Alternatively, it could be "I hate the pressure of facing exams when I have not studied for them".

Now, think of this pressure situation again. This time, however, I would like you to *restructure* it in your head so that you think about it differently:

"I love the challenge of ..."

Please note that you are not allowed to simply repeat what you wrote before. For example, you cannot say "I love the challenge of serving for the match when playing tennis". Instead, you have to pick something else to focus on in that pressure situation besides the fear of making mistakes. As we shall see in Chapter 4, the secret of maintaining your focus under pressure is to concentrate on something that is specific, relevant and under your own control. Usually, that means concentrating on some aspect of your *preparation* for the feared situation. For example, you could write "I love the challenge of preparing in the same way for every serve – no matter what the score is in the match". Notice how restructuring a situation can make you feel differently about it. You no longer see it as something to fear but as something which challenges your skills.

Becoming more aware of anxiety: interpreting arousal signals constructively

Having learned how athletes can restructure pressures as challenges, our next step is to examine some practical techniques for reducing anxiety in pressure situations. Despite their talent and experience, many athletes have a poor understanding of what their body is telling them when they are anxious. In particular, they need to be educated to realize that anxiety is not necessarily a bad thing but merely a sign that they *care* about the results of what they are doing. Without such education, athletes tend to make the mistake of misinterpreting physical signs of *readiness* (e.g., a rapid heart beat, a surge of adrenaline) as harbingers of impending disaster. Therefore, sport performers must learn to perceive somatic arousal as an essential prerequisite of a good performance. Some players realize this intuitively when they concede that they cannot play well unless they feel appropriately "juiced" or pumped up for a contest. Interestingly, Thomas et al. (2007) investigated the effects of a psychological skills training programme on elite hockey players' anxiety symptoms. Results showed that the intervention was successful in helping these players to interpret their symptoms more constructively. In summary, the first step in helping athletes to cope with anxiety is to educate them as to what it means and how to detect it. The psychological principle here is that awareness precedes control of psychological states.

Using physical relaxation techniques: lowering shoulders, slowing down and breathing deeply

Earlier in the chapter, we explained that anxiety causes certain behavioural character-istics. For example, anxious athletes tend to speed up their behaviour. The obvious solution to this problem is to encourage them to breathe deeply, slow down and relax whenever tension strikes. For example, after his defeat of Jay Haas (USA) on the eighteenth hole in the 1995 Ryder Cup at the Oak Hill Club, Pittsford, New York, Europe golfer Philip Walton revealed how he had used a diaphragmatic breathing technique to counteract his anxiety. "What saved me ... was something I learned ... about how to breathe properly in a stressful situation. You do it from your belly not high up in your chest" (cited in L. Kelly, 1998). Of course, any advice on relaxation must be tailored to the demands of the particular sport in question. Indeed, the feasibility of using physical relaxation techniques such as progressive muscular relaxation (see practical tips offered by J. Williams, 2010) depends heavily on the amount of "break time" offered by the sport in question. For example, in stop-start, untimed sports like golf or tennis, there are moments where it may be possible to lower one's shoulders, flap out the tension from one's arms and engage in deep-breathing exercises. Interestingly, some professional tennis players use a relaxation strategy whereby they visualize an imaginary area (e.g., behind the baseline of a tennis court) which serves as a relaxation zone where they can switch off mentally during breaks in play (for a discussion of mental **imagery** in sport, see also Chapter 5). However, this procedure may be impossible to use in athletic activities where play is fast and continuous (e.g., hockey). Also, another caution is necessary when teaching relaxation skills to athletes. In my experience, relaxation CDs do not work effectively with many sport performers as they are perceived as being too passive. A comprehensive account of relaxation techniques in sport may be found in J. Williams (2010).

Giving oneself specific instructions

Anxiety is unhelpful because it makes people focus on what might go *wrong* (i.e., possible negative consequences) rather than on what exactly they have to do (the immediate challenge of the situation). Therefore, a useful way to counteract pressure in a competition is to ask oneself: "What exactly do I have to do right now?" By focusing on what they have to do, athletes can learn to avoid the trap of confusing the *facts* of the situation (e.g., "We're 1–0 down with ten minutes to go") with an anxious *interpretation* of those facts ("It's no use, we're going to lose"). Therefore, when athletes experience pressure, they should give themselves specific commands which help them to focus on actions that can be performed immediately.

Adhering to pre-performance routines

Most athletes use **pre-performance routines** (PPRs), or systematic sequences of preparatory thoughts and actions, in an effort to concentrate optimally before they execute important skills (e.g., golf putts, penalty kicks; see also Chapter 4). Briefly, these routines serve as a cocoon against the adverse effects of anxiety. In particular, by concentrating on each step of the routine, athletes learn to focus on only what they can control – a vital principle of anxiety management. Mesagno and Mullane-Grant (2010) investigated the efficacy of different PPRs in attempting to alleviate choking behaviour in a sample of Australian Rules football players as they performed free kicks under low- and high-pressure conditions. Results showed that choking was *least* likely when the footballers' attention was taken up by task-relevant thoughts. Based on this finding, Mesagno and Mullane-Grant (2010, p. 358) recommended that choking can be reduced if athletes use a non-automated PPR that "occupies attention prior to execution and decreases involuntary shifts to pressure-related threat".

Constructive thinking: encouraging oneself

When sports performers are anxious, their **self-talk** (i.e., what they say to themselves inside their heads; see also Chapter 4) tends to become hostile and sarcastic. Although such frustration is understandable, it is *never* helpful to the person involved and may even make the situation worse. So, athletes need to talk to themselves with two objectives: to encourage themselves for their efforts (positive reinforcement) and to instruct themselves on what to do next (guidance). For example, an anxious tennis player might say, "Come on, this point now: go cross-court on my next return".

Simulation training

If anxiety in athletes is associated with a fear of the unknown, then one way of counteracting it is by reducing uncertainty through the use of **simulation training** (i.e., practising under conditions that replicate key aspects of an impending challenge; see also Chapter 4). This idea is supported by both anecdotal and descriptive evidence. To illustrate the former, many coaches of elite athletes try to inoculate their performers against the unwanted effects of anticipated anxiety. Miller (1997) described how the Australian women's hockey team, as part of their training for gold medal success in the 1988 Olympics, practised under such adversity as games-manship (especially verbal taunting or "sledging") and adverse umpiring decisions. More recently, the renowned swimming coach Bob Bowman admitted deliberately breaking the goggles of Michael Phelps (who has won more Olympic gold medals than any other athlete) during practice so that he could learn to swim calmly without them if necessary in a competition. Remarkably, this situation actually arose in the 2008 Olympics when Phelps won the 200 metres butterfly event even though his goggles had been broken for the last 100 metres of the race (Whitworth, 2008). Descriptive evidence on the value of simulation training comes from Uphill and Jones (2004) who reported that athletes used "what if?" scenarios in an effort to minimize the likely anxiety that would be prompted by imminent pressure situa-tions. Although these sources of evidence are interesting, they are not compelling. But an experiment by Oudejans and Pijpers (2010) may fill this gap in the relevant research literature. The question addressed by these researchers was as follows. Can simulating mild levels of anxiety in practice conditions help to prevent athletes from choking in a subsequent competitive situation? See Box 3.8.

Box 3.8 Thinking critically about … whether or not simulation training can prevent choking

Sometimes, players and coaches claim that it is difficult to prepare for the anxiety experienced by athletes in real-life competition because the pressure situations in question are too intense and/or too sport-specific to be replicable in practice. Until 2010, this proposition was untested empirically in psychology. But using an experimental paradigm, Oudejans and Pijpers (2010) investigated whether or not simulation training helps to counteract choking behaviour in athletes. In this study, a sample of novices was assigned to one of two groups. In the experimental group, participants practised darts throwing under experi-mentally induced levels of mild anxiety – achieved by requiring participants to hang high rather than low on an indoor climbing wall. In the control group, participants practised without any additional anxiety. Manipulation checks using heart rate (an index of arousal/anxiety) were conducted to ensure that the anxiety manipulation had been effective. State anxiety was measured before and after the training programme using visual-analogue anxiety scale called the "anxiety thermometer" (Oudejans and Pijpers, 2010). After training, parti-cipants were tested under conditions of low, mild and high anxiety. Results showed that despite systematic increases in anxiety, heart rate and effort from low to mid to high anxiety, the experimental group (i.e., the one that had trained under mild anxiety) performed *equally well* on all three tests whereas the performance of the control group *deteriorated* in the high anxiety condition. Oudejans and Pijper (2010) interpreted their results to indicate that training with mild anxiety helps to prevent choking under conditions of high anxiety. They acknowledged, however, that this apparently beneficial simulation effect is short term, and that additional research is required to explore its efficacy over longer periods of time.

Critical thinking questions

Do you think that Oudejans and Pijpers' (2010) conclusions are warranted by the experimental method that they used? Specifically, are you satisfied that heart rate (an index of arousal) was used as one of the anxiety manipulation measures? Do you think that the ecological validity of this study is questionable in view of the rather contrived nature of experimental task – namely, throwing darts while *hanging* from a climbing wall? If you were a member of the University Ethics Committee faced with the task of evaluating the protocol of this study before it was conducted, would you have any concerns? If so, what specific changes would you recommend to the authors?

In summary, this section of the chapter suggests that athletes can learn to cope with pressure situations by using at least four psychological strategies. First, they must be trained to believe that pressure lies in the eye of the beholder. Therefore, they must be taught to cognitively restructure competitive events so that they can be perceived as opportunities to display their talents (the challenge response) rather than as potential sources of failure (the fear response). Second, athletes must learn for themselves that systematic preparation tends to reduce pressure. One way of doing this is to use simulation training and mental rehearsal (or "visualization" – see also Chapter 5) to inure themselves against anticipated difficulties. Third, anxious athletes can benefit from using self-talk techniques to guide themselves through pressure situations. Fourth, when anxiety strikes, athletes must be prepared to deepen their routines and to use physical relaxation procedures in accordance with the temporal demands of the sport that they are performing. We now consider the second objective of this section – to explore some recent research on the coping strategies of elite athletes and coaches.

Research on coping strategies of elite athletes and coaches

Recent years have seen an upsurge of research interest in the coping strategies used by elite athletes and coaches (e.g., see A. Nicholls and Polman, 2007). For example, N. Weston et al. (2009) used in-depth interviews to explore the stressors faced, and coping strategies employed, by five single-handed, round-the-world sailors. Among the stressors experienced by these sailors were environmental hazards (e.g., isolation and sleep deprivation), competitive stressors (e.g., yacht-related difficulties) and personal issues (e.g., family problems). In response to these stressors, the sailors reported using a combination of problem-focused coping strategies (e.g., making detailed plans for what to do in various hypothetical scenarios) and emotion-focused coping strategies (e.g., relying on social support from family and supporters to counteract the isolation of single-handed sailing). Interestingly, N. Weston et al. (2009) acknowledged that their research did not establish specific causal or temporal links between the stressors experienced by these sailors and the resulting coping strategies adopted. However, they suggested that future research in this field could benefit from equipping participants with electronic diaries to log the time-course of their stressor-coping strategy interactions. Qualitative methodology was also used by Olusoga et al. (2010) to explore the responses to stress of, and coping techniques used by, a sample of world-class UK coaches from a range of sports (e.g., swimming, field hockey). Thematic analysis showed that the most frequently reported coping strategy was "structuring and planning" – a problem-focused approach that involved using past experience to anticipate and circumvent likely stressors. Attending coaching courses and seeking continuous professional development were also widely cited as preferred coping strategies.

How effective are coping strategies in sport? According to A. Nicholls and Polman (2007, p. 15), coping effectiveness refers to "the extent to which a coping strategy, or combination of strategies, is successful in alleviating the negative emotions caused by stress". Unfortunately, there has been a dearth of theoretically-driven attempts to evaluate the efficacy of coping strategies in athletes. Nevertheless, some sport psychology researchers have tested Folkman's (1991) "goodness of fit" proposal that problem-focused coping techniques should be used when people face personally *controllable* stressors (e.g., those arising from their own behaviour) whereas emotion-focused strategies may be more appropriate when the stressful situations are *uncontrollable* (e.g., in sport, those arising from an opponent's performance). This hypothesis was corroborated by Anshel (1996), who reported that high perceived controllability was linked to problem-focused coping strategies whereas low perceived controllability was associated with emotion-focused coping strategies in competitive athletes. Similarly, Kim and Duda (2003) discovered that when stressors were perceived to be controllable, athletes tended to use problem-based coping strategies. Despite such findings, little progress has been made in understanding the theoretical mechanisms underlying the apparent efficacy of problem-focused and emotion-focused coping strategies. Clearly, additional studies are required in which theoretically derived hypotheses concerning coping strategies are tested using longitudinal research designs.

Unresolved issues and new directions in research on anxiety in athletes

Despite a long tradition of research on anxiety in athletes, many issues remain unresolved in this field. Identification of these issues can help us to outline six areas for further research on anxiety in sport performers. First, the fact that researchers tend to use terms such as arousal, fear, anxiety and stress interchangeably in sport psychology suggests that greater conceptual rigour is required throughout this field. Fortunately, some progress in this regard is evident with the development of a model designed to clarify the relationship between arousal-related constructs (see Gould et al., 2002c; Thomas et al., 2009). Second, idiographic research designs (i.e., ones which reflect the uniqueness or individuality of the phenomena of interest: Cashmore, 2008) are required to augment the traditional nomothetic approach (i.e., the search for general principles of psychology based on large samples of participants) to anxiety in sport. A good example of the idiographic approach comes from an interview study by Edwards et al. (2002) on the catastrophic experiences of elite athletes when choking competitively. Single-case research designs (see Barker et al., 2011) and qualitative methodology such as focus groups (see Chapter 1) could be especially useful in exploring the meaning of anxiety to athletes. Third, some researchers (e.g., Wilson et al., 2007a) have questioned the validity of the **dual-task paradigm** used in many studies of anxiety on the grounds that the difficulty of secondary tasks is hard to evaluate independently. Fourth, little research has been conducted to date on the question of how cognitive anxiety, somatic anxiety and physiological arousal interact to affect performance in sport. Fifth, apart from anecdotal insights yielded by athletes and coaches, virtually nothing is known about the effects of emotions like anger or revenge on sport performance. Finally, relatively little research has been conducted on the anxiety experienced by athletes close to and during competitive performance (but see Hanton et al., 2004). Field studies in this area are particularly welcome.

Ideas for research projects on anxiety in athletes

Here are five ideas for research projects on anxiety in athletes.

1   Based on the research of Hanton et al. (2004), you could investigate possible changes in the intensity and direction of athletes' experiences of cognitive and somatic anxiety in the days preceding a competitive match. As yet, little is known about the time course of these constructs among athletes in field settings. Of course, in such a study, you would have to be extremely careful to be as unobtrusive as possible in your data collection to prevent possible interference with the athletes' preparation.

2   Compared to athletes, sports officials have received little research attention from psychologists. Therefore, by extending the interview approach adopted by Thatcher (2005) in her research on stress and challenge responses of Rugby League officials, it would be interesting to use psychometric measures to investigate possible differences in the coping techniques reported by experienced and novice umpires in various sports.

3   Few studies have evaluated theoretically based interventions designed to alleviate choking behaviour in athletes. In order to address this gap in the research literature, you could extend Mesagno and Mullane-Grant's (2010) novel attempt to investigate which components of a pre-performance routine are most effective in reducing anxiety in athletes required to perform self-pace skills (e.g., golf putting, tennis serving) under pressure conditions.

4   You could evaluate the psychometric adequacy of one of the self-report anxiety scales described in this chapter (e.g., the Revised Competitive State Anxiety Inventory-2: Cox et al., 2003). Surprisingly few data on these tests have been gathered from elite athletes.

5   If you have access to eye-tracking technology in your academic department's research laboratory, it would be intriguing to test the prediction from attentional control theory (ACT: Eysenck et al., 2007) that anxious penalty takers in soccer are more likely to fixate on the goalkeeper rather than the target compared with less anxious players (see M. Wilson et al., 2009).

Summary

- It is widely agreed that athletic success depends significantly on the ability to regulate one's arousal levels effectively. Put simply, sport performers need to know how and when to either psych themselves up or to calm themselves down in competitive situations.
- The second section examined the nature, causes and types of anxiety experienced by athletes. It also distinguished between anxiety and related constructs such as fear and arousal and explored the question of whether anxiety facilitates or impairs performance in sport.
- The third section reviewed the most popular instruments available for the measurement of anxiety in athletes.
- Theories and research on the relationship between arousal, anxiety and performance were examined in the fourth section, which also contained a brief discussion of the nature and causes of choking under pressure in sports.
- The fifth section addressed the practical issue of how to control anxiety and cope effectively with pressure situations in sport.
- Finally, some unresolved issues on anxiety in athletes were identified along with several potentially fruitful new directions for future research in this field.

Chapter 4

Staying focused in sport: concentration in sport performers

I never think too far ahead. How can you think three days
ahead when you've got two days in-between? That's how
you cock things up. I'll just keep going, day by day.
(Bradley Wiggins, Britain's Olympic cycling gold
medallist in Beijing, 2008; cited in R. Williams, 2009)

Introduction

Many coaches and athletes believe that "concentration", or the ability to focus effectively on the task at hand while ignoring distractions, is a vital prerequisite of successful performance in sport. This idea applies both to team and individual sports. For example, Alex Ferguson (Manchester United) proclaimed that in soccer, "without question, at the top level, concentration is a big part of a player's game – whether they're a keeper or outfield" (cited in Northcroft, 2009, p. 12) (see Figure 4.1). This view is shared by Petr Cech, the Czech Republic goalkeeper who, having set a record for his club, Chelsea, in 2005 by keeping twenty-four "clean sheets" in the Premier League, revealed that "everything is about concentration" (cited in Szeczepanik, 2005, p. 100). Interestingly, Cech's comment was prompted by his observation that opposing teams invariably get at least one chance to score during a game and "it's difficult to be concentrated for the right moment". Not surprisingly, in individual sporting activities, the ability to dwell only on the present moment is also crucially important. Trevor Immelman, the South African golfer, remarked that

Figure 4.1 According to Alex Ferguson, concentration is vital for success in sport
Source: Courtesy of Inpho photography

he had been "so totally in the present" (cited in McRae, 2008, p. 7) during his triumph at the US Masters tournament in 2008. In this regard, perhaps the epitome of a present-centred awareness is that displayed by Michael Johnson, a three times Olympic gold medallist in 400 metres, and nine times a world athletics gold medallist. Remarkably, he claimed that he had

> learned to cut out all the unnecessary thoughts ... on the track. I simply concentrate. I concentrate on the tangible – on the track, on the race, on the blocks, on the things I have to do. The crowd fades away and the other athletes disappear and now it's just me and this one lane.
>
> (cited in Miller, 1997, p. 64)

Such extraordinary powers of concentration were also evident in Garry Sobers, the former West Indies cricket star, who once remarked that "on the cricket field, you have to have a concentration that you can rely on to take you beyond the average" (cited in White, 2002a, p. 20). By contrast with the preceding examples, an *inability* to focus effectively can mean the difference between success and failure in competitive sport. For example, at the 2008 Olympic Games in Beijing, the US rifle-shooter Matthew Emmons missed an opportunity to win a gold medal in the 50 metre three-position target event due to a lapse in concentration. Leading his nearest rival Qiu Jian (China) by 3.3 points as he took his last shot, Emmons lost his focus momentarily and inexplicably misfired, ending up with a 4.4 for his efforts – and fourth place. This example dramatically illustrates how concentration can mean the difference between winning and losing an Olympic gold medal. Similarly, Novak Djokovic, the current (2011) world number 1 tennis player, cited a lapse in concentration as one of the causes of his defeat by Rafael Nadal in the 2010 US Open final (see Figure 4.2). Specifically, he said: "I was playing really well for most of the match but there were moments in the third and fourth set where I dropped my focus" (cited in Mitchell, 2010b). Arising from such experiences, top athletes not only realize the importance of focusing skills but also have developed informal theories about how their concentration systems work in competitive situations. To illustrate, Garry Sobers proposed:

> concentration's like a shower. You don't turn it on until you want to bathe ... You don't walk out of the shower and leave it running. You turn it off, you turn it on ... It has to be fresh and ready when you need it.
>
> (cited in White, 2002a, p. 20)

Often, these intuitive theories about how the mind works are accompanied by idiosyncratic concentration techniques – especially in individual sports. Andy Roddick, the US tennis star, revealed that during his 2007 Wimbledon match against his compatriot and friend, Justin Gimmelstob, he avoided making any eye contact with him in case he might lose his concentration as a result (Muscat, 2007). Similarly, the snooker player Mark Williams raised a few eyebrows when he revealed that he had sung a song silently to himself in an effort to block out negative thoughts towards the end of his classic defeat of Ken Doherty in the 2003 world championship

Figure 4.2 Novak Djokovic discovered that a lapse in concentration can prove costly in tennis
Source: Courtesy of Inpho photography

final. As he said: "At 16–16, I was singing songs in my head. I was singing Tom Jones' Delilah. I just tried to take my mind off the arena, the crowd, everything" (cited in Everton, 2003, p. 31). Strange as it may seem, however, this curious strategy actually makes psychological sense. To explain, singing to oneself as a deliberate distraction may "dampen" the effects of anxiety by preventing an athlete from thinking too much. It may also help athletes to counteract their tendency to use their working memory to control their procedural memory when attempting to exert conscious control over actions that are better performed automatically (Beilock, 2010a). Using a similar strategy, the snooker star Ronnie O'Sullivan, who won the 2007 UK Championship, counted dots on a spoon to maintain his focus while his semi-final opponent (Mark Selby) was playing. As he said:

> My head was going so I had to find a way to keep it. They won't let me put a towel over my head any more so when Mark was at the table I picked up a spoon. If I lost count of the dots, I just started all over again. My thanks go to the spoon!
>
> (cited in Yates, 2007)

These examples and incidents raise a number of questions. For example, can psychological techniques help athletes to turn on and turn off their concentration systems like a shower? What other strategies can they use to achieve and maintain an optimal focus for competition? What is "concentration" anyway and why do athletes lose it so easily in competitive situations?

The purpose of this chapter is to answer these and other relevant questions using the principles and findings of **cognitive sport psychology** – that part of the discipline that is concerned with understanding how the mind works in athletic situations. In order to achieve this objective, the chapter is organized as follows. In the next section, I explore the nature, dimensions and importance of concentration in sport psychology. In the third section, I outline briefly the principal methods used by psychologists to measure attentional processes (including concentration) in athletes. The fourth section of the chapter summarizes some key principles of effective concentration that have emerged from research on attention in sport performers. The fifth section addresses the question of why athletes are vulnerable to lapses or loss of concentration. In the sixth section, I review various practical exercises and psychological techniques that are alleged to improve concentration skills in athletes. The seventh section outlines some old problems and new directions for research in this field. Finally, I suggest some ideas for possible research projects on concentration in athletes.

Nature and importance of concentration in sport psychology

In cognitive sport psychology, concentration is regarded as one component of the multidimensional construct of "attention" (Moran, 1996). For cognitive psychologists, attention involves "focusing on specific features, objects or locations or on certain thoughts or activities" (Goldstein, 2011, p. 391). It is a cognitive system that facilitates the selection of some information for further processing while inhibiting the selection of other information for processing (E. Smith and Kosslyn, 2007). Put simply, it is "a concentration of mental activity" (Matlin, 2009, p. 67). Let us now consider the main dimensions and types of attention before examining a topic that we mentioned earlier – namely, the special importance of concentration in sport.

Research on attention is central to cognitive sport psychology because the ability to focus mental effort effectively is associated with optimal athletic performance (see later in this chapter for a discussion of flow states). Attentional research is also one of the fastest growing fields in cognitive **neuroscience**. Broadly, it explores the mechanisms by which "voluntary control and subjective experience arise from and regulate our behaviour" (Posner and Rothbart, 2007, p. 1). For psychologists, attention is paradoxical because it is *familiar* but yet *mysterious*. To explain, the term attention is *familiar* because it is used frequently in everyday life – as happens, for example, when a coach asks her students to "pay attention" to something important that she is about to say or demonstrate to her athletes. Indeed, based on such apparent familiarity, William James (1890) remarked famously:

> Everyone knows what attention is. It is the taking possession by the mind, in clear and vivid form, of one of what may seem several simultaneously possible objects or trains of thought. Focalization, concentration, of consciousness are

of its essence. It implies withdrawal from some things in order to deal effectively with others.

(W. James, 1890, pp. 403–404)

Attention is also *mysterious* because it refers to many different types and levels of psychological processes ranging from biological arousal or alertness to high level conscious awareness. Not surprisingly, therefore, James' "folk-psychology" approach to attention (i.e., one based on unsystematic but compelling insights drawn from everyday life: Pashler, 1998) has been criticized for its limited scope. And so, despite more than a century of research in the field, there is still a great deal of confusion concerning the nature of attention and the mechanisms underlying it. For example, Ashcraft (2006) identified *six* different meanings of this term. Commenting on the multiplicity of approaches and definitions in this field, Pashler (1998, p. 1) subverted James' quotation by observing that perhaps "no one knows what attention is, and … there may not even be an 'it' to be known about". Of course, brain scanning techniques (e.g., see J. Ward, 2010) can help to establish the neural mechanisms associated with the "it" of attention – if not the actual phenomenon itself. So, undaunted by Pashler's somewhat pessimistic conclusion, we can see that a great deal of progress has been made in attentional research since the late 1990s. First, most theorists in the field accept that the hallmark of attention is the concentration of mental activity (Matlin, 2009). Second, neuroscientific studies have identified a number of different brain regions activated during attentional processing. Corbetta and Shulman (2002) concluded that the task of searching for your friend in a crowded room involves activation of frontal and dorsal parietal brain regions. By contrast, redirecting your attention to an unexpected stimulus (e.g., the sound of breaking glass) involves the activation of the ventral frontal cortex (see also E. Smith and Kosslyn, 2007). Third, researchers agree on the *multidimensional* nature of this construct and can distinguish between several different dimensions of attention.

Dimensions of attention

At least three separate dimensions of attention have been identified by cognitive psychologists. The first one is called "concentration" and refers to a person's ability to exert deliberate mental effort on what is most important in any given situation. For example, football players concentrate when they attempt to absorb coaching instructions delivered before an important match. The second dimension of attention denotes a skill in selective perception – namely, the ability to zoom in on task-relevant information while ignoring potential distractions. This dimension refers to the ability to discriminate relevant stimuli (targets) from irrelevant stimuli (distractors) that tend to compete for our attention. To illustrate, a tennis player who is preparing to smash a lob from his or her opponent must learn to focus only on the flight of the ball, not on the distracting movement of the player(s) on the other side of the net. As a test of your selective attentional skill, can you focus only on the vocals of a song on the radio, disregarding the instrumental backing? Interestingly, research suggests that one way of capturing people's attention is through the use of sudden onset stimuli and movement. For example, the blinking cursor on a computer monitor makes it stand out from the static display of text that the user is typing on the screen. Similarly, internet "pop up" advertising exploits this perceptual principle by trying to "steal" computer users' attention. The third dimension of attention involves a form of mental time-sharing ability whereby athletes learn, as a result of extensive practice, to perform two or more concurrent actions equally well. For example, a skilful basketball player can dribble with the ball while simultaneously looking around for a teammate who is in a good position to receive a pass. As you can see, the construct of attention refers to at least three different cognitive processes: concentration or effortful awareness, selectivity of perception, and/or the ability to coordinate two or more actions at the same time. A possible fourth dimension of attention called vigilance has also been postulated (De Weerd, 2002). This dimension designates a person's ability to orient attention and respond to randomly occurring relevant stimuli over an extended period of time. Unfortunately, the multidimensional nature of attention has occasionally spawned conceptual confusion among sport psychologists. Gauron (1984, p. 43) appeared to suggest that mental time-sharing is a *weakness* rather than a skill when he claimed that athletes could "*suffer* from divided attention" (italics mine). Perhaps this author failed to grasp the fact that repeated practice enables people to spread their attentional resources between concurrent activities – often without any deterioration in performance. Incidentally, research shows that people are capable of doing two or more things at the same time provided that at least one of them is highly practised and the tasks operate in different sensory modalities (Matlin, 2009). If neither task has been practised sufficiently and/or if the concurrent activities in question take place in the same sensory system, errors will probably occur. Box 5.3 in Chapter 5 examines a practical implication of this principle when I explain why it is dangerous to drive a car while listening to a football match on the radio.

Just like other scientists, cognitive psychology researchers have used various metaphors to understand how the mind works. Since the 1950s, a number of metaphors have been coined by cognitive psychologists to describe the selective and divided dimensions of attention (see review by Fernandez-Duque and Johnson, 1999). The earliest metaphors of attention ("filter" approaches) were largely auditory in nature but as a greater range of experimental procedures emerged, attention metaphors became mainly visual. More recently, resource metaphors have dominated cognitive research on attention. One of the most influential metaphors of attention is the "spotlight" metaphor (e.g., Posner, 1980). According to this metaphor, **selective attention** resembles a mental beam which illuminates targets that are located either in the external world around us or else in the subjective domain of our own thoughts and feelings. This idea of specifying a target for one's attentional spotlight is important practically as well as theoretically because it is only relatively recently that sport psychologists have begun to explore the question of what exactly athletes should focus on when they are exhorted to "concentrate" by their coaches (see Mallett and Hanrahan, 1997; MacPherson et al., 2008). Unfortunately, the spotlight metaphor of attention is plagued by a number of problems. First, it has not adequately explained the mechanisms by which executive control of one's attentional focus is achieved. Put simply, who or what is directing the spotlight at its target? This question is difficult to answer without postulating a homunculus. Second, the spotlight model assumes that people's attentional beam sweeps through space en route to its target. However, this assumption is challenged by research evidence that "attention is not influenced by the presence of spatially intervening information" (E. Smith and Kosslyn, 2007, p. 131). Third, the spotlight metaphor neglects the issue of what lies *outside* the beam of our concentration. In other words, it ignores the possibility that unconscious factors can affect people's attentional processes. Interestingly, such factors have attracted increasing scrutiny from cognitive scientists. Nadel and Piattelli-Palmarini (2002, p. xxvi) remarked that although cognitive science began with the assumption that cognition was limited to conscious processes, "much of the domain is now concerned with phenomena that lie behind the vale of consciousness". Interestingly, there is evidence that perception without conscious awareness can occur in vision (Merikle, 2007). I shall return to this issue later in the chapter when I consider how unconscious sources of distraction can affect athletes. Fourth, the spotlight model of attention has been concerned mainly with *external* targets – not internal ones. Again, I shall return to this issue later in the chapter when considering how and why *internal* distractions disrupt our concentration. A fifth weakness of the spotlight metaphor is that it neglects emotional influences on attentional processes. For example, anxiety can narrow one's mental spotlight and encourage performers to shine it inwards. Interestingly, as we learned in Chapter 3, attentional control theory (ACT: Eysenck et al., 2007) was developed to account for the effects of anxiety on cognitive performance.

Metaphors have also been coined for **divided attention**. The fact that people can sometimes do two or more concurrent tasks equally well suggests that attention is a "resource" or pool of mental energy (Kahneman, 1973). This pool is believed to be available for allocation to competing tasks depending on various strategic principles. For example, motivation, practice and arousal are held to increase spare attentional capacity whereas task difficulty is believed to reduce it (Kahneman, 1973). Unfortunately, the resource metaphor of divided attention is somewhat simplistic. Navon and Gopher (1979) have argued that people may have multiple attentional resources rather than a single pool of undifferentiated mental energy. Each of these multiple pools may have its own functions and limits. For example, R. Schmidt and Lee (1999) discovered that the attentional resources required for a motor skill such as selecting a finger movement may be separate from those which regulate a verbal skill such as the pronunciation of a word. Although intuitively appealing, multiple resource theories of attention have been criticized on the grounds of being "inherently untestable" (Palmeri, 2002, p. 298). To explain, virtually any pattern of task interference can be "explained" *post hoc* by attributing it to the existence of multiple pools of attentional resources.

In general, cognitive models of attention, whether based on spotlight or resource metaphors, have two major limitations. First, they have focused mainly on external (or environmental) determinants of attention and have largely overlooked internal factors (e.g., thoughts and feelings) which can distract athletes. Consider what happened to former athlete Sonia O'Sullivan, the 2000 Olympic silver medallist in the 5,000 metre event in Sydney, who allowed her concentration to slip in the 10,000 metre race at the Games. According to her post-event interview, the thought of the medal she had won prevented her from focusing properly in the next race:

If I hadn't already got a medal, I might have fought a bit harder. But when you have a medal already, maybe you think about that medal for a moment. It probably was only for a lap ... but that is all it takes for a race to get away from you.

(cited in Curtis, 2000)

Of course, as I indicated in Chapter 1, athletes' insights into their own mental processes are not always reliable or valid from a researcher's perspective. The second weakness of cognitive models of attention is that they ignore the influence of emotional states. This neglect of the affective dimension of behaviour is lamentable because it is widely known in sport psychology that anxiety impairs attentional processes. The phenomenon of choking under pressure (whereby nervousness causes a sudden deterioration of athletic performance; see also Chapter 3) illustrates how the beam of one's attentional spotlight can be directed *inwards* when it should be focused only on the task at hand. For a comprehensive account of the role of emotional factors in sport, see Thatcher et al. (2011).

To summarize, this section of the chapter highlighted two important ideas. First, concentration is just one aspect of the multidimensional construct of attention. In particular, it refers to the ability to pay attention to the task at hand while ignoring distractions from internal as well as external sources. Second, despite their plausibility, cognitive metaphors of attention have certain limitations which hamper theories and research on concentration in athletes. Having sketched the nature of concentration, let us now consider its importance for optimal athletic performance.

Importance of concentration in sport

The importance of concentration in sport is indicated by at least three sources of evidence: anecdotal, descriptive and experimental (see Chapter 1 for a discussion of the main research methods used in sport and exercise psychology).

First, as the anecdotal examples and anecdotes at the beginning of this chapter reveal so graphically, many top managers (e.g., Alex Ferguson) and athletes (e.g., Petr Cech) attest to the value of focusing skills in sport. Such anecdotal insights are supported by objective evidence in the form of athlete surveys indicate the importance of concentration to sport performance. For example, Durand-Bush et al. (2001) found that a large sample (n=335) of athletes perceived "focusing" as a vital mental skill in determining successful performance in their sport. Unfortunately, this survey did not explore in depth what the term "focusing" meant to athletes. Therefore we cannot be sure that athletes and researchers were referring to the same cognitive construct in this study.

The second source is descriptive evidence on the value of concentration in sport which comes from studies of "flow" states or "peak performance" experience of athletes (e.g., see reviews by Harmison, 2007; S. Jackson and Kimiecik, 2008). These experiences refer to coveted yet elusive occasions during which the physical, technical, tactical and psychological components of sporting performance (see Figure 1.2) intertwine perfectly for the athlete in question. Given the importance of such experiences to athletes and musicians, it is not surprising that they have attracted considerable research interest from psychologists (e.g., see S. Jackson and Kimiecik, 2008; Sinnamon et al., 2012; Stavrou et al., 2007). A key finding from such research is that flow experiences emanate mainly from a *cognitive* source – namely, a heightened state of concentration. Indeed, S. Jackson et al. (2001, p. 130) defined flow as a "state of concentration so focused that it amounts to absolute absorption in an activity". Overall, studies of peak performance suggest that athletes tend to perform optimally when they are totally absorbed in the task at hand. This state of mind is epitomized in a quote from the golfer Darren Clarke, who remarked after a tournament victory that his ball had seemed to be "on the club-face for so long I could almost tell it where I wanted it to go" (cited in Kimmage, 1998). Unfortunately, research on flow states in sport is plagued by a variety of conceptual and methodological problems that are summarized in Box 4.1.

Box 4.1 Thinking critically about … flow states in sport

Flow states or **peak performance experiences** tend to occur when people become absorbed in challenging tasks that demand intense concentration and commitment (see review in S. Jackson and Kimiecik, 2008). In such desirable but fleeting states of mind, performers become so deeply immersed in the activities of the present moment that they lose track of time, feel highly alert and experience a temporary sense of euphoria and joy. Research in this field was pioneered by a Hungarian psychologist named Mihalyi Csikszentmihalyi (pro-nounced "chick-sent-me-hai") who set out to explore the reasons why some people pursue activities (e.g., painting, mountain-climbing) that appear to offer minimal extrinsic rewards (Csikszentmihalyi, 1975). Briefly, he argued that they do so because of the *intrinsic* feeling of satisfaction that arises whenever there is a perfect match between the challenge of the task at hand and the skill level of the performer. Since the 1980s, sport psychologists have explored the nature and characteristics of flow states in athletes (e.g., Schuler and Brunner, 2009). According to A. Martin and Jackson (2008), there are nine putative dimensions of flow. These dimensions include

> challenge-skill balance (feeling competent enough to meet the high demands of the situation), action-awareness merging (doing things spon-taneously and automatically without having to think), clear goals (having a strong sense of what one wants to do), unambiguous feedback (know-ing how well one is doing during the performance itself), concentration on the task at hand (being completely focused on the task at hand), sense of control (having a feeling of total control over what one is doing), loss of self-consciousness (not worrying what others think of oneself), transfor-mation of time (having the sense that time passes in a way that is different from normal), and autotelic experience (feeling the experience to be extremely rewarding).

> (A. Martin and Jackson, 2008, p. 146)

Given the ephemeral nature of these states of mind, however, it is not surprising that research on flow has encountered a number of conceptual and methodological difficulties. First, consider the proliferation of different terms that have been used to refer to the construct. Although "flow", "peak performance" and "peak experience" are often used synonymously, there are important differences between them. If peak performance is defined as a performance that exceeds a person's previous levels of performance, then, as S. Jackson and Kimiecik (2008, p. 382) pointed out, "a peak performance may not lead to a peak experience and an athlete can probably have a peak experience without having a peak performance". Second, how universal is the flow experience? Turning to methodological problems, there is evidence that people are not always reliable judges of their own mental processes. Brewer et al. (1991) discovered that when people were given spurious feedback concerning their performance on certain tasks, they unwittingly distorted their subsequent recall of the way in which they had performed these tasks. In other words, their recollections of task performance were easily contaminated by "leading" information. Is there a danger of similar contamination of athletes' retrospective accounts of flow states?

Critical thinking questions
Why is it so difficult to predict when flow states are likely to occur? Why, in your view, are these states so rare in sport? Do you think that athletes could experience flow states in practice – or do they happen only in competition? Is it possible to study flow states without disrupting them? Can you think of one advantage and one disadvantage of using questionnaires to assess athletes' peak performance experiences (see S. Jackson et al., 2008)? Apart from psychometric tests, what other methods could you use to study flow states? Do you think that a flow state comes *before* or *after* an outstanding athletic performance? Give reasons for your answer. Finally, do you think that athletes can be trained to experience flow states more regularly (see also Box 4.2)?

One of the critical thinking questions in Box 4.1 concerned the apparent rarity of peak experiences in sport. One possible reason why flow states are not more common in sport is that our concentration system is too fragile to maintain the type of absorption that is necessary for them. To explain, psychologists believe that concentration is controlled mainly by the "central executive" component of our working memory system (whose main objective is to keep a small amount of information active in our minds while we make a decision about whether or not to process it further: see Logie, 1999). This component of the memory system regulates what we consciously attend to, such as holding a telephone number in our heads before we write it down. Unfortunately, the working memory system is very limited in its capacity and duration. This limitation helps to explain why people are easily distracted. Put simply, we find it very difficult to focus on our intentions when there is a lot of activity going on around us. Other causes of distractibility are examined briefly later in the chapter. In any case, as soon as we begin to pay attention to *task-irrelevant* information – something other than the job at hand – our mental energy is diverted and we lose our concentration temporarily. Despite the issues raised in Box 4.1, there is little doubt that athletes who perform at their peak tend to report focusing only on *task-relevant* information – which is a sign of effective concentration.

The third source of evidence on the importance of concentration in sport comes from experimental research on the consequences of manipulating athletes' attentional focus in competitive situations. For example, a review by Wulf (2007) concluded that an *external* focus of attention (in which performers direct their attention at the effects that their movements have on the environment) is more effective than an *internal* one (in which performers focus on their own body movements) in improving the learning and performance of motor skills. There is also experimental evidence on the efficacy of attentional focus manipulations among athletes. Mallett and Hanrahan (1997) found that sprinters who had been trained to use race plans that involved deliberately focusing on task-relevant cues ran faster than those in baseline (control) conditions. Similarly, the use of "associative" attentional techniques (see explanation of term in Morgan and Pollock, 1977) in which athletes are trained to focus on bodily signals such as heart beat, respiratory signals and kinaesthetic sensations has been linked with faster performance in running (K. Masters and Ogles, 1998; Morgan, 2000) and swimming (Couture et al., 1999) in comparison with "dissociative" techniques such as paying attention to thoughts other than those concerned with bodily processes. Overall, K. Masters and Ogles (1998) concluded that whereas associative techniques are typically related to comparatively faster performances by athletes, dissociative techniques are usually linked to a reduction in perceived exertion in endurance events. However, the validity of this conclusion was challenged by Salmon et al. (2010) in a comprehensive review of the research literature in this field. Briefly, these researchers argued that a variety of conceptual and methodological difficulties hamper traditional studies of associative and dissociative attentional techniques. For example, they pointed out that the psychodynamic theory underlying original use of the term "dissociation" has been largely discredited and supplanted by cognitive constructs. Methodologically, many studies in this field are flawed because they are based on non-validated measures of association and dissociation. In view of these problems, Salmon et al. (2010) proposed that future research on the relationship between attentional strategies and sustained physical activity could benefit from adopting the theoretical model of **mindfulness** – a theory and practice derived from Buddhist meditation. For an account of a study on mindfulness training in sport, see Box 4.2.

Box 4.2 Mindfulness training in sport: helping athletes to focus on the here-and-now

Earlier in this chapter, I explained how important it is for athletes to focus on the task at hand while ignoring distractions. But how exactly can athletes develop this rather unnatural type of present-centred awareness? One emerging technique for this purpose is "mindfulness" training – an attentional focusing strategy that originated in the Buddhist meditative tradition (Erisman and Roemer, 2010). According to one of its leading proponents Kabat-Zinn (2005, p. 24), mindfulness involves "an openhearted, moment-to-moment, non-judgmental awareness" of oneself and of the world. This emphasis on adopting a non-judgemental orientation to distractions is important because it distinguishes mindfulness training from more active cognitive control techniques such as thought suppression. By urging *acceptance* rather than attempted elimination of intrusive, unwanted thoughts and feelings, mindfulness training purports to help performers to concentrate on the here-and-now. In an experiment, Aherne et al. (2011) investigated the effects of a six-week, CD-based mindfulness training programme on elite athletes' flow experiences in training. Results showed that athletes who underwent this training programme experienced greater flow than a control group who received no mindfulness instruction. Although this result is interesting, additional research employing larger samples and controlling for the potential effects of increased attention by the experimenter is needed before firm conclusions can be reached regarding the efficacy of mindfulness training on flow experiences in athletes.

To summarize, the three preceding strands of evidence (anecdotal, descriptive and experimental) converge on the conclusion that concentration is vital for success in sport. This conclusion has been echoed by researchers such as Abernethy et al. (2007, p. 245), who proclaimed that "it is difficult to conceive of any aspect of psychology that may be more central to the enhancement of skill learning and expert performance than attention". But how can psychologists measure people's attentional skills?

Measurement of attentional processes in athletes

As concentration is a hypothetical construct, and hence unobservable, it cannot be measured directly. Nevertheless, attentional processes can be assessed *indirectly* using methods drawn from three main paradigms: the psychometric (or individual differences), experimental and neuroscientific traditions in psychology. Due to space restrictions, I can provide only a brief overview of these paradigms here. For a more detailed review of these methodological approaches, see Summers and Moran (2011).

Psychometric approach

Some sport psychologists have attempted to measure individual differences in attentional processes in athletes through the use of specially designed paper-and-pencil tests. For example, the Test of Attentional and Interpersonal Style (TAIS: Nideffer, 1976) has been used as a screening device in several applied sport psychology settings, such as in the Australian Institute for Sport (Nideffer et al., 2001). It contains 144 items, broken down into 17 subscales, which purport to measure people's attentional processes in everyday situations (e.g., "When I read, it is easy to block out everything but the book"). Although the original version of this test was not intended for use with athletic populations, several sport-specific versions of the TAIS have emerged. The TAIS is based on Nideffer's model of attention, which can be outlined briefly as follows. According to Nideffer (1976), people's attentional focus varies simultaneously along two independent dimensions – namely, "width" and "direction". With regard to width, attention is believed to range along a continuum from a broad focus (where one is aware of many stimulus features at the same time) to a narrow one (where irrelevant information is excluded effectively). Attentional "direction" refers to the target of one's focus: whether it is external or internal (for a review of external and internal attention, see Chun et al., 2011). These dimensions of width and direction may be combined factorially to yield four hypothetical attentional styles. To illustrate, a narrow external attentional focus in sport is implicated when a golfer looks at the hole before putting. By contrast, a narrow internal focus is required when a gymnast mentally rehearses a skill such as back-flip while waiting to compete. Nideffer (1976) proposed that athletes have to match the attentional demands of a given sport skill or situation with the appropriate attentional focus. Some evidence to support this idea comes from a study by Kress and Statler (2007) on the strategies used by former Olympic cyclists to cope with exertion pain. Depending on what was required at the time, these cyclists reported using a broad external focus (e.g., concentrating on getting to the finish line), a broad internal focus (concentrating on pedalling and body movements), a narrow external focus (e.g., "staying on the wheel in front of me") or a narrow internal focus (concentrating on a smooth pedalling stroke). Despite its plausibility and popularity, however, the TAIS has several flaws which are discussed in Box 4.3.

Box 4.3 Thinking critically about ... the Test of Attentional and Interpersonal Style

The Test of Attentional and Interpersonal Style (TAIS: Nideffer, 1976) has been used in sport psychology to investigate the relationship between attentional processes and athletic performance. Unfortunately, its validity and utility have been questioned. So, what are the strengths and weaknesses of this test? On the positive side, the TAIS has a plausible theoretical rationale and considerable face validity because its assumptions make "intuitive sense to coaches and athletes" (Bond and Sargent, 1995, p. 394). Also, there is some empirical support for its construct validity. Nideffer (1976) reported that unsuccessful swimmers were attentionally "overloaded" when compared to successful counterparts. Similarly, V. Wilson et al. (1985) discovered that volleyball players who had been rated by their coaches as "good concentrators" under competitive stress scored significantly lower on the broad external focus (BET) and broad internal focus (BIT) subscales than did "poor concentrators". Unfortunately, such strengths must be weighed against the following weaknesses of this test. First, it is questionable whether athletes are reliably capable of evaluating their own attentional processes using self-report instruments

(Boutcher, 2008). Second, the TAIS assesses *perceived*, rather than actual, attentional skills. Accordingly, we cannot be sure that athletes who complete it are differentiating between what they *actually* do and what they would like us to believe that they do in everyday situations requiring attentional processes. Third, the factor structure of the TAIS has not been replicated consistently across different cultural setting (Wada et al., 2003). Fourth, the TAIS fails to differentiate between athletes of different skill levels in sports in which selective attention is known to be important (Summers and Ford, 1990). Fifth, Nideffer's theory is conceptually flawed because it does not distinguish between task-relevant and task-irrelevant information in sport situations. Finally, Boutcher (2008) raised doubts about the predictive validity of the test. Specifically, based on a review of relevant evidence, he concluded that the TAIS has "limited validity and predictive properties for sport performance" (Boutcher, 2008, p. 330). This conclusion echoes that of Cratty (1983, p. 100), who said that the test was only "marginally useful, and the data it produces are not much better than the information a coach might obtain from simply questioning athletes or observing their performance".

Critical thinking questions
From the evidence above, what conclusions would you draw about the validity of the TAIS? If you were redesigning this test, what changes would you make to its content and format? Can a psychological test be useful in applied settings even if its construct validity is questionable? More generally, do you think that paper-and-pencil tests of attention should be augmented by other measurement paradigms? If so, which ones would you suggest and why?

As you can see, the psychometric paradigm, as epitomized by the TAIS, is a popular if somewhat flawed approach to the measurement of attentional processes in athletes. Nevertheless, this approach has yielded several promising new instruments which claim to measure concentration skills. Hatzigeorgiadis (2002) and Hatzigeorgiadis and Biddle (2000) have developed psychometric tools to measure "cognitive interference" or task-irrelevant, self-preoccupied thinking in sport performers. The Thought Occurrence Questionnaire for Sport (TOQS: Hatzigeorgiadis and Biddle, 2000) is a seventeen-item test that measures athletes' performance worries, situation-irrelevant thoughts, and thoughts about escape. Its factorial validity for use among adolescent sports performers was supported in a study by Lane et al. (2005).

Neuroscientific approach

The second measurement paradigm in attentional research comes from cognitive neuroscience – a field that is concerned broadly with the identification of the neural substrates of mental processes (Ward, 2010). Since 2000, a variety of neuroscientific techniques such as **electroencephalography (EEG), functional magnetic** resonance imaging (fMRI), and **positron emission tomography** (PET scanning) have been used to reveal which parts of the brain "light up" when a person is paying attention to designated stimuli (Kolb and Whishaw, 2009). Interestingly, a neuroscientific study using functional imaging technology has revealed that compared to expert golfers, the brains of relative novices have difficulty in filtering out irrelevant information (Milton et al., 2007). Let us now summarize some key findings arising from neuroscientific studies of athletes' attentional processes.

Psychophysiological indices of attention such as heart rate have been monitored in athletes as they perform self-paced skills in target sports like archery, pistol-shooting and rifle-shooting (see reviews by Hatfield and Kerick, 2007; Janelle and Hatfield, 2008). An early finding that emerged from this line of research is that cardiac *deceleration* (or a slowing of the heart rate) tends to occur among elite rifle-shooters in the seconds before they pull the trigger of their guns. This finding is interesting in the light of Garry Sobers's comments in the first section of this chapter because it suggests that expert target sport performers can indeed "switch on" their concentration processes at will. Interestingly, a study by Radlo et al. (2002) reported that dart-throwers' heart rates may vary in accordance with the type of attentional focus that they adopted. For example, when they used an external attentional strategy, their heart rates tended to decline just before they threw the darts. As yet, however, the psychophysiological significance of this heart rate change is unknown.

The next methodological innovation in this paradigm occurred with the development of equipment designed to measure continuous patterns of electrical activity in the brain. This "brain wave" technology included electroencephalographic methods and those based on **event-related potentials (ERPs)**. In a typical EEG experiment, an electrode is attached to a person's scalp in order to detect the electrical activity of neurons in the underlying brain region. Another electrode is then attached to the person's earlobe, where there is no electrical activity to detect. Then the EEG is recorded to indicate the difference in electrical potentials detected by the electrodes (Kolb and Whishaw, 2009). Since the late 1990s, a considerable amount of research has been conducted on EEG activity in athletes (Hatfield and Hillman, 2001). From such research, certain cerebral asymmetry effects are evident. For example, in keeping with previous findings from heart rate studies, research suggests that just before expert archers and pistol performers execute their shots, their EEG records tend to display a distinctive shift from left-hemisphere to right-hemisphere activation (Hatfield and Hillman, 2001). This shift is believed to reflect a change in executive control from the verbally based left hemisphere to the visuo-spatially specialized right hemisphere. Put differently, target-shooters display a marked reduction in the extent of their verbal-analytical processes (including self-talk) prior to shot execution. In the light of this finding, perhaps the snooker player Mark Williams's strategy of covert singing (see first section of chapter) was not so daft after all because it may have helped him to avoid thinking too much – which can cause paralysis-by-analysis – prior to shot execution (for an explanation of R. Masters' (1992) "conscious processing" or reinvestment hypothesis, see Chapter 3). More generally, EEG research findings suggest that top-class athletes know how to regulate their physiological processes as they prepare for the performance of key skills (for a discussion of **expertise** in sport, see also

Chapter 6). Unfortunately, this theory has not been tested systematically to date as the EEG is a relatively blunt instrument because its data are confounded with the brain's *global* level of electrical activity. Nevertheless, EEG research in sport has had at least one practical implication. Specifically, it has led to the use of **biofeedback** techniques designed to help athletes to become more effective at controlling their cortical activity. Staying with brain wave measurement in sport, event-related potentials are brief changes in EEG signals that are synchronized with or "time locked" to some eliciting event or stimulus. Unlike the EEG, which is a measure of continuous electrical activity in the brain, ERPs reflect transient cortical changes that are evoked by certain information-processing events. Typically, ERPs display characteristic peaks of electrical activity that begin a few milliseconds after the onset of a given stimulus (e.g., a loud noise) and continue for up to a second afterwards (for more details, see Kolb and Whishaw, 2009).

A methodological wave in neuroscientific research on attention concerns the use of functional brain imaging techniques. With these procedures (e.g., positron emission tomography and functional magnetic resonance imaging; see also Chapter 5), researchers can obtain clear and dynamic insights into the specific brain regions that are activated when people perform specific cognitive tasks. Since about 2007, the neural processes underlying athletic expertise have attracted increasing research interest from cognitive neuroscientists (e.g., see Nakata et al., 2010; Wei and Luo, 2010; Yarrow et al., 2009). For example, **transcranial magnetic stimulation** (TMS, a technique in which the functioning of a specific area of the brain is temporarily disrupted through the application of pulsating magnetic fields to the skull using a stimulating coil) has been employed to study attentional processes (e.g., Aglioti et al., 2008; Thomson et al., 2008). Such research has allowed investigators to link several functions of attention to specific anatomical areas in the brain. So far, three separable attention-related neural networks have been identified linked to the functions of achieving and maintaining high sensitivity to incoming stimuli (alerting); selecting information from sensory input (orienting); and monitoring and resolving conflict (executive attention) (for a review, see Posner and Rothbart, 2007).

Although fMRI scans can answer questions concerning the "where" of attention, issues concerning the "how" of attention require methods (such as the EEG) that assess changes in patterns of the brain's neurological activity over time. In this regard, a considerable amount of research has accumulated on the pre-event patterns of EEG activity in certain athletes (Hatfield and Kerick, 2007). For example, there is evidence that just as expert shooters and archers prepare to fire, their EEG records reveal a marked shift from left hemisphere to right hemisphere activation. This shift may signify a change in executive control from the verbally based left hemisphere to the visuo-spatially specialized right hemisphere. Perhaps a reduction in left-hemisphere activity may indicate a deliberate suppression of "self-talk" on the part of the shooters in an effort to achieve a truly focused state of automaticity. In summary, the major advantage of neuroscientific techniques over their psychometric counterparts is that they yield *objective* data on biological processes which can be recorded *while* the athlete is performing his or her skills. Unfortunately, the major drawbacks associated with the neuroscientific paradigm are cost and practicality.

143

Experimental approach

The third approach to the measurement of attentional processes in athletes comes mainly from capacity theory (Kahneman, 1973) in experimental psychology. Briefly, this theory suggests that attention may be defined operationally in terms of the interference between two tasks (a primary task and a secondary task) that are performed simultaneously. To explain this "dual-task paradigm", if the two tasks can be performed as well simultaneously as individually, it may be concluded that at least one of them was automatic (i.e., demanding minimal attentional resources). However, if the primary task is performed less well when it is combined with the secondary task, then both tasks are believed to require attentional resources. Adopting this experimental approach, the dual-task method of measuring attention requires participants to perform two tasks over three conditions. In condition one, the person has to perform the primary task on its own. Likewise, in condition two, the person must perform the secondary task on its own. In condition three, however, the person is required to perform both tasks concurrently.

When the dual-task paradigm is used in sport psychology, the primary task usually consists of a self-paced or "closed" skill (i.e., one that can be performed without interference from others such as target-shooting in archery) whereas the secondary task typically requires the subject to respond to a predetermined probe signal (e.g., an auditory tone). Following comparison of performance between these three conditions, conclusions may be drawn about the attentional demands of the primary and secondary tasks. Using this method, sport psychologists are usually interested in people's performance in condition three – the concurrent task situation. In this condition, participants are required to perform a primary task which is interrupted periodically by the presentation of the probe stimulus. When this probe is presented, the person has to respond to it as rapidly as possible. It is assumed that the speed of responding to the probe is related inversely to the momentary attention devoted to the primary task. Therefore, if a primary task is cognitively demanding, a decrement should be evident in secondary task performance. However, if the performance of the secondary task in the dual-task condition does not differ significantly from that evident in the relevant control condition, then it may be assumed that the primary task is relatively effortless (or automatic).

In summary, the dual-task paradigm is an attempt to measure the spare mental capacity of a person while he or she is engaged in performing some task or mental activity. To illustrate this approach, consider a study by M. Wilson et al. (2007a), which was designed to investigate the effects of anxiety on skilled performance. These researchers used a dual-task design to examine the effects of manipulating people's focus of attention (either explicitly on their own driving performance or on a distracting secondary task) on performance on a driving simulator under low-anxiety or high-anxiety experimental conditions. In this study, participants were required to perform a primary task (i.e., simulated rally driving) as fast as possible while responding as accurately as possible to one of two theoretically derived secondary tasks. The skill-focused secondary task required participants to respond to an auditory tone by indicating at that moment whether their left hand on the steering wheel was higher, lower or at the same height as their right hand. The distraction secondary task required participants to remember the pitch of an auditory tone presented while they were driving. Each condition was completed under evaluative and non-evaluative instructional sets that were designed to manipulate the level of anxiety experienced by the drivers. Results showed that racing performance effectiveness (as measured by lap times) was maintained under anxiety-provoking conditions, although is occurred at the expense of reducing processing efficiency (recall our discussion of processing efficiency theory in Chapter 3). Unfortunately, despite its ingenuity, the dual-task paradigm has not been used widely to measure attentional processes in athletes, although it may offer researchers a way of validating athletes' reports of their imagery experiences (see Chapter 5).

To summarize this section of the chapter, the self-report approach to the measurement of concentration processes is favoured by most sport psychologists for reasons of brevity, convenience and economy. Given the issues raised in Box 4.3, however, the results yielded by psychological tests of concentration must be interpreted cautiously. Also, few if any of the available measures of attention deal explicitly with *concentration* skills. Moreover, no consensus has emerged about the best combination of these methods to use when assessing athletes' attentional processes in applied settings. Now that we have explained the nature, importance and measurement of concentration in sport, let us consider some psychological principles which govern an optimal focus in athletes.

Principles of effective concentration

Based on general reviews of the relationship between attention and athletic performance (e.g., Moran, 1996), at least five theoretical principles of effective concentration in sport may be identified (Kremer and Moran, 2008a; see Figure 4.3). Three of them concern the establishment of an optimal focus and the other two describe how it may be disrupted or lost.

The first principle of effective concentration is that a focused state of mind requires deliberate mental effort and intentionality on the part of the athlete concerned. In short, one must *prepare* to concentrate rather than hope that it will occur by chance. This principle was endorsed by Ronan O'Gara, the Ireland and Lions' rugby out-half, who claimed that:

> I have to be focused. I have to do my mental preparation. I have to feel that I'm ready. I don't want to be putting myself out there for credit but I have a big impact on how Munster perform. When it's coming up to a big match, rugby is the only thing in my head. Driving around, I visualize certain scenarios, different positions on the pitch, different times when the ball is coming to me.
>
> (cited in English, 2006, p. 70)

Not surprisingly, many athletes use imaginary "switch on" and "switch off" zones in their sports. For example, when top tennis players look for towels behind the

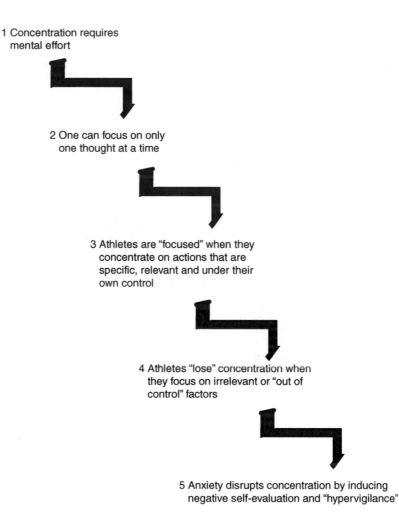

1 Concentration requires mental effort

2 One can focus on only one thought at a time

3 Athletes are "focused" when they concentrate on actions that are specific, relevant and under their own control

4 Athletes "lose" concentration when they focus on irrelevant or "out of control" factors

5 Anxiety disrupts concentration by inducing negative self-evaluation and "hypervigilance"

Figure 4.3 Concentration principles
Source: based on Moran (1996, 2004)

baseline during a game to mop up perspiration, they are in their switch off zone. But when they step forward to begin their pre-service routine, they move into their switch on zone. Second, one has to be single-minded. To explain, athletes can focus on only *one thought* at a time – even though they can divide their attention between two or more concurrent actions (see earlier discussion). Indeed, this "one thought" principle may be hard-wired into our brains because research shows that the working memory system which regulates conscious awareness (see Logie, 1999) is fragile and limited in duration (unless extensive practice occurs; see also Chapter 6). Third, as I indicated earlier in the chapter, research on the phenomenology of peak performance states indicates that athletes' minds are focused optimally when they are *doing* what they are *thinking*. In other words, there is no difference between what athletes are thinking about and what they are doing. By implication, sport performers tend to concentrate most effectively when they direct their mental spotlight (recall our earlier discussion of various metaphors of attention) at actions that are specific, relevant and, above all, under their own control. Fourth, athletes need to refocus regularly in order to keep their minds on track. Research shows that athletes tend to "lose" their concentration when they focus on factors that are outside their control (Moran, 1996). I shall return to this issue in the next section. The fifth principle of effective concentration suggests that athletes should focus *outwards* when they become anxious. This principle acknowledges the potentially disruptive influence of emotions such as anxiety. In particular, anxiety impairs concentration systems in several distinctive ways. First, it overloads working memory with worries (or cognitive anxiety; see Chapter 3). Second, it tends to restrict the beam of one's mental spotlight and also shifts its focus onto self-referential stimuli. Baumeister (1984) invoked this principle in attempting to explain the psychological mechanisms underlying the phenomenon of choking under pressure (see Chapter 3). Briefly, he postulated that anxiety causes people to monitor their own skills excessively, thereby leading to a sudden deterioration of performance. Third, anxiety precipitates task-irrelevant information processing. Janelle et al. (1999) discovered that anxious drivers who participated in a motor-racing simulation were especially likely to attend to irrelevant cues. Fourth, another way in which anxiety affects sport performance is by its influence on the *direction* of athletes' attentional focus. In particular, anxiety may encourage them to dwell on real or imagined personal weaknesses (self-focused attention) and on potential threats in the environment, thereby inducing a state of hypervigilance. Interestingly, the conscious processing (or reinvestment) hypothesis postulates that anxiety hampers performance by inducing performers to rely too much either on explicit monitoring (Beilock and Carr, 2001) or on conscious control (Masters, 1992) of their skills (see also Chapter 3). It is clear, therefore, that anxiety affects the content, direction and width of athletes' concentration beam (see also Moran et al., 2002).

In summary, at least five principles govern either the maintenance or loss of an optimal focus for athletes. But why do sport performers lose their concentration in the first place?

Why do athletes lose their concentration?

As we learned from Figure 4.3, when people focus on factors that are either irrelevant to the job at hand or beyond their control, they lose concentration and their performance deteriorates. However, psychologists believe that concentration is never really "lost", but merely *redirected* at some target that is irrelevant to the task at hand. For example, have you ever had the experience of realizing suddenly that you have been reading the same sentence in a book over and over again without any understanding simply because your mind was "miles away"? If so, then you have distracted yourself by allowing a thought, daydream or feeling to become the target of your attention. By the way, this problem can be overcome by writing down two or three specific study questions before you approach a textbook or notes (see advice in

Moran, 2000b). Let us now consider the question of why athletes appear to lose their concentration.

Competitive sport is replete with a variety of distractions that can disrupt athletes' concentration. In general, these distractions fall into two main categories – external and internal (Moran, 1996, 2004). Whereas external distractions are objective stimuli which divert our attentional spotlight away from its intended target, internal distractions include a vast array of thoughts, feelings and/or bodily sensations (e.g., pain, fatigue) which impede athletes' efforts to concentrate on the job at hand. Typical external distractions include such factors as crowd movements, sudden changes in ambient noise levels (e.g., the click of a camera – as happened to the golfer, Ian Poulter, who lost his chance to win the 2009 French Open when a camera click caused him to hit his ball into the water on the fifteenth hole: Irish Times, 2009), gamesmanship by opponents (e.g., at corner-kicks in football, opposing forwards often stand in front of the goalkeeper to prevent him or her from tracking the incoming ball) and unpredictable playing surface or weather conditions (e.g., a golfer may become distracted by windy conditions). As an example of the last of these factors, the Swiss cyclist Fabian Cancellara complained about the distracting effect of the heat he experienced during the 2009 Tour de France: "With the heat like that, ... there's a lack of concentration among the riders" (cited in Associated Press, 2009). Interestingly, a study by Larrick et al. (2011) analysed data from over 57,000 Major League baseball games on the relationship between ambient temperature and retaliatory aggression among pitchers. Results showed that, when many relevant variables were controlled for, the probability of a pitcher hitting a batter increased significantly during high temperatures. More generally, distractions lead to impaired performance at the worst possible moment for the performer concerned. For example, the Brazilian marathon runner Vanderlei De Lima was leading the race in the 2004 Olympics in Athens when an unstable spectator suddenly jumped out from the crowd and wrestled him to the ground. Stunned and naturally distracted, De Lima eventually finished third in the event (Goodbody and Nichols, 2004). By contrast, internal distractions are self-generated concerns arising from one's own thoughts and feelings. Typical factors in this category include wondering what might happen in the future, regretting what has happened in the past, worrying about what other people might say or do and/or feeling tired, bored or otherwise emotionally upset (Figure 4.4). A classic example of a costly internal distraction occurred in the case of the golfer Doug Sanders, who missed a putt of less than three feet that would have earned him victory at the 1970 British Open championship in St. Andrews, Scotland. This error not only prevented him from winning his first major tournament, but also deprived him of an estimated £10 million in prize money, tournament invitations and advertising endorsements. Remarkably, Sanders' attentional lapse was precipitated by a cognitive error – thinking too far ahead or in this case, making a victory speech before the putt had been taken. Intriguingly, over thirty years later, he revealed what had gone through his mind at the time: "I made the mistake about thinking which section of the crowd I was going to bow to!" (cited in Gilleece, 1999b). Clearly, Sanders had inadvertently distracted *himself* by allowing his mental spotlight to shine into the future instead of at the task in hand. As he explained:

I had the victory speech prepared before the battle was over … I would give up every victory I had to have won that title. It's amazing how many different things to my normal routine I did on the eighteenth hole. There's something for psychologists there, the way that the final hole of a major championship can alter the way a man thinks.

(cited in G. Moran, 2005, p. 21)

Unfortunately, despite such vivid accounts of attentional lapses in sport, little research has been conducted on the phenomenology of distractibility – although Gouju et al. (2007) explored athletes' attentional experiences in a hurdle race, especially those arising from the "felt presence" of rival competitors. This general neglect of distractibility is attributable to a combination of theoretical and metho-dological factors. First, since the 1960s, cognitive researchers have assumed falsely that information flows into the mind in only one direction – from the outside world inwards. In so doing, they ignored the possibility that information (and hence distractions) could travel in the opposite direction – from long-term memory into working memory or current awareness. A second reason why researchers focused on external distractions is simply because they were easier to measure than were their self-generated equivalents. As a result of this combination of factors, the theoretical mechanisms by which internal distractions disrupt concentration are still rather mysterious. Nevertheless, a promising approach to this problem may be found in Wegner's (1994) "ironic processes" model. This model is interesting because it addresses the question of why people often lose their concentration at the most *inopportune* moment. Briefly, Wegner's (1994) theory proposed that the mind

Figure 4.4 Internal distractions can upset athletes' concentration in competitive situations

wanders *because* we try to control it. Put simply, when we are anxious or tired, the decision *not* to think about something may paradoxically increase the prominence of that phenomenon in our consciousness. In such circumstances, the attempt to block out a certain thought from one's mind may lead to a "rebound" experience whereby the suppressed thought becomes even more prominent in consciousness. In other words, when we are anxious or tired, trying *not* to think about something may paradoxically increase its prominence in our consciousness. For example, if you try to focus on falling asleep, you will probably achieve only a prolonged state of wakefulness! Similarly, if you attempt to block a certain thought from entering your mind, you may end up becoming more preoccupied with it. This tendency for a suppressed thought to come to mind more readily than a thought that is the focus of intentional concentration is called "hyperaccessibility" and is especially likely to occur under conditions of mental load. Clearly, there are many situations in sport in which such ironic self-regulation failures occur. For example, issuing a negative command to your doubles partner in tennis (such as "whatever you do, don't double-fault") may produce counter-intentional results. What theoretical mechanisms could account for this phenomenon? Briefly, Wegner's (1994) theory proposed that the mind wanders *because* we try to control it; when people try to suppress a thought, they engage in a controlled (conscious) search for thoughts that are different from the unwanted thought. At the same time, however, our minds conduct an automatic (unconscious) search for any signs of the unwanted thought. In other words, the intention to suppress a thought activates an automatic search for that very thought in an effort to monitor whether or not the act of suppression has been successful. Normally, the conscious intentional system dominates the unconscious monitoring system. But under certain circumstances (e.g., when our working memories are overloaded or when our attentional resources are depleted by fatigue or stress), the ironic system prevails and an ironic intrusion of the unwanted thought occurs. Wegner (1994) attributes this rebound effect to cognitive load. But although this load is believed to disrupt the conscious mechanism of thought control, it does not interfere with the automatic (and ironic) monitoring system. Wegner (1994) proposed that the intention to concentrate creates conditions under which mental load can enhance the monitoring of irrelevant information. To summarize, Wegner's (1994) research helps us to understand why athletes may find it difficult to suppress unwanted or irrelevant thoughts when they are tired or anxious.

Perhaps not surprisingly, Wegner (2002) has investigated ironies of *action* as well as those of thought. For example, consider what happens when people who are asked *not* to overshoot the hole in a golf putt are given tasks which impose a heavy mental load on them. In such situations, the unwanted action (overshooting the hole) is exactly what occurs.

Since the late 1990s, the **ironic theory of mental control** has attracted considerable research attention and some empirical support within sport psychology (e.g., see Binsch et al., 2009; Janelle, 1999). Dugdale and Eklund (2002) asked participants to watch a series of videotapes of Australian Rules footballers, coaches and umpires. In one experiment, results revealed that participants became *more* aware of the umpires when instructed *not* to pay attention to them. Clearly, this finding raises doubts about the validity of asking anxious athletes *not* to worry about an important forthcoming athletic event or outcome. Woodman and Davis

(2008) showed that ironic processes impair athletic performance. Specifically, they discovered that the imposition of a cognitive load manipulation (based on the opportunity to win a financial prize for proficiency in putting) resulted in increased ironic errors in a golf putting task. Interviews with athletes have also revealed that ironic errors are common in elite sport. To illustrate, in a study by Bertollo et al. (2009) on the mental preparation strategies used by Italy's 2004 Olympic pentathlon squad, one of the athletes explained: "In some circumstances my intention is not to do the best but to avoid making a bad shot. That is when I make a bad shot. *When I think about avoiding the error, I make the error*" (Bertollo et al., 2009, p. 252; italics mine).

At this stage, it might be helpful to do some research on distractions. So, if you are interested in exploring the factors that cause athletes to lose their focus, try the exercise in Box 4.4.

Box 4.4 Exploring distractions in sport

The purpose of this exercise is twofold. First, you will find out what the term "concentration" means to athletes. Second, you will try to classify the distractions which they perceive to have affected their performance.

To begin with, find three athletes who compete regularly in different sports (e.g., golf, soccer, swimming). Request their permission to record your interview with them on an electronic voice-recorder. Then, ask them the following questions:

1 What does the term "concentration" mean to you?
2 On a scale of 0 (meaning "not at all important") to 5 (meaning "extremely important"), how important do you think that the skill of concentration is for successful performance in your sport?
3 What sort of distractions tend to upset your concentration *before* a game/ match? Describe the situation and the distraction which results from it.
4 What distractions bother you *during* the event itself? Describe the situation and the distraction which results from it.
5 Please give me a specific example of how a distraction changed your focus and/or affected your performance. Tell me what the distraction was, how it occurred and how you reacted to it.
6 What techniques do you use, if any, to cope with distractions?

Analysis
Compare and contrast the athletes' answers to your questions. The word "focus" will probably feature in responses to Q 1. Try to establish exactly what athletes mean by this word. You should also find that athletes regard concentration as being very important for successful performance in their sport (Q 2). After you have compiled a list of distractions (Qs 3 and 4), you will probably find that they fall into two main categories: external and internal. Is there any connection between the type of sport which the athletes perform and the distractions that they reported?

Concentration training exercises and techniques

Having explored what concentration is, how to measure it and why we often lose it, we should now examine the various strategies recommended by sport psychologists for improving focusing skills. Applied sport psychology is replete with strategies which claim to improve concentration skills in athletes (Greenlees and Moran, 2003). Typically, the purpose of these strategies is to help athletes to achieve a focused state of mind in which there is no difference between what they are thinking about and what they are doing (see Figure 4.3). If this happens, the athlete's mind is "cleared of irrelevant thoughts, the body is cleared of irrelevant tensions, and the focus is centred only on what is important at that moment for executing the skill to perfection" (Orlick, 1990, p. 18). But what concentration strategies do sport psychologists recommend to athletes and what do we know about their efficacy?

In general, two types of psychological activities have been alleged to enhance focusing skills in sport performers: concentration training exercises and concentration techniques (Moran, 1996, 2003b). The difference between these activities is that whereas the former ones are intended for use mainly in athletes' training sessions, the latter are designed primarily for competitive situations. Among the plethora of concentration exercises recommended by sport psychologists are such activities as the "concentration grid" (a **visual search task** endorsed by Schmid and Peper (1998), in which the participant is required to scan as many digits as possible within a given time limit), watching the oscillation of a pendulum (which is alleged to show how "mental concentration influences your muscle reactions": Weinberg, 1988, p. 87) and looking at a clock "and saying 'Now' to yourself every alternate 5 and 10 seconds" (L. Hardy and Fazey, 1990, p. 9). Unfortunately, few of these activities are supported by either a coherent theoretical rationale or adequate evidence of empirical validity. For example, take the case of the ubiquitous concentration grid. Surprisingly, no references were cited by Weinberg and Gould (2007) to support their claim that it was used "extensively in Eastern Europe as a pre-competition screening device" or that "this exercise will help you learn to focus your attention and scan the environment for relevant cues" (Weinberg and Gould, 2007, pp. 391 and 392). Despite the absence of such evidence, the grid is recommended unreservedly by Schmid and Peper (1998, p. 324) as a "training exercise for practising focusing ability" and also by Weinberg and Gould (2007) and J. Williams et al. (2010). These endorsements are contradicted by empirical evidence, however. Greenlees et al. (2006) examined the validity of the grid as a concentration exercise over a nine-week period with a sample of collegiate soccer players. Results showed no significant effects of the grid on the athletes' concentration skills relative to a control group. Therefore, these authors concluded that the grid "lacks the efficacy that has been ascribed to it in previous literature and anecdotal accounts" (Greenlees et al., 2006, p. 36).

In summary, there appears to be little empirical justification for the use of generic visual search and/or vigilance tasks in an effort to improve athletes' concentration skills. Indeed, research suggests that visual skills training programmes are not effective in enhancing athletes' performance in sports such as soccer (Starkes et al., 2001) – a finding which challenges the validity of using visual search tasks like the concentration grid as a training tool.

In contrast to the previous concentration exercises, simulation training (Orlick, 1990; Moran 2003a) appears to have a satisfactory theoretical rationale (for a discussion of the use of simulation training to counteract anxiety, see Chapter 3). This exercise, which is also known as dress rehearsal (Schmid and Peper, 1998), simulated practice (Hodge and McKenzie, 1999) and distraction training (Maynard, 1998), proposes that athletes can learn to concentrate more effectively in real-life pressure situations by simulating them in practice conditions. A number of anecdotal testimonials to the value of this practice have emerged since 2000. Earl Woods, the father and initial coach of Tiger Woods, used such methods on him when he was a boy. Woods Senior claimed:

> all the strategies and tactics of distraction I'd learned I threw at that kid and he would just grit his teeth and play ... and if anyone tries pulling a trick on him these days he just smiles and says "my dad used to do that years ago".
>
> (cited in Evening Herald, 2001)

Javier Aguirre, the coach of the Mexican national soccer team, instructed his players to practise penalty-taking after every friendly match in the year leading up to the 2002 World Cup in an effort to prepare for the possibility of penalty shootouts in that competition. As he explained: "there will always be noise and that is the best way to practise" (cited in M. Smith, 2002). Another example of simulation training comes from rugby football. Here, in preparation for an away match against Stade Français where a capacity crowd (80,000 people) were expected to attend, the Harlequins team trained at home under a giant screen playing loud music and YouTube clips. Harlequins won the match (Casey, 2011). As we discovered in Chapter 3, Bob Bowman helped the swimmer Michael Phelps (multiple Olympic champion) to prepare for possible adverse conditions (e.g., having to swim without goggles) in competition by deliberately breaking Phelps' goggles in training races.

Unfortunately, despite its intuitive appeal, simulation training has received little or no empirical scrutiny as a concentration strategy. Nevertheless, some support for its theoretical rationale may be found in cognitive psychology. Research on the "encoding specificity" principle of learning shows that people's recall of information is facilitated by conditions which resemble those in which the original encoding occurred (Matlin, 2009). Based on this principle, the simulation of competitive situations in practice should lead to positive transfer effects to the competition itself. In addition, adversity training may counteract the tendency for novel or unexpected stimuli to distract athletes in competition. The simulation of these factors in training should reduce their attention-capturing qualities subsequently. To summarize, there is some theoretical justification for the belief that simulation training could enhance athletes' concentration skills, but this conclusion is tentative for one important reason. Specifically, even the most ingenious simulations cannot replicate completely the *actual* arousal experienced by athletes in competitive situations. For example, Ronan O'Gara, the Ireland and Lions' rugby out-half, admitted that although he can practise taking penalty kicks in training, "it's completely different in a match where my heartbeat is probably 115 beats a minute whereas in training it's about 90–100" (cited in Fanning, 2002). Clearly, it is difficult to simulate accurately the emotional aspects of competitive action.

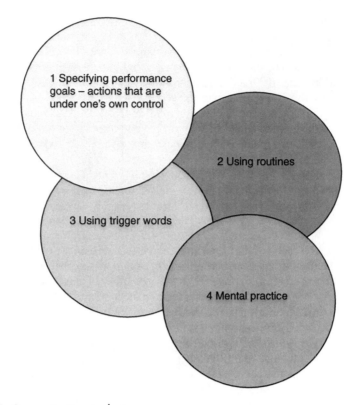

Figure 4.5 Concentration techniques
Source: based on Moran (1996)

Having reviewed some popular concentration exercises, we should now turn to the second type of attentional skills intervention used in sport psychology – namely, concentration techniques listed in Figure 4.5.

Specifying performance goals

In Chapter 2, I explained the theory and practice of goal-setting. As you may recall, a "goal" is a future valued outcome (Locke and Latham, 2006). Sport psychologists (e.g., L. Hardy and Jones, 1994) commonly distinguish between result goals (e.g., the outcome of a sporting contest), performance goals (or specific end-products of performance that lie within the athlete's control, attempting to achieve 90 per cent accuracy in one's serve in tennis) and process goals (or specific behavioural actions that need to be undertaken to achieve a goal – such as tossing the ball up high for greater service accuracy). Using this distinction, some researchers (e.g., G. Winter and Martin, 1991) have proposed that specifying performance goals can improve athletes' concentration skills. According to this theory, tennis players could improve their concentration on court by focusing solely on such performance goals as seeking

100 per cent accuracy on their first serves. This suggestion seems plausible theoretically because performance goals encourage athletes to focus on task-relevant information and on controllable actions. Additional support for this idea springs from studies on the correlates of people's best and worst athletic performances. S. Jackson and Roberts (1992) found that collegiate athletes performed worst when they were preoccupied by result goals. Conversely, their best displays coincided with an explicit focus on performance goals. Similarly, Kingston and Hardy (1997) discovered that golfers who focused on specific action goals improved both their performance and their concentration. In summary, there seems to be some support for the idea that performance goals can facilitate concentration skills in athletes.

Using pre-performance routines

Sport is a highly ritualized activity. Thus most top-class athletes display characteristic, self-consistent sequences of preparatory actions before they perform key skills. For example, tennis players tend to bounce the ball a preferred number of times before serving and rugby place-kickers like to go through a systematic series of steps before striking the ball (see Figure 4.6).

These preferred action sequences and/or repetitive behaviours are called pre-performance routines (PPRs: for a comprehensive review of research on this topic, see Cotterill, 2010) and are typically conducted prior to the execution of self-paced skills (i.e., actions that are carried out largely at one's own speed and without interference from other people). According to Harle and Vickers (2001), such routines are often used in an effort to improve concentration and performance.

Figure 4.6 Pre-performance routines help players to concentrate
Source: Courtesy of University College Dublin, Sport

At least three types of routines are common in sport. First, pre-event routines are preferred sequences of actions in the run-up to competitive events. Included here are stable preferences for what to do on the night before, and on the morning of, the competition itself. Second, pre-performance routines are characteristic sequences of thoughts and actions which athletes adhere to prior to skill execution – as in the case of tennis players bouncing the ball before serving. Third, post-mistake routines are action sequences which may help performers to leave their errors in the past so that they can refocus on the task at hand. For example, a golfer may "shadow" the correct swing of a shot that had led to an error.

Support for the value of pre-performance routines as concentration techniques comes from both theoretical and empirical sources. Theoretically, pre-performance routines may improve concentration for at least three reasons. First, they are intended to encourage athletes to develop an appropriate mental set for skill execution by helping them to focus on task-relevant information. For example, many soccer goalkeepers follow pre-kick routines in an effort to block out any jeering that is directed at them by supporters of opposing teams. Second, such routines may enable athletes to concentrate on the present moment rather than on past events or on possible future outcomes. Third, pre-performance routines may prevent athletes from devoting too much attention to the mechanics of their well-learned skills – a habit which can unravel automaticity (see Beilock and Carr, 2001; see also Chapter 3). Thus routines may help to suppress the type of inappropriate conscious control that often occurs in pressure situations. A useful five-step pre-performance routine for self-paced skills is described by Singer (2002) and Lidor and Singer (2003).

Augmenting the preceding arguments is empirical evidence derived from case studies which show that routines can improve athletes' concentration skills and performance. For example, Crews and Boutcher (1986) compared the performances of two groups of golfers – those who had been given an eight-week training programme of only swing practice and those who had participated in a "practice-plus-routine" programme for the same duration. Results revealed that the more proficient golfers benefited more from using routines than did the less skilled players. An important issue in research on the efficacy of pre-performance routines concerns the degree to which they are *actually* consistent in competitive situations. Some studies have raised doubts about such consistency. For example, R. Jackson and Baker (2001) analysed the pre-strike routine of the prolific former Welsh international and Lions rugby kicker, Neil Jenkins, who scored 1,049 points in 87 games for his country. As expected, Jenkins reported using a variety of concentration techniques (such as thought-stopping and mental imagery) as part of his pre-kick routine. However, what surprised Jackson and Baker (2001) was that Jenkins *varied* the timing of his pre-kick behaviour as a function of the difficulty of the kick he faced. This finding shows that routines are not as rigid or stereotyped as was originally believed. Subsequently, R. Jackson (2003) reported that goal-kickers at the 1999 rugby World Cup varied the duration of their pre-kick routine in accordance with the perceived difficulty of the task. Lonsdale and Tam (2008) examined the consistency of the pre-performance routines of a sample of elite National Basketball Association (NBA) players whose "free throw" behaviour was analysed from television footage. Results showed that, contrary to expectations, the temporal consistency of the basketball players' pre-performance routines was not associated with accurate skill execution. However, there was evidence that behavioural consistency was related to accurate performance. Specifically, Lonsdale and Tam (2008) found that the basketball players were more successful when they adhered to their dominant behavioural sequence prior to their free throws. Having considered research on the relationship between pre-performance behaviour and skilled performance, is there any empirical evidence on the attentional importance of pre-shot routines? Unfortunately, there is a dearth of studies on this issue. However, a case study by D. Shaw (2002) reported that a professional golfer experienced some attentional benefits arising from the use of a pre-shot routine. Although this evidence is anecdotal, the golfer reported that "the new routine had made him more focused for each shot and therefore less distracted by irrelevancies" (D. Shaw, 2002, p. 117). Cotterill et al. (2010) conducted in-depth interviews with a sample of amateur international golfers in an effort to understand the nature and perceived benefits of their PPRs. Results showed that these golfers used routines for attentional purposes such as attempting to "switch on and off" and "staying in the present and not dwelling on the past or engaging in fortune telling" (Cotterill et al., 2010, p. 55).

What theoretical mechanisms could explain the poularity of ritualized behaviour (such as pre-performance routines) in sport? According to R. Jackson and Masters (2006), such behaviour probably serves two purposes simultaneously. First, it consumes working memory resources and hence prevents the performer from "reinvesting" conscious control over skills that are more effectively executed automatically. Second, pre-competitive rituals may provide some temporary relief from excessive anxiety on the part of the performer.

Apart from their apparent variability in different situations, pre-performance routines give rise to other practical issues that need to be addressed here. They may lead to superstitious rituals on the part of the performer. For example, consider the mixture of routines and rituals used by the Australian tennis player Jelena Dokic. Apparently, she never steps on white lines, she always blows on her right hand while waiting for her opponent to serve and she bounces the ball five times before her own first serve and twice before her second serve (Edworthy, 2002). Furthermore, she insists that "the ball boys and girls always have to pass me the ball with an underarm throw, which is luckier than an overarm throw" (cited in Edworthy, 2002). Clearly, this example highlights the rather fuzzy boundaries between pre-performance routines and superstitious rituals in the minds of some athletes. A study by D. Foster et al. (2006) highlighted the overlap between these two types of ritualized behaviour. Briefly, these authors evaluated the effect of removing superstitious behaviour (e.g., kissing the tape covering a wedding ring on the shooter's hand) and introducing a pre-performance routine (of bouncing the ball, taking a deep breath, visualizing the perfect shot and then using a cue word before executing the skill) for a group of basketballers engaged in free-throw skill execution. Contrary to what was predicted, there was very little difference between performance following either superstitious behaviour or a pre-performance routine – perhaps because many of the basketballers had been using superstitious behaviour for years prior to the study whereas the routine was only a recent addition to their mental preparation for skill execution.

At this stage, it may occur to you that routines are merely superstitions in disguise. To explore this issue further, read Box 4.5.

Box 4.5 Thinking critically about ... routines and superstitions in sport: helpful or harmful?

Pre-performance routines (PPRs: see Cotterill, 2010) are consistent sequences of thoughts and behaviour displayed by athletes as they prepare to execute key skills. Given some apparently compulsive features of this behaviour, however, it may be argued that routines are not really concentration techniques but merely *superstitions*. Is this allegation valid?

Superstition may be defined as the belief that, despite scientific evidence to the contrary, certain actions are causally related to certain outcomes. Furthermore, we know that athletes are notoriously superstitious – largely because of the capricious nature of sport (Vyse, 1997). Rafael Nadal must have two water bottles beside the court, perfectly aligned and with the labels facing the baseline. Tiger Woods typically wears a "lucky" red shirt on the last day of a golf tournament. The South African golfer Ernie Els never plays with a ball marked with the number two because he associates it with bad luck. The former tennis player Martina Hingis refused to step on the lines on the tennis court for fear of misfortune (Laurence, 1998). In general, sport psychologists distinguish between routines and superstitious behaviour on two criteria: control and purpose. First, consider the issue of control. The essence of superstitious behaviour is the belief that one's fate is governed by factors that lie *outside* one's control. But the virtue of a routine is that it allows the player to exert complete control over his or her preparation. Indeed, players often shorten their pre-performance routines in adverse circumstances (e.g., under unfavourable weather conditions). Unfortunately, the converse is true for superstitions. Thus they tend to grow *longer* over time as performers "chain together" more and more illogical links between behaviour and outcome. A second criterion which may be used to distinguish between routines and rituals concerns the technical role of each behavioural step followed. To explain, whereas each part of a routine should have a rational basis, the components of a superstitious ritual may not be justifiable objectively. Despite these neat conceptual distinctions, the pre-shot routines of many athletes are often invested with magical thinking and superstitious qualities. Schippers and Van Lange (2006) analysed the psychological benefits of superstitious rituals among elite athletes. Based on an examination of the circumstances in which such rituals are displayed before games, these investigators concluded that superstitious behaviour was most likely to occur when games were perceived as especially important. In addition, these researchers reported that players with an external locus of control tended to display more superstitious rituals than those with an internal locus of control.

As a final point, evidence has emerged to suggest that despite their irrational origins, superstitions may be helpful sometimes to performers. Damisch et al. (2010) conducted a series of intriguing experiments which appear to highlight

---

some benefits of superstitions to motor and cognitive task performance. Specifically, they showed that playing with a ball described as "lucky" seems to improve participants' golf putting accuracy and that the presence of a personal charm enhances participants' performance on memory and anagram tests. Volunteers who kept their fingers crossed finished a dexterity task faster than did participants in a control condition. In an effort to explain these results, Damisch et al. (2010) postulated that "good-luck" superstitions may have increased participants' self-efficacy (or belief in their own ability to succeed on the tasks in question) which, in turn, may have improved their performance. In short, although carrying a lucky charm is irrational, it may boost one's confidence.

Critical thinking questions
Do you think that athletes really understand the difference between routines and rituals? What do you think of the idea that it does not really matter that athletes are superstitious – as long as it makes them feel mentally prepared for competition? Can you think of any other explanation – besides one involving a possible boost in self-efficacy – for the results reported by Damisch et al. (2010)?

Another problem with routines is that they need to be reviewed and revised regularly in order to avoid the danger of automation. To explain, if athletes maintain the same pre-performance routines indefinitely, their minds may begin to wander as a consequence of growing accustomed to them or tuning out. Clearly, an important challenge for applied sport psychologists is to help athletes to attain an appropriate level of conscious control over their actions before skill execution. Too much control, however, can cause "reinvestment" – a problem which occurs when relatively automated motor processes are disrupted if they are run using consciously accessed knowledge to control the mechanics of the movements (R. Masters and Maxwell, 2008).

Trigger words as cues to concentrate

Trigger words are short, vivid and positively phrased verbal reminders designed to help athletes to focus on a specific target or perform a given action. For example, the British Olympic athlete Paula Radcliffe, who won the 2007 New York City Marathon, reported using a strategy whereby she counted her steps silently to herself in an effort to maintain her concentration in a race. As she indicated, "When I count to 100 three times, it's a mile. It helps me to focus on the moment and not to think about how many miles I have to go. I concentrate on breathing and striding, and I go within myself" (cited in Kolata, 2007) (see Figure 4.7). Similarly, consider the use of covert verbal cues by Michael Lynagh, the former Australian international rugby player, as he prepared to take a penalty kick during the World Cup final against England in 1991: "Five steps back, three to the left, and kick through the ball" (cited in Brolly, 2007). In a similar vein, consider an incident that

Figure 4.7 Paula Radcliffe counts silently to herself in order to maintain her concentration in a race
Source: Courtesy of Inpho photography

occurred during the 2002 Wimbledon Ladies' Singles tennis final between the Williams sisters, Serena and Venus. Briefly, Serena (who defeated Venus 7–6, 6–3) was observed by millions of viewers to be reading something as she sat down during the change-overs between games. Afterwards, she explained that she had been reading notes that she had written to herself as trigger words or instructional cues to remind her to "hit in front" or "stay low" (R. Williams, 2002b). She used a similar strategy in 2007 in Wimbledon when she defeated Daniela Hantuchova in the fourth round of the tournament. On this occasion, she used phrases like "get low", "add spin" and "move up" (A. Martin, 2007). A self-report scale designed to measure athletes' use of such self-talk was developed by Zervas et al. (2007). Another example of the use of triggers comes from golf. Louis Oosthuizen, the 2010 British Open champion, used a red dot on his glove to remind him to concentrate (L. Kelly, 2010).

Many sport performers talk to themselves either silently or out loud when they compete – usually in an effort to motivate themselves. This covert self-talk may involve praise (e.g., "Well done! That's good"), criticism ("You idiot – that's a stupid mistake") and/or instruction ("Swing slowly"). Accordingly, self-talk may be positive, negative or neutral. As a cognitive self-regulatory strategy, self-talk may enhance concentration skills (J. Williams and Leffingwell, 2002). In particular, Landin and Herbert (1999) discovered that tennis players who had been trained to use instructional cues or trigger words (such as "split, turn") attributed their improved performance to enhanced concentration on court. A survey of the nature and uses of self-talk in athletes was conducted by L. Hardy et al. (2001). One of the findings reported in this study was that athletes used it for such mastery reasons as staying "focused" (L. Hardy et al., 2001, p. 315).

Can self-talk improve athletes' concentration? Unfortunately, no published research on this question could be located. However, it is possible that positive and/or instructional self-statements could enhance attentional skills by reminding athletes about what to focus on in a given situation. For example, novice golfers may miss the ball completely on the fairway in the early stages of learning to swing the club properly. In an effort to overcome this problem, golf instructors may advise learners to concentrate on sweeping the grass rather than hitting the ball. This trigger phrase ensures that learners stay "down" on the ball instead of looking up to see where it went. In general, trigger words must be short, vivid and positively phrased to yield maximum benefits. They should also emphasize positive targets (what to aim for) rather than negative ones (what to avoid).

Mental practice

The term **mental practice** (MP) or visualization refers to the systematic use of mental imagery in order to rehearse physical actions. It involves seeing and feeling a skill in one's imagination before actually executing it (Moran, 2002a). Although there is considerable empirical evidence that MP facilitates skill-learning and performance (see Chapter 5), its status as a concentration technique remains uncertain. However, from anecdotal evidence, it is clear that mental imagery is used widely by athletes for the purpose of focusing. For example, visualization can be valuable in blocking out distracting thoughts, as Darren Clarke, the Irish Ryder Cup golfer, revealed:

> Visualizing things is massively important. If you don't visualize, then you allow other negative thoughts to enter your head. Not visualizing is almost like having a satellite navigation system in your car, but not entering your destination into it. The machinery can only work if you put everything in there.
>
> (Clarke, 2005, p. 3)

In a similar vein, Ronan O'Gara, the Ireland and Lions' rugby out-half, used imagery to concentrate on executing his last minute drop-goal to help Ireland to win the 2009 Grand Slam in the final match against Wales: "I had the imagery and visualized the kick going over ... I just had to get the ball up as opposed to drive it up" (cited in Souter, 2009).

Despite such anecdotal insights, there have been few studies of mental imagery as a concentration technique. In summary, we have reviewed four psychological techniques that are used regularly in an effort to improve athletes' concentration skills. Unfortunately, few studies have evaluated the efficacy of these techniques in enhancing concentration skills. Despite the absence of such evidence, these four concentration techniques appear to be both plausible and useful in sport settings.

Old problems and new directions in research on concentration in athletes

Despite a considerable amount of research on attentional processes in athletes, some old problems remain. The purpose of this section of the chapter is to identify these unresolved issues and to sketch some potentially fruitful new directions for research in this field.

First, as is evident from the insights of some leading sports performers earlier in this chapter, further research is required on the **meta-attentional** processes of athletes or their intuitive theories about how their own concentration systems work. Such research is important because concentration skills enhancement in applied sport psychology is really an exercise in meta-attentional training whereby athletes learn to understand, and gain some control over, their apparently capricious concentration system. As yet, however, we know very little about the nature, accuracy and/or malleability of athletes' theories of how their own mental processes operate. Second, we need to address the question of why athletes misdirect their concentration spotlight so easily and so frequently in competitive situations. Unfortunately, few studies addressed this topic. Therefore, little or nothing was known about the influence of internal distractions – those which arise from athletes' own thoughts and feelings – on performance. However, with the advent of Wegner's (1994, 2002) ironic processes model and the development of novel ways of assessing athletes' susceptibility to cognitive interference (e.g., see the test developed by Hatzigeorgiadis and Biddle, 2000), a greater understanding has emerged of the mechanisms underlying athletes' internal distractions. Third, in the late 1990s, Simons (1999) raised the question of whether or not sport performers know precisely what they *should* be concentrating on in different sport situations. This question is often neglected by sport psychologists in their enthusiasm to provide practical assistance to athletes. As a solution, Simons (1999) recommended that instead of exhorting players to "watch the ball", sport psychology consultants should ask such questions as "What way was the ball spinning as it came to you?" or "Did you guess correctly where it would land?" Fourth, what is the best way to measure concentration skills in athletes? Although three different approaches to this question have been proposed in sport psychology (i.e., the psychometric, neuroscientific and experimental: see earlier in chapter), there is a dearth of validation data on tests of concentration in sport. This situation is disappointing because unless concentration skills can be measured adequately, it is impossible to evaluate whether or not they have been improved by the exercises and techniques discussed earlier. A related problem is that few tests have been devised explicitly to assess concentration skills in athletes. This situation is puzzling given the importance of this construct for successful performance in sport. Fifth, additional research is required on the relationship between the *structure* of various athletic activities and their attentional demands (see also Chapter 1 for a discussion of this issue). For example, do untimed games such as golf place different cognitive demands on athletes' concentration systems as compared with those imposed by timed activities (e.g., soccer)? If so, what theoretical mechanisms could account for such differences? A related issue concerns the *type* of concentration skills required for success in various sports. Intuitively, it seems reasonable to expect that sports such as weight-lifting may require short periods of intense concentration while others (e.g., cycling) may demand sustained alertness for a longer duration. Indeed, this ability to *sustain* attention is vital, for example, for tennis players during a gruelling match (e.g., at the 2010 Wimbledon tennis championship, the United States' John Isner took 11 hours and 5 minutes to defeat France's Nicolas Mahut 6–4, 3–6, 6–7, 7–6, 70–68) and for the wicket keeper in cricket whose team spends an entire day on the field (as this player has to pay attention to every ball as it is bowled). Given the variety of different attentional demands in different sports, is it reasonable to expect that the same concentration intervention packages should work equally well in all sports? Unfortunately, at present, many applied sport psychologists seem to endorse a "one-size-fits-all" approach in advocating the same toolbox of psychological strategies (e.g., goal-setting, self-talk) for a variety of different athletic problems. Sixth, additional research is needed to establish the precise mechanisms by which emotions (such as anxiety) affect athletes' concentration processes. One way to address this question is to explore the visual search behaviour of anxious athletes as they tackle laboratory simulations of sport-relevant tasks (see Moran et al., 2002). A seventh fruitful avenue for research on attention in sport comes from cognitive neuroscience. As mentioned earlier, this field is concerned with understanding the biological substrates of cognitive processes through the use of psychophysiological measures (e.g., EEG, ERP, PET scanning, fMRI, and TMS) collected during "real-time" performance of various tasks. Already, such techniques have proved valuable in identifying the main attentional networks in the brain (Posner and Rothbart, 2007). Although these techniques have limitations (e.g, they are likely to be most beneficial when guided by psychological theories; see Cacioppo et al., 2008), they offer intriguing possibilities for the study of attentional processes in athletes. Finally, additional theoretically driven research is needed to establish the precise mechanisms by which emotions (such as anxiety) affects athletes' concentration processes. An interesting example of such research is an attempt by Wilson et al. (2007a) to arbitrate empirically between different theoretical accounts of choking in athletes (see also Chapter 3).

Ideas for research projects on concentration in athletes

Here are six ideas for possible research projects on attentional processes in athletes.

1   It would be interesting to investigate precisely what athletes of different levels of ability, and also from different sports, understand by the term "focusing". Unfortunately, many studies in this field assume that athletes interpret this term in the same way as researchers. Is this assumption valid?

2   You could fill a gap in the field by exploring the nature and extent of expert–novice differences in athletes' "meta-attentional awareness" (i.e., their

understanding of, and control over, how their concentration system works).
Little is known about this topic so far.

3   You could address some of the unresolved questions in research on flow
     states in athletes. For example, do athletes ever experience such states when
     practising or training? Or do they occur only in competitive situations?

4   It would be a good idea to evaluate the reliability and validity of Nideffer's
     (1976) Test of Attentional and Interpersonal Style (TAIS) using a large sample
     of athletes.

5   It would be helpful to test Wegner's (1994) theory of ironic control in a sport
     setting. For example, using the methodology developed by Dugdale and
     Eklund (2002), can ironic rebound effects be reduced by manipulating athletes'
     attentional focus?

6   Do concentration techniques such as pre-performance routines (PPRs) actually
     improve athletes' performance of self-paced skills such as golf putting, tennis
     serving or rugby place-kicking in actual sport settings? Surprisingly few field
     studies have been conducted in this area (for a review of research on this topic,
     see Cotterill, 2010).

Summary

- The term "concentration" refers to the ability to focus mental effort on what is
  most important in any situation while ignoring distractions. This ability is a
  crucial prerequisite of successful performance in sport. Research suggests that
  the ability to focus effectively is associated with peak performances in athletes. Unfortunately, despite a century of empirical studies on attentional
  processes, there is still a great deal of confusion about what concentration is
  and how it can be measured and improved in athletes. Therefore, the purpose
  of this chapter was to alert you to the progress and prospects of research in
  this field.
- The second section examined the nature, dimensions and importance of the
  construct of concentration in sport.
- The third section outlined briefly three approaches to the measurement of
  attentional processes (including concentration) in athletes.
- The fourth section explained the main principles of effective concentration
  that have emerged from research on the ideal performance states of athletes.
- The fifth section explored the question of why athletes lose their concentration
  so easily.
- The sixth section reviewed various practical exercises and psychological
  techniques that are purported to enhance concentration skills in athletes.
- The seventh section outlined some unresolved issues concerning attentional
  processes in sport performers.
- Finally, some potentially fruitful new directions for research in this field were
  suggested.

Chapter 5

Using imagination in sport: mental imagery and mental practice in athletes

You have to see the shots and feel them through your hands.

(Tiger Woods, quoted in Pitt, 1998b)

Introduction

Many top athletes have discovered that "mental imagery", or the ability to simulate in the mind information that is not currently being perceived by the sense organs, is helpful for the learning and performance of sport skills. For example, "seeing" and "feeling" oneself performing one's skills in one's mind's eye is widely evident among world-class performers in rugby, athletics and swimming. When Ronan O'Gara, the Ireland and Lions' rugby out-half, had scored a last-minute drop goal against Wales to help Ireland to win the 2009 Six Nations' championship, he revealed how he had simulated the kick in his mind:

> I picked out three numbers in the stand behind the posts. I can still picture them perfectly. That was my target. I visualized the ball going through and kept that image. I played it in my mind a few times ... this is what it comes down to now. One chance.
>
> (cited in Walsh, 2009)

When British athlete Paula Radcliffe (a world record holder for the marathon event) trained for the 2012 Olympic Games, she visualized herself running up the final stretch of the race venue in London. As she said at the time, "I try to imagine that I'm in the closing stages of the marathon in London ... I just visualize myself running up The Mall" (cited in Hart, 2011). Just like Tiger Woods (see quotation above), Michael Phelps, fourteen times Olympic gold medallist in swimming, high-lighted the importance of kinaesthetic or "feeling oriented" imagery (see Figure 5.1). He said:

> swimmers like to say they can "feel" the water. Even early on, I felt it. I didn't have to fight the water. Instead, I could feel how I moved in it. How to be balanced. What might make me go faster or slower.
>
> (Phelps, 2008a)

Not surprisingly, the value of using mental imagery to rehearse actions and move-ments is also recognized in other fields of skilled performance. Imagery has been shown to enhance performance in musicians (Meister et al., 2004) and surgeons (Arora et al., 2010, 2011) and can even be used to augment the physical rehabilitation of people who have suffered neurological damage (e.g., see review of the use of imagery with stroke patients: Braun et al., 2006; McEwen et al., 2009). Perhaps not surprisingly, mental imagery techniques are used extensively by athletes, coaches and sport psychologists to improve motor learning and skilled performance (see review by Weinberg 2008) and, as a result, are widely recommended by sport psychologists (e.g., see Cumming and Ramsey, 2009; Vealey and Greenleaf, 2010). To illustrate Caliari (2008) found that table tennis players who used imagery to mentally rehearse a stroke (the forehand drive) improved significantly relative to a control group. Furthermore, Mellalieu et al. (2009) found that imagery can improve psychological skills such as self-confidence in rugby players. Arising from such research, imagery has become such a common component of sport psychological

Figure 5.1 Michael Phelps uses kinaesthetic imagery to "feel" the water
Source: Courtesy of Inpho photography

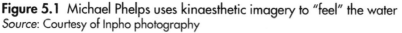

interventions (e.g., see P. Holmes and Collins, 2002) that it has been acclaimed as a "central pillar of applied sport psychology" (T. Morris et al., 2004, p. 344). Nevertheless, athletes who practise imagery may be regarded as rather eccentric. For example, when the England goalkeeper David James rehearses his skills imaginatively during traffic delays, he often receives puzzled glances from other drivers. As he says, "I have had a few strange looks when people see my head nodding from side to side but I firmly believe that it is part of the repetitive process that every sportsman requires" (D. James, 2003). In summary, athletes, dancers and sport psychologists endorse the value of imagery as a cognitive tool for giving performers a winning edge in their chosen field. But is this belief in the power of imagery supported by empirical evidence in psychology? Or does it merely reflect some "New Age", pseudo-scientific mysticism?

In attempting to answer these challenging questions, this chapter explores a variety of intriguing issues at three different levels: practical, methodological and theoretical. For example, if mental imagery *does* improve athletic performance, is it possible that athletes could practise their skills in their heads without leaving their armchairs? Or are the alleged benefits of systematic mental rehearsal too small to be of any practical significance to sport performers? Turning to methodological issues, how can we measure people's mental images? After all, they are among the most private and ephemeral of all our psychological experiences. At a theoretical level, many fascinating questions have emerged in this field. For example, what happens in our brains when we imagine something? Also, what psychological mechanisms could account for the effects of mental rehearsal on skilled performance? More generally, can research on imagery processes in athletes provide us with any valuable insights into how the mind works? For example, could it be that imagery is not something that we "have" in our minds but something that we "do" with our brains? Perhaps the best way to address these questions is to explore the main psychological theories, findings and issues in research on mental imagery in sport performers. In order to achieve this objective, I have organized this chapter as follows.

In the next section, I investigate the nature and types of mental imagery and also explain what the term "mental practice" means in sport psychology. The third section reviews the main findings, theories and issues arising from research on mental practice in sport. The fourth section considers briefly the measurement of mental imagery skills in sport. The fifth section describes what researchers have learned about the ways in which athletes use mental imagery in various athletic situations. In the sixth section, I sketch some new directions for research on imagery in athletes, with a special emphasis on **motor imagery** or a dynamic mental state during which the representation of a given motor act or movement is rehearsed in working memory without any overt motor output (Moran et al., in press). Finally, a few ideas for possible research projects in this field are provided.

What is mental imagery?

Historically, the term "mental imagery" has been used in two ways (Wraga and Kosslyn, 2002). First, it designates the content of one's imagination such as the subjective experience of "seeing with the mind's eye" or "hearing with the mind's ear", for example. Second, imagery refers to "an internal representation that gives rise to the experience of perception in the absence of the appropriate sensory input" (Wraga and Kosslyn, 2002, p. 466). It is this latter understanding of the term that guides this chapter.

One of the most remarkable features of the mind is its capacity to mimic or simulate experiences. Psychologists use the term mental imagery to describe this cognitive (or knowledge-seeking) process which we use every day in order to represent things (e.g., people, places, experiences, situations) in working memory in the absence of appropriate sensory input (Moran, 2002a). For example, if you close your eyes, you should be able to imagine a set of traffic lights changing from green to red (a visual image), the sound of an ambulance siren (an auditory image) or maybe even the muscular feelings evoked by running up steep stairs (a kinaesthetic image). Theoretically, imagery involves perception without sensation. Specifically, whereas perception occurs when we interpret sensory input, imagery arises from our inter-pretation of stored, memory-based information. Thus the process of generating a mental image may be understood crudely as running perception backwards (Behrmann, 2000). As we shall see later, the term "mental practice" refers to a particular application of mental imagery in which performers "practise" in their heads, or rehearse their skills symbolically, before actually executing them.

If imagery resembles perception, there should be similarities between the measurable cortical activity involved in these psychological processes. Put simply, similar parts of the brain should "light up" when we imagine things as when we actually perceive them. For example, visual imagery should be associated with neural activity in the cortical areas that are specialized for visual perception. Until the 1990s, this hypothesis remained untested simply because no technology was available to allow researchers to peer into the brain in order to measure the neural substrates of "real time" or ongoing cognitive activities. Since about 2000, however, a variety of neuroimaging techniques have been developed to allow brain activation to be measured objectively. What are these dynamic brain techniques and how do they work?

According to Kolb and Whishaw (2009), the modern era of brain imaging began in the early 1970s with the development of an X-ray procedure called "computerised tomography" (derived from the word "tomo" meaning "cut") or the CT scan. The logic of this approach is that a computer may be used to draw a three-dimensional map of the brain from information yielded by multiple X-rays directed through it. With the advent of more sophisticated computational strategies to reconstruct images, three other brain imaging procedures emerged: positron emission tomography (PET scanning), functional magnetic resonance imaging (fMRI) and transcranial magnetic stimulation (TMS). These procedures are designed to detect changes in metabolism or blood flow in the brain as people are engaged in cognitive tasks. Such changes are correlated with neural activity. Briefly, in the PET scan, people are given radioactively labelled compounds such as glucose which are metabolized by the brain. This radioactivity is subsequently recorded by special detectors. For reasons of convenience, however, PET scan measurement of metabolism was replaced by the measurement of blood flow. Magnetic resonance imaging is a less invasive technique and is based on two key principles. First, blood oxygenation levels tend to change as a result of neural activity. Second, oxygenated blood differs from non-oxygenated blood in its magnetic properties. When combined, these principles allow researchers to detect changes in brain activity using special magnets. TMS is a procedure in which a magnetic coil is placed over the skull either to stimulate or to inhibit selectively certain areas of the cortical surface.

Using these neuroimaging techniques, research shows that the occipital cortex or visual centre of the brain (which is located at the back of our heads) is activated when people are asked to imagine things (Kosslyn et al., 2001). In addition, these brain-imaging studies have also shown that, contrary to what most people believe, mental imagery is *not* a single undifferentiated ability but, instead, a collection of different cognitive capacities localized in different brain regions. To illustrate, brain imaging studies show that when we "rotate" images in our mind (as happens, for example, when we try to imagine what an object would look like if it were turned upside down), neural activity is detected in the **parietal lobes** (which are located behind the frontal lobe and above the temporal lobe). By contrast, visualizing previously memorized patterns tends to elicit neural activity in the occipital lobes at the back of our heads where vision is coordinated (Kosslyn et al., 2001). Similarly, research on brain-damaged patients shows that if the ventral pathways from the

occipital lobes are impaired, people often lose their ability to recognize and/or imagine shapes. But if damage occurs in the dorsal system, the person may suffer deficits in his or her ability to visualize the locations of objects.

Before concluding this section, it is important to mention a conceptual issue that has been debated vigorously by imagery researchers since the late 1970s. Briefly, this debate concerns the nature of the mental representations that underlie imagery experiences. Specifically, does visual mental imagery reply on mental representations that *depict* things or on ones that *describe* things? Championing the former position, Kosslyn and his colleagues (e.g., see Kosslyn, 1994; Kosslyn et al., 2006) argue that images are visuo-spatial brain representations or depictions ("pictures in the head") and that visual mental images are structurally analogous to visual perceptual representations. Supporting this position is evidence that mental imagery activates significant fronto-parietal and occipito-temporal neural networks in the brain (e.g., Sack et al., 2008). Opposing this view is Pylyshyn (1973, 1981), who argues that visual mental imagery relies on representations that are largely propositional or language-like and that any structural or phenomenal similarities between imagery and perception are illusory. Another point of disagreement between these rival theorists is whether or not mental imagery plays a functional role in cognitive processing. Whereas Kosslyn and his colleagues use neurocientific evidence to support their argument that visuo-spatial depictions play a crucial role in human cognition, Pylyshyn (1973, 1981) argues that imagery is epiphenomenal – an accidental byproduct of abstract cognitive processing but not a central part of it – like the pilot light of a CD player.

Types and dimensions of mental imagery

At the outset, at least four general points can be made about mental imagery types and dimensions. First, depending on the sensory modality and cognitive systems involved, different types of mental imagery have been identified. Second, research suggests that imagery is a multisensory experience. In other words, we have the capacity to imagine "seeing", "hearing", "tasting", "smelling" and "feeling" various stimuli and/or sensations. Third, the greater the number of sensory modalities that we use to create our mental representation of the non-present information, the more *vivid* is the resulting mental imagery experience. Fourth, images differ from each other in dimensions such as **vividness** and controllability (Callow and Hardy, 2005; Moran, 1993). Let us now explore each of these points briefly.

First, whereas sport psychology researchers tend to differentiate between different types of imagery based on their predominant sensory modality (e.g., visual, auditory, gustatory) cognitive neuroscientists tend to use more theoretically based distinctions – such as those between visual, spatial and motor imagery processes. To explain, researchers have discovered two distinct cognitive systems that encode and process visual information in different ways (Blajenkova et al., 2006). Whereas object-based imagery represents the shape and colour information of objects, spatial imagery represents location information. More precisely, "visual object imagery" involves mental representations of "the literal appearances of individual objects in terms of their precise form, size, shape, colour and brightness"

(Blajenkova et al., 2006, p. 239) and "spatial imagery" involves the mental representations of "the spatial relations amongst objects, parts of objects, locations of objects in space, movements of objects and object parts and other complex spatial transformations" (Blajenkova et al., 2006, pp. 239–240). Cognitive researchers have identified "motor imagery" as "a mental/neuronal simulation of an overt movement without muscle contraction" (Hohlefeld et al., 2011, p. 186). This largely proprioceptive or kinaesthetic process is used whenever people imagine actions without engaging in the actual physical movements involved (see also Box 5.2, later in the chapter).

As I mentioned, imagery is a multisensory experience. Thus L. Hardy et al., (1996, p. 28) defined it as "a symbolic sensory experience that may occur in any sensory mode". Of the various senses contributing to imagery experiences in daily life, vision is the most popular. Thus diary studies (Kosslyn et al., 1990) showed that about two-thirds of people's mental images in everyday life are visual in nature. For example, have you ever had the experience of trying to remember where you parked your car as you wandered around a large, congested carpark? If so, then the chances are that you tried to form a mental map of the location of your vehicle. Interestingly, some neuroscientific studies corroborate the primacy of the visual modality over other types of imagery. To explain, Kosslyn et al. (2001) reported that visual images rely on about two-thirds of the same brain areas that are used in visual perception. Specifically, the areas that appear to be most active during visual imagery lie in the occipital lobe (especially areas 17 and 18 or "V1" and "V2"). Evidence to support this conclusion comes from the fact that when people visualize things with their eyes closed, the "V1" and "V2" areas of the brain become active. Also, if these areas are temporarily impaired by the effects of strong magnetic pulses, the person's visual imagery abilities are disrupted (Kosslyn et al., 2001). Despite this phenomenological and neurological evidence that most of our images are visual in nature, our imagination is not confined solely to the visual sense. To illustrate, if you pause for a moment and close your eyes, you should also be able to imagine the sensations evoked by feeling the fur of a cat (a tactile image), hearing the sound of your favourite band or song (an auditory image) or experiencing the unpleasant grating sensation of a nail being scraped across a blackboard (a combination of tactile and auditory images).

Visual and auditory sensations are easily imagined in sport (e.g., can you "see" yourself taking a penalty and then "hear" the crowd roar as your shot hits the net?), but the type of feeling-oriented imagery that Tiger Woods referred to earlier in the chapter is more difficult both to conceptualize and to investigate empirically (see Figure 5.2).

Although few studies have been conducted on feeling-oriented imagery in sport, Moran and MacIntyre (1998) and Callow and Hardy (2005) have investigated **kinaesthetic imagery** processes in elite athletes (see Box 5.1).

To summarize, we have learned that although mental imagery is a multisensory construct, most studies of imagery processes in athletes have been confined to the visual sensory modality.

Turning to the third and fourth points – how images differ from each other – as explained earlier, it is clear that images vary in controllability as well as vividness. "Controllability" refers to the ease with which mental images can be manipulated by the person who creates them. To illustrate, can you imagine a feather falling down

Figure 5.2 Tiger Woods uses kinaesthetic imagery to "feel" his shots before he plays them
Source: Courtesy of Inpho photography

from the ceiling of your room, slowly wafting this way and that before gently landing on your desk? Now, see if you can imagine this feather reversing its path – floating back up towards the ceiling like a balloon, as if carried higher by a sudden current of air. If you found these mental pictures easy to create, then you probably have reasonably good control over your imagery. As another example of this skill, try to imagine yourself standing in front of where you live. How many windows can you see? Count them. Now, using your imagination as a camera with a zoom lens, try to get a close-up picture of one of the windows. What material are the frames made of? What colour are the frames? Can you see them in a different colour? If you can "see" these details of your windows accurately, then you have good imagery control skills.

Box 5.1 Exploring "feel": investigating kinaesthetic imagery in athletes

As research on mental imagery in athletes has focused almost exclusively on the visual sensory modality, other types of imagery experiences in sport have been relatively neglected. This oversight is unfortunate because elite performers in sports such as golf (e.g., Tiger Woods), swimming (e.g., Michael Phelps), canoe slalom and horse-racing rely greatly on "touch" and "feel" when rehearsing their skills and movements in their minds before they actually execute them. Such kinaesthetic imagery processes involve feelings of force and motion or the mental simulation of sensations associated with bodily movements. More precisely, kinaesthetic imagery denotes "the sensations of how it feels to perform an action, including the force and effort involved in movement and balance, and spatial location (either of a body part or piece of sports equipment) (Callow and Waters, 2005, pp. 444–445). Since the late 1990s, some progress has been made in understanding and using this type of imagery in athletes (e.g., see Callow and Hardy, 2005; Moran and MacIntyre, 1998). Moran and MacIntyre (1998) used a combination of qualitative and quantitative methods to investigate the kinaesthetic imagery experiences of a sample (n=12) of elite canoe slalomists participating in World Cup competitions. These athletes were first interviewed about their understanding and use of feeling-oriented imagery in their sport. Then they were assessed using a battery of measures which included specially devised Likert rating scales and the Movement Imagery Questionnaire-Revised (C. Hall and Martin, 1997). Next, in an effort to validate the athletes' subjective reports on their imagery experiences (see later in the chapter for a discussion of this problem), the canoe slalom competitors were timed as they engaged in a "mental travel" procedure during which they had to visualize a recent race in their imagination and execute it as if they were paddling physically. The time taken to complete these mental races was then compared with actual race times. As expected, there was a significant positive correlation between mental and physical race times ($r=0.78$, $p<0.05$). Callow and Waters (2005) investigated the efficacy of a kinaesthetic imagery intervention on the confidence of three flat-race jockeys. Using a single-case, multiple-baseline design (for a comprehensive account of single-case research in sport and exercise psychology, see Barker et al., 2011), Callow and Waters (2005) found that the kinaesthetic imagery intervention was associated with a significant increase in confidence for two of the three jockeys involved. An interesting implication of this latter finding is that a delay is likely to occur between athletes' use of imagery and any subsequent benefits that may accrue from it. Presumably, this time lag occurs simply because athletes need to learn to use imagery properly before any of its advantages become evident. Unfortunately, as Shane Murphy et al. (2008, p. 321) noted, "the expected duration of this time lag is unknown".

Mental imagery representations have three important characteristics. First, they are multisensory constructs that enable us to bring to mind experiences of absent objects, events and/or experiences. Second, they are believed to be functionally equivalent to percepts in the sense that they share a great deal of the same brain machinery or neural substrates with perception. Third, mental images vary in their vividness and controllability – two dimensions which facilitate their measurement (see the fourth section of this chapter). Having explained the nature and types of imagery, let us now consider the topic of mental practice.

Mental practice

As I explained earlier, MP refers to a systematic form of covert rehearsal in which people imagine themselves performing an action without engaging in the actual physical movements involved (Driskell et al., 1994). Because it relies on simulated movements (see Decety and Ingvar, 1990), MP is sometimes known as visuo-motor behavioural rehearsal (VMBR: Suinn, 1994). It has also been called: symbolic rehearsal, imaginary practice, implicit practice, mental rehearsal, covert rehearsal, mental training and cognitive practice (see Shane Murphy and Jowdy, 1992) as well as motor imagery (Decety and Michel, 1989).

Psychological interest in mental practice is as old as the discipline of psychology itself. W. James (1890) suggested rather counter-intuitively that by anticipating experiences imaginatively, people actually learn to skate in the *summer* and to swim in the *winter*! Interestingly, the 1890s witnessed various expressions of an idea called the **ideo-motor principle** which suggested that all thoughts have muscular concomitants. For example, in 1899 Henri-Etienne Beaunis (cited in Washburn, 1916, p. 138) proposed that "it is well known that the idea of a movement suffices to produce the movement or make it tend to be produced". Similarly, Carpenter (1894) claimed that low-level neural impulses are similar in imagined movement. Furthermore, he argued that these impulses are similar in nature, but lower in amplitude, to those emitted during actual movement. I shall return to this ideo-motor hypothesis later in the chapter when evaluating theories of mental practice.

Although research on MP was vibrant in the wake of Galton's (1883) research on imagery vividness, it declined in popularity shortly afterwards as a result of the Behaviourist manifesto (Watson, 1913) which attacked "mentalistic" constructs such as imagery because they were too subjective to be amenable to empirical investigation. Fortunately, a resurgence of research on mental practice occurred in the 1930s with the work of Jacobson (1932), H. Perry (1939) and Sackett (1934). These studies continued in a rather sporadic, atheoretical manner until the 1960s, when the first comprehensive reviews of mental practice were published by A. Richardson (1967a, 1967b). Unfortunately, despite (or maybe, because of!) more than a century of research on imagery, criticisms have been levelled at both the definition of MP and at the typical research designs used to study it. Shane Murphy and Martin (2002) identified a contradiction at the heart of this construct. Specifically, the term mental practice conveys an implicit, dualistic distinction between physical and mental practice that is at variance with current neuroscientific understanding of how the brain works. Thus the fact that visualizing something in the mind's eye usually elicits measurable brain activity in the visual cortical areas (Kosslyn et al., 2001) suggests that mind and body are not really separate processes but function as an integrated unit. Murphy and Martin (2002) also criticized the assumption that mental practice is a standardized, homogeneous intervention. It is not. To illustrate, visualizing a perfect tennis serve could mean either seeing *yourself* playing this stroke or perhaps seeing someone else (e.g., Rafael Nadal) performing this action. It seems likely that there will be many differences between these two types of MP. Further criticism of MP research will be considered in the next section of the chapter. Now that we have examined the nature of mental imagery and mental practice, let us explore research methods and findings on MP. Research on athletes' use of mental imagery will be examined in the fifth section of the chapter.

Research on mental practice in sport

For over a century, the effects of MP on skilled performance have attracted research attention from psychologists. Reviews of this large research literature (amounting to several hundred studies) have been conducted, in chronological order, by A. Richardson (1967a, 1967b), Feltz and Landers (1983), Grouios (1992), Shane Murphy and Jowdy (1992), Driskell et al. (1994), Shane Murphy and Martin (2002), van Meer and Theunissen (2009) and Schuster et al. (2011). Before I summarize the general findings of these reviews, here is a brief explanation of the typical research paradigm used in studies of MP.

Typical research design and findings

In general, the experimental paradigm in MP research involves a comparison of the pre- and post-intervention performance of the following groups of participants: those who have been engaged only in physical practice of the skill in question (the physical practice group, PP); those who have mentally practised it (the mental practice group, MP); those who have alternated between physical and mental practice (PP/MP); and, finally, people who have been involved in a control condition. Historically, the target skills investigated in MP research have largely been relatively simple laboratory tasks (e.g., dart-throwing or maze-learning) rather than complex sports skills. After a pre-treatment baseline test has been conducted on the specific skill involved, participants are randomly assigned to one of these conditions (PP, MP, PP/MP, or control). Normally, the cognitive rehearsal in the MP treatment condition involves a scripted sequence of relaxing physically, closing one's eyes, and then trying to see and feel oneself repeatedly performing a target skill (e.g., a golf putt) successfully in one's imagination. After this MP intervention has been applied, the participants' performance on this skill is tested again. Then, if the performance of the MP group exceeds that of the control group, a positive effect of mental practice is reported.

Based on this experimental paradigm, a number of general conclusions about mental practice have emerged. First, relative to not practising at all, MP appears to improve skilled performance. However, MP is less effective than is physical practice. More precisely, a meta-analytic review by Driskell et al. (1994) showed that physical practice (PP) treatment conditions produced greater statistical effect sizes than was evident in mental rehearsal conditions (recall from Chapter 2 that meta-analysis is a statistical technique which combines the results of a large number of studies in order to determine the overall size of a statistical effect). Statistically, the relative effect sizes of physical practice and mental practice were estimated by these researchers as 0.382 and 0.261 (both Fisher's Z), respectively. These figures can be interpreted with reference to J. Cohen's (1992) suggestion that values of 0.20, 0.50 and 0.80 represent effect sizes that are small, medium and large, respectively. The second general finding from the research literature is that MP, when combined and alternated with physical practice, seems to produce superior skill-learning to that resulting from either mental or physical practice conducted alone. Third, research suggests that mental practice improves the performance of cognitive skills (i.e., those that involve sequential processing activities; e.g., mirror drawing tasks) more than it does for motor skills (e.g., as balancing on a stabilometer). Fourth, there seems to be an interaction between the level of expertise of the performer and the type of task which yields the best improvement from mental rehearsal (Driskell et al., 1994). Specifically, expert athletes tend to benefit more from MP than do novices, regardless of the type of skill being practised (either cognitive or physical). Fifth, the positive effects of MP on task performance tend to decline sharply over time. Indeed, according to Driskell et al. (1994), the beneficial effects of visualization are reduced to *half* of their original value after approximately two weeks of time has elapsed. A practical implication of this finding is that in order to gain optimal benefits from mental practice, "refresher" training should be implemented after this critical two-week period. Finally, there is evidence that imagery ability mediates the relationship between MP and motor skill performance. More precisely, athletes who display special skills in generating and controlling vivid images tend to benefit more from visualization than do counterparts who lack such abilities. In summary, there is now considerable evidence (much of it experimental) to support the efficacy of mental practice as a technique for improving the performance of a variety of sport skills. These skills include not only "closed" actions (i.e., ones which are self-paced and performed in a relatively static environment) such as golf putting or placekicking in rugby but also "open" or reactive skills. For example, the rugby tackle (McKenzie and Howe, 1991) and the counter-attacking forehand in table tennis (Lejeune et al., 1994) have shown improvements under mental rehearsal training.

Critical evaluation of research on mental practice

At first glance, the preceding evidence on the efficacy of mental practice conveys the impression of a vibrant and well-established research field in cognitive sport psychology. But closer inspection reveals a less satisfactory picture. Specifically, as I mentioned in the previous section, MP research has encountered many conceptual and methodological criticisms over its century-long history (Shane Murphy and Martin, 2002). Of these criticisms, perhaps the two most persistent concerns have been the "validation" problem and an issue stemming from a lack of field research in the area. The validation problem can be conveyed by a simple question. How do we know that people who claim to be visualizing a target skill are actually using mental imagery? In other words, how can we validate people's subjective reports about their imagery processes? The problem stemming from the neglect of field research concerns the fact that few published studies of MP have been conducted on athletes engaged in learning and performing sport skills in real life settings. Let us now sketch these problems in more detail.

The validation problem: how do we know that athletes are actually using imagery?

At the beginning of this chapter, we encountered a quotation from Tiger Woods, which provided an anecdotal testimonial to the value of mental imagery. As critical psychologists, however, should we accept at face value what athletes and performers tell us about their imagery experiences? After all, cognitive researchers (e.g., Nisbett and Wilson, 1977) and sport psychologists (e.g., Brewer et al., 1991) have warned us that people's retrospective reports on their own mental processes are susceptible to a variety of memory biases and other distortions (e.g., "response sets" whereby people may wish to convey the impression that they have a good or vivid imagination). Unfortunately, few researchers over the past century have attempted either to keep precise records of the imagery scripts used by participants in MP studies or otherwise to validate athletes' reports of their alleged imagery experiences. This neglect is probably attributable to the fact that in order to validate these latter reports, sport psychology researchers require either objective methods (e.g., functional brain imaging techniques to find out if the imagery centres in the brain are activated when the person claims to be visualizing; see Kosslyn et al., 2001) or experimental procedures (e.g., manipulation checks such as asking people detailed questions about their images; see Shane Murphy and Martin, 2002).

Although the use of brain imaging technology with athletes is prohibited by cost and inconvenience at present, progress has been made in devising theoretically based procedures to check if athletes are really using imagery when they claim to be doing so. For example, Moran and MacIntyre (1998) checked the veracity of canoe slalomists' imagery reports (see Box 5.1) by using a theoretical principle derived from Decety et al. (1989) and MacIntyre (1996). Specifically, this proposition suggests that the greater the congruence between the imagined time and "real" time to complete a mental journey, the more likely it is that imagery is involved. This mental **chronometric paradigm** offers an intriguing way to check whether or not athletes are actually using imagery when claiming to do so. To explore what can be learned from comparing the time it takes to complete actual and imaginary tasks, try the exercise in Box 5.2.

Box 5.2 Mental chronometry in action: experiencing your imagination

What is the relationship between imagining an action and actually doing it? Using the mental chronometric paradigm (see Guillot and Collet, 2005, 2010), it is now possible to investigate motor imagery objectively by comparing the duration required to execute real and imagined actions. The logic here is as follows. If imagined and executed actions rely on similar motor representations and activate certain common brain areas (e.g., the parietal and prefrontal cortices, the pre-motor and primary cortices; see Gueugneau et al., 2008), the temporal organization of imagined and actual actions should also be similar. If that is so, there should be a close correspondence between the time required to *mentally* perform a given action and that required for its *actual* execution. Using this logic, Calmels et al. (2006) examined the temporal congruence between actual and imagined movements in gymnastics. They found that the overall times required to perform and imagine a complex gymnastic vault were broadly similar, regardless of the imagery perspective used (i.e., imagining oneself from a first person perspective or from a third person perspective). However, the temporal congruence between actual and imagined actions is mediated by a number of factors. Guillot and Collet (2005) concluded that when the skills to be performed are largely automatic (e.g., reaching, grasping) or occur in cyclical movements (e.g., walking, rowing), there is usually a high degree of temporal congruence between actual and imagined performance. But when the skills in question involve complex, attention-demanding movements (e.g., golf putting, tennis serving), people tend to *overestimate* their imagined duration. Although this use of mental chronometry has proved very helpful in motor imagery research, it needs to be augmented by other techniques in order to identify the cognitive mechanisms mediating the relationship between imagined and actual skilled performance. One possible solution to this problem is to use eye-tracking technology (see Chapter 6) as an objective method for investigating online cognitive processing during "eyes open" motor imagery. By comparing the eye movements of people engaged in mental and physical practice, we may be able to investigate the cognitive processes (especially those concerned with attention) that are activated by imaginary action (see Heremans et al., 2008).

To experience the mental chronometry in action, try this exercise (adapted from Robertson, 2002) at home. Imagine that you are about to write down your name, address and phone number on a sheet of paper. Before you begin this mental task, make sure the second hand of your watch is at the zero position. Then, make a note of how long it took you to write the three pieces of information in your mind's eye. Next, find another piece of paper and repeat the writing exercise. Now, compare the two times that you recorded. If you were to repeat this exercise several times, you would find that the time it takes to write down your name, address and phone number is about the same as it takes to complete this task mentally.

Perhaps not surprisingly, the temporal congruence between actual and imagined movements seems to be affected by intervening variables such as the nature of the skill being performed and the level of expertise of the performers. Reed (2002) compared physical execution times for springboard dives with the time taken to execute this skill mentally. Three groups of divers were used: experts, intermediate performers and novices. Results revealed that, in general, visualization time increased with the complexity of the dives. Also, by contrast with the experts and novices, visualized dive execution time was slower than physical dive execution time. A further complication within this field of mental chronometry emerged from a study by Orliaguet and Coello (1998). Briefly, these researchers found little or no similarity between the timing of actual and imagined putting movements in golfers. Until recently, most research on the congruence between actual and imagined movement execution used skilled tasks (e.g., canoe slalom, diving) in which there were no environmental constraints imposed on the motor system of the performer. However, Papaxanthis et al. (2003) conducted a remarkable study in which cosmonauts were tested on actual and imagined motor skills (e.g., climbing stairs, jumping and walking) before and after a six-month space flight. The specific issue of interest to these researchers was the degree to which a long exposure to microgravity conditions could affect the duration of actual and imagined movements. Results showed that, in general, the cosmonauts performed the actual and imagined movements with similar durations before and after the space flight. Papaxanthis et al. (2003) interpreted this finding to indicate that motor imagery and actual movement execution are affected by similar adaptation processes and share common neural pathways. In summary, the fact that the timing of mentally simulated lengthy actions tends to resemble closely the actual movement times involved suggests that motor imagery is functionally equivalent to motor production. Let us now return to the issue of how to assess the veracity of athletes' imagery reports. Another possibility in this regard is to validate such experiences through **functional equivalence theory**. To explain, until the 1980s, the mechanisms underlying mental imagery were largely unknown. However, important theoretical progress on this issue occurred with the discovery that imagery shares some neural pathways and mechanisms with like-modality perception (Farah, 1984; Kosslyn, 1994) and with the preparation and production of motor movements (Jeannerod, 2001). This postulated overlap of neural representations between imagery, perception and motor execution is known as the functional equivalence hypothesis (e.g., Finke, 1979; Jeannerod, 1994). To illustrate, P. Johnson (1982) investigated the effects of imagined movements on the recall of a learned motor task and concluded that "imagery of movements has some functional effects on motor behaviour that are in some way *equivalent* to actual movements" (P. Johnson, 1982, p. 363; italics mine). Other studies (e.g., Roland and Friberg, 1985) suggested a functional equivalence between imagery and perception because "most of the neural processes that underlie like-modality perception are also used in imagery" (Kosslyn et al., 2001, p. 641). According to the functional equivalence hypothesis, mental imagery and perception are functionally equivalent in the sense that they are mediated by similar **neuropsychological** pathways in the brain. Accordingly, interference should occur when athletes are required to activate perceptual and imagery processes concurrently in the same sensory modality. This interference should manifest itself in errors and longer response times when athletes face this dual-task situation. Interestingly, as Figure 5.3 shows, interference can also occur between mental imagery and perception in other situations in everyday life such as driving a car while listening to the radio. Why is it so difficult to use perception and imagination in the same sensory modality? See Box 5.3.

The idea of using cognitive interference to validate imagery reports has certain obvious limitations, however. For example, apart from being modality-specific, it is rather unwieldy if not impractical as it depends on finding a suitable pair of perceptual and imagery tasks. Let us now turn to the second problem afflicting MP research. Why have there been so few imagery studies conducted on elite athletes who have to learn and perform sport skills in field settings?

Figure 5.3 It is dangerous to listen to a football match while driving a car

Box 5.3 Why you should not listen to football commentaries while driving: interference between imagery and action

It has long been known that people have great difficulty in perceiving and imagining information presented in the same sensory modality. Indeed, research by the British Transport Research Laboratory showed that listening to sport on the radio can affect drivers more than being drunk at the wheel (Massey, 2010). Furthermore, during simulated driving scenarios, there were nearly 50 per cent more incidents involving hard braking while motorists were listening to sport commentaries on the radio than when drivers were driving without the presence of distractions. To experience this difficulty of trying to engage in perception while imagining, try to form a mental image of a friend's face while reading this page. If you are like most people, you should find this task rather difficult because the cognitive activities of forming a visual image and reading text on a page draw upon the same neural pathways. Another example of this "like-modality" interference problem occurs if you try to imagine your favourite song in your "mind's ear" while listening to music on the radio. Just as before, auditory perception and auditory imagery interfere with each other because both tasks compete for the same processing pathways on the brain. An interesting practical implication of this interference phenomenon is that you should not listen to football matches while driving your car because both tasks require visual processing. This time, unfortunately, cognitive interference could result in a nasty accident (see Figure 5.3). Similar interference could occur if you try to visualize an action while driving.

Lack of field research problem in MP research

Earlier in this chapter, I indicated that most research on mental practice has been carried out in laboratories rather than in real-life settings. Unfortunately, this trend has led to a situation in which few studies on MP have used "subjects who learned actual sport skills, under the same conditions and time periods in which sport activities are typically taught" (Isaac, 1992, p. 192). This neglect of field research is probably attributable to the fact that studies of this type are very time-consuming to conduct – which is a major drawback for elite athletes whose training and travel schedules are usually very busy. In addition, laboratory studies offer a combination of convenience and experimental control which is not easily rivalled in research methodology (see Chapter 1 for a brief summary of research methods in sport and exercise psychology). Since about 2000, there has been an upsurge of interest in "single-case" multiple-baseline research designs (for a comprehensive review of these designs, see Barker et al., 2011). In this paradigm, all participants not only receive the treatment but also act as their own controls because they are required to spend some time earlier in a baseline condition. A major advantage of these research designs is that they cater for individual differences because the intervention in question is administered at different times for each of the different participants in the study. As yet, however, only a handful of imagery studies in sport (e.g., Casby and Moran, 1998) have used single-case research designs.

Despite the conceptual and methodological criticisms discussed above, few researchers deny that MP is effective in improving certain sport skills in certain situations. So, what theoretical mechanisms could account for this MP effect?

Theories of mental practice: overview

Although many theories have been proposed since the 1930s to explain MP effects (see review by Moran, 1996), the precise psychological mechanisms underlying symbolic rehearsal remain unclear. One reason for this equivocal state of affairs is that most MP studies are "one-shot" variations of a standard experimental paradigm (described in the previous section) rather than explicit hypothesis-testing investigations. In spite of this problem, three main conceptual approaches have been postulated to explain MP effects: the **neuromuscular theory of mental practice** (e.g., Jacobson, 1932), the **cognitive or symbolic theory of mental practice** (e.g., Denis, 1985) and the **bio-informational theory of imagery** (e.g., Lang, 1979). As we shall see, the neuromuscular perspective proposes that mental practice effects are mediated mainly by faint activity in the peripheral musculature whereas the cognitive model attributes causal mechanisms to a centrally stored representation in the brain. The bio-informational theory postulates that MP effects reflect an interaction of three different factors: the environment in which the movement in question is performed (stimulus information), what is felt as the movement occurs (response information) and the perceived importance of this skill to the performer (meaning information). Let us now outline and evaluate each of these theories briefly (but for a more detailed review see Murphy and Martin, 2002) before proposing a possible compromise between these rival models of mental practice.

Neuromuscular theories of mental practice

The earliest theories of mental rehearsal (e.g., ideo-motor principle: Carpenter 1894; Washburn, 1916) contained two key propositions. First, they suggested that imagination of any physical action tends to elicit a pattern of faint and localized muscle movements. Second, they claimed that such muscular activity can provide kinaesthetic feedback to the performer which enables him or her to make adjustments to this skill in future trials. This version of neuromuscular theory was supported by Jacobson (1932) who suggested that visualization causes tiny innervations to occur in the muscles that are actually used in the physical performance of the skill being rehearsed covertly. Such minute subliminal muscular activity was held to be similar to, but of a lower magnitude than, that produced by actual physical execution of the movements involved. A subsequent term for this theory is the inflow explanation approach (Kohl and Roenker, 1983) whereby the covert efferent activity patterns elicited by imagery are held to "facilitate appropriate conceptualizing for future imagery trials" (Kohl and Roenker, 1983, p. 180).

In order to corroborate neuromuscular theories of MP, evidence would have to be found which shows that there is a strong positive relationship between the muscular activity elicited by imagery of a given skill and that detected during the actual performance of this skill. Unfortunately, there is very little empirical support for neuromuscular theories of mental practice. For example, there is no convincing evidence that the faint muscular activity which occurs during imagery of a given skill is similar to that recorded during its overt performance. W. Shaw (1938) found that increased **electromyographic (EMG) activity** during motor imagery was distributed across a variety of muscle groups in the body – including some which were not directly related to the imagined action. In other words, the muscular innervations elicited by imagery may merely reflect *generalized* arousal processes. Doubts have surfaced about the type of muscular activity elicited by imagery. Despite using nuclear magnetic resonance (NMR) spectroscopy to monitor what happens in people's muscles during imaginary performance of a specific skill, Decety et al. (1993) could not detect any change in relevant muscular metabolic indices. Finally, in a test of some predictions from neuromuscular theory, Slade et al. (2002) reported that the EMG pattern of activation in biceps and triceps for two types of imagined movements (namely, dumbbell and "manipulandum" curls) did not match the EMG pattern detected during actual movement. The authors of this study concluded that it added to "the mounting research evidence against the psychoneuromuscular theory" (Slade et al., 2002, p. 164). On the basis of the preceding evidence, Shane Murphy and Martin (2002) concluded that there is little or no empirical support for a relationship between the muscular activity elicited by MP and subsequent performance of sport skills. This conclusion was supported by Lutz (2003). Briefly, this investigator used a sample of novice darts players to test the relationship between covert muscle excitation elicited during motor imagery and subsequent performance in dart-throwing. Results showed that although motor imagery led to elevations in covert muscle excitation (as predicted by neuromuscular theory), the *pattern* of activation did not match that shown by the participants during actual dart-throwing. Also, this covert muscle excitation did not predict motor skill acquisition or retention errors. Therefore, Lutz (2003) concluded that covert muscle excitation is an outflow from the central generation of motor imagery rather than an inflow from peripheral structures.

Cognitive theories of mental practice

Cognitive (or symbolic) accounts of visualization propose that mental practice facilitates both the coding and rehearsal of key elements of the task. One of the earliest proponents of this approach was Sackett (1934), who discovered that people's performance on a finger-maze task improved following mental rehearsal of the movement patterns involved. This finding was held to indicate that imagery facilitates the symbolic coding of the mental representation of the movements involved. For example, if you are a keen tennis player you could use imagery to practise a top-spin serve in your mind. This might involve seeing yourself in your mind's eye standing at the service line, feeling yourself bouncing the ball a few times before tossing it upwards and then feeling the strings of your racket brushing up behind it as you hit the ball and move onto the court.

By contrast with neuromuscular accounts of MP, cognitive models attach little importance to what happens in the peripheral musculature of the performer. Instead, they focus on the possibility that mental rehearsal strengthens the brain's central representation or cognitive blueprint of the skill or movement being visualized. In general, two types of evidence have been cited in support of cognitive theories of MP (Murphy and Martin, 2002). First, central representation theories may explain why visualization is especially suitable for mastering tasks (e.g., mirror drawing) which contain many cognitive or symbolic elements such as planning sequential movements (see research findings on MP discussed previously). Interestingly, some anecdotal evidence complementing this finding comes from athletes who use mental imagery to anticipate what might happen in a forthcoming competitive situation (see the quote from Ronan O'Gara in Chapter 4). Second, a cognitive explanation of MP is corroborated by certain research findings on the transfer of learned skills. Specifically, Kohl and Roenker (1980) investigated the role of mental imagery in the bilateral transfer of rotary pursuit skill from participants' right hands to their left hands. Results showed that such transfer of learning occurred even when the training task (involving the contralateral limb) was imagined.

Despite receiving some empirical support, symbolic theories of mental practice have been criticized on at least four grounds. First, they cannot easily explain why MP sometimes enhances motor or strength tasks (see Budney et al., 1994) which, by definition, contain few cognitive components. Remarkably, since the early 1990s, evidence has emerged that imagery training can lead to enhanced muscular strength. Yue and Cole (1992) used a variation of the mental practice research design to show that imagery training could increase finger strength. Subsequently, Yue and his colleagues extended this paradigm to other types of strength training. Uhlig (2001) reported that Yue and his research team required ten volunteers to take part in an imagery-training exercise involving a mental work-out five times a week. This "mental gym" exercise, which consisted of the imaginary lifting of heavy weights with their arms, increased the bicep strength of the participants by 13.5 per cent! Control participants, who missed such mental work-outs, did not show any significant gains in muscle strength. Second, in contrast to these studies, Herbert et al. (1998) discovered that imagined training produces increases in the strength of the elbow flexor muscles which did not differ significantly from those attained by a control group. Third, another problem for symbolic theories is that they find it difficult to explain how MP enhances the performance of experienced athletes who, presumably, already possess well-established blueprints or motor schemata for the movements involved. Fourth, and perhaps most worryingly, most cognitive theories of MP are surprisingly vague about the theoretical mechanisms which are alleged to underlie imagery effects.

Bio-informational theory of mental practice

The bio-informational theory of imagery grew out of Lang's (1979) attempt to understand how people respond emotionally and psychophysiologically to feared objects. It was subsequently applied to research on MP in motor skills by Bakker et al. (1996).

Influenced by the ideas of Pylyshyn (1973), Lang (1979) began with the claim that mental images are not "pictures in the head" but propositional representations in long-term memory. These propositional representations are abstract, language-like cognitive codes that do not physically resemble the stimuli to which they refer. Three types of information about the imagined object or situation are coded in these propositional representations. First, stimulus propositions are statements that describe the content of the scene or situation being imagined. For example, if one were to visualize a penalty kick in football, stimulus information might include the sight of the opposing goalkeeper, the sound of the crowd, and the feel of the ball in one's hands as one places it on the penalty spot. Second, response propositions are statements that describe how and what the person feels as he or she responds to the scenario imagined. For example, stepping up to take a penalty kick is likely to cause some degree of tension and physiological arousal in the player. Images that are composed of response propositions tend to be more vivid than those containing only stimulus propositions (Bakker et al., 1996). Third, meaning propositions refer to the perceived importance to the person of the skill being imagined. For example, if there were only a few seconds left in the match, and one's team is a goal down, the hypothetical penalty kick is imbued with great significance. Lang's (1979) theory postulates that information from these three types of propositions is organized in an associative network in the mind.

Within this network, the response propositions are of special interest to imagery researchers. This is so because these propositions are believed to be coded as bodily responses which are primed by efferent outputs to the muscles of the body. In other words, the propositions regulating imagined responses reflect how a person would actually react in the real-life situation being imagined. Lang (1977, 1979) suggested that response propositions are modifiable. Therefore, based on this theory, it should be possible to influence athletes' mental practice by using imagery scripts that are heavily laden with response propositions. Unfortunately, with the exception of studies by researchers such as Bakker et al. (1996) and Hecker and Kaczor (1988), this hypothesis has not been tested systematically in sport psychology. Nevertheless, there is some evidence that imagery scripts emphasizing response propositions elicit greater physiological activation than do those containing stimulus propositions predominantly (Lang et al., 1980). This conclusion was supported by Cremades (2002), who recorded the EEG activity of golfers during imagery of a putting task using different types of visualization scripts. Analysis of alpha activity in these participants revealed that greater arousal and effort were needed during the golfers' imagery emphasizing response propositions as compared with that apparent during imagery emphasizing stimulus propositions.

In summary, according to bio-informational theory, imagery not only allows people to rehearse what they would do in certain hypothetical situations but also leads to measurable psychophysiological changes associated with the response and meaning propositions triggered by the situation being imagined. Although this theory has not been widely tested in sport and exercise psychology, it has at least three interesting implications for MP research. First, it encourages researchers to regard imagery as more than just a "picture in the head". To explain, Lang's (1977, 1979) theories postulate that for MP to be effective, both stimulus and response propositions must be activated by the imagery script used (Gould et al., 2002a). Second, it highlights the value of "individualizing" imagery scripts so that they take account of the personal meaning which people attribute to the skills or movements that they wish to rehearse. For an application of this idea to sport psychology, see the discussion of the PETTLEP model of P. Holmes and Collins (2001, 2002) in Box 5.4. Third, bio-informational theory emphasizes the need to consider emotional factors when designing imagery scripts – an issue which has been largely neglected by advocates of neuromuscular and cognitive theories of mental practice. There is now compelling evidence that visualizing a stimulus has an effect on the body similar to that when actually seeing it. Lang et al. (1993) discovered that people who imagine threatening objects experience the same signs of emotional arousal (e.g., increased heart rate, shallow breathing) as they do when actually looking at them.

Box 5.4 An applied checklist for mental practice in sport: the PETTLEP model

In an effort to develop a theoretically based checklist for the effective implementation of mental imagery intervention in sport, P. Holmes and Collins (2001) drew upon Lang's (1977, 1979) bio-informational theory and the functional equivalence hypothesis in neuroscience (described above) to produce the PETTLEP model. PETTLEP is an acronym, with each letter representing a key practical issue to be considered when designing imagery scripts and implementing imagery interventions for optimal efficacy in sport. Specifically, these issues are **p**hysical, **e**nvironmental, **t**ask, **t**iming, **l**earning, **e**motional and **p**erspectival. Thus "P" refers to the athlete's physical response to the sporting situation, "E" is the environment in which the imagery is performed, "T" is the imagined task, "T" refers to timing – or the pace at which the imagery is performed, "L" is a learning or memory component of imagery, "E" is the emotions elicited by the imagery and "P" designates the type of visual imagery perspective used by the practitioner (either first person or third person). Overall, the PETTLEP model proposes that in order to produce optimal functional equivalence between imagery and motor production, and thereby to enhance subsequent sport performance, imagery interventions should replicate not only athletes' sporting situation but also the emotions that they experience when performing their skills. For example, P. Holmes and Collins (2002) proposed various practical ideas to "enhance the physical dimensions of an athlete's imagery. These include using the correct stance, holding any implements that would usually be held, and wearing the correct clothing" (D. Smith and Wright, 2008, p. 145). Furthermore, in accordance with bio-informational theory, the PETTLEP model recommends that imagery scripts should include stimulus (i.e., the information describing the stimuli in the environment), response (i.e., the cognitive, affective and behavioural responses of the person to a given stimulus), and meaning (i.e., the perceived importance of the behaviour) propositions (Cumming and Ramsey, 2009). Although the predictions of the PETTLEP model have not been tested extensively to date, available empirical results are generally supportive. For example, D. Smith et al. (2007) compared the use of PETTLEP imagery training with traditional mental practice techniques and also with physical practice in developing gymnastics jump skills. Results showed that the PETTLEP group improved its proficiency in these skills whereas the traditional imagery group did not.

A note of caution about PETTLEP

Sometimes, theories in psychology become distorted through a slippage in the meaning of key terms. This problem is evident among some researchers who have attempted to test the PETTLEP model. For example, consider the claim by Ramsey et al. (2008, p. 209) that "the degree of equivalence between the imagery experience and the physical experience is a major determinant of imagery's effectiveness at modulating behaviour". This claim can be challenged on at least two grounds. First, it is inaccurate to postulate that functional equivalence occurs at the *phenomenological* level – between the "experience" of imagining a skill or movement and that of performing it. Early proponents of the concept of functional equivalence (e.g., Finke, 1979; P. Johnson, 1982) were at pains to suggest that the hypothesized equivalence occurred either at the *neural* or *mental representational* levels– not experientially. Clearly, imagining running a marathon does not make one feel as tired as if one actually ran this event! Second, there is no agreed index of "degree of equivalence" as it is difficult to measure objectively. This apparent misunderstanding of functional equivalence is also evident in Cumming and Ramsey's (2009, p. 20) suggestion that "imagery more functionally equivalent to actual performance will have more pronounced effects on subsequent performance compared to less functionally equivalent imagery". Again, the problem with this claim is that there is no independent measure of the "amount" of functional equivalence between imagery and motor production. This is a problem for all studies of functional equivalence in psychology.

An integrated model of mental practice: functional equivalence theory

Having considered the strengths and limitations of three traditional theories of mental practice (namely, the neuromuscular, cognitive and bio-informational models), it may be helpful to propose an integrated, compromise position that takes account of neuropsychological research on mental imagery namely, functional equivalence theory. Briefly, two key propositions underlying this integrated position may be expressed as follows. First, neuroimaging studies suggest that imagery is functionally equivalent to perception because these two types of cognitive activity share similar neural pathways in the brain (Kosslyn et al., 2001). Second, research indicates that mental practice is functionally equivalent to physical practice in the sense that imagery is guided by the same kinds of central mental representations as are motor movements (C. Hall, 2001). Evidence to support this proposition comes from several sources. For example, neuroscientific studies show that there is a great deal of overlap between the neural substrates of physical and imagined movement execution (see Moran et al., in press). Specifically, motor imagery and movement execution activate such neural regions as the premotor cortex, primary motor cortex, basal ganglia and cerebellum (Jeannerod, 2001). This overlap of neural substrates is not complete, though. Thus Carrillo-de-la-Peña et al. (2008) found that there were significant differences between the event-related potentials elicited during motor imagery and motor execution. Indeed, Dietrich (2008) claimed that there are a number of brain areas that show *increased* activation while participants are engaged in imagery of a skill but not during its actual performance. The converse also appears to be true. Thus there are certain brain areas that are activated during physical performance but not during mental imagery. Based on such neuroscientific evidence, it seems plausible that mental practice is best understood, at present, as a centrally mediated cognitive activity that mimics perceptual, motor and certain emotional experiences in the brain. This view integrates the strengths of all three theories of mental practice – the neuromuscular account (because MP has neural substrates even though these are regulated neither centrally nor peripherally), the cognitive model (because MP is believed to be mediated by a central mental representation) and the bio-informational approach (because MP elicits emotional reactions as well as cognitive and neural activity). Influenced by recent developments in neuroscience, Shane Murphy et al. (2008, p. 308) have proposed "a neurocognitive model of imagery for movement disciplines". This model is based on the functions that imagery serves in regulating action (e.g., motor control, regulation of emotional and motivational processes) and allocates a central role to working memory. Empirical validation of this model is awaited.

Conclusions about research on mental practice in athletes

In summary, research on MP has shown that the systematic covert rehearsal of motor movements and sport skills has a small but significant positive effect on their actual performance. But this conclusion must be tempered by at least three cautionary notes. First, as Box 5.5 shows, mental practice effects are influenced by a number of intervening variables.

Box 5.5 Thinking critically about ... the effects of mental practice on sport performance

Despite an abundance of research on mental practice since the 1960s, relatively few studies have been conducted on the nature of, and cognitive mechanisms underlying, motor imagery processes in athletes. Therefore, any conclusions about the effects of MP on sporting performance – especially at the elite level – must be regarded as somewhat tentative because they reflect extrapolations from a body of research literature that was developed using rather different tasks and research designs from those employed in sport psychology. For example, for reasons of convenience and control, the criterion tasks employed by most MP researchers tend to be laboratory tasks (e.g., maze-learning) rather than complex sport skills (e.g., the golf drive). In addition, traditional studies of mental practice have adopted "between groups" experimental designs in laboratory settings rather than either single-case studies or field experiments. Clearly, future studies of mental practice in athletes will benefit from the use of more complex and ecologically valid sport skills than those used to date and also from the adoption of a wider range of experimental research designs than has been evident until now. Nevertheless, there is at least one important lesson to be learned by motor imagery researchers in sport psychology from traditional studies of MP. Specifically, investigators in the latter field have evaluated a range of intervening variables that affect the relationship between MP and skilled performance. These intervening variables offer crucial clues to the design of successful motor imagery interventions. Schuster et al. (2011) conducted a systematic review of the research literature on mental practice in an effort to identify the key elements of successful motor imagery interventions reported in 133 studies in five different disciplines – sport (i.e., research using athlete populations), psychology (i.e., research using healthy participants who were not athletes), education, medicine and music. Schuster et al. (2011) discovered that, in general, successful imagery interventions had a number of key training elements. For example, the imagery training was conducted in individual sessions and added after physical practice of the skill being targeted. In addition, the participants received acoustic and detailed imagery instructions and kept their eyes closed while imagining the execution of the skill. The imagery perspective that seemed to work best was an internal/kinaesthetic one.

Critical thinking questions

All too often, studies on mental practice in sport fail to include either an imagery test or a manipulation check on whether or not participants actually adhered to the imagery instructions provided. Why do you think it is important to evaluate the imagery skills of participants in mental practice research? (As a hint, would it be helpful to find out if people's imagery scores changed over the course of the intervention? If so, why?) Is it possible to evaluate an imagery intervention in the absence of a manipulation check that imagery instructions were followed adequately? Do you think that the duration of a motor imagery intervention affects its efficacy? Give reasons for your answer – and then check your ideas with what Schuster et al. (2011) found in their review.

Second, research on imagery processes in athletes is hampered by inadequate theoretical explanation of the psychological mechanisms underlying MP effects. In this regard, however, the weight of evidence at present tends to favour the functional equivalence model of mental rehearsal. The third cautionary note arises from the possibility that MP research may constrain our understanding of imagery use in athletes. To explain, as Shane Murphy and Martin (2002) observed, research on the symbolic rehearsal of movements and skills may blind us to the many other ways in which athletes use imagery in sport. Put differently, MP research "offers little guidance regarding the many uses of imagery by athletes beyond simple performance rehearsal" (Shane Murphy and Martin, 2002, p. 417). I shall return to this last point in the fifth section of this chapter.

Measuring mental imagery skills in sport

Research on the measurement of mental imagery has a long and somewhat controversial history in psychology. It goes back to the earliest days of experimental psychology when Galton (1883) asked people to describe their images and to rate them for vividness. Not surprisingly, this introspective, self-report strategy proved contentious. In particular, as I explained earlier in the chapter, Behaviourists like Watson (1913) attacked it on the grounds that people's imagery experiences could neither be verified independently nor linked directly with observable behaviour. Fortunately, theoretical advances in cognitive psychology (see Kosslyn et al., 2006) and the advent of brain imaging techniques in neuroscience (discussed earlier in this chapter) overcame these methodological objections and led to a resurgence of interest in imagery research. Thus imagery is now measured via a combination of techniques that include experimental tasks (e.g., asking people to make decisions and solve problems using imagery processes), timing of behaviour (e.g., comparing imagined with actual time taken to execute an action), neuroscientific procedures (e.g., recording what happens in brain areas activated by imagery tasks) and psychometric tools (e.g., for the assessment of imagery abilities and imagery use in athletes). Arising from these empirical strategies, two questions are especially relevant to this chapter. First, how can psychologists measure people's private experience of mental imagery? Second, what progress has been made in assessing imagery processes in athletes? In order to answer these questions, a brief theoretical introduction is necessary.

Earlier in this chapter, we learned that although mental images are ephemeral constructs, they differ from each other along at least two psychological dimensions: vividness and controllability. Over the past century, these two dimensions of imagery have been targeted by psychologists in their attempt to measure this construct. Throughout this period, two different strategies have been used to assess these imagery dimensions. Whereas the subjective approach is based on the idea of asking people about the nature of their images, the objective approach requires people to complete visualization tasks that have right or wrong answers. The logic here is that the better people perform on these tasks, the more imagery skills they are alleged to possess.

These approaches to imagery measurement can be illustrated as follows. The vividness of an image (which refers to its clarity or sharpness) can be assessed using self-report scales in which people are asked to comment on certain experiential aspects of their mental representation. For example, close your eyes and form an image of a friend's face. On a scale of 1 (meaning "no image at all") to 5 (meaning "as clear as in normal vision"), how vivid is your mental image of this face? Similarly, the clarity of an auditory image might be evaluated by asking people such questions as: "If you close your eyes, how well can you hear the imaginary sound of an ambulance siren?" Unfortunately, subjective self-report scales of imagery have certain limitations (Moran, 1993). For example, they are subject to contamination from response sets such as social desirability. Put simply, most people are eager to portray themselves as having a good or vivid imagination regardless of their true skills in that area. For this reason, objective tests of imagery have been developed. Thus the controllability dimension of a visual mental image (which refers to the ease and accuracy with which it can be transformed symbolically) can be measured objectively by requesting people to complete tasks which are known to require visualization abilities. In the Group Mental Rotations Test (GMRT: Vandenberg and Kuse, 1978), people have to make judgements about whether or not the spatial orientation of certain three-dimensional target figures matches (i.e., is congruent with) or does not match (i.e., is incompatible with) various alternative shapes. The higher people's score is on this test, the stronger are their image control skills. For a more comprehensive account of the history of imagery measurement, as well as of the conceptual and methodological issues surrounding it, see J. Richardson (1999).

Let us now turn to the second question guiding this section. What progress has been made in assessing imagery processes in athletes? The most comprehensive account of imagery measurement in sport psychology to date is that provided by T. Morris et al. (2005). In general, two types of instruments have been developed in this field: tests of athletes' imagery *abilities* and tests of their imagery *use* (see T. Morris et al., 2005). Although an exhaustive review of these measures lies beyond the scope of this chapter, some general trends and issues in imagery measurement may be summarized as follows.

First, among the most popular and psychometrically impressive tests of imagery skills in athletes are the Vividness of Movement Imagery Questionnaire (VMIQ: Isaac et al., 1986) and the revised version of the Movement Imagery Questionnaire (MIQ-R: C. Hall and Martin, 1997). The VMIQ is a twenty-four-item measure of "visual imagery of movement itself and imagery of kinaesthetic sensations" (Isaac et al., 1986, p. 24). Each of the items presents a different movement or action to be imagined (e.g., riding a bicycle). Respondents are required to rate these items in two ways: "watching somebody else" and "doing it yourself". The ratings are given on a five-point scale where 1 = "perfectly clear and as vivid as normal vision" and 5 = "no image at all". Although not extensive, available evidence suggests that the VMIQ satisfies conventional standards of psychometric adequacy. Eton et al. (1998) reported that it had high internal consistency coefficients (e.g., 0.97 for the total scale) and a test-retest reliability score of 0.64 (for the "other" subscale) to 0.80 (for the "self" score) over a two-week interval. Lequerica et al. (2002) reported a high internal consistency value of 0.95 for the visual imagery subscale and 0.97 for the kinaesthetic imagery subscale. An amended version of this test called the Vividness of Movement Imagery Questionnaire-2 (VMIQ-2) was published by R. Roberts et al. (2008) (see Box 5.6).

Box 5.6 A new test of movement imagery in athletes: revising the Vividness of Movement Imagery Questionnaire

Although the Vividness of Movement Imagery Questionnaire (VMIQ: Isaac et al., 1986) has been one of the most popular and psychometrically sound imagery tests used in sport psychology, it has several limitations that were identified by R. Roberts et al. (2008). First, the VMIQ appears to confound two different imagery modalities – visual and kinaesthetic. Thus it requires respondents to imagine performing movements themselves but does not instruct them to use the kinaesthetic modality rather than the visual one, even though first person visual imagery (IVI) and kinaesthetic imagery are regarded as separate modalities (Fourkas et al., 2006b). Second, as the visual imagery subscale of the VMIQ requests respondents to imagine someone else performing actions (as distinct from watching oneself performing these actions), it fails to measure adequately external self-imagery. Third, the VMIQ has not been subjected to confirmatory factor analysis – a technique commonly used to investigate the construct validity of a psychometric test. To address these problems, R. Roberts et al. (2008) developed the Vividness of Movement Imagery Questionnaire – 2 (VMIQ-2). This test consists of twelve items and assesses the ability to form mental images of a variety of movements visually and kinaesthetically. The visual component is further subdivided into "external" and "internal" visual imagery. Respondents are required to imagine each of the twelve movements and to rate the vividness of each item on a Likert-type scale from 1 ("perfectly clear and vivid") to 5 ("no image at all"). The VMIQ-2 displays impressive factorial validity and acceptable concurrent and discriminate validity.

Turning to the MIQ-R (C. Hall and Martin, 1997), this test is especially interesting for sport researchers because it was designed to assess individual differences in *kinaesthetic* as well as visual imagery of movement. Briefly, this test contains eight items which assess people's ease of imaging specific movements either visually or kinaesthetically. In order to complete an item, respondents must execute a movement and rate it on a scale ranging from "1" (meaning "very hard to see/feel") to 7 (meaning "very easy to see/feel"). Imagery scores are calculated as separate sums of the two subscales of visual and kinaesthetic imagery skills. Available evidence indicates that the MIQ-R displays adequate reliability and validity. Abma et al. (2002) reported an internal consistency value of 0.87 for the visual scale and a value of 0.88 for the kinaesthetic scale.

The second point to note about imagery assessment in sport is that the Sport Imagery Questionnaire (SIQ: C. Hall et al., 1998, 2005) is a popular, theory-based and reliable tool for measuring the frequency with which athletes use imagery for motivational and cognitive purposes. Based on Paivio's (1985) theory that imagery affects behaviour through motivational and cognitive mechanisms operating at general and specific levels, the SIQ is a thirty-item instrument (with five sub-scales) that asks respondents to rate on a seven-point scale (where 1 = "rarely" and 7 = "often") how often they use five specific categories of imagery: *motivational general-mastery* (e.g., imagining appearing mentally tough, self-confident and in control in front of others), *motivational general-arousal* (e.g., imagining the anxiety, stress and/or excitement associated with competition), *motivational specific* (e.g., imagining achieving an individual goal, such as winning a medal), *cognitive general* (e.g., imagining various strategies, game plans or routines for a competitive event) and *cognitive specific* (e.g., mentally practising specific sport skills). Sample items from these subscales include "I imagine myself appearing self-confident in front of my opponents" (motivational general-mastery), "I imagine the stress and anxiety associated with competing" (motivational general-arousal), "I imagine myself winning a medal" (motivational specific), "I image alternative strategies in case my event/game plan fails" (cognitive general) and "I can mentally make corrections to physical skills" (cognitive specific).

The six items that comprise each subscale are averaged to yield a score that indicates to what extent respondents use each of the five functions of imagery. According to C. Hall et al. (2005), this test has acceptable psychometric character-istics. This claim is supported by Cumming and Ste-Marie (2001), who reported internal consistency values of 0.75 to 0.91 for the various subscales. Beauchamp et al. (2002) reported internal consistency values ranging from 0.72 (for a scale measuring motivational general-arousal) to 0.94 (for a scale assessing motivational general-mastery) for a modified version of the SIQ. Mellalieu et al. (2009) reported internal consistency values for the scale that ranged from 0.77 (for the motivational general-arousal subscale) to 0.83 (for the cognitive specific subscale).

Unfortunately, despite the preceding progress in imagery measurement, a number of conceptual and methodological issues remain in this field (see also T. Morris et al., 2005). First, even though evidence has accumulated from neuroima-ging techniques that imagery is a multidimensional construct, most imagery tests in sport and exercise psychology rely on a single imagery scale score. Second, until recently, few imagery tests in sport psychology had either an explicit or an adequate theoretical rationale. This issue prompted Shane Murphy et al. (2008, p. 298) to proclaim that "researchers and theorists need to develop a comprehensive model that will guide imagery investigations". Third, much of the psychometric evidence cited in support of imagery tests in sport psychology comes from the research teams that developed the tests in the first place – which is hardly ideal an ideal scientific development. A brief summary of some other issues in the field is contained in Box 5.7.

Box 5.7 Thinking critically about … imagery tests in sport psychology

Many tests of imagery abilities and imagery use are available in sport psychology (see T. Morris et al., 2005). Which one should you use? Although the answer to this question depends partly on the degree to which the test matches your specific research requirements (e.g., are you studying visual or kinaesthetic imagery or both?), it also depends on psychometric issues. These issues are expressed below in the critical thinking questions.

Critical thinking questions
If the psychometric adequacy of the imagery test is unknown, how would you assess its reliability? What value of a reliability coefficient is conventionally accepted as satisfactory by psychometric researchers? How would you establish the construct validity of an imagery test in sport? Specifically, what other measures of this construct would you use to establish the "convergent validity" of the test? Also, how would you establish the "discriminant validity" of the test (i.e., what measures should your test be unrelated to statistically)? If you were designing an imagery test for athletes from scratch, what precautions would you take to control for response sets (e.g., social desirability) or acquiescence (i.e., the tendency to apply the same rating to all items regardless of the content involved)?

Athletes' use of mental imagery

Having analysed how mental imagery processes have been measured in sport performers, let us now consider how they are used by athletes. People use mental imagery for many purposes in everyday life. Kosslyn et al. (1990) asked a sample of university undergraduates to keep a diary or log of their imagery experiences over the course of a week. Results revealed that imagery was used for such functions as problem solving (e.g., trying to work out in advance whether or not a large suitcase would fit into the boot of a car), giving and receiving directions (e.g., using mental maps to navigate through the physical environment), recall (e.g., trying to remember where they had left a lost object), mental practice (e.g., rehearsing what to say in an important interview on the way to work) and motivation (e.g., using images of desirable scenes for mood enhancement purposes). This type of research raises several interesting questions. How widespread is imagery use among athletes (see review by Munroe et al., 2000)? Do elite athletes use it more frequently than less proficient counterparts? For what specific purposes do athletes employ imagery?

Before we explore empirical data on these questions, let us consider briefly some anecdotal reports and textbook accounts of reports on imagery use in sport. In this regard, many testimonials to the value of imagery have emerged from interviews with, and profiles on, athletes in different sports. For example, current and former world-class performers such as Michael Jordan (basketball), Tiger Woods and Jack Nicklaus (golf), John McEnroe and Andre Agassi (tennis), George Best and David James (football) all claim to have seen and felt themselves performing key actions successfully in their imagination before or during competition (Begley, 2000). As critical thinkers, however, we should be careful not to be too easily influenced by anecdotal testimonials. A critic once remarked acerbically about another psychologist's work which was heavily based on colourful examples, the plural of anecdote is not data! In other words, examples do not constitute empirical evidence. As I explained in Chapter 1, psychologists are wary of attaching too much importance to people's accounts of their own mental processes simply because such insights are often tainted by biases in memory and distortions in reporting. Athletes may recall more cases of positive experiences with imagery (i.e., occasions on which their visualization coincided with enhanced performance) than negative experiences with it (where visualization appeared to have no effect).

Turning to the textbooks, many applied sport psychologists have compiled lists of alleged uses of imagery in sport (see Box 5.8).

Box 5.8 Thinking critically about ... athletes' use of mental imagery

Many applied sport psychologists provide lists of assumed applications of mental imagery by athletes. Vealey and Greenleaf (2010) suggested that athletes use imagery to enhance three types of skills: physical (e.g., a golf putt), perceptual (e.g., to develop a strategic game plan) and psychological (e.g., to control arousal levels). Within these three categories, imagery is alleged to be used for the following purposes:

- Learning and practising sport skills (e.g., rehearsing a tennis serve mentally before going out to practise it on court)
- Learning strategy (e.g., formulating a game plan before a match)
- Arousal control (e.g., visualizing oneself behaving calmly in an anticipated stressful situation)
- Self-confidence (e.g., "seeing" oneself as confident and successful)
- Attentional focusing/refocusing (e.g., focusing on the "feel" of a gymnastics routine)
- Error correction (e.g., replaying a golf swing slowly in one's mind in order to rectify any flaws in it)
- Interpersonal skills (e.g., imagining the best way to confront the coach about some issue)
- Recovery from injury or managing pain (e.g., visualizing healing processes).

Critical thinking questions
Sometimes, speculation goes beyond the evidence in sport psychology. To explain, there is a big difference between speculating about what athletes *could* use imagery for and checking on what they *actually* use it for in sport situations. For example, few studies have found any evidence that athletes use imagery to enhance either interpersonal skills or recovery from injury. Therefore, despite the unqualified enthusiasm which it commonly receives in applied sport psychology, mental imagery is not a panacea for all ills in sport. Clearly, it is advisable to adopt a sceptical stance when confronted by claims about the alleged use of mental imagery by athletes.

How can we test the claims made in Box 5.8? To answer this question, two main research strategies have been used by sport psychologists: descriptive and theoretical. Whereas the descriptive approach has tried to establish the *incidence* of general imagery use in athletes, the theoretical approach has examined specific *categories* of imagery use (e.g., imagery as an aid to motivation and cognition) in these performers. These two approaches to imagery use can be summarized as follows.

Using the descriptive approach, special survey instruments have been designed to assess imagery use in various athletic populations. This approach has led to some interesting findings. For example, successful athletes appear to use imagery more frequently than do less successful athletes (Durand-Bush et al., 2001). We should not be surprised at this discovery because Shane Murphy (1994) reported that 90 per cent of a sample of athletes at the US Olympic Training Centre claimed to use imagery regularly. Ungerleider and Golding (1991) found that 85 per cent of more than 600 prospective Olympic athletes employed imagery techniques while training for competition. Clearly, imagery is used extensively by expert athletes. By contrast, Cumming and Hall (2002b) found that recreational sport performers used imagery less than did more proficient counterparts (namely, provincial and international athletes) and also rated it as being less valuable than did the latter group. This trend was apparent even out of season (Cumming and Hall, 2002a). Moreover, as one might expect, visual and kinaesthetic imagery are more popular than other kinds of imagery in athletes (C. Hall, 2001).

Although this type of descriptive research provides valuable baseline data on imagery use among athletes, it does not elucidate the precise tasks or functions for which athletes employ their visualization skills. To fill this gap, a theoretically derived conceptual model of imagery use in athletes was required. Craig Hall et al. (1998) postulated a taxonomy of imagery use in athletes based on Paivio's (1985) theory that imagery affects both motivational and cognitive processes. As indicated in the previous section, this taxonomy of C. Hall et al. (1998) proposed five categories of imagery use. First, motivational general-mastery involved the imagination of being mentally tough and focused in a forthcoming competitive situation. Second, motivational general-arousal involved imagining the feelings of excitement that accompany an impending competitive performance. Third, motivational specific was implicated in visualizing the achievement of a goal such as winning a race.

Fourth, cognitive general imagery occurred when athletes imagined a specific strategy or game plan before or during a match. Fifth, cognitive specific imagery involved mentally rehearsing a skill such as a golf putt or a penalty kick in football.

At first glance, this taxonomy is helpful not only because it distinguishes between imagery *function* and imagery *content* but also because it allows researchers to explore the relationship between these variables and subsequent athletic performance. Short et al. (2002) discovered that both imagery direction (i.e., whether imagery was positive or negative) and imagery function (motivational general-mastery and cognitive specific) can affect people's self-efficacy and performance in golf putting. Despite its heuristic value, however, the classification system by C. Hall et al. (1998) has been criticized for conceptual vagueness. To illustrate, Abma et al. (2002) pointed out that athletes who use cognitive specific imagery regularly (e.g., in rehearsing a particular skill) may be classified as using motivational general-mastery if they believe that mental practice is the best way to boost their confidence. Another limitation of this taxonomy is that it offers no explanation of the cognitive mechanisms underlying imagery processes. Despite such criticisms, the theoretically driven taxonomies developed by C. Hall et al. (1998) and K. Martin et al. (1999) offer greater scope for research on imagery use by athletes than do the intuitive classifications promulgated by applied sport psychologists (e.g., Vealey and Greenleaf, 2010).

Let us now summarize some general findings on imagery use in athletes. According to C. Hall (2001), three general trends may be detected in this field. First, athletes tend to use imagery more in pre-competitive than in practice situations – a fact which suggests that they tend to visualize more frequently for the purpose of mental preparation or performance enhancement in competition than for skill acquisition. Second, available evidence suggests that, as predicted by Paivio (1985), imagery is used by athletes for both motivational and cognitive purposes. Although the former category is rather fuzzy and ill-defined, it includes applications like seeing oneself achieving specific goals and feeling oneself being relaxed in competitive situations. It is precisely this latter application that the British Olympic champion shooter, Richard Faulds, pursued in creating the image of an ice-man prior to winning the 2000 Olympic gold medal for trap-shooting: "The image is the ice-man. You walk like an ice-man and think like an ice-man" (quoted in Nichols, 2000, p. 7). With regard to cognitive uses of imagery by athletes, two main applications have been discovered by researchers. First, as is evident from anecdotal and survey evidence, imagery is widely used as a tool for mental rehearsal (a "cognitive specific" application). Second, imagery is often used as a concentration technique. The former England cricket batsman Mike Atherton used to practise in his mind's eye in an effort to counteract anticipated distractions on the big day. This involved visualizing "What's going to come, who's going to bowl, how they are going to bowl, what tactics they will use, what's going to be said to try and get under my skin so that nothing can come as a surprise" (cited in Selvey, 1998). A third general research finding in this field concerns the *content* of athletes' imagery. In this regard, C. Hall (2001, p. 536) claims that athletes tend to use positive imagery (e.g., seeing themselves winning competitive events) and "seldom imagine themselves losing". But is this really true? After all, everyday experience would suggest that many club-level golfers are plagued by negative mental images such as hitting bunkers or striking the ball out of bounds. Nevertheless, C. Hall (2001) concluded that athletes' imagery is generally accurate, vivid and positive in content.

New directions for research on imagery in athletes

Two questions dominate this section of the chapter. First, what new directions can be identified in research on imagery processes in athletes? Second, does this research shed any light on how the mind works?

At least seven new directions may be identified for imagery research on athletes. First, despite its obvious importance for skilled performance (e.g., see the quotes from Tiger Woods and Michael Phelps near the beginning of the chapter), motor imagery has been relatively neglected by imagery researchers in sport psychology and cognitive psychology. Fortunately, this trend has changed and significant interdisciplinary progress has been made in understanding motor imagery processes since 2000 (see Box 5.9).

Box 5.9 Exploring motor imagery: some progress ... but still some confusion apparent

As we discovered earlier in the chapter, people have the capacity to mentally simulate *actions* as well as experiences. The term "motor imagery" refers to people's imagination of actions without engaging in actual physical movements involved or the "mental rehearsal of voluntary movement without accompanying bodily movement" (Milton et al., 2008a, p. 336). For reviews of research in this field, see Guillot and Collet (2010) and Moran et al. (in press). In general, two types of information – kinaesthetic/proprioceptive and visual information – contribute significantly to the capacity to simulate actions mentally. Indeed, research suggests that visual and kinaesthetic imagery are mediated by separate neural networks (Guillot et al., 2009; Solodkin et al., 2004). What is not clear, however, is how these components of imagery interact with each other. Influenced by M. Mahoney and Avener's (1977) research on imagery perspective, Decety (1996, p. 87) suggested that motor imagery "corresponds to the so-called internal imagery (or first person perspective) of sport psychologists". Similarly, Jeannerod (1997, p. 95) distinguished between visual or "external" imagery and motor imagery, which was defined as "a 'first-person' process where the self feels like an actor rather than a spectator ('internal' imagery)". Although intuitively appealing, these suggestions by Decety (1996) and Jeannerod (1997) have been challenged by imagery research findings in sport psychology. As Fourkas et al. (2006a) pointed out, people can form motor images using either a first-person perspective (whereby people imagine themselves performing a given action) or a third-person perspective (whereby people imagine seeing either themselves or someone else performing the action). Furthermore, there is evidence from qualitative studies (Moran and MacIntyre, 1998), descriptive research (e.g., Callow and Hardy, 2004; Callow and Roberts, 2010) and experiments (e.g., L. Hardy and Callow, 1999) in sport psychology that motor imagery representations can be accessed consciously using a third-person visual perspective. Thus L. Hardy and Callow (1999) investigated the effects of different imagery perspectives on the performance of tasks involving form-based movements (e.g., a gymnastic floor routine). Results showed that an "external" (third-person) visual imagery perspective was superior to an "internal" (first-person) perspective in facilitating performance of such movements.

Second, very little is known about athletes' **meta-imagery** processes – or their beliefs about the nature and regulation of their own imagery skills (see Moran, 1996). Within this topic, it would be interesting to discover if expert athletes have greater insight into, or control over, their imagery processes than do relative novices (see MacIntyre and Moran, 2007a, 2007b). Third, additional research is required to establish the extent to which athletes use mental imagery in the period immediately prior to competition (Beauchamp et al., 2002). Fourth, we need to tackle the old issue of how to validate athletes' reports of their imagery experiences. As I mentioned early in this chapter, however, we may be approaching this task with the wrong theory in mind. Put simply, what if imagery were not so much a characteristic that people "have" but something – a cognitive process – that they "do"? If, as Kosslyn et al. (2001) propose, imagery and perception are functionally equivalent, interference should occur when athletes are required to use these processes concurrently in the same modality. As I indicated earlier, this possibility of creating experimental analogues of this type of interference could help to discover whether athletes are really using imagery when they claim to be mentally practising their skills. Psychophysiological indices may also be helpful in "tracking" athletes' imagery experiences. Fifth, Cumming and Hall (2002b) raise the intriguing proposition that the theory of **deliberate practice** (see Chapter 6) can be explored in athletes using research on imagery processes. This idea, which is based on C. Hall's (2001) speculation that mental and physical practice are equivalent in certain ways, could be a profitable avenue for future research. Sixth, not enough studies have been conducted on the issue of how top-level athletes use mental imagery in learning and performing complex sport skills. Seventh, Collet et al. (2011) argued that the multidimensional construct of motor imagery is best measured using a combination of psychometric, behavioural and psychophysiological tools. Furthermore, they proposed a way of combining these different imagery measures into an integrated "motor imagery index". Clearly, this new measure requires additional validation before it can be used in research on motor imagery processes.

Let us now turn to the issue of whether or not imagery research has any implications for the pursuit, in mainstream cognitive psychology, of how the mind works. Moran (2002a) considered several ways in which research on mental imagery in athletes can enrich mainstream cognitive psychology. Up to now, however, cognitive psychology has devoted little attention to the world of athletic performance (although Frederick Bartlett used tennis and cricket examples when explaining his theory of schemata in the early 1930s). Nevertheless, imagery research in sport may help to enrich cognitive theory in at least three ways. First, it can provide a natural laboratory for the study of neglected topics such as kinaesthetic and meta-imagery processes. Second, it offers a sample of expert participants (top-class athletes) and a range of imagery tests (T. Morris et al., 2005) which may help researchers to make progress in understanding individual differences in cognitive processes. Interestingly, Kosslyn et al. (2001) observed that the issue of why people differ so much in imagery abilities remains largely unresolved. Third, research on athletes could facilitate our understanding of the neural substrates of imagery. To explain, some studies (Behrmann, 2000; Kosslyn et al., 2001) show that people with vivid imagery show significantly increased blood flow in the occipital region when visualizing. Does this pattern also emerge when functional brain-mapping techniques are applied to athletes skilled in the use of imagery? What neural activation is elicited by kinaesthetic imagery processes in sport performers? These are just some of the cognitive issues raised by research on imagery processes in athletes.

Ideas for research projects on imagery in athletes

Here are five suggestions for possible research projects on the topic of mental imagery in sport and exercise psychology.

1   It would be interesting to explore the relationship between imagery perspective (i.e., the viewpoint that a person takes during imagery – either a first-person or a third-person perspective) and the performance of a closed skill such as a tennis serve. To illustrate the difference between these rival perspectives, consider two different ways of visualizing the serve. For this skill, an "external" imagery would involve watching oneself serving from the perspective of an outside observer (e.g., as if one were looking at someone else performing this skill on television). Conversely, an internal perspective would entail the simulation of what one would *actually* experience if one were physically serving the ball. According to M. Mahoney and Avener (1977), task performance should improve when participants adopt an internal (or first-person) rather than an external (or third-person) imagery perspective. However, L. Hardy and Callow (1999) found that the adoption of an external visual imagery perspective was superior to that of an internal perspective when learning skills in which correct "form" is important (e.g., karate, gymnastics). It would be useful to design a study that could arbitrate empirically between these rival theoretical predictions using the skill of tennis serving. In conducting such a study, however, it is essential to match participants for motor imagery ability as measured by a scale such as the revised version of the Vividness of Movement Imagery Questionnaire (VMIQ-R: R. Roberts et al., 2008).

2   Using the mental chronometric paradigm (see Guillot and Collet, 2005), it would be interesting to investigate the extent to which the level of *expertise* of the performer affects the congruence between his or her imagined and actual time taken to execute a given skilled action.

3   Given the relative dearth of mental practice studies on elite athletes in field settings, it would be interesting to conduct a field study with athletes such as elite rugby or basketball players on the efficacy of mental practice in enhancing skills such as place-kicking or free-throwing, respectively.

4   What is the effect of the mental image *speed* on their performance of a self-paced action like golf putting? It would be interesting to extend O and Munroe-Chandler's (2008) research addressing this question.

5   It would be interesting to investigate the nature and types of mental imagery used by expert and novice athletes from different sports (see Nordin and Cumming, 2008).

Summary

• Mental imagery is a cognitive process which enables us to represent in our minds experiences of things which are not physically present. Although this ability is valuable in many everyday situations (e.g., in reminding you to perform a certain task), it is especially useful for the planning of future actions. So, the term mental practice (MP) or visualization refers to a form of symbolic rehearsal in which people "see" and "feel" themselves executing a skilled action in their imagination, without overt performance of the physical movements involved.

• The second section outlined the nature and characteristics of mental imagery, and explained the term mental practice.

• The third section explored research on mental practice in athletes; special attention was devoted to the imagery validation problem (namely, how do we know that athletes are really using imagery when they purport to be engaged in mental rehearsal?) as well as to the relative dearth of field studies on MP in athletes.

• The third section also featured a review of three main theories of mental practice – the neuromuscular, cognitive and bio-informational models.

• The fourth section examined the measurement of mental imagery skills in athletes.

• The fifth section assessed the main research findings on athletes' imagery use.

• The sixth section evaluated some old problems and new directions in research on imagery processes in athletes.

• Finally, five ideas for possible research projects on imagery processes in sport and exercise psychology were suggested.

What lies beneath the surface? Investigating expertise in sport

Expert performance is similar to an iceberg ... only one
tenth of the iceberg is visible above the surface of the water
and the other nine tenths are hidden below it.

(Ericsson, 2001, p. 2)

chapter 6

Introduction

Whether out of envy or admiration, we have long been fascinated by the exploits of outstanding performers in any field – people who display exceptional talent, knowledge and/or skills in a particular area of human achievement (such as sport). For example, many of us would love to be able to sprint like Usain Bolt, dribble a football like Lionel Messi, drive a golf ball with the power of Tiger Woods or serve a tennis ball with the skill of Serena Williams. But all we can do is sit and watch as these experts perform apparently impossible athletic feats. In psychology and cognitive neuroscience, research on expertise investigates the mental and neural processes that underlie such exceptional performance – originally, in cognitively rich domains such as chess, but more recently, in perceptual-motor activities such as sport. Regardless of the domain under scrutiny, however, certain questions arise when we marvel at the gifts of such expert performers as Bolt, Messi, Woods and Williams. For example, are champion athletes born or made? Put differently, what is the relationship between talent, expertise and success in sport? At first glance, the answer to this question seems obvious. If someone has sufficient innate talent and is lucky enough to have received instruction from an excellent coach, then he or she will develop expertise and become successful. But as we shall discover in this chapter, this "talent myth" has largely been discredited by empirical research on the role of practice in the development of expertise (for a review of research in this field, see Hodges and Baker, 2011).

For well over a century, scientists have investigated the nature and determinants of expertise. Whereas some early researchers such as Galton (1869) held that genius in any field comes mainly from inherited abilities, others (perhaps most prominently, Anders Ericsson – whose ideas we shall examine in more detail later) have postulated that practice and experience are what really matter. As research findings have accumulated, several flaws have appeared in the "inherited talent" explanation of athletic excellence. First, just like the rest of us, sports stars are often unreliable judges of the factors which influenced their career success. For example, in seeking to explain how they reached the top of the athletic ladder, they may inadvertently *overestimate* the influence of natural ability and *underestimate* the influence of other influences such as environmental factors (see Box 6.8 later in the chapter), physical training regimes and/or the time they spent practising their skills. Second, as coaches and psychologists have discovered, *quality* is better than quantity when it comes to practice. For example, there is a big difference between mindless drills (where athletes repeat basic skills without any specific purpose in mind) and *mindful* practice (also known as "deliberate practice" – where athletes strive purposefully and single-mindedly to achieve specific and challenging goals in a deliberate attempt to improve their skills; discussed later in the chapter). To explain this idea of deliberate practice, consider what Anders Ericsson, the man who coined this term, says about it: "When most people practise, they focus on things they can do effortlessly. Expert practice is different. It entails considerable, specific, and sustained efforts to do something you can't do well – or even at all" (cited in Syed, 2010, pp. 73–74). Third, as is evident from the research cited in this book, success in sport is determined as much by psychological factors (e.g., motivation) and by strategic planning (e.g., anticipating one's opponent's actions, having a "game plan" for a competition) as by innate technical skill. When combined, these three points highlight the importance of experience and practice in determining athletic expertise. This combination of experience and practice lies beneath the surface in Ericsson's (2001) iceberg metaphor of athletic expertise. Thus when we observe a moment of apparently spontaneous genius by Lionel Messi, Tiger Woods or Serena Williams, we should not overlook the fact that this action is a consequence of lots of practice and hard work – amounting to at least 10,000 hours or more (see below for an explanation of how this figure was estimated). Similar sentiments were expressed by the former golf champion Gary Player, who quipped paradoxically, "You must work very hard to become a natural golfer!" (cited in MacRury, 1997, p. 95). Although this remark is not intended to dismiss the influence of innate skills in sport, it challenges us to understand the complex interplay that occurs between talent, motivation, practice habits, quality of coaching and family support (see J. Baker and Horton, 2004; Farrow et al., 2007) in shaping athletic expertise. In this regard, as we shall see later in this chapter, some researchers (e.g., Ericsson, 2001, 2002) have gone so far as to proclaim that practice is the *foremost* cause of expert performance in any field. And so, Ericsson and his colleagues have challenged the "talent myth" – the idea that innate ability rather than practice habits is what determines athletic success (Syed, 2010).

Against this background of claims and controversies, this chapter investigates the nature and determinants of athletic expertise. Therefore, it addresses a number of intriguing questions. For example, what makes someone an expert in a given field? Is athletic expertise simply a matter of being endowed with the right genetic "hardware" (e.g., visual acuity skills above the average) or do "software" characteristics such as practice habits and psychological skills play an important role? If sporting excellence lies partly in the mind, how do the knowledge and skills of expert athletes differ from those of less successful counterparts? What stages of learning and development do novice athletes pass through on their journey to expertise? Finally, can research on expertise illuminate any significant principles that might help us to understand how the mind works?

In order to answer these questions, the chapter is organized as follows. In the next section, I explain what "expertise" means and indicate why it has become such an important topic in psychology. The third section addresses the general question of whether athletic success is determined more by hardware or by software characteristics of sport performers. In the fourth section, I outline and evaluate research methods and findings on expert–novice differences in the domain of sport. One of the issues that is raised in this section is the degree to which athletic expertise transfers effectively from one domain to another within a given sport. Specifically, do former top-class football players make expert managers? The fifth section explores the development of expertise in sport performers. Included in this section is an explanation and critique of Ericsson's (1996, 2001) theory that expertise is due mainly to a phenomenon called "deliberate practice". In the sixth section of the chapter, I examine the significance of, and some problems and new directions in, research on expertise in athletes. Finally, some suggestions are provided for possible research projects in this field.

The nature and study of expertise in sport

Expertise, or the growth of specialist knowledge and skills through effortful experience, is currently a "hot topic" both in cognitive psychology (Gobet et al., 2011), cognitive neuroscience (e.g., Didierjean and Gobet, 2008; Yarrow et al., 2009) and sport psychology (e.g., Moran, 2009; Williams and Ericsson, 2008). Researchers from both of these disciplines have generated a considerable volume of studies on the cognitive processes and structures that underlie the skilled performance of experts in various fields ranging from chess to athletic pursuits. To illustrate this trend, expertise has attracted special editions of academic journals such as *Journal of Experimental Psychology: Applied* (Ericsson and Williams, 2007) and *Applied Cognitive Psychology* (Ericsson, 2005), a comprehensive handbook (Ericsson et al., 2006), an entire section of the *Handbook of Sport Psychology* (Tenenbaum and Eklund, 2007), and interest from popular science writers (e.g., Colvin, 2010; Ross, 2006; Syed, 2010). One index of this trend is evident from the coverage devoted to expertise research in recent handbooks of sport psychology. Specifically, whereas the first edition of the *Handbook of Sport Psychology* (published in 1993) had no chapters on expertise and the second edition (in 2001) had just one chapter, the third edition (2007) has *five* chapters on it. For cognitive psychologists, research on expert–novice differences in sport is important because it provides an empirical window on the topic of knowledge-based perception. Specifically, it can reveal the role of cognitive processes in mediating the relationship between visual perception and skilled action in dynamic yet constrained environments. For psychologists, the study of athletic expertise (see reviews by Hodges and Baker, 2011; Hodges et al., 2006; A. Williams and Ford, 2008) presents at least two intriguing challenges. Theoretically, it raises the question of how certain people (such as elite athletes) manage to circumvent information-processing limitations when performing complex motor skills (Müller et al., 2009). Methodologically, it poses the challenge of developing objective and valid measures of expert–novice differences. Before we consider the reasons for its popularity among researchers in these disciplines, however, we need to explain precisely what the term expert actually means.

In everyday life, the term "expert" is used in a variety of different ways. For example, at a humorous level, it could refer to someone who is wearing a suit, carrying a laptop computer and who is more than 50 km from home! More seriously, this term is often used to refer to the possession of specialist knowledge in a designated field (e.g., medical pathology). For example, an "expert witness" may be summoned to appear in court in order to offer an informed opinion about some legally contentious issue. On other occasions, the term is ascribed to someone who is deemed to be exceptionally skilful in performing a specific task such as tuning a piano or repairing a watch. What these two definitions have in common is the idea that expertise depends on some combination of experience and specialist training in a given field. But how much experience and what duration of training qualifies one as an expert?

In an attempt to answer this question, cognitive psychologists tend to invoke Hayes' (1985) **ten-year rule** when defining expertise. Briefly, Hayes discovered from his study of geniuses in different fields (e.g., musicians, chess players) that nobody had reached expert levels of performance without investing approximately ten years of sustained practice in the field in question. According to Daniel Levitin, a neurologist and musician, "it takes the brain this long to assimilate all that it needs to know to achieve true mastery" (cited in Gladwell, 2009, p. 40). Using this temporal criterion, we can define an expert as someone who has displayed consistent evidence of a high level of proficiency in a specific field as a result of at least *ten years* of sustained training and experience in it (Ericsson and Charness, 1997). By convention, this criterion is deemed equivalent to about 10,000 hours of practice in the field in question. Interestingly, by contrast with many other guidelines in psychology, this ten-year rule (or its "10,000 hours of practice" equivalent) appears to be remarkably consistent across a range of different activities within the domains of music and sport. Ericsson et al. (1993) found that expert pianists and violinists had conducted over 10,000 hours of practice between the ages of 8 and 20 years. This figure may be contrasted with about 8,000 hours of practice for the good performers and about 4,000 hours of practice for the average performers. Similar corroboration of this rule has emerged from research in sport with evidence that elite soccer players (Helsen et al., 1998), figure skaters (Starkes et al., 1996) and wrestlers (Hodges and Starkes, 1996) satisfied the stated criterion. Consider the case of Roger Federer, whose record of achieving sixteen Grand Slam men's tennis titles is unsurpassed. He won his first Wimbledon singles title in 2003 at the age of 22 years – about ten years after he had begun to specialize in this sport. Also in tennis, Steffi Graf, who won twenty-two Grand Slam titles in her career, began to dominate her rivals consistently in her early to mid twenties – about ten years after she had played her first professional match as a 13 year old. In golf, Tiger Woods had clocked up about 10,000 hours of dedicated practice by his mid-teen years (Syed, 2010). In fact, by the age of 3 years, he was playing nine holes of golf. At the age of 15, he became the youngest winner of the US junior amateur golf championship (Lehrer, 2010). In summary, it seems that some of the best athletes in these sports have accumulated about 10,000 hours of practice within ten or twelve years of specialization in their chosen sport. Additional support for this rule comes from Ericsson (2002), who claimed that the typical age at which most sport stars reach their peak is between the mid and late twenties – which is approximately ten years after most young athletes have begun to practise seriously for their sport.

Despite the canonical status of the ten-year rule (or its equivalent, the 10,000 hours of practice rule), many sport psychology researchers have identified problems with it and some exceptions to it. First, research suggests that practice, on its own, is not a sufficient condition for the development of expertise. Gobet and Campitelli (2007) investigated the determinants of expertise among chess players in Argentina. Although results confirmed the importance of practice for the attainment of excellence in this game, considerable variability was also evident (e.g., slower players needed a lot more practice than faster players to attain the status of chess master). Overall, Gobet and Campitelli (2007) argued that practice is a necessary but not sufficient condition for the development of expertise. Second, as we mentioned earlier, the *quality* of practice undertaken to become an expert is at least as important as the quantity of practice. In other words, it is probably more important to explore what types of practice work best than simply to count the duration of such practice in hours or years. Third, many people develop expertise in certain complex skills (e.g., learning to cycle) in less than the requisite ten years. Again, this point has not been adequately addressed by proponents of the rule. Fourth, there are obvious exceptions to the ten-year rule in certain domains. For example, in music, Mozart began composing pieces for the violin and piano at the age of 5 years (although it has been estimated that he had accumulated about 3,500 hours of musical practice before he was 6: Syed, 2010). Similarly, Bobby Fischer had attained the status of an international chess master by the age of 16, after playing for only nine years – a remarkable feat (Cloud, 2008). More formally, Hodges et al. (2004) found that length of involvement in sport was not related to subsequent performance by athletes in swimming and triathlon. Regardless of these caveats, however, most researchers agree that the ten-year rule is a robust and useful criterion for distinguishing between expertise and average levels of performance in any given domain of inquiry. In summary, expertise in sport refers to consistently superior performance in athletic activities that takes at least ten years to develop.

Although the ten-year rule has been promulgated in a largely uncritical manner in cognitive neuroscience, it has received considerable scrutiny in sport psychology. Such scrutiny has led to alternative ways of defining athletic expertise. Starkes (2001) suggested that an expert athlete was someone who competed at an international level and whose performance is generally at least two standard deviations above average. However, she acknowledged an obvious limitation of this approach – namely, the fact that this status is easier to achieve in sports where the level of participation (and hence competition) is relatively low. Thus it is easier to be acknowledged as an expert in a little-known sport such as curling as compared with one which is truly global in popularity such as soccer. For this reason, it is unlikely that this alternative approach to defining expertise in sport will supplant the ten-year rule. Unfortunately, there is a great deal of inconsistency among researchers in the definition of expertise. For example, despite the ten-year rule,

Figure 6.1 Phil "The Power" Taylor – the greatest darts player of all time?
Source: Courtesy of Inpho photography

Werner and Thies (2000, p. 166) defined "experts" in their study as "individuals who had at least three years of extensive experience playing, coaching, or refereeing football".

Having considered the nature of expertise from a theoretical perspective, we should now explore the human face of an expert sport performer – the multiple world champion darts player, Phil "The Power" Taylor (see Figure 6.1). What is so special about this man? For a brief profile of Phil Taylor, see Box 6.1.

Box 6.1 Profile of an expert sport performer: Phil "The Power" Taylor

Despite its stereotypical association with overweight, tattooed beer-swilling men in noisy pubs (and they are just the performers!), darts is a popular and skilful game that requires a surprising amount of implicit knowledge of geometry and considerable computational prowess. To explain, the objective of this game, which probably dates back to the Middle Ages, is to throw a set of projectiles (darts) at a board which is placed about eight feet away (approximately 237 cm). Put simply, it involves propelling a 27 gramme projectile through the air at a target that is about the size of an AAA battery. Different locations on the board yield different points for the dart thrower. It is easy to see that success in darts requires a high degree of concentration, eye–hand coordination and fine motor control skills. To illustrate, players need to be able to stand completely still while controlling the speed, angle and spin of the darts. Apart from these skills, some mathematical proficiency is also required. Indeed, top darts players must be adept at making rapid mental calculations (Smyth, 2009). For example, in most darts tournaments, players start on 501 points and count down to zero. They have to be able to finish with a double that takes them to zero. Thus if they are on 59, they may aim for a single 19 and then a double 20. All of the ingredients of expertise in darts are epitomized in abundance in the career of Phil "The Power" Taylor, fifteen times world champion, who is widely regarded as one of the most successful individual sports performers of all time. To illustrate, apart from his world championship success, he has won the World Matchplay eleven times, the World Grand Prix nine times and over a hundred ranking tournaments in his career spanning more than twenty years (O'Sullivan, 2010). So, who is this star performer and what makes him so successful?

Born in Stoke, Phil Taylor was working as a tool machinist when his wife gave him a birthday present of a set of darts in 1986 when he was 26. He began to play once a week and showed enough skill at this sport to represent his county after a mere two years. One day, Eric Bristow (the most famous darts player of his generation) saw him practising and offered to advise him about the game. This advice soon paid off because in 1990, Taylor entered the world darts championship – and won it. Ironically, he defeated his mentor, Bristow, in the final! This victory was the first of a series of stunning performances that saw him demolish opponent after opponent with remarkable displays of accurate dart-throwing under intense competitive pressure. Famed for his eye–hand coordination (which he honed as a child by throwing a golf ball against the garden wall), dedication to physical and mental fitness (e.g., he practises for six hours a day: Hughes, 2002), and for his ruthless ability to finish matches when he gets the chance, he deliberately refuses to socialize with his fellow competitors in case he loses his competitive edge. For him, darts is a battle:

> familiarity breeds contempt … I can see when people play me that they're worried. I can see the fear in their eyes and I know I've got them then … As soon as he (the opponent) shows weakness, I'm in there, humiliating him. It's like boxing. You need to get your guy on the ropes.
>
> (cited in Kervin, 2001)

Continuing this confrontational theme, he claimed that success in darts is about "reading the body language … I can see when people's minds are wrong … In darts you wait for that dip and them you hit them hard" (cited in Ronay, 2008).

Why does the topic of expertise in sport appeal equally to popular science (e.g., see Ross, 2006) as to researchers (e.g., Hodges et al., 2006)? Three main reasons are apparent. First, the existence of athletic expertise gives us a tantalizing glimpse of the benefits which people have attained through dedicated practice and self-development. By implication, our admiration of other people's expertise beguiles us into believing that *we too* could have untapped potential which could be turned to our advantage.

In capturing this idea, an adage from the study of attentional skills comes to mind: there is no such thing as a difficult task, only an unpractised task. Second, the study of expert athletic performance is appealing because it enables researchers to examine how skills are acquired and perfected over time in real-life rather than artificial contexts. This distinction is an important point because traditional laboratory studies of human skill-learning were confined mainly to short-term activities (e.g., maze-learning) that had little relevance to everyday life. By contrast, contemporary researchers are striving to understand how people become proficient at complex everyday skills such as swimming or playing tennis. Of course, there is also a methodological explanation for the upsurge of research interest in athletic expertise. Specifically, the scientific study of skill-learning in sport is facilitated by the profusion of ranking and rating systems available to researchers – a fact which enables investigators to define and measure "success" in this field with some degree of objectivity. The same point holds true for chess which may explain why it is so popular among problem-solving researchers in cognitive psychology. Third, expert athletes are admired not only for their speed, economy of movement, and timing but also because they appear to transcend the limits of what is humanly possible. For example, the Spanish rider Miguel Indurain, who won five *successive* Tour de France cycling titles between 1991 and 1995, had a resting heart rate of only 28 beats per minute (bpm) (Shontz, 1999). To put this figure in perspective, the average resting heart rate is between 77 and 72 bpm whereas that of an experienced endurance athlete is around 40 bpm. (The advantage of having a well-trained heart is that it is significantly larger and can pump more blood with each beat than can an untrained heart.) Other sporting champions who have attained extraordinary records in their careers include Tiger Woods (who won four consecutive major golf championships in the 2000–2001 season), Carl Lewis (who won four Olympic long-jump titles in succession between 1984 and 1996), Sir Steve Redgrave (who won an unprecedented five Olympic gold medals at consecutive Games between 1984 and 2000), Michael Phelps (who has already won a record fourteen Olympic gold medals, so far, in his athletic career) and Martina Navratilova (who, apart from her brilliant tennis career as a singles player, won an all-time record of thirty-one Grand Slam doubles titles). The existence of such outstanding competitors suggests that the horizons of human physical achievements are expanding. This impression is supported by historical analyses of sporting records. To illustrate, top amateur swimmers and marathon runners at present can routinely beat the records set by Olympic gold medallists in the early 1900s – even though the times recorded by the latter athletes were regarded in that era as being close to the impermeable boundaries of human performance (Ericsson, 2002). Interestingly, the French Institute of Sport in a study of performance improvements in sport over the past century suggested that world records in athletics will probably hit a ceiling around 2060 (Naish, 2009). The Institute analysed over 3,000 world records since the Olympics began in 1896 and concluded that athletes were operating at about 75 per cent of their potential at that time but at about 99 per cent of their potential by 2008. Extrapolating from such estimates, athletes in track and field events should reach their full potential by about 2060.

Analysis of the horizons of human performance in sport can help cognitive scientists to understand how the mind achieves some of its remarkable feats. For example, how do skilled athletes such as Andy Murray (who is widely regarded as the tennis player with one of the best returns of serve in the world today) manage to hit winning returns off tennis balls that travel towards him at over 193 kilometres per hour (kph) or about 120 miles per hour (mph), which is faster than the eye can see? By the way, the current world record for the fastest serve in tennis is held by the Croatian player Ivo Karlovic, who hit a serve of 251 kph (or 156 mph) in a Davis Cup match against Germany in Zagreb in March 2011. Theoretically, the feat of returning such a serve is impossible because there is about a 200 millisecond time-lag between noticing a stimulus and responding to it. To explain this delay, it takes about 100 milliseconds for a nerve impulse to travel from the eye to the brain and about another 100 milliseconds for a motor message to be sent from the brain back to the muscles. Remarkably, therefore, expert athletes in fast-ball, reactive sports like tennis, hurling (a type of aerial hockey that is played in Ireland and regarded as being one of the fastest games in the world), baseball and cricket manage to overcome the severe time-constraints imposed by this "hard-wired" delay in the human information-processing system. In short, they effortlessly achieve the impossible feat of responding to fast-flying balls *before* they have any conscious knowledge of them! But this feat may not be as paradoxical as it seems. After all, some neuroscientists claim that our conscious awareness of *any* neural event is delayed by several hundred milliseconds although we do not normally notice this time-lag because we refer this awareness back in time – so that we convince ourselves that we were aware of the stimulus from its onset (Gazzaniga et al., 2002). For an account of the neuroscience of fast-ball sports, see Box 6.2.

Box 6.2 The neuroscience of expertise in fast-ball sports

What neural processes underlie the ability of expert baseball players to hit deliveries that are pitched at them at speeds of over 100 miles an hour? According to Milton et al. (2008b), the baseball hitter's brain has to coordinate two main tasks in striking the ball successfully – preparing to swing the bat and interpreting the kinematic movements of the pitcher in an effort to predict the direction of the pitched ball. In order to understand the neural substrates of these skills, Milton et al. (2008b) have used brain-imaging technology (e.g, fMRI) to investigate expert–novice differences in baseball players as they *imagine* swinging their bats to hit the ball. From such research, a number of fascinating insights into the neuroscience of fast-ball sports have emerged. Perhaps the most important one is that expert players typically show *less* brain activation but greater cortical efficiency than novice counterparts. For example, whereas expert baseball hitters tend to activate mainly the supplementary motor areas of the brain when they imagine hitting, novice players tend to activate the limbic regions (e.g., the amygdala and basal forebrain complex) which generally regulate emotions such as fear and anxiety (see Chapter 3). This activation of the limbic region suggests that novice players have a difficulty in filtering out irrelevant information as they prepare to execute their swings.

The discovery that fast reactions in sport lie mainly in the unconscious mind of the athlete has at least one surprising implication. Specifically, it suggests that contrary to coaching wisdom, top players in fast-ball sports do *not* actually watch the ball in flight. Instead, they use early signals or "advance cues" from their opponents' body position and/or limb movements to anticipate the type of delivery, trajectory and likely destination of the speeding ball (e.g., see Müller et al., 2009). Perhaps not surprisingly, this capacity to extrapolate accurately from the information yielded by advance cues appears to be a distinctive characteristic of expert athletes. Abernethy and Russell (1987) found that top-class squash players based their predictions about ball flight on early signals from opponents' movements (e.g., from both the position of the racquet and the racquet arm) when watching film simulations of squash matches. However, squash beginners tended to adopt a more constrained visual search process – looking only at those cues that were yielded by the racquet itself. The significance of this finding is clear. Expert athletes have a *knowledge-based* rather than an innate speed advantage over less proficient rivals. In general, therefore, speed of reaction in sport depends as much on the mind (because it depends on game-specific knowledge and anticipation skills) as on the body. Put differently, research on anticipatory cue usage suggests that expert athletes have a *cognitive* rather than a physical advantage over less successful counterparts. This finding raises the contentious question of whether hardware or software explanations of athletic expertise are more plausible scientifically.

What makes an expert in sport? Hardware or software characteristics?

Are sport stars born or made? Unfortunately, it is not really possible to answer this general question scientifically because genetic and environmental factors are inextricably intertwined (see Davids and Baker, 2007). Indeed, as modern neuroscientific research has shown, the activity of acquiring and storing knowledge (a software process) can actually change structural aspects (hardware processes) of the brain. In a remarkable study, Maguire et al. (2000) found that the posterior hippocampi (brain regions that are specialized for the storage of spatial representations of environmental knowledge) of London taxi drivers were significantly larger than those of a matched group of people who did not drive taxis. These authors interpreted this finding as indicating that the thousands of hours spent by taxi drivers in mastering "the knowledge" (i.e., accurate representation of the spatial layout of London's maze of streets) had resulted in structural change to the "map storage" regions of their brains. Building on such research, some progress has been made in identifying the relative contributions of physical (or hardware) and mental (or software) processes to expertise in sport (Yarrow et al., 2009). To start with, let us consider the popular idea that athletic expertise is largely a matter of being born with the right physical hardware such as a muscular physique, fast reactions, acute vision and exceptional sensitivity to peripheral visual information. According to this intuitively appealing theory, success in sport is attributable to the possession of some fixed and prototypical constellation of physiological attributes (which we could call a "superior" nervous system) as well as to exceptional perceptual-motor skills (e.g., rapid reflexes, dynamic visual acuity). Furthermore, it is assumed that by using these advantages, top athletes can run faster, see more clearly and display sharper reactions than average performers. At first glance, this approach is persuasive because it is easily exemplified in sport. To illustrate, Yao Ming, the Chinese basketball player who stands 7 feet 6 inches and weighs 310 pounds (ESPN NBA, 2010), has obvious natural advantages in his sport. Indeed, he has been selected for the National Basketball Association's (NBA) "all star" team on a number of occasions since 2003. Similarly, Venus Williams, who won four Grand Slam events in one season, stands at an impressive height of 6 feet 1 inch (1.85m) and can hit tennis serves that travel at over 120 miles per hour (193kph) (The Economist, 1999). In fact, she has been credited with the fastest recorded serve in women's tennis history. Clearly, the hardware possessed by Williams and others is as impressive as their athletic achievements. By contrast, the appearance and actions of most sporting novices seem ungainly, poorly coordinated and badly timed – even to an untutored eye. But this physical theory of athletic expertise is flawed by several problems. First, even at an anecdotal level, "bigger" does not always mean "better" in sport (see Box 6.3).

Box 6.3 Does size really matter? Is bigger always better in sport?

Does an athlete's physical "hardware" determine his or her success in sport? How important are the three S's of athletic ability – size, strength and speed? Is bigger always better? At first glance, few could argue against the claim that

Figure 6.2 Usain Bolt has a wonderful physique that facilitates his prodigious speed
Source: Courtesy of Inpho photography

physical factors such as size and strength matter in competitive sport. For example, consider athletics, swimming and rugby. In athletics, Usain Bolt, the Jamaican triple Olympic champion sprinter who broke his own 100m and 200m world records in 2009, has a physique which facilitates his prodigious speed (Gibson, 2009) (see Figure 6.2). Specifically, his height (6 feet 5 inches or 1.96m) enables him to cover the 100m in just 40 or 41 strides – which is between 5 and 7 strides less than that taken by his shorter competitors. Put simply, Bolt's longer leg muscles generate more speed and velocity than that of his rivals. What is even more remarkable about Bolt is that he was born with a condition (scoliosis or curvature of the spine) that could easily have made it impossible for him to play sport at a high level. Indeed, this condition resulted in one of his legs being half an inch shorter than the other (Hattenstone, 2010). More generally, research indicates that elite sprinters have grown by about 6.4 inches over the past century compared with an average population growth of about 2 inches. Perhaps more tellingly, Bolt is a full 11 inches (27.94cm) taller than the world sprint champion of 1929 (Gibson, 2009). Turning to swimming, Michael Phelps, the most successful athlete in Olympic history (because he is a sixteen-time medal winner), not only is very tall (at 6 feet 4 inches or 1.93m) but also has enormous hands and very large feet (he takes size 14 shoes). These physical attributes enable him to "hold onto" the water as he swims. In addition, Phelps has a long torso in relation to his legs (he is almost all "back") which helps him to "plane" on the water like a boat. Also, he has a huge "wingspan" (6 feet 7 inches or 2.01m), long arms (which enables him to take fewer strokes in a single lap), flexible ankles (that act like fins) and a very high endurance capacity in his heart and lungs (Phelps, 2008b). In rugby, the sheer bulk of modern players can be illustrated by comparing the height and weight of some of the backs of the 2009 British and Irish Lions squad with their counterparts from the 1974 squad (Hands, 2009). For example, at centre, Ian McGeechan (1974 squad) was 5 feet 9 inches (1.75m) and weighed 11 stone 3 pounds (71.21kg) whereas Jamie Roberts (2009 squad) is 6 feet 4 inches (1.93m) and weighs 16 stone 9 pounds (105.69kg). Similarly, at scrum half, Gareth Edwards (1974) was 5 feet 8 inches (1.73m) and weighed 12 stone 9 pounds (80.29kg) whereas Mike Phillips (2009) is 6 feet 3 inches (1.91m) and weighs 16 stone 3 pounds (102.97kg). Clearly, from these three sporting examples, we can conclude that today's athletes are generally taller, stronger and fitter than their predecessors. Perhaps it is this fact that explains why so many of the athletic records set in the early 1900s have been smashed a century later. For example, whereas the men's world record for throwing the hammer in 1900 was 51.10 metres (set by an Irish athlete called John Flanagan), it was 86.74 metres in 2000 (set by a Russian performer named Yuri Sedykh) – a figure which represents an increase of almost 70 per cent in the distance involved! Interestingly, the current female hammer-throwing record is held by Anita Wlodarczyk (Poland), who threw a distance of 77.96 metres in the IAAF World Athletics Championships in Berlin in 2009. But bigger is certainly *not* always better in sport: big athletes may be clumsier than their smaller counterparts. In sports such as tennis, tall players may have trouble in playing shots aimed at their feet. In addition, tall or strong players may tend to neglect other parts of their game. So, in modern tennis, despite the increasing prevalence of tall (i.e., over 1.8m or 6 feet) stars such as Ivo Karlovic (who, at 6 feet 10 inches or 2.08m, is the tallest player ever on the professional tour), shorter players like Lleyton Hewitt (Australia) and David Ferrer (Spain) (both under 5 feet 11 inches or 1.8m in height) have won as many, if not more, singles titles than their taller counterparts. Of course, there are distinct advantages to being tall and strong in the majority of sports. Big athletes tend to have large lungs and powerful hearts – physical assets which increase their cardiovascular efficiency in pumping oxygenated blood around the body. Larger limbs are advantageous in certain sports: in swimming, long arms can give an athlete leverage for speedy passage through the water. Similarly, long legs are essential for high-jumpers. Of course, there are also sports in which a small stature and a wiry physique are mandatory. Accordingly, marathon runners tend to be slight, if not scrawny, in build and they usually have "slow twitch" muscles. Likewise, successful jockeys are usually small, light, wiry and strong.

Second, there is little or no empirical evidence that top-class sports performers possess hardware characteristics, such as unusually fast reflexes or extreme visual acuity, that differentiate them significantly from less successful counterparts (A. Williams and Davids, 1998). For example, elite adult athletes do not perform consistently better than novices on tests of visual abilities (A. Williams, 2002b). The same principle seems to apply also to younger athletes. P. Ward and Williams (2003, p. 108) found that elite and sub-elite soccer players were "not meaningfully discriminated on nonspecific tests of visual function throughout late childhood, adolescence or early adulthood". Furthermore, Mann et al. (2007) found that optimal vision is not essential for optimal performance in interceptive tasks (such as batting in cricket) because the human perceptual-motor system can compensate for significant alterations in visual input. More generally, there is little reliable evidence of expert–novice differences in simple reaction time. In fact, as explained earlier, it takes about 200 milliseconds for *anyone* to react to a given stimulus – regardless of whether that person is an expert athlete or an unfit "couch potato". Remarkably, this finding suggests that there is little or no difference between the average reaction time of a tennis star like Andy Murray and that of a spectator picked randomly from a courtside seat. The implication of this point is clear. The rapid reactions exhibited by top athletes in sport situations do *not* reflect hard-wired, innate talents but are probably due instead to acquired skills (such as the ability to read and anticipate what an opponent is likely to do next). In short, expert athletes have a distinct *anticipatory* advantage over everyone else, which makes it *seem* as if their reaction times are exceptionally fast (e.g., see Müller et al., 2006, 2009).

The third problem for hardware theories of sporting expertise comes from research findings on the age at which athletes tend to reach their peak level of performance (see Ericsson, 2001). Briefly, if expertise were limited mainly by biological factors, such as the functional capacity of the brain and body, then we would expect that the age at which athletes reach their peak would be around the time that they reach physical maturation – namely, in their late teens. However, research shows that the age at which most athletes attain peak levels of performance occurs many years later – usually, in the mid to late twenties. This latter finding has challenged the validity of hardware theories of athletic expertise.

In the light of the preceding evidence, expertise in sport appears to be "dependent on perceptual and cognitive skills as well as on physical and motor capabilties" (A. Williams, 2002b, p. 416). Put differently, knowledge-driven factors (software processes) can account significantly for differences between expert and novice athletes in a variety of sports (Starkes and Ericsson, 2003; A. Williams, 2002b; A. Williams et al., 1999). To illustrate the extent to which exceptional athletic performance is cognitively driven, consider how an expert tennis player and a relative novice might respond to the same situation in a match. Briefly, if a short, mid-court ball is played to an expert performer, she will probably respond to it with an attacking drive either cross-court or down the line followed by an approach to the net in order to volley the anticipated return shot from the opponent. In similar circumstances, however, a novice player is likely to be so preoccupied with the task of returning the ball anywhere back over the net that she will fail to take advantage of this attacking opportunity. In other words, the weaker player is handicapped *cognitively* (i.e., by an inability to recognize and respond to certain patterns of play) as well as technically. I shall return to this point in the next section of the chapter.

Despite its flaws, the hardware theory of sporting expertise has some merit. There is evidence that people's performance in certain athletic events is facilitated by the type of musculature that they possess (Andersen et al., 2000). Top-class sprinters tend to possess an abundance of "fast twitch" muscles which provide the explosive power which they need for their event. Conversely, "slow" muscle fibres have been shown to be helpful for endurance sports such as long-distance running and cycling. M. Reid and Schneiker (2008) have provided a thorough review of research on the importance of strength and conditioning in top-level professional tennis. In the future, the field of hardware research in sport may serve in future as a natural laboratory for testing the effects of genetic engineering. For example, in an effort to boost their chances of success, sprinters could be equipped genetically with more "fast twitch" muscles, long-distance runners could be given the genes that create the blood-enhancing hormone erythropoietin, and basketball players may seek artificial height increases! Fortunately for legislators and sports associations, this type of genetic therapy for athletes is not a feasible proposition at present.

In summary, despite its intuitive plausibility, the hardware approach is inadequate for the task of explaining the theoretical mechanisms that underlie athletic expertise. But what about the software approach? Can research on expert–novice differences in cognitive processes help us to understand the nature of athletic expertise?

Expert–novice differences in sport: research methods and findings

After the pioneering research of de Groot (1965) and Chase and Simon (1973) on the cognitive characteristics of chess grand-masters, cognitive psychology researchers have used laboratory simulations of various real-life tasks in order to determine how expert performers differ from novices (see review by P. Ward et al., 2006). Initially, the main fields of expertise investigated were formal knowledge domains such as chess and physics where problem-solving processes and outcomes can be measured objectively. The archetypal research in this regard was a set of studies conducted by de Groot (1965) on chess expertise (for a detailed account of this work, see Gobet and Charness, 2006).

In one of these experiments, de Groot (1965), who was a chess master player, explored how performers of different abilities planned their moves. Briefly, he found that the grand-masters made *better* moves than less skilled experts – even though they did not appear to consider more moves than the latter players. Some years later, Chase and Simon (1973) discovered that although chess experts were superior to novices in recalling the positions of chess pieces from real or meaningful games, they did not differ from this group in their memory for chess pieces that had been randomly scattered around the board. The evidence for this conclusion came from two key findings. First, whereas chess masters could recall, on average, about sixteen of the twenty-four chess pieces displayed on the board in their correct positions after a single five-second glance, novices could recall only about four such pieces correctly. Second, when the chess pieces were presented in random or meaningless configurations on the board, the experts were no better than the novices at recalling their positions correctly. Indeed, neither group could recall more than two or three chess pieces in their correct location. This classic study shows that expert chess players do not have superior memories to those of novices – but that they use their more extensive knowledge base to **chunk** or code the chess config-urations in meaningful ways. Another conclusion from this study is that the cognitive superiority of expert chess players over novices is knowledge based and context specific – not indicative of some general intellectual advantage. In the light of this finding, research on expertise since the 1990s has shifted away from formal knowledge domains (such as chess) towards informal, everyday domains such as sport, music and dance (see coverage of these topics in Ericsson et al., 2006).

Research methods in the study of expertise

Within the domain of sport, a variety of research methods have been used to study expert–novice differences. These methods include both qualitative techniques (such as in-depth interviews, **think aloud verbal protocols** and **thought sampling techniques**) and quantitative procedures (e.g., pattern recall and **pattern recognition tasks**, video-based methods such as the **temporal occlusion paradigm** and **spatial occlusion paradigm**, and eye-tracking technology). Although I shall describe each of these techniques briefly below, additional information on their strengths and weaknesses is available in Hodges et al. (2006, 2007) and Lavallee et al. (2012).

In-depth interviews

Intensive interviews are widely used by researchers in an effort to elicit experts' knowledge and opinions about different aspects of their sports. The advantages and disadvantages of the interview method were mentioned briefly in Box 1.4 in Chapter 1 (see also Côté et al., 2007). Interestingly, Eccles et al. (2002) interviewed the British orienteering squad (n = 17) in an attempt to develop a "grounded theory" of how expert performers in this sport manage to divide their attention successfully between three key sources of information: the map, the environment and the travel path. Grounded theory is a qualitative approach in psychology in which researchers build a conceptual model inductively from the data yielded by participants rather than deductively from the researcher's assumptions about the phenomenon in question.

Think aloud verbal protocols and thought sampling techniques

As we learned in Chapter 1, interviews are limited as research tools because of their reliance on people's retrospective reconstructions of their past experiences – a procedure which is known to be flawed (Brewer et al., 1991). An alternative to this approach is the "think aloud" verbal protocol method whereby people are required to talk about and/or give a running commentary on their thoughts and actions as they tackle real or simulated problems in their specialist domain (for a thorough review of research on **protocol analysis**, see Ericsson, 2006; M. Fox et al., 2011). This technique was pioneered by de Groot (1965) in an effort to explore the cognitive processes of chess masters as they contemplated their next move in a simulated game. It is a valuable tool as it helps researchers to represent not only what people know (**declarative knowledge**) but also how they perform skilled behaviour (**procedural knowledge**). Of course, there are certain limitations associated with the collection and analysis of verbal protocols. First, an editing problem arises from the sheer volume of data collected. Second, protocols are limited to consciously accessible processes on the part of the person studied. Third, a difficulty arises from the fact that recording what people say as they solve a problem may inadvertently distort the quality of the data obtained. Put simply, people may become more self-conscious, guarded and/or spuriously rational if they know that their every utterance is being analysed by a researcher. In spite of these limitations, verbal protocols are useful because they are not vulnerable to the retrospective recall biases that afflict interviews.

Thought sampling or experience sampling methods (based on Csikszentmihalyi, 1990; Nakamura and Csikszentmihalyi, 2002; see also the method of descriptive experience sampling: Hurlburt and Akhter, 2006) involve equipping athletes with electronic beepers during training or competitive encounters and cueing them randomly to pay attention to their thoughts and experiences at the precise moment in question. Thus athletes are prompted electronically to respond to such questions as "What were you thinking of just now?" Using this technique, researchers can keep track of athletes' thoughts, feelings and focus of attention in real-life situations. In a variation of this procedure, McPherson (2000) asked expert and novice tennis players questions such as "What were you thinking about while playing that point?" and "What are you thinking about now?" during the period between points in competitive tennis matches. Unfortunately, despite its ingenuity, certain flaws in this method are apparent. First, there are obvious practical and ethical constraints surrounding athletes' willingness to be "thought sampled" during competitive situations. Second, little or no data have been gathered to evaluate the reliability of this procedure (for a review, see Hodges et al., 2007).

Pattern recall and recognition tasks

Pattern recall recognition tasks are based largely on the classic studies of de Groot (1965) and Chase and Simon (1973) on chess experts' memories for briefly presented chess patterns. When these tasks are adapted for use in sport situations, athletes and/or coaches are tested on their ability to remember precise details of rapidly presented, game-relevant information such as the exact positions of players depicted briefly in a filmed sport sequence. In the Chase and Simon (1973) study, expert and novice chess players were asked to study chessboards with pieces on them for five seconds. Next, they had to reconstruct the positions of these pieces on another board. As I indicated previously, results showed that the chess masters were superior to the novices in recalling the pieces – but only if these pieces came from structured game situations. No differences between the groups were evident when the pieces were randomly presented initially. In a typical sport psychological modification of this paradigm, participants may be shown a slide or a video sequence of action from a game-specific situation for a brief duration. Then, they are asked to recall as accurately as possible the relative position of each player in the slide or sequence. Interestingly, the ability to recall and recognize evolving patterns of play seems to be an excellent predictor of athletes' anticipatory skills in team sports (A. Williams, 2002b; for an investigation of the transfer of pattern recall skills between athletes in basketball, netball and hockey, see Abernethy et al., 2005).

As a practical illustration of this pattern recall paradigm applied to the sport of rugby, consider the configurations of players displayed in Figure 6.3a and Figure 6.3b. In both cases, the aim of the diagrams is to depict a "three-man defence" tactical strategy. But only one of these patterns is meaningful. Can you identify which of them makes sense and which of them is random or meaningless? Take a moment to examine the diagrams carefully.

If you are not knowledgeable about rugby, you should find this task very difficult, if not impossible! But if you were an expert rugby coach, you would quickly realize that Figure 6.3b is the meaningless pattern. To explain, Figure 6.3a portrays an orthodox three-man defence in which the number 10 player covers the opposing number 10, the number 12 takes the opposing number 12, the number 13 covers the opposing number 13 with the winger taking the last person. By contrast, in Figure 6.3b there is no obvious pattern to the defensive alignment. In fact, the only defensive player who is in the correct position is the number 10.

Extrapolating from Chase and Simon's (1973) study, we would expect that expert rugby players or coaches would be able to memorize the pattern of players depicted in the orthodox three-man defence (Figure 6.3a) much better than the meaningless pattern depicted in Figure 6.3b.

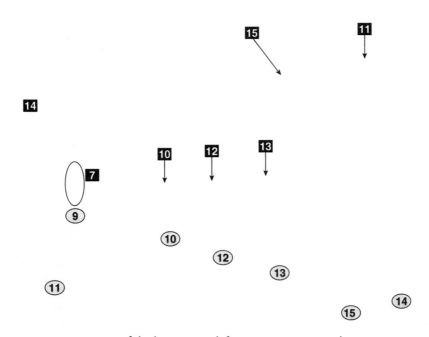

Figure 6.3a A meaningful "three-man defence" pattern in rugby

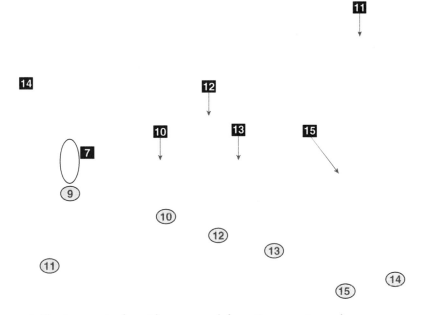

Figure 6.3b A meaningless "three-man defence" pattern in rugby

Video-based temporal occlusion paradigm

As the term "occlusion" means to hide or to obscure from view, the "occlusion paradigm" involves presenting participants with predictive tasks (e.g., guessing the likely direction of a shot in tennis) based on obscured or incomplete information. By analysing how experts differ from novices in extrapolating from such incomplete information, researchers can establish the relative importance of different cues in making predictive decisions. Typically, two different types of occlusion paradigms are used in sport psychology research – *temporal* occlusion and *spatial* occlusion (Hodges et al., 2007).

The temporal occlusion paradigm (e.g., for more details, see Yarrow et al., 2009) is a method which requires participants to guess "what happens next" when asked to view video or film sequences in which key time-based, sport-related information has been occluded deliberately (e.g., by disguising the ball flight-path). Participants are then asked to make anticipatory judgements based on the varying levels of information that they had seen. For example, in an attempt to investigate anticipation skill in soccer goalkeepers, A. Williams and Burwitz (1993) presented participants with video footage that was occluded at four successive points around the point at which the player's foot struck the ball. At the early cut-off points that occurred (prior to foot on ball impact), expert goalkeepers performed significantly better than relative novices in their ability to use what they had seen to make accurate predictions about where the ball would go. Müller et al. (2006) used the temporal occlusion approach to examine anticipation skills in cricket players of different levels of expertise. Results showed that the expert batsmen were significantly better than their less skilled counterparts in picking up advance information about ball flight from early cues such as the position of the arm and hand of the bowlers. Similarly, Rowe et al. (2009) used the temporal occlusion paradigm to explore the effects of deliberately disguising tennis ground strokes on expert and novice players' anticipation skills. Results showed that, as expected, disguise reduced anticipatory accuracy – but more for the novices than the expert tennis players.

In an ecological variation of the temporal occlusion method, liquid crystal occlusion glasses may be used to replicate film occlusion procedures in actual sport settings. To illustrate, a tennis player may be asked to wear such glasses while receiving a serve on court. Both variations of this paradigm are especially useful for assessing expert–novice differences in advance cue usage (A. Williams, 2002b). For example, a top-class tennis player can guess which side of the court his or her opponent is likely to serve to by making predictions from the direction of the server's ball toss. A right-handed server tossing the ball to his or her right will probably swing the serve to the right of the receiver. The occlusion paradigm has also been used to study how soccer goalkeepers anticipate the direction of penalty kicks against them in the actual pitch environment. Early anticipation of the direction of a penalty kick is vital as goalkeepers have less than half a second to decide which way to dive in an effort to save the shot. Researchers at the Australian Institute of Sport in Canberra have used occlusion goggles with goalkeepers in an effort to vary the amount and type of pre-contact cue information available to them. In this way, the goalkeeper's use of early visual cues from the penalty taker (e.g., his or her posture, foot angle and arm swing) can be analysed (M. Smith, 2003; for a study that investigated anticipation and visual search skills in goalkeepers, see Savelsbergh et al., 2005). From such research, it should be possible to develop anticipatory training programmes for goalkeepers. Unfortunately, little is known as yet about the efficacy of instructional programmes designed to improve athletes' knowledge of situational probabilities in specific sports (A. Williams, 2003). Before concluding this brief discussion of the laboratory version of the occlusion paradigm, we need to acknowledge that its fidelity or realism is open to question. For example, to what extent is watching a video sequence of a tennis serve on a large screen equivalent to being on the receiving end of it on court during windy conditions? A detailed discussion of the advantages and disadvantages of this technique may be found in A. Williams et al. (1999).

Video-based spatial occlusion paradigm

Although the temporal occlusion paradigm is helpful in providing insights into the issue of *exactly when* participants extract certain information from a filmed sequence of movements, the *spatial occlusion* approach attempts to answer the *"where?"* question – namely, the issue of *exactly which areas* of the filmed scene are perceived as most important by viewers. In this spatial occlusion paradigm, specific portions of the visual scene are typically removed or occluded from view and their effects on viewers' accuracy scores are analysed (for more details, see Yarrow et al., 2009).

The logic of this method is that if there is a performance decrement when a particular spatial element or area of the stimulus display (e.g., the hips or shoulders of a tennis player model during a simulated serve) is occluded from participants, that area of interest could prove to be especially informative to viewers. Special software packages are now available to enable researchers to be more precise in determining exactly which areas of the stimulus display they wish to occlude. Using these packages, researchers can "clone" the background of any scene and overlay it on the element to be occluded. In this way the element "disappears" or becomes invisible to the participant for as long as is necessary. To illustrate this method, R. Jackson and Mogan (2007) investigated expert–novice differences in tennis players' ability to judge the direction of a serve. Participants of different ability levels were required to look at video clips of tennis serves under various conditions of spatial occlusion and to make appropriate predictions about the likely direction of the ball. Results showed that, as expected, the expert players were more attuned to early advances cues (e.g., from ball toss and serving arm position) than were less proficient counterparts. One recurrent criticism of this spatial occlusion technique, however, concerns the issue of experimenter bias. To explain, the potential areas of interest are rarely specified on theoretical grounds but are usually designated in advance by the researchers themselves. Clearly, this practice raises the question of whether or not experimenters' preconceptions may influence the data collected using this paradigm. Slattery (2010) addressed this problem by basing the areas of interest on empirical data rather than on experimenters' theories.

Eye-tracking technology

If, as an old proverb says, the eyes serve as windows to the mind, the study of eye movements can provide insights into the relationship between "looking" (or visual fixation) and "seeing" (or paying attention). Two main types of eye movements have been identified (Kowler, 1999). First, **saccadic eye movements** are conjugate, high-speed jumps of the eyes which shift people's gaze from one location to another (e.g., notice how your gaze is moving from one word to the next while you read this sentence). Second, **smooth pursuit eye movements** help people to fixate on a given target (e.g., a ball) during the intervals between the saccades. These smooth pursuit movements are important because they enable perceivers to compensate for any displacements on the retina that may be caused by variations in either head or object position. Typically, people display about three fixations per second when viewing a scene that is unfamiliar to them (Goldstein, 2011).

A variety of eye trackers (or eye-movement registration systems) have been developed in psychology (for a review, see Duchowski, 2007). Among the most popular of these approaches in sport psychology are the Applied Science Laboratories' (ASL) 5000 SU eye-tracking system and the Tobii system (depicted in Figure 6.4). The Tobii eye-glasses have heralded the arrival of the latest generation of mobile eye-trackers. The ASL system is a video-based monocular corneal-reflection system that measures the perceiver's point of gaze with respect to video images recorded by an infra-red eye camera and a scene camera (which is usually floor mounted). This system works by detecting two features, namely, the position of

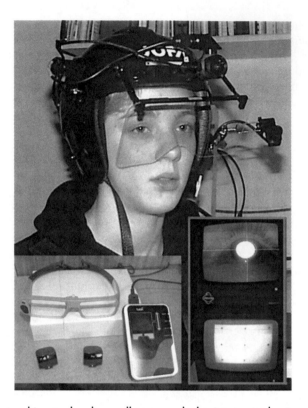

Figure 6.4 Eye-tracking technology allows psychologists to study visual search behaviour in athletes
Source: Courtesy of Andrew Flood, University College Dublin, School of Psychology

the pupil and the corneal reflex, in a video image of the eye. The relative position of these features is used to compute the visual point of gaze. The infra-red eye camera records displacement data from the left or right pupil and cornea.

Using such eye-tracking systems, a considerable amount of research has been conducted on the eye movements of athletes since the late 1990s. Typical stimuli used in these studies include static slides depicting schematic sport situations as well as dynamic video presentations of similar material (see review by A. Williams et al., 1999). Certain inferences are drawn from the location and duration of the perceiver's visual fixations. First, the location of a fixation is usually regarded as an index of the relative importance of a given cue within a stimulus display. Second, the number and duration of fixations recorded (which define "search rate") are believed to reflect the information-processing demands placed on the perceiver. Using such variables, expert–novice differences in visual search strategies have been discovered in such sports as soccer (Helsen and Starkes, 1999; Savelsbergh et al., 2005), tennis (Singer et al., 1996), boxing (Ripoll et al., 1993), golf (Vickers, 1992), basketball (Vickers, 1996) and ice-hockey (Martell and Vickers, 2004).

A prediction that is frequently tested in this field is that expert athletes will display a more efficient visual search strategy than relatively less skilled counterparts when inspecting sport-specific displays (e.g., see A. Williams et al., 2004). This means that they will show fewer visual fixations of longer length – and focus more on "information rich" areas of the display than will relative novices. To find out if this prediction is supported in cricket, see Box 6.4.

Box 6.4 Expert–novice differences in the eye movements of cricket batsmen

Cricket is an exciting and skilful sport in which batsmen face the task of striking balls bowled to them at fast speeds with uncertain spins and bounces. This task is made all the more difficult by the fact that cricket balls travel in an arc, change speed when they bounce and rarely arrive at the eye-level of the batsman. Despite such difficulties, expert batsmen can judge the arrival time of the ball surprisingly precisely. How is this remarkable perceptual feat achieved? Do they *actually* look at the ball – as is commonly believed? If so, how is this possible given the speed involved? In a classic study, Land and McLeod (2000) tried to answer these questions using eye-tracking technology. Briefly, these authors measured the eye movements of three batsmen as they faced balls bowled at them at speeds of 25 metres per second. Results showed that in accordance with previous studies, the cricketers did *not* keep their eyes continuously on the ball throughout its flight. Instead, they followed the initial ball delivery closely for approximately the first 200 milleseonds. Then, they made predictive saccades to the place where they expected it to bounce, waited for it to hit the ground and then tracked its trajectory after the bounce. In other words, they used their cricket knowledge and experience to make predictions about the likely destination of the ball *before* preparing to execute an attacking or defensive stroke. Interestingly, the expert batsmen were distinguished from their less competent players by the speed and accuracy of anticipatory saccades. In other words, they saw the ball early. To summarize, the skill of batting in cricket and also in sports like baseball (for a fascinating popular account of anticipation in this sport, see Stadler, 2008) seems to lie as much in the *head* of the performer as in his or her hands.

Research findings on expert–novice differences in athletes

Using a combination of the preceding methods, a number of expert–novice differences in sport have been identified. The following research findings summarize what is known about the differences between expert and novice athletes at present. For a more detailed discussion of these research trends, see Beilock (in press), Ericsson and Williams (2007), Hodges et al. (2007) and A. Williams and Ford (2008).

Experts have a more extensive knowledge base of sport-specific information

Expert athletes and coaches *know more* about their specialist domain than do relative novices but as we shall see later, this knowledge tends to be "domain specific" or restricted to one specific field. In the case of chess masters, the size of this chess database or "vocabulary" has been estimated at approximately 50,000 "chunks" of information (Simon and Gilmartin, 1973), where a chunk is defined as a meaningful grouping of chess piece positions.

This quantitative advantage associated with expertise means that experienced athletes and coaches possess a larger and better cross-referenced knowledge base about their chosen sport than do relative novices. Typically, this cognitive superiority is evident in three different areas: declarative knowledge (i.e., factual knowledge about the sport in question such as knowing its rules), procedural knowledge (i.e., the ability to perform basic technical skills in this sport accurately and efficiently) and **strategic knowledge** (i.e., the ability to recognize and respond optimally to various patterns of play in the sport). P. Morris et al. (1985) found that people who knew a lot about soccer displayed significantly greater recall of match results than did less knowledgeable participants. Hyllegard (1991) discovered that expert batters were better than novices in predicting the type of pitch they were about to receive in a simulated baseball situation. Abernethy et al. (1994) found that expert snooker players were more adept than novices at planning future shots.

Experts use their knowledge more efficiently to identify, remember and manipulate relevant information

Apart from knowing more about their specialist sport than novices, expert athletes can *do more* with information deemed relevant. Chase and Simon (1973) discovered that top chess players were better than novices at encoding and recalling meaningful (but not random) patterns from actual game situations. This cognitive advantage of experts over novices has been replicated extensively in sport situations. Thus top athletes and coaches are adept at recognizing and memorizing patterns of play in their sport. Bedon and Howard (1992) found that expert karate practitioners were significantly superior to beginners in memorizing various strategic techniques which had been presented to them. There is also evidence that experts tend to represent problems at a deeper level than novices because they search for principles and rules rather than superficial features of the tasks in question (Woll, 2002).

One explanation of the cognitive superiority of experts over novices comes from skilled memory theory (Chase and Ericsson, 1981). This theory proposes that experts use their long-term memory advantages to enrich the coding of new information. In other words, their rich database of knowledge appears to guide their **chunking** of new information. This proposition is significant for two reasons. First, it highlights a paradox of expertise (E. Smith et al., 1978). Put simply, this paradox concerns the fact that although experts have more knowledge to search through in their database than have novices, they can retrieve information in their specialist domain more quickly. Perhaps the reason for this difference in speed of search and retrieval is that experts' knowledge tends to be extensively cross-referenced whereas that of novices is usually compartmentalized. The second reason that skilled memory theory is significant psychologically is that it challenges a common misconception about the way in which our memory system is designed. Briefly, many people believe that our minds resemble containers which fill up with the knowledge we acquire but which may overflow if we are exposed to too much information. Research on experts, however, shows that our memory system is not passive but expands to accommodate new information. Put simply, the more we know about a given field, the *more* we can remember in it (Moran, 2000b). In summary, the study of expert–novice differences in memory yields several interesting findings about the way in which our minds work.

Experts are faster, more consistent and have better anticipation skills than novices

Classical studies on expertise showed that elite performers are usually faster at solving problems in their specialist field than are novices (Woll, 2002). Experts also tend to be more consistent than novices in performing their skills accurately. For example, top golfers are able to perform basic skills like driving or putting several times more consistently than are average players (Ericsson, 2001). As indicated earlier, a number of laboratory studies of ball sports have shown that expert athletes are superior to novices in using advance cues from opponents to predict accurately shot placement and destination ("What will happen next?") in simulated sport-specific situations. Typically, in these studies, participants are presented with specially prepared video sequences in which key ball-flight information has been occluded selectively. The task is to predict the likely destination or flight-path of the ball in the film. For example, A. Williams and Burwitz (1993) reported that expert soccer players were better able to predict the destination of filmed penalty kicks than novices – but only during conditions of minimal exposure (40 milliseconds after impact). Arising from these findings on expert–novice differences in advance cue utilization, a practical question arises. Do anticipatory abilities in athletes develop over time? This issue is examined in Box 6.5.

Box 6.5 Do anticipatory abilities develop over time?

In sport, the term "anticipation" refers to an athlete's ability to predict task-relevant events accurately. Although it is well known that top performers are adept at this skill (Slattery, 2010; A. Williams and Ward, 2007), little research has been conducted on whether or not this skill can be developed over time. Therefore, in an effort to fill this gap in the literature, Tenenbaum et al. (2000) explored how visual anticipatory abilities developed in young tennis players of different skill levels over time. Using a temporal occlusion paradigm (described earlier in the chapter), high- and low-skilled tennis players from the Israeli

Academy of Tennis watched specially prepared video segments and had to predict the final ball location after various tennis strokes (e.g., a backhand down the line, a serve) had been executed by model players. Results showed that, as expected, the more skilful players anticipated ball location more accurately than did less proficient performers. However, contrary to the theory of Ericsson et al. (1993) (see later in the chapter) some differences in visual anticipatory abilities were found to exist between the players of different skill levels from the earliest stages of their development. These latter differences suggest that deliberate practice alone cannot account for differences in anticipation skills in young tennis players. Tenenbaum et al. (2000, p. 126) concluded that "extensive practice is a necessary but not a sufficient condition for developing highly skilled performance". Extending this research on anticipation in tennis, Smeeton et al. (2005) investigated the relative efficacy of different instructional approaches to the task of improving anticipation skills in intermediate-level players. More precisely, they compared the effectiveness of explicit instruction, guided discovery, and discovery learning techniques in teaching anticipation skills to these athletes. Results showed that the three intervention groups improved their anticipation performance relative to a control condition, thereby highlighting the benefits of perceptual-cognitive training. However, in comparison with the other two groups, the explicitly instructed group showed a significant deterioration in anticipation performance under anxiety provoking conditions. Based on these results, Smeeton et al. (2005) recommended guided discovery methods for teaching anticipation skills in pressure situations.

Expertise in sport is domain-specific

Research suggests, as mentioned earlier in this section, that the skills of expert athletes tend to be "domain-specific" or confined to one area. In other words, few of the specialist skills acquired by expert athletes transfer to other sporting fields. At first glance, this finding is surprising as it challenges the existence of sporting "all rounders" or athletes who appear to be capable of achieving expert-level performance in several different sports simultaneously. For example, Jim Thorpe, won a gold medal as a decathlete and pentathlete in the 1912 Olympic Games before going on to play basketball and baseball professionally. A more recent example of the "all rounder" is Rebecca Romero, who became an individual world champion in two unrelated Olympic sports – rowing and cycling. More precisely, in 2008, she became the first British woman to win Olympic medals in two different sports when she added a gold medal in cycling (won at the Beijing Games in 2008) to the silver medal that she had won in rowing at the Athens Games in 2004. On closer scrutiny, however, the domain-specificity of athletic skills is not completely surprising. Consider the case of Michael Jordan, who was one of the greatest basketballers of all time. In the late 1990s, he retired from basketball and tried to become a professional baseball player with the Chicago White Sox. Unfortunately, his involvement with this new sport was not a success by his standards and he failed to attain his desired level of expertise in it. Anecdotally, similar experiences are evident in the case of several world-class athletes who tried to become successful golfers on the professional tour (Capostagno, 2002). Among these former athletes are Nigel Mansell (former Formula One world champion) and Ivan Lendl (a former world number 1 tennis player in the 1980s). Of course, as I explained in Chapter 1, we must be cautious about extrapolating from anecdotal examples. Also, we need to be careful to point out that some sports stars do indeed become skilled exponents of another game. John Surtees is the only person to have won world championships on both two and four wheels, in both motorcycle racing and Formula One motor racing (Gallagher, 2008). Despite these last few examples, research suggests that top athletes rarely achieve equivalent levels of expertise in sports outsider their own specialist domain – unless there is a substantial level of overlap between the skills required by the sports in question. An interesting test case of the "transferability" of athletic skills concerns the question of whether or not expert football players also make expert coaches or managers (see Box 6.6).

Box 6.6 Thinking critically about … whether or not expert soccer players become successful managers?

Docs expertise transfer from one specialist role to another within a given sport? This question comes to mind when we explore whether or not expert footballers become successful managers (Lawrenson, 2008; Marcotti, 2001; Moore, 2000). At the outset, we need a definition of expertise in playing sport. An obvious possibility in this regard is to use the ten-year rule explained earlier in the chapter. The difficulty with this criterion, however, is that it does not distinguish between players who excel consistently over a period of time and those whose performance is more variable and/or short-lived. In view of this problem, another definition of success could be postulated – namely, whether or not one is selected to represent one's country. This latter criterion is promising because research suggests that less than 1 per cent of professional players will be selected for their countries' national teams (Marcotti, 2001). As regards a definition for "success" in management, coaching one's team to win a league championship or cup competition may suffice. Initially, it is easy to think of some excellent football players who subsequently became successful managers. Kenny Dalglish was a star for Liverpool and subsequently managed that club to league championship honours. Similarly, on the international stage, Jack Charlton, who won a World Cup medal with England in 1966, managed the unheralded Republic of Ireland team to a quarter-final place in the World Cup finals in Italy in 1990. Also, legendary stars like Franz Beckenbauer won World Cup medals both as a player and as a manager. From these examples, it is clear that one advantage of possessing playing experience at an elite level is that it adds credibility to one's views on coaching. However, managers who achieved success with teams in the British Premier League such as Arsenal (under Arsène Wenger), Liverpool (under Rafael Benitez) and Manchester United (under Alex Ferguson) were only moderately successful as players.

Analysing the archives, Moore (2000) calculated that of the twenty-six managers who had coached winning teams in the Premier League in England between 1945 and 2000, only *five* had won more than six caps for their countries. Surprisingly, even acknowledged expert managers like Bob Paisley and Bill Shankly (both of Liverpool) and Alex Ferguson (manager of Manchester United – perhaps the most successful club manager in England since the early 1960s) – were *never* capped by their native country, Scotland. In addition, statistics reveal that only one (Jack Charlton) of the eight English World Cup-winning team of 1966 who went into management was subsequently successful in this role. Additional support for the idea that one does not have to be a great player to become a great manager comes from the fact that top managers such as Arsène Wenger (Arsenal), Rafael Benitez (former manager of Inter Milan) and José Mourinho (manager of Real Madrid) were never capped for their countries at senior international level either. But let us leave the last word on this issue to Arigo Sacchi, who won the Italian league and two European Cups with AC Milan even though he had never even played professional soccer! He said:

> What's the problem here? So I never played. I was never good enough. But so what? If you want to be a good jockey, it's not necessary to have been a horse earlier in your career. In fact, sometimes it's a hindrance.
>
> (cited in Marcotti, 2001)

A key lesson from the preceding discussion is that playing and managing are completely different tasks with different requirements. As Lawrenson (2008) pointed out, a key skill in managing players is the ability to assess talented players with the right mentality. This skill is not part of a player's repertoire – regardless of his or her ability.

Critical thinking questions

Do you agree with the definitions of success that were used above? How could you analyse scientifically whether or not great players become great managers? Is it enough merely to stack up examples on both sides of the question – or is there another way to proceed? One possibility is to elicit the views of a large sample of expert coaches on this question. An alternative method is to devise a checklist of managerial skills and to survey the views of players and managers on the relative importance of each of these factors. Why do you think that expertise in playing may not transfer to expertise in coaching or management? Remember that coaching largely involves teaching – and it is often quite difficult to teach a skill that one learned intuitively.

Experts have more insight into, and control over, their own mental processes

The term **metacognition** refers to people's insight into, and control over, their own mental processes (Matlin, 2009). It has long been assumed that experts are superior to novices in this area. If this principle holds true in sport, then expert athletes and coaches should have greater insight into, and more control over, their minds than do novices. Although few studies have tested this hypothesis, there is some evidence to support it with regard to planning behaviour. McPherson (2000) found that expert collegiate tennis players generated *three times* as many planning concepts as novices during "between point" periods in tennis matches. Cleary and Zimmerman (2001) discovered significant differences between expert, non-expert and novice basketball players in self-regulatory processes exhibited during practice sessions. Specifically, the expert players planned their practice sessions better than did other groups by choosing specific, technique-oriented processes (e.g., "to bend my knees").

In summary, research shows that expert adult athletes differ consistently from relative novices with regard to a variety of perceptual, cognitive and strategic aspects of behaviour. This conclusion appears to apply equally to young athletes. P. Ward and Williams (2003) discovered that perceptual and cognitive skills discriminated between elite and sub-elite soccer players between the ages of 9 and 17 years. These general findings are consistent with those derived from more formal domains like chess and physics where experts have been shown to display both quantitative and qualitative knowledge advantages over novices. Thus experts' knowledge is better organized and largely domain-specific and is probably represented differently from that of novices. But how do people become athletic experts in the first place? In order to answer this question, we need to consider the role of practice in the acquisition of expertise.

Becoming an expert athlete: Ericsson's theory of "deliberate practice"

Earlier in this chapter, we mentioned the joy of watching expert athletes such as Lionel Messi and Serena Williams. Why do we find it almost impossible to emulate the skills of these players? At one level, the answer to this question is obvious. Most of us lack the hardware and/or sufficient athletic talent to do so. But there is another possibility. Perhaps we simply do not *practise* hard enough, long enough or *well* enough to fulfil our potential (see Hodges et al., 2004). This "nurturist" possibility raises an intriguing issue. How important is practice in the development of expertise in any field?

Surprisingly, it is only since the mid-1980s that this question has begun to receive sustained empirical attention in psychology. In this era, several stage theories were developed to account for the development of expertise in young performers in different fields (e.g., see Bloom, 1985; Dreyfus, 1997). Of these approaches, the work of Ericsson has generated the greatest volume of research in recent years.

According to Ericsson et al. (1993, 2006), innate talent is a necessary but not sufficient condition for the development of expertise in a given domain. Instead, top-level performance is believed to be an acquired skill that is attributable largely to the quantity and quality of the performer's practice schedule (where "practice" is understood as any exercise that is designed to fulfil the goal of improving the person's performance). This claim about the primacy of practice is based on two main sources of evidence – first, research which highlights the **plasticity** or amenability of many cognitive characteristics to practice effects, and second, studies on the practice habits of elite musicians. Let us now consider each of these two strands of evidence in more detail.

For a long time, it was assumed that many of our mental limitations (e.g., the fact that our **short-term memory** is very brief and fragile) were caused by flaws in the design of our brain. For example, early cognitive research (see details in Matlin, 2009) showed that the average person's short-term memory span is restricted to between seven and nine units of information – which probably explains why we find it difficult to remember people's mobile phone numbers. However, this structural limitation principle was challenged by Chase and Ericsson (1981) who showed that with between 200 and 400 hours of practice, a person could be trained to remember up to *80* randomly presented digits. Details of this remarkable case study are presented in Box 6.7.

Box 6.7 How practice can improve your memory

One of the oldest tasks in experimental psychology is the memory-span test. This test requires people to recall a number of random digits (e.g., 1, 9, 6, 6, 2, 0, 0, 1) in the precise sequence in which they were presented. Early research (e.g., see details in Matlin, 2009) showed that most people can remember between seven and nine such digits – hence the estimation of the apparent limit on our short-term memory span. But what if one were trained to group or chunk these digits together so that they could be transformed into meaningful units? For example, the previous digit sequence could be segmented into two composite units rather than eight separate digits (e.g., "1966" or the year that England won the World Cup and "2001" or the title of a famous science-fiction film directed by Stanley Kubrick). Using this chunking approach, Chase and Ericsson (1981) trained a volunteer referred to as "SF" (whose original memory span was about the average of seven units) in 230 practice sessions spanning almost two years to achieve a remarkable memory span whereby he could recall accurately *82* digits presented randomly! How was this feat accomplished? What chunking strategies were exploited? Interestingly, although SF's memory was no better than average, he was a keen varsity track athlete who used his knowledge of running times to chunk the digits to be remembered into familiar units of 3–4 digits. For example, he might break up six digits such as 2 2 0 3 4 9 2 into two chunks using the time taken to run a marathon (2 hours and 20 minutes) followed by a near-world record time to run a mile (3 minutes and 49.2 seconds). Remarkably, in keeping with the domain specificity principle explained earlier, SF's extraordinary memory skill was confined to numbers only. Thus he was no better than average in his ability to recall long strings of *letters*. The clear implication of this study is that people's memory span can be increased if they practise chunking techniques based on specialist knowledge or personal interest. Thus SF managed to increase his short-term memory span for digits *tenfold* by practising extensively. The lesson is clear. According to Anders Ericsson, "there are apparently no limits to improvements in memory skill with practice" (cited in Syed, 2010, p. 22).

Box 6.7 shows us that practice can circumvent certain information-processing limitations of the mind. Put differently, Chase and Ericsson's (1981) study showed that remarkable changes in performance (albeit in one field only) could be produced in otherwise unexceptional performers simply by practising rigorously over time. Augmenting this line of evidence was other research which showed that practice could induce actual *anatomical* changes in athletes. For example, evidence indicates that years of intensive practice can increase the size and endurance of athletes' hearts as well as the size of their bone structure (Ericsson, 2002). Thus the playing arm of a professional tennis player is often more heavily muscled and larger boned than his or her non-dominant arm. In summary, a recurring theme of research in modern neuroscience is the malleability or plasticity of anatomical and physiological mechanisms.

The second important influence on Ericsson's work emerged from studies which his research team conducted on the practice habits of eminent musicians (Gladwell, 2009). Specifically, Ericsson et al. (1993) investigated the nature, type and frequency of violinists at the Berlin Academy of Music. They divided the Academy's violinists into three groups – the elite performers (students who were judged to have the potential to become world-class musicians), good performers (students who were predicted to become regular professional performers) and average performers (who were judged to have the potential to become music teachers). Each of these violinists was asked how many hours they had practised since they had first taken up their instrument. Results showed that almost all these performers had started at about the same age (around 5 years old) and had reportedly practised for about 2–3 hours per week until they were about 8 years of age. However, significant differences between the groups began to emerge at that time. In particular, the elite performers reported practising for longer durations than their counterparts in the other two groups – 6 hours a week by the age of 9, 8 hours per week by the age of 12, 16 hours per week by the age of 14 and over 30 hours per week by the age of 20. By this latter age, the elite violinists had clocked up an average of about 10,000 hours of practice (recall the ten-year rule that we explained earlier in this chapter). In contrast, the "good" group of violinists had accumulated about 8,000 hours of practice and the potential music teachers had aggregated about 4,000 hours of practice. Ericsson and his colleagues then compared the practice habits of professional and amateur pianists. Results showed that not only did the expert group practise longer than their less successful counterparts, but also they practised *differently* – spending more time on perfecting their skills (4–5 hours a day on average) than in mindlessly repeating elementary drills. From this evidence, Ericsson et al. (1993, p. 392) concluded that "across many domains of expertise, a remarkably consistent pattern emerges: The best individuals start practice at earlier ages and maintain a higher level of daily practice". Furthermore, these researchers proposed that *practice*, rather than innate talent, was the main cause of expertise or achievement level – not a correlate of it. More precisely, Ericsson and Charness (1994, p. 738) suggested that expertise is a direct function of the total amount of *deliberate practice* (or "individualized training on tasks selected by a qualified teacher") that has been undertaken by performers. This proposition is the cornerstone of Ericsson's theory. But what exactly is deliberate practice and how does it change over time?

Deliberate practice

Earlier in the chapter, I highlighted the idea that mindful practice (working deliberately to overcome one's weaknesses rather than engaging in mindless drills) is the key to success in sport. But what exactly does this type of practice involve? According to Ericsson et al. (1993), deliberate practice is a highly structured, focused, purposeful and (typically) not inherently enjoyable form of practice that is particularly relevant to the improvement of performance in any domain. It involves individualized training on tasks that are highly structured by skilled instructors in order to provide "optimal opportunities for learning and skill acquisition" (Ericsson and Charness, 1994, p. 739). The goal of such practice is to challenge the learner to go beyond his or her current level of performance. It may be contrasted with mechanical practice which is characterized solely by mindless repetition of basic drills (see A. Williams et al., 2008a). Interestingly, based on the findings of Maguire et al. (2000), some commentators (e.g., Syed, 2010) claim that deliberate practice can build neural connections and increase the size of specific brain areas.

What are the characteristics of deliberate practice? Ericsson et al. (1993, p. 373) suggested that deliberate practice activities are "very high on relevance for performance, high on effort, and comparatively low on inherent enjoyment". More precisely, four criteria of such practice may be specified as follows. First, deliberate practice targets specific skills that can improve performance. Second, it requires hard work and intense concentration on the part of the learner. A practical implication of this feature is that the duration of deliberate practice is determined mainly by the ability of the performer to sustain his or her concentration during the training session. Third, Ericsson believes that deliberate practice activities are not intrinsically rewarding. For example, in sport, a top tennis player may have to spend an hour working repetitively on the ball toss for his or her serve rather than engaging in the more pleasant task of rallying with a partner. A fourth criterion of deliberate practice is that it requires feedback from a specialist coach or instructor. This feedback helps the performer to monitor discrepancies between his or her current level of performance and some designated target standard. In summary, deliberate practice consists of activities that require effort and attention but are not play, not enjoyable intrinsically and not part of one's paid employment. Let us now turn to the issue of how expertise is held to develop from sustained engagement in deliberate practice.

Stages in the development of expertise

People are not born experts in anything: they become that way as a function of practice and instruction. Based on this assumption, several stage theories of expertise have been postulated. Dreyfus (1997) proposed a five-stage model of the transition from novice to expert. These stages are novice (stage 1), advanced beginner (stage 2), competent (stage 3), proficient (stage 4) and expert (stage 5). An alternative approach was proposed by Ericsson and his colleagues (e.g., see Ericsson and Charness, 1994). This model can be explained as follows.

Inspired by the theories of Bloom (1985), Ericsson and his colleagues postulated three stages in the development of expertise. These stages are distinguished from each other largely on the basis of the type of practice engaged in at each phase of development. They may be described in relation to athletic expertise as follows. In stage 1, a child is introduced to a given sport and may display some athletic talent which is recognized by his or her parents. At this stage, practice usually takes the form of "play", which may be defined as an unstructured and intrinsically enjoyable activity. During this era, the child's parents may facilitate skill development by encouraging him or her to take some lessons in the activity in question. Stage 2 can extend over a long period. It is here that a protracted period of preparation occurs during which the young learners are taught to perform their skills better. Therefore, "deliberate practice" begins in earnest in stage 2. As explained previously, this form of practice stems from having a well-defined task with an appropriate level of difficulty for the individual concerned, informative feedback, and opportunities for the correction of errors. During this stage, the young athlete's performance usually improves significantly. Usually, the stage ends with some commitment from the performer to pursue activities in the domain on a full-time basis. Finally, in stage 3, the average amount of daily deliberate practice increases and specialist or advanced coaches are sought by the parents to assist the young performer. Indeed, on occasion, parents of some performers may move home in order to live closer to specialist coaches or advanced training facilities. Stage 3 usually ends either when the performer becomes a full-time competitor in the sport in question or when he or she abandons the sport completely. A fourth stage has been recognized by Ericsson and his colleagues. Here, certain outstanding performers may go beyond the competence (skills and knowledge) of their coaches to achieve exceptional levels of success in their chosen sport. One interesting implication of Ericsson's stage theory is that it suggests that mere exposure to a given sport will not make someone an expert performer in it. Research shows that the ability to perform to an expert standard in sport does not come from merely watching it but requires instead active interaction with its structure.

A four-stage model of the development of expertise has been postulated by Hodges and Baker (2011). The first stage involves early engagement in sport and typically occurs at about 5 years of age. In this stage, children learn fundamental athletic skills, usually in the context of play. In the second stage or intermediate phase of athlete development, playful involvement in sport changes to more structured and specialized activities. The third stage is expertise or demonstrated world-class performance. The fourth stage involves "masters involvement" in sport for people who continue, or at some later time in their lives, begin or resume competing in events for middle-aged and elderly athletes. Relatively few studies have been conducted on athletes in this age category (Medic, 2010).

Testing the theory of deliberate practice in sport

As we learned above, Ericsson (2001, 2002; Ericsson et al., 1993) postulated that expert performance in sport is largely determined by the amount of domain-specific deliberate practice accumulated by the athletes in question. How well has this proposition been supported in the domain of sport?

Overall, a growing number of studies on this issue lend qualified support to Ericsson's belief in the importance of deliberate practice as a determinant of expertise in sport. For example, consider two reviews of research in this area since 2001. In her review, Starkes (2001) concluded:

> in every sport we have examined to date, we have found that level of skill has a positive linear relationship with amount of accumulated practice throughout one's sports career. The best athletes … have put in significantly more practice than their lesser skill [*sic*] counterparts.
>
> (Starkes, 2001, p. 198)

Hodges et al. (2006, p. 481) reached a similar conclusion when they proclaimed that "across a number of sports, ranging from figure skating to wrestling, from hockey to karate, sport-specific practice has been shown to be a significant predictor of skill-based differences in sport". But some caution is necessary when interpreting these conclusions. In particular, certain aspects of Ericsson's theory of deliberate practice appear to be problematic when applied to sport settings. Consider the fact that the theory of deliberate practice emerged originally from research on musicians. There are at least two key differences between the deliberate practice schedules of musicians and those of athletes. First, whereas most musicians tend to practise on their own, athletes tend to train with teammates or practice partners (Summers, 1999). Second, the concept of deliberate practice in sport may differ from that in the domain of music. To illustrate, recall that one of the criteria of such practice stipulated by Ericsson is that the activity in question should be relatively *unenjoyable* (as well as being purposeful and requiring effort). In sport, however, there is evidence that many athletes (e.g., wrestlers: Hodges and Starkes, 1996) seem to *enjoy* engaging in mundane deliberate practice activities. This finding was confirmed by Helsen et al. (1998), who analysed the practice habits of soccer and hockey players of various levels of ability. The results of this study revealed two key findings and an anomaly. First, the ten-year rule was confirmed. Specifically, results showed that after this period of time, both the soccer and hockey players realized that a significantly greater investment of training time would be required to enable them to achieve further success. Second, as expected, there was a direct linear relationship between the amount of deliberate practice undertaken by these athletes and the level of proficiency that they attained. But an anomaly also emerged from this study. In particular, these researchers found that contrary to Ericsson's model, those practised activities which were deemed to be *most relevant* to skill development were also seen by the soccer and hockey players as being *most enjoyable*. Again, this finding contradicts Ericsson's assertion that deliberate practice of basic skills is not inherently enjoyable. Influenced by such findings, Young and Salmela (2002) assessed middle-distance runners' perceptions of Ericsson's definition of deliberate practice.

Briefly, these researchers asked the runners to rate various practice and training activities on the amount of effort and concentration required to perform them and the degree of enjoyment to which they gave rise. Contrary to what Ericsson's theory predicted, Young and Salmela (2002) found that these runners rated the most relevant and most effortful of these training activities as also being the *most* inherently enjoyable. This finding led these authors to conclude that the construct of deliberate practice in sport should be redefined to refer to activities that are highly relevant for performance improvement, highly demanding of effort and concentration – and *highly enjoyable* to perform. In summary, there is evidence that top athletes differ from expert musicians by appearing to *enjoy* the routine practice of basic skills in their domain. Interestingly, a substantial body of evidence has accumulated from researchers such as Côté et al. (2007) to suggest that time spent in "deliberate play" activities (i.e., actions that people engage in purely for the sake of enjoyment such as playing football on the street) is related to athletic success. Another problem encountered in trying to apply or test Ericsson's theory of deliberate practice in sport concerns the phenomenon of early specialization – or prioritizing one activity or sport at a young age. Ericsson et al. (1993) argued that early specialization is crucial for later success in any domain because the sooner one adheres to a systematic regime of deliberate practice, the quicker one will attain expertise. However, in sport, researchers such as J. Baker et al. (2009) have pointed out that early intensive training (e.g., deliberate practice) is potentially hazardous to athletes because it is associated with a pattern of negative developmental outcomes such as increased risk of physical injury, decreased enjoyment of sport, burnout (i.e., a withdrawal from a formerly pursued and enjoyable sport, often accompanied by feelings of exhaustion and depersonalization: Cashmore, 2008) and impaired social skills. Beilock (2010b) highlighted some benefits of "sampling" a number of sporting activities rather than specializing in one of them at an early age. Specifically, she remarked that sampling not only reduces the chances of burnout but also lowers the likelihood of incurring overuse injuries. Clearly, the vexed issues of "practice" versus "play" and "early specialization" versus "sampling" have both theoretical and practical implications in sport psychology. To summarize, empirical research is generally supportive of Ericsson's claim that deliberate practice is crucial to athletic success. Nevertheless, doubts remain about the validity of extrapolating certain key propositions of Ericsson's theory of deliberate practice to the domain of sport.

Implications of Ericsson's research

At least six interesting implications arise from Ericsson's research on deliberate practice. First, his stage theory of expertise suggests that practice *by itself* is not sufficient to achieve excellence. Specialist advice and corrective feedback from a skilled instructor are essential for the development of expertise (Ericsson et al., 1993). Second, Ericsson's research raises the intriguing possibility that continuous improvement is possible in skill-learning – even among people who have already achieved the proficiency level of experts. This proposition challenges conventional accounts of skill-learning in at least one significant way. In the past, automaticity, or fluent, effortless and unconscious performance, was regarded as the end point of all skill-learning: it was believed that once this state has been achieved, no further progress is possible. This assumption is challenged by Ericsson, who suggests that experts' performance "*continues* to improve as a function of increased experience and deliberate practice" (Ericsson, 2001, p. 18; italics mine). In this regard, Ericsson's theory is controversial because it suggests that "expert performance is not fully automated" (Ericsson, 2001, p. 39) because most experts prepare consciously, deliberately and strategically for impending competitive encounters. The fact that experts can also remember their performances in great detail also challenges the idea that expertise is completely automated (Ericsson, 2001). As yet, little research has been conducted to test the proposition that experts can continue to improve their performance beyond automaticity. Nevertheless, Ericsson's theory purports to explain why most recreational golfers and tennis players do not improve beyond a certain level in spite of practising regularly: "The key challenge for aspiring expert performers is to avoid the arrested development associated with automaticity that is seen with everyday activities and, in addition, to acquire cognitive skills to support continued learning and improvement of their performance" (Ericsson, 2001, p. 12). Third, Ericsson's theories offer suggestions as to why continuous practice is so important to experts. Briefly, if elite performers fail to practise continuously, they will lose the "feel" or kinaesthetic control that guides their skills (see Ericsson, 2001, p. 42). Fourth, Ericsson's research on expertise highlights the role of *acquired knowledge* rather than innate talent in shaping top-level performance: if someone can master the knowledge and skills required for expertise, expert performance should occur. Ericsson concedes that there may well be individual differences in the degree to which people are motivated to engage in deliberate practice, but a key theme of Ericsson's research is that expertise is inextricably linked to knowledge compilation. Syed (2010) captures this idea neatly by arguing that deliberate practice is *transformative*. Fifth, research on deliberate practice shows us that concentration is essential for optimal learning (Ericsson, 2001; see also Young and Salmela, 2002). Sixth, the theory of deliberate practice has some interesting implications for talent identification programmes (Summers, 1999). For example, it suggests that instead of attempting to identify precociously talented young performers, sports organizations may be better advised to concentrate instead on searching for youngsters who display the types of psychological qualities (e.g., dedication to practice, determination to improve) which are likely to facilitate and sustain requisite regimes of deliberate practice.

Some criticisms of Ericsson's theories

As one might expect of such an environmentalist approach, Ericsson's theory of expertise has aroused as much controversy as enthusiasm within sport psychology. At a practical level, a recurring theme is that many coaches baulk at the claim that practice is more important than innate talent in determining athletic success. Against this background of controversy, what are the principal criticisms directed at Ericsson's research on deliberate practice?

At least six criticisms of Ericsson's theories and research may be identified in sport psychology. First, an early objection to the theory of deliberate practice concerned apparently invalid extrapolation from the field of music to that of sport. The argument here is that there are important differences between these fields which Ericsson and his colleagues may have neglected. For example, as I mentioned earlier, deliberate practice is usually undertaken alone by musicians but in pairs or collectively in sport. As a result of this contextual difference, the nature of the practice activities undertaken may differ significantly. For example, the camaraderie generated among teammates who spend a lot of time training together may explain why athletes differ from musicians in their tendency to enjoy performing basic practice drills in their specialist domain (see Young and Salmela, 2002). A second criticism of Ericsson's theory is that it is based on evidence that is *correlational* rather than experimental in nature. According to this argument, these data may merely indicate that people who are highly motivated in a given field will spend more time practising in it and hence are more likely to become experts. Unfortunately, correlational research designs cannot control adequately for possible intervening variables such as motivation. Therefore, somewhat surprisingly, "it is still unclear how crucial motivation and commitment are as factors necessary to promote practice and engender skill development" (Hodges and Baker, 2011, p. 43). Third, like many theories in psychology, Ericsson's stage theory of expertise may be criticized for ignoring important contextual and socioeconomic variables. In particular, this theory lacks a precise analysis of the effects of different resource constraints (e.g., access to suitable training facilities or specialist instructors) on people's progress through the three postulated stages of expertise. In a similar vein, Ericsson has not addressed adequately the impact of socioeconomic variables on the maintenance of deliberate practice schedules. Duffy et al. (2006) have highlighted the importance of environmental factors in determining athletic success (see Box 6.8). A fourth criticism is that Ericsson's claims are difficult to falsify or disprove empirically because it is very difficult to find a performance domain in which people have managed to attain expertise *without* engaging in extensive practice (Duffy et al., 2006). Fifth, another methodological issue is that Ericsson's theory relies heavily on people's retrospective accounts of their practice schedules. Data obtained retrospectively are potentially contaminated by exaggerations, memory biases and various kinds of response sets. Sixth, Ericsson's research may be criticized for his failure to include control groups in his studies. Despite these criticisms, the theory of deliberate practice has proved to be rich and insightful in helping researchers to understand the nature and development of expertise in sport (see also Davids and Baker, 2007). It has also stimulated much popular interest in athletic success (e.g., see Colvin, 2010; Gladwell, 2009; Syed, 2010). Before concluding this section, it may be helpful to address another relevant question. What factors are perceived by expert sports performers to have contributed to their success (see Box 6.8)?

Box 6.8 How did we get here? What expert athletes tell us about the factors that determined their success

Despite scientific advances that have occurred in understanding the complex determinants of athletic success, two key questions remain largely ignored in this field. First, until the early 2000s, most researchers have tended to focus on "solitary determinants of expertise, often in contrived settings" (Janelle and Hillman, 2003, p. 25), thereby neglecting the impact of real-life environmental influences on athletes such as coaches, family members and national sporting governing bodies. This neglect is surprising because it seems plausible that the amount of familial support and coaching advice that an aspiring athlete receives is likely to have a significant bearing on his or her future success. Second, an unresolved issue in expertise research is the relative neglect of athletes' perceptions of, and insights into, the barriers that they have overcome on their journey to elite-level performance. In an attempt to address these two oversights in the literature, Duffy et al. (2006) administered a questionnaire to a large (n=191) sample of international athletes to investigate the factors that were perceived to have either facilitated or inhibited their sporting development and success. Results confirmed that although the athletes acknowledged the importance of natural ability and motivation to their success, family support and dedicated coaches were also regarded as pivotal – especially in the early years of the athletes' careers. At a later stage, specialist coaching, sport science assistance and funding from national governing bodies were perceived as being crucially important. Among the main perceived inhibitors to athletic success were factors such as inadequate sport science support, insufficient funding and poor training facilities. Overall, Duffy et al.'s (2006) research highlighted the relatively neglected influence of *environmental* factors on the trajectory of athletes' careers.

Evaluating research on expertise in sport: significance, problems and new directions

Research on expertise in athletes is important both for theoretical and practical reasons. Theoretically, expertise is one of the few topics that bridge the gap between sport psychology and mainstream cognitive psychology. Indeed, until the advent of research on everyday cognition (see Woll, 2002), research on athletic expertise was seen as falling between two stools in the sense that it was perceived as being too "physical" for cognitive psychology and too "cognitive" for sport psychology (Starkes et al., 2001). However, since about 2001, largely as a result of Ericsson's research programme on the relationship between practice and exceptional perfor- mance, athletic skills have begun to attract the interest of researchers from cognitive psychology. Meanwhile, at a practical level, research on athletic expertise is valuable because it has highlighted the need for greater understanding of the practice habits of sport performers of different levels of ability (Starkes, 2001). In addition, it has raised the intriguing practical question of whether or not perceptual training programmes can accelerate the skills of novices so that they can "hasten the journey" to expertise (Starkes, 2001). With regard to this issue, research suggests that cognitive interventions designed to develop the knowledge base underlying exper- tise are probably more effective in facilitating elite performance than are perceptual skills training programmes (see A. Williams, 2002b, 2003).

Despite its theoretical and practical significance, however, research on athletic expertise is hampered by at least four conceptual and methodological problems (see Hodges et al., 2007; Starkes et al., 2001). First, a great deal of confusion surrounds the use of the term "expert" at present. This term has been applied in a rather cavalier fashion to such heterogeneous groups as inter-varsity level athletes, provincial team members, professional performers and members of national squads – without any obvious recourse to the ten-year rule or 10,000 hours of practice criterion. Indeed, "experts" in sport psychology may comprise college level, national level or international level athletes, which raises serious questions about the validity of this term (recall our earlier discussion of the unusual definition of expertise used by Werner and Thies, 2000). Even if the ten-year rule is applied stringently, anomalies are evident. For example, although a scratch-handicap golfer and a touring golf professional may be described as equivalent "experts", there are usually enormous qualitative differences between the skills of these players. Therefore, greater precision and consistency are required in the operational definitions of the term expert. Second, little is known at present about the retention of expertise in sport skills over time. In other words, how long does expertise in a given sport last? The paucity of evidence on this question is a consequence of the fact that most research on athletic expertise uses retro-spective recall paradigms rather than longitudinal research designs. Third, the methods used to study expertise in sport (reviewed in the fourth section of this chapter) have been challenged on the grounds that they are often borrowed uncritically and without modification from mainstream psychology. For example, can researchers extrapolate validly from methods in which two-dimensional static slides are used to present dynamic three-dimensional sporting information? Fourth, Hodges et al. (2006) recommended that sport psychology researchers should define expertise not only in terms of years of experience but also with regard to the precise competitive level and performance level that the athletes in question have attained.

Ideas for research projects on expertise in sport

Here are five suggestions for possible research projects on expertise in sport performers.

1   It is implicitly assumed in sport psychology that the term "expert" applies equally to athletes and coaches. But few studies have examined the similarities and differences between these two types of experts (performers and instruc-tors, respectively) on the recall of sport-specific information presented to them. Therefore, it would be interesting to explore "expert versus *expert*" differences between athletes and coaches from a particular sport using the pattern recognition paradigm explained earlier in this chapter.

2   It would be valuable to seek the views of expert athletes and coaches on the main tenets of Ericsson's theory of the stages of expertise and the nature of deliberate practice. A special questionnaire could be designed for this purpose. So far, little or no published research is available on this issue.

3   Additional research is required on the application of thought-sampling techniques to explore expertise in sport situations. For example, it would be interesting to equip snooker players with "beepers" in order to investigate possible expert–novice differences in thinking as players are forced to sit in their chairs while their opponents are competing at the table (see earlier discussion of this phenomenon in Chapter 1).

4   In the light of the discovery by Young and Salmela (2002) that Ericsson's criteria of deliberate practice may not always apply to athletes, it would be interesting to investigate systematically the degree to which athletes enjoy the basic practice drills required by their sport. Few studies have been conducted in which the "enjoyability" of practice activities has been compared using an expert–novice paradigm across different sports. A good place to start is by reading McCarthy et al. (2008), who have investigated enjoyment of sport from a developmental perspective.

5   Relatively few studies been conducted on expertise in masters level athletes. As Hodges and Baker (2011, p. 44) concluded: "we know very little about the training and development of elite older athletes". It would be interesting to address this unresolved issue because it can provide us with valuable information about the relationship between ageing and skill maintenance (see also Medic, 2010).

Summary

- We have long been fascinated by the exploits of expert performers in any field – those who display exceptional talent, knowledge and/or outstanding skills in a particular domain such as sport. Until the early 1990s, however, little was known about the psychological differences between expert and novice athletes. The purpose of this chapter was to investigate the nature and significance of research on athletic expertise in sport psychology.
- The second section explained the meaning of the term "expertise" and indicating some reasons for its current popularity as a research topic.
- The third section explored the general question of whether athletic success is determined more by hardware (i.e., physical) or by software (i.e., psychological) characteristics of sport performers. As we learned, available evidence largely supports the latter approach.
- The fourth section reviewed a variety of research methods and findings on expert–novice differences in sport.
- The fifth section examined the question of how athletic expertise develops over time. A special feature of this section was an explanation and critique of Ericsson's theory that expertise is largely due to the amount of deliberate practice accumulated by the performer.
- The sixth section evaluated the significance of, as well as some problems and new directions in, research on expertise in athletes.
- Finally, some ideas were provided for research projects in this field.

TEAM COHESION

Overview

Part one of the book examined the nature of the discipline and profession of sport and exercise psychology. Part two investigated the various psychological processes (e.g., motivation, anxiety, concentration, imagery) that affect *individual* athletes in their pursuit of excellence. But athletes rarely compete on their own in sport. Part three acknowledges the fact that *group* processes are crucial to success in sport. Oddly, however, group phenomena have been somewhat neglected in sport psychology. Carron and Brawley (2008, p. 230) concluded: "the amount of sport and exercise group research is surprisingly limited compared with the amount of research focused on the individual". Chapter 7 explores the main theories, findings and issues arising from research on one vital group process – team cohesion – in sport.

Exploring team cohesion in sport: a critical perspective

I wouldn't want to win five matches out of five and the team lose. I'd happily take no points if we had a European victory.

(Irish three times golf major winner, Pádraig Harrington, on playing for Europe in the 2010 Ryder Cup, cited in Gilleece, 2010)

Introduction

Few athletes compete alone in their sports. Instead, most of them interact either *with* or *against* other athletes collectively. Indeed, even in quintessentially individual sports such as golf or tennis, competitive action is often assessed or aggregated as a team game (e.g., the Ryder Cup in golf or the Davis Cup in tennis). Furthermore, many top individual sports performers travel and work with support groups of specialist advisers. For example, three times golf major winner Pádraig Harrington had a back-up team of *seven* people when he won the Open Championship in 2007 – a caddie, an agent, a coach, a psychologist, a fitness consultant, a sport scientist and a physiotherapist (Kremer and Moran, 2008a). Top tennis players have similar teams of advisers. Little wonder, then, that when Novak Djokovic lost to Rafael Nadal in the final of the 2010 US Open tennis championship, he congratulated his opponent *"and his team"* (cited in Evening Herald, 2010; italics mine). But what exactly is a "team"? And is "team spirit" essential for the achievement of sporting excellence? In relation to this latter question, many athletes and coaches believe in the importance of a sense of collective unity when competing in team competitions. At first glance, there is plenty of anecdotal evidence to support this latter belief. For example, according to Sven-Göran Eriksson, the former Leicester City and former England soccer manager, "the creation of team spirit and the building of 'the good team' is ... one of the coach's most important jobs" (Eriksson, 2002, p. 116). And such team-building by skilful managers can be highly effective. To illustrate, consider the remarkable achievement of Otto Rehhagel's Greece in winning the European Championship in soccer in 2004 despite the absence of individual star players. Similarly, Barcelona, the 2011 Champions' League winners, earned universal praise not only for their brilliant passing game but also for their extraordinary team cohesion (see Figure 7.1).

Figure 7.1 Barcelona FC, winners of the 2011 Champions' League, displayed remarkable team cohesion
Source: Courtesy of Inpho photography

For players this cohesion is often forged in the crucible of competition. Jeremy Guscott, the former British and Irish Lions rugby player, claimed:

> tours are about bonding together ... Success depends on whether you come together or you split into factions ... There were times with this Lions squad when we felt invincible – that we could take on the whole world and beat them.
>
> (cited in Guscott, 1997, p. 153)

Although these quotations seem persuasive, they need to be tested against relevant scientific evidence. In this regard, attempts to forge team spirit have led to some rather bizarre practices (e.g., see Boxes 7.5 and 7.6 later in the chapter). So, do team-building exercises really work? Is it true that young people's involvement in school sports builds their "character" and imbues them with a healthy respect for team spirit? It has long been believed that sport develops leadership qualities. For example, the Duke of Wellington is alleged to have remarked that the battle of Waterloo "was won on the playing fields of Eton" (Knowles, 1999, p. 810). But scandals involving cheating in sport are ubiquitous (e.g., see J. Perry, 2007). Consider the infamous "bloodgate" incident in which a rugby club doctor admitted deliberately cutting the lip of a Harlequins player, Tom Williams, in order to cover up an earlier bogus injury (contrived by having the player bite a fake blood capsule) which enabled a specialist place-kicker to replace him as a substitute at a vital stage of his team's match against Leinster in a Heineken quarter-final in 2009 (Carter, 2010). In order to answer these and other relevant questions, this chapter is organized as follows.

In the next section, I explain how psychologists define key terms such as groups, teams and **group dynamics**. In the third section, I introduce the concept of team spirit, which has been defined operationally by sport psychologists as "cohesion" (also known as "cohesiveness") or the extent to which a group of athletes or players is united by a common purpose and bonds together in pursuit of that objective. This section also examines the measurement of cohesion and its relationship to athletic performance. Given the assumption that cohesion can be enhanced, the fourth section of the chapter investigates the nature and efficacy of team-building activities in sport psychology. In the fifth section, I briefly evaluate the commonly held belief that team sports foster desirable psychological qualities in participants. The sixth section of the chapter outlines some new directions for research on team cohesion in sport. Finally, suggestions are provided for possible research projects in this field.

Unfortunately, due to space restrictions, this chapter is not able to deal with other questions concerning the impact of groups on individual athletic performance. For example, the issue of how the presence of other people such as spectators and/or fellow competitors affects athletes' performance lies beyond the scope of this chapter. This latter topic, which was mentioned briefly in Chapter 1, is called social facilitation, and was first studied empirically by Triplett (1898). Review of research on social facilitation have been provided by Strauss (2002) and Uziell (2007). Similarly, the converse phenomenon of **social loafing** in sport, or the reduction in individual effort seen when individuals work in groups compared to when they work alone (Carron et al., 2009, p. 65), also lies beyond the boundary of this chapter.

Groups, teams and group dynamics in sport

In everyday life, we tend to see any collection of people as a group. However, social psychologists are much more precise in their usage of this term. Alderfer (1977) defined a "group" as "an intact social system, complete with boundaries, interdependence for some shared purpose, and differentiated member roles" (cited in Hackman and Katz, 2010, p. 1210). It is this sense of mutual interaction or interdependence for a common purpose that distinguishes the members of a group from a mere aggregation of individuals. As Hodge (1995) observed, a collection of people who happen to go for a swim after work on the same day each week does not, strictly speaking, constitute a "group" because these swimmers do not interact with each other in a structured manner. By contrast, a squad of young competitive swimmers who train every morning before going to school *is* a group because they not only share a common objective (training for competition) but also interact with each other in formal ways (e.g., by warming up together beforehand). It is this sense of people coming together to achieve a common objective that really defines the term "team".

According to Carron and Hausenblas (1998), a sports *team* is a special type of group. In particular, teams have four key characteristics – apart from having the defining properties of mutual interaction and task interdependence – that serve to differentiate then from aggregates of strangers (see also Carron et al., 2009). First, they have a collective sense of identity – a "we-ness" rather than a collection of "I-ness". This collective consciousness emerges when individual team members and non-team members agree that the group is distinguishable from other groups ("us" versus "them"). For example, the leaders of the successful Wimbledon soccer team of the late 1980s called themselves the "crazy gang" and their manager Dave Bassett used this self-styled identity as a cohesive force when preparing his team to compete against higher ranked football clubs. Often, this type of social bonding led to enhanced team performance. The former Liverpool player Alan Hansen was amazed at the intimidatory tactics and "all-for-one" spirit which the Wimbledon players showed in the tunnel before they defeated his team in the 1988 FA Cup Final (Hansen, 1999). Second, sports teams are characterized by a set of distinctive *roles*. As Carron et al. (2009, p. 64) explained, group members "develop a generalized expectation for those individuals who through ability or experience assume specific responsibilities". For example, soccer and rugby teams have acknowledged roles for creative players who generate or exploit scoring opportunities as well as for tough-tackling "enforcers" whose job it is to prevent opponents from playing creatively. The third feature of sports teams is their use of *structured modes of communication* within the group. This type of communication often involves nicknames and short-hand instructions for teammates. Fourth, teams develop *norms* or social rules that prescribe what group members either should or should not do in certain circum-stances. Individual performers learn to ignore the idiosyncratic routines of their teammates as they prepare for important competitive events. Having explained the key characteristics of teams, a sports team may be defined as

> a collection of two or more individuals who possess a common identity, have consensus on a shared, purpose, share a common fate, exhibit structured

patterns of interaction and communication, hold common perceptions about group structure, are personally and instrumentally interdependent, and consider themselves to be a group.

(Carron and Brawley, 2008, p. 215)

In view of the preceding characteristics, teams are regarded as *dynamic* entities by sport and exercise psychologists (for reviews of research in this field, see Beauchamp and Eys, 2008; Eys et al., 2010). Interestingly, the term "dynamic" comes from the Greek word *dunamikós*, which means "powerful". Perhaps not surprisingly, certain aspects of team behaviour change over time. Tuckman (1965) has identified four hypothetical stages in the development of any team. In the first stage, *forming*, the team's members come together and engage in an informal assessment of each other's strengths and weaknesses. Second, the *storming* stage is postulated in which interpersonal conflict is common as the players compete for the coach's attention and strive to establish their rank in the pecking order of the team. Third, the *norming* stage occurs when group members begin to see themselves as a team united by a common task and by interpersonal bonds. Finally, the *performing* stage occurs when the members of the team resolve to channel their energies as a cohesive unit into the pursuit of agreed goals. A similar account of the way in which teams change over time has been offered by Whitaker (1999), who identified three stages of evolution: *inclusion* (where new members are preoccupied with how to become a part of the team), *assertion* (where members struggle to establish their position within the hierarchy of the team) and *cooperation* (where members strive to work together to fulfil team goals). Unfortunately, although both of these hypothetical stage models of team development seem plausible intuitively, they have not been validated adequately by empirical evidence.

Having explained that teams are dynamic entities and hence change over time, it is important to clarify what psychologists mean by the term "group dynamics". In general, sport psychologists use this term in at least three different ways (Carron and Hausenblas, 1998; Widmeyer et al., 2002). First, it denotes the scientific study of how athletes behave in groups, especially in face-to-face situations (e.g., when coaches address players in team talks). Second, "group dynamics" refers broadly to a host of factors (e.g., confidence) that are believed to play a role in determining team performance. Third, this term designates the processes that generate *change* in groups (Cashmore, 2008). It is mainly the second and third of these meanings that are explored in this chapter – especially, the question of how team spirit or cohesion is related to team performance. Let us now explore this idea of team spirit in more detail.

Team spirit or social cohesion: from popular understanding to psychological analysis

It has long been believed that successful sports teams have a unique spirit or sense of unity that transcends the simple aggregation of their individual components. This idea is captured by an old Irish proverb which states "ní neart go cur le chéile" (there is no strength without unity). An example of this unity was the extraordinary sense

Figure 7.2 Team spirit helped the European team to victory over the United States in the 2011 Ryder Cup
Source: Courtesy of Inpho photography

of togetherness displayed by the victorious European team during its 2002 Ryder Cup golf match against the United States. Illustrating this spirit, Darren Clarke, a member of the European team, revealed that "we played as a team, we dined as a team, we talked as a team and we won as a team … The team spirit this week has been the best that I have experienced in this, my third Ryder Cup" (cited in O'Sullivan, 2002b). This sense of togetherness among Ryder Cup golfers is epitomized by the quotation from Pádraig Harrington at the beginning of the chapter in which he states that he would prefer to sacrifice individual victories for team success (see Figure 7.2). Before we analyse what team spirit means in sport, however, let us pause for a moment to consider the benefits of teamwork in a rather unusual domain – the animal kingdom. Have you ever wondered why birds fly in a peculiar "V"-like formation? According to Mears and Voehl (1994), this pattern is adaptive because as each bird in the "V" flaps its wings, it creates an "uplift" current for the bird behind it. This uplift enables the entire flock of birds to fly significantly further than any of the individual birds could fly alone. But how can this idea of synergy among flocks of bird apply to sports behaviour? In order to answer this question, we need to analyse what team spirit or cohesion means to athletes, coaches and sport psychologists.

Athletes' and coaches' views on cohesion

As the quotations at the beginning of this chapter indicate, team cohesion is valued highly by coaches and sports performers. This high regard is supported by research evidence. For example, team cohesion is associated positively with increased positive affect, increased effort, decreased role ambiguity, decreased cognitive anxiety and decreased social loading (mentioned earlier) (Statler, 2010). Perhaps not surprisingly, many team managers believe that it can be *enhanced* through instruction and experience. Sam Torrance, the manager of the European Ryder Cup golf team in 2002, sought advice from two successful soccer managers – Alex Ferguson (manager of Manchester United) and Sven-Göran Eriksson (then coach of England) (R. Williams, 2002a) – in an effort to enrich the **task cohesion** and **social cohesion** of his players before the match. The key message delivered by these managers was to treat all the golfers in the team in the same way (R. Williams, 2002c). This principle was appreciated greatly by the players: in commenting on Torrance's captaincy, Pádraig Harrington said, "everybody got the same treatment, there were no stars in the team ... he kept the spirits up all the way" (cited in A. Reid, 2002). By contrast with this egalitarian approach, Curtis Strange, the captain of the US team, showed evidence of preferential treatment for certain players. For example, he allowed Tiger Woods to engage in his customary early morning practice round on his own before the match whereas he insisted that the other players had to practise together. Some studies on university athletes suggests that perceived inequity, or favouritism on the part of coaches towards certain individuals, decreased team cohesion (Turman, 2003).

In addition to believing that team cohesion can be increased (see later in the chapter for some practical techniques in this regard), many athletes and coaches claim that individual performers must learn to subordinate their skills and efforts to the goals of the team. Consider the views of Michael Jordan on this issue. Jordan, who won six world basketball championships with the Chicago Bulls, remarked that "if you think and achieve as a team, the individual accolades will take care of themselves. Talent wins games but teamwork and intelligence win championships" (www.quotesandpoem.com/quotes/listquotes/author/michael-jordan). This view supports the old coaching adage that "there is no I in team" (although – according to the comedian Ricky Gervais's character, David Brent, "there is a 'ME' if you look hard enough" (see www.bioteams.com/2006/02/05/managing_teams_david.html).

Despite this adage, however, there are situations in which the "I" in teams becomes apparent. As an extreme example of this phenomenon, consider what happens when the *captain* of a team challenges the authority of its coach or manager. Two interesting case studies of this problem occurred in World Cup soccer finals since 2002. The first incident occurred in May 2002 shortly before the World Cup soccer finals in Japan and Korea when Roy Keane, who was then the captain of the Republic of Ireland team, was sent home after a heated argument with his manager, Mick McCarthy. This incident happened in Saipan, the location of the team's training camp for the finals.

By way of background, the relationship between Keane and Mick McCarthy was never cordial. Despite this coolness between the captain and the manager, the team had played very well in qualifying for the World Cup finals. But the relationship between these men changed dramatically in Saipan when Roy Keane gave a controversial interview to a journalist in which he criticized both the training facilities and preparation methods of the Irish squad.

Following this interview, he was summoned to attend a "clear the air" meeting with McCarthy and the rest of the players. At this meeting, Keane not only questioned the adequacy of the Irish team's facilities (citing a lack of training gear and footballs as well as deficient medical support) but also publicly rebuked his manager in a vitriolic speech. Not surprisingly, this speech and its consequences attracted media coverage around the world. More significantly, it raised a debate about an important psychological issue – namely, whether or not one player's striving for perfection can impede the progress of the team. For the manager (and some of the team's senior players), Keane's speech was inexcusable and had to be punished by instant dismissal from the rest of the tournament. This is precisely what happened. Unfortunately, as no physical injury had been involved in prompting Keane's departure, the dismissal left the Ireland squad one player short of the quota permitted by the World Cup organizers. It also left the players emotionally drained by the shock of losing their captain in such highly controversial circumstances.

Although there are two sides to this incident (e.g., why did the manager not try to resolve his differences with his captain privately or through an agreed intermediary before summoning him to a specially convened squad meeting?), McCarthy's decision to dismiss Roy Keane reflects a popular coaching belief that any potential threat to team harmony must be removed instantly. Weinberg and Gould (2007, p. 201) urge players and coaches "to respond to the problem quickly so that negative feelings don't build up". Similarly Sven-Göran Eriksson, the manager of England, warned about the danger of negative thinking within a squad: "A bad atmosphere can spread quickly, particularly if one of the 'leaders of opinion' in the team represents the negative thinking – the captain, for instance" (Eriksson, 2002, p. 116). Curiously, the Irish team performed exceptionally well during this competition in spite of losing its most influential player, and was defeated in the knockout stages by Spain only after a penalty shootout.

The second incident involving a mutiny by a national soccer team's captain occurred in South Africa in June 2010 when Patrice Evra (captain of France) and the other twenty-two players in the national squad refused to participate in a training session organized by the team's manager, Raymond Domenech, after a heated disagreement about tactics. Following a temporary resolution of this problem, the players returned to training but subsequently performed poorly and France was eliminated from the tournament. Several months later, the French Football Federation suspended Evra and the other perceived ringleaders of the team's rebellion (namely, Nicolas Anelka, Franck Ribery and Jeremy Toulalan). Anelka was suspended for *eighteen matches*, thereby effectively ending his international career (L. Davies, 2010). These two incidents show that team captains can sometimes rebel against coaches on the eve of championship finals, but the outcome of such dissent is not always clearcut. Whereas the Ireland team appeared to "pull together" after its captain's departure, the French squad continued to perform poorly after its mutiny against the national coach.

In this section, we have seen that team spirit or cohesion is important to athletes and coaches. But what progress have psychologists made in understanding and measuring the construct of team cohesion? Also, what does research reveal about the relationship between the cohesion and performance of a team? The remainder of this section addresses these questions.

Cohesion (or cohesiveness) in psychology

Until now, I have used the term "cohesion" to refer to a form of social bonding between individuals in order to achieve a common purpose. Let us now analyse this term in more depth. According to the *New Penguin English Dictionary*, the word "cohesion" comes from the Latin word *cohaerere*, meaning "to stick together" (R. Allen, 2000). In popular expression, cohesion refers to acting or working together as a unit. In physics, however, the term has a slightly different meaning: it designates the molecular attraction by which the particles of a body are united together (R. Allen, 2000). Psychologists have combined the common sense and physicists' approach to cohesion when describing it as "the total field of forces which act on members to remain in the group" (Festinger et al., 1950, p. 164). Historically, this definition emerged from psychological research on group integration processes evident in accommodation units for returned US veterans of the Second World War. Apart from Festinger and his colleagues, another seminal figure in research on cohesion was the social psychologist Kurt Lewin, a refugee from German Nazi oppression, who was fascinated by the powerful ways in which groups affect people's behaviour. Adopting a "field of forces" model of human behaviour, Lewin (1935) regarded cohesion as a set of ties (including forces of attraction and repulsion) that bind members of a group together. He proposed that the main objectives of any group were to maintain cohesion and to enhance performance – two recurrent themes throughout the team cohesion literature.

This idea of cohesion as the "glue" that integrates members of a group was echoed subsequently by sport psychologists but with one important modification – namely, the idea that cohesion is a *multidimensional* rather than a unidimensional construct. Carron et al. (1998, p. 213) defined cohesion as "a tendency for a group to stick together and remain united in the pursuit of its instrumental objectives and/or for the satisfaction of member affective needs". Based on this proposition, Carron and his colleagues postulated a conceptual framework to account for the construct of cohesion (see reviews by Carron and Brawley, 2008; Carron et al., 2007). In this framework, these researchers proposed that cohesion emerges from two kinds of perceptions: those arising from group members' perceptions of the group as a totality ("group integration") and those generated by members' perceptions of the personal attractiveness of the group ("individual attractions to group"). Put simply, these dimensions reflect a bifurcation between "task" and "social" components of any group. Carron's analysis of cohesion implies that it is a desirable state; if cohesion reflects people's tendency to stick together in order to pursue common goals, it should be associated with team success.

But is this hypothesis supported by empirical evidence? I shall address this question later in the chapter. Before that, let us quickly sketch some key features of cohesiveness in sport psychology. First, cohesion is a multidimensional construct. As Carron and his colleagues have suggested, two dimensions of this construct are important – a desire of group members to complete a given task (task cohesion) as well as a need by team members to form and maintain interpersonal bonds (social cohesion). Based on this proposition, Carron et al. (1998) developed a theoretical model of group cohesion similar to that displayed in Figure 7.3.

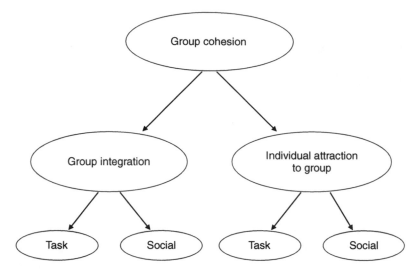

Figure 7.3 Carron's model of group cohesion
Source: adapted, by kind permission, from A.V. Carron, W.N. Widmeyer, and
L. R. Brawley (1985) The development of an instrument to assess cohesion in sport teams:
The Group Environment Questionnaire. *Journal of Sport Psychology, 7*, 244–266, p. 248

As Figure 7.3 shows, Carron et al. (1998) distinguished between two over-arching strands of cohesion: "group integration" and "individual attraction to group". Group integration represents each team member's perception of the close-ness, bonding and degree of unity in the group as a totality. Individual attraction to the group refers to each team member's perception of what encourages him or her to remain in the group. Figure 7.3 also shows that both types of perceptions may be divided into "task" and "social" orientations. Combining these various aspects, four dimensions of cohesion were proposed by Carron et al. (1998). These four dimensions of cohesion are group integration-task (GI-T), group integration-social (GI-S), indi-vidual attractions to the group-task (ATG-T) and individual attractions to the group-social (ATG-S). According to S. Burke et al. (2008), these four dimensions are believed to account for the majority of variance in cohesiveness. Applying this model to sport, Hodge (1995) and Hodge and McKenzie (1999) suggested that "task" and "social" cohesion are synonymous with "teamwork" and "team spirit", respectively.

The second characteristic of group cohesion is that it is a *dynamic* process. Cohesion is not a fixed property of a group but changes over time as a function of a number of variables such as the degree of success or failure experienced by the team. A soccer team could score highly on cohesion if it has won a considerable number of games in succession, but this cohesion might diminish if the team were to lose one or two important matches. Unfortunately, despite acknowledging the dynamic nature of this construct, few researchers in sport psychology have monitored changes in team cohesion over the course of a competitive season. One exception to this trend is a study by Holt and Sparkes (2001), who followed a university soccer squad throughout a season and found that when the team was eliminated from a mid-season tournament, the players revised their goals for the remainder of the period. This result is not surprising because when a team competes in two tournaments simultaneously, some confusion is likely about which of these tournaments is more important. Holt and Sparkes' (2001) research also shows that team cohesion can vary considerably over a competitive season.

The third property of cohesion is that it is characterized by "instrumentality". People join or become a team for utilitarian reasons, to achieve a common purpose. Finally, Carron et al. (1998) proposed that the construct of cohesion has an emotional dimension which is derived from social relationships and feelings of togetherness among the players. In summary, cohesion is a multidimensional construct whose practical importance for team performance can be gauged from the variety of contexts in which it has been studied, such as in military settings (Ahronson and Cameron, 2007; Siebold, 2006), in the industrial/organizational sphere (Cannon-Bowers and Bowers, 2011; Mathieu et al., 2010) and, of course, in the world of sport (Heuzé and Fontayne, 2002; Rovio et al., 2009).

Despite the apparent clarity of the preceding theoretical analysis, the construct of cohesion has been criticized on both conceptual and methodological grounds (see reviews by Casey-Campbell and Martens, 2009; Friedkin, 2004). First, Casey-Campbell and Martens (2009, p. 235) pointed out that the widespread assumption that group cohesion is a dynamic construct "has still to be tested". Second, Mudrack (1989a, p. 38) noted a dilemma at the heart of this construct – the fact that although cohesion is alleged to be a property of groups, the group itself "as a distinct entity is beyond the grasp of our understanding and measurement". The problem is that the "field of forces" approach to cohesion is difficult to operationalize and the "attractions to the group" approach is conceptually inadequate because "it focuses exclusively on individuals at the expense of the group, and therefore may not entirely capture the concept of group cohesiveness" (Mudrack, 1989a, p. 42). Later in the chapter, I shall return to this thorny issue of how to select the most appropriate unit of analysis (group or individual) when studying cohesion in teams. Third, another criticism of research on cohesion comes from Mudrack (1989a), who complained that studies in this field have been plagued by "confusion, inconsistency, and almost inexcusable sloppiness". To illustrate this allegation, he listed a variety of meanings spawned by the term cohesion. These include interpersonal attraction, group resistance to break-up, a desire to remain in the group, feelings of group membership, and the value that people place on group membership. As these referents do not share many common features, the meaning of the term "cohesion" is elusive. A similar problem was noted by Widmeyer et al. (2002, p. 298) who concluded that "there is no conceptual or theoretical model that can be used as the basis for defining and measuring cohesion". As an illustration of this difficulty, Mudrack (1989b) reported that of twenty-three investigations conducted between 1975 and 1985, no two studies used the same operational indices of cohesiveness. Unfortunately, there has been little progress in achieving a consensus definition of cohesion. Casey-Campbell and Martens (2009, p. 224) lamented the "lack of consistent definitions and operationalizations" in the field. Finally, Shapcott and Carron (2010) highlighted a recurrent conceptual problem in this field in the form of "reification" – the fallacy of treating an abstraction as a concrete entity. They warned that "reification can arise when individual member responses are summed to reflect a group property without first determining whether some degree of consensus is present" (Shapcott and Carron, 2010, p. 96). For example, they cite the case of two members of a doubles team whose responses are at opposite ends of a continuum of cohesiveness scores. Shapcott and Carron (2010) suggest that it is wrong to reify this property of the team by averaging these extreme scores to indicate that the doubles team has a "moderate" level of cohesiveness. Given such conceptual problems in defining cohesion, what is the best way to measure this construct?

Measuring team cohesion

The profusion of different definitions of cohesion is matched by a plethora of different ways of measuring this construct. Indeed, so plentiful are such measures that Casey-Campbell and Martens (2009, p. 224) remarked wryly that "there are approximately as many methods for assessing cohesion as there are researches investigating the construct itself". Although the perceived cohesion of a group can be assessed using methods such as **sociograms** (techniques in which members are asked confidentially to name other group members whom they either like or dislike), specially developed self-reports scales are more popular among researchers in this field. One of the earliest of these scales was a measure developed by Martens et al. (1972) called the Sport Cohesiveness Questionnaire (SCQ). This seven-item test requires respondents to rate perceived cohesion in terms of friendship (interpersonal attraction), personal power or influence, enjoyment, closeness, teamwork, sense of belonging, and perceived value of membership. Unfortunately, despite its superficial plausibility or face validity, this test has never been validated adequately for use with athletes. Also, it is limited to the extent that it focused more on social cohesion (or the closeness between players) than on task cohesion (or the degree of common purpose between players). To overcome such limitations, two other measures of team cohesion were developed – the Team Cohesion Questionnaire (TCQ: Gruber and Gray, 1982) and the Multidimensional Sport Cohesion Instrument (MSCI: Yukelson et al., 1984). The TCQ contains thirteen items which provide measures of six different factors: satisfaction with team performance, satisfaction with one's own performance, task cohesion, affiliation cohesion, desire for recognition, and value of group membership. Unfortunately, as with its predecessor, little evidence is available on the psychometric adequacy of this test. The MSCI is a twenty-two-item self-report scale which asks people to rate perceived cohesion in terms of such factors as attraction to the group, unity of purpose, quality of teamwork and valued roles (which is alleged to reflect identification with group membership). As with its predecessor, however, the validity of the MSCI is unknown, and it is hampered by the fact that its items relate only to basketball. Apart from their psychometric shortcomings, the TCQ and MSCI suffer from another problem – namely, a flimsy theoretical basis. This problem arose from the fact that many of their items were borrowed from other instruments without adequate theoretical justification (Widmeyer et al., 2002).

By contrast with the preceding measures, the Group Environment Questionnaire (GEQ: Carron et al., 1985) has become the most widely used instrument in research on team cohesion. The dominance of this test is attributable mainly to two factors: it is based on an explicit conceptual model of cohesion (e.g., see Carron and Brawley, 2008; see also Figure 7.3) and it has impressive psychometric qualities. The GEQ is an eighteen-item self-report questionnaire scale which purports to measure the four key dimensions of team cohesion described in the previous section. First in this test, which was developed for athletic populations between the ages of 18 and 30 years (Eys et al., 2009), "group integration-task" (GI-T: five items) refers to an individual member's perceptions of the similarity, closeness, and bonding within the group as a whole with regard to the task it faces. It is measured by items such as "our team is united in trying to reach its goals for performance" or "we all take responsibility for any loss or poor performance by our team". Second, "group integration-social" (GI-S: four items) refers to an individual member's feelings about the similarity and unification of the group as a social unit. A sample item here is that "members of our team would rather go out on their own than get together as a team" (reverse scored) or "our team would like to spend time together in the off-season". Third, "individual attractions to the group-task" (ATG-T: four items) designates a team member's feelings about his or her personal involvement with the group's task. It is typically assessed using items like "I'm not happy with the amount of playing time I get" (reverse scored) or "I do not like this team's style of play" (reverse scored). Fourth, "individual attractions to the group-social" (ATG-S: five items) describes an individual team member's feelings about his or her personal social interactions with the group. A sample item to assess this component of cohesion is "I am not going to miss the members of this team when the season ends" (reverse scored) or "some of my best friends are on this team".

Responses to these items are indicated by choosing the appropriate answer on a nine-point Likert scale ranging from "strongly disagree" (1) to "strongly agree" (9). Negative items are reverse scored to ensure that relatively higher scores on the GEQ reflect stronger perceptions of team cohesiveness among group members. Not surprisingly, it has become very popular in sport psychology and has been translated into French (Heuzé and Fontayne, 2002). It has also been used in exercise settings. Estabrooks and Carron (1999) investigated the relationship between exercise intentions, attitudes and behaviour among a sample of elderly adults in an exercise group. Results showed that, as expected, both social cohesion and task cohesion were associated positively with the participants' attitudes to, and frequency of attendance at, the exercise classes (for a discussion of exercise psychology, see Chapter 8).

In general, the psychometric characteristics of the Group Environment Questionnaire are impressive (Dion, 2000). Specifically, with regard to test reliability, the internal consistency coefficients of the four cohesion subscales range from 0.64 (in the case of "individual attractions to the group-social") to 0.75 (for "individual attractions to the group-task"). Several studies have reported solid factorial validity and satisfactory reliability (with alpha values ranging from 0.63 to 0.81) for the test (Spink et al., 2010). Perhaps more importantly, Carron et al. (1998) supported the construct validity of the GEQ on the basis of evidence that the four dimensions of cohesion were significantly positively associated with such variables as role clarity in teams and adherence to exercise programmes. They were also significantly negatively correlated with variables like social loafing – defined earlier in this chapter as a tendency for some people within a group to "slacken off" when working towards a common goal. Unfortunately, reviewers (e.g., Casey-Campbell and Martens, 2009; Dion, 2000) have noted that the factorial structure of the test remains unclear due to equivocal research findings. Whereas Li and Harmer (1996) replicated Carron's four-factor model in their analysis of cohesion processes in baseball and softball players, Dyce and Cornell's (1996) factor analysis of cohesion data from musicians yielded a three-factor structure. Specifically, these latter investigators concluded "the results support social-task distinctions ... but not the group integration-individual attractions to the group distinctions" (Dyce and Cornell, 1996, p. 264). Carless and De Paola (2000) also reported a three-factor structure for the GEQ – with these factors being task cohesion, social cohesion and attraction to the group. Similar doubts about the factorial validity of the GEQ were raised by Schutz et al. (1994), who discovered that different factor structures emerged depending on the gender of the participants. In an effort to resolve the criticism that the GEQ is not valid for use with young athletes (those aged under 18 years), Eys et al. (2009) developed the Youth Sport Environment Questionnaire (YSEQ), a measure which appears to have promising psychometric qualities. Taken together, available evidence provided reasonable empirical support the construct validity of the Group Environment Questionnaire.

Befoer concluding this section, we should consider the issue of the most appropriate level of analysis to adopt in studying team cohesion (see also Dion, 2000). Put simply, is cohesion investigated best as a property of a *group* (Carless and DePaola, 2000), as a characteristic of its *individual members* (e.g., Hogg, 1992), or perhaps as some *combination* of these different units of analysis (e.g., Widmeyer et al., 1985)? Depending on how this question is answered, different interpretations of the cohesion–performance relationship may emerge. In their meta-analysis of the relationship between cohesion and performance, Gully et al. (1995) discovered that the correlations between these variables was stronger for studies that had used the *group* rather than the individual as the unit of analysis. In an effort to resolve this issue about which unit of analysis to use, Carron et al. (2002a) and Carron and Brawley (2008) provided the following practical suggestions for researchers. First, one should consider the research question being asked. For example, if researchers are interested in exploring the relationship between cohesion and individual adherence behaviour in an exercise group, the individual's perception of group cohesion is crucial. By contrast, if a researcher wishes to explore the relationship between perceived cohesion and team performance in a sport setting, the average level of cohesion in the group is the variable of most interest. Second, cohesion researchers need to consider the type of theory being tested. For example, if such a theory concerns social influences within groups, then the group itself is the most appropriate level of analysis. Third, statistical considerations are important. For example, appropriate statistical procedures need to be used to analyse individual team members' responses because these responses are nested within groups. Having highlighted the complexity of analysing cohesion, let us now turn to a more practical question. What is the relationship between team cohesion and performance?

Team cohesion and performance

For many years, sport psychologists have assumed that team cohesion is positively associated with desirable outcomes such as improved communication between athletes/players, increased expenditure of effort and enhanced team success (Carron and Spink, 1993). But is this assumption supported by empirical evidence? Do cohesive teams really achieve more success than teams in which disharmony reigns? Unfortunately, there is no easy answer to this question because the relationship between team cohesion and success is complex. Indeed, there are many anecdotal accounts of sports teams that were highly successful *in spite* of enmity and disharmony between teammates. The former basketball star Dennis Rodman was frequently at odds with his fellow players in the Chicago Bulls team of the late 1990s, yet he managed to contribute significantly to this team's extraordinary success in that era (Weinberg and Gould, 2007). Similarly, there are many examples in soccer of teammates coming to blows during a competitive match. In April 2005, two Newcastle Football Club players, Kieron Dyer and Lee Bowyer, traded punches while playing against Aston Villa. In January 2008, two Arsenal players, Emmanuel Adebayor and Nicklas Bendtner, punched each other during their Carling Cup match against Tottenham Hotspur. Syer (1986) suggested that the existence of friendship-based cliques in a team may sometimes impede rather than facilitate its success (see also Box 7.2 later in the chapter). This speculation has received little or no empirical scrutiny. However, M. Klein and Christiansen (1969) reported that basketball players who were close friends tended to pass the ball disproportionately frequently to each other – often to the relative neglect of team efficacy. But in general, what conclusions have emerged from studies of the link between team cohesion and performance?

Before reviewing the literature on this issue, it is important to comment briefly on the research paradigms used in cohesion research. In general, studies of the relationship between cohesion and success have adopted either a correlational or an experimental research paradigm (Mullen and Copper, 1994). The correlational approach is more popular among investigators in this field and consists of studies in which perceived levels of team cohesion are elicited from individual members and subsequently correlated with team performance or success. Carron et al. (2002a) investigated the relationship between the perceived cohesiveness of elite basketball and soccer teams and their winning percentages in competitive games. Results revealed quite a strong relationship between team cohesion and success, with correlation values ranging between 0.55 and 0.67. The experimental research paradigm, by contrast, involves evaluation of the effect on team performance of some intervention designed to manipulate the level of cohesion in the group. Few studies in the field have used this paradigm, however. A possible explanation for this neglect is that sport researchers tend to be reluctant to use the artificial and ad-hoc groups that are required by the experimental approach. Instead, they prefer to use actual sports teams.

Using the correlational approach, some evidence emerged to indicate that teams could achieve success in spite of enmity between their members. Lenk (1969) suggested that cohesion was not necessary for team success in rowing. Briefly, he investigated the cohesiveness of two teams of German rowers – the 1960 Olympic gold medal winning eight and the 1962 world champions. Although he did not measure team cohesion explicitly, Lenk (1969) assessed group unity by participant observation of social relationships among team members. The results were counter-intuitive because they showed that team success occurred in spite of considerable disharmony among the rowers. Accordingly, this study refuted the traditional view that cohesion is an essential prerequisite of team success; the results challenged "a thesis that seems to have been taken for granted ... [namely that] only small groups, which are low in conflict, or highly integrated can produce especially high performances" (Lenk, 1969, p. 393). Subsequently, he concluded that "sports crews can, therefore, perform top athletic achievements in spite of strong internal conflicts" (Lenk, 1977, p. 38). Of course, as critical consumers of research, we should be cautious about extrapolating too boldly from the results of this study for at least two reasons. First, it is possible that these results are attributable partly to the nature of the sport of rowing. To explain, Syer (1986) noted that it is not too damaging for members of a rowing eight to dislike each other because each one of them has a specific task to perform and is focused on the cox rather than on each other. Thus no matter how much bickering the rowers engaged in with each other, the nature of their sport prevented them from forming cliques that might impede collective performance of the task. Second, Carron et al. (1998) reinterpreted Lenk's results on the grounds that although the rowers in the study had not been socially cohesive, they had been *task* cohesive. So, Lenk's research findings are ambiguous as they have different meanings depending on which aspect of cohesion one examines.

Despite its flaws, Lenk's (1969) study was pivotal in challenging the assumption that cohesion is crucial to team success. Some subsequent studies (e.g., Melnick and Chemers, 1974) found no relationship between cohesiveness and team success whereas others discovered negative relationships between these two variables (e.g., Landers and Luschen, 1974). Research by Carron and Ball (1977) and J. Williams and Hacker (1982) found that team cohesion was associated positively with athletic performance. A review by Widmeyer et al. (1993) claimed that 83 per cent of studies in this field corroborated a positive relationship between team cohesion and performance. Most of these studies found that athletes in successful teams tend to perceive their team as scoring highly in cohesion whereas the converse is true among athletes of unsuccessful teams. But a note of caution regarding this relationship was expressed by Aronson et al. (2002). Briefly, these researchers observed that team cohesion facilitates success *only* if the task facing the team requires close cooperation between members. Furthermore, they warned that team cohesion can impair performance if members of a group are so close emotionally that they allow their social bonds to obscure their critical awareness.

Overall, sport psychologists have shown that the relationship between team cohesion and performance is neither simple nor predictable. Let us consider each of these two points separately. First, as the work of Aronson et al. (2002) indicates, the cohesion–performance relationship is mediated by a host of intervening variables. Consider how the type of sport played may moderate the cohesion–performance relationship. Carron and Chelladurai (1981) speculated that in interactive sports (e.g., basketball, soccer), where team members have to rely on each other, cohesion is likely to be associated with enhanced team success. By contrast, in co-active sports, where athletes play for a team but where individual performance does not depend on teamwork (e.g., golf, rifle-shooting), team cohesiveness should either have no effect or be associated with less team success. This theory was challenged by Matheson et al. (1995), who failed to discover any significant interaction between team cohesion and sport type (a finding supported by Mullen and Copper, 1994). A subsequent review of the literature by Carron and Hausenblas (1998) concluded that in general, team cohesion is positively associated with performance. Similarly, as indicated earlier in the chapter, Carron et al. (2002a) reported that in a large sample of athletes (n = 294) from twenty-seven different basketball and soccer teams, cohesion was correlated positively with team success (with r values ranging from 0.55 to 0.67). Nevertheless, other variables that are believed to mediate the cohesion–performance relationship include such factors as goal clarity and acceptance (Brawley et al., 1987) and "collective efficacy" or group members' shared beliefs in their conjoint capacity to organize and execute actions to produce a desired goal (Bandura, 1997). According to Feltz and Lirgg (2001), teams with a relatively high degree of team self-efficacy beliefs should perform better, and persist longer when behind, than teams with lower levels of such beliefs. But a team's collective efficacy is thought to be more than the simple aggregate of individual levels of self-efficacy (Spink, 1990). Not surprisingly, therefore, the relationship between team cohesion and performance may be moderated by this intervening variable of collective self-efficacy.

The second counter-intuitive conclusion from the research literature is that team cohesion may be a *consequence* rather than a cause of team success. In other words, the relationship between cohesion and performance may be *circular* rather than linear. This possibility is supported by Mullen and Copper (1994) who concluded that "although cohesiveness may indeed lead the group to perform better, the tendency for the group to experience greater cohesiveness *after* successful performance may be even stronger" (Mullen and Copper, 1994, p. 222; italics mine). If this is so, perhaps there is some truth in the old idea that "team spirit" is what a team gains *after* it achieves success! A review by Casey-Campbell and Martens (2009, p. 228) concluded that "existing research appears to provide evidence that the 'performance leads to cohesion' effect seems to be stronger than the 'cohesion leads to performance' effect". A critical perspective on the issue of distinguishing between cause and effect is presented in Box 7.1.

Box 7.1 Thinking critically about ... the direction of causality in cohesion–performance research

Every psychology student is taught that "correlation does not imply causality". In other words, just because two variables are related to each other does not mean that one *caused* the other. After all, there could be a third, confounding factor which is the real cause of the correlation in question. Nevertheless, certain correlational research designs allow investigators to draw conclusions about causal relationships between variables in the absence of experimental manipulations or controls. To illustrate, a "cross-lagged panel correlation" research design (Rozelle and Campbell, 1969) can provide useful clues to the question of causality. Briefly, this design is based on the assumption that analysis of the pattern of correlations between variables at different times (note that the term "lagged" means that there is a time-lag between the collection of some of the correlations) allows certain inferences to be drawn about possible causal links between these variables. In particular, if one variable causes another, it seems likely that it should be more strongly related to the second variable *later* in time – because it is assumed that causes take time to produce effects. Using this cross-lagged research design, Bakeman and Helmreich (1975) measured cohesion and performance in water-sports teams on two separate occasions. Results showed that "first-segment" cohesiveness was highly associated with "second-segment" cohesiveness but not with second-segment performance. Accordingly, these authors concluded that team cohesion was not a good predictor of team performance but that successful performance may have contributed to the development of strong cohesiveness.

Critical thinking questions
Why is it important for researchers to indicate the precise time at which team cohesiveness and performance data were collected? Can you think of any flaws in the logic underlying cross-lagged panel research designs? If performance influences cohesion more than cohesion influences performance, what mechanisms could explain this finding? What are the practical implications of this idea that performance affects team cohesion?

Apart from the preceding conclusions, what other findings have emerged from the research literature on cohesion and performance? One way of answering this question is by augmenting narrative reviews (i.e., those in which researchers draw informal conclusions from reviewing relevant evidence) with meta-analytic reviews of available research. As indicated in Chapter 2, a meta-analysis is literally an analysis of analyses, or a quantitative synthesis of published research on a particular question (e.g., "Does team cohesion affect athletic performance?") in order to determine the effect of one variable on another variable across many different studies and samples. The extent of this effect is indicated by the effect size statistic – a number which represents the average strength of the effect in standard score units, independent of sample size. Using this statistical technique, Mullen and Copper (1994) examined forty-nine studies of groups derived from a broad cross-section of settings including industrial, military, social and sport psychology. At least five conclusions emerged. First, the authors concluded that the cohesion–performance relationship was small but positive and significant. Interestingly, this relationship was stronger for sports teams than for any other groups (e.g., ad-hoc, artificial groups) in the sample. The authors attributed this trend to the fact that sports groups tend to have a unique sense of collective identity, and they differ from other groups by virtue of being formally organized according to explicit rules of competition. Second, Mullen and Copper (1994) found that stronger cohesion–performance relationships existed among "real" (i.e., naturally formed) groups than among "artificial" groups. Third, they concluded that performance was more strongly related to cohesion than was cohesion to performance (see also Box 7.1). Fourth, the type of athletic activity (e.g., interactive versus co-active sports) did not seem to mediate the relationship between cohesion and performance in sports teams. Fifth, Mullen and Copper (1994) claimed that commitment to the *task* was the primary component of cohesiveness in the cohesion–performance relationship. This conclusion suggests that team-building techniques aimed at enhancing the other components of cohesion (see Figure 7.3) may not be effective. Mullen and Copper (1994) were sceptical of the merit of fostering interpersonal attraction among members and/ or attempting to "pump up" the group in an effort to enhance team performance. Incidentally, the next section examines the nature and efficacy of some popular team-building techniques in sport.

In 2002, Carron et al. (2002b) updated the preceding meta-analytic review by focusing on studies conducted only in the domain of sport. Using a database of forty-six published studies, they discovered that there was a "significant moderate to large" effect size of 0.655 for cohesion on performance – indicating that cohesiveness was significantly associated with team performance in sport. In contrast to the findings of Mullen and Copper (1994), Carron et al. (2002b) found that both task *and* social cohesion were significantly related to athletic performance. Another notable finding emerging from this study was that cohesiveness in female teams was more strongly related to performance than was cohesiveness in male teams.

So far, we have examined the relationship between cohesion and performance only in relation to the variable of objective team success. But as Kremer and Scully (2002) observed, the focus on only one type of outcome is too narrow as it neglects other ways in which cohesion may affect team dynamics. For example, the cohesion of a group may affect subjective variables such as team satisfaction, team identity and the perceived self-efficacy of a team. These variables could be included fruitfully in future research in this field, although it should be pointed out that "satisfaction" may be either a cause or a consequence of team cohesion. In a longitudinal field study of cohesion, Holt and Sparkes (2001) explored the factors that contributed to the cohesion of a university soccer team over an eight-month season. Using a variety of ethnographic methods (such as participant observation and interviews), Holt and Sparkes (2001) identified four main factors that shaped team cohesiveness. These factors were, first, clear and meaningful roles (e.g., in mid-season, some of the teams' midfield players wanted to play a more attacking game to the relative neglect of their defensive duties), second, team goals (in late season, the fact that the team was eliminated from one competition helped to refocus the team for the league campaign), third, personal sacrifices (e.g., the team captain made a three-hour train journey in order to play in the final match of the league) and fourth, communication (especially "on-field" communication among the players).

Before concluding this section, it may be interesting to explore two intriguing questions. First, can group cohesion ever be harmful (see Box 7.2)? Second, would you be surprised to learn that cohesion does not feature in a list of the characteristics of a successful team – at least in the opinion of one successful coach (see Box 7.3)?

Box 7.2 Thinking critically about … whether or not team cohesion can ever be harmful

It has long been assumed that high levels of team cohesion are associated with better performance and improved results. In general, empirical research supports this putative connection between cohesion and performance. Carron et al. (2002a) suggested that the relationship between cohesion and performance is reciprocal – with high cohesion leading to improved performance and successful performance in turn increasing cohesion. But Rovio et al. (2009) challenged this conclusion. Briefly, these authors investigated the relationship between the performance of a junior ice-hockey team and various social psychological phenomena (including team cohesion). They used a mixed methodology involving interviews, observational data, a diary and psychometric testing, with the Group Environment Questionnaire (GEQ: Carron et al., 1985). Results showed that despite high social cohesion, the team's performance deteriorated during the season. Based on this finding, Rovio et al. (2009) concluded that cohesion is not always beneficial to team performance.

Critical thinking questions
In the light of the complex relationship between team cohesion and team performance, are you surprised by the findings reported by Rovio et al. (2009)? Can you think of any other explanation of their findings above – besides the one that claims that team cohesion is overvalued? Do you think that the authors' conclusion were justified by the methodology that they used? If you wanted to replicate or extend this study, what methods would *you* choose?

Box 7.3 presents former England coach Sven-Göran Eriksson's views on the ingredients of a successful team.

Box 7.3 Thinking critically about … a coach's view of successful teams

According to the former England soccer manager Sven-Göran Eriksson (2002), who has coached championship winning teams in three countries (Sweden, Portugal and Italy: Every, 2002), there are eight key characteristics of a successful team in sport.

First, the members of the team must have a common vision. Second, they should have a clear understanding of the team's goals. Third, they must have a good understanding of team strategy and tactics. Fourth, they must have "inner discipline" – which involves both knowing and adhering to the rules of the team (e.g., with regard to time-keeping). Fifth, successful teams must have players who complement each other. For example, Eriksson claims that more than one player like Messi in a team could cause problems because of the unpredictability of their skills. Sixth, effective teams require a division of roles – but the coach must respect each of them equally. Seventh, players in a successful team must learn to put the common good before their own interests. Finally, the members of a successful team must accept collective responsibility and think of "we" instead of "me".

Critical thinking questions
Notice that Eriksson did not specify "social cohesion" as one of his criteria of successful teams. Do you agree with this decision? If not, why not? Do you think that all of Eriksson's eight team characteristics can be developed psychologically in players? Which ones are the most difficult to develop?

Team-building in sport

Having established the nature, measurement and correlates of team cohesion in sport, let us now consider the main methods by which coaches, managers and psychologists have attempted to enhance it. One popular method in this regard is through team-building activities or experiences that are intended to enhance aspects of team harmony such as trust, communication and leadership (Statler, 2010). According to Martin et al. (2009, p. 3), the purpose of team-building is "to help a group become more cohesive while working toward its common goals". Increasingly, sports teams try to achieve this latter objective by the use of special training camps – often held away from home either before the competitive season starts or during it. Although such trips are often useful, they may also prove to be counterproductive in generating adverse publicity for the team involved as a result of unruly antics. In 2004, eight Leicester City footballers on a mid-season "bonding session" in Spain were taken into custody by local police (and subsequently released) following allegations of rape by two women (Kremer and Moran, 2008a). Similarly, a team-building trip to Portugal by Liverpool Football Club in February 2007 in preparation for an important Champions' League match turned sour when one of the players (Craig Bellamy) asaulted a teammate (John Arne Riise) with a golf-club during a karaoke session in a local bar (Wallace, 2007). Although anecdotal in nature, these examples highlight the danger of assuming that "away days" inevitably foster team cohesion. Howard Wilkinson, a former manager of Leeds United and Sunderland, showed commendable awareness of this problem when he pointed out that there is a big difference between facilitating a temporary form of camaraderie and generating an abiding sense of team cohesion among players. Specifically, he noted that "going out and getting drunk generates a feel-good factor which is different to real team-spirit. I think real team spirit is much more enduring – that (other) feel-good factor cracks under pressure" (cited in Fanning, 2004b). Moving on from anecdotal examples, it is evident that relatively little empirical research has been conducted on the nature and efficacy of team-building techniques in sport psychology (but see the special issue of the *Journal of Applied Sport Psychology* edited by C. Hardy and Crace, 1997). From the research literature available, however, it is possible to identify some principles and findings as follows.

To begin with, a definition of team-building is required. Several possibilities are available. B. Newman (1984, p. 27) defined this term as an attempt to "promote an increased sense of unity and cohesiveness and enable the team to function together more smoothly and effectively". Bettenhausen (1991, p. 369) described team-building as an attempt "to improve group performance by improving communication, reducing conflict, and generating commitment among work group members". In a similar vein, C. Hardy and Crace (1997) suggested that team-building involves interventions that purport to enhance team performance by positively affecting team processes or team synergy. Echoing this view, Brawley and Paskevich (1997, p. 13) defined team-building as "a method of helping the group to (a) increase effectiveness, (b) satisfy the needs of its members, or (c) improve work conditions". More recently, C. Klein et al. (2009, p. 183) defined team-building as "formal and informal team-level interventions that focus on improving social relations and clarifying roles, as well as solving task and interpersonal problems that affect team functioning". In summary, a common theme running through these definitions is the idea that team-building is designed explicitly to enhance team cohesion.

Does team-building actually work? In an attempt to answer this question, C. Klein et al. (2009) reviewed the effects of four team-building strategies – goal-setting, interpersonal relations, problem solving and role clarification – on various indices of team performance, mainly in organizational settings. The results were encouraging in being "suggestive of the idea that team-building does improve team performance" (C. Klein et al., 2009, p. 212). Nevertheless, at least three caveats must be noted when evaluating research and practice in this field (Crace and Hardy, 1997; McLean, 1995). First, team-building should not be regarded as a type of "quick fix, pep talk" which ensures team harmony through the cursory application of some arcane psychological strategies. Instead, it involves a long-term commitment to the development of task-related and interpersonal dynamics of a team in the interests of enhancing its performance. Emphasizing this point, McLean (1995, p. 424) claimed that team-building "is not a set of exercises that get wheeled out from time to time, but it is a way of thinking which pervades every interpersonal interaction within that group". Second, team-building is not designed to increase similarity or agreement between group members but to enhance mutual respect among teammates. As Yukelson (1997) suggested, sports teams resemble families in the sense that although teammates may not always like or agree with each other, they know that they belong to the same "household". Third, we should acknowledge that most of the principles and strategies of team-building in sport are derived from research on organizational development in business settings (see C. Klein et al., 2009). Although this cross-fertilization of ideas between business and sport has been valuable in certain areas of sport psychology (most notably, perhaps, in goal-setting; see Chapter 2), it has also generated activities (e.g., participation in outdoor adventure weekends) whose appeal is based more on intuition than on empirical evidence. Put simply, the fact that a team-building technique is popular in business does not make it either valid or effective in sport settings. Bearing these caveats in mind, let us now consider the theory and practice of team-building interventions in sport psychology.

Developing team cohesion: from theory to practice

As we learned in the previous section, the main objective of team-building interventions is to increase the effectiveness of a group by enhancing the cohesiveness of its members (Carron et al., 1997). But as cohesion is a multidimensional construct (see earlier in chapter), what aspects of it should team-builders focus on in designing interventions? More generally, what team-building exercises are most effective in strengthening cohesion? Let us now consider each of these two questions.

According to Mullen and Copper (1994), the three most important dimensions of cohesion are interpersonal attraction, commitment to a common task and pride in the group itself. Most cohesion theorists have explored the first and second of these aspects of cohesion but have tended to neglect the "pride in the group" aspect. Naturally, these different aspects of cohesion have different implications for team-building initiatives. First, if one wishes to strengthen the interpersonal determinants of cohesion, team-building techniques should focus on increasing mutual liking and affiliation among team members. Second, if one wishes to increase group members' commitment to a given task, team-building exercises should be directed at helping them to increase the intrinsic enjoyment of tackling this task. Third, if group pride is seen as the most important dimension of cohesion, activities that "psych up" the group may be appropriate (see also Chapter 3).

In general, two types of team-building interventions may be distinguished in sport and exercise psychology – direct and indirect interventions (Eys et al., 2005). In the direct interventions paradigm, the coach, manager or sport psychology consultant works *directly* with the athletes in the team in an effort to increase cohesion among them and to foster a communal vision and sense of identity. In the indirect interventions paradigm, the consultant instructs coaches and managers in the skills of team-building rather than working directly with the athletes or players concerned.

Usually, team-building in sport is conducted through the *indirect* intervention paradigm for three main reasons (Carron and Hausenblas, 1998; Estabrooks and Dennis, 2003). First, most coaches and managers like to be involved in mediating the interventions of consultants to their team members because they tend to know the individual athletes well. Second, many coaches are reluctant to relinquish their control over the team to an outside consultant. Third, some coaches may be wary of the possibility that the consultant in question may use his or her work with the team for personal promotional purposes. Let us now consider some examples of direct and indirect team-building interventions.

Direct team-building interventions

Based on his experience as a sport psychology consultant to a variety of university athletes, Yukelson (1997) delineated four stages of direct team-building work with athletes: assessment, education, **brainstorming** and goal-setting. First, he suggested that the consultant must assess the current team situation as accurately as possible. This step requires the consultant to meet relevant coaching staff and listen to and observe the athletes or players in order to determine the goals, expectations and concerns of the entire team. Second, in the education stage, the consultant should provide the team with some elementary information about how groups develop over time. In the third stage, Yukelson (1997) proposed that the consultant should use brainstorming techniques to help the team to generate and prioritize its current needs. In the fourth stage, these needs should be analysed to determine the goals of the team-building intervention. Across these four stages, a number of practical team-building techniques are recommended. These techniques are evaluated in Box 7.4.

Box 7.4 Thinking critically about ... building a great team

Veach and May (2005) proposed the MAPS framework for building a successful team. The acronym MAPS stands for **M**ission, **A**ssessment, **P**lan and **S**ystematic evaluation. Here is a summary of the steps involved in this approach.

- *Mission*: What does the team stand for? What are its values and how strongly is it committed to achieving excellence? Following discussions with the team and its coaches, develop a concise mission statement that tries to answer these questions as clearly as possible.
- *Assessment*: Try to assess team strengths and weaknesses by observing how well players work together, communicate with each other and respond to feedback from coaches during practice sessions and competitive matches. Regular appraisal of these qualities is crucial to effective team-building.
- *Plan*: Help the team members and coaches to develop an action plan designed to improve individual and team efforts. This can be done by facilitating team goal-setting meetings and by encouraging open and honest communication about how best to achieve team goals.
- *Systematic evaluation*: You need to review the entire "road map" regularly.

Critical thinking questions
Imagine that you are a sport psychologist hired to engage in direct team-building work with a squad of athletes and coaches. How could you use the MAPS approach to facilitate this task? Do you think that it would be difficult to devise a mission statement for the team if there are lots of conflicting goals among the players? How would you handle a situation in which some of the players rejected the coach's goals for the team? Can you see any contradiction between teaching team members to be self-reliant and yet encouraging them to depend on each other? How would you like to be introduced to the team – as a sport psychologist or as a team-building consultant? Give reasons for your answer.

Apart from the suggestions contained in Box 7.4, a variety of other team-building exercises have been used by coaches and managers in sport. Some of the more unusual ones are described in Box 7.5.

Box 7.5 Team-building exercises in soccer: bingo, bathing, drinking and ... injecting monkey-testicles!

Soccer coaches and managers have used many unusual strategies in an effort to foster team spirit among their players. Don Revie, who managed the highly successful Leeds United team of the 1960s and 1970s, used to organize games of bingo for his players. In addition, former players claim that he often used to personally soap and massage them in baths after training and matches! Apart from such hands-on techniques, other favourite bonding strategies include playing practical jokes on teammates and engaging in drinking games. The "crazy gang" members of the Wimbledon team of the 1980s used to cut each other's suits, set their clothes on fire and pack talcum powder into teammates' motor-cycle helmets as initiation rites. D. Taylor (2003) reported that when Neil Warnock was manager of Bury, he used to encourage his players to drink cocktails made of raw eggs and sherry after training every Friday. According to Dean Kiely, Bury's goalkeeper at the time, this technique was Warnock's way of saying "we stand and fall together". Perhaps the strangest technique used to enhance team performance was that involving the injection of monkey-testicle serum – allegedly pioneered by Major Frank Buckley (manager of Wolverhampton Wanderers from 1927 to 1944) (Norrish, 2009).

Incidentally, Don Revie was ahead of his time in extolling the psychological value of bingo because research by Julie Winstone (cited in Horwood, 2002) revealed that this activity can yield measurable cognitive benefits. Specifically, she reported that people who played bingo regularly tended to perform faster and more accurately on visual search tasks than those who did not.

Direct team-building techniques are increasingly evident in sport – even in games which are regarded as quintessentially individual activities such as golf. Consider the various practical strategies used by the captains of the 2002 and 2006 Europe teams in their matches against the United States in the Ryder Cup. Sam Torrance (captain of the 2002 Europe team) used the thirteen months period between the date on which the European team was selected and the match itself (recall that the long delay was caused by the cancellation of the 2001 Ryder Cup match in the wake of the September 11 terrorist attacks) to boost the confidence of his players. He circulated catchy inspirational statements such as "out of the shadows come heroes" and "Curtis has one Tiger – but I've got twelve lions". These motivational phrases were delivered regularly at team meetings and were accompanied by video screenings in which the players were encouraged to view themselves holing putts, hitting wonderful shots and winning tournaments (A. Reid, 2002). He also appealed to his players emotionally: just before the match itself, Torrance addressed the team with the words, "this is going to be the best day of your life. You were born to do this. This is what we practise for. This is what we live for" (cited in A. Reid, 2002). Turning to Europe's team preparation for the 2006 Ryder Cup, a rather different approach was used by the captain, Ian Woosnam, who recruited Jamil Qureshi, a former professional cricketer turned hypnotist and stage entertainer, to help the team of golfers. Qureshi staged a 45-minute show for the golfers after Woosnam had delivered his opening speech to the team (Donegan, 2006).

Perhaps the most bizarre example of team-building techniques in modern sport is that used by the South African rugby union in preparing its national team for the 2003 World Cup – the infamous Kamp Staaldrad (Kremer and Moran, 2008a; Ray, 2003a). Box 7.6 provides some details of this extraordinary boot camp for the South African rugby squad.

Box 7.6 Team-building exercises in rugby: Kamp Staaldraad – a (jack) boot camp that failed

Kamp Staaldraad (from the Afrikaans meaning "Camp Barbed Wire") was a military-type boot camp established under the direction of South Africa's national rugby coach, Rudolf Straeuli, and his assistant Adriaan Heijns (a former Special Services military man from the country's apartheid era). Its goal was to develop team spirit and cohesiveness among the South African rugby squad prior to the 2003 World Cup.

At this camp, the players were forced to undergo a series of torturous and humiliating exercises in an effort to forge team spirit and mental toughness. In particular, the players were allegedly:

- forced to stand naked in a freezing lake and pump up rugby balls underwater (and those who tried to climb out were forced back literally at gunpoint)
- ordered to climb into a foxhole naked and sing the South African national anthem while ice-cold water was poured over their heads (recordings of *God Save the Queen* (England's national anthem) and the New Zealand All Blacks pre-match haka were played at full volume)
- made to crawl naked across gravel
- coerced into carrying tyres, poles and bags branded with the flag emblems of England and New Zealand
- made to spend a night in the bush, including killing animals and cooking meals.

These unconventional team-building strategies (or alleged human rights violations: see Ray, 2003b) were of little benefit to South Africa as the team lost in the quarter-final of the tournament to New Zealand. Shortly afterwards, Straeuli resigned. The South African public was shocked by revelations surrounding the camp and one of the country's most respected religious figures, Archbishop Ndungane, was reported to have said: "You don't motivate people with jackboot tactics, and the proof is certainly in the World Cup pudding" (cited in Wildman, 2003). Curiously, despite the absence of any scientific evidence to support the strategies used in Kamp Staaldraad, and the worldwide outrage it generated, the team captain, Corne Kriege, claimed that "most of the stuff was really good for team spirit" (cited in Evening Herald, 2003, p. 8).

Before concluding this section, we should remember that a great deal of caution is necessary when evaluating the impact of direct team-building interventions. Specifically, when comparing the preparation techniques used by the European and US teams we must be careful not to fall into the trap of assuming that team success means that team preparation must have been ideal. In other words, we should be wary of *post-hoc* reasoning when attempting to determine the possible causes of a given sporting outcome. This problem is also called the "glow of success" bias and reflects the invalid reasoning procedure by which people think "we won – so we must have been cohesive" (Diane Gill, 2000).

Indirect team-building interventions

As explained previously, indirect team-building involves the sport psychologist working with the coaching staff rather than the team members. Within this paradigm, Carron et al. (1997) developed an influential theoretical model which proposed a four-step intervention process. In the first stage, which typically lasts for less than twenty minutes, the consultant outlines for the team coach or manager both the nature and benefits of team-building. Second, in the "conceptual stage", which takes about the same length of time, the goal of enhanced team cohesion is explained as being the result of three main factors: the team's environment (e.g., the distinctiveness of the team), the team's structure (e.g., norms) and its communication processes. Third, the "practical stage", which takes place in collaboration with the team coach or manager, involves the practical work of generating as many team-building strategies as possible. Fourth, in the "intervention stage", the team-building methods are implemented by the coach or manager with the assistance of trained assistants, if necessary. Box 7.7 presents examples of the various team-building exercises advocated by Carron et al. (1997, 2009).

Box 7.7 Theory and practice of team-building (based on Carron et al., 1997, 2009)

Team-building objective	*Possible strategy*
Enhancing team distinctiveness	Emphasize unique history or traditions of team and design special team T-shirts or sportswear (e.g., warm-up tracksuits) for players and coaches
Increasing team togetherness	Organize social outings for teammates and design team drills in the lead-up to matches
Clarifying team goals and norms	Set goals in consultation with team members and encourage "goals for the day" exercises
Facilitating team communication	Arrange regular meetings for team members and alternate the role of "social organizer" within team

---

Evaluating team-building interventions

How effective are the direct and indirect team-building interventions described above? As Pain and Harwood (2009, p. 523) pointed out, despite the importance of team-building to coaches and psychologists, "surprisingly little sport-specific research has been conducted". Of the handful of published studies on this topic, results are equivocal. Prapavessis et al. (1996) assigned soccer teams to one of three conditions: a team-building intervention condition, an attention-placebo condition, or a control condition. The attention-placebo condition consisted of an intervention strategy which involved soccer-specific information (e.g., nutrition) rather than team-building information. The soccer players' perceptions of team cohesion were evaluated before the beginning of the season and also after an eight-week intervention period. Surprisingly, results indicated no significant difference in cohesiveness between the players in the various conditions: the team-building intervention was not effective in this study. By contrast, Pain and Harwood (2009) evaluated a team-building intervention (based on structured team meetings) with a soccer team during a competitive season. Using a single-case research design (see Chapter 1; see also Barker et al., 2011), these researchers reported that their intervention had led to increased team cohesion and improvements in team performance. In the domain of exercise, team-building interventions have also been shown to be moderately effective (Carron and Hausenblas, 1998; L. Martin et al., 2009). Carron et al. (1997) explained how team-building strategies were successful in developing cohesion in, and adherence to, exercise classes for young adults. Estabrooks and Carron (1999, 2000) reported similar results for more elderly exercisers. One possible reason for this apparent discrepancy between team-building effects in sports teams and exercise groups is that a "ceiling effect" may be at work. To explain, the cohesiveness among sport team members is probably greater than that among exercise group members and so interventions designed to enhance cohesion may produce less change in the former than in the latter participants. As Carron and Hausenblas (1998, p. 342) speculated, the "opportunities for increased cohesiveness through team-building are greater in exercise groups". L. Martin et al. (2009) conducted a meta-analysis of research on the efficacy of team-building interventions in sport. Following a review of seventeen relevant studies, the authors concluded that team-building had "a significant moderate effect" on cohesion and performance (L. Martin et al., 2009, p. 11). Furthermore, results showed that the most successful interventions used goal-setting techniques and lasted between two and twenty weeks in duration.

Perhaps a more interesting question for the layperson is: how do athletes themselves react to team-building interventions? Although little or no research data exist on this issue, some relevant insights can be gleaned from athletes' autobiographical accounts of their experiences of team-building. Typically, these accounts reveal considerable scepticism about the merit of team-building activities. Jeremy Guscott, the former England international rugby player who travelled on a seven-week tour of South Africa with the British and Irish Lions in 1997, was very wary of the management consultants who were hired to engage in team-building exercises with the squad prior to its departure. He revealed:

rugby players are not the most receptive audiences to new-fangled ideas ... I shared the scepticism. I'm a bit old-fashioned about these things and, as far as I'm concerned, a quick drink down the pub would have been enough for me to get to know everyone.

(Guscott, 1997, pp. 19–20)

One of the exercises which was the target of his derision involved the attempt by a subgroup of players to balance a long bamboo cane on the edges of their fingertips before lowering it to the floor. Canoeing and crate-stacking exercises were also used in an effort to develop team spirit among the Lions squad members. As I indicated previously, however, such techniques lack both a coherent theoretical rationale and evidence of empirical validity. Martin Johnson, who captained the England rugby team to victory in the 2003 World Cup, provided some fascinating insights into the motivational ideas and techniques used by the manager, Clive Woodward. Johnson claimed:

some of the ideas were good, some OK and some just plain crazy – like the computer system (designed to identify true winners) from Mossad ... There was a joystick and you had to line up all these targets and fire things ... At that point, we thought Clive had completely lost it ... we used the program for a couple of months, then we never saw it again.

(cited in Kervin, 2005, p. 72)

Clearly, Johnson was not impressed by fads like the use of computer game playing as a team-bonding exercise. In passing, scepticism about team-building is also pre-valent in professional soccer. Recall the story (in Chapter 1) of what happened when a management consultant used an exercise involving plasticine in an attempt to promote team-building among the Sunderland club's soccer players (Dickinson, 2007). Statler (2010) examined some common pitfalls in team-building activities; she noted that some athletes do not feel comfortable in sharing their thoughts with others in a public discussion of team goals. Similarly, sport psychologists engaged in team-building must be sensitive to the possibility that some players will give socially desirable suggestions (i.e., will say what they think the coach wants to hear) rather than honest feedback in group brainstorming sessions. Finally, Statler (2010, p. 333) pointed out that the task of developing a group identity or a team vision is a lengthy process and is "only as great as the commitment to working on it".

Implicationof team-building techniques for coaches

At least five practical implications for coaches may be identified from theories of effective team-building (Weinberg and Gould, 2007). First, coaches should try to create a team environment in which open channels of communication exist among teammates and between team members and the coaching or management staff. The assumption here is that clear communication processes foster mutual trust among team members. Practical ways of improving communication in teams include arranging regular team meetings to discuss issues that can be filled into sentences such as "It would be better if …". Second, although many coaches proclaim that "there is no 'I' in team", it is essential that they recognize the importance of individual roles within groups of athletes. At the very least, all players should be told exactly how they can contribute to the success of the team. Also, if individual players know what skills they have to work on, they are likely to work harder for team objectives. Third, coaches must learn to set challenging group goals for their teams. Fourth, a collective sense of team identity can be strengthened by encouraging teammates to wear similar team clothing. Fifth, successful coaches tend to spend a lot of time in getting to know their players as well as possible (for some practical advice on team-building techniques, see also Estabrooks and Dennis, 2003).

School sports: helpful or harmful?

School sports are among the earliest and most powerful ways in which young people are introduced to athletic activities, but what are the psychological benefits and hazards associated with playing competitive sports in school? Does sport build character – or merely *reveal* it? Let us now consider these questions briefly.

Many people have happy memories of their youthful days on the playing field. Samuel Beckett, a Nobel Prize-winner for literature, wrote fondly of the time he spent playing cricket for Portora Royal School in Enniskillen, Northern Ireland. At inter-varsity level, the sheer delight of winning a rowing race is captured in the faces of the young women in Figure 7.4.

Figure 7.4 Jumping for joy … University College Dublin women's rowing team celebrate victory
Source: Courtesy of The Irish Examiner and University College Dublin, Sport

We must remember that for every winner in competitive sport, there has to be a loser. So, not surprisingly, cheers can quickly turn to tears for young athletes when they equate "winning" with "success" and "losing" with "failure". This problem is exacerbated if excessive emphasis is placed by parents and coaches on winning (Shane Murphy, 1999). Psychologically, there are several problems with the assumption that "winning" is the sole, or even primary, goal for sports performers of any age. Apart from being outside one's control, this goal may encourage the view that victory can come only at someone else's expense. But as we learned in Chapter 2, many of the world's top athletes are motivated not by a desire to defeat others but by the goal of improving upon their *own* performance. This idea of seeking to improve one's skills lies at the heart of the developmental models of sport coaching developed by psychologists such as R. Smith and Smoll (2002a) and Smoll and Smith (2005, 2010). These researchers postulate that "success" in sport transcends winning – and instead involves enjoying the challenge of expending maximum effort to develop one's skills. Put simply, according to Ronald Smith:

> the best way to maximize performance is by creating an environment in which athletes are having fun, are highly motivated, they're trying to improve, they're giving maximum effort, and you have a good relationship with them, so they're more likely to listen to what you tell them. That's the way you get to winning.

(cited in Munsey, 2010, p. 59)

More generally, what do we know about the psychological consequences of participation in youth sports?

The long-term effects of competitive athletic activity in young people have attracted relatively little research attention from psychologists. Therefore, it is difficult to evaluate the widely held assumption that school/youth sports develop "character", team spirit and/or the virtues of sportspersonship (which may be defined broadly as "sport behaviours that carry moral connotations because of their connections to fundamental issues of fairness and respect": Shields et al., 2007, p. 747). In an early review of the literature in this field, Shields and Bredemeier (2001) proposed that sport does not *automatically* build character – a conclusion echoed by Gould and Carson (2008: see below). Shields and Bredemeier (2001, p. 599) also proposed that "the longer one stays in sport, and the higher the competitive level reached, the more winning becomes the dominant value". This conclusion is endorsed by Shane Murphy (1999), who suggested that the longer athletes remain in sport, the less sportingly they behave and the more likely they are to condone cheating and violent behaviour on the field of play! In a similar vein, Miracle and Rees (1994) found no support for the claim that sport builds character in school or anywhere else. Given such research findings, it is not surprising that Shields and Bredemeier (2007) question the evidence underlying the common assumption that participation in sport builds moral attitudes that transfer to other domains in life. Although such a conclusion seems controversial, it has played a valuable role in stimulating popular and scientific debate about the advantages and disadvantages of youth sport involvement. Fortunately, advances have been made in the development of coaching programmes that are designed to enhance enjoyment and to promote moral and ethical development in young athletes (see R. Smith and Smoll, 2002b). Progress is also evident in the measurement of the construct of sportspersonship. Vallerand et al. (1997) reported the development and validation of a psychometric scale to assess a general commitment to fair play in sport as well as a respect for the rules, officials, social conventions and opponents encountered in the specific game in question. Shields et al. (2007), M. Lee et al. (2007) and Kavussanu and Boardley (2009) have developed other potentially valuable questionnaires to measure aspects of sportspersonship/moral behaviour in sport.

Although the link between sport and character development is tenuous, what of the claim that athletic involvement can forge a sense of identity and cohesion among competitors? As before, little or no research exists on this issue, but there is some historical evidence to corroborate the idea that sport fosters cohesion. In Ireland, Sean Moran (2001) showed how Gaelic games in the nineteenth century played a significant role in strengthening people's sense of identity in their struggle to establish independent political rule. Unfortunately, problems can arise when this sense of identity becomes rigid or entrenched. In Northern Ireland, allegiance to various sports and teams has a distinctive sectarian dimension (McGinley et al., 1998). A graphic example of the depth of this sectarianism occurred in August 2002 when Neil Lennon, the Northern Ireland player, was forced to retire from international soccer after he had received death threats from "supporters" of his own national team (McIntosh, 2002). These death threats were believed to have been prompted by Lennon's affiliation with the predominantly Catholic team for which he played at the time – Glasgow Celtic.

Finally, can life skills be developed though sport? Although a detailed analysis of this question is beyond the scope of this chapter, research in this field has been reviewed by Gould and Carson (2008). Having defined "life skills" as "those personal assets, characteristics and skills such as goal setting, emotional control, self-esteem, and hard work ethic that can be facilitated or developed in sport and transferred for use in non-sport settings", these authors found that such skills do not automatically result from mere participation in competitive sport: "life skills are taught not caught" (Gould and Carson, 2008, pp. 60, 75).

To summarize, it may be argued that school sports offer potential health, social and psychological benefits to young people. They can help children to discover the benefits of systematic practice (A. Moran, 2001), but to achieve these benefits fully, young sports performers need to be exposed to an enlightened coaching philosophy rather than a "win at all costs" mentality that causes stress to athletes of all ages and levels of ability.

New directions for research on team cohesion

Based on some comprehensive reviews of the empirical literature (e.g., Carron and Brawley, 2008; Carron et al., 2007), at least six new directions can be suggested for research on team cohesion in sport. First, in view of formidable definitional problems in this field, there is an urgent need for conceptual clarification of such key terms as group, team, social cohesion and task cohesion. Second, there is a need for empirical studies designed to test explicit hypotheses about, and/or possible explanations for, group processes in athletes. This type of hypothesis-testing research is preferable to descriptive, atheoretical studies. Third, there is a paucity of knowledge at present about possible *changes* in group dynamics within sports teams over time; additional longitudinal studies (e.g., extending the research of Pain and Harwood, 2009) are required in which such key variables as athletes' social and task cohesion could be measured at various stages over a competitive season. This type of research would rectify the danger of over-reliance on data obtained from "snapshot" studies in this field. Fourth, in examining the relationship between team cohesion and athletic performance, it is important either to measure or to control for the moderating influence of such variables as sport type, group structure and intra-group relationships. Fifth, just as in many other areas of sport and exercise psychology, there has been a dearth of field studies using top-level athletes. Sixth, the field of sportspersonship and moral behaviour in sport is ripe for investigation. Kavussanu (2008) pointed out that few studies have investigated the consequences of morally relevant behaviour in sport for such variables as team cohesion, team performance and enjoyment.

Ideas for research projects on team cohesion in sport

Here are six ideas for research projects on group processes in athletes.

1   According to Carron and Brawley (2008), studies on group processes in sport are hampered by the use of static, "snapshot" research designs. The problem with this latter approach is that it fails to examine the dynamic nature of groups. Therefore, these authors recommend the use of prospective, longitudinal studies. In order to fill this gap in the field, it would be interesting to investigate possible changes in social and task cohesion in a sports team over the course of a competitive season (see Pain and Harwood, 2009).

2   Given the equivocal nature of the evidence surrounding the psychometric characteristics of the Group Environment Questionnaire (GEQ: Carron et al., 1985), it would be interesting to conduct a systematic attempt to validate this measure for adults in sport and exercise settings.

3   It would be intriguing to examine the relationship between team cohesion and individual cognitive processes such as decision making in sport situations. As yet, little or nothing is known about this topic.

4   Few studies have been conducted on the relationship between a coach's leadership style and the cohesion of his or her team.

5   Given the substantial research literature that has accumulated on expert–novice differences in sport (see Chapter 6), it would be interesting to examine the effects of expertise on the type of team-building strategies used by coaches in different sports.

6   Additional research is required on the nature, correlates and development of sportspersonship in young athletes (e.g., see Shields et al., 2007). For example, do athletes' perceptions of team cohesion and coaching climate/values affect their level of sportspersonship?

Summary

- Despite the importance of group processes in athletic performance, less research has been conducted on team-related processes in sport than on the individual characteristics of the performers. To rectify this trend, this chapter examined the nature, measurement and correlates of one of the most popular constructs in this field – team spirit/cohesion (or the degree of closeness and collaboration between teammates).
- The second section explained the meaning of such terms as group, team and group dynamics.
- The third section reviewed psychological research on the measurement and correlates of team cohesiveness (or the degree to which team members stick together) and teamwork (or the productive cooperation between group members) in sport.
- The fourth section examined the nature and efficacy of team-building activities in sport psychology. This section concluded with a summary of the practical implications of these activities for coaches.
- The fifth section described the advantages and disadvantages of young people's participation in school sports.
- The sixth section sketched some potentially fruitful new directions for future research on team dynamics in athletes.
- Finally, six ideas for possible research projects in this field were outlined.

EXPLORING HEALTH, EXERCISE AND INJURY

Overview

Part one of the book examined the nature of the discipline and profession of sport and exercise psychology. Parts two and three examined individual and collective components of athletic performance. Part four returns to the "exercise" aspect of sport and exercise psychology. Chapter 8 investigates the positive and negative health consequences of engaging in regular physical activity. Chapter 9 explores some psychological aspects of physical injury.

Does a healthy body always lead to a healthy mind? Exploring exercise psychology

(with the assistance of James Matthews and Tadhg MacIntyre)

Throughout most of human history and outside the first world nowadays, food has been relatively scarce and physical exercise abundant; only when the status of these two things is reversed does "exercise" make sense.

(Solnit, 2001, p. 261)

Introduction

Psychological aspects of physical activity have long intrigued eminent scholars in various fields. The French philosopher Jean-Jacques Rousseau claimed that "I can only meditate when I am walking. When I stop, I cease to think; my mind only works with my legs" (Rousseau, 1953/1781, p. 382). The American author and naturalist Henry David Thoreau celebrated the relationship between walking and thinking when he observed that "the moment my legs begin to move, my thoughts begin to flow" (cited in Healthcare News of Western Massachusetts, 2010). The nineteenth-century psychologist William James highlighted the emotional effects of physical activity when he wrote that "our muscular vigour will ... always be needed to furnish the background of sanity, serenity, and cheerfulness to life ... and make us good-humoured" (W. James, 1899, pp. 205–207). Although these epigrams offer interesting insights into the relationship between physical activity and mental processes, we need to check how well they accord with scientific research findings; that is why we turn to the growing field of exercise psychology.

According to Dishman and Chambliss (2010, p. 563), exercise psychology is concerned with the "social-cognitive antecedents of leisure-time physical activity and the psychological consequences of being physically active". A great deal of research evidence has accumulated to show that regular physical activity not only is associated with a range of physical and mental health benefits (Biddle and Mutrie, 2008; US Department of Health and Human Services, 2010; see also later in this chapter) but also can help to counteract the effects of chronic diseases such as cardiovascular problems and diabetes. Despite the compelling nature of this research evidence, many people appear to be reluctant to take up leisure-time physical activity (a phenomenon known as the exercise initiation problem) and/or are easily dissuaded from continuing with it (the exercise adherence or maintenance problem). To illustrate, in 2001, surveys showed that only about 25 per cent of the adult population of most industrialized countries were regularly active and that only 10 per cent of such populations exercise either sufficiently vigorously (e.g., by jogging, running) or often enough to obtain significant benefits in fitness (Dishman, 2001). Little has changed in recent years. Pleis and Lucas (2009) reported that 39 per cent of the US adult population may be considered inactive physically and that 61 per cent *never* engage in any vigorous-intensity exercise at all. Furthermore, 35–40 per cent of Americans report that they participate in no leisure-time physical activity (Centres for Disease Control and Prevention, 2007). Little wonder, therefore, that two-thirds of adults in the United States and almost one-third of children are overweight or obese (US Department of Health and Human Services, 2010). Taken together, these statistics suggest not only that physical inactivity is a significant concern for many communities but also that intervention campaigns are required to promote exercise initiation and adherence (Marcus and Forsyth, 2003). Unfortunately, such interventions face formidable barriers. Despite the fact that most people report feeling refreshed or invigorated after they have exercised (Gauvin and Rejeski, 1993; Gauvin et al., 2000), about half of those who commence a supervised physical activity programme drop out of it within six months (Dishman, 2001). Although these twin difficulties of exercise initiation and exercise adherence have been acknowledged by scholars for several decades, little agreement exists about their causes, consequences or solution (Morgan and Dishman, 2001). The main reason is that historically, research on physical activity has been descriptive in nature rather than theory driven. It is only since 2001 that formal conceptual models of physical activity (e.g., see Spence and Lee, 2003) have begun to replace intuitive models. Compounding this difficulty, critics such as Solnit (2001) have even questioned the degree to which our modern preoccupation with exercise makes sense from an evolutionary perspective (see her quotation at the beginning of this chapter). Happily, in response to the atheoretical nature of much research in exercise psychology, in 2011 a special issue of the journal *Psychology of Sport and Exercise* was devoted to understanding the mechanisms underlying physical activity behaviour change, as well as the methods used to study such theoretical mechanisms (see Nigg et al., 2011a).

Against this background, the purpose of this chapter is twofold. Not only does it review psychological research findings on the benefits and hazards of engaging in regular physical activity, but also it summarizes some key discoveries and unresolved issues in the study of people's exercise behaviour. These two themes are linked by the paradox to which I referred earlier. Although most people realize that physical activity is good for them, they appear to be reluctant to engage in it habitually. This problem has a long history. For every advocate of exercise (such as Rousseau, Thoreau or James), there are mischievous sceptics like Henry Ford and Al Pacino who extol the merits of indolence and a sedentary lifestyle. Although these latter sentiments are usually intended to be humorous, they remind us that certain kinds of exercise are potentially hazardous. If people's involvement in physical activity becomes excessive, they may develop a maladaptive pattern of compulsive behaviour known as **exercise dependence** (see later in the chapter). Given the physical and psychological distress which this syndrome can cause the afflicted person, it is important to learn about its aetiology and treatment. In summary, the main objective of this chapter is to investigate the "exercise" part of the discipline of sport and exercise psychology. This task involves analysis of the benefits, costs and psychological issues arising from people's involvement in physical activity.

In the next section, I explain the nature and goals of the discipline of exercise psychology. This section includes an analysis of the meaning of key terms such as physical activity, exercise and physical fitness. In the third section of the chapter, I provide a summary and critical appraisal of research on the main health benefits associated with regular physical activity. To balance this discussion, two potential problems linked to habitual exercise (namely, **overtraining** and exercise dependence) are also examined. In the fourth section, I outline the main theories and research findings on the issues of exercise initiation (the take-up problem) and exercise adherence (the keeping it up problem). This section includes a brief analysis of why people drop out from physical activity programmes and some practical advice on how to build up an effective habit of exercise. Finally, a number of ideas for possible research projects in this field are sketched.

What is exercise psychology? Exploring physical activity, exercise and physical fitness

Exercise psychology emerged as a distinct field of academic study in the 1980s (K. Fox, 2001). According to a classic definition by Buckworth and Dishman

(2002, p. 17), this discipline explores "the brain and behaviour in physical activity and exercise settings". Although research on the correlates of physical activity has a long if somewhat chequered history, it is only since the late 1980s that exercise psychology became an accepted subdiscipline of sport psychology. In 1988 the *Journal of Sport Psychology* was renamed the *Journal of Sport **and Exercise** Psychology* (Diane Gill, 1987; my emphasis) in recognition of the emergence of a distinct field of research pertaining to physical activity, exercise and fitness. This change heralded the official arrival of "exercise" as a scientifically respectable construct for research psychologists. More importantly, it showed that the traditional goal of the discipline of sport psychology – namely, performance enhancement in athletes (see also Chapter 1) – had expanded to include a concern for the promotion of exercise behaviour in the general population. The prominence of "exercise" in sport and exercise psychology can be gauged from the fact that Division 47 of the American Psychological Association is called "*Exercise* and Sport Psychology" (my italics) – not the other way around. In summary, whereas the traditional focus of sport and exercise psychology was on performance enhancement, there has been an upsurge of interest since the late 1980s in the relationship between people's participation in exercise and their health and well-being (Singer and Burke, 2002).

Although exercise psychology is a relatively new field, it has a venerable ancestry. One of the progenitors of this field was Hippocrates, the Greek physician, who emphasized the health benefits associated with regular physical activity. Influenced by such ancient ideas as well as by subsequent developments in sport psychology, physical education and sports medicine, exercise psychology is concerned broadly with two main research questions. First, what are the psychological effects of exercise? Second, what factors are associated with people's participation in physical activity? This latter question involves the study of the adoption, maintenance and consequences of exercise behaviour. According to K. Fox (2001), the origin of these two seminal questions can be traced as follows. The first of them arose mainly from curiosity about the scientific basis of the "feel good" phenomenon whereby people who exercise regularly tend to experience positive mood changes and an enhanced sense of well-being which they usually attribute to the physical activity in question. The second objective of exercise psychology emerged largely from a concern with certain health-related benefits of regular exercise. Specifically, if exercise is associated with a reduced susceptibility to coronary heart disease, obesity and high blood pressure, how can people be persuaded to take up and maintain the habit of taking exercise regularly? These twin aims of exercise psychology are addressed later in the chapter. Before doing so, however, some conceptual clarification is necessary.

So far this chapter has used the terms "physical activity" and "exercise" synonymously, but there are important differences between these terms which need to be elucidated. Perhaps most significantly, although exercise is a type of physical activity, not all physical activity may be classified as exercise: the construct of "physical activity" is broader than that of "exercise". Caspersen (1985) defined physical activity as any bodily movement that is produced by the skeletal muscles and which results in the expenditure of energy. Of course, for any significant health benefits to be derived from such energy expenditure, the activity would have to be well above resting levels. Physical activity may be divided informally into such categories as "moderate" (e.g., walking briskly) and "vigorous" (e.g., jogging, running). Another popular distinction within this construct is that between leisure-time physical activity (where people choose to expend energy in the service of some hobby or interest) and occupational physical activity (which is undertaken in the context of one's job or domestic setting). "Exercise" is usually regarded as being a subcategory of physical activity. It is understood as a leisure-time physical activity that people engage in for the purpose of developing physical fitness (which can be defined broadly as "the ability to perform work satisfactorily": Gauvin and Spence, 1995, p. 435). More precisely, exercise is the "planned, structured and repetitive bodily movement done to improve or maintain one or more components of physical fitness" (American College of Sports Medicine, 2006, p. 3). Of course, there is considerable overlap between the terms "physical activity" and "exercise". So, in keeping with the recommendation of Biddle and Mutrie (2008), this chapter uses the term "exercise" to designate such structured, leisure-time types of physical activity as walking, running, keep fit activities and participation in recreational sports. By the way, psychologists distinguish between two types of exercise behaviour: acute and chronic activity. Acute exercise refers to a single, relatively short bout of exercise, while chronic exercise is conducted several times a week for relatively long periods of time. They also distinguish between the intensities with which the exercise is conducted. Westerterp (2001) suggested that short bursts of high-intensity exercise (e.g., "working out" in the gym) may not be as beneficial to health as is engaging in low-intensity physical activities such as walking. Apparently, strenuous exercisers tend to compensate for bouts of energy expenditure by doing less activity for the remainder of the day!

Having distinguished between the terms "physical activity" and "exercise", let us now turn to another important question. How do we measure physical activity behaviour? In Box 8.1, this question is addressed.

Box 8.1 How can we assess physical activity? Subjective and objective measures

Accurate measurement of physical activity is crucial to theoretical and practical progress in sport and exercise psychology. There are two main ways to assess physical activity – subjective and objective measures (Ainsworth, 2009; Marshall and Welk, 2008), which assess the caloric energy expenditure that results from physical activity in different ways.

Subjective measures
Among the most widely used psychological techniques for assessing physical activity are self-report measures such as questionnaires (Warren et al., 2010). These measures require respondents to assess or recall their own physical activity level over a designated period of time (see Sallis and Saelens, 2000; Shepard, 2003). Although these measures have the same limitations as all self-report instruments (e.g., threats to validity and reliability arising from problems such as recall biases and social desirability response sets), they are easy

and convenient to use with large samples of people. Increasingly, self-report measures are validated against objective tools for the assessment of physical activity.

Objective measures
Objective measures of physical activity include the use of direct observation of the behaviour in question, motion-sensor devices such as pedometers (small devices worn at the waist that are triggered when the person walks) and accelerometers (devices for measuring acceleration at the vertical plane), and heart rate monitors (for a review of objective measures of activity, see Dale et al., 2002). Of these measures, accelerometers are perhaps the widely used objective indices of physical activity (Marshall and Welk, 2008; Troiano et al., 2008).

Accelerometers are electronic devices that include electronic sensors designed to detect accelerations in various planes (anteroposterior, mediolateral and vertical). The data from across these planes are recorded by the internal memory of the device and can be downloaded to a computer (Chen and Bassett, 2005). Accelerometers are typically used to collect data on habitual physical activity over a number of days. Although they yield precise data, they suffer from certain limitations such as their inability to detect upper body movement when worn at the waist (Warren et al., 2010). They are also very costly – a fact which can be prohibitive in large-scale studies (Livingstone et al., 2003). A good discussion of the strengths and weaknesses of questionnaires and objective methods for measuring physical activity is in Ainsworth (2009).

Critical thinking questions
Which of these types of measures do you think would be more suitable for a large scale survey of adolescent physical activity levels? Which ones would work best for an in-depth analysis of a small sample of residents in a care home for elderly people? Give reasons for your answers. Would you expect to find a close correspondence between the data yielded by subjective and objective measures? If not, why not? Can sedentary behaviour be measured in the same way as physical activity behaviour is assessed (see Marshall and Welk, 2008)?

In general, psychology researchers regard exercise as a multifaceted construct. It can include various types of physical behaviour which people perform alone (e.g., a set of fitness exercises that one engages in before going to work) or in groups (e.g., dance classes). It also includes activities that are categorized as being either competitive (e.g., sport) or non-competitive (e.g., leisure pursuits) and **aerobic exercise** (e.g., vigorous actions such as jogging which stimulate pulmonary and cardiovascular systems) or **anaerobic exercise** (e.g., less intense activities such as golf). In summary, despite its wide variety of referents, the term "exercise" always involves the idea of exertion. This exertion can be undertaken either as a means to an end (e.g., when climbing the stairs to one's office because the lift is broken) or as an end in itself (e.g., going for a long walk for the intrinsic pleasure of the activity itself;

see also Chapter 2). We shall see later in the chapter that the question of whether or not exercise has a *purpose and context* has important implications for people's willingness to adhere to it. Morgan (2001) argued that "Factor P" – a sense of purpose – is missing from many exercise regimes that people adopt at present. He criticized much of the exercise behaviour that people undertake in gyms as being "non-purposeful" because it involves a great deal of "walking or running on a treadmill to nowhere, climbing stairs to nowhere, cycling and rowing ... to nowhere" (Morgan, 2001, p. 372). It is not surprising that such exercise soon becomes boring for many people. By contrast, he exhorted people to rediscover the joy of "purposeful" physical activity such as walking one's dog or commuting actively (e.g., cycling) to work. Some of these ideas are echoed in Solnit's (2001) analysis of the significance of modern gyms, drawn from her book *Wanderlust: A History of Walking* (see Box 8.2).

Box 8.2 On treadmills, gyms and the myth of Sisyphus ... thinking about the modern meaning of exercise

In a fascinating book called *Wanderlust: A History of Walking*, Rebecca Solnit (2001) meditated on the question of what it means to go for a walk. As this is no longer possible in many urban areas due to road design and traffic congestion, gyms have arisen as places of exercise. But what happens symbolically in such places? In a chapter entitled "Aerobic Sisyphus", Solnit draws an analogy between people's exercise behaviour in gyms (especially their use of treadmills) and the psychological experience of repetitive labour captured in the ancient Greek myth of Sisyphus. According to this myth, the Gods punished Sisyphus, who had robbed and murdered people, by condemning him to push a boulder up a hill for eternity. Extending this analogy, Solnit (2001, p. 261) argued that just as the suntan became fashionable when poor people moved from outdoor work to the factories, muscular development has now become a status symbol simply because most jobs no longer require bodily strength. Muscles, like tans, are "an aesthetic of the obsolete". Based on this assumption, the gym becomes something more than a convenient location in which to engage in exercise behaviour. It is a "factory for the production of muscles, or of fitness" (Solnit, 2001, p. 262). Viewed from this perspective, the treadmill becomes "a Sisyphean contraption" that prevents people from walking anywhere – a device which celebrates people's alienation because it allows them "to go nowhere in places where there is now nowhere to go". The treadmill has replaced the outdoor environment that people used to walk in naturally: "space – as landscape, terrain, spectacle, experience – has vanished" (Solnit, 2001, pp. 264, 266).

Critical thinking questions
Do you agree with Solnit's provocative views that gyms are really just shrines to narcissism or "factories" concerned with the production of fashionable body shapes? Is she correct when she attacks the mindless glorification of exercise in gyms? What are the advantages and disadvantages of exercising indoors? Do you think that the myth of Sisyphus is a valid analogy for certain kinds of

exercise? After all, in the original version of the myth, Sisyphus varied the absurd and repetitive task of pushing the boulder up the hill by changing the *pace* of the activity. He trained himself to change the way in which he tackled the task so that it would never be boring (Ravizza, 2002).

An important theme emerging from the criticisms of Morgan (2001) and Solnit (2001) is that in order to yield optimal benefits, physical activity requires both a sense of purpose and a natural context. It is not surprising, therefore, that the potential advantages of exercising *outdoors* have attracted increasing interest from the scientific community. For example, a general practitioner, Dr William Bird (cited in Sam Murphy, 2001) established the "Green Gym", a conservation project that combines the idea of ecological work with purposeful physical activity. The Green Gym requires people to work out by undertaking tasks such as building stiles, cutting trees and repairing fences in natural surroundings. Extending this idea, researchers have begun to explore the potential benefits of exercising in relatively natural environments – a field known as "green exercise" (Pretty et al., 2007). In an early study in this field, Bodin and Hartig (2003) investigated the relative effects of different environmental contexts on the benefits yielded by a bout of vigorous exercise. They conducted a field experiment in which twelve regular runners exercised alternately in park and urban environments. These environments differed with regard to such factors as the extent of greenery encountered, proximity to water and amount of motor traffic apparent. The hypothesis was that the psychological benefits of running would be stronger for the runners in the park than in the urban condition. Results showed that although the runners preferred the park to the urban environment, and perceived it as being more psychologically "restorative", no significant effect of exercise environment was evident on psychometric indices of emotional and attentional variables. Mackay and Neill (2010) investigated the short-term effects of "green exercise" on state anxiety (for a detailed treatment of anxiety, see Chapter 3). Results showed that there was a significant reduction in anxiety among people who had engaged in outdoor exercise. The mechanisms underlying this effect remain unclear, however.

Having raised some questions about the symbolic meaning of exercise in modern life, let us consider what the term "physical fitness" means. According to Biddle and Mutrie (2008, p. 10), this concept of fitness refers to people's capacity "to perform muscular work". The President's Council on Physical Fitness (2003, p. 1) defined it as "the ability to perform daily tasks vigorously and alertly, with energy left over for enjoying leisure-time activities and meeting emergency demands. It is the ability to endure, to bear up, to withstand stress". Also it is "a major basis for good health and well-being". There are four main components of fitness. First, *cardio-respiratory endurance* or aerobic fitness refers to the ability of the circulatory and respiratory systems to supply oxygen and nutrients to body tissues during sustained physical activity. It is an index of the efficiency with which one's heart, lungs and caridiovascular system work. It is assessed in the laboratory using the "VO_2 max" test (which measures the body's maximal oxygen uptake or its aerobic capacity for endurance exercise) and in field settings by tests like the "one mile run" or the "one mile walk". Second, *muscular strength* is the ability of the muscles to exert force for brief periods of time. It is assessed commonly by the "handgrip" test. Third, *muscular endurance* refers to the ability of the muscles to sustain repeated contractions and to exert force against a fixed object, without fatigue. It is usually measured using isokinetic machines. Fourth, fitness is also indicated by *muscular flexibility*, understood as the range of motion available to a joint without discomfort or pain. It may be measured in the lab using apparatus like the "goniometer" and in field contexts using various "sit-and-reach" exercises. Another putative index of fitness is *body composition* as assessed by the ratio of fat to lean body mass (LeUnes and Nation, 2002). In summary, the health-related components of physical fitness include cardiovascular fitness, muscular strength, muscular endurance, muscular flexibility and body composition.

Given the importance of regular physical activity for a healthy lifestyle, how does **health psychology** fit into the picture? According to Buckworth and Dishman (2002, p. 10), this latter discipline is concerned with "the scientific understanding of how behavioural principles relate to health and illness". It differs from exercise psychology in at least one significant way: whereas the latter field is concerned mainly with the study of physical activity, exercise behaviour and/or physical fitness as *dependent* variables (typically indicated by measures such as VO$_2$ max), health psychology has traditionally explored these processes as *independent* variables (Rejeski and Thompson, 1993).

Exploring the benefits and hazards of physical activity

The idea that physical exercise confers a number of health benefits on people dates back at least as far as the fourth or fifth centuries BCE (Buckworth and Dishman, 2002). Thus the Greek physicians Herodicus (*c.* 480 BCE), Hippocrates (*c.* 460–377 BCE) and Galen (*c.* 199–129 BCE) advocated the importance of exercise in treating various forms of illness. This "gymnastic medicine" approach continues to the present day, but with one important difference. Contemporary physicians do not just recommend exercise as a form of treatment for illness but as a *preventive* measure in an effort to counteract the health risks posed by people's increasingly sedentary lifestyles. Individuals are usually deemed as being "sedentary" if they engage in little or no physical activity. The health risks associated with such a lifestyle include coronary artery disease, colon cancer, depression, hypertension, osteoporosis and strokes (A. Bauman, 2004). Indeed, so worried are many health scientists about these problems that the insidious effects of an inactive lifestyle have been called "the silent enemy" or "sedentary death syndrome" (A. Bauman, 2004). The prevalence of this problem can be gauged from certain epidemiological trends. Caspersen and Merritt (1995) discovered that less than 10 per cent of a sample of almost 35,000 adults in the United States exercised enough to obtain significant fitness benefits from their efforts. The problem of physical inactivity has been reported to be more common among women than men, among older than younger adults and among less affluent than more affluent people in most developed countries (Kruger et al., 2005; US Department of Health and Human Services, 1996). As a consequence of such data, a picture is emerging of a lifestyle in the twenty-first century whereby people have to *plan* to exercise simply because they no longer expend enough physical energy to achieve health benefits through manual work or even as result of walking or cycling to work on a daily basis. But as we shall see later in this chapter, planning or having an intention to exercise is no guarantee of actually doing it. Another problem that we shall encounter concerns the fact that exercise prescription should not be undertaken naively. Sime (2002) warned that, for this practice to be effective, the physician in question must set realistic goals and provide regular supervision or guidance to the patient. Otherwise, this patient may not achieve his or her exercise targets and hence end up feeling more depressed and guilty than beforehand.

Before reviewing the research literature on the effects of regular physical activity, it is important to point out that there have been far more studies on the *positive* effects (i.e., the benefits) of exercise on physical and psychological processes than on its negative consequences – a trend which I hope to rectify in this chapter. Let us now summarize the principal research findings on the benefits of exercise for both physical and mental health processes. After that, a brief evaluation of some important conceptual and methodological issues in this field will be provided.

Physical benefits of regular activity

People who are habitually sedentary can increase their level of physical activity in two main ways. First, they can take up exercise classes or engage in such traditional fitness pursuits as walking briskly, cycling, running or swimming. Second, they can increase their level of physical activity by adopting a lifestyle approach whereby they make active choices to engage in exercise in everyday situations. For example, they might decide to walk or cycle to work and/or to take the stairs to their office rather than using the lift. Regardless of the mode of physical activity chosen, a considerable volume of research has accumulated on the health benefits arising from regular physical activity (see reviews by Biddle and Mutrie, 2008; Landers and Arent, 2007; Warburton et al., 2006).

Much of the research on this topic is summarized in various reports of the Surgeon General since the 1990s. For example, three conclusions regarding the physical benefits of regular exercise were evident in the 1996 Surgeon General's report (US Department of Health and Human Services, 1996). First, people of all ages can derive significant health benefits from cumulative amounts of moderately intense physical activity (e.g., thirty minutes of brisk walking or fifteen minutes of running) undertaken on several days per week. This finding is important because it shows that physical activity does not have to be strenuous in order to be advantageous – a point to which I shall return later. So, it looks as though the popular phrase "no pain, no gain" is seriously mistaken. Mutrie et al. (2002) demonstrated that a self-help, active commuting intervention called the "walk in to work out" programme was successful in increasing people's walking behaviour (but not cycling) in travelling to work. Culos-Reed et al. (2008) discovered that an eight-week "mall-walking" programme helped to increase the physical activity behaviour and fitness of a group of middle-aged to elderly participants. Research cited by the Surgeon General's report also indicates that additional health benefits can be achieved by taking part in physical activity that is of a longer duration or of a more vigorous intensity than the minimal "thirty minutes a day" criterion. Second, physical activity reduces the risk of such common and costly problems as premature mortality, coronary heart disease, high blood pressure, colon cancer, obesity and non-insulin-dependent diabetes mellitus. It is also important for maintaining the health of people's bones, muscles and joints – and and is a useful aid in the prevention of osteoarthritis. Third, activities which develop muscular strength ("resistance training") should be performed at least twice per week in order to yield significant fitness benefits. Ideally, at least eight to ten such exercises should be performed at each session, with at least ten repetitions of the relevant exercise required each time. In summary, physical activity is associated with a reduction in a number of risk-factors for health. The magnitude of this relationship is quite strong and can be gauged from the fact that the Surgeon General's report (US Department of Health and Human Services, 1996) claims that the link between physical inactivity and cardiovascular illness is approximately equivalent to that between smoking and coronary heart disease. The Surgeon General's *Vision for a Healthy and Fit Nation* (US Department of Health and Human Services, 2010, p. 6) reiterated that "physical activity can help control weight, reduce risk for many diseases ... strengthen your bones and muscles, improve your mental health, and increase your chances of living longer". Based on such evidence, the Surgeon General recommends that adults should engage in at least 150 minutes of moderate intensity physical activity per week.

What physiological mechanisms underlie the positive effects of physical activity on health? Not surprisingly, the answer to this question depends on the type of medical condition involved (see Ogden, 2000). Regular activity seems to reduce coronary heart disease either by stimulating the muscles that support the heart or by increasing the electrical activity of the heart itself. Also, it lowers blood pressure, thereby decreasing the chances of a stroke. Because exercise improves glucose metabolism, it is associated with a reduction in people's susceptibility to diabetes (a medical condition in which one's body either fails to produce enough insulin to power the muscles or else uses prevailing insulin inefficiently). Physical exercise can act like insulin for people who suffer from diabetes (P. Weston, 2002). Regular exercise also strengthens the skeletomuscular system by improving joint and muscle flexibility. On account of these benefits, people who exercise regularly are "functionally younger in these various physical capacities and aerobic power than their sedentary age-mates" (Bandura, 1997, p. 407). By contrast, sedentary adults age twice as fast as nature intended (O'Brien Cousins, 2003).

Psychological health benefits of regular physical activity

In accordance with the intuitive insights of William James (see first section of this chapter), regular activity appears to produce a number of mental as well as physical health benefits for people of all ages. The purpose of this section is to summarize some of these psychological (affective and cognitive) benefits (but for more extensive reviews, see Biddle and Mutrie, 2008; Buckworth and Dishman, 2002; Landers and Arent, 2007). Before doing so, however, an important caution must be expressed. Briefly, due to their ephemeral nature, the affective aspects of people's exercise behaviour – namely, their feelings, moods and emotions – are difficult to conceptualize and measure. As a result, research in this area is bedevilled by semantic confusion. Consider the phenomenology of "feelings". Is a feeling *of* something (e.g., fatigue after a run) the same as a feeling *about* something (e.g., apprehension before a race)? Many definitional issues need to be clarified in this field (Gauvin and Spence, 1998). For the purpose of this chapter, I use the term "mood" to refer to an emotional state that is characterized by the experience or anticipation of either pleasure or pain (Buckworth and Dishman, 2002); one can be in a positive mood (when anticipating pleasure) or a negative mood (when anticipating pain).

First, research suggests that people who perform moderate amounts of physical activity regularly (e.g., at least three times a week for approximately thirty minutes each time) tend to experience significantly improved mood states, as measured by such self-report instruments as the Profile of Mood States (POMS: McNair et al., 1992) and/or reductions in anxiety (e.g., Berger and Motl, 2000; Folkins and Sime, 1981). In a meta-analysis of forty studies on this topic, Long and van Stavel (1995) reported that exercise had a significant effect on anxiety levels, with an effect size of 0.36 standard deviations relative to control conditions. Other research shows that, in practical terms, self-rated levels of state anxiety (see Chapter 3) are lowered by about one-quarter of a standard deviation within twenty minutes of participation in acute bouts of continuous exercise such as cycling, swimming or running (O'Connor et al., 2000). Berger and Motl (2000) recommended that in order to maximize exercise-induced mood enhancement, the physical activity undertaken should be enjoyable, aerobic, non-competitive and performed at moderate intensity for at least twenty to thirty minutes. This relationship between exercise and mood is complex because it is mediated by several factors. Consider the intensity with which the physical activity is conducted. Mutrie (2001) reported that moderate levels of such activity (e.g., taking a brisk walk) tend to produce more positive effects on people's sense of well-being than do more vigorous activities such as jogging or running.

Second, research suggests that frequent exercise is associated with a reduction in reported symptoms of depression (e.g., France et al., 2004; Martinsen and Morgan, 1997). To evaluate this relationship more rigorously, Lawlor and Hopker (2001) conducted a meta-analysis of studies in this field. Adopting strict inclusion criteria, these authors focused solely on studies which had used randomized controlled trials in their research design. By combining relevant results from fourteen such studies, Lawlor and Hopker (2001) discovered that physical activity had a relatively large effect on depression scores when compared with data yielded by control conditions. The results also showed that the effects of such activity on depression were similar to those of cognitive therapy – a finding which raises the intriguing possibility that exercise can be prescribed as a form of therapy for people who are depressed (see also Sime, 2002). Even though studies have shown that exercise can be as effective as cognitive therapy, only 21 per cent of general practioners reported that they tend to prescribe a supervised programme of exercise as a treatment for mild to moderate depression (Mental Health Foundation, 2009). This figure has increased significantly from only 4 per cent five years earlier, in 2004 (see Mental Health Foundation, 2009). Among the putative mechanisms for this effect is the neurobiological possibility that exercise triggers the release of "morphine-like", pain-reducing **neurotransmitters** in the brain. Animal research shows that aerobic exercise improves brain function by stimulating new capillary growth, increasing blood flow and boosting the production of proteins that improve neuron functioning (Azar, 2010). Of course, exercise may also work by giving people a "time out" from their daily stresses and/or boost their self-esteem. Box 8.3 explores these rival explanations of the psychological effects of exercise behaviour.

Box 8.3 Explaining the beneficial effects of physical activity: is it all in the mind?

It is widely agreed that people who are physically active tend to report significantly lower rates of anxiety and depression than do their more sedentary counterparts. What theoretical mechanisms could account for this finding?

Since the 1990s, exercise psychologists have proposed at least three possible explanations for the beneficial effects of physical activity on problems such as anxiety and depression. These three explanations – the neurobiological, cognitive and self-efficacy theories – may be summarized as follows. First, advocates of the neurobiological approach argue that both acute and chronic physical activity triggers the release of neurotransmitters such as norepinephrine or **serotonin** in the brain (e.g., Chauloff, 1997; Hoffmann, 1997). This release is alleged to reduce the painful effects of exercise while enhancing concomitant pleasurable sensations. Although the **endorphin hypothesis** has great popular appeal, it is poorly supported scientifically; few studies have reported any evidence of empirical associations between exercisers' mood changes and their release of **endorphins** (Buckworth and Dishman, 2002). Second, proponents of cognitive explanations of exercise effects (e.g., Morgan, 1985) tend to emphasize a "distraction" or "time out" effect. The idea here is that exercise offers participants a period of respite from the stresses and worries of everyday life. One implication of this theory is that it is not the exercise itself but the change in context in which it occurs that enhances people's sense of psychological well-being. Unfortunately, as the evidence bearing upon this theory is somewhat equivocal (e.g., see Bodin and Hartig, 2003), its explanatory value is questionable. Third, another explanation of beneficial exercise effects comes from research on self-efficacy or people's beliefs in their "capabilities to organize and execute the courses of action required to produce given attainments" (Bandura, 1997, p. 3). According to this theory, exercise is beneficial because it helps people in a practical way to increase their sense of mastery over their behaviour. Some support has been reported for the theory that self-efficacy mediates the relationship between exercise and health (see Bozoian et al., 1994).

Critical thinking questions

Which of these explanations do you think is most plausible? Why do you think the endorphin explanation of exercise benefits is so popular given its rather shaky scientific foundations? Can you think of any other ways (besides that of Bodin and Hartig, 2003) of testing the theory that physical activity offers people some respite from the stress and tedium of everyday life?

A third finding from relevant research is that regular physical activity seems to enhance people's sense of self-esteem. In evaluating research on this topic, K. Fox (2000) reviewed thirty-six randomized controlled studies on the relationship between physical activity and self-esteem. Of these thirty-six studies, twenty-eight (78 per cent) reported evidence of positive changes in self-perception or self-esteem – especially with regard to body image. Also, greater benefits were apparent among those who were initially relatively low in self-esteem.

Overall, these data led K. Fox (2002, p. 95) to conclude that the relationship between exercise and self-esteem is a "robust and significant finding". Unfortunately, the psychological mechanisms underlying this beneficial effect remain largely unknown.

The fourth documented benefit of habitual exercise on mental processes concerns apparent improvements in cognitive functioning – especially in elderly people. This conclusion emerged from empirical studies (e.g., L. Baker et al., 2010) as well as from narrative (e.g., Erickson and Kramer, 2010; Kramer and Erickson, 2007) and meta-analytic reviews of relevant research (Etnier et al., 1997). Moderate physical activity performed in middle age or later seems to be associated with a reduced risk of cognitive impairment (L. Baker et al., 2010). In their review of 134 relevant studies, Etnier et al. (1997) discovered that exercise had a small but significant positive impact (overall adjusted mean effect size of 0.29) on such cognitive variables as memory, mathematical ability, verbal ability, reasoning skills, reaction time and creativity. This beneficial effect was larger for chronic exercise (effect size of 0.33) than for acute exercise (effect size of 0.16). Harada et al. (2001) discovered a link between regular jogging and improved performance on certain working memory tasks. Briefly, seven healthy students jogged for thirty minutes a day (a recommended "dose" of exercise for health benefits – see previous section), three times a week for twelve weeks. The joggers took a series of cognitive tests at three different stages during the study: at the start, after six weeks, and again after twelve weeks. For comparison purposes, seven sedentary participants also took these cognitive tests. Results showed that after the study, the joggers scored significantly higher than their sedentary counterparts on the cognitive tests. These results were interpreted by Harada et al. (2001) as indicating that jogging somehow stimulates the prefrontal areas of the brain. Chang and Etnier (2009) reported that an acute bout of resistance exercise improved participants' cognitive functioning. Furthermore, regular engagement in high-intensity aerobic exercise may improve cognitive functioning in middle-aged and elderly participants (L. Baker et al., 2010).

Before concluding this section, it may be useful to explore the effects of music on physical activity behaviour (see Box 8.4).

Box 8.4 The effects of music on physical activity: exercise for the iPod generation

Many people wear headphones and listen to music as they engage in physical activities such as exercising in the gym, walking in the park, or jogging along the road. In the light of such habits, psychology researchers (e.g., Karageorghis, 2008; Karageorghis et al., 2009, 2010) have examined the effects of various aspects of music on sport and exercise behaviour. Consider the synchronization between musical tempo and human movement. Is it beneficial to exercise in time with the rhythm of the music to which one is listening? Put differently, do synchronous music conditions (i.e., those in which the exerciser's movement is performed consciously *in time* with the rhythm of the music) affect people differently from asynchronous music conditions (i.e., those in which there is no conscious synchronization between the exercisers and the music to which they are listening)? Karageorghis et al. (2009) examined the effects of motivational music (i.e., music with a fast tempo and a strong rhythm), neutral music (or *oudeterous* music as Karageorghis described it) and no music on the performance of university students on a treadmill walking task. Results indicated that endurance was increased in both music conditions and that motivational music had a greater ergogenic (or performance-enhancing) effect than did neutral music. The motivational qualities of music can affect how long an exerciser can endure a repetitive activity. Karageorghis et al. (2009) also found that motivational music increased the positive emotions of the walkers while they walked on the treadmill – but not afterwards. Based on this study, we can conclude that listening to synchronous music can enhance our endurance in exercise situations.

Evaluation of research on the benefits of physical activity

Now that we have identified the main research findings on the health benefits of regular physical activity, we need to take a step back in order to evaluate the quality of research evidence in this field. This critical appraisal is necessary because it goes to the heart of any claim that habitual exercise is good for us. Researchers and practitioners in the field of exercise psychology must be satisfied that the alleged health benefits described above are caused solely by physical activity rather than by other factors. These factors could include intervening variables such as people's expectations about the likely effects of exercise interventions, contextual factors like the environment in which the physical activity occurs (see Bodin and Hartig, 2003) and a host of methodological flaws such as researchers' failure to use non-exercise control groups or to match people for their fitness histories. To prevent inaccurate interpretation of research in this field, therefore, at least five conceptual and methodological issues concerning the benefits of physical activity can be specified as follows.

First, consider the familiar direction of causality issue. In simple terms, are such experiences as "feeling well" and "thinking clearly" the cause or the consequence of people's involvement in regular exercise? As with all causal issues in psychology, this is a complex issue which can be addressed only by the use of controlled experimental research designs. Ideally, such designs would involve a chronic exercise programme in which sedentary participants are assigned randomly to physical activity or control conditions. Unfortunately, the prevalence of correlational research designs in this field makes it difficult to test causal hypotheses about the relationship between exercise and mental processes. In any case, there is a vast array of intervening variables in this relationship. Research indicates that the motives of exercisers and the behaviour of their instructors may affect health experiences. Grant (2000) suggested that the physical activity tends to have its strongest effect on people's mood and sense of well-being when exercisers have a task orientation (see Chapter 2), in which they focus on mastering the exercise activity for its own sake rather than in an effort to exercise better or faster than others in the group (thereby reflecting an ego orientation). In structured exercise situations, the behaviour of the instructor could modify the health benefits yielded by the activity undertaken. Turner et al. (1997) explored the effect of an exercise teacher's leadership style on the affective states of exercise participants. Briefly, these authors asked a sample of female university students to complete a scale designed to measure "exercise-induced" feeling states (see Gauvin and Rejeski, 1993). The women were assigned randomly either to an "enriched" or to a "bland" exercise instruction condition, then they were tested on the inventory once again. Results revealed that participants in the enriched condition scored significantly higher than did those in the bland condition on the affective dimensions of "revitalization" and "positive engagement". This finding was interpreted as showing that the social environment created by an activity instructor may influence the benefits produced by the exercise activity itself. Unfortunately, many exercise psychology researchers have failed either to eliminate or to measure the effects of such intervening variables. Few studies have controlled for the expectations of participants about the efficacy of exercise interventions. This is a pity because Desharnis et al. (1993) found that when people were led to believe that they were receiving exercise which had been designed to improve their well-being, their self-esteem levels actually increased as much as those who had been involved in "real" exercise interventions. There was a self-fulfilling prophecy among people who had volunteered to take part in an exercise programme. For this reason, experimental controls for placebo effects are mandatory in this field.

Second, another conceptual issue in this field stems from terminological confusion. Researchers do not always treat physical fitness as a multidimensional construct and may not distinguish between its different forms – aerobic and anaerobic fitness. The construct of "subjective well-being" is a semantic minefield: it is sometimes defined by positive characteristics (e.g., the presence of feelings of happiness or satisfaction) but on other occasions by the absence of negative emotions such as depression or mood disturbance. Such conceptual vacillation leads to problems of measurement. Several reviewers (e.g., see Berger and Motl, 2001) have lamented the usage of idiosyncratic, unstandardized measures of key variables (e.g., psychological well-being) in exercise psychology. This criticism also applies to measures of affective constructs like anxiety and depression. Thus it is debatable whether available psychometric measures of these constructs are sufficiently sensitive to detect actual changes in these variables as a result of exercise interventions (Buckworth and Dishman, 2002).

Third, one flaw affecting research on the effects of physical activity is that many researchers in this field have combined results obtained from different participant populations. This cavalier attitude is unfortunate because there are significant differences between elite athletes, non-athletic university students, patients in psychiatric settings and people being treated for coronary heart disease. Fourth, a problem encountered in this field concerns the fact that few researchers have bothered to conduct "follow-up" studies on their participants in an effort to assess the long-term effects of exercise activity. A fifth difficulty is the relative neglect by researchers of possible negative consequences of exercise. It is to this issue that we now turn.

Exploring some adverse effects of exercise on health

So far in this chapter, I have argued that physical exercise is a healthy habit, but research suggests that occasionally this habit can have adverse consequences. Injury is a significant risk for people who exercise vigorously or who participate in competitive sports (see Chapter 9). For certain vulnerable people (especially young women), exercise is associated with specific psychopathologies arising from eating disorders and distortions of body image (Buckworth and Dishman, 2002). A variety of physiological health hazards have been found to be associated with habitual physical activity and/or sport. These hazards include metabolic abnormalities (e.g., hypothermia in swimmers or dehydration in marathon runners), blood disorders (e.g., anaemia in endurance athletes) and cardiac problems (e.g., arryhthmia as a result of prolonged vigorous activity). As these conditions fall largely within the realm of sports medicine, they lie outside the scope of this book. Instead, this section is concerned with the issue of what happens when people's exercise habits become excessive, compulsive or otherwise maladaptive. Therefore, I now consider briefly two health hazards that are associated with exercise behaviour – overtraining and exercise dependence. Although the symptoms of these problems are similar, there is one important difference between the conditions: whereas overtraining is largely confined to sports performers, exercise dependence can also occur in non-athlete populations (Buckworth and Dishman, 2002).

It has long been known that intensive training regimes do not always enhance athletic performance. When the nature, intensity and/or frequency of athletic training exceed the body's adaptive capacity and lead to a deterioration in sport performance, overtraining has occurred (Cashmore, 2008). Commonly regarded as a generalized stress response of the body to an extended period of overload, overtraining may be defined as "an abnormal extension of the training process culminating in a state of staleness" (Weinberg and Gould, 1999, pp. 434–435). Other terms for this syndrome include staleness, burnout and "failing adaptation" (Hooper et al., 1993). A theoretical model of this state was proposed by Tenenbaum et al. (2003).

Overtraining has been attributed to a combination of excessive levels of high-intensity training and inadequate rest or recovery time. Although no single, universally agreed diagnostic index of this problem exists, a host of typical physiological and psychological symptoms have been identified. Physiological signs of overtraining include suppressed immune function (with an increased incidence of upper respiratory tract infection), increases in resting heart rate, decreases in testosterone and increases in cortisol concentration and decreases in maximal blood lactate concentration. Apart from a deterioration in athletic performance, common psychological symptoms of this disorder include mood disturbances, feelings of chronic fatigue, loss of appetite, repetitive loading injuries (e.g., shin-splints) and sometimes insomnia (Cashmore, 2008; Morgan et al., 1987). The prevalence of this syndrome can be gauged from the claim by Morgan (2000) that over 50 per cent of all elite male and female marathon runners have overtrained in their careers.

Paradoxically, overtrained athletes tend to perform progressively worse as they try harder. We encountered this phenomenon of diminishing returns in sport performance earlier in the section on choking (Chapter 3). But overtraining differs from choking because it appears to be caused by factors other than excessive anxiety. These factors include inadequate recovery time between bouts of training, prolonged or over-intense training regimes, personal problems and inadequate coping resources (Weinberg and Gould, 2007). Although overtraining has been recognized by sports scientists for decades, little research has been conducted on the putative psychological mechanisms underlying this problem. One mechanism that has been proposed in this regard is mood state. Morgan (2000) claimed that mood disturbance in athletes, as measured by the Profile of Mood States (POMS: McNair et al., 1992), may be causally related to overtraining. Unfortunately, this speculation has received only limited empirical scrutiny, and little theoretical progress has been made in understanding either the precise causes of this problem or the best way to overcome it. Despite the fact that this state is poorly understood, its very existence highlights the need to be sceptical of the adage that "more is better" when it comes to training regimes in sport and exercise.

The second psychological hazard associated with habitual physical activity is exercise dependence (for a comprehensive overview of research in this field, see Kerr et al., 2007). According to Hausenblas and Downs (2002, p. 90), such dependence refers to "a craving for leisure-time physical activity, resulting in uncontrollable excessive exercise, that manifests in physiological (e.g., tolerance/withdrawal) and/ or psychological (e.g., anxiety/depression) symptoms". Other terms for this compulsive behavioural syndrome, which has been studied mainly in runners, include obligatory exercise, excessive exercise and exercise addiction (see detailed review by Hausenblas and Downs, 2002). The last-mentioned of these terms is proposed on the basis that obligatory exercisers may experience withdrawal symptoms if they are deprived of the required physical activity. Despite such withdrawal symptoms, exercise dependence has not yet been classified as an addiction by clinicians.

People who exercise excessively tend to report such symptoms as mood changes, restlessness, irritability, lack of appetite, insomnia and feelings of guilt if a twenty-four to thirty-six hour duration passes by without vigorous physical activity (Sachs, 1981). Support for the addictive nature of this compulsive exercise syndrome in runners was provided by Morgan (1979), who described eight case studies. One index of the strength of this compulsion to exercise came from the fact that the runners in Morgan's (1979) study regarded this activity as being more important than their jobs or than interacting with their spouses, children or friends. These obligatory runners reported that they had sometimes exercised even when in pain and when acting against the advice of their physicians. Despite such case studies of this problem, several questions remain. Can people really become addicted to aerobic exercise in the same way as they might become addicted to drugs? If so, what are the symptoms of this problem? Are there any distinctive psychological factors (e.g., personality characteristics) that make exercisers vulnerable to this problem? In order to answer these questions, we need to examine the research literature on exercise dependence (which amounts to almost eighty published studies: Hausenblas and Downs, 2002).

First, we consider the nature and criteria of exercise dependence. According to Hausenblas and Downs (2002), this construct refers to a multidimensional, maladaptive pattern of physical activity which leads to clinically significant impairments or distress in the exerciser. Precise diagnostic criteria include evidence of *three or more* of the following seven features:

- *tolerance* (i.e., either a need for significantly increased amounts of exercise to achieve the desired effect or diminished effects with the same amount of exercise)
- *withdrawal* (i.e., evidence of withdrawal symptoms such as anxiety or fatigue when the person is deprived of exercise)
- *intention effects* (i.e., exercise is often taken in greater amounts or for longer durations than was intended)
- *loss of control* (whereby unsuccessful efforts are made to reduce the amount of exercise taken)
- *time* (a large amount of time is taken up by the activity)
- *conflict* (i.e., important occupational or social activities are given up because of exercise)
- *continuance* (i.e., the person continues to exercise even when confronted by physical or psychological impediments, such as injury).

Second, in addition to these diagnostic criteria, another distinction is required when analysing exercise dependence. Hausenblas and Downs (2002) indicated that if obligatory exercise is performed as an end in itself, it is classified as *primary* exercise dependence. However, if it is undertaken in order to control body composition or shape, as happens in the case of eating disorders (see Blumenthal et al., 1984), it is regarded as *secondary* exercise dependence. In sport and exercise settings, at least two forms of secondary exercise dependence have been identified – the first associated with eating disorders and the second with a condition called muscle dysmorphia (i.e., a chronic preoccupation with the belief that one is insufficiently muscular: Pope et al., 1997, p. 550; see a review by Tod and Lavallee, 2010). Research suggests that the proposed link between eating disorders and high levels of exercise is somewhat controversial (Biddle and Mutrie, 2008). Adams (2009) reported that excessive exercise habits are found among patients with anorexia or bulimia. However, Szabo's (2000) review of sixteen studies examining the relationship between eating disorders and exercise behavior was inconclusive. Intriguingly, Cook and Hausenblas (2008) suggested that it is the *symptoms* of exercise dependence rather than the behaviour itself that is predictive of disordered eating behaviors such as bulimia nervosa. The amount of exercise (e.g., frequency, duration or intensity) being undertaken by the person might not be as important in predicting eating disorders as is the person's *motivation* for engaging in exercise in the first place. Turning to muscle dysmorphia, this disorder is the primary condition and the secondary issue is the person's dependence on the exercise behaviour in question, which is usually weightlifting (Biddle and Mutrie, 2008). Although research on this topic is sparse, there are indications that the condition tends to appear in late adolescence and may involve individuals spending more than three hours per day thinking about their muscularity (Cafri et al., 2008).

Having explained the nature and types of exercise dependence, we should now return to an important conceptual issue in this field. To what extent is the obligatory exerciser suffering from an addiction? Superficially, the concept of exercise addiction seems plausible for several reasons. First, as we learned earlier in this chapter, chronic exercise is associated with changes in the brain levels of neurotransmitters like norepinephrine and serotonin – substances which are known to influence people's moods. Thus exercise addiction may have a neurobiological basis. Second, just like people who are addicted to drugs of any kind, exercise addicts may develop a tolerance for their habit. In this case, "tolerance" is indicated when people require longer, more intense and more frequent physical work-outs in order to maintain the same levels of satisfaction with their exercise. However, as Aidman and Woollard (2003) pointed out, this tolerance criterion may apply only to the *later* stages of exercise dependence, which makes it unsuitable as a diagnostic indicator. However, this objection does not apply to the third criterion of exercise addiction – namely, the existence of post-deprivation withdrawal symptoms such as increased fatigue, depression, anger and irritability (Sachs, 1981). Remarkably, some studies suggest that these symptoms can be detected in athletes after only *one day* without exercise. Aidman and Woollard (2003) discovered that club runners who abstained from their daily training run experienced significantly more withdrawal symptoms than did runners who maintained their normal training regime. This finding is somewhat counter-intuitive because it suggests that committed runners who have an extra rest day may end up feeling more tired than those who exercise every day! This addiction criterion of withdrawal symptoms is by no means clear-cut, however. For example, cocaine dependence does not always yield withdrawal symptoms (Aidman and Woollard, 2003). In summary, doubts exist about the validity of classifying compulsive exercise behaviour as an addiction.

Some critics are sceptical of the value of debating the addictive status of exercise dependence. Morgan (2000) suggested that it does not really matter whether a runner is said to be "addicted" to, "dependent" on, or "abusing" exercise. What does matter, he claimed, is that when such runners are prevented from exercising, they usually experience significant distress – a phenomenon which "exercise evangelicals" (Morgan, 2000, p. 304) have been slow to acknowledge. And so, we come to the question of whether compulsive exercise behaviour is ultimately helpful or harmful. This question is considered in Box 8.5.

Box 8.5 Thinking critically about … the dangers of compulsive exercise behaviour

Regular physical activity not only is an enjoyable habit but also confers such important health benefits on its practitioners as strengthening muscles, controlling weight and increasing endurance. Unfortunately, some people appear to become addicted to physical activity and engage in compulsive exercise that is extreme in its frequency and often conducted at inappropriate times and in inappropriate places (for a more detailed list of symptoms of this problem, see Hausenblas and Giaccobi, 2004). Although the prevalence of compulsive exercise behaviour in the general population is not known precisely, a study by Villella et al. (2011) reported that it affected about 8.5 per cent of a large sample (n=2,853) of Italian adolescents. Against this background, what do we know about compulsive exercise behaviour? Is it just a harmless fad or a potentially serious problem for its practitioners?

In the 1970s, at the boom of the "jogging generation", Glasser (1976) referred to obligatory running as a "positive addiction" because he believed that it produced psychological benefits such as increased alertness, an improved sense of well-being and control, and feelings of euphoria. Several years later, however, Morgan (1979) challenged this optimistic view by describing compulsive exercise behaviour as a "negative addiction" on the grounds that it not only was characterized by punishing schedules of daily physical training but also resulted in withdrawal symptoms (e.g., depression, fatigue and restlessness) when prevented. Which of these theoretical perspectives is more accurate? As usual in psychology, research has shown that there is some truth on both sides of the argument. For example, J. Kerr (1997) observed that there are probably two distinct types of exercise-dependent people. First, some people engage in excessive exercise as a means of achieving a particular state of mind (e.g., a feeling of tiredness yet satisfaction after a period of strenuous physical activity). Second, a small minority of people engage in excessive exercise for psychopathological reasons (e.g., associated with eating-disordered behaviour: see Taranis and Meyer, 2011).

Critical thinking questions
What are the advantages and disadvantages of regarding the construct of compulsive exercise behaviour as a continuum rather than as a single phenomenon? What research methods could you use to investigate people's motivation for engaging in apparently compulsive exercise behaviour? Do you think that gender differences are likely to be apparent among compulsive exercisers? Give reasons for your answer and then check the research literature using a database such as PsycINFO.

Having considered some important conceptual issues surrounding exercise dependence, I now sketch some research findings in this field.

First, attempts to measure exercise dependence rely mostly on self-reported assessments of the frequency, duration and/or intensity of the physical activity under scrutiny. Whereas earlier scales were unidimensional (e.g., the Obligatory Running Questionnaire: Blumenthal et al., 1984), more recent measures of exercise dependence have been multidimensional. The Exercise Dependence Questionnaire (Ogden et al., 1997) measures both neurobiological (e.g., tolerance, withdrawal) and psychosocial symptoms (e.g., interference with social and occupational commitments) of the problem. Unfortunately, many of these self-report scales are inadequate psychometrically. Also, due to a paucity of relevant normative data, most measures of exercise dependence cannot be used validly for diagnostic purposes (Hausenblas and Downs, 2002). Second, another general finding is that in spite of speculation about the association between compulsive physical activity and such personality characteristics as perfectionism, no distinctive profile of the "exercise addict" has yet emerged. Third, little progress has been made in identifying precisely what exercise-dependent people miss when they are prevented from habitual physical activity. Is it the aerobic activity itself, or the context in which it is undertaken, or some combination of these factors? Until this issue has been resolved, it will be difficult to understand how people's apparent addiction to exercise develops (Aidman and Woollard, 2003). To summarize, given the many gaps in the research literature in this field, it is not surprising that there are no agreed criteria for either diagnosing or treating this problem of compulsive exercise behaviour (Hausenblas and Downs, 2002).

This section of the chapter has explored two health hazards associated with habitual physical activity. Of course, we should not exaggerate these problems as the phenomena of overtraining and exercise dependence affect only a small minority of people. For the majority of the population, two questions are probably far more pressing. First, why do so many people fail to take up the healthy habit of regular physical activity? Second, why do they find it so difficult to maintain the habit of exercise?

Exploring people's exercise behaviour

At the beginning of this chapter, we learned that most people in industrialized countries do not take enough physical activity to gain significant health benefits. This finding is as perplexing to health promotion campaigners (who have bombarded the public for decades with information about the advantages of regular physical activity) as it is to exercise psychologists. Nevertheless, these groups differ in their approach to the problem of exercise initiation. Whereas health promotion campaigners rely mainly on descriptive methods (e.g., surveys) to identify demographic correlates of people's propensity to engage in physical activity, exercise psychologists have developed sophisticated theoretical models in an effort to understand why people vary in their levels of physical activity. To illustrate the latter approach, Spence and Lee (2003) pointed out that analysis of "individual" barriers to exercise account for at best 20 per cent to 40 per cent of the variance in physical activity. Accordingly, these researchers suggest that an ecological approach to the problem of exercise initiation may prove fruitful. This approach is based on the assumption that a person's level of physical activity is determined not only by individual intentions but also by environmental factors such as the availability of safe and pleasant spaces in which to engage in exercise behaviour. Until relatively recently, this ecological perspective on physical activity has been neglected.

Although health promotion campaigners and exercise psychologists adopt different theoretical perspectives on the issue of exercise initiation, they have similar views about the desired outcome of any physical activity programme – namely, the inculcation of an active lifestyle (Buckworth and Dishman, 2002). This shift from fitness to health as the optimal goal of physical activity occurred gradually between the 1970s and the 1990s. Thus Blair et al. (1992) distinguished between exercise that improves fitness and that which promotes an active and healthy lifestyle. This latter type of exercise consists mainly of a moderate type of physical activity that can be accumulated over the course of a given day.

Taking up exercise: reasons and barriers

Having sketched some background information on the exercise initiation problem, we should now consider what research psychologists have discovered about people's reasons for, and barriers to, an active lifestyle. As one might expect, people take up exercise for a wide variety of reasons. According to Biddle and Nigg (2000), among the most popular reasons given by exercisers are that it is enjoyable and challenging, potentially beneficial to health, and that it offers new social outlets and opportunities. Perhaps not surprisingly, these reasons tend to vary with age and gender. Whereas younger adults tend to be motivated by perceived fitness benefits, older adults are more concerned with the apparent *health* advantages arising from physical activity. Also, more women than men tend to emphasize the value of exercise for weight control and improved appearance.

Turning to the barriers which hamper people's exercise behaviour, Buckworth and Dishman (2007) identified a number of demographic and psychological impediments to the initiation of physical activity. These barriers include demographic factors such as habitual smoking, obesity, lower socioeconomic status and poor education as well as personal issues like medical problems, insufficient motivation and an apparent lack of time. Curiously, this "lack of time" explanation for physical inactivity has been challenged by research in a number of ways. First, even in environments (e.g., prisons) where time constraints are minimal, people's exercise behaviour is not much different from that in the general population (Morgan, 1977). Second, it is possible that the reported barrier of "lack of time" may be simply a socially acceptable excuse for not exercising – one that masks the individual's real reason(s) for inactivity, such as a lack of motivation, low self-confidence, and/or unhealthy body image issues (Brawley et al., 1998). Although the descriptive approach has been helpful in identifying barriers to exercise initiation and in providing baseline data for public health initiatives, it suffers from the limitation that we referred to in the previous section – its atheoretical nature (Biddle and Nigg, 2000). In other words, it does not explain the psychological processes (e.g., attitudes, intentions) that determine people's level of involvement in habitual physical activity. Fortunately, several theories have emerged in exercise psychology to fill this gap. These theories are borrowed mainly from models of social cognition but have been modified for use in exercise settings. Although they differ from each other in significant ways, these theories share a common assumption that people are rational and goal directed in their pursuit of physical activity.

Theories of exercise behaviour

Although many theories of exercise behaviour have been developed (for reviews, see Biddle and Mutrie, 2008; Biddle et al., 2007), space limitations prevent us from examining all but the most popular ones in this chapter. Of these theories, four deserve special consideration. These approaches are the **theory of reasoned action**, the **theory of planned behaviour**, **self-determination theory** and the **transtheoretical model of behaviour change**.

Although these approaches have certain similarities (e.g., in assuming that people's intentions predict their behaviour: Ogden, 2000), they differ in important ways. Whereas the theories of reasoned action and planned behaviour are largely static in attempting to predict exercise behaviour, the transtheoretical model of change is a *dynamic* model which assumes that people move in a spiral fashion through a sequence of qualitatively different stages on their journey from inactivity to activity. This latter approach assumes that at any point in this cycle, people can fall back to an earlier stage – as if they were playing an exercise version of the game of snakes and ladders. I now examine these three theories of exercise behaviour in more detail.

Theory of reasoned action

The theory of reasoned action (TRA) was developed by Ajzen and Fishbein (1974) to explore the degree to which people's voluntary behaviour reflects their intentions. It was subsequently extended by Ajzen (1988) into the theory of planned behaviour (TPB). The relationships between the key constructs of these theories are depicted in Figure 8.1.

The TRA postulates that people behave in a rational manner by taking into account available information before they act, and it proposes that the best predictor of people's volitional behaviour is their intention to act. This construct of *intention* represents a person's immediate behavioural inclination to engage in a given target behaviour such as physical activity. It is alleged to be determined by two social-cognitive variables – first, the person's attitude to performing the behaviour in

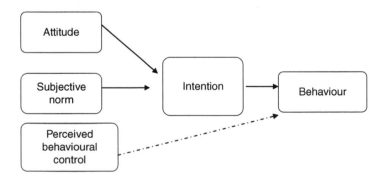

Figure 8.1 Theories of reasoned action and planned behaviour
Source: reprinted, by kind permission, from H. A. Hausenblas, A. V. Carron, and D. E. Mack (1997) Application of the theories of reasoned action and planned behaviour: A meta-analysis. *Journal of Sport and Exercise Psychology, 19*, 36–51, p. 37

question, and second, the subjective norms which surround it. *Attitude* represents the person's beliefs about the target behaviour (exercise) as well as his or her evaluation of the consequences of this behaviour. For example, a student might believe that although exercise is good for her health, it takes away from her study time. *Subjective norms* comprise the person's beliefs about the degree to which significant others want him or her to engage in the target behaviour; they represent social pressures to behave in a certain way. For example, if a person believes that his family thinks he should take more exercise, and he usually follows his family's wishes, then he will experience a positive subjective norm for exercising.

These two variables – attitudes and norms – are held to play a crucial role in determining people's involvement in physical activity. Indeed, the theory of reasoned action suggests that the question of whether or not people take up exercise is influenced more by attitudes and norms than by such demographic variables as their educational level or socioeconomic status (see the barriers to exercise described in the preceding section). An age effect is also evident. A research review by Hagger et al. (2002) concluded that older people are more likely to implement their intentions than are younger adults. Overall, the TRA has received solid empirical support. Research suggests that attitudinal factors account for up to 30 per cent of the variance generated by people's intentions to exercise (Buckworth and Dishman, 2002). A meta-analysis by Hausenblas et al. (1997) of relevant research showed that intention had a relatively large effect on exercise behaviour (effect size of 1.09) and that attitude had a large effect on intention (effect size of 1.22). A problem for the TRA is the fact that a person's decision about whether or not to engage in exercise behaviour is not always under his or her voluntary control. For example, physical injury or adverse weather conditions may make it difficult to implement one's intention to exercise.

Theory of planned behaviour

The theory of planned behaviour (TPB) is a modification of the TRA resulting from the addition of a single variable – *perceived behavioural control* – which refers to one's belief about how easy or difficult it is to perform the target behaviour. Azjen (2005) suggested that this variable affects people's intentions in any social situation. If people want to exercise but have little opportunity to do so due to certain barriers, they are unlikely to engage in physical activity, regardless of any positive attitudes to exercise or the existence of favourable social norms. The TPB suggests that exercise behaviour is guided by behavioural, normative and control beliefs. According to Hyde et al. (2010), the TPB postulates that evaluative attitudes towards exercise behaviour, perceived social pressures, and belief in one's ability to control such behaviour combine to predict intentions, which, in turn, predict the exercise behaviour in question. This theory has been successful in predicting physical activity behaviour in participants of different ages and ethnic groups (e.g., see Nigg et al., 2009). Anderson and Lavallee (2008) found that the TPB was a significant predictor (accounting for 24 per cent of variance) of adherence to training by elite athletes. Keats and Culos-Reed (2009) discovered that an intervention programme based on this theory was helpful in encouraging physical activity in a group of adolescent cancer survivors.

To summarize, reviews of relevant research (e.g., Biddle and Mutrie, 2008) indicate that the TRA and TPB models have been quite useful in predicting people's exercise intentions and any subsequent physical activity. When compared, however, the TPB seems to be superior to the TRA in its explanatory scope. A meta-analytic review by Hagger et al. (2002) concluded that there are strong positive relationships among the TPB components of attitudes, subjective norms, perceived behavioural control, behavioural intentions and exercise behaviour. Briefly, this review showed that the TPB accounted for more variance in physical activity intentions and behaviour than did the TRA. At least one important practical implication stems from this finding: it seems that in order to optimize the likelihood of taking up physical activity, interventions should concentrate on fostering a sense of control and/or self-efficacy in participants. Unfortunately, despite their explicit analysis of the links between intentions, attitudes and behaviour, the TRA and TPB have been criticized on three grounds. First, because they are unidirectional models, they do not envisage the possibility that engaging in exercise behaviour may cause people to change their attitudes to exercise (Biddle and Nigg, 2000). Second, these theories do not provide many formal guidelines on how key beliefs can be targeted using interventions (Keats and Culos-Reed, 2009). Third, they are not especially helpful in explaining behavioural *change*. Consideration of this latter problem will lead us to consider shortly an alternative conceptual approach in exercise psychology – the transtheoretical model. But first, I examine a model of exercise behavior that has become very popular in the field – self-determination theory.

Self-determination theory

Self-determination theory (SDT), which was developed by Deci and Ryan (e.g., see Deci and Ryan, 1985, 2000, 2008), is a meta-theory or broad conceptual approach to the study of human motivation – especially the autonomous control of behaviour. It is a "dialectical framework" (Weiss and Amorose, 2008, p. 129) because it argues that motivation emerges from constant interaction between human nature and social contextual factors. According to Hagger and Chatzisarantis (2008, p. 80), self-determination theory attempts "to explain human motivation and behaviour based on individual differences in motivational orientations, contextual influences on motivation, and interpersonal perceptions".

A key proposition of SDT is the idea that optimal performance and maximal subjective well-being tend to occur when people's innate needs for *relatedness* (i.e., feeling connected with, and close to, others in one's community), *competence* (i.e., feeling proficient in producing desired outcomes) and *autonomy* (i.e., feeling that one has a sense of agency in, or control over, one's actions – which provides a sense of self-determination) are satisfied (P. Wilson and Rodgers, 2007). Put simply, having meaningful personal relationships, being able to perform proficiently in different situations, and feeling in control of one's actions tend to promote health and happiness. Ryan and Deci (2000) postulated that social-contextual factors (or "autonomy suppor-tive" environments) that satisfy these three basic needs are more likely to increase people's effort, persistence and sense of well-being than are environments that inhibit these needs. This hypothesis has been supported by empirical research in sport and exercise psychology (see reviews by Hagger and Chatzisarantis, 2007, 2008; Ryan and Deci, 2007). Vallerand (2007) reported that self-determined (or autonomously regulated) behaviour such as intrinsic motivation is associated with positive outcomes such as increased effort and persistence and enhanced well-being when compared with more "controlling" environments (e.g., where behaviour is motivated by consequences that are extrinsic to, or separate from, the activity in question). Thus a crucial distinction in SDT is between autonomous (or self-determined) motivation and non-self-determined (or controlling) motivation. It is notable that since about the mid-1990s, SDT has shifted its emphasis away from the old distinction between intrinsic and extrinsic motivation (see also Chapter 2) and towards the newer one between *autonomous* and *controlled* motivation (Deci and Ryan, 2008). Evidence is accumulating to suggest that the benefits of "self-control" training can generalize from one domain to another. Oaten and Cheng (2006) found that students who had learned self-control skills through a regime of daily exercise and regular study habits became more adept at self-regulation in other environments (e.g., when sitting examinations).

Self-determination theory comprises a number of mini-theories – most prominently, cognitive evaluation theory (CET), organismic integration theory (OIT) and basic needs theory (BNT). Although a detailed treatment of these theories is beyond the scope of this chapter (but see Hagger and Chatzisarantis, 2008; Ryan and Deci, 2002), here is a brief summary of their relevance to exercise behaviour. First, CET was postulated to account for the effects of social contextual factors (e.g., rewards) on people's intrinsic motivation (or behaviour based on the inherent satisfaction associated with the activity itself). It proposes that if people believe that a given task (e.g., performing a particular form of exercise in a gym) lies within their capacity, they will be intrinsically motivated to perform it (Cashmore, 2008). However, if an extrinsic reward is offered for successful performance of the exercise behaviour in question, their intrinsic motivation will decrease. This "undermining effect" of rewards is well known in psychology. Lepper and Greene (1975) showed that providing rewards to individuals for activities that they *already* find interesting and challenging tends to lead to a *decrease* in their reported intrinsic motivation. This phenomenon has been termed the "over-justification effect" and refers to a "tendency to devalue those activities that we perform in order to get something else" (Gilovich et al., 2011, p. 222). You may recall that we encountered this phenomenon in Chapter 2 (see Box 2.2). The second mini-theory of the SDT framework is organismic integration theory, which attempts to explain the process by which people assimilate behaviour that is initially *externally* regulated into their own repertoire. Consider the motivational processes at work when a young athlete is told by her coach that she needs to increase her weight training regime in the gym before going to college (an example borrowed from Weiss and Amorose, 2008). She might comply with this request not only because she was advised to do so (external regulation) but also because she feels that she would not like to let her coach down (introjected regulation). In this way, OIT examines the psychological processes by which social-contextual factors may be internalized by people. Third, as with SDT in general, basic needs theory postulates that the origin of self-determined motivation lies in satisfaction of the three universal psychological needs described earlier – relatedness, competence and autonomy. A considerable amount of research has tested BNT propositions in exercise contexts. For example, the hypothesized relationship between need satisfaction and subjective well-being has been tested with gymnasts and dancers. Gagné et al. (2003) found that changes in gymnasts' sense of well-being from pre-practice to post-practice sessions changed in accordance with satisfaction of the needs that they experienced during practice. Quested and Duda (2010) discovered that need satisfaction according to self-determination theory predicted positive emotions among dancers.

In summary, Hagger and Chatzisarantis (2008) claimed that SDT has contributed significantly to increased theoretical understanding of factors both in the environment and in the person that predict exercise behaviour. Nevertheless, they also highlighted certain issues that need to be addressed by proponents of this approach. Few experimental or intervention studies have been conducted on SDT in exercise behaviour. Also, further research is required on the role of implicit processes in self-determined motivation. As Hyde et al. (2010) pointed out, an exclusive focus on conscious motivational factors neglects the automatic processes that may influence exercise behaviour.

Transtheoretical model of behaviour change

It has long been known that people can improve their health not only by giving up hazardous activities (e.g., smoking) but also by adopting constructive habits such as exercising regularly. But how can people change from being in a sedentary state to active engagement in a healthy lifestyle? The transtheoretical model of behaviour change (TTM) was developed originally by Prochaska and DiClemente (1983) in an effort to account for the success of "self-changers" in smoking: people who managed to reduce this addictive behaviour without the aid of any professional intervention. The term "transtheoretical" reflects the fact that the concepts and principles of this approach are borrowed from a variety of theories of behaviour change within the fields of psychotherapy and health psychology. The TTM is a dynamic approach because it assumes that intentional behaviour change is not an all or nothing phenomenon but reflects a process that unfolds gradually over time. This dynamic approach arose from the observation that people who quit smoking tended to go through a distinctive pattern of behavioural changes as they gradually gave up cigarettes. Not surprisingly, therefore, the TTM is also known as the "stages of change" model. Since the early 1990s, this model has been applied to *preventive* health issues, especially those concerning exercise initiation and maintenance (Marcus and Simkin, 1993).

The TTM has four main components:

1 The idea of stages of change.
2 The hypothetical processes by which such change occurs.
3 The concept of self-efficacy (or one's belief in one's ability to perform the required behaviour; see also Box 8.3).
4 The theory of "decisional balance" (i.e., an evaluation of the positive and negative aspects of changing one's target behaviour).

Although a detailed analysis of these components is beyond the scope of this chapter (but see a review by Nigg et al., 2011b), I now consider the "when" (time-course) and "how" (transformation mechanisms) of the transtheoretical model of behaviour change as it applies to physical activity. The first main component of the TTM postulates that people progress through a series of five stages before they achieve a desired and sustained change in their behaviour. The first stage is *precontemplation*, a sedentary stage in which the person has no intention of becoming physically active in the immediate future (usually measured operationally as within the next six months). The second stage is *contemplation*, where the person does not currently exercise but has some intention of becoming more active physically within the next six months. The third stage is *preparation*, where the person engages in some physical activity but not on a regular basis (usually understood as less than three times a week). The fourth stage is *action*, where the person is physically active regularly but has only been so for less than six months. The fifth stage is *maintenance*, which occurs when the person is physically active regularly and has been exercising for at least six months. These stages are described in Box 8.6.

Box 8.6 The transtheoretical model of behaviour change as applied to physical activity

Stage	What happens?
Precontemplation	Person is not active physically and has no intention of exercising over the next six months.
Contemplation	Person is still inactive but intends to start exercising regularly within next six months.
Preparation	Person is active physically but below the criterion level of regularity required for health benefits (i.e., at least three times per week for twenty or thirty minutes or longer per session).
Action	Person is engaged in regular physical activity but has been doing so at the criterion level for less than six months.
Maintenance	Person is engaged in regular physical activity and has been exercising regularly for more than six months.

As you can see from Box 8.6, each of these hypothetical stages of change is defined by a unique combination of intentionality and behaviour and can be measured using self-report instruments (see Marcus and Simkin, 1993). Note that the stages are assumed to be cyclical rather than linear because many people do not maintain their intended changes but regress to an earlier stage. These relapses to previous stages of change are common among people who wish to become more physically active and are often caused by injury, illness and by the vicissitudes of travel and personal or business issues. Many successful "self-changers" proceed in a spiral fashion several times through the preliminary stages before they achieve the maintenance stage (see Figure 8.2).

Although the above stages describe how people's exercise behaviour changes over time, the *process* by which these changes occur requires a separate explanation. Thus the second main component of the TTM postulates ten different strategies to account for a person's transformation from a state of inactivity to one of regular physical activity. These strategies are defined as actions that are "initiated or

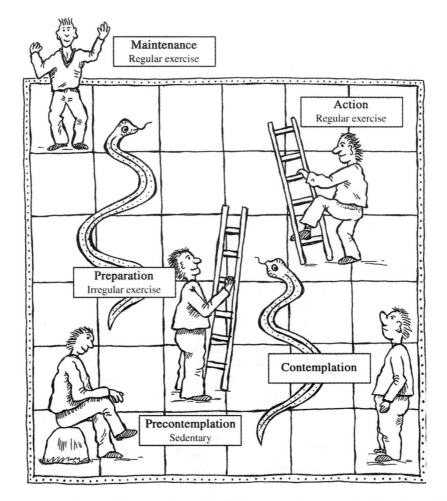
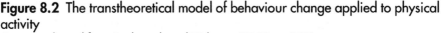

Figure 8.2 The transtheoretical model of behaviour change applied to physical activity
Source: adapted from Buckworth and Dishman (2002, p. 220)

experienced by an individual in modifying affect, behaviour, cognition, or relationships" (Prochaska and DiClemente, 1984, p. 7). Among these strategies are experiential processes like *consciousness raising* (whereby the person tries to learn more about the benefits of regular physical activity) and *dramatic relief* (whereby the person may be moved emotionally by warnings about the dangers of not taking regular exercise). Also, behavioural strategies such as *stimulus control* may be used. Here, the exerciser may try to avoid any situations that promote physical inactivity. Another popular behavioural change mechanism is the use of *helping relationships* in which exercisers seek social support to encourage them to continue with their planned physical activity.

The third main component of the TTM is the construct of self-efficacy, which, as we learned earlier in this chapter, refers to people's confidence in their ability to perform a certain action. Theoretically, people with high levels of self-efficacy are confident of being able to exercise even when they encounter barriers such as bad weather, fatigue or other adverse circumstances. The fourth main component of the TTM is the hypothetical decisional balance or cost–benefit analysis in which the person is believed to weigh up the pros and cons of taking part in regular physical activity. For example, an advantage of exercise could be that "I know I'll meet my friends in the gym tonight" but a disadvantage might arise from apprehension of the fatigue that is likely to follow vigorous physical activity. In general, the TTM predicts that the pros should increase as people move from the precontemplation to the contemplation stages, whereas the cons should diminish as people go from the action to the maintenance stages.

Overall, the TTM appears to offer a plausible and fruitful account of people's exercise behaviour. It acknowledges the difficulties that many people experience in attempting to change their exercise habits. It also recognizes the fact that people differ from each other in their readiness for becoming more active physically. This idea offers the possibility of matching a particular exercise intervention to a particular state of individual behavioural change. But does available research evidence support the validity of the transtheoretical model? Unfortunately, the data bearing upon this issue are equivocal. Although Callaghan et al. (2002) summarized a number of predictions from the TTM that have been corroborated by researchers, there are several flaws and inconsistencies in the research literature in this field. To illustrate these contrasting perspectives on the TTM, consider the following evidence. First, on the positive side, T. Peterson and Aldana (1999) reported that a "stage-matched" intervention to increase exercise behaviour (i.e., those in which people are encouraged to use processes of change that correspond to, or match, their current stage of change) was more effective than a generic intervention. Second, on the negative side, the TTM has been criticized for failing to specify the precise psychological mechanisms facilitating successful change from one stage to another. It is also open to criticism for its neglect of individual differences that may account for stage relapses. A third problem for the TTM is that the instruments designed to test both stages and processes of change have been poorly validated (Buckworth and Dishman, 2002). Fourth, in the field of physical activity, TTM research has focused mainly on middle-aged populations rather than on people of a younger age, despite the fact that this latter group is increasingly sedentary (Trost et al., 2002; Catherine Woods et al., 2002). In view of these limitations, the popularity of the TTM may be somewhat greater than is warranted by available empirical evidence.

The way forward: combining theories of exercise behaviour?

As we have seen in this section, psychology researchers have tended to use a *single* theoretical approach, such as theory of planned behaviour (TPB) or self-determination theory (SDT), when investigating motivational issues in exercise behaviour (Biddle et al., 2008). Since 2008, however, some leading figures in the field (e.g., Biddle and Fuchs, 2009; Biddle et al., 2008) have raised the intriguing possibility that by *combining* theories, we can not only overcome certain gaps in individual approaches to understanding exercise behaviour (e.g., the vexed question in SDT of how self-determined motivation is converted into intentions and then translated into action) but also increase our predictive power. In an effort to test this idea, Hagger and Chatzisarantis (2009) conducted a meta-analysis of studies to assess possible predictive improvements gained by integrating two prominent theories of health behaviour – the theory of planned behavior and self-determination theory. The results of their analysis supported the predictive utility of an integrated theoretical approach. The effects of self-determined motivation on intentions and behaviour were mediated by predictors derived from TPB. Clearly, further research is required to establish the complementarity of the various theories of exercise behaviour.

Exercise attrition: why do people drop out of physical activity programmes?

As we learned at the beginning of this chapter, as many as half of the people who join exercise programmes in gyms or elsewhere tend to drop out of them within months. Why are these attrition rates so high? Two ways of answering this question can be identified. First, the descriptive research approach tries to identify a range of factors that are associated with dropping out from physical activity programmes. Second, the theoretical approach uses conceptual models of relapse behaviour in an effort to understand people's *reasons* for giving up exercising regularly. Let us now consider each of these approaches briefly.

With regard to the descriptive approach, research suggests that dropping out from exercise activities is associated with variables like low socioeconomic status, habitual smoking, limited coping skills, low motivation and/or the belief that physical activity requires too much effort, and a perceived lack of facilities (but see Box 8.7). By contrast, exercise adherence is associated with intrinsic motivation – enjoying exercise for its own sake (Ogden, 2000). Unfortunately, research in this field is hampered by methodological limitations. Few studies on exercise attrition have followed up drop-outs to make sure that they are not continuing to take exercise spontaneously or on their own. As regards the theoretical approach to understanding exercise attrition, Marcus et al. (2002) proposed various principles governing effective "relapse prevention" interventions. The first principle emphasizes the importance of identifying high-risk situations which are likely to precipitate dropping out. A common example of such situations is a change in work routine or unexpected travel demands. Second, an effective relapse prevention intervention should equip exercisers with psychological strategies designed to cope with the demands of these risky situations. For example, a woman whose travel demands force her to miss her weekly aerobics class may change the location of her next session. Thus she may decide to go for a run while she is away rather than missing her exercise completely. Further details of the causes of, and proposed solutions for, exercise attrition are found in Biddle and Mutrie (2008) and Morgan and Dishman (2001). Before concluding this section, it is worth exploring the possible relevance of **exergaming**, that is playing electronic motion-control games for increasing exercise behaviour in adolescents (see Box 8.7).

Box 8.7 Thinking critically about … exergaming: is it even *better* than the real thing?

Video game playing is ubiquitous among children and adolescents in many countries (Mellecker and McManus, 2008). Ever since Nintendo invented motion-control computer games such as the Wii in 2006, a new generation of active video games (AVGs) has offer the opportunity to contribute to young people's energy expenditure (EE) and thereby to transform sedentary leisure time into time spent being physically active. So, is exergaming as good as, or even better than, the real thing? Daley (2009) and Biddiss and Irwin (2010) carried out systematic reviews of the empirical evidence concerning the effects of active video games on physical activity and EE. Encouragingly, these reviews concluded that AVGs *do* lead to greater energy expenditure when compared to non-AVGs and result in low- to moderate-intensity physical activity. Perhaps not surprisingly, available evidence suggests that engaging in the *actual* physical activity has a substantially larger effect on EE than engaging in the video game simulation of it (Graves et al., 2007).

The research shows that much depends on the type of AVG being played and for how it is long played. To illustrate, if the AVG focuses primarily on upper body movement (e.g., bowling and tennis), physical activity is significantly less intense than the level of activity which occurs when the game focuses either on lower body movement (e.g., dancing) or on both upper and lower body movement (e.g., boxing) (Biddiss and Irwin, 2010). In order to satisfy conventional physical activity guidelines, the most "intense" AVGs would have to be played for at least thirty minutes per day (Daley, 2009). In conclusion, it appears that although exergaming provides greater energy expenditure than does sedentary video games, it is *not* actually better than the real thing!

Critical thinking questions
What claims do commercial manufacturers make for the benefits of exergaming? In the light of the evidence above, do you think that such claims are warranted? In practical terms, what are some of the benefits of playing active video games? Could they be useful for people whose physical disabilities may prevent them from actual performance of the simulated activity? Are there any disadvantages to exergaming? Could familiarity with particular AVG influence how much energy is expended by the player? How might exergaming help people who have low self-confidence in their ability to engage in exercise behaviour?

Practical tips on becoming more active physically

So far in this chapter, we have learned about the nature and health consequences of exercise as well as the obstacles that can prevent people from engaging in habitual physical activity. After examining relevant theories and findings, it is time to apply what you have learned. Here are some classic practical tips on exercising effectively

(Baron and Kalsher, 2002; DeAngelis, 2002). See also Chapter 2 for some practical advice on effective goal-setting.

- *Put a "p (ep)" in your step: make your exercise purposeful*
  The gym is not the only place to exercise. Instead, try to include some natural physical activity in your daily list of things to do. For example, go for a walk with your dog, rake the leaves in your garden or cycle down to the shops. Try to accumulate at least thirty minutes of moderate intensity physical activity per day.
- *Think big but start small*
  If the thought of exercising puts you off, try to take one small step at a time. For example, instead of saying to yourself, "I'm going to walk every day this week for at least an hour", try to say, "I'll build it up in five-minute periods from Sunday to Thursday".
- *Establish an exercise routine*
  Try to develop a habit of physical activity by exercising at the same time every day.
- *Make it sociable and enjoyable*
  It is easy to maintain an exercise regime if you enjoy it and are supported by other people in the same activity. So, if possible, try to make a social occasion of your physical activity so that you and your friends can have fun while exercising.
- *If you start at an older age, take exercise gradually*
  If you are a recent convert to the joy of exercising, begin gradually: slowly but surely is the best advice here.
- *Get on your bike*
  Try to cycle as often as possible. Cycling not only uses all the main muscles of the legs but also tones the buttocks through the repeated "push down" phase of the pedalling action.
- *Develop an active lifestyle*
  You will reap the greatest benefits from exercise if you regard it as just one part of an active lifestyle rather than as an isolated task that you feel compelled to perform a few times per week.

Ideas for research projects on exercise psychology

Here are five suggestions for research projects on aspects of the psychology of exercise behaviour.

1   Although it has long been known that regular exercise can elevate people's moods, relatively few studies have been conducted to find out the nature and extent of these changes over time. Using a standardized test of mood such as the Profile of Mood States (POMS: McNair et al., 1992) as well as a diary of people's feelings at different times of the day, can you think of a way of testing the relationship between mood and exercise over a period of several months?

2   Arising from discussion of "green exercise" (see earlier in this chapter), does the physical environment in which one conducts one's physical activity affect

its perceived benefits? It would be interesting to extend the study by Bodin and Hartig (2003) described earlier in the chapter by comparing the relative effects of different types of walking routes (e.g., urban, suburban and rural) on people's mood and well-being.

3   Among adolescents, the popularity of social networking sites (SNS: R. Baker and White, 2010) such as Twitter and Facebook has grown exponentially in recent years. Based on a suggestion by Matthews (2009), are such sites effective in helping sedentary adolescents to overcome certain perceived barriers (e.g., absence of social support) to engaging in regular physical activity? It would be interesting to investigate this possibility empirically.

4   Research suggests that adolescents (Matthews, 2009) and older adults are among the least physically active groups in the general population (Troiano et al., 2008). So, based on the research of Buman et al., 2010), it would be interesting to examine the similarities and differences between the perceived barriers to physical activity reported by these two groups of people.

5   Arising from Box 8.7, and given the apparently inexorable rise of interactive video and computer games (e.g., the Wii), it would be interesting to investigate the nature and types of physical injuries suffered by people who play them – and to compare such injury profiles with those experienced by athletes playing the "real" sports.

Summary

- Although many people realize that physical activity is associated with a range of health benefits, they appear to be reluctant either to engage in or to persist with regular exercise. This paradox lies at the heart of exercise psychology – a discipline which is concerned with people's involvement in physical activity in various everyday settings. Given this background, this chapter set out to investigate the benefits, hazards and psychological issues arising from people's exercise behaviour.

- The second section explained the nature and goals of exercise psychology.

- The third section provided a critical evaluation of research on the health benefits associated with regular physical activity as well as some potential hazards (e.g., overtraining and exercise dependence).

- The fourth section examined the main theories and research findings on the issues of exercise initiation (the take-up problem) and exercise maintenance (the keeping it up problem).

- The final section presented several ideas for possible research projects on exercise psychology.

Chapter 9

Helping athletes to cope with injury: from theory to practice

There were days in his clinic when I broke down, my body couldn't take it. My mind was making demands that my body couldn't meet. I went through every emotion from hope to despair and back.

(Ronan O'Gara, Ireland and Lions' rugby out-half, on his successful rehabilitation from an anterior cruciate ligament injury with Ger Hartmann, physical therapist, cited in Foley, 2010)

Introduction

In Chapter 8, we explored the health benefits and potential hazards of engaging in regular physical activity. Continuing this theme, this chapter examines another drawback associated with regular engagement in sport and exercise – namely, physical injury. Unfortunately, people who take part in regular competitive physical activity inevitably run the risk of sustaining injury (see Figure 9.1). This point is well illustrated both by quotations from leading athletes in a variety of different sports and by some remarkable facts about sporting injuries. Andre Agassi, the former world number 1 tennis player, described in his autobiography the constant struggle that he faces in coping with the chronic injuries he experienced throughout his career: "I've been negotiating with my body, asking it to come out of retirement for a few hours here, a few hours there. Much of this negotiation revolves around a cortisone shot that temporarily dulls the pain" (Agassi, 2009, p. 4). Steffi Graf, also a former world number 1 tennis player, revealed the emotional impact of enforced absence from the game due to injury: "I couldn't do anything. No work-outs, nothing, I was angry, moody, frustrated" (cited in Miller, 1997, p. 124). Turning to the facts about sports injuries, Tony McCoy, the jump jockey who won the 2010 Grand National and who is the only rider to have won over 3,000 races, has suffered an extraordinary range of problems including broken ankles, broken arms, a broken leg and a fractured back (BBC Sport, 2010). Lewis Moody, a former captain of the

Figure 9.1 Injury is almost inevitable in sport
Source: Courtesy of Inpho photography

England rugby team, has had three shoulder reconstruction operations, hip surgery, repair of a ruptured Achilles tendon, and a broken ankle so far in his career (Media Planet, 2010). These latter injuries are not really surprising, however, given the fact that modern professional rugby players are fitter, stronger and faster than their counterparts from the amateur era. Commenting on the damage caused by collisions between highly conditioned athletes in international rugby, Dr James Robson, the chief medical officer to the Great Britain and Ireland Lions teams, remarked that "if people on one side are fitter and more powerful than ever before, and they meet people on the other side who have developed along similar lines, the impacts are necessarily greater" (cited in Hewett, 2004, p. 54).

Sports injuries can be represented on a continuum formed by a combination of magnitude (i.e., extent of damage to body tissues) and duration of impact. They range from minor (e.g., twisting a finger while attempting to catch a ball) via moderate (e.g., damaging ankle ligaments) to severe (e.g., suffering brain damage in a boxing match – as happened to Michael Watson, who was in a coma for forty days after he had been injured in his world super-middle-weight title fight against Chris Eubank in 1991). As an illustration of the severe end of the spectrum, consider the case of Shane Duffy, the Everton and Republic of Ireland international Under-21 soccer player who almost died after a freak training ground injury in 2010. Having lacerated his liver in an accidental collision with the opposing team's goalkeeper, Duffy was just seconds from death until he was rushed to hospital for emergency surgery (C. Dunn, 2010). Although the vast majority of sports injuries are not life threatening, they represent a significant impediment to athletic success. Junge et al. (2009) analysed the prevalence of sports injuries at the 2008 Olympic Games in Beijing. Physicians and/or therapists of nine national teams (representing 88 per cent of the nations competing at the Games) completed a standardized injury report form. Results revealed an incidence of 96.1 injuries per 1,000 athletes – a prevalence of almost 10 per cent among the Olympic athletes concerned. Half of these injuries were expected to prevent the athletes from participating in competition or training, which seriously jeopardized their chances of achieving success. Perhaps not surprisingly, this study also showed that the risk of injury was greatest in physical contact sports such as soccer and boxing and lowest in sports such as sailing, rowing, diving, fencing and swimming. As the quote above from Dr James Robson (medical officer to the Lions rugby team) suggests, there is anecdotal evidence that the severity of physical injuries experienced by international rugby players is linked directly to improvements in their physical conditioning (Hewett, 2004). A good example of the extent of the injuries suffered by top-class rugby players comes from Jonny Wilkinson, the England and Great Britain and Ireland Lions out-half. Between 2002 and 2008, Wilkinson suffered such injuries as ankle ligament damage (which ruled him out of the 2002–2003 season), shoulder damage (which ruled him out of the 2004 Six Nations Championship), knee ligament damage (which forced him out of the 2006 autumn test series) and chronic shoulder problems (which forced him out of England's summer tour of New Zealand) (see The Times, 2008). In the general population, sports injuries constitute a significant volume of acute admissions to hospitals. In 1999 about 750,000 people reported to the casualty wards of British hospitals seeking treatment for injuries which they had received while playing sports or engaging in exercise (Hoey, 2002). Indeed, the level of injury risk for professional sports performers is significantly higher than for other occupational groups. To illustrate this disparity, Drawer and Fuller (2002) reported that whereas employees in the UK suffer, on average, 0.36 reportable injuries per 100,000 working hours, professional footballers suffer an average of 710 reportable injuries per 100,000 hours of training and competition. Sports injuries comprise approximately one-third of all injuries reported to medical agencies in the UK (Uitenbroek, 1996). Not all of these ailments reflect sudden-impact injuries, however. It is increasingly evident that certain types of long-term physical deterioration can occur as a consequence of habitual sporting activity. Degenerative joint conditions in rugby players can take up to twenty years to develop (A. Lee et al., 2001). Cases of chronic brain damage have been detected in former professional soccer players. Some of this damage has been attributed to repeated heading of the ball. In November 2002, a coroner in England ruled that Jeff Astle, one of the most famous football strikers of his generation, had died at the age of 59 from a degenerative condition that had probably been caused by his prowess in heading. Apparently, the twenty years which Astle had spent in heading rapidly delivered, water-sodden leather balls had damaged his brain irrevocably (McGrory, 2002). As Box 9.1 shows, we must be careful to avoid uncritical acceptance of the claim that heading in soccer causes brain damage. After all, in Astle's era, leather footballs were more likely to cause head injuries because they became about 20 per cent heavier than normal during wet conditions. By contrast, modern footballs are not only lighter but also waterproof and hence do not absorb rain as a match progresses. Thus it appears that available evidence is not adequate to justify the claim that deliberate heading (as distinct from accidental collisions involving the head) causes brain damage.

Box 9.1 Thinking critically about ... the link between heading and brain damage: are footballers heading for injury?

The ability to head the ball accurately while standing, running, jumping or diving is a highly valued skill in soccer because it demands excellent technique and precise timing. But can repeated execution of this skill of heading cause brain damage, or traumatically induced alteration in brain function, in footballers? This is an important and controversial question (e.g., see Webbe and Salinas, 2011). In 2001, in an attempt to answer this question, Kirkendall and Garrett (2001) and Kirkendall et al. (2001) reviewed available research evidence from over fifty studies on the nature and causes of head injuries in soccer. At least four key conclusions emerged. First, Kirkendall and his colleagues established that head injuries are most likely to occur within the penalty area when defenders and attackers compete for crosses or corner-kicks or around the halfway line when midfield players challenge each other for aerial clearances from the goalkeeper. Second, they found some evidence that the higher the skill level of the players involved, the more frequent were the incidents in which concussion occurred. Third, they concluded that although a significant number of retired soccer players show signs of cognitive dysfunctions and various neuropsychological impairments, the causes of these problems are difficult to determine. For example, these maladies may be caused by accidental collisions with other players or with stationary objects (e.g., the goalposts, advertising hoardings) rather than by repeated heading of the ball. Fourth, they concluded that the research literature on heading and brain damage is marred by a host of methodological weaknesses. Many studies in this field have failed to control for such factors as inconsistencies in the criteria used to define brain damage, unreliable estimates of the frequency of heading engaged in during a match and variations in the age, neurological histories and possible alcohol intake of the players involved. In summary, Kirkendall et al. (2001, p. 384) conclude that "the use of the head for controlling and advancing the ball is not likely to be a significant factor in mild traumatic brain injury" in soccer players. In spite of this conclusion, a neuropsychological study by Witol and Webbe (2003, p. 414) found that cumulative experience (or lifetime frequency) of heading among male soccer players was associated with poor performance on tests of attention/concentration, cognitive flexibility and general intellectual functioning. These researchers argued that "players who head the ball frequently may carry a higher risk of neurobehavioural sequelae". A contrary view on the danger of heading was proposed by Straume-Naesheim et al. (2005), who investigated the relationship between previous concussions, self-reported number of heading actions per match and performance on various neuropsychological tests for a sample of Norwegian professional soccer players. Surprisingly, results showed no evidence of neuropsychological impairment due to repeated experience of heading or of previous concussion. Koutures et al. (2010) challenged the prevailing view that heading is associated with problems such as cognitive dysfunction. Indeed, they concluded that "a critical review of the literature does not support the contention that purposeful heading contacts are likely to lead to either acute or cumulative brain damage" (Koutures et al., 2010, p. 412). Interestingly, Billy McPhail, the former Scottish international footballer, lost a legal action to claim benefits for dementia that he alleged had been caused by head injuries that he had suffered in his playing days (MacRae, 2006).

Critical thinking questions

Do you think that the statistics on head injuries in professional soccer are really accurate? After all, many players may be unwilling to report symptoms arising from such injuries in order to avoid being dropped from their teams. How many times in a game do you think that defenders, midfielders and attackers head the ball during a competitive match? Check your guess by recording a televised match and then counting the appropriate totals for a random fifteen-minute sequence of play. Given the fact that young soccer players are less skilled technically and have less developed brains, do you think that heading should be banned in children's football? Can you think of any changes in football equipment (e.g., using only plastic-coated footballs; making goalposts softer) and/or coaching practices (e.g., teaching children to head the ball only when they have developed sufficient coordination to make use of his or her head, trunk and neck muscles) that could reduce the likelihood of head injuries in soccer?

In summary, the preceding strands of anecdotal and descriptive evidence suggest that sports injuries pose significant national public health concerns. Naturally, such problems have serious economic consequences. For example, in 2001 in Britain alone, soccer injuries cost the taxpayer about £1 billion through direct treatment costs and indirect loss of production through the resultant problem of time off work (Rahnama et al., 2002). Leaving aside the medical and economic issues, how do athletes react to, and cope with, the injuries that they experience? Is there a psychological dimension to injury rehabilitation as some of the quotes at the beginning of this chapter would suggest? In addressing these questions, my objectives in this chapter are twofold. First, I try to summarize what is known about current theory and research on the psychological factors involved in athletic injuries. Second, I try to provide some practical insights into the strategies used by sport psychologists to facilitate rapid and effective injury rehabilitation in athletes.

The chapter is organized as follows. In the next section, I trace the shift from a physical to a psychological perspective on injuries in sport. In the third section, a brief analysis of the nature, prevalence and causes of sports injuries is presented. The fourth section of the chapter outlines and evaluates two theoretical models which purport to describe how athletes react psychologically to injuries: the **grief stages model of injury reaction** theory and the cognitive appraisal model. In the fifth section, I sketch some practical strategies used by sport psychologists in the rehabilitation of injured athletes. The sixth section examines some new directions for research on the psychological aspects of injury. Finally, suggestions are provided for possible research projects in this field.

The psychological approach to injuries in athletes

Until the 1980s, most sports medicine specialists believed that because injuries were caused by physical factors, they required only physical forms of treatment. Furthermore, it was assumed that athletes who had attained minimal levels of physical rehabilitation were "fully prepared for a safe and successful return to competition" (J. Williams et al., 1998, p. 410). Since the 1990s, however, sports scientists and sports medicine practitioners have acknowledged the important role that psychological factors play in injury rehabilitation. This increased awareness of the "mind-body" approach to injury rehabilitation is largely due to the impact of three converging strands of evidence ranging from anecdotal to scientific.

First, interviews with many injured athletes (e.g., see the quotes from the former Wimbledon tennis champions Steffi Graf and Andre Agassi near the beginning of this chapter) revealed the significant emotional consequences of their physical problems. Anger and depression are common reactions to the discovery that one is prevented from pursuing one's hobby or livelihood. In this regard, a study by Mainwaring et al. (2010) compared and contrasted the emotional consequences for athletes of two different types of serious physical trauma – concussion and anterior cruciate ligament (ACL) injury. Having measured the pre-injury, post-injury and longer-term emotional functioning of these injured athletes using the Profile of Mood States (POMS: McNair et al., 1992), Mainwaring et al. (2010) discovered that athletes who had been concussed did not report as much emotional disturbance as did athletes who had suffered ACL injuries. Unfortunately, not all coaches or managers are sensitive to the mental repercussions of sports injuries. Consider the way in which injured soccer players used to be treated at Liverpool Football Club during the managerial reign of Bill Shankly in the late 1960s and early 1970s. Apparently, Shankly believed that the best way to hasten the rehabilitation of such players was to ignore them completely until they had recovered (Bent et al., 2000)! This curious practice of scapegoating injured athletes was revealed by the former Liverpool team captain, Tommy Smith, who recalled that his manager used to speak to him via a third party (the club trainer) whenever he was injured. Shankly's attitude to injured players was shared by Gordon Strachan, the former manager of Middlesbrough, who admitted that "one thing I have tended to do is to blank out injured players ... the idea is that they will think 'I better get back quickly or I'll be forgotten'" (Strachan, 2004, p. 37). Fortunately, a more enlightened approach to injuries has emerged with the advent of specialist medical staff and sophisticated treatment facilities in leading Premiership clubs.

A second strand of evidence to support a psychological approach to injury management comes from surveys of the opinions and experiences of treatment specialists in this field. By way of background, in the mid-1990s several surveys of athletic trainers revealed a growing awareness of the significance of the "mental side" of injuries. For example, 47 per cent of a large (almost 500) sample of trainers in the United States recognized that injured athletes tend to suffer significant psychological distress as result of their physical trauma (Larson et al., 1996). Francis et al. (2000) asked a sample of physiotherapists about the psychological characteristics which facilitated recovery in injured athletes. Among the most important perceived prerequisites of successful rehabilitation were such factors as a willingness to listen to physiotherapists' advice and effective interpersonal communication skills. Hemmings and Povey (2002) investigated the way in which English chartered physiotherapists perceived psychological aspects of their professional work. Results showed that the physiotherapists reported using a variety of psychological techniques (e.g., creating variety in rehabilitation exercises, setting short-term goals and encouraging positive self-talk) with injured athletes. A rather surprising finding was the discovery that few of the physiotherapists in the study had ever referred a patient to an accredited sport psychologist. This finding was echoed in a study by Arvinen-Barrow et al. (2010), who used semi-structured interviews to investigate physiotherapists' personal experiences of using psychological techniques as part of injury rehabilitation training programmes. Results showed that these physiotherapists believed in the value of psychological techniques as part of the rehabilitation process. Despite a lack of formal training in psychology, the physiotherapists were knowledgeable about, and confident in using, techniques such as goal-setting during their work with injured athletes. However, they were more cautious about using mental imagery and self-talk (see Box 9.5 later in the chapter) as rehabilitation tools. Arvinen-Barrow et al. (2010) also found that the physiotherapists showed an intuitive awareness of the "stage-like" nature of athletes' recovery from injury (see the discussion of "stage models" later in this chapter).

The third boost for a psychological approach to injury management came from research findings in sport science. Since about 2005, there has been a profusion of studies both on the psychosocial antecedents of sports injuries (J. Williams and

Andersen, 2007) and on the psychological consequences of these problems (e.g., Brewer, 2007, 2010a; Udry and Andersen, 2008). To illustrate the volume of this research, Brewer (2010a) included twenty-six studies in his review of the psychological correlates of athletic injury. This body of literature has generated some interesting findings on the interaction between motivation, fatigue and injury in athletes. Rahnama et al. (2002) proposed that the increased risk of injury experienced by soccer players near the beginning (first fifteen minutes) or end (last fifteen minutes) of football matches may be due to the effects of initial intensity of tackling combined with subsequent fatigue later in the game. Also, the fusion of athletic accomplishments and personal identity is apparent from evidence that injured runners had significantly lower levels of self-esteem than did fully fit athletes in control groups (Chan and Grossman, 1988). More recent research has shown that a fear of re-injury is associated with poor rehabilitation outcomes for athletes suffering from anterior cruciate ligament injuries (Tripp et al., 2007). To summarize, at least three strands of evidence have converged to highlight the importance of psychological factors in the causes and treatment of injury in athletes.

Nature, prevalence and causes of injuries in sport

So far, I have introduced the mental side of physical trauma in athletes without actually explaining what the term **sports injury** actually means. This problem is rectified below. Unfortunately, as we shall see, there are no universally agreed criteria available to define sports injuries. Therefore, any analysis of sports injuries raises certain conceptual and methodological issues that need to be addressed.

What is a sports injury? Nature, types and severity

In sports science, an injury may be defined as any physical or medical condition that prevents a player from participating in a match or training session (Orchard and Seward, 2002). More generally, it may be regarded as any "involuntary, physically disruptive experience" (Cashmore, 2008, p. 230) encountered by an athlete. Despite their apparent clarity, these definitions gloss over several important conceptual issues. For example, as Udry and Andersen (2008) observed, athletes often incur injuries which originate *outside* sporting contexts. For example, what if an athlete is involved in a car crash while driving to the training ground? Does this disruptive experience constitute a sports injury? In an effort to deal with such objections, some sports scientists (e.g., Noyes et al., 1988) postulated the enforced or unexpected time lost from participation in sport as a key criterion in defining athletic injuries. But once again, this definition was criticized on two grounds. First, some athletes try to play their sport even though they are technically injured (Flint, 1998). One explanation for this phenomenon is that such performers may have higher pain thresholds than others. The second problem with the criterion of time loss is that it neglects the fact that injuries have *medical* as well as temporal consequences for athletes (Kujala, 2002). It may be wise to augment time loss with the requirement that to qualify as an "injury" a given problem should require medical attention. In summary, it is clear that despite several decades of research in this field, there does not seem to be any universally agreed definition of sports injury.

Despite some vagueness about the criteria used to define sports injuries, we know that the tissue damage which characterizes them varies considerably in type and severity. There is a clear distinction between acute and chronic injuries. Acute injuries refer mainly to "direct trauma" or injuries stemming from a known cause such as a sudden impact which may produce a bone fracture, muscle strain or a ligament sprain. Chronic injuries are relatively diffuse conditions that develop slowly and which only gradually lead to tissue breakdown. An example of such problems is tendonitis in the wrist of a regular tennis player – an injury which has no single identifiable cause. Given the fact that sports injuries vary along temporal dimensions (acute versus chronic), do they also vary in severity? Although there is no agreed method of measuring objectively the seriousness of an injury, a variety of possible indices of severity have been proposed. The seriousness of an athletic injury has been operationally defined in terms of the amount of time lost from participation in the sport, the degree of pain experienced by the athlete in the injured limb or area, the range of motion available for the injured body part, and the estimated time for recovery (G. Kerr and Miller, 2001). To illustrate the last of these criteria, Rahnama et al. (2002) distinguished between minor, moderate and severe types of injury in soccer players on the basis of the length of time needed for recovery. Nevertheless, no consensus exists about the best way to measure injury severity in sports. Having sketched the nature of sports injuries, we should now consider their prevalence.

Prevalence of injuries in sport

In general, the prevalence of injuries across different sports is difficult to assess because of factors such as variations in the criteria used to define and report physical trauma in athletes as well as inconsistencies in the use of protective equipment in a given sport (Junge and Dvorak, 2000; Walter et al., 1985). According to sports team physicians, injury rates for elite athletes can be as high as 50 per cent (Brewer, 2009). Dr Nathan Gibbs, club doctor to the famous Sydney Swans Australian Rules football team, said: "out of 22 players, we would have, on average, any week, five players who don't play due to injury. But then out of the 22 that are picked, there are probably eight or ten who are taking an injury into the game" (cited in C. Murphy, 2010, p. 24). More formal evidence on the prevalence of injury comes from UK research on two popular sports: cricket (a non-contact sport) and rugby (a contact sport). Hopps (2002) reported that between 2000 and 2002, England's top cricket players were almost *twice* as likely as their Australian counterparts to experience back injuries which had rendered participants unfit to play. This disparity in injury prevalence between cricketers from different countries is difficult to explain but may reflect the arduous, non-stop nature of the modern cricket season in Britain as compared to that in the southern hemisphere. With regard to injury prevalence in rugby, statistics released by the Rugby Football Union in England in 2002 showed that serious injuries (defined operationally as enforced time loss from the sport for a period of more than twenty-one days) had increased significantly from a figure of

1,058 (for the 1992–1993 season, before rugby union became a professional sport) to between 2,120 and 2,461 per year over a five-year period (1997–2002). Again, this apparent increase in injuries in rugby has been attributed to external factors – in this case, the increasing demands of professionalism in this sport (Starmer-Smith, 2002). Unfortunately, little is known about whether or not injuries in soccer have increased to a similar degree. What is known, however, is that at any one time, about 10 per cent of the players in the ninety-two professional football squads in Britain are unable to train because of injury (Caroline Woods et al., 2002). About 47 per cent of professional footballers are forced to retire from the game as a result of injury (Drawer and Fuller, 2002). These figures highlight the extent of the problem of injury in soccer. In summary, research evidence suggests that injuries are widespread in such popular sports as cricket, rugby and soccer.

The apparent growth of sports injury incidence is attributable mainly to a combination of social and/or professional influences. Consider the growing emphasis in our society on the pursuit of optimal health and fitness: in order to look and feel better, one has to work harder on one's fitness and appearance. Unfortunately, working harder may cause physical injury unless one's training programmes are individually tailored to one's current level of fitness (see also discussion of over-training in Chapter 8) and one is properly conditioned physically to undertake the exercise in the first place. In relation to this latter point, stretching before exercising has long been regarded as a popular and effective conditioning technique. It is widely believed that runners who stretch their calves and hamstrings before a race not only increase their flexibility but also reduce their chance of incurring injury. But does the research evidence support the validity of stretching exercises? Remarkably, a study by Herbert and Gabriel (2002) raised doubts about this matter by questioning the extent to which "warming up" and "warming down" by stretching reduces the risk of muscle injuries (see Box 9.2).

Box 9.2 Thinking critically about ... the value of stretching before and after exercising

Although certain strategies are useful in preventing sports injuries (e.g., the wearing of helmets is believed to protect cyclists from head trauma), others are of doubtful value. Although improvements in helmet design in the 1960s led to a reduction in deaths from head injuries in American football players, they were also associated with an *increase* in spine fractures following tackles in the game (Kujala, 2002). Given this uncertainty about the value of certain injury prevention techniques, how useful is the ubiquitous strategy of stretching before engaging in exercise? It seems heretical to question the value of stretching because virtually all athletes are taught that stretching before and after exercise is beneficial in at least three ways. First, it is alleged to reduce muscle soreness. Second, as stretching is believed to enhance muscle flexibility, it should lessen the likelihood of musculoskeletal injury. Third, stretching is reckoned to enhance athletic performance. But where is the empirical evidence to support any of these three claims?

In an attempt to answer this question, Herbert and Gabriel (2002) conducted a systematic review of the research literature on stretching. Results revealed that across five relevant studies, there was no significant effect of stretching before or after exercise on delayed-onset muscle soreness. Next, a review of two studies conducted on army recruits indicated that stretching before undertaking exercise does not yield useful reductions in the risk of incurring injury. However, this conclusion applies strictly to the military setting in which the relevant data had been gathered. A review by Thacker et al. (2004) concluded that pre-exercise stretching did not prevent injury among either recreational or competitive athletes. Perhaps not surprisingly, Kujala (2002, p. 36) claimed that stretching "lacks scientific evidence". Surprisingly, no empirical studies could be located on the issue of whether or not stretching improves athletic performance. In summary, the work of Herbert and Gabriel (2002) highlights the value of evidence based research in attempting to disentangle the myths of the locker room from prescriptions based on sound empirical principles. As a consequence of the above studies, sports scientists are beginning to evaluate the optimal time in which to conduct stretching exercises. As a person's body temperature tends to increase *after* exercise, with concomitant enhanced extensibility of ligaments, tendons and muscles, it may make more sense to stretch at this stage (Cottell, 2003). Of course, a key issue that needs to be addressed in this field is the extent to which researchers are really comparing "like with like" when evaluating stretching exercises across different sports. After all, the static stretching displayed by a runner (where each muscle is held to the point of resistance for a given duration) is different from a more dynamic method of stretching that can be found in martial arts (e.g., where short, sharp kicks are practised before combat).

Critical thinking questions

Can you think of any psychological reasons why pre-performance stretching may be helpful to athletes? Could it be regarded as part of their routine to help them to get into the right frame of mind to compete? How could you persuade sports performers to stretch while "warming down" after they have competed?

A second possible explanation for the apparent increase in sports injuries among active people is that at the elite level, professional performers are pushing their bodies to the limits of their abilities in pursuit of athletic success. This theory is supported anecdotally by observation of injury trends in tennis and golf. Bill Norris, the principal trainer on the American Tennis Professionals' tour, observed that problems of injury and burnout (see also Chapter 2) stem from a combination of the "never-ending pursuit of achievement and the inability of coaches to understand that the human body can only take so much for so long" (cited in R. Evans, 2002, p. 24). A similar picture has long been evident in golf. As the golf swing and hunched stance of the putting action place great strain on golfers' backs, it is not surprising that back injuries are very common in this sport. McHardy et al. (2007) discovered that lower back problems accounted for about 25 per cent of all golf-related injuries sustained by a large sample of Australian players. It is difficult to know whether or not athletic injuries are increasing because of the dearth of injury surveillance data from national sports organizations. What *can* be explored, however, is the issue of whether or not sports vary in the injury risks that they pose for participants.

Do sports differ in their levels of "dangerousness"? Intuitively, it seems plausible that one could place sports along a continuum of riskiness with apparently safe activities at one end (e.g., endurance events such as marathon running) and high-risk sports at the other end. Indeed, in motor racing, sixty-nine drivers from Formula One died as a result of on course accidents between 1950 and 1994 (Kujala, 2002). Somewhere in the middle of this hypothetical injury risk continuum lie popular sports such as basketball and soccer. Another way of investigating the "danger" of sports is to elicit risk ratings of them from the performers themselves. Using this approach, D. Pedersen (1997) asked more than 400 people to assess the risks posed by various sporting activities. Results revealed that motorcycle racing was perceived as the most dangerous sport, followed by cliff-jumping, hang-gliding, sky-diving, bungee-jumping, rock-climbing, scuba-diving and, last of all, skiing. Perhaps not surprisingly, D. Pedersen (1997) found that there was an inverse relationship between the perceived dangerousness of these sports and people's willingness to participate in them. Despite such risks, many people are attracted to dangerous leisure activities (see also Chapter 2 for discussion of people's motivation for participating in dangerous sports). Additional research on the riskiness of sports comes from Grimmer et al. (2000), who examined a sample of Australian adolescents in an effort to identify the seven most common sports which were associated with elevated risks of injury. In decreasing order of injury potential, these sports were martial arts, hockey, Australian Rules football, roller-blading, netball, soccer and basketball. Most of these activities are team games in which there is a high degree of bodily contact with opponents and a lot of jumping and landing. In summary, reasonable progress has been made in assessing the riskiness of various sports and in classifying them according to their perceived level of dangerousness. Having analysed the nature, types and prevalence of injuries, we should now consider their causes.

Causes of injuries in sport

Although a detailed analysis of the aetiology of athletic injuries is beyond the scope of this chapter, certain obvious causes can be pinpointed. In this regard, Kirkby (1995) compiled a list of precipitating factors which included inadequate physical conditioning and/or warm up procedures (but see Box 9.2), faulty biomechanical techniques used by athletes, deficient sports equipment, poor quality protective apparel, dangerous sports surfaces and, of course, illegal and aggressive physical contact from opponents. In passing, it is notable that one of these factors – deficient sports equipment – was blamed for a spate of injuries among professional footballers in Britain. To illustrate, Caroline Woods et al. (2002, p. 439) claimed that modern football boots contribute to the occurrence of injuries due to their "inadequate heel lift, soft and high heel counter, and rigid sole". But apart from these precipitating factors, there are plenty of other ways in which athletes can incur injury. Some of these factors are surprising if not bizarre (see Box 9.3).

Research on the causes of sports injury has identified two broad classes of risk variables: extrinsic and intrinsic factors (Kujala, 2002). Among the extrinsic factors are the type of sport played (with high-risk activities like motorcycle racing standing in contrast with safer pursuits like tennis), methods of training undertaken, typical environment in which the sport is played and the nature and amount of protective equipment used. By contrast, the intrinsic factors include personal characteristics of the participants such as age, gender and possible congenital abnormalities. Andre Agassi, the former world number 1 tennis player, was born with spondylolisthesis (or congenital displacement of the vertebrae), a condition that led to chronic sciatica and increased vulnerability to back injuries, and ultimately to his retirement (Agassi, 2009). Other intrinsic injury determinants include a previous history of physical injury and a vulnerability to stress. The idea that psychosocial factors could serve as antecedents of athletic injury may be traced back at least as far as T. Holmes and Rahe (1967). Briefly, these investigators found that people who had experienced stressful life events were more likely to suffer adverse health subsequently than were those who had experienced less stress in their lives. Evidence to support this theory in sport comes from the fact that injured athletes tend to have experienced higher levels of stress during the year preceding their injury than have athletes who had not been injured (Cryan and Alles, 1983). Such research has been criticized by Petrie and Falkstein (1998), however, for its reliance on subjective reports of injury severity and also for failing to consider the possible influence of intervening variables such as the social support mechanisms available to the injured athletes. In a review of research in this field, J. Williams and Roepke (1993) concluded that eighteen out of twenty studies had found a significant positive relationship between stress and injury in athletes. In the light of such conclusions, let us now explore the psychological significance of athletes' reactions to the injuries that they experience.

Box 9.3 Yes, it really happened! Unusual causes of injury among athletes

Athletic injuries are not always incurred on the sports field. Here are some unusual causes of injury in various sports (Edgar, 2006; Rooney, 2007).

- Marc Warren (Scottish golfer) was practising golf swings in his hotel room, wearing only a towel, when he accidentally hit a chandelier which cut him badly (Donegan, 2007).
- Alan Wright (former soccer player with Aston Villa and Blackburn Rovers) strained his neck by stretching out to reach the accelerator of his new Ferrari.
- Vijay Singh (Fijian former world number 1 golfer and three times major winner) withdrew from the Deutsche Bank Open because he had hurt his back playing table tennis with his son.
- Mike Tindall (England rugby player) missed the start of the 2005 Six Nations Championship due to a hand injury incurred when his hand had got stuck between two weights.

- David Seaman (former Arsenal and England goalkeeper) damaged his knee ligaments when bending down to pick up a remote control unit for his television.
- Volkan Demirel (Fenerbache goalkeeper) dislocated his shoulder when he fell over after he had thrown his shirt to a fan after his team had defeated Galatasaray.

How do athletes react psychologically to injury? Contrasting theoretical models

According to Udry and Andersen (2008), two main theories have been postulated to explain the way in which sport performers react cognitively and emotionally to physical setbacks. The first approach is the grief stages model, which focuses mainly on the *emotional* consequences of injury for the afflicted athlete. The second approach is the cognitive appraisal model, which concentrates on *cognitive* aspects of the injury experience and is influenced by studies of the way in which people perceive and cope with stress. One advantage of this latter approach over the grief stages model is that it tries to take into account personal and situational factors that determine athletes' emotional reactions to injuries. A second advantage is that it addresses the extent and quality of coping resources available to the injured athlete.

Stage models

Grief stages models (e.g., Rotella, 1985) are based on the assumption that injury is experienced as a form of symbolic *loss* by athletes. As a result of such loss, injured athletes are assumed to go through a predictable sequence of emotional changes on their way to recovery. As Cashmore (2008, p. 230) put it, "not only do they lose a physical capability, they also lose a salient part of their self". But how valid is this assumption of injury as a form of loss? More generally, what are the consequences of this loss for the rehabilitation of the athlete?

The experience of loss is widespread in sport. Lavallee et al. (1998) analysed the various forms of loss that athletes encounter in sport, ranging from competitive defeat to the loss of self-esteem that is often associated with physical injury. According to Ford and Gordon (1999), injured athletes may experience losses affecting factors such as mobility, independence, sense of control, virility, social relationships, income and financial rewards. Among the earliest proponents of the grief response theory of athletes' reactions to injury was P. Pedersen (1986), who suggested that sport performers may display a form of grief similar to that exhibited by people who suffer the loss of a loved one. This theory was based on the seminal work of Elizabeth Kübler-Ross (1969), a Swiss psychiatrist who had witnessed much death and suffering in the Second World War as a young adult and who had subsequently worked as a physician with cancer patients in the Unites States

(Derek Gill, 1980). Based on interviews with these patients, and observations of the way in which they dealt with their terminal illness, Kübler-Ross proposed that people go through five hypothetical stages of emotional response after they have been told of their impending death. These stages are denial, anger, bargaining, depression and acceptance. *Denial* occurs when patients refuse to accept the diagnosis offered to them or deny its implications. *Anger* results from an attempt to address the apparent unfairness of the situation by asking the question "Why me?" *Bargaining* happens when patients say prayers or offer to make changes in their lifestyle in an exchange for a postponement of their death. *Depression* occurs when patients start to grieve deeply. Finally, but not always, *acceptance* emerges when patients resign themselves with dignity to their fate. The interpretation of this last stage is somewhat controversial. L. Hardy et al. (1996) pointed out that acceptance does not mean resignation. In Kübler-Ross's model, the stage of acceptance seems to have the connotation of capitulation or giving up. This reaction is rarely the case with injured athletes, because the final stage of their reaction involves a readiness to engage in physical activity again.

Although this five-stage theory seems plausible, it has been criticized on the grounds of poor methodology (Kübler-Ross's recording of data was unsystematic and there are no independent empirical data to validate it) and for unreliable findings (e.g., see Aronoff and Spilka, 1984–1985). Doka (1995) argues that the alleged reactions of terminally ill patients to bad news are not typical of people facing death in other situations. Despite such criticisms of loss theory, Kubler-Ross's work has exerted a major influence on sport psychologists' understanding of how athletes react to injuries (Brewer, 2001a). According to this grief stages model, athletes who experience a significant injury or a career-threatening illness tend to go through a predictable sequence of stages as part of their recovery process. At first glance, however, this claim seems fanciful not only because illness and injury are not the same as death but also because there are many differences between the worlds of terminal illness and sport. Nevertheless, there is no doubt that injury generates doubt and loss in athletes. Sports performers who suffer serious injury are not only precluded from engaging in the activity that they love but also vulnerable to significant losses of income, mobility, independence and social status.

Kübler-Ross's (1969) five stages may be translated into the sporting domain as follows. First, an injured athlete's denial is captured by such statements as "I'll be fine – it can't be very serious". Second, anger may begin when athletes realize the amount of time they will miss as a result of the injury. Third, some bargaining may occur in which athletes may offer to make compromises to their lifestyle in an attempt to regain lost fitness. Fourth, depression may arise when afflicted athletes make pessimistic predictions about their future in sport. This feeling is epitomized by such expressions as "This is hopeless – I'll never be as good as I was in the past". Finally, acceptance should arrive as athletes come to terms with the adverse circumstances which they have encountered. For example, they may say, "It's no use moaning – I'll just have to work myself back to fitness". Heil (1993) proposed a sport-related modification of Kübler-Ross's five-stage model. Briefly, his affective cycle model suggested that athletes go through three broad stages on the way to recovery. First, they are held to experience distress (e.g., shock, anger, depression). Second, they are believed to engage in denial. Third, they experience determined coping, whereby realism sets in and athletes accept their responsibility in the rehabilitation process.

Typically, stage theories of injury reaction have been tested in two ways (Brewer, 2001b). First, quantitative studies have used questionnaires and standardized psychological tests to assess athletes' emotional responses to injury and to compare them with the normal emotional fluctuations experienced by matched participants in control groups. In this regard, the Profile of Mood States (McNair et al., 1992) has been used extensively to measure six affective states in athletes: tension/anxiety, depression/dejection, anger/hostility, vigour, fatigue, and confusion/bewilderment. In this test, a total mood disturbance score may be calculated by adding the negative mood scale scores (tension, depression, anger, fatigue and confusion) and subtracting the positive mood scale (vigour). An abbreviated, sport-specific version of this instrument has been developed by Grove and Prapavessis (1992). The second approach in this field uses qualitative methodology (see brief account in Chapter 1). Adopting this approach, researchers have used such techniques as in-depth interviews and focus groups to examine athletes' beliefs about, and emotional reactions to, their injuries over a given period of time (Hurley et al., 2007). Briefly, Hurley et al. (2007) found that whereas most athletes initially viewed their injuries negatively, some of them reported positive interpretations of them over time. For example, they spoke of "learning new lessons" or "gaining a different perspective" (Hurley et al., 2007).

At least four interesting findings have emerged from the research literature on psychological aspects of injury rehabilitation. First, according to Brewer (2001b), higher levels of emotional disturbance (e.g., depression, anger, frustration) have been detected in athletes suffering from injuries than in control groups. Chan and Grossman (1988) discovered that injured runners displayed significantly more depression, anxiety and confusion than did non-injured counterparts. According to Kishi et al. (1994), patients who had experienced amputations or spinal cord injuries became depressed and even suicidal afterwards. Using a longitudinal research design, Leddy et al. (1994) found that injured athletes showed greater depression and anxiety than athletes in control groups immediately after injury occurrence. Perhaps more significantly, these authors discovered that this disparity in distress was still evident as long as two months later. Overall, Brewer (1999) suggested that between 5 and 13 per cent of injured athletes suffer emotional disturbance of clinically significant proportions.

The second general finding in the research literature is that physical trauma appears to be associated with elevated levels of emotional distress. Indeed, such distress has been reported in between 5 and 24 per cent of injured athletes who have been tested (Brewer, 1999). Nevertheless, Brewer (2001b) urges caution as such evidence does not prove that injury actually *causes* emotional disturbance.

The third general finding in this field is that, not surprisingly, the emotional reactions of injured athletes tend to change from negative to positive during the course of their rehabilitation. Quinn and Fallon (1999) administered the POMS to 136 elite injured athletes and discovered that a variety of initially negative emotional states (e.g., anger, depression) decreased significantly over time. Johnston and Carroll (2000) discovered that the degree of emotional confusion precipitated by injury varied directly with athletes' level of involvement in their sport. Following up athletes at different stages of rehabilitation, they found that those performers who had been more involved in sport and exercise before incurring injury reported higher levels of confusion and lower perceptions of recovery during rehabilitation than did colleagues who had been less involved in their sport.

The fourth general trend in the literature is the surprising discovery that occasionally, the experience of injury may *benefit* the athletes afflicted (Udry, 1999). Among the common benefits cited by athletes in this regard are opportunities for personal growth, development of interests outside sport, and increased motivation (Brewer, 2001b). If viewed constructively, recuperation time from a serious injury not only may allow athletes to learn more about themselves and how their bodies work but also may help them to develop interests outside sport. Consider the benefits that Roy Keane, the former captain of Manchester United and the Republic of Ireland, derived from the time he spent in solitary reflection as he recovered from the cruciate knee ligament injury which he experienced in 1998: "a bleak period in my professional life had changed me considerably even if I hadn't been fully aware of what was happening or what it meant. Time spent alone helped me figure myself out" (Keane, 2002, p. 181). Commonly, a cruciate injury is career-threatening as it usually requires reconstruction of the knee and precludes the afflicted athlete from active participation in the sport for up to a year afterwards. Athletes who undergo reconstruction of their anterior cruciate ligament may lose up to 1.5 inches of girth size in their quadriceps muscles – a fact which explains why they have to work so hard in rehabilitation (A. Smith et al., 2001). During this rehabilitation period, Roy Keane worked on his upper-body strength in the gym, reduced his alcohol intake and planned his life more effectively (Keane, 2002). A similarly constructive use of injury down-time was evident in the case of Robert Pires, the Arsenal and French international soccer player. This player experienced a seven-month injury in 2002 which forced him to miss the World Cup finals in Japan and Korea. During this recovery time, Pires claimed:

> you see things differently after something like that. Compared to people who have really bad accidents, what happened to me was nothing so at a certain point I need to be aware just how lucky I am. I can keep doing what I've always loved doing … Life goes on, I still have two legs, and I'll play again.
> (cited in Fotheringham, 2002a)

Of course, another aspect of athletes' emotional reactions to injury concerns the possible "secondary gains" (Heil, 1993) which they may experience. Sometimes athletes gain sympathy or social support simply as a result of adopting the role of an injured patient. Ironically, this type of secondary benefit could delay the rehabilitation of these athletes concerned because it encourages them to become passive and dependent on others.

Critical evaluation of the grief stages model

Although the grief stages model of injury reaction seems eminently plausible, it has been criticized on at least five grounds (see reviews by Brewer et al., 2002; L. Evans and Hardy, 1995).

First, at a conceptual level, there are obvious and significant differences between the type of loss which people tend to experience when bereaved and those that often follow a physical injury. While the former loss is irrevocable due to death, the latter loss is usually only a temporary phenomenon. Similarly, if the hypothetical emotional reactions of injured athletes are accepted as facts, certain problems may develop in the patient–physician relationship (Brewer, 2001b). Sport medicine specialists may perceive injured athletes as being "in denial" when they have got over the initial feelings of distress that accompany any physical trauma. Therefore, we should be cautious in extrapolating from theories based on terminal illness to the world of sport. Second, researchers disagree about the extent to which the alleged sequence of stages in grief reaction models is fixed. Some critics claim that these stages are *circular* rather than linear (L. Evans and Hardy, 1995). If so, regression to earlier stages in the sequence may occur among certain athletes. Clearly, this possibility makes it difficult to specify testable predictions from grief reaction models of injury. Third, at least one of the hypothetical stages in the grief reaction may be difficult to measure psychometrically (Udry and Andersen, 2008). Specifically, if denial is an unconscious process, how can it be assessed validly using self-report scales or interviews that are limited to experiences that are consciously accessible? Fourth, stage models tend to ignore substantial individual differences between athletes in emotional reaction to injuries (Brewer et al., 2002). Although some athletes tend to perceive all ailments pessimistically, others (e.g., Roy Keane – see quote earlier in this chapter) may view the period of enforced rest that follows an injury as being an opportunity for self-discovery. Similarly, stage theories tend to ignore the mediating influence of situational factors (Brewer, 2001b). The degree of emotional upset caused by an athletic injury appears to depend on such factors as the type of ailment (with acute injuries eliciting greater emotional reactions than chronic injuries) and the stage in the sporting season in which the damage occurs. The pattern of emotional reactions displayed by injured athletes varies as a function of individual differences and situational factors. Fifth, grief stages models lack a clear specification of the possible theoretical mechanisms by which psychological factors influence athletes' reactions to injury. In summary, psychological research has not supported all of the major tenets of grief reaction stage theories. Udry and Andersen (2008) concluded that it is difficult to draw firm conclusions regarding the utility of these models. Interestingly, L. Evans and Hardy (1995, p. 233) remarked that "contemporary theorists have spent more time and effort criticizing … classical approaches to grief … than in proposing models of grief that can be empirically tested and verified". In view of the flaws of stage theories, alternative approaches have been postulated to account for the way in which athletes react to injury. Perhaps the most popular and influential of these approaches are the cognitive appraisal models developed by Brewer (1994) and Wiese-Bjornstal et al. (1998). It is to these models that we now turn.

Cognitive appraisal models of injury reaction

Cognitive appraisal models of injury reaction (also known as "stress and coping" approaches: Udry and Andersen, 2008) are based on the idea that people's emotional and behavioural reactions to any type of physical trauma are determined principally by their *interpretation* (or appraisal) of it (Lazarus, 1993). Put differently, cognitive appraisal theorists propose that individual differences in how people perceive injuries influence their reactions to, and recovery from, them. But what exactly does the term appraisal mean? For psychologists, it refers to a subjective interpretation of an event or situation. Any everyday experience can be appraised either as a threat or as a challenge. Thus some people get annoyed while queueing in a bank whereas others appear to be immune to feelings of frustration in this situation. This happens, according to Lazarus and Folkman (1984), because of individual differences in cognitive appraisal. Specifically, if people perceive every second spent in a queue as a waste of time, they are likely to feel stressed by the experience. But if they appraise the same situation more constructively (e.g., "Waiting in this queue will give me a chance to slow down, catch my breath and plan the rest of my day"), it will not be as stressful to them. So, for cognitive theorists, stress is transactional because it involves two processes: the tendency for people to perceive a situation as a threat to their well-being and also the feeling that they will not be able to cope with its demands. Based on this analysis, two types of appraisal processes may be identified. First, **primary appraisal** occurs when one decides that because a given situation poses a threat, it requires a coping response. Second, **secondary appraisal** occurs when one asks oneself whether or not one has the ability to cope with the situation in question. In any case, when people perceive an event as a challenge to their abilities, and are confident that they have sufficient mental resources to overcome it, they tend to react positively to the situation in question.

Injured athletes' appraisal processes are believed to be determined by a number of factors. These factors include the amount of previous experience that athletes have had of similar injuries, the adequacy of their coping resources, the degree of uncertainty in the situation (e.g., is there much consensus among medical specialists about the nature and prognosis of the injury?) and the amount of perceived control that injured athletes can exert over their physical setback. Taking these factors into consideration, appraisal theorists propose that athletes with a history of injuries, a way of looking at things pessimistically and a lack of coping resources will be most at risk for slow recovery from whatever injuries they experience. In summary, cognitive appraisal theorists suggest that the way in which athletes interpret their injury determines not only their emotional response to it but also the degree to which they adhere to prescribed rehabilitation programmes.

Theoretically, the psychological variables which determine athletes' emotional and behavioural reactions to injury fall into three main categories. First, *personal* factors include such variables as whether or not athletes have experienced a similar injury before, their motivation and the way in which they typically cope with stress in general. Second, *situational* influences include the level at which athletes compete, the time of the season in which the injury occurred and the amount of social support available to the injured athletes. Third, *cognitive appraisal* characteristics include athletes' ability to perceive the injury experience as manageable and to identify the specific challenges that lie ahead. There is some evidence that cognitive appraisal is affected by situational factors such as the type of injury incurred by the sports performer. For example, athletes are more likely to experience post-traumatic reactive distress when the injuries are acute, severe and relatively

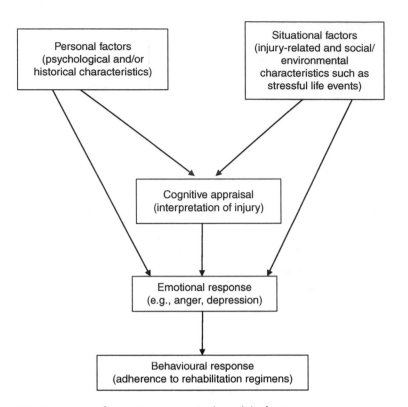

Figure 9.2 Diagram of cognitive appraisal model of injury reaction

uncommon (Brewer, 2001a). A generic cognitive appraisal model of athletes' injury reactions is presented in Figure 9.2.

According to this model, personal and situational factors interact with cognitive and emotional factors to influence the way in which sport performers respond to injuries. Athletes' emotional reactions to physical trauma are influenced by a combination of *pre-injury* variables such as their history of previous injuries, motivation, and coping skills, and various *post-injury* factors like the way in which they perceive the nature and implications of the injury. This model does not take account of possible gender differences in athletes' reactions to injury (see Box 9.4).

Box 9.4 Thinking critically about ... the role of gender in athletes' reactions to injury

Are there gender differences in the way in which athletes react to injuries? In an effort to answer this question, Granito (2002) interviewed thirty-one intercollegiate athletes (sixteen females and fifteen males) about their experiences of sports injuries. Results revealed differences between the male and female athletes in three key areas. First, the female athletes tended to be less satisfied than the male athletes with regard to their post-injury relationship with their coaches. Many of the female performers felt ignored by their coaches after the injury had occurred. Also, they reported feeling unhappy about an apparent lack of sympathy from their coaches. Second, by contrast with the male athletes interviewed, few of the female athletes in the study felt that they had received sufficient emotional support from their partners, friends and/or from family members. Third, the female athletes in this study were more likely than the males to express concern over how their injuries might affect their future health.

Critical thinking questions

Are you satisfied that gender differences are the only possible explanation for these findings? If not, what other variables (e.g., the gender of the coach, the nature of the sport) might have affected the results of this study? Given the reliance of this study on retrospective recall by the athletes interviewed, what potential biases could have affected the findings? Granito (2002) acknowledged that the time between injury onset and athletes' interviews was not standardized. How could this factor have affected the results? How could you test the theory that coaches communicate differently with female and male athletes after these performers have incurred injuries?

At the heart of Figure 9.2 is the assumption that injury is a form of stress for athletes. How valid is this assumption? Intuitively, it could be argued that a vulnerability to stress may render athletes susceptible to injury because muscle tension increases the possibility of sprains and other musculoskeletal damage (Gould et al., 2000). Unfortunately, this theory has not been tested adequately so far. Indeed, few researchers have sought to identify the precise theoretical mechanisms by which psychological factors like stress influence athletes' vulnerability to injury. Nevertheless, as we learned earlier in this chapter, there is evidence that certain kinds of life stress are associated with athletic injury. J. Williams (2001) observed that athletes who had experienced a relatively high degree of stressful life events were between two and five times more likely to be injured than were athletes who had experienced relatively low levels of such stress. Let us now evaluate the cognitive appraisal model of injury reaction in more detail.

Critical evaluation of the cognitive appraisal model of injury reaction

From a cursory inspection of relevant research literature, it seems that the cognitive appraisal approach to injury reaction has generated more research than its predecessor, the grief stages model. This research may be classified into two broad categories (Brewer et al., 2002): first, studies of the aetiology of injuries, and second, research on the role of psychological factors in people's recovery from injuries. These two strands of research converge on a number of conclusions.

First, as predicted by the generic model, stressful life events are associated with increased vulnerability to injury. Bramwell et al. (1975) discovered that the risk of injury to American football players grew in direct proportion to the amount of stressful life events that they had experienced. Similar findings were reported by Cryan and Alles (1983), but the results of these studies should be interpreted cautiously, because they used retrospective data collection procedures which are vulnerable to memory biases and other cognitive distortions. Second, there is evidence that the way in which athletes think about, or try to make sense of, their injuries is related to their reactions to the trauma (see also Chapter 2 for a discussion of attributional processes in athletes). Specifically, athletes who attribute their injuries to internal factors (e.g., "It was entirely my fault") which have global consequences (e.g., "This injury has ruined my life") tend to experience more distress than do athletes with more optimistic explanatory styles. By contrast, athletes' adherence to physical rehabilitation programmes is associated with attributions to stable and personally controllable factors (e.g., "If I work hard on my exercises every day, I can get back to full fitness soon"). Third, research on the relationship between athletes' coping strategies for stress and the speed and/or success of their physical rehabilitation has produced mixed results. Udry (1997) explored the relationship between injured athletes' coping skills, the social support which they received from others, and their adherence to post-surgery rehabilitation programmes. The injury studied in this research was a cruciate ligament rupture. Results showed that although "instrumental" coping strategies (e.g., attempting to locate as much information as possible about the injury) were related to adherence, social support was not associated with any rehabilitation outcome measures.

Despite receiving reasonable empirical support, cognitive appraisal models of injury reaction have at least two notable limitations. First, these models may be more appropriate in describing athletes' reactions to acute than to chronic injuries (J. Williams, 2001). To explain, whereas acute injuries are usually caused by sudden and potentially stressful incidents, chronic injuries have unknown causes and are probably not mediated by stress-related mechanisms. Second, the profusion of variables included in cognitive appraisal models (see Figure 9.2) makes it difficult to test causal relationships. In short, these models appear to be too all-embracing to serve as heuristic devices for hypothesis testing.

Conclusions about theories of injury reaction

Until the 1990s, psychological understanding of the way in which athletes react to injuries was based largely on intuition and clinical case studies. Subsequently, this picture changed with the advent of two important theories in this field – namely, the grief stages and the cognitive appraisal models. Having explained these approaches separately in the previous sections, let us consider how they compare.

At first glance, there are certain similarities between these two models. Both of them claim that athletes' psychological reactions to injuries vary over time. On closer inspection, however, these models differ from each other in at least three ways. First, whereas grief stages models tend to neglect individual differences between athletes in reactions to injury, cognitive appraisal approaches begin with the assumption that athletes differ considerably in how they perceive and interpret their injuries. Second, whereas grief stages models dwell primarily on emotional factors, cognitive appraisal models claim that injuries affect athletes also at the cognitive and behavioural levels. Third, the two approaches differ with regard to postulated theoretical mechanisms. In particular, whereas grief stages models appeal to the mediating influence of constructs such as emotional loss, cognitive appraisal models propose that stress mediates athletes' reactions to injury. Unfortunately, as both loss and stress are rather nebulous constructs, little explanatory value has been achieved using either of these theoretical models. Despite these criticisms, the grief stages and cognitive appraisal models of injury reaction have been helpful to sport science researchers. Udry and Andersen (2008) concluded that the grief stages model has been useful in illuminating not only "what" athletes experience after injury but also "when" they do so, while the cognitive appraisal approach may offer investigators some ideas about the reasons why athletes differ from each other in their emotional reactions to injuries.

At this stage, having reviewed available theoretical approaches, we need to consider an important practical question. Specifically, what psychological techniques are useful in facilitating the rehabilitation of injured athletes? In accordance with the theme of this book, I believe that the best techniques are those which combine theoretical rigour with practical utility.

Rehabilitation of injured athletes: from psychological theory to practice

The principal objective of any injury rehabilitation programme is to help afflicted athletes to return to full fitness and active involvement in their chosen sport as quickly and as safely as possible. In this regard, a growing body of research has investigated the factors influencing athletes' adherence to the rehabilitation advice of, and exercises prescribed by, their injury treatment specialists. Having reviewed such research, Brewer (2010b) highlighted three main types of factors that are associated with adherence to sport injury rehabilitation programmes: personal characteristics, contextual/environmental characteristics, and rehabilitation-related beliefs (such as locus of control beliefs, i.e., whether one thinks that important outcomes in one's life are determined largely by internal or external factors). First, among athletes' personal characteristics that are associated with their rehabilitation compliance are self-motivation, high pain tolerance, and strong identification with athletic identity. Second, key contextual environmental factors that affect adherence to rehabilitation include perceived supportiveness of others and convenient scheduling of rehabilitation activities. Third, with regard to rehabililitation-related or locus of control beliefs research evidence suggests that athletes who think that they can exert control over their rehabilitation outcomes tend to adhere better to the advice that they receive from treatment specialists than do athletes who believe that they can do little to influence their health. More generally, a number of theoretically based injury management principles and practical techniques may be identified as follows.

First, the cognitive appraisal model of injury reaction emphasizes the importance of taking into account cognitive and perceptual factors such as the way in which the afflicted person makes sense of what has happened to him or her. A practical implication of this theoretical approach is that athletes' beliefs about the causes and likely course of the injuries from which they are suffering should be addressed explicitly by the treatment specialist. Therefore, as early as possible, incorrect assumptions or naive theories about the injury should be elicited and challenged. Influenced by this approach, A. Smith et al. (2001) stressed the need for therapists to convey to their patients an accurate understanding of the nature and prognosis of the injury in question. It is also important for treatment specialists to assess the degree to which injured athletes believe that they can exert control over the pace of the rehabilitation process. The theory here is that the more control that athletes perceive they have over the injury, the more likely they are to take personal responsibility for adhering to the prescribed treatment regime. Conversely, athletes who fail to understand the nature of their injury, and/or who believe that they are helpless to overcome it, will probably take longer to recover from it than will counterparts who have more accurate knowledge about it. In summary, the first principle of injury management is the idea that accurate knowledge and perceived control will help to reduce the stress generated by physical injuries.

Second, based on the grief stages model, it seems likely that afflicted athletes will tend to experience a characteristic sequence of emotional reactions as they work their way through the rehabilitation programme. Therefore, treatment is likely to be more effective if it is matched to the athlete's current position in this emotional sequence. Advice such as "cheer up, it could be worse" is ineffective and insensitive if the injured athlete is not ready to accept such comments (e.g., due to the fact that the athlete is in the denial stage).

Third, another injury management principle is concerned with the behavioural level of the injury experience. Perhaps the biggest danger for recovering athletes is to make a premature return to their sport. As Robert Pires, the former Arsenal and French international soccer star admitted after his long layoff through cruciate knee damage, "You need to be patient, not precipitate your return. You want to come back, that's natural, but it has to be all in good time" (cited in Fotheringham, 2002b, p. 2). Clearly, any unrealistic expectations of an early return to action must be dealt with sensitively during the rehabilitation programme. The therapist should try to help athletes to discuss any fears which they may have about their impending return to sport. There is evidence that athletes who are passive and/or uncooperative tend to recover more slowly and less successfully than athletes who take a more active role in the process. Fisher et al. (1988) studied the differences between athletes who adhered to their rehabilitation programme and those who did not. Not surprisingly, results showed that the "adherers" scored higher on self-motivation and also worked harder to recover from their injuries than did the "non-adherers". A final treatment principle stems from research findings on the importance of helping athletes to develop constructive interpretations of their injuries in order to minimize the stress experienced. The key objective here is to encourage injured athletes to restructure depressive thinking ("This is the end of my career") in more optimistic terms (e.g., "This injury gives me the opportunity to work on my weaknesses").

Turning to practical psychological techniques used in injury rehabilitation, mental practice (see Chapter 5) is an obvious candidate. Many applied sport psychologists recommend that injured athletes should be encouraged to "see" and "feel" themselves performing their sport skills fluently and effortlessly. This type of healing-oriented imagery is common in applied sport medicine (Brewer, 2009; Waters, 2007). In 2002 Jarrod Cunningham, the former London Irish rugby player, was diagnosed with amyotrophic lateral sclerosis, a form of motor neurone disease. One of the methods he used to tackle this condition was imagery. In particular, he claimed that he tried to "visualize sluggish electrons in the brain and spinal cord and to use mental imagery to inject energy and power into them" (quoted in Gallagher, 2002). Apart from mental practice, physical relaxation techniques may also be useful in helping athletes to counteract muscular tension experienced in the site of the injury.

In Box 9.5, a number of psychological techniques used in psychological interventions with injured athletes are presented (see also J. Williams and Scherzer, 2010).

Box 9.5 Psychological techniques used in injury rehabilitation programmes

Goal-setting
Working backwards from the long-term goal of recovery from the injury and participation in sport, a number of intermediate stepping-stones to full fitness should be agreed with the injured athlete. In general, positively phrased short-term goals are recommended to ensure optimal motivation for the daily rehabilitation schedule.

Constructive thinking
Injured athletes should be trained to acknowledge that although their injury is unfortunate and frustrating, it can provide them with an opportunity to take time out from their sport in order to rest, clarify their goals and regroup mentally.

Positive self-talk
Injured athletes can benefit from talking to themselves encouragingly using such phrases as "I can work out a plan to deal with this problem" or "I've been through situations like this before – this time is no different".

Mental imagery
Injured athletes should be trained to "see" and "feel" their injured limbs performing the skilled actions that they wish to regain. In a qualitative study, Driediger et al. (2006) interviewed ten athletes about their use of imagery during injury rehabilitation. Results showed that these athletes reported using imagery for rehabilitation purposes. An injured badminton player remarked that in attempting to recover from a muscle tear, "I would try to imagine what the tear looked like and I think about how it feels and how it's going to heal" (Driediger et al., 2006, p. 266).

Relaxation
Training injured athletes to breathe properly and to practise progressive muscular relaxation can be useful in counteracting the stress of injury.

Social support

Injury rehabilitation can be a rather lonely enterprise. Therefore, it is important to help athletes to identify people (e.g., friends, teammates and family) who can provide support and encouragement during the recovery process. For example, a fit teammate could attend the rehabilitation session of an injured colleague in order to provide him or her with some advice or encouragement. Social support serves as a buffer against the emotional distress typically caused by injuries. A good example here is the support given to each other by two injured French international athletes – the soccer star Robert Pires (then of Arsenal), who had been out of action for seven months between April and October 2002 due to a cruciate knee injury, and Thomas Castaignède (then of Saracens), a rugby player who was out for two years due to a ruptured Achilles tendon, before resuming in autumn 2002. Pires visited Castaignède in hospital in Paris and Castaignède visited Pires in London during their long spells of rehabilitation: "When you're injured, there's a certain level where there's not much you can say, it's just a question of being there" (cited in Fotheringham, 2002b, p. 2).

How effective are these psychological techniques when applied to the rehabilitation of injured athletes? Although research evidence on this issue is sparse, some evaluative data are available. Ievleva and Orlick (1991) studied thirty-two athletes who had attended a sports medicine clinic for rehabilitation treatment for knee and ankle injuries. Results showed that the techniques which were most strongly associated with fast recovery were positive self-talk (see also Chapter 4), goal-setting and "healing" imagery. In a similar study, Davis (1991) evaluated the effects of using relaxation and imagery exercises with collegiate swimmers and football players. Results indicated that there was a 52 per cent reduction in injuries to the swimmers and a 33 per cent reduction in injuries to the football players. L. Evans et al. (2000) used a longitudinal case study approach with three injured rugby players who were each receiving treatment for serious injuries. Results showed that the perceived efficacy of the psychological techniques used depended on the stage at which they were applied. Whereas emotional support was perceived as being important to the athletes in the initial stages of rehabilitation, task support was seen as being more useful in the middle to late stages of this process. An interesting feature of this study was that the researchers tackled the neglected question of *re-entry* for injured athletes. Briefly, they found that two key determinants of successful re-entry were gaining confidence in the injured body part and gaining confidence in overall fitness. L. Evans et al. (2006) interviewed four injured athletes about their use of imagery at three different stages of their rehabilitation. Results showed that imagery was used both for healing and pain management during the recovery process. Despite the apparent efficacy of many psychological techniques in injury rehabilitation settings, few researchers have explored the possible theoretical mechanisms that underlie these effects. However, one possible mechanism in this regard is self-efficacy. Put simply, these techniques may work simply because they strengthen athletes' sense of personal control over their physical condition. In this regard, imagery may help athletes to simulate successful rehabilitation outcomes, thereby enhancing their self-efficacy. Overall, it is evident from the preceding evidence that effective injury rehabilitation is a collaborative enterprise involving the treatment specialist, the athlete, other health-related professionals (e.g., a physiotherapist, a psychologist), the coach and other significant members of the athlete's life and family. Indeed, research suggests that the importance of these team members may vary with the stage of athletic rehabilitation in question. Gilbourne and Taylor (1998) suggested that early in the treatment phase, the medical staff and the physiotherapist play a significant role. Later in the recovery process, however, the coach of the injured athlete may assume a special significance as the performer begins to contemplate the possibility of participation in the sport once again.

Based on his experience, Petitpas (2002) recommended that the following four steps are necessary when working psychologically with injured athletes. In the first step, the therapist must attempt to build up a rapport with the athlete in question. To do so, the therapist must listen carefully to the athlete in order to find out what the injury means to him or her. The second step involves providing accurate and up-to-date information to the injured athlete on the nature of the injury, the medical and rehabilitation procedures required, and the goals of the rehabilitation programme. The third step of effective counselling for injured athletes involves identifying the nature and types of coping resources available to the athlete. The fourth step sees the therapist and athlete collaborating in working out specific, relevant and achievable "goal ladders" for the rehabilitation programme (for advice about goal-setting techniques, see also Chapter 2).

Before concluding this section of the chapter, it might be helpful to read about a case study using a psychological approach to injury rehabilitation (see Box 9.6).

Box 9.6 Thinking critically about … a case study of injury rehabilitation in rugby

Cecil et al. (2009) described a multidisciplinary approach to the rehabilitation of an injured international female rugby player referred to as "TJ". This player had damaged her medial collateral ligament in her knee after a collision with another player in a game. As a result of this injury, TJ had developed negative thoughts ("Will I favour my knee?") and shown signs of anxiety when watching rugby (e.g., she winced when viewing collisions between players). Following an initial assessment of the extent of TJ's injury, a three-month, multidisciplinary rehabilitation programme was designed in which the traditional methods of physiotherapy and strength and conditioning exercises were augmented by psychology sessions involving techniques such as "reframing" (i.e., replacing negatively phrased thoughts with positive expressions), mental imagery, relaxation and goal-setting. By the end of the programme, TJ had achieved full fitness, played for her country in the 2006 World Cup, and had regained her self-confidence.

Critical thinking questions
What are the advantages and disadvantages of working in an interdisciplinary team? For example, do you think that principles such as client confidentiality are considered equally important by the different disciplines involved in rehabilitation? Can you find any published studies in which sport psychology researchers acknowledge the difficulties of working in multidisciplinary teams?

New directions for research on the mental side of injuries

At least five new directions can be identified for research on psychological aspects of injuries in sport. First, given the dearth of prospective studies in this field, Kirkby (1995) and J. Williams (2001) suggested that future researchers should use longitudinal designs in order to explore the physical and psychological consequences of rehabilitation programmes for athletes over the course of a competitive season. Of course, these studies would have to ensure that the athletes involved had been matched for age and type of injury beforehand. Most research on the psychological consequences of injury has been hampered by a significant methodological problem – the failure to specify the pre-injury psychological characteristics of the athletes concerned (Quinn and Fallon, 1999). Second, little is known at present about either the nature or the efficacy of the coping strategies used by athletes during the course of injury rehabilitation. Therefore, future studies should attempt to establish which strategies are most useful at which stages of physical rehabilitation regimes. Third, in an effort to counteract naive expectations about the relationship between stress and injury, J. Williams (2001) urged future researchers to take into account such potentially important variables as type of sport, competitive level and gender. Fourth, research is required to explore expert–novice differences in injured athletes' "mental models" (i.e., their cognitive representation or understanding) of their problems. This type of research could address several important questions. Do elite athletes have a richer or more accurate understanding of their injuries than do less successful counterparts? Is there any relationship between the accuracy of athletes' understanding of their injuries and the success of their physical rehabilitation? Qualitative methods (such as in-depth interviews and focus groups) could help researchers to address these questions. Fifth, research is needed to establish the degree to which injured athletes can derive any significant benefits from their period of enforced absence from their chosen sports.

Ideas for research projects on injuries in sport

Here are four ideas for possible research projects on the psychology of injury in athletes.

1   Although considerable research exists on the psychosocial correlates of injury rehabilitation, relatively few studies have been conducted on the cognitive, emotional and behavioural issues experienced by athletes who have returned

to full involvement in sport and exercise activity. To fill this gap in the literature, you could replicate or extend Podlog and Eklund's (2009) analysis of elite athletes' perceptions of success in returning to sport from prolonged injuries.

2   Based on the research of Arvinen-Barrow et al. (2010), it would be interesting to find out if experienced chartered physiotherapists (say, those who have been working for at least ten years) differ from relatively inexperienced colleagues in the psychological techniques that they use during the rehabilitation programmes that they implement with injured athletes.

3   Based on the research of Hurley et al. (2007), can you think of a way of establishing whether or not there is a relationship between the accuracy of athletes' understanding of their injury and their subsequent compliance with prescribed rehabilitation exercises?

4   Based on the qualitative research methods and ideas of B. Smith (2010) and B. Smith and Sparkes (2009), it would be interesting to compare and contrast the experiences of athletes who have faced different types of injuries.

Summary

- Injury is an inevitable consequence of regular participation in sport and exercise, especially if vigorous physical contact occurs between athletes. Unfortunately, until relatively recently, little was known about the ways in which sports performers tend to perceive and/or react to the injuries which they experience. Therefore, the purpose of this chapter was to explore the mental side of sports injuries.

- The second section attempted to trace the shift from a physical to a mental perspective on injuries in sport.

- The third section provided a brief analysis of the nature, prevalence and causes of athletic injuries. In this section, a number of conceptual and methodological issues were addressed. For example, no clear consensus exists about how to either define or measure the severity of a sports injury.

- Despite this problem, the fourth section offered two main theories to describe how athletes react psychologically to injuries. These theories are the grief stages model and the cognitive appraisal approach. The section reviewed the strengths and limitations of these theories of injury reaction in athletes.

- The fifth section explained some practical psychological strategies used in the rehabilitation of injured athletes.

- The sixth section outlined several potentially fruitful new directions for research on psychological aspects of injury.

- Finally, four suggestions were provided for possible research projects in this field.

Glossary

Achievement goal theory (also known as goal orientation theory) A theory that postulates two types of motivational orientations in athletes – namely, ego orientation (i.e., focusing mainly on demonstrating one's competence in a given skill by performing better than others) and task orientation (i.e., focusing mainly on acquiring a certain level of competence in a given skill) – depending on how they interpret the meaning of achievement or success. See also **ego orientation** and **task orientation**.

Achievement motivation The tendency to strive for success or to expend effort and display persistence in attempting to attain a desirable goal.

Aerobic exercise Physical activities that elevate heart rate and increase the ability of the cardiovascular system to take up and use oxygen.

Anaerobic exercise Physical activities that are relatively high in intensity and short in duration.

Anecdotal evidence Subjective evidence derived from examples or personal experience.

Anxiety An emotional state characterized by worry, feelings of apprehension and/or bodily tension that tends to occur in the absence of real or obvious danger. See also **behavioural anxiety**, **cognitive anxiety** and **somatic anxiety**.

Arousal A diffuse pattern of alertness and physiological activation that prepares the body for action.

Attention The concentration of mental effort on sensory or mental events. See also **divided attention** and **selective attention**.

Attentional control theory A theory that postulates that anxiety hampers skilled performance by disrupting attentional control mechanisms in working memory such as attentional inhibition (the process which enables people to ignore irrelevant stimuli) and attentional shifting (the process by which people can switch attention from one task to another depending on changing task requirements).

Attribution The process of drawing inferences from, or seeking explanations for, events, experiences and behaviour.

Attribution theory The study of people's explanations for the causes of events or behaviour in their lives.

Attributional style The characteristic manner in which people make sense of, or offer similar explanations for, different events in their lives.

Autonomic nervous system (ANS) Part of the peripheral nervous system that regulates the body's involuntary muscles (e.g., the heart) and internal organs.

Behavioural anxiety A component of anxiety that is typically evident in such behaviour as tense facial expressions, changes in communication patterns (e.g., unusually rapid speech delivery) and jerky and inefficient body movements. See also **cognitive anxiety** and **somatic anxiety**.

Biofeedback A technique that allows people to monitor and gain control over certain bodily functions through the use of specialized equipment.

Bio-informational theory of imagery A theory that mental images are not "pictures in the head" but consist of stimulus, response and meaning propositions. See also **cognitive or symbolic theory of mental practice** and **neuromuscular theory of mental practice**.

Brainstorming The generation of ideas or suggestions by members of a group in an effort to solve a problem.

Burnout A state of withdrawal from a valued activity that is usually caused by chronic stress and accompanied by feelings of physical and mental exhaustion.

Case study A research method that involves in-depth description or detailed examination of a single person or instance of a situation.

Catastrophe theory A theory which postulates that high levels of cognitive and somatic anxiety will produce a sudden and dramatic (hence "catastrophic") deterioration in performance.

Choking under pressure A phenomenon in which athletic performance deteriorates suddenly and significantly as a result of anxiety.

Chronometric paradigm A method in experimental psychology in which the time-course of information-processing activities is used to draw inferences about possible underlying cognitive mechanisms.

Chunk A well-learned, cognitive unit of information in memory that may contain several smaller components.

Chunking The process of combining individual items into larger, more meaningful units as an aid to remembering them.

Cognitive anxiety Worry – or having negative expectations about some current or impending task or situation. See also **behavioural anxiety** and **somatic anxiety**.

Cognitive appraisal The process of interpreting or making judgements about a given event or situation. See also **primary appraisal** and **secondary appraisal**.

Cognitive evaluation theory A theory of motivation which postulates that rewards which are perceived as controlling tend to impair intrinsic motivation whereas those which are perceived as informative tend to strengthen it.

Cognitive or symbolic theory of mental practice The theory that mental practice facilitates attention to, and coding and retention of, key elements of the task or skill being learned through imagination. See also **bio-informational theory of imagery** and **neuromuscular theory of mental practice**.

Cognitive processes Mental activities, such as thinking, by which people acquire, store and use their knowledge.

Cognitive restructuring A psychological technique that helps people to change the way in which they think so that they can learn to perceive feared situations as controllable challenges.

Cognitive sport psychology A branch of sport psychology that is concerned with understanding how the mind works in athletic situations.

Cohesion (also known as team cohesion) The extent to which a group of people is united by a common purpose and bonds together to achieve that objective. See also **social cohesion** and **task cohesion**.

Concentration The ability to focus effectively on the task at hand, or on what is most important in any situation, while ignoring distractions. See also **focus**.

Confidence A belief in one's ability to perform a certain skill or to achieve a specific goal regardless of prevailing circumstances. See also **self-efficacy**.

Conscious processing hypothesis A theory which proposes that performance may deteriorate when people try to exert conscious control over skills that had previously been automatic. See also **reinvestment hypothesis**.

Construct An abstract or theoretical idea in psychology representing something that cannot be observed directly.

Construct validity The extent to which a psychological test actually measures what it purports to measure.

Controllability The ease with which mental images can be manipulated by the person who experiences them.

Correlational research A research method that measures the relationship or degree of association between two or more variables. See also **descriptive research** and **experimental research**.

Declarative knowledge Knowledge of facts and rules that can be consciously retrieved and declared explicitly.

Deliberate practice A highly structured, purposeful and individualized form of practice in which the learner tries to improve a specific skill under the guidance of a specialist instructor. See also **expertise**.

Descriptive research A group of research methods designed to record and analyse certain aspects of behaviour in natural settings. This category includes such methods as case studies (which are intensive or in-depth analyses of individuals, groups or events), naturalistic observation (where researchers observe behaviour as it occurs in its own natural environment), survey research (where information is collected about the behaviour, experiences or attitudes of many people using a series of questions about the topic of interest) and psychometric testing (where differences between people on some psychological construct are assessed using specially designed, standardized instruments). See also **correlational research** and **experimental research**.

Direction of anxiety The extent to which a person perceives anxiety to be either facilitative or debilitative of his or her performance.

Dispositional attributions Explanations of behaviour that invoke personality characteristics as the causes of a given outcome.

Divided attention The ability to perform two or more tasks equally well as a result of extensive practice. See also **selective attention**.

Drive theory A theory of motivation which suggests that behaviour is fuelled from within by drives stemming from basic biological needs.

Dual-task paradigm A research method for studying divided attention in which participants are required to perform two tasks at once.

Effect size Statistical estimation of the effect of one variable on another variable.

Ego orientation A type of motivation in which an athlete perceives success as performing better than others on a given task or skill. See also **achievement goal therapy**.

Electroencephalography (EEG) A neuroscientific technique for recording electrical activity in the brain using special electrodes placed on the scalp.

Electromyographic (EMG) activity A recording of the electrical activity of the muscles.

Endorphin A naturally occurring, opiate-like peptide substance in the brain that serves to reduce pain and increase pleasure.

Endorphin hypothesis The theory that the mood-enhancing effects of exercise are attributable to the effects of endorphins which are released during physical activity.

Epinephrine A neurotransmitter (also known as adrenaline) that is secreted by the adrenal gland when people are afraid or angry (during the "fight or flight" response) and causes increased heart rate and opening of air passages into the lungs in preparation of the body for strenuous activity. See also **norepinephrine**.

Event-related potential (ERP) A neuroscientific technique for measuring transient electrical changes in the brain evoked by certain information processing events.

Exercise Planned, structured and repetitive bodily movements that people engage in to improve or maintain physical fitness and/or health.

Exercise dependence (also known as exercise addiction) A desire for leisure-time physical activity that may result in uncontrollable bouts of excessive exercise.

Exercise psychology The scientific study of the psychological antecedents, correlates and consequences of physical activity. It has also been defined as the systematic investigation of the brain and behaviour in physical activity settings.

Exergaming The use of active, motion-control computer games to increase people's physical activity levels.

Experimental research A research method in which investigators examine the effects of manipulating one or more independent variables, under controlled conditions, on a designated dependent variable. See also **correlational research** and **descriptive research**.

Expertise Exceptional skills and/or knowledge in a specific area as a result of at least ten years of deliberate practice in it. See also **deliberate practice**.

Extrinsic motivation The impetus to engage in an activity for external rewards rather than for the satisfaction or enjoyment yielded by the activity itself. See also **intrinsic motivation**.

Eye-tracking technology The use of special computerized equipment to record and analyse the location, duration and order of people's visual fixations when asked to inspect a given scene.

Fitness See **physical fitness**.

Flow states See **peak performance experiences**.

Focus A figurative term that is commonly used in everyday life to refer to the convergence of one's mental spotlight or concentration system on a given target. In this sense, to focus is to pay specific attention to something. See also **concentration**.

Focus group A qualitative data collection technique which involves a group discussion led by a trained facilitator and which attempts to understand participants' attitudes, experiences and perceptions of designated ideas or topics. See also **qualitative research**.

Functional equivalence theory The theory that mental imagery and perception share similar neural mechanisms and pathways in the brain.

Functional magnetic resonance imaging (fMRI) A neuroscientific imaging technique that detects changes in the activity of the brain by measuring the amount of oxygen brought to a particular location in it.

Goal See **mastery goals, performance goals, process goals** and **result goals**.

Goal orientation theory See **achievement goal theory**.

Goal-setting The process by which people establish targets or objectives to attain.

Grief stages model of injury reaction The theory that athletes react to injury as a form of loss and hence go through a predictable sequence of emotions during their physical rehabilitation process.

Grounded theory A qualitative research method that uses a systematic set of procedures to generate a theory from the data collected.

Group Two or more people who interact with, and exert mutual influence on, each other. See also **team**.

Group dynamics Psychological processes that generate change in groups.

Hardiness A set of psychological characteristics that appear to protect people against stress by increasing their commitment to, and perceived control over, pressure situations.

Health psychology A field of psychology that is concerned with the promotion and maintenance of health as well as the prevention and treatment of physical illness.

Ideo-motor principle The theory that all thoughts have muscular concomitants.

Idiographic An approach in psychology that emphasizes the uniqueness or individuality of behaviour rather than its general principles. See also **nomothetic**.

Imagery The cognitive ability to simulate in the mind information that is not currently being perceived by the sense organs. See also **mental practice**.

Individual zone of optimal functioning (IZOF) A theory which suggests that optimal performance in sport occurs within a unique and individualized zone of arousal for the athlete concerned.

Internal consistency coefficient A type of reliability coefficient which assesses the degree to which the items of a test correlate with each other and hence measure the same construct. See also **reliability coefficient**.

Intrinsic motivation The impetus to engage in an activity for internal rewards such as enjoyment or satisfaction. See also **extrinsic motivation**.

Inverted-U hypothesis A theory that postulates that the relationship between arousal and performance is curvilinear and takes the form of an inverted-U shape.

Ironic theory of mental control A theory which proposes that under certain circumstances, the attempt to consciously suppress a specific thought or action can result in an ironic rebound effect whereby that thought or action becomes even more accessible than before.

Kinaesthetic imagery Feeling-oriented imagery or the mental simulation of sensations associated with limb positions and bodily movements. See also **motor imagery**.

Likert scale A numerical rating scale used in tests or questionnaires in which respondents are required to choose a value that represents their attitude or belief concerning a specific topic.

Mastery goals Goals that are self-referenced (i.e., involve personal improvement rather than comparison with the performance of other people) and that involve the cultivation of a designated level of competence in a given skill. See also **performance goals**.

Mental imagery See **imagery**.

Mental practice The systematic use of mental imagery to rehearse an action in the mind's eye without engaging in the actual physical movements involved. See also **imagery**.

Mental toughness An informal term used loosely to describe athletes' resilience, ability to cope with pressure and determination to persist in the face of adversity.

Meta-analysis A technique which enables researchers to analyse and combine the results of a number of separate studies on the same topic in order to determine the overall size of a statistical effect.

Meta-attention People's knowledge about, and control over, their own attentional processes.

Metacognition People's knowledge about, and control over, their own cognitive processes.

Meta-imagery People's knowledge about, and control over, their own mental imagery processes.

Mindfulness An attentional focusing strategy that originated in the Buddhist meditative tradition and that advocates a present-centred, non-judgemental awareness and acceptance (rather than attempted suppression) of external and internal distractions.

Motivation Factors that initiate, guide and/or sustain behaviour. See also **self-determination theory**.

Motivational climate The type of learning environment which a coach establishes for an athlete – namely, either ego-oriented or mastery-oriented.

Motor imagery The cognitive rehearsal of voluntary movement without accompanying bodily movement. It may also be defined as a dynamic mental state during which the representation of a motor action or movement is rehearsed in working memory without any overt motor output. See also **kinaesthetic imagery**.

Narrative inquiry A form of qualitative research that investigates the stories that people create and use over time in order to make sense of themselves and their experience of the world.

Naturalistic observation A research method in which the investigator observes behaviour in its natural setting and attempts to avoid influencing the participants or behaviour being observed.

Neuromuscular theory of mental practice The theory that imagination of any physical action elicits a faint pattern of activity in the muscles used to perform that action. See also **bio-informational theory of imagery** and **cognitive or symbolic theory of mental practice**.

Neuropsychology The study of the relationship between brain function, behaviour and experience.

Neuroscience An interdisciplinary field of research that is concerned mainly with the identification of the neural substrates of mental processes.

Neuroscientific imaging Brain-scanning techniques that produce pictures of the structure and/or functioning of specific parts of the brain.

Neurotransmitter A chemical substance that carries signals across synapses from one neuron to another.

Nomothetic An approach in psychology that seeks to establish general laws of behaviour using data obtained from group comparisons. See also **idiographic**.

Norepinephrine A type of neurotransmitter in the brain. See also **epinephrine**.

Occipital lobe A region of the cerebral cortex at the back of the head that is concerned with visual information processing.

Overtraining Any abnormal extension of the training process that leads to feelings of staleness and fatigue in athletes or exercisers.

Paradigm The detailed framework of principles, theories, methods and assumptions that is shared by a group of researchers in a given field.

Paratelic dominance A state of mind in which the person's behaviour is adventurous, playful and fun-loving. See also **reversal theory** and **telic dominance**.

Parietal lobe A brain region at the top and rear centre of the head which is believed to be involved in regulating spatial attention and motor control.

Pattern recognition tasks An experimental technique used by researchers to investigate expert–novice differences in people's ability to remember briefly presented patterns of information in a particular field.

Peak performance experiences (also known as flow states) Coveted but elusive experience in sport where an athlete performs to the best of his or her ability mainly as a result of being totally focused on the task at hand.

Perfectionism A person's tendency to strive for flawlessness and to set excessively high standards for one's performance.

Performance goals Behavioural outcomes or targets (such as serving accurately in tennis) that are largely under the control of the performer. See also **mastery goals**.

Physical activity Bodily movements that are produced by the skeletal muscles and result in the expenditure of energy.

Physical fitness The capacity to respond successfully to the physical challenges of life.

Plasticity A property of the brain that allows it to be moulded by experience and enables it to adapt to and/or compensate for loss of function due to damage.

Positron emission tomography (PET scanning) A neuroscientific imaging technique that measures the metabolic activity of the brain by tracking radioactive substances injected into the bloodstream.

Pre-performance routines Preferred sequences of preparatory thoughts and actions that athletes use in an effort to concentrate effectively before the execution of key skills.

Primary appraisal One's initial perception of a situation as benign, neutral or threatening. See also **cognitive appraisal** and **secondary appraisal**.

Procedural knowledge Implicit knowledge of how to perform actions and cognitive and/or motor skills.

Process goals Goals that specify the precise actions or behavioural strategy required in order to execute a particular skill or to attain a specific performance outcome.

Processing efficiency theory A theory that seeks to explain how anxiety affects skilled performance by distinguishing between performance *effectiveness* (i.e., the quality of task performance) and processing *efficiency* (i.e., the relationship between performance effectiveness and the use of processing resources – in short, performance effectiveness divided by effort) and by postulating that anxiety impairs processing efficiency to a greater extent than it does processing effectiveness.

Protocol analysis A research method which involved recording what people say as they think aloud while solving a problem. See also **think aloud verbal protocols**.

Psychometric data Information that is yielded by psychological tests and measures.

Psychometric testing The use of standardized psychological tests to measure people's abilities, beliefs, attitudes, preferences or activities.

Psychophysiology A field of psychology that explores the physiological processes underlying behaviour and experience.

Qualitative research A broad range of data collection techniques used by researchers in an attempt to understand and represent the quality, meaning or richness of people's lived experiences. See also **focus group**.

Quantitative research A range of research methods which are concerned with measuring and drawing statistical inferences from the data rather than with attempting to understand the subjective meaning or experience of this information.

Reinvestment hypothesis A theory that postulates that skilled performance breaks down when performers "reinvest" in, or attempt to exert conscious control over, actions and movements that are normally performed automatically. See also **conscious processing hypothesis**.

Reliability coefficient A statistic that is used in psychological measurement to indicate the consistency of a test or the degree to which it can be expected to yield the same results on different occasions. See also **internal consistency coefficient**.

Response set A tendency to respond to a survey, questionnaire or test in a particular way regardless of the person's actual attitudes or beliefs.

Result goals Behavioural outcomes or targets that can be defined objectively (such as winning a race or defeating an opponent) but which are not directly under one's own control.

Reversal theory A theory of personality which suggests that people alternate or reverse between paired metamotivational states such as telic and paratelic dominance. See also **paratelic dominance** and **telic dominance**.

Saccadic eye movements A series of high-speed, involuntary jumps of the eye which shift people's gaze from one fixation location to another. See also **smooth pursuit eye movements**.

Secondary appraisal One's perception of the adequacy of one's personal resources in dealing with a source of stress. See also **cognitive appraisal** and **primary appraisal**.

Selective attention The ability to focus on task-relevant information while ignoring distractions. See also **divided attention**.

Self-determination theory A general theory of motivation that distinguishes between autonomous motivation (where people experience a sense of volition over, and intrinsic interest in, their actions) and controlled motivation (in which one's behaviour is a function of external contingencies such as rewards). See also **motivation, theory of planned behaviour, theory of reasoned action** and **transtheoretical model of behaviour change**.

Self-efficacy People's expectations about their ability to perform a given task. See also **confidence**.

Self-serving attributional bias A tendency for people to attribute their successes to internal causes and their failures to external causes.

Self-talk The internal or covert dialogue which people engage in when they "talk" to themselves inside their heads.

Sensation seeking A variable which refers to people's need for, and willingness to take risks in pursuing, various novel, complex or adventurous experiences.

Serotonin A type of neurotransmitter in the brain.

Short-term memory The traditional term for the temporary memory store that can hold a limited amount of information for a brief period of time (usually less than 30 seconds) in the absence of rehearsal. Since the mid-1970s, this term has been largely replaced by "working memory" to reflect an important change in emphasis from a passive store to an active system for the conscious processing and manipulation of temporarily stored information. See also **working memory**.

Simulation training The theory that athletes can learn to concentrate more effectively in real-life pressure situations if they have practised under simulated versions of these conditions.

Single-case research design A group of quasi-experimental research methods that can be used to study the effects, time-course or variability of an independent variable (e.g., an intervention programme) on a designated dependent variable (e.g., behaviour or performance). Although the units in single-case research are typically individual participants, they can also be dyads, small-groups (e.g., teams) or even institutional populations.

Situational attributions Explanations of behaviour that invoke environmental factors as the causes of a given outcome.

Smooth pursuit eye movements Eye movements that are activated when a moving target appears within the visual field. These movements serve to centre and stabilize the image of the moving object of interest on the fovea, thereby guaranteeing its high-acuity inspection. See also **saccadic eye movements**.

Snooker A game played on a billiard table in which people use a cue to hit a white ball to send twenty-one coloured balls in a set order into the pockets around the table.

Social cohesion The desire by team members to form and maintain interpersonal bonds. See also **cohesion, task cohesion** and **team spirit**.

Social desirability A bias that occurs when people who are answering questions try to make themselves look good rather than responding truthfully.

Social facilitation The improvement in people's performance that can occur when they are either part of a group or are being observed by other people.

Social loafing The tendency of people to work less hard on a task when they are part of a group than as individuals due to diffusion of responsibility.

Sociogram A technique that is used to measure social cohesion by asking group members confidentially to indicate their like or dislike of other members.

Somatic anxiety An unpleasant state of bodily tension that is usually accompanied by increased heart rate, rapid breathing and "butterflies" in the stomach. See also **behavioural anxiety** and **cognitive anxiety**.

Spatial occlusion paradigm A research method commonly used in eye-tracking research in which viewers are required to make judgements about a visual scene from which certain parts have been either occluded from view or removed altogether. See also **temporal occlusion paradigm**.

Sport and exercise psychology An academic discipline and profession in which the principles, methods and findings of psychology are applied to sport and exercise settings.

Sports injury Any physical or medical condition that prevents an athlete from participating in a training session or competitive encounter.

State anxiety Transient, situation-specific feelings of fear, worry and physiological arousal.

Strategic knowledge The ability to recognize and respond to various patterns of play in a given sport.

Survey research A research method in which questionnaires or interviews are used to obtain information from a sample of people about specific beliefs, attitudes, preferences or activities.

Task cohesion The desire by group members to complete a common task. See also **cohesion** and **social cohesion**.

Task orientation A type of motivation in which an athlete perceives success as mastering a given skill or task to a self-defined standard of excellence. See also **achievement goal theory**.

Team A task-related group which is characterized by a collective sense of identity and a set of distinctive roles. See also **group**.

Team-building The attempt to improve team performance by developing communication and cohesion among team members.

Team cohesion See **cohesion**.

Team goal-setting The process by which teams plan to achieve certain targets.

Team spirit A term that is used loosely to indicate the degree of social cohesion that is apparent. See also **social cohesion**.

Telic dominance A state of mind in which a person's behaviour is serious and goal-directed. See also **paratelic dominance** and **reversal theory**.

Temporal occlusion paradigm A research method commonly used in eye-tracking research in which people are asked to guess what happens next when viewing information presented in slides, film or video. See also **spatial occlusion paradigm**.

Ten-year rule The theory that it takes approximately ten years (or approximately 10,000 hours) of sustained deliberate practice to become an expert in any field.

Theory of planned behaviour A theory that postulates that individual behaviour is guided by a combination of behavioural, normative and control beliefs. Behavioural beliefs concern the likely consequences of engaging in the behaviour in question. Normative beliefs concern the perceived expectations of others about the behaviour in question. Control beliefs concern the perceived ease with which the behaviour in question can be performed. See also **self-determination theory**, **theory of reasoned action** and **transtheoretical model of behaviour change**.

Theory of reasoned action Widely regarded as a special case of the theory of planned behaviour, the theory of reasoned action postulates that the best predictor of people's behaviour is their intention to act. This intention is itself determined by two key factors – people's attitude to performing the behaviour in question and the subjective norms that surround the performance of such behaviour. See also **self-determination theory**, **theory of planned behaviour** and **transtheoretical model of behaviour change**.

Think aloud verbal protocols A method in which data are collected from what people say as they talk about or give a running commentary on their thoughts and actions as they tackle a cognitive task or problem in their specialist domain. See also **protocol analysis**.

Thought sampling techniques A research method in which people are equipped with electronic beepers and cued to reveal their thoughts and feelings at specific moments.

Trait anxiety A consistent and pervasive tendency to perceive certain situations as threatening.

Transcranial magnetic stimulation (TMS) A neuroscientific technique in which a high-intensity magnetic coil is placed over a person's skull in an effort to stimulate neural activity in the brain.

Transtheoretical model of behaviour change (TTM) A theory of long-term behaviour change which proposes that people go through certain stages and use certain psychological processes when they attempt to implement relevant intentions. See also **self-determination theory**, **theory of planned behaviour** and **theory of reasoned action**.

Trigger words Instructional cues used by athletes and coaches to help them to concentrate on what is most important when executing a skill.

Validity See **construct validity**.

Visual search task An experimental technique used by researchers to determine people's speed and accuracy in detecting target stimuli presented in complex arrays containing distractors.

Visualization See **imagery**.

Vividness The apparent clarity, realism or richness of a mental image.

Working memory Part of the conscious memory system that stores, retrieves and manipulates transient formation for current use (formerly known as short-term memory). See also **short-term memory**.

References

Abernethy, B., and Russell, D. G. (1987) The relationship between expertise and visual search strategy in a racquet sport. *Human Movement Science, 6,* 283–319.

Abernethy, B., Neal, R. J., and Koning, P. (1994) Visual-perceptual and cognitive differences between expert, intermediate, and novice snooker players. *Applied Cognitive Psychology, 8,* 185–211.

Abernethy, B., Baker, J., and Côté, J. (2005) Transfer of pattern recall skills may contribute to the development of sport expertise. *Applied Cognitive Psychology, 19,* 705–718.

Abernethy, B., Maxwell, J. P., Masters, R. S. W., Van der Kamp, J., and Jackson, R. C. (2007) Attentional processes in skill learning and expert performance. In G. Tenenbaum and R. C. Eklund (eds) *Handbook of sport psychology* (3rd edn, pp. 245–263). New York: Wiley.

Abma, C. L., Fry, M. D., Li, Y., and Relyea, G. (2002) Differences in imagery content and imagery ability between high and low confident track and field athletes. *Journal of Applied Sport Psychology, 14,* 67–75.

Adams, J. (2009) Understanding exercise dependence. *Journal of Contemporary Psychotherapy, 39,* 231–240.

Agassi, A. (2009) *Open: An autobiography.* London: HarperCollins.

Aglioti, S. M., Cesari, P., Romani, M., and Urgesi, C. (2008) Action anticipation and motor resonance in elite basketball players. *Nature Neuroscience, 11,* 1109–1116.

Aherne, C., Moran, A., and Lonsdale, C. (2011) The effects of mindfulness training on athletes' flow: An initial investigation. *Sport Psychologist, 25,* 177–189.

Ahronson, A., and Cameron, J. E. (2007) The nature and consequences of group cohesion in a military sample. *Military Psychology, 19,* 9–25.

Aidman, E. V., and Woollard, S. (2003) The influence of self-reported exercise addiction on acute emotional and physiological responses to brief exercise deprivation. *Psychology of Sport and Exercise, 4,* 225–236.

REFERENCES

Ainsworth, B. E. (2009) How do I measure physical activity in my patients? Questionnaires and objective methods. *British Journal of Sports Medicine, 43*, 6–9.

Aitken, M. (2008) Els rediscovers route to Big Easy street. *The Scotsman*, 4 March. Retrieved from http://thescotsman.scotsman.com/sport/Els-rediscovers-route-to-Big.3838345.jp on 16 December 2008.

Ajzen, I. (1988) *Attitudes, personality and behaviour*. Chicago, IL: Dorsey Press.

Ajzen, I. (2005) *Attitudes, personality and behaviour* (2nd edn). Milton Keynes, Buckinghamshire: Open University Press.

Ajzen, I., and Fishbein, M. (1974) Factors influencing intentions and the intention-behaviour relation. *Human Relations, 27*, 1–15.

Alderfer, C. P. (1977) Group and intergroup relations. In J. R. Hackman and J. L. Suttle (eds) *Improving life at work* (pp. 227–296). Santa Monica, CA: Goodyear.

Allen, M. S., Jones, M. V., and Sheffield, D. (2011) Are the causes assigned to unsatisfactory performances related to the intensity of emotions experienced after competition? *Sport and Exercise Psychology Review, 7*, 3–9.

Allen, R. (2000) *The new Penguin English dictionary*. London: Penguin.

American College of Sports Medicine (2006) *ACSM's guidelines for exercise testing and prescription* (7th edn). Philadelphia, PA: Lippincott, Williams & Wilkins.

Ames, C. (1992) Achievement goals, motivational climate, and motivational processes. In G. Roberts (ed.) *Motivation in sport and exercise* (pp. 161–176). Champaign, IL: Human Kinetics.

Andersen, J. L., Schjerling, P., and Saltin, B. (2000) Muscle, genes and athletic performance. *Scientific American*, September, pp. 48–55.

Anderson, A. (2002) The Assessment of Consultant Effectiveness instrument. *Newsletter – Sport and Exercise Psychology Section (British Psychological Society), 17*, 4–7.

Anderson, A., and Lavallee, D. (2008) Applying the theories of reasoned action and planned behaviour to athlete training adherence behaviour. *Applied Psychology, 57*, 304–312.

Anshel, M. (1995) Anxiety. In T. Morris and J. Summers (eds) *Sport psychology* (pp. 29–62). Brisbane: Wiley.

Anshel, M. (1996) Coping styles among adolescent competitive athletes. *Journal of Social Psychology, 136*, 311–324.

Aronoff, S. R., and Spilka, B. (1984–1985) Patterning of facial expressions among terminal cancer patients. *Omega: Journal of Death and Dying, 15*, 101–108.

Aronson, E., Wilson, T. D., and Akert, R. M. (2002) *Social psychology* (4th edn). Upper Saddle River, NJ: Prentice-Hall.

Arora, S., Aggarwal, R., Sevdalis, N., Moran, A., Sirimanna, P., Kneebone, R., and Darzi, A. (2010) Development and validation of mental practice as a training strategy for laparoscopic surgery. *Surgical Endoscopy, 24*, 179–187.

Arora, S., Aggarwal, R., Sirimanna, P., Moran, A., Grantcharov, T., Kneebone, R., Sevdalis, N., and Darzi, A. (2011) Mental practice enhances surgical technical skills: A randomized controlled study. *Annals of Surgery, 253*, 265–270.

Arvinen-Barrow, M., Penny, G., Hemmings, B., and Corr, S. (2010) UK chartered physiotherapists' personal experiences in using psychological interventions with injured athletes: An interpretative phenomenological analysis. *Psychology of Sport and Exercise, 11*, 58–66.

Ashcraft, M. (2006) *Cognition* (4th edn). Upper Saddle River, NJ: Pearson.

Associated Press (2009) Cavendish springs to Stage 2 victory. Associated Press, 5 July 2009. Retrieved from http://sports.espn.go.com/oly/tdf2009/news/story?id=4307025 on 30 September 2010.

Augé, W. K., and Augé, S. M. (1999) Naturalistic observation of athletic drug-use patterns and behaviour in professional-calibre bodybuilders. *Substance Use and Misuse, 34,* 217–249.

Azar, B. (1996) Researchers explore why some athletes "choke". *American Psychological Association Monitor on Psychology, 27,* July, 21.

Azar, B. (2010) Another reason to break a sweat. *American Psychological Association Monitor on Psychology, 41,* June, 36–38.

Bakeman, R., and Helmreich, R. (1975) Cohesiveness and performance: Covariation and causality in an undersea environment. *Journal of Experimental Social Psychology, 11,* 478–489.

Baker, J., and Horton, S. (2004) A review of primary and secondary influences on sport expertise. *High Ability Studies, 15,* 211–228.

Baker, J., Cobely, S., and Fraser-Thomas, J. (2009) What do we know about early sport specialization? Not much! *High Ability Studies, 20,* 77–89.

Baker, L. D., Frank, L. L., Foster-Schubert, K., Green, P. S., Wilkinson, C. W., McTiernan, A., Plymate, S. R., Fishel, M. A., Watson, G. S., Cholerton, B. A., Duncan, G. E., Mehta, P. D., and Craft, S. (2010) Effects of aerobic exercise on mild cognitive impairment. *Archives of Neurology, 67,* 71–79.

Baker, R. K., and White, K. M. (2010) Predicting adolescents' use of social networking sites from an extended theory of planned behaviour perspective. *Computers in Human Behaviour, 26,* 1591–1597.

Bakker, F. C., Boschker, M. S. J., and Chung, T. (1996) Changes in muscular activity while imagining weight lifting using stimulus or response propositions. *Journal of Sport and Exercise Psychology, 18,* 313–324.

Bandura, A. (1997) *Self-efficacy: The exercise of control.* New York: Freeman.

Barker, J., McCarthy, P., Jones, M., and Moran, A. (2011) *Single-case research designs in sport and exercise psychology.* London: Routledge.

Barnes, S. (2009) The unfashionable truth about success. *The Times,* 1 June. Retrieved from www.timesonline.co.uk/tol/sport/columnists/simon_barnes/article6401625.ece on 10 March 2011.

Baron, R. A., and Kalsher, M. J. (2002) *Essentials of psychology* (3rd edn). Boston, MA: Allyn & Bacon.

Bauman, A. E. (2004) Updating the evidence that physical activity is good for health: An epidemiological review 2000–2003. *Journal of Science and Medicine in Sport, Physical Activity Supplement, 7,* 6–19.

Bauman, J. (2008) Sport psychology at the Olympics. *Div47 News: Exercise and Sport Psychology Newsletter, 21,* 2. Retrieved from http://apa47.org/pdfs/summer08newsletter.pdf on 10 March 2011.

Baumeister, R. F. (1984) Choking under pressure: Self-consciousness and the paradoxical effects of incentives on skilled performance. *Journal of Personality and Social Psychology, 46,* 610–620.

Baumeister, R. F., and Showers, C. J. (1986) A review of paradoxical performance effect: Choking under pressure in sports and mental tests. *European Journal of Social Psychology, 16,* 361–383.

BBC (2003) *Snooker: The World Championship.* Coverage of the 2003 World Championship, Sheffield. Presented by Hazel Irvine with Steve Dabikd and John Parrott. BBC2, 5 May.

BBC Sport (2008) Little makes Wrexham blunder plea. Retrieved from http://news.bbc.co.uk/sport2/hi/football/teams/w/wrexham/7291542.stm on 21 September 2011.

BBC Sport (2010) Tony McCoy – injuries. Retrieved from http://news.bbc.co.uk/sport2/hi/other_sports/horse_racing/7861452.stm on 24 August 2010.

REFERENCES

Beattie, S., Hardy, L., Savage, J., Woodman, T., and Callow, N. (2011) Development and validation of a trait measure of self-confidence. *Psychology of Sport and Exercise, 12*, 184–191.

Beauchamp, M. R., and Eys, M. A. (eds) (2008) *Group dynamics in exercise and sport psychology*. Champaign, IL: Human Kinetics.

Beauchamp, M. R., Bray, S. R., and Albinson, J. G. (2002) Pre-competition imagery, self-efficacy and performance in collegiate golfers. *Journal of Sports Sciences, 20*, 697–705.

Bedon, B. G., and Howard, D. E. (1992) Memory for the frequency of occurrence of karate techniques: A comparison of experts and novices. *Bulletin of the Psychonomic Society, 30*, 117–119.

Begley, S. (2000) Mind games. *Newsweek*, 25 September, pp. 60–61.

Behrmann, M. (2000) The mind's eye mapped onto the brain's matter. *Current Directions in Psychological Science, 9*, 50–54.

Beilock, S. (2010a) *Choke*. New York: Free Press.

Beilock, S. (2010b) How to create a sports superstar. *Psychology Today*, 2 August. Retrieved from www.psychologytoday.com/blog/choke/201008/how-create-sports-superstar?utm_source=twitterfeed&utm_medium=twitter on 8 September 2010.

Beilock, S. (in press) Expert performance: From action to perception to understanding. In J. J. Staszewski (ed.) *Expertise and skill acquisition: The impact of William G. Chase*. New York: Psychology Press.

Beilock, S. L., and Carr, T. H. (2001) On the fragility of skilled performance: What governs choking under pressure? *Journal of Experimental Psychology: General, 130*, 701–725.

Bensley, D. A. (2010) A brief guide for teaching and assessing critical thinking in psychology. *The Observer (Association for Psychological Science), 23*, 49–53.

Bent, I., McIlroy, R., Mousley, K., and Walsh, K. (2000) *Football confidential*. London: BBC.

Berger, B. G., and Motl, R. W. (2000) Exercise and mood: A selective review and synthesis of research employing the Profile of Mood States. *Journal of Applied Sport Psychology, 12*, 69–92.

Berger, B. G., and Motl, R. W. (2001) Physical activity and quality of life. In R. N. Singer, H. A. Hausenblas, and C. M. Janelle (eds) *Handbook of sport psychology* (2nd edn, pp. 636–671). New York: Wiley.

Bertollo, M., Saltarelli, B., and Robazza, C. (2009) Mental preparation strategies of elite modern pentathletes. *Psychology of Sport and Exercise, 10*, 244–254.

Bettenhausen, K. L. (1991) Five years of group research: What we have learned and what needs to be addressed. *Journal of Management, 17*, 345–381.

Biddiss, E., and Irwin, J. (2010) Active video games to promote physical activity in children and youth: A systematic review. *Archives of Pediatric Adolescent Medicine, 164*, 664–672.

Biddle, S. J. H., and Fuchs, R. (2009) Exercise psychology: A view from Europe. *Psychology of Sport and Exercise, 10*, 410–419.

Biddle, S. J. H., and Hanrahan, S. (1998) Attributions and attributional style. In J. L. Duda (ed.) *Advances in sport and exercise psychology measurement* (pp. 3–19). Morgantown, WV: Fitness Information Technology.

Biddle, S. J. H., and Mutrie, N. (2008) *Psychology of physical activity: Determinants, well-being and interventions* (2nd edn). London: Routledge.

Biddle, S. J. H., and Nigg, C. R. (2000) Theories of exercise behaviour. *International Journal of Sport Psychology, 31*, 290–304.

Biddle, S. J. H., Hanrahan, S. J., and Sellars, C. N. (2001) Attributions: Past, present and future. In R. N. Singer, H. A. Hausenblas, and C. M. Janelle (eds) *Handbook of sport psychology* (2nd edn, pp. 444–471). New York: Wiley.

Biddle, S. J. H., Hagger, M. S., Chatzisarantis, N. L. D, and Lippke, S. (2007) Theoretical frameworks in exercise psychology. In G. Tenenbaum and R. C. Eklund (eds) *Handbook of sport psychology* (3rd edn, pp. 537–559). New York: Wiley.

Biddle, S. J. H., Treasure, D. C., and Wang, C. K. J. (2008) Motivational characteristics. In A. L. Smith and S. J. H. Biddle (eds) *Youth physical activity and sedentary behavior: Challenges and solutions* (pp. 193–214). Champaign, IL: Human Kinetics.

Binsch, O., Oudjeans, R. R. D., Bakker, F. C., and Savelsberrgh, G. J. P. (2009) Unwanted effects in aiming actions: The relationship between gaze behaviour and performance in a golf putting task. *Psychology of Sport and Exercise, 10*, 628–635.

Bishop, D. T., Karageorghis, C. L., and Loizou, G. (2007) A grounded theory of young tennis players' use of music to manipulate emotional state. *Journal of Sport and Exercise Psychology, 29*, 584–607.

Blair, S. N., Kohl, H. W., Gordon, N. F., and Paffenbarger, R. S. (1992) How much physical activity is good for health? *Annual Review of Public Health, 13*, 99–126.

Blajenkova, O., Kozhevnikov, M., and Motes, M. (2006) Object-spatial imagery: A new self-report imagery questionnaire. *Applied Cognitive Psychology, 20*, 239–265.

Blau, E. (1998) Nervous issues. *Guardian* (Review), 2 October, pp. 16–17.

Bloom, B. S. (1985) Generalizations about talent development. In B. S. Bloom (ed.) *Developing talent in young people* (pp. 507–549). New York: Ballantine.

Blumenthal, J. A., O'Toole, L. C., and Chang, J. L. (1984) Is running an analogue of anorexia nervosa? An empirical study of obligatory running and anorexia nervosa. *Journal of the American Medical Association, 14*, 145–154.

Bodin, M., and Hartig, T. (2003) Does the outdoor environment matter for psychological restoration gained through running? *Psychology of Sport and Exercise, 4*, 141–153.

Bond, J., and Sargent, G. (1995) Concentration skills in sport: An applied perspective. In T. Morris and J. Summers (eds) *Sport psychology: Theory, applications and issues* (pp. 386–419). Chichester, West Sussex: Wiley.

Boutcher, S. H. (2008) Attentional processes and sport performance. In T. S. Horn (ed.) *Advances in sport psychology* (3rd edn, pp. 325–338). Champaign, IL: Human Kinetics.

Bozoian, S., Rejeski, W. J., and McAuley, E. (1994) Self-efficacy influences feeling states associated with acute exercise. *Journal of Sport and Exercise Psychology, 16*, 326–333.

Bramwell, S. T., Masuda, M., Wagner, N. N., and Holmes, T. H. (1975) Psychosocial factors in athletic injuries: Development and application of the Social and Athletic Readjustment Rating Scale (SARRS). *Journal of Human Stress, 1*, 6–20.

Braun, S. M., Beurskens, A. J., Borm, P. J., Schack, T., and Wade, D. (2006) The effects of mental practice in stroke rehabilitation: A systematic review. *Archives of Physical Medicine and Rehabilitation, 87*, 842–852.

Brawley, L. R., and Paskevich, D. M. (1997) Conducting team building research in the context of sport and exercise. *Journal of Applied Sport Psychology, 9*, 11–40.

Brawley, L. R., Carron, A. V., and Widmeyer, W. N. (1987) Assessing the cohesion of teams: Validity of the Group Environment Questionnaire. *Journal of Sport Psychology, 9*, 275–294.

Brawley, L. R., Martin, K. A., and Gyurcsik, N. C. (1998) Problems in assessing perceived barriers to exercise: Confusing obstacles with attributions and excuses. In J. L. Duda (ed.) *Advances in sport and exercise measurement* (pp. 337–350). Morgantown, WV: Fitness Information Technology.

Brewer, B. W. (1994) Review and critique of models of psychological adjustment to athletic injury. *Journal of Applied Sport Psychology, 6*, 87–100.

Brewer, B. W. (1999) Causal attribution dimensions and adjustment to sport injury. *Journal of Personal and Interpersonal Loss, 4*, 215–224.

Brewer, B. W. (2001a) Emotional adjustment to sport injury. In J. Crossman (ed.) *Coping with sports injuries: Psychological strategies for rehabilitation* (pp. 1–19). Oxford: Oxford University Press.

Brewer, B. W. (2001b) Psychology of sport injury rehabilitation. In R. N. Singer, H. A. Hausenblas, and C. M. Janelle (eds) *Handbook of sport psychology* (2nd edn, pp. 787–809). New York: Macmillan.

Brewer, B. W. (2007) Psychology of sport injury rehabilitation. In G. S. Tenebaum and R. C. Eklund (eds) *Handbook of sport psychology* (3rd edn, pp. 404–424). Hoboken, NJ: Wiley.

Brewer, B. W. (2009) Injury prevention and rehabilitation. In B. W. Brewer (ed.) *Sport psychology (handbook of sports medicine and science)* (pp. 75–86). Oxford: Wiley-Blackwell.

Brewer, B. W. (2010a) The role of psychological factors in sport injury rehabilitation outcomes. *International Review of Sport and Exercise Psychology, 3,* 40–61.

Brewer, B. W. (2010b) Adherence to sport injury rehabilitation. In S. J. Hanrahan and M. B. Andersen (eds) *Routledge handbook of applied sport psychology* (pp. 233–241). Abingdon, Oxfordshire: Routledge.

Brewer, B. W., and Van Raalte, J. (in press) Introduction to sport and exercise psychology. In B. Brewer and J. Van Raalte (eds) *Exploring sport and exercise psychology* (3rd edn). Washington, DC: American Psychological Association.

Brewer, B. W., Van Raalte, J. L., Linder, D. E., and Van Ralte, N. S. (1991) Peak performance and the perils of retrospective introspection. *Journal of Sport and Exercise Psychology, 8,* 227–238.

Brewer, B. W., Andersen, M. B., and Van Raalte, J. L. (2002) Psychological aspects of sport rehabilitation: Toward a biopsychosocial approach. In D. L. Mostofsky and L. D. Zaichkowsky (eds) *Medical and psychological aspects of sport and exercise* (pp. 41–54). Morgantown, WV: Fitness Information Technology.

Brolly, J. (2007) How to win Sam or Liam? Start as you aim to finish. *Irish Mail on Sunday,* 14 January, p. 93.

Browne, P. J. (2008) *Reading the green: The inside line on the Irish in the Ryder Cup.* Dublin: Currach Press.

Brustad, R. J. (2008) Qualitative research approaches. In T. S. Horn (ed.) *Advances in sport psychology* (3rd edn, pp. 31–43). Champaign, IL: Human Kinetics.

Buckley, W. (2005) Black knight of the fairway. *Sunday Independent* (Sport), 10 July, p. 12.

Buckworth, J., and Dishman, R. K. (2002) *Exercise psychology.* Champaign, IL: Human Kinetics.

Buckworth, J., and Dishman, R. K. (2007) Exercise adherence. In G. Tenenbaum and R. C. Eklund (Eds) *Handbook of sport psychology* (3rd edn, pp. 509–535). New York: Wiley.

Budney, A. J., Murphy, S. M., and Woolfolk, R. L. (1994) Imagery and motor performance: What do we really know? In A. A. Sheikh and E. R. Korn (eds) *Imagery in sports and physical performance* (pp. 97–120). Amityville, NY: Baywood.

Bull, S. J., Albinson, J. G., and Shambrook, C. J. (1996) *The mental game plan.* Eastbourne, East Sussex: Sports Dynamics.

Buman, M. P., Yasova, L. D., and Giaccobi, P. R., Jr (2010) Descriptive and narrative reports of barriers and motivators to physical activity in sedentary older adults. *Psychology of Sport and Exercise, 11,* 223–230.

Burke, K. L., Sachs, M. L., Fry, S. J., and Schweighardt, S. L. (2008) *Directory of graduate programs in applied sport psychology* (9th edn). Morgantown, WV: Fitness Information Technology.

Burke, S. M., Carron, A. V., and Shapcott, K. M. (2008) Cohesion in exercise groups: An overview. *International Review of Sport and Exercise Psychology, 1,* 107–123.

Burton, D. (1989) Winning isn't everything: Examining the impact of performance goals on collegiate swimmers' cognitions and performance. *Sport Psychologist, 32*, 105–132.

Burton, D. (1998) Measuring competitive state anxiety. In J. L. Duda (ed.) *Advances in sport and exercise psychology measurement* (pp. 129–148). Morgantown, WV: Fitness Information Technology.

Burton, D., and Naylor, S. (2002) The Jekyll/Hyde nature of goals: Revisiting and updating goal-setting in sport. In T. Horn (ed.) *Advances in sport psychology* (2nd edn, pp. 459–499). Champaign, IL: Human Kinetics.

Burton, D., and Weiss, C. (2008) The fundamental goal concept: The path to process and performance success. In T. S. Horn (ed.) *Advances in sport psychology* (3rd edn, pp. 339–375). Champaign, IL: Human Kinetics

Burton, D., Naylor, S., and Holliday, B. (2001) Goal setting in sport. In R. N. Singer, H. A. Hausenblas, and C. M. Janelle (eds) *Handbook of sport psychology* (2nd edn, pp. 497–528). New York: Wiley.

Butler, R. (1996) *Sport psychology in action.* Oxford: Butterworth-Heinemann.

Cacioppo, J. T., Berntson, G. G., and Nusbaum, H. C. (2008) Neuroimaging as a new tool in the toolbox of psychological science. *Current Directions in Psychological Science, 17*, 62–67.

Cafri, G., Olivaridia, R., and Thompson, K.J. (2008) Symptom characteristics and psychiatric comorbidity among males with muscle dysmorphia. *Comprehensive Psychiatry, 49*, 374–379.

Caliari, P. (2008) Enhancing forehand acquisition in table tennis: The role of mental practice. *Journal of Applied Sport Psychology, 20*, 88–96.

Callaghan, P., Eves, F. F., Norman, P., Chang, A. M., and Yuk Lung, C. (2002) Applying the transtheoretical model of change to exercise in young Chinese people. *British Journal of Health Psychology, 7*, 267–282.

Callow, N., and Hardy, L. (2004) The relationship between the use of kinaesthetic imagery and different visual imagery perspectives. *Journal of Sports Sciences, 22*, 167–177.

Callow, N., and Hardy, L. (2005) A critical analysis of applied imagery research. In D. Hackfort, J. Duda and R. Lidor (eds) *The handbook of research in applied sport and exercise psychology: International perspectives* (pp. 21–42). Morgantown, WV: Fitness Information Technology.

Callow, N., and Roberts, R. (2010) Imagery research: An investigation of three issues. *Psychology of Sport and Exercise, 11*, 325–329.

Callow, N., and Waters, A. (2005) The effect of kinaesthetic imagery on the sport confidence of flat-race horse jockeys. *Psychology of Sport and Exercise, 6*, 443–459.

Calmels, C., Holmes, P., Lopez, E., and Naman, V. (2006) Chronometric comparison of actual and imaged complex movement patterns. *Journal of Motor Behavior, 38*, 339–348.

Cannon-Bowers, J. A., and Bowers, C. (2011) Team development and functioning. In S. Zedeck (ed.) *APA handbook of industrial and organisational psychology, Vol. 1: Building and developing the organization* (pp. 597–650). Washington, DC: American Psychological Association.

Capostagno, A. (2002) Wegerle pitches up in a whole new ball game. *Guardian*, 17 January, p. 31.

Carless, S. A., and De Paola, C. (2000) The measurement of cohesion in work teams. *Small Group Research, 13*, 71–88.

Carpenter, W. B. (1894) *Principles of mental physiology*. New York: Appleton-Century-Crofts.

Carrillo-de-la-Peña, M. T., Galdo-Alvarez, S., and Lastra-Barreira, C. (2008) Equivalent is not equal: Primary motor cortex (MI) activation during motor imagery and execution of sequential movements. *Brain Research, 1226*, 134–143.

REFERENCES

Carron, A. V., and Ball, J. R. (1977) Cause-effect characteristics of cohesiveness and participation motivation in intercollegiate hockey. *International Review of Sport Sociology, 12*, 49–60.

Carron, A. V., and Brawley, L. R. (2008) Group dynamics in sport and physical activity. In T. S. Horn (ed.) *Advances in sport psychology* (3rd edn, pp. 213–237). Champaign, IL: Human Kinetics.

Carron, A. V., and Chelladurai, P. (1981) Cohesion as a factor in sport performance. *International Review of Sport Sociology, 16*, 2–41.

Carron, A. V., and Hausenblas, H. (1998) *Group dynamics in sport* (2nd edn). Morgantown, WV: Fitness Information Technology.

Carron, A. V., and Spink, K. S. (1993) Team building in an exercise setting. *Sport Psychologist, 7*, 8–18.

Carron, A. V., Widmeyer, W. N., and Brawley, L. R. (1985) The development of an instrument to assess cohesion in sport teams: The Group Environment Questionnaire. *Journal of Sport Psychology, 7*, 244–266.

Carron, A. V., Spink, K. S., and Prapavessis, H. (1997) Team building and cohesiveness in the sport and exercise setting: Use of indirect interventions. *Journal of Applied Sport Psychology, 9*, 61–72.

Carron, A. V., Brawley, L. R., and Widmeyer, W. N. (1998) The measurement of cohesiveness in sport groups. In J. L. Duda (ed.) *Advances in sport and exercise psychology measurement* (pp. 213–226). Morgantown, WV: Fitness Information Technology.

Carron, A. V., Bray, S. R., and Eys, M. A. (2002a) Team cohesion and team success in sport. *Journal of Sports Sciences, 20*, 119–126.

Carron, A. V., Colman, M. M., Wheeler, J., and Stevens, D. (2002b) Cohesion and performance in sport: A meta analysis. *Journal of Sport and Exercise Psychology, 24*, 168–188.

Carron, A. V., Eys, M. A., and Burke, S. M. (2007) Team cohesion: Nature, correlates and development. In S. Jowett and D. Lavallee (eds) *Social psychology in sport* (pp. 91–101). Champaign, IL: Human Kinetics.

Carron, A. V., Burke, S. M., and Shapcott, K. M. (2009) Enhancing team effectiveness. In B. W. Brewer (ed.) *Sport psychology: Handbook of sports medicine* (pp. 64–74). Oxford: Wiley-Blackwell.

Carter, H. (2010) Doctor in "bloodgate" rugby scandal cleared to go back to work. *Guardian*, 1 September, p. 12.

Cary, T. (2010) "Team orders" debacle spoils Alonso's victory. *Irish Independent* (Sport), 26 July, p. 21.

Casby, A., and Moran, A. (1998) Exploring mental imagery in swimmers: A single-case study design. *Irish Journal of Psychology, 19*, 525–531.

Casey, B. (2011) Power of the mind key to curing a team with a stutter. *The Irish Times* (Sport), 21 February, p. 5.

Casey-Campbell, M., and Martens, M. L. (2009) Sticking it all together: A critical assessment of the group cohesion-performance literature. *International Journal of Management Reviews, 11*, 223–246.

Cashmore, E. (2008) *Sport and exercise psychology: The key concepts* (2nd edn). London: Routledge.

Caspersen, C. J. (1985) Physical activity, exercise, and physical fitness: Definitions and distinctions for health-related research. *Physician and Sportsmedicine, 13*, 162.

Caspersen, C. J., and Merritt, R. K. (1995) Physical activity trends among 26 states, 1986–1990. *Medicine and Science in Sports and Exercise, 27*, 713–720.

Castaneda, B., and Gray, R. (2007) Effects of focus on attention on baseball batting performance in players of different skill levels. *Journal of Sport and Exercise Psychology, 29*, 59–76.

Cecil, S., Brandon, R., and Moore, J. (2009) An integrated multi-disciplinary support service for an injured rugby union lock. In B. Hemmings and T. Holder (eds) *Applied sport psychology: A case-based approach* (pp. 203–222). Oxford: Wiley-Blackwell.

Centres for Disease Control and Prevention (2007) Prevalence of regular physical activity among adults – United States, 2001 and 2005. *MMWR (Morbidity and Mortality Weekly Report)*, *56*, 23 November, 1209–1212.

Chan, C. S., and Grossman, H. Y. (1988) Psychological effects of running loss on consistent runners. *Perceptual and Motor Skills*, *66*, 875–883.

Chang, Y. K., and Etnier, J. L. (2009) Effects of an acute bout of resistance exercise on cognitive performance in middle-aged adults. A randomized controlled trial study. *Psychology of Sport and Exercise*, *10*, 19–24.

Chase, W. G., and Ericsson, K. A. (1981) Skilled memory. In J. R. Anderson (ed.) *Cognitive skills and their acquisition* (pp. 141–189). Hillsdale, NJ: Lawrence Erlbaum Associates.

Chase, W. G., and Simon, H. A. (1973) Perception in chess. *Cognitive Psychology*, *4*, 55–81.

Chauloff, F. (1997) The serotonin hypothesis. In W. P. Morgan (ed.) *Physical activity and mental health* (pp. 179–198). Washington, DC: Taylor & Francis.

Chen, K. Y., and Bassett, D. R., Jr (2005) The technology of accelerometry-based activity monitors: Current and future. *Medicine and Science in Sports and Exercise*, *37*, S490–S500.

Chun, M. M., Golomb, J. D., and Turk-Browne, N. B. (2011) A taxonomy of external and internal attention. *Annual Review of Psychology*, *62*, 73–101.

Clark, T. P., Tofler, I. R., and Landon, M. T. (2005) The sport psychiatrist and golf. *Clinics in Sports Medicine*, *24*, 959–971.

Clarke, D., with K. Morris (2005) *Golf – The mind factor*. London: Hodder & Stoughton.

Cleary, T. J., and Zimmerman, B. J. (2001) Self-regulation differences during athletic practice by experts, non-experts and novices. *Journal of Applied Sport Psychology*, *13*, 185–206.

Clerkin, M. (2010) Pressure makes diamonds and golfers like Harrington. *Sunday Tribune* (Sport), 19 September, p. 2.

Clews, G. J., and Gross, J. B. (1995) Individual and social motivation in Australian sport. In T. Morris and J. Summers (eds) *Sport psychology: Theory, applications and issues* (pp. 90–121). Brisbane: Wiley.

Cloud, J. (2008) The science of experience. *Time*. Retrieved from www.time.com/time/health/article/0,8599,1717927-2,00.html on 19 June 2009.

Clough, P., Earle, K., and Sewell, D. (2002) Mental toughness: The concept and its measurement. In I. Cockerill (ed.) *Solutions in sport psychology* (pp. 32–45). London: Thomson.

Coaching Excellence (1996) Mental toughness questions answered: Tim Henman and Greg Rusedski. *Coaching Excellence*, *13*, p. 3.

Cohen, A., Pargman, D., and Tenenbaum, G. (2003) Critical elaboration and empirical investigation of the cusp-catastrophe model: A lesson for practitioners. *Journal of Applied Sport Psychology*, *15*, 144–159.

Cohen, J. (1992) A power primer. *Psychological Bulletin*, *112*, 155–159.

Collet, C., Guillot, A., Lebon, F., MacIntyre, T., and Moran, A. (2011) Measuring motor imagery using psychometric, behavioural, and psychophysiological tools. *Exercise and Sport Sciences Reviews*, *39*, 85–92.

Colvin, G. (2010) *Talent is overrated: What really separates world-class performers from everybody else*. London: Penguin.

Connaughton, D., and Hanton, S. (2009) Mental toughness in sport: Conceptual and practical issues. In S. D. Mellalieu and S. Hanton (eds) *Advances in applied sport psychology: A review* (pp. 317–346). Abingdon, Oxfordshire: Routledge.

Connaughton, D., Wadey, R., Hanton, S., and Jones, G. (2008) The development and maintenance of mental toughness: Perceptions of elite performers. *Journal of Sports Sciences*, *26*, 83–95.

Connaughton, D., Hanton, S., and Jones, G. (2010) The development and maintenance of mental toughness in the world's best performers. *Sport Psychologist*, *24*, 168–193.

Conroy, D. E., Kaye, M. P., and Schantz, L. H. (2008) Quantitative research methodology. In T. S. Horn (ed.) *Advances in sport psychology* (3rd edn, pp. 15–30). Champaign, IL: Human Kinetics.

Cook, B. J., and Hausenblas, H. A. (2008) The role of exercise dependence for the relationship between exercise behavior and eating pathology: Mediator or moderator? *Journal of Health Psychology*, *13*, 495–502.

Cooper, T. (2003) Join the human race. *Daily Telegraph* (Weekend), 12 April, p. 15.

Corbetta, M., and Shulman, G. L. (2002) Control of goal-directed and stimulus-driven attention in the brain. *Nature Reviews Neuroscience*, *3*, 201–215.

Corrigan, P. (2007) Countdown to the US PGA: What next for Sergio Garcia? *The Independent*, 4 August. Retrieved from www.independent.co.uk/sport/golf/countdown-to-the-us-pga-what-next-for-sergio-garcia-460200.html on 16 December 2008.

Côté, J., Baker, J., and Abernethy, B. (2007) Practice and play in the development of sport expertise. In G. Tenenbaum and R. C. Eklund (eds) *Handbook of sport psychology* (3rd edn, pp. 184–202). New York: Wiley.

Cottell, C. (2003) Don't stretch. *The Times* (T2), 18 April, p. 9.

Cotterill, S. T. (2010) Pre-performance routines in sport: Current understanding and future directions. *International Review of Sport and Exercise Psychology*, *3*, 132–153.

Cotterill, S. T., Sanders, R., and Collins, D. (2010) Developing effective pre-performance routines in golf: Why don't we ask the golfer? *Journal of Applied Sport Psychology*, *22*, 51–64.

Couture, R. T., Jerome, W., and Tihanyi, J. (1999) Can associative and dissociative strategies affect the swimming performance of recreational swimmers? *Sport Psychologist*, *13*, 334–343.

Cox, R. H., Martens, M. P., and Russell, W. D. (2003) Measuring anxiety in athletes: The revised Competitive State Anxiety Inventory-2. *Journal of Sport and Exercise Psychology*, *25*, 519–533.

Crace, R. K., and Hardy, C. J. (1997) Individual values and the team building process. *Journal of Applied Sport Psychology*, *9*, 41–60.

Craft, L. C., Magyar, T. M., Becker, B. J., and Feltz, D. L. (2003) The relationship between the Competitive State Anxiety Inventory-2 and sport performance: A meta-analysis. *Journal of Sport and Exercise Psychology*, *25*, 44–65.

Cratty, B. J. (1983) *Psychology in contemporary sport*. Englewood Cliffs, NJ: Prentice-Hall.

Cremades, J. G. (2002) The effects of imagery perspective as a function of skill level on alpha activity. *International Journal of Psychophysiology*, *43*, 261–271.

Crews, D. J., and Boutcher, S. H. (1986) Effects of structured preshot behaviours on beginning golf performance. *Perceptual and Motor Skills*, *62*, 291–294.

Crust, L. (2008) A review and conceptual re-examination of mental toughness: Implications for future researchers. *Personality and Individual Differences*, *45*, 576–583.

Cryan, P., and Alles, W. (1983) The relationship between stress and college football injuries. *Journal of Sports Medicine and Physical Fitness*, *23*, 52–58.

Csikszentmihalyi, M. (1975) *Beyond boredom and anxiety*. San Francisco, CA: Jossey-Bass.

Csikszentmihalyi, M. (1990) *Flow: The psychology of optimal experience*. New York: Harper & Row.

Culos-Reed, S. N., Stephenson, L., Doyle-Baker, P. K., and Dickinson, J. A. (2008) Mall walking a physical activity option: Results of a pilot project. *Canadian Journal on Aging*, *27*, 81–87.

Culver, D. M., Gilbert, W. D., and Trudel, P. (2003) A decade of qualitative research in sport psychology journals: 1990–1999. *Sport Psychologist, 17,* 1–15.

Cumming, J., and Hall, C. (2002a) Athletes' use of imagery in the off-season. *Sport Psychologist, 16,* 160–172.

Cumming, J., and Hall, C. (2002b) Deliberate imagery practice: The development of imagery skills in competitive athletes. *Journal of Sports Sciences, 20,* 137–145.

Cumming, J., and Ramsey, R. (2009) Imagery interventions in sport. In S. D. Mellalieu and S. Hanton (eds) *Advances in applied sport psychology: A review* (pp. 5–36). Abingdon, Oxfordshire: Routledge.

Cumming, J., and Ste-Marie, D. M. (2001) The cognitive and motivational effects of imagery training: A matter of perspective. *Sport Psychologist, 15,* 276–288.

Curtis, R. (2000) Sydney 2000. *The Mirror,* 2 October, p. 29.

Dale, D., Welk, G. W., and Matthews, C. E. (2002) Methods for assessing physical activity and challenges for research. In G. Welk (ed.) *Physical activity assessment for health related research* (pp. 19–34). Champaign, IL: Human Kinetics.

Daley, A. J. (2009) Can exergaming contribute to improving physical activity levels and health outcomes in children? *Pediatrics, 124,* 763–771.

Damisch, L., Stoberock, B., and Musseweiler, T. (2010) Keep your fingers crossed! How superstition improves performance. *Psychological Science, 21,* 1014–1020.

Davids, K., and Baker, J. (2007) Genes, environment and sport performance: Why the nature–nurture dualism is no longer relevant. *Sports Medicine, 37,* 961–980.

Davies, D. (2001) Relaxed Woods identifies the major pressure points. *Guardian,* 6 April, p. 26.

Davies, D. (2003) Psychology forms a closer Love. *Guardian,* 1 April, p. 30.

Davies, L. (2010) Nicolas Anelka suspended for 18 matches by France over World Cup revolt. *Guardian,* 17 August. Retrieved from www.guardian.co.uk/football/2010/aug/17/nicolas-anelka-banned-for-18-matches-france on 2 September 2010.

Davis, J. O. (1991) Sports injuries and stress management: An opportunity for research. *Sport Psychologist, 5,* 175–182.

DeAngelis, T. (1996) Seligman: Optimism can be a vaccination. *American Psychological Association Monitor on Psychology, 27,* October, p. 33.

DeAngelis, T. (2002) If you do just one thing, make it exercise. *American Psychological Association Monitor on Psychology, 33,* July–August, 49–51.

Decety, J. (1996) Do imagined and executed actions share the same neural substrate? *Cognitive Brain Research, 3,* 87–93.

Decety, J., and Ingvar, D. H. (1990) Brain structures participating in mental simulation of motor behaviour: A neuropsychological interpretation. *Acta Psychologica, 73,* 13–34.

Decety, J., and Michel, F. (1989) Comparative analysis of actual and mental movement times in two graphic tasks. *Brain and Cognition, 11,* 87–97.

Decety, J., Jeannerod, M., and Prablanc, C. (1989) The timing of mentally represented actions. *Behavioural and Brain Research, 34,* 35–42.

Decety, J., Jeannerod, M., Durozard, M., and Baverel, G. (1993) Central activation of autonomic effectors during mental simulation of motor actions. *Journal of Physiology, 461,* 549–563.

Deci, E. L. (1971) Effects of externally mediated rewards on intrinsic motivation. *Journal of Personality and Social Psychology, 18,* 105–115.

Deci, E. L., and Ryan, R. M. (1985) *Intrinsic motivation and self-determination in human behavior.* New York: Plenum.

Deci, E. L., and Ryan, R. M. (1991) A motivational approach to self: Integration in personality. In R. Dienstiber (ed.) *Nebraska symposium on motivation: Perspectives on motivation* (Vol. 38, pp. 37–288). Lincoln, NE: University of Nebraska Press.

Deci, E. L., and Ryan, R. M. (2000) Self-determination theory and the facilitation of intrinsic motivation, social development, and well-being. *American Psychologist, 55*, 68–78.

Deci, E. L., and Ryan, R. M. (2008) Facilitating optimal motivation and psychological well-being across life's domains. *Canadian Psychology, 49*, 14–23.

de Groot, A. D. (1965) *Thought and choice in chess*. The Hague, Netherlands: Mouton.

Delingpole, J. (2001) Anything to escape the tyranny of comfort. *Sunday Times* (News Review), 5 August, p. 8.

Denis, M. (1985) Visual imagery and the use of mental practice in the development of motor skills. *Canadian Journal of Applied Sport Sciences, 10*, 4s–16s.

Derakshan, N., and Eysenck, M. W. (2009) Anxiety, processing efficiency, and cognitive performance: New developments from Attentional Control Theory. *European Psychologist, 14*, 168–176.

Desharnis, R., Jobin, J., Côte, C., Lévesque, L., and Godin, G. (1993) Aerobic exercise and the placebo effect: A controlled study. *Psychosomatic Medicine, 55*, 149–154.

De Weerd, P. (2002) Attention, neural basis of. In L. Nadel (ed.) *Encyclopaedia of cognitive science* (Vol. 1, pp. 238–246). London: Nature Publishing Group.

Dickinson, M. (2007) Hypnotist? Bolton better off with a miracle worker. *Irish Independent*, 21 August, p. 26.

Didierjean, A., and Gobet, F. (2008) Sherlock Holmes – an expert's view of expertise. *British Journal of Psychology, 99*, 109–125.

Dietrich, A. (2008) Imaging the imagination: The trouble with motor imagery. *Methods, 45*, 319–324.

Dion, K. L. (2000) Group cohesion: From "field of forces" to multidimensional construct. *Group Dynamics, 4*, 7–26.

Dishman, R. K. (1983) Identity crises in North American sport psychology: Academics in professional issues. *Journal of Sport Psychology, 5*, 123–134.

Dishman, R. K. (2001) The problem of exercise adherence: Fighting sloth in nations with market economies. *Quest, 53*, 279–294.

Dishman, R. K., and Chambliss, H. O. (2010) Exercise psychology. In J. M. Williams (ed.) *Applied sport psychology: Personal growth to peak performance* (6th edn, pp. 563–595). New York: McGraw-Hill.

Dixon, L. (2002) Wenger's formula based on science. *Daily Telegraph* (Sport), 24 December, p. S2.

Dixon, P. (2008) Pádraig Harrington the champion of mind games. *The Times*, 16 July. Retrieved from www.timesonline.co.uk/tol/sport/golf/article4340348.ece on 16 December 2008.

Dixon, P., and Kidd, P. (2006) The golf pro who missed from 3ft and lost £230,000. *The Times*, 21 March, p. 5.

Dobson, R. (1998) In the grip of the yips. *Guardian* (Sport), 31 March, p. 16.

Doka, K. J. (1995) Coping with life-threatening illness: A task model. *Omega: Journal of Death and Dying, 32*, 111–122.

Donegan, L. (2006) How a swing doctor and a mind reader bolster the home defence. *Guardian* (Supplement: Golf-Ryder Cup countdown), 20 September, p. 7.

Donegan, L. (2007) Chandelier falls on Warren as Montgomerie hits glass ceiling. *Guardian* (Sport), 29 September, p. 7.

Dowthwaite, P. K., and Armstrong, M. R. (1984) An investigation into the anxiety levels of soccer players. *International Journal of Sport Psychology, 15*, 145–159.

Drawer, S., and Fuller, C. W. (2002) Evaluating the level of injury in English professional football using a risk based assessment process. *British Journal of Sports Medicine, 36*, 446–451.

Dreyfus, H. (1997) Intuitive, deliberative, and calculative models of expert performance. In C. E. Zsambok and G. Klein (eds) *Naturalistic decision making* (pp. 17–28). Mahwah, NJ: Lawrence Erlbaum Associates.

Driediger, M., Hall, C., and Callow, N. (2006) Imagery use by injured athletes: A qualitative analysis. *Journal of Sports Sciences, 24,* 261–272.

Driskell, J. E., Copper, C., and Moran, A. (1994) Does mental practice enhance performance? *Journal of Applied Psychology, 79,* 481–492.

Duchowski, A. T. (2007) *Eye tracking methodology: Theory and practice* (2nd edn). New York: Springer.

Duda, J., and Hall, H. (2001) Achievement goal theory in sport. In R. N. Singer, H. A. Hausenblas, and C. M. Janelle (eds) *Handbook of sport psychology* (pp. 417–443). New York: Wiley.

Duda, J., and Nicholls, J. G. (1992) Dimensions of achievement motivation in schoolwork and sport. *Journal of Educational Psychology, 84,* 290–299.

Duda, J., and Pensgaard, M. (2002) Enhancing the quantity and quality of motivation: The promotion of task involvement in a junior football team. In I. Cockerill (ed.) *Solutions in sport psychology* (pp. 49–57). London: Thomson.

Duda, J., and Whitehead, J. (1998) Measurement of goal perspectives in the physical domain. In J. L. Duda (ed.) *Advances in sport and exercise psychology measurement* (pp. 21–48). Morgantown, WV: Fitness Information Technology.

Duffy, P. J., Lyons, D. C., Moran, A. P., Warrington, G. D., and MacManus, C. P. (2006) How we got here: Perceived influences on the development and success of international athletes. *Irish Journal of Psychology, 27,* 150–167.

Dugdale, J. R., and Eklund, R. C. (2002) Do not pay any attention to the umpires: Thought suppression and task-relevant focusing strategies. *Journal of Sport and Exercise Psychology, 24,* 306–319.

Dunn, C. (2010) Shane Duffy undergoes life-saving surgery. *The Times,* 22 May. Retrieved from www.timesonline.co.uk/tol/sport/football/article7133786.ece on 16 August 2010.

Dunn, J. G. H. (1999) A theoretical framework for structuring the content of competitive worry in ice hockey. *Journal of Sport and Exercise Psychology, 21,* 259–279.

Dunn, J. G. H., and Syrotuik, D. G. (2003) An investigation of multidimensional worry dispositions in a high contact sport. *Psychology of Sport and Exercise, 4,* 265–282.

Dunn, J. G. H., Causgrove Dunn, J., Wilson, P., and Syrotuik, D. G. (2000) Re-examining the factorial composition and factor structure of the Sport Anxiety Scale. *Journal of Sport and Exercise Psychology, 22,* 183–193.

Durand-Bush, N., Salmela, J., and Green-Demers, I. (2001) The Ottawa Mental Skills Assessment Tool (OMSAT-3*). *Sport Psychologist, 15,* 1–19.

Dyce, J. A., and Cornell, J. (1996) Factorial validity of the Group Environment Questionnaire among musicians. *Journal of Social Psychology, 136,* 263–264.

Earle, K., Earle, F., and Clough, P. (2008) Mental toughness and its application for golfers. *Sport and Exercise Psychology Review, 4,* 22–27.

Eccles, D. W., Walsh, S. E., and Ingledew, D. K. (2002) A grounded theory of expert cognition in orienteering. *Journal of Sport and Exercise Psychology, 24,* 68–88.

Economist, The (1999) Freaks under pressure. *The Economist,* 18 December, pp. 90–92.

Edgar, B. (2006) Bearing up under the strain. *The Times,* 10 February, p. 91.

Edwards, T., Kingston, K., Hardy, L., and Gould, D. (2002) A qualitative analysis of catastrophic performances and the associated thoughts, feelings, and emotions. *Sport Psychologist, 16,* 1–19.

Edworthy, S. (2002) Brazil buoyant in World Cup final rehearsal. *Daily Telegraph* (Sport), 28 June, p. S4.

Elliott, A. J., and Conroy, D. E. (2005) Beyond the dichotomous model of achievement goals in sport and exercise psychology. *Sport and Exercise Psychology Review, 1*, 17–25.

English, A. (2006) *Munster: Our road to glory.* Dublin: Penguin.

Erickson, K. I., and Kramer, A. F. (2009) Aerobic exercise effects on cognitive and neural plasticity in older adults. *British Journal of Sports Medicine, 43*, 22–24.

Ericsson, K. A. (ed.) (1996) *The road to excellence: The acquisition of expert performance in the arts and sciences, sports and games.* Mahwah, NJ: Lawrence Erlbaum Associates.

Ericsson, K. A. (2001) The path to expert golf performance: Insights from the masters on how to improve performance by deliberate practice. In P. R. Thomas (ed.) *Optimising performance* (pp. 1–57). Brisbane: Australian Academic Press.

Ericsson, K. A. (2002) Attaining excellence through deliberate practice: Insights from the study of expert performance. In M. Ferrari (ed.) *The pursuit of excellence through education* (pp. 21–55). Hillsdale, NJ: Lawrence Erlbaum Associates.

Ericsson, K. A. (2005) Recent advances in expertise research: A commentary on the contributions to the special issue. *Applied Cognitive Psychology, 19*, 233–241.

Ericsson, K. A. (2006) Protocol analysis and expert thought: Concurrent verbalizations of thinking during experts' performance on representative tasks. In Ericsson, K. A., Charness, N., Feltovich, P. J., and Hoffman, R. R. (eds) *The Cambridge handbook of expertise and expert performance* (pp. 223–241). New York: Cambridge University Press.

Ericsson, K. A., and Charness, N. (1994) Expert performance: Its structure and acquisition. *American Psychologist, 49*, 725–747.

Ericsson, K. A., and Charness, N. (1997) Cognitive and developmental factors in expert performance. In P. J. Feltovich, K. M. Ford, and R. R. Hoffman (eds) *Expertise in context* (pp. 3–41). Cambridge, MA: MIT Press.

Ericsson, K. A., and Williams, A. M. (2007) Capturing naturally occurring superior performance in the laboratory: Translational research on expert performance. *Journal of Experimental Psychology: Applied, 13*, 115–123.

Ericsson, K. A., Krampe, R. T., and Tesch-Romer, C. (1993) The role of deliberate practice in the acquisition of expert performance. *Psychological Review, 100*, 363–406.

Ericsson, K. A., Charness, N., Feltovich, P. J., and Hoffman, R. R. (eds) (2006) *The Cambridge handbook of expertise and expert performance.* New York: Cambridge University Press.

Eriksson, S.-G., with Willi Railo (2002) *On management.* London: Carlton.

Erisman, S. M., and Roemer, L. (2010) A preliminary investigation of the effects of experimentally induced mindfulness on emotional responding to film clips. *Emotion, 10*, 72–82.

ESPN NBA (2010) Yao Ming stats. ESPN NBA. Retrieved from http://sports.espn.go.com/nba/players/profile?playerId=1722 on 28 August 2010.

Estabrooks, P., and Carron, A. V. (1999) The influence of the group with elderly exercisers. *Small Group Research, 30*, 438–452.

Estabrooks, P., and Carron, A. V. (2000) The Physical Activity Group Environment Questionnaire: An instrument for the assessment of cohesion in exercise classes. *Group Dynamics, 4*, 230–243.

Estabrooks, P., and Dennis, P. W. (2003) The principles of team building and their application to sport teams. In R. Lidor and K. P. Henschen (eds) *The psychology of team sports* (pp. 99–113). Morgantown, WV: Fitness Information Technology.

Etnier, J. L., Salazar, W., Landers, D. M., Petruzzello, S. J., Han, M. W., and Nowell, P. (1997) The influence of physical activity, fitness, and exercise upon cognitive functioning: A meta-analysis. *Journal of Sport and Exercise Psychology, 19*, 249–277.

Eton, D. T., Gilner, F. H., and Munz, D. C. (1998) The measurement of imagery vividness: A test of the reliability and validity of the Vividness of Visual Imagery and the Vividness of Movement Imagery Questionnaire. *Journal of Mental Imagery, 22*, 125–136.

Eubank, M., Niven, A., and Cain, A. (2009) Training routes to registration as a Chartered Sport and Exercise Psychologist. *Sport and Exercise Psychology Review, 5*, 47–50.

Evans, L., and Hardy, L. (1995) Sport injury and grief responses: A review. *Journal of Sport and Exercise Psychology, 17*, 227–245.

Evans, L., Hardy, L., and Fleming, S. (2000) Intervention strategies with injured athletes: An action research study. *Sport Psychologist, 14*, 186–206.

Evans, L., Hare, R., and Mullen. R. (2006) Imagery use during rehabilitation from injury. *Journal of Imagery Research in Sport and Physical Activity, 1*, article 1, 1–21.

Evans, R. (2002) Breaking point. *Sunday Times* (Sport), 19 May, p. 24.

Evening Herald (2001) One Tiger that will never crouch. *Evening Herald*, 9 April, p. 61.

Evening Herald (2003) Starved and terrorised – that's rugby. *Evening Herald*, 17 November, p. 8.

Evening Herald (2010) Unbelievable win for Nadal. *Evening Herald*, 14 September, p. 66.

Everton, C. (2003) Williams' bareknuckle victory. *Guardian*, 7 May, p. 31.

Everton, C. (2009) O'Sullivan snaps cue and claims circuit needs repair. *Guardian* (Sport), 12 January, p. 12.

Everton, C. (2011) Psychologist helped save O'Sullivan. *Guardian* (Sport), 20 April, p. 8.

Every, D. (2002) UEFA pro licence mid season master class. *Insight: The FA Coaches Association Journal, 2*, 1–4.

Eys, M., Patterson, M. M., Loughead, T. M., and Carron, A. V. (2005) Team building in sport. In D. Hackfort, J. Duda and R. Lidor (eds) *The handbook of research in applied sport and exercise psychology: International perspectives* (pp. 219–231). Morgantown, WV: Fitness Information Technology.

Eys, M., Loughead, T., Bray, S. R., and Carron, A. V. (2009) Development of a cohesion questionnaire for youth: The Youth Sports Environment Questionnaire. *Journal of Sport and Exercise Psychology, 31*, 390–408.

Eys, M., Burke, S. M. Carron. A. V., and Dennis, P. W. (2010) The sport team as an effective group. In J. M. Williams (ed.) *Applied sport psychology: Personal growth to peak performance* (6th edn, pp. 132–148). New York: McGraw-Hill.

Eysenck, M. W., and Calvo, M. (1992) Anxiety and performance: The processing efficiency theory. *Cognition and Emotion, 6*, 409–434.

Eysenck, M. W., Derakshan, N., Santos, R., and Calvo, M. G. (2007) Anxiety and cognitive performance: Attentional control theory. *Emotion, 7*, 336–353.

Fanning, D. (2002) Coping with a stress factor. *Sunday Independent* (Sport), 6 October, p. 6.

Fanning, D. (2004a) Arsène aims to mix war and serenity. *Sunday Independent* (Sport), p. 5.

Fanning, D. (2004b) Wilko a deep thinker trapped by his image. *Sunday Independent* (Sport), 16 November, p. 5.

Farah, M. J. (1984) The neurological basis of mental imagery: A componential analysis. *Cognition, 18*, 245–272.

Farrow, D., Baker, J., and MacMahon, C. (2007) *Developing sport expertise: Researchers and coaches put theory into practice*. Abingdon, Oxfordshire: Routledge.

Feltz, D. L., and Landers, D. M. (1983) The effects of mental practice on motor skill learning and performance: A meta-analysis. *Journal of Sport Psychology, 5*, 25–57.

Feltz, D. L., and Lirgg, C. D. (2001) Self-efficacy beliefs of athletes, teams, and coaches. In R. N. Singer, H. A. Hausenblas, and C. M. Janelle (eds) *Handbook of sport psychology* (2nd edn, pp. 340–361). New York: Wiley.

REFERENCES

Fenz, W. D., and Epstein, S. (1967) Gradients of physiological arousal in parachutists as a function of an approaching jump. *Psychosomatic Medicine, 29*, 33–51.

Fernandez-Duque, D., and Johnson, M. L. (1999) Attention metaphors: How metaphors guide the cognitive psychology of attention. *Cognitive Science, 23*, 83–116.

Festinger, L., Schacter, S., and Back, K. (1950) *Social pressures in informal groups*. Stanford, CA: Stanford University Press.

Finke, R. A. (1979) The functional equivalence of mental images and errors of movement. *Cognitive Psychology, 11*, 235–264.

Fisher, A. C., Damm, M. A., and Wuest, D. A. (1988) Adherence to sports injury rehabilitation programs. *Physician and Sportsmedicine, 16*, 47–51.

Flatman, B. (2009) "Grunt and you're out", Wimbledon players told. *Sunday Times*, 14 June, p. 9.

Flatman, B. (2010) Holding court. *Sunday Times* (Sport), 4 July, p. 14.

Fletcher, D., Hanton, S., and Mellalieu, S. D. (2006) An organisational stress review: Conceptual and theoretical issues in competitive sport. In S. Hanton and S. D. Mellalieu (eds) *Literature reviews in sport psychology* (pp. 321–374). Hauppauge, NY: Nova Science.

Flett, G. L., and Hewitt, P. L. (2005) The perils of perfectionism in sports and exercise. *Current Directions in Psychological Science, 14*, 14–18.

Flint, F. (1998) Integrating sport psychology and sports medicine in research: The dilemmas. *Journal of Applied Sport Psychology, 10*, 83–102.

Foley, C. (2010) "Ger took me apart and then built me back up". *Irish Independent* (Sport), 28 August, p. 7.

Folkins C., and Sime, W. (1981) Physical fitness training and mental health. *American Psychologist, 36*, 373–389.

Folkman, S. (1991) Coping across the life span: Theoretical issues. In E. M. Cummings, A. L. Greene, and K. H. Karraker (eds) *Life-span developmental psychology: Perspectives on stress and coping* (pp. 3–19). Hillsdale, NJ: Lawrence Erlbaum Associates.

Ford, I., and Gordon, S. (1999) Coping with sport injury: Resource loss and the role of social support. *Journal of Personal and Interpersonal Loss, 4*, 243–256.

Forrester, M. (ed.) (2010) *Doing qualitative research in psychology: A practical guide*. London: Sage.

Foster, C., Cowburn, G., Allender, S., and Pearce-Smith, N. (2007) *Physical activity and children review 3: The view of children on the barriers and facilitators to participation in physical activity. A review of qualitative studies*. London: NICE Public Health Collaborating Centre – Physical Activity.

Foster, D. J., Weigand, D. A., and Baines, D. (2006) The effect of removing superstitious behaviour and introducing a pre-performance routine on basketball free-throw performance. *Journal of Applied Sport Psychology, 18*, 167–171.

Fosterling, F. (1988) *Attribution theory in clinical psychology*. Chichester, West Sussex: Wiley.

Fotheringham, W. (2002a) Rushed return gives Pires the taste for more. *Guardian* (Sport), 26 October, p. 3.

Fotheringham, W. (2002b) Shared pain that sealed a French connection. *Guardian* (Sport), 26 October, pp. 2–3.

Fourkas, A. D., Avenanti, A., Urgesi, C., and Aglioti, S. M. (2006a) Corticospinal facilitation during first and third person imagery. *Experimental Brain Research, 168*, 143–151.

Fourkas A. D., Ionta, S., and, Aglioti, S.M. (2006b) Influence of imagined posture and imagery modality on corticospinal excitability. *Behavioural Brain Research, 168*, 190–196.

370

Fox, K. R. (2000) The influence of exercise on self-perceptions and self-esteem. In S. J. H. Biddle, K. R. Fox, and S. H. Boutcher (eds) *Physical activity and mental well-being* (pp. 78–111). London: Routledge.

Fox, K. R. (2001) Exercise psychology and the world of health services research, policy, and practice. In B. Cripps, S. Drew, and S. Woolfson (eds) *Activity for life: Theoretical and practical issues for exercise psychologists* (pp. 35–42). Leicester: British Psychological Society.

Fox, K. R. (2002) Self-perceptions and sport behaviour. In T. S. Horn (ed.) *Advances in sport psychology* (2nd edn, pp. 83–99). Champaign, IL: Human Kinetics.

Fox, M. C., Ericsson, K. A., and Best, R. (2011) Do procedures for verbal reporting of thinking have to be reactive? A meta-analysis and recommendations for best reporting methods. *Psychological Bulletin, 137*, 316–344.

France, C., Lee, C., and Powers, J. (2004) Correlates of depressive symptoms in a representative sample of young Australian women. *Australian Psychologist, 39*, 228–237.

Francis, S. R., Andersen, M. B., and Maley, P. (2000) Physiotherapists' and male professional athletes' views on psychological skills for rehabilitation. *Journal of Science and Medicine in Sport, 3*, 17–29.

Fraser, A (2009) For Laura. *Daily Mail*, 23 June, p. 77.

Friedkin, N. E. (2004) Social cohesion. *Annual Review of Sociology, 30*, 409–425.

Frost, R. O., and Henderson, K. J. (1991) Perfectionism and reaction to athletic competition. *Journal of Sport and Exercise Psychology, 13*, 323–335.

Funday Times (2002) Sachin Tendulkar. *The Funday Times* (Supplement to *Sunday Times*), 678, 8 September, p. 12.

Gagné, M., Ryan, R. M., and Bargmann, K. (2003) Autonomy support and need satisfaction in the motivation and well-being of gymnasts. *Journal of Applied Sport Psychology, 15*, 372–389.

Gallagher, B. (2002) Cunningham imagines the comeback of his life. *Daily Telegraph* (Sport), 27 November, p. S5.

Gallagher, B. (2008) Six of the best British sporting all-rounders. *Daily Telegraph*, 29 March. Retrieved from www.telegraph.co.uk/sport/columnists/brendangallagher/2295734/Six-of-the-best-British-sporting-all-rounders.html on 30 August 2010.

Galton, F. (1869) *Hereditary genius*. London: Macmillan.

Galton, F. (1883) *Inquiries into human faculty*. London: Dent.

Garrod, M. (2011) Rory's major meltdown. *Evening Herald*, 11 April, 64–65.

Garside, K. (2008) Fitter means faster. *Sunday Times*(Sport), 2 March, p. 15.

Gauron, E. (1984) *Mental training for peak performance*. Lansing, NY: Sport Science Associates.

Gauvin, L., and Rejeski, W. J. (1993) The Exercise-Induced Feeling Inventory: Development and initial validation. *Journal of Sport and Exercise Psychology, 15*, 403–423.

Gauvin, L., and Spence, J. C. (1995) Psychological research on exercise and fitness: Current research trends and future challenges. *Sport Psychologist, 9*, 434–448.

Gauvin, L., and Spence, J. C. (1998) Measurement of exercise-induced changes in feeling states: Affect, mood, and emotions. In J. L. Duda (ed.) *Advances in sport and exercise psychology* (pp. 325–350). Morgantown, WV: Fitness Information Technology.

Gauvin, L., Rejeski, J. W., and Reboussin, B. A. (2000) Contributions of acute bouts of vigorous physical activity to explaining diurnal variations in feeling states in active, middle-aged women. *Health Psychology, 19*, 365–375.

Gazzaniga, M. S., Ivry, R. B., and Mangun, G. R. (2002) *Cognitive neuroscience: The biology of the mind* (2nd edn). New York: Norton.

REFERENCES

Gee, C. J. (2010) How does sport psychology actually improve athletic performance? A framework to facilitate athletes' and coaches' understanding. *Behavior Modification, 34*, 386–402.

Geoghegan, T. (2009) What a racket. *BBC News Magazine*, 22 June. Retrieved from http://news.bbc.co.uk/2/hi/uk_news/magazine/8110998.stm on 22 September 2010.

Gibson, O. (2009) From man to superman ... how fast will we be by 2030? *Guardian*, 18 August, p. 3.

Gilbourne, D., and Smith, B. (2009) Editorial. *Qualitative Research in Sport and Exercise, 1*, 1–2.

Gilbourne, D., and Taylor, A. H. (1998) From theory to practice: The integration of goal perspective theory and life development approaches within an injury-specific goal-setting program. *Journal of Applied Sport Psychology, 10*, 124–139.

Gill, Derek L. (1980) *Quest: The life of Elizabeth Kübler-Ross*. New York: Harper & Row.

Gill, Diane L. (1987) Journal of Sport (and Exercise) Psychology. *Journal of Sport Psychology, 9*, 1–2.

Gill, Diane L. (2000) *Psychological dynamics of sport and exercise* (2nd edn). Champaign, IL: Human Kinetics.

Gilleece, D. (1996) Breathe deeply and be happy with second. *The Irish Times*, 27 September, p. 7.

Gilleece, D. (1999a) Qualifiers do it for themselves. *The Irish Times* (Sport), 19 June, p. 2.

Gilleece, D. (1999b) So near and yet so far. *The Irish Times*, 6 July, p. 23.

Gilleece, D. (2010) "I'd happily take no points if we had a European victory". *Sunday Independent* (Sport), 26 September, p. 7.

Gilovich, T., Keltner, D., and Nisbett, R. E. (2011) *Social psychology* (2nd edn). New York: Norton.

Gladwell, M. (2009) *Outliers: The story of success*. London: Penguin.

Glasser, W. (1976) *Positive addiction*. New York: Harper & Row.

Gobet, F., and Campitelli, G. (2007) The role of domain-specific practice, handedness and starting age in chess. *Developmental Psychology, 43*, 159–172.

Gobet, F., and Charness, N. (2006) Expertise in chess. In Ericsson, K. A., Charness, N., Feltovich, P. J., and Hoffman, R. R. (eds) *The Cambridge handbook of expertise and expert performance* (pp. 523–538). New York: Cambridge University Press.

Gobet, F., Chassy, P., and Bilalic, M. (2011) *Foundations of cognitive psychology*. Maidenhead, Berkshire: McGraw-Hill.

Gola, H. (2008) Tiger Woods entering a zone where few athletes have ever travelled. *Daily News*. Retrieved from www.nydailynews.com/sports/more_sports/2008/03/16/2008-03-16_tiger_woods_entering_a_zone_where_few_at.html?page=0 on 15 December 2008.

Goldenberg, S. (2003) Footballers who paid the penalty for failure. *Guardian*, 19 April, p. 6.

Goldstein, E. B. (2011) *Cognitive psychology* (3rd edn). Belmont, CA: Wadsworth/Cengage.

Goodbody, J., and Nichols, P. (2004) Marathon marred by invader's attack on race leader. *The Times* (Sport), 30 August, p. 1.

Goodger, K., Lavallee, D., Gorely, T., and Harwood, C. (2010) Burnout in sport: Understanding the process – from early warning signs to individualized intervention. In J. M. Williams (ed.) *Applied sport psychology: Personal growth to peak performance* (6th edn, pp. 492–511). New York: McGraw-Hill.

Gordin, R. D. (2003) Ethical issues in team sports. In R. Lidor and K. P. Henschen (eds) *The psychology of team sports* (pp. 57–68). Morgantown, WV: Fitness Information Technology.

Gordon, S. (2008) Appreciative inquiry coaching. *International Coaching Psychology Review, 3*, 19–31.

Gotwals, J. K., and Dunn, J. G. H. (2009) A multi-method multi-analytic approach to establishing internal construct validity evidence: The Sport Multidimensional Perfectionism Scale 2. *Measurement in Physical Education and Exercise Sciences, 13,* 71–92.

Gotwals, J. K., Dunn, J. G. H., Causgrove-Dunn, J., and Gamache, V. (2010) Establishing validity evidence for the Sport Multidimensional Perfectionism Scale-2 in intercollegiate sport. *Psychology of Sport and Exercise, 11,* 423–432.

Gouju, J.-L., Vermersch, P., and Bouthier, D. (2007) A psycho-phenomenological approach to sport psychology: The presence of the opponents in hurdle races. *Journal of Applied Sport Psychology, 19,* 173–186.

Gould, D. (1998) Goal setting for peak performance. In J. M. Williams (ed.) *Applied sport psychology: Personal growth to peak performance* (3rd edn, pp. 182–196). Mountain View, CA: Mayfield.

Gould, D. (2010) Goal-setting for peak performance. In J. M. Williams (ed.) *Applied sport psychology: Personal growth to peak performance* (6th edn, pp. 201–220). New York: McGraw-Hill.

Gould, D., and Carson, S. (2008) Life skills development through sport: Current status and future directions. *International Review of Sport and Exercise Psychology, 1,* 58–78.

Gould, D., Petlichkoff, L. M., Prentice, B., and Tedeschi, F. (2000) Psychology of sports injuries. *Sports Science Exchange Roundtable, 11,* no. 2.

Gould, D., Damarjian, N., and Greenleaf, C. (2002a) Imagery training for peak performance. In J. L. Van Raalte and B. W. Brewer (eds) *Exploring sport and exercise psychology* (2nd edn, pp. 49–74). Washington, DC: American Psychological Association.

Gould, D., Dieffenbach, K., and Moffett, A. (2002b) Psychological characteristics and their development in Olympic champions. *Journal of Applied Sport Psychology, 14,* 172–204.

Gould, D., Greenleaf, C., and Krane, V. (2002c) Arousal-anxiety and sport. In T. S. Horn (ed.) *Advances in sport psychology* (2nd edn, pp. 207–241). Champaign, IL: Human Kinetics.

Goulding, N. (2011) Allen facing the toughest fight of his life. *Irish Mail on Sunday* (The Title), 27 March, p. 21.

Granito, V. J., Jr (2002) Psychological responses to injury: Gender differences. *Journal of Sport Behaviour, 25,* 243–259.

Grant, T. (ed.) (2000) *Physical activity and mental health: National consensus statements and guidelines for practice.* London: Health Education Authority.

Graves, L., Stratton, G., and Cable, N. T. (2007) Comparison of energy expenditure in adolescents when playing new generation and sedentary computer games: cross sectional study. *British Medical Journal, 335,* 1282–1284.

Green, C. D. (2003) Psychology strikes out: Coleman R. Griffith and the Chicago Cubs. *History of Psychology, 6,* 267–283.

Green, C. D., and Benjamin, L. T., Jr (2009) *Psychology gets in the game: Sport, mind and behaviour, 1880–1960.* Lincoln, NE: University of Nebraska Press.

Greenlees, I., and Moran, A. (eds) (2003) *Concentration skills training in sport.* Leicester: British Psychological Society (Sport and Exercise Psychology Section).

Greenlees, I., Graydon, J., and Maynard, I. (2000) The impact of individual efficacy beliefs on group goal selection and group goal commitment. *Journal of Sports Sciences, 18,* 451–459.

Greenlees, I., Thelwell, R., and Holder, T. (2006) Examining the efficacy of the concentration grid exercise as a concentration enhancement exercise. *Psychology of Sport and Exercise, 7,* 29–39.

Greenspan, M. J., and Feltz, D. L. (1989) Psychological interventions with athletes in competitive settings: A review. *Sport Psychologist, 3,* 219–236.

Grimmer, K. A., Jones, D., and Williams, J. (2000) Prevalence of adolescent injury from recreational exercise: An Australian perspective. *Journal of Adolescent Health, 27,* 266–272.

REFERENCES

Grouios, G. (1992) Mental practice: A review. *Journal of Sport Behaviour, 15,* 42–59.

Grove, J. R., and Prapavessis, H. (1992) Preliminary evidence for the reliability and validity of an abbreviated profile of mood states. *International Journal of Sport Psychology, 23,* 93–109.

Gruber, J. J., and Gray, G. R. (1982) Responses to forces influencing cohesion as a function of player status and level of male varsity basketball competition. *Research Quarterly for Exercise and Sport, 53,* 27–36.

Guardian (2005) How relaxed Chelsea took complete control. *Guardian* (Sport), 15 October, p. 3.

Guardian (2009) Guardian and Observer guides to getting fit with Britain's medal winners. *Guardian,* 11 January, p. 35.

Gucciardi, D. F., and Dimmock, J. A. (2008) Choking under pressure in sensorimotor skills: Conscious processing or depleted attentional resources? *Psychology of Sport and Exercise, 9,* 45–59.

Gucciardi, D. F., and Mallett, C. J. (2010) Mental toughness. In S. J. Hanrahan and M. B. Andersen (eds) *Routledge handbook of applied sport psychology* (pp. 547–556). Abingdon, Oxfordshire: Routledge.

Gucciardi, D. F., Gordon, S., and Dimmock, J. A. (2009a) Advancing mental toughness research and theory using personal construct psychology. *International Review of Sport and Exercise Psychology, 2,* 54–72.

Gucciardi, D. F., Gordon, S., and Dimmock, J. A. (2009b) Development and preliminary validation of a mental toughness inventory for Australian football. *Psychology of Sport and Exercise, 10,* 201–209.

Gucciardi, D. F., Gordon, S., and Dimmock, J. A. (2009c) Evaluation of a mental toughness training program for youth-aged Australian footballers: I. A quantitative analysis. *Journal of Applied Sport Psychology, 21,* 307–323.

Gueugneau, N., Crognier, L., and Papaxanthis, C. (2008) The influence of eye movements on the temporal features of executed and imagined arm movements. *Brain Research, 1187,* 95–102.

Guillot, A., and Collet, C. (2005) Duration of mentally simulated movement: A review. *Journal of Motor Behavior, 37,* 10–20.

Guillot, A., and Collet, C. (eds) (2010) *The neurophysiological foundations of mental and motor imagery.* Oxford: Oxford University Press.

Guillot, A., Collet, C., Nguyen, V. A., Malouin, F., Richards, C., and Doyon, J. (2009) Brain activity during visual versus kinaesthetic imagery: An fMRI study. *Human Brain Mapping, 30,* 2157–2172.

Gully, S. M., Devine, D. J., and Whitney, D. J. (1995) A meta-analysis of cohesion and performance: Effects of level of analysis and task interdependence. *Small Group Research, 26,* 497–520.

Guscott, J., with N. Cain (1997) *The Lions' diary.* London: Michael Joseph.

Gustafsson, H., Hassmén, P., Kenttä, G., and Johansson. M. (2008) A qualitative analysis of burnout in elite Swedish athletes. *Psychology of Sport and Exercise, 9,* 800–816.

Gustafsson, H., Kenttä, G., and Hassmén, P. (2011) Athlete burnout: An integrated model and future research directions. *International Review of Sport and Exercise Psychology, 4,* 3–24.

Hackman, J. R., and Katz, N. (2010) Group behaviour and performance. In S. T. Fiske, D. T. Gilbert and G. Lindzey (eds) *Handbook of social psychology* (5th edn, Vol. 2, pp. 1208–1251). Hoboken, NJ: Wiley.

Hagger, M. S., and Chatzisarantis, N. L. D. (2007) Advances in self-determination theory research in sport and exercise. *Psychology of Sport and Exercise, 8,* 597–599.

Hagger, M. S., and Chatzisarantis, N. L. D. (2008) Self-determination theory and the psychology of exercise. *International Review of Sport and Exercise Psychology, 1,* 79–103.

Hagger, M. S., and Chatzisarantis, N. L. D. (2009) Integrating the theory of planned behaviour and self-determination theory in health behavior: A meta-analysis. *British Journal of Health Psychology*, *14*, 275–302.

Hagger, M. S., Chatzisarantis, N. L. D., and Biddle, S. J. H. (2002) A meta-analytic review of the theories of reasoned action and planned behaviour in physical activity: Predictive validity and the contributions of additional variables. *Journal of Sport and Exercise Psychology*, *24*, 3–32.

Hagtvet, K. A., and Hanin, Y. L. (2007) Consistency of performance-related emotions in elite athletes: Generalizability theory applied to the IZOF model. *Psychology of Sport and Exercise*, *8*, 47–72.

Hall, C. R. (2001) Imagery in sport and behaviour. In R. N. Singer, H. A Hausenblas, and C. M. Janelle (eds) *Handbook of sport psychology* (2nd edn, pp. 529–549). New York: Wiley.

Hall, C. R., and Martin, K. A. (1997) Measuring movement imagery abilities: A revision of the Movement Imagery Questionnaire. *Journal of Mental Imagery*, *21*, 143–154.

Hall, C. R., Mack, D., Paivio, A., and Hausenblas, H. A. (1998) Imagery use by athletes: Development of the Sport Imagery Questionnaire. *International Journal of Sport Psychology*, *29*, 73–89.

Hall, C. R., Stevens, D. E., and Paivio, A. (2005) *Sport Imagery Questionnaire: Test manual.* Morgantown, WV: Fitness Information Technology.

Hall, H. K., and Kerr, A. W. (2001) Goal setting in sport and physical activity: Tracing empirical developments and establishing conceptual direction. In G. C. Roberts (ed.) *Advances in motivation in sport and exercise* (pp. 183–233). Champaign, IL: Human Kinetics.

Hands, D. (2009) Ever-growing list of injuries puts emphasis on menace of incredible bulk. *The Times*, 6 July, p. 56.

Hanin, Y. (1997) Emotions and athletic performance: Individual zones of optimal functioning hypothesis. *European Yearbook of Sport Psychology*, *1*, 29–72.

Hankes, D. (in press) Sport and performance psychology: Ethical issues. In S. M. Murphy (ed.) *Handbook of sport and performance psychology.* Oxford: Oxford University Press.

Hannigan, M. (2003) Keeping sensible. *The Irish Times*, 20 October, p. 7.

Hanrahan, S. J., and Cerin, E. (2009) Gender, level of participation, and type of sport: Differences in achievement goal orientation and attributional style. *Journal of Science and Medicine in Sport*, *12*, 508–512.

Hanrahan, S. J., and Grove, J. R. (1990) A short form of the Sport Attributional Style Scale. *Australian Journal of Science and Medicine in Sport*, *22*, 97–101.

Hanrahan, S. J., Grove, J. R., and Hattie, J. A. (1989) Development of a questionnaire measure of sport-related attributional style. *International Journal of Sport Psychology*, *20*, 114–134.

Hansen, A., with J. Thomas (1999) *A matter of opinion.* London: Bantam.

Hanton, S., and Jones, G. (1999) The acquisition and development of cognitive skills and strategies: I. Making the butterflies fly in formation. *Sport Psychologist*, *13*, 1–21.

Hanton, S., Thomas, O., and Maynard, I. (2004) Competitive anxiety responses in the week leading up to competition: The role of intensity, direction and frequency dimensions. *Psychology of Sport and Exercise*, *15*, 169–181.

Harada, T., Okagawa, S., and Kubota, K. (2001) Habitual jogging improves performance of prefrontal tests. *Society for Neuroscience Abstracts*, program number 311.17, 12 November, 31st Annual Meeting, San Diego, CA.

Hardy, C. J., and Crace, R. K. (1997) Foundations of team building: Introduction to the team building primer. *Journal of Applied Sport Psychology*, *9*, 1–10.

Hardy, L. (1990) A catastrophe model of anxiety and performance. In G. Jones and L. Hardy (eds) *Stress and performance in sport* (pp. 81–106). Chichester, West Sussex: Wiley.

REFERENCES

Hardy, L. (1996) Testing the predictions of the cusp catastrophe model of anxiety and performance. *Sport Psychologist, 10*, 140–156.

Hardy, L. (1997) The Coleman Roberts Griffith address: Three myths about applied consultancy work. *Journal of Applied Sport Psychology, 9*, 277–294.

Hardy, L., and Callow, N. (1999) Efficacy of external and internal visual imagery perspectives for the enhancement of performance on tasks in which form is important. *Journal of Sport and Exercise Psychology, 21*, 95–112.

Hardy, L., and Fazey, J. (1990) *Concentration training: A guide for sports performers.* Headingley, Leeds: National Coaching Foundation.

Hardy, L., and Jones, J. G. (1994) Current issues and future directions for performance-related research in sport psychology. *Journal of Sports Sciences, 12*, 61–92.

Hardy, L., and Nelson, D. (1988) Self-regulation training in sport and work. *Ergonomics, 31*, 1573–1583.

Hardy, L., and Parfitt, C. G. (1991) A catastrophe model of anxiety and performance. *British Journal of Psychology, 82*, 163–178.

Hardy, L., Jones, G., and Gould, D. (1996) *Understanding psychological preparation for sport: Theory and practice of elite performers.* Chichester, West Sussex: Wiley.

Hardy, L., Gammage, K., and Hall, C. (2001) A descriptive study of athletes' self-talk. *Sport Psychologist, 15*, 306–318.

Hardy, L., Beattie, S., and Woodman, T. (2007) Anxiety-induced performance catastrophes: Investigating effort required as an asymmetry factor. *British Journal of Psychology, 98*, 15–31.

Hare, R., Evans, L., and Callow, N. (2008) Imagery use during rehabilitation from injury: A case study of an elite athlete. *Sport Psychologist, 22*, 405–422.

Harle, S. K., and Vickers, J. N. (2001) Training quiet eye improves accuracy in the basketball free throw. *Sport Psychologist, 15*, 289–305.

Harlow, J. (1999) Fear drives actors from the stage. *Sunday Times*, 14 February, p. 13.

Harman, N. (2006) Inner drive is key to Murray's hopes of joining greats. *The Times*, 5 July, p. 67.

Harman, N. (2009) Djokovic winning battle between body and soul. *The Times* (Wimbledon 09 supplement), 22 June, p. 5.

Harmison, R. J. (2007) Peak performance in sport: Identifying ideal performance states and developing athletes' psychological skills. *Professional Psychology: Research and Practice, 37*, 233–243.

Harris, D. V. (1973) *Involvement in sport: A somatopsychic rationale for physical activity.* Philadelphia, PA: Lea & Febiger.

Hart, S. (2011) London 2012 Olympics: Paula Radcliffe's amazing race for the summit. *Daily Telegraph*, 28 March. Retrieved from www.telegraph.co.uk/sport/othersports/olympics/8394951/London-2012-Olympics-Paula-Radcliffes-amazing-race-for-the-summit.html on 8 April 2011.

Harwood, C. (2002) Assessing achievement goals in sport: Caveats for consultants and a case for contextualisation. *Journal of Applied Sport Psychology, 14*, 106–119.

Harwood, C., and Biddle, S, (2002) The application of achievement goal theory in youth sport. In I. Cockerill (ed.) *Solutions in sport psychology* (pp. 58–73). London: Thomson.

Harwood, C., Spray, C. M., and Keegan, R. (2008) Achievement goal theories in sport. In T. S. Horn (ed.) *Advances in sport psychology* (3rd edn, pp. 157–185, 444–449). Champaign, IL: Human Kinetics.

Hatfield, B. M., and Hillman, C. H. (2001) The psychophysiology of sport. In R. N. Singer, H. A. Hausenblas, and C. M. Janelle (eds) *Handbook of sport psychology* (2nd edn, pp. 362–386). New York: Wiley.

Hatfield, B. M., and Kerick, S. E. (2007) The psychology of superior performance: A cognitive and affective neuroscience perspective. In G. Tenenbaum and R. C. Eklund (eds) *Handbook of sport psychology* (3rd edn, pp. 84–109). New York: Wiley.

Hattenstone, S. (2010) Fast and loose. *Guardian* (Weekend), 28 August, pp. 30–37.

Hatzigeorgiadis, A. (2002) Thoughts of escape during competition: Relationships with goal orientation and self-consciousness. *Psychology of Sport and Exercise, 3*, 195–207.

Hatzigeorgiadis, A., and Biddle, S. J. H. (2000) Assessing cognitive interference in sport: Development of the Thought Occurrence Questionnaire for Sport. *Anxiety, Stress, and Coping, 13*, 65–86.

Hausenblas, H. A., and Downs, D. S. (2002) Exercise dependence: A systematic review. *Psychology of Sport and Exercise, 3*, 89–123.

Hausenblas, H. A., and Giacobbi, P. R, Jr (2004) Relationship between exercise dependence symptoms and personality. *Personality and Individual Differences, 36*, 1265–1273.

Hausenblas, H. A., Carron, A. V., and Mack, D. E. (1997) Application of the theories of reasoned action and planned behaviour to exercise behaviour: A meta-analysis. *Journal of Sport and Exercise Psychology, 19*, 36–51.

Hayes, J. (1985) Three problems in teaching general skills. In J. Segal, S. Chipman, and R. Glaser (eds) *Thinking and learning skills, Vol. 2: Research and open questions* (pp. 391–406). Hillsdale, NJ: Lawrence Erlbaum Associates.

Healthcare News of Western Massachusetts (2010) BFMC senior class presents walk this way, August. Retrieved from http://healthcarenews.com/article.asp?id=2531 on 17 September 2010.

Hecker, J. E., and Kaczor, L. M. (1988) Application of imagery theory to sport psychology: Some preliminary findings. *Journal of Sport and Exercise Psychology, 10*, 363–373.

Heider, F. (1958) *The psychology of interpersonal relations.* New York: Wiley.

Heil, J. (1993) *Psychology of sport injury.* Champaign, IL: Human Kinetics.

Helsen, W. E., and Starkes, J. L. (1999) A multidimensional approach to skilled perception and performance in sport. *Applied Cognitive Psychology, 13*, 1–27.

Helsen, W. E., Starkes, J., and Hodges, N. J. (1998) Team sports and the theory of deliberate practice. *Journal of Sport and Exercise Psychology, 20*, 12–34.

Hemmings, B., and Povey, L. (2002) Views of chartered physiotherapists on the psychological content of their practice: A preliminary study in the United Kingdom. *British Journal of Sports Medicine, 36*, 61–64.

Hemmings, B., Mantle, H., and Ellwood, J. (2007) *Mental toughness for golf: The minds of winners.* London: Green Umbrella.

Henderlong, J., and Lepper, M. R. (2002) The effects of praise on children's intrinsic motivation: A review and synthesis. *Psychological Bulletin, 128*, 774–795.

Herbert, R. D., and Gabriel, M. (2002) Effects of stretching before and after exercising on muscle soreness and risk of injury: Systematic review. *British Medical Journal, 325*, 468–470.

Herbert, R. D., Dean, C., and Gandevia, S. C. (1998) Effects of real and imagined training on voluntary muscle activation during maximal isometric contractions. *Acta Physiologica Scandinavica, 163*, 361–368.

Heremans, E., Helsen, W. F., and Feys, P. (2008) The eyes as a mirror of our thoughts: Quantification of motor imagery of goal-directed movements through eye movement registration. *Behavioural and Brain Research, 187*, 351–360.

Heuzé, J.-P., and Fontayne, P. (2002) Questionnaire sur l'Ambiance du Groupe: A French-language instrument for measuring group cohesion. *Journal of Sport and Exercise Psychology, 24*, 42–67.

REFERENCES

Hewett, C. (2004) Modern power game puts future of players and rugby at risk. *The Independent*, 28 October, pp. 54–55.

Hill, D., Hanton, S. M., Matthews, N., and Fleming, S. (2010) Choking in sport: A review. *International Review of Sport and Exercise Psychology*, 3, 24–39.

Hoberman, J. D. (1992) *Mortal engines: The science of performance and the dehumanization of sport*. New York: Free Press.

Hodge, K. (1995) Team dynamics. In T. Morris and J. Summers (eds) *Sport psychology: Theory, application and issues* (pp. 190–212). Brisbane: Wiley.

Hodge, K. (2010) Working at the Olympics. In S. J. Hanrahan and M. B. Andersen (eds) *Routledge handbook of applied sport psychology* (pp. 405–413). Abingdon, Oxfordshire: Routledge.

Hodge, K., and McKenzie, A. (1999) *Thinking rugby: Training your mind for peak performance*. Auckland: Reed.

Hodges, N. J., and Baker, J. (2011) Expertise: The goal of performance development. In D. Collins, A. Button, and H. Richards (eds) *Performance psychology: A practitioner's guide* (pp. 31–46). Edinburgh: Churchill Livingstone/Elsevier.

Hodges, N. J., and Starkes J. L. (1996) Wrestling with the nature of expertise: A sport specific test of Ericsson, Krampe and Tesch-Romer's theory of deliberate practice. *International Journal of Sport Psychology*, 27, 1–25.

Hodges, N. J., Kerr, T., Starkes, J. L., Weir, P., and Nananidou, A. (2004) Predicting performance from deliberate practice hours for triathletes and swimmers: What, when and where is practice important? *Journal of Experimental Psychology: Applied*, 10, 219–237.

Hodges, N. J., Starkes, J. L., and MacMahon, C. (2006) Expert performance in sport: A cognitive perspective. In K. A. Ericsson, N. Charness, P. J. Feltovich and R. R. Hoffman (eds) *The Cambridge handbook of expertise and expert performance* (pp. 471–488). Cambridge: Cambridge University Press.

Hodges, N. J., Huys, R., and Starkes, J. L. (2007) A methodological review and evaluation of research of expert performance in sport. In G. Tenenbaum and R. C. Eklund (eds) *Handbook of sport psychology* (pp. 161–183). New York: Wiley.

Hodgkinson, M. (2002) The top 10 worst sporting excuses. *Sunday Times* (Sport), 6 October, p. 24.

Hoey, K. (2002) UK is still way behind when it comes to sports medicine. *Daily Telegraph* (Sport), 18 November, p. S7.

Hoffmann, P. (1997) The endorphin hypothesis. In W. P. Morgan (ed.) *Physical activity and mental health* (pp. 163–177). Washington, DC: Taylor & Francis.

Hogg, M. A. (1992) *The social psychology of group cohesiveness*. Toronto: Harvester Wheatsheaf.

Hohlefeld, F. U., Nikulin, V. V., and Curio, G. (2011) Visual stimuli evoke rapid activation (120 ms) of sensorimotor cortex for overt but not for covert movements. *Brain Research*, 1368, 185–195.

Holmes, P., and Collins, D. (2001) The PETTLEP approach to motor imagery: A functional equivalence model for sport psychologists. *Journal of Applied Sport Psychology*, 13, 60–83.

Holmes, P., and Collins, D. (2002) Functional equivalence solutions for problems with motor imagery. In I. Cockerill (ed.) *Solutions in sport psychology* (pp. 120–140). London: Thomson.

Holmes, T. H., and Rahe, R. H. (1967) The Social and Readjustment Rating Scale. *Journal of Psychosomatic Research*, 11, 213–218.

Holt, N. L., and Sparkes, A. C. (2001) An ethnographic study of cohesiveness in a college soccer team over a season. *Sport Psychologist*, 15, 237–259.

Honigsbaum, M. (2004) Sitting pretty. *Observer Sport Monthly*, August, pp. 15–20.

Hooper, S. L., MacKinnon, L. T., Gordon, R. D., and Bachmann, A. W. (1993) Hormonal responses of elite swimmers to overtraining. *Medicine and Science in Sports and Exercise, 25*, 741–747.

Hopps, D. (2002) It's official: England's injuries are the worst in the world. *Guardian*, 3 September, p. 22.

Hopps, D. (2011) Another player in distress reopens debate on the "black wings" of illness. *Guardian* (Sport), 25 March, p. 2.

Horwood, J. (2002) Sick of work? Bingo! *The Psychologist, 15*, p. 544.

Hudson, J., and Walker, N. C. (2002) Metamotivational state reversals during matchplay golf: An idiographic approach. *Sport Psychologist, 16*, 200–217.

Hughes, S. (2002) Darts feels the power of Taylor's tungsten. *Daily Telegraph* (Sport), 7 January, p. S7.

Hull, C. L. (1943) *Principles of behaviour*. New York: Appleton-Century-Crofts.

Hurlburt, R. T., and Akhter, S. A. (2006) The descriptive experience sampling method. *Phenomenology and the Cognitive Sciences, 5*, 271–301.

Hurley, O. A., Moran, A., and Guerin, S. (2007) Exploring athletes' experience of their injuries: A qualitative investigation. *Sport and Exercise Psychology Review, 3*, 14–22.

Hyde, A. L., Doerksen, S. E., Ribeiro, N. F., and Conroy, D. E. (2010) The independence of implicit and explicit attitudes toward physical activity: Introspective access and attitudinal concordance. *Psychology of Sport and Exercise, 11*, 387–393.

Hyllegard, R. (1991) The role of baseball seam pattern in pitch recognition. *Journal of Sport and Exercise Psychology, 13*, 80–84.

Ievleva, L., and Orlick, T. (1991) Mental links to enhanced healing: An exploratory study. *Sport Psychologist, 5*, 25–40.

Ievleva, L., and Terry, P. C. (2008) Applying sport psychology to business. *International Coaching Psychology Review, 3*, 8–18.

Irish Times (2008) Fear pushes me and keeps me practising. *The Irish Times*, 22 July, p. 25.

Irish Times (2009) Poulter blames photographer. *The Irish Times*, 6 July, p. 5.

Isaac, A. (1992) Mental practice: Does it work in the field? *Sport Psychologist, 6*, 192–198.

Isaac, A., Marks, D., and Russell, E. (1986) An instrument for assessing imagery of movement: The Vividness of Movement Imagery Questionnaire (VMIQ). *Journal of Mental Imagery, 10*, 23–30.

Jackson, J. (2010) Wenger wants Arsenal to play without fear. *The Irish Times* (Sport), 8 December, p. 3.

Jackson, R. C. (2003) Pre-performance routine consistency: Temporal analysis of goal kicking in the Rugby Union World Cup. *Journal of Sports Sciences, 21*, 803–814.

Jackson, R. C., and Baker, J. S. (2001) Routines, rituals, and rugby: Case study of a world class goal kicker. *Sport Psychologist, 15*, 48–65.

Jackson, R. C., and Masters, R. S. W. (2006) Ritualized behaviour in sport. *Behavioural and Brain Sciences, 29*, 621–622.

Jackson, R. C., and Mogan, P. (2007) Advance visual information, awareness, and anticipation skill. *Journal of Motor Behavior, 39*, 341–351.

Jackson, R. C., Ashford, K. J., and Norsworthy, G. (2006) Attentional focus, dispositional reinvestment and skilled motor performance under pressure. *Journal of Sport and Exercise Psychology, 28*, 49–68.

Jackson, S. A., and Kimiecik, J. C. (2008) The flow perspective of optimal experience in sport and physical activity. In T. S. Horn (ed.) *Advances in sport psychology* (3rd edn, pp. 377–399, 474–477). Champaign, IL: Human Kinetics.

Jackson, S. A., and Roberts, G. C. (1992) Positive performance states of athletes: Toward a conceptual understanding of peak performance. *Sport Psychologist, 6*, 156–171.

Jackson, S. A., Thomas, P. R., Marsh, H. W., and Smethurst, C. J. (2001) Relationships between flow, self-concept, psychological skills, and performance. *Journal of Applied Sport Psychology, 13*, 129–153.

Jackson, S. A., Martin, A. J., and Eklund, R. C. (2008) Long and short measures of flow: The construct validity of FSS-2, DFS-2, and new brief counterparts. *Journal of Sport and Exercise Psychology, 30*, 561–587.

Jacob, G. (2003) The game. *The Times*, 19 May, p. 5.

Jacobson, E. (1932) Electrophysiology of mental activities. *American Journal of Psychology, 44*, 677–694.

James, D. (2003) "I am ready and able to handle the real thing". *The Times* (Sport), 22 March, p. 36.

James, W. (1890) *Principles of psychology*. New York: Holt, Rinehart & Winston.

James, W. (1899) *Talks to teachers on psychology: And to students on some of life's ideals*. New York: H. Holt.

Janelle, C. M. (1999) Ironic mental processes in sport: Implications for sport psychologists. *Sport Psychologist, 13*, 201–220.

Janelle, C. M., and Hatfield, B. D. (2008) Visual attention and brain processes that underlie expert performance: Implications for sport and military psychology. *Military Psychology, 20* (supplement 1), S39–S69.

Janelle, C. M., and Hillman, C. H. (2003) Expert performance: Current perspectives. In J. L. Starkes and K. A. Ericsson (eds) *Expert performance in sports: Advances in research on sport expertise* (pp. 19–47). Champaign, IL: Human Kinetics.

Janelle, C. M., Singer, R. N., and Williams, A. M. (1999) External distractions and attentional narrowing: Visual search evidence. *Journal of Sport and Exercise Psychology, 21*, 70–91.

Jeannerod, M. (1994) The representing brain: Neural correlates of motor intention and imagery. *Behavioural and Brain Sciences, 17*, 187–245.

Jeannerod, M. (1997) *The cognitive neuroscience of action*. Oxford: Blackwell.

Jeannerod, M. (2001) Neural simulation of action: A unifying mechanism for motor cognition. *NeuroImage, 14*, S103–S109.

Johnson, D. W., and Johnson, F. P. (1987) *Joining together: Group therapy and group skills* (3rd edn). Englewood Cliffs, NJ: Prentice-Hall.

Johnson, P. (1982) The functional equivalence of imagery and movement. *Quarterly Journal of Experimental Psychology, Section A, 34*, 349–365.

Johnston, L., and Carroll, D. (2000) The psychological impact of injury: Effects of prior sport and exercise involvement. *British Journal of Sports Medicine, 34*, 436–439.

Jones, G. (1995) More than just a game: Research developments and issues in competitive anxiety in sport. *British Journal of Psychology, 86*, 449–478.

Jones, G., and Hanton, S. (2001) Pre-competitive feeling states and directional anxiety interpretations. *Journal of Sports Sciences, 19*, 385–395.

Jones, G., and Swain, A. B. J. (1992) Intensity and direction as dimensions of competitive state anxiety and relationships with competitiveness. *Perceptual and Motor Skills, 74*, 467–472.

Jones, G., and Swain, A. B. J. (1995) Predispositions to experience debilitative and facilitative anxiety in elite and non-elite performers. *Sport Psychologist, 9*, 201–211.

Jones, G., Hanton, S., and Swain, A. B. J. (1994) Intensity and interpretation of anxiety symptoms in elite and non-elite sports performers. *Personality and Individual Differences, 17*, 756–663.

Jones, G., Hanton, S., and Connaughton, D. (2002) What is this thing called mental toughness? An investigation of elite sport performers. *Journal of Applied Sport Psychology, 14,* 205–218.

Jones, G., Hanton, S., and Connaughton, D. (2007) A framework of mental toughness in the world's best performers. *Sport Psychologist, 21,* 243–264.

Jones, M. V., and Uphill, M. (2004) Responses to the Competitive State Anxiety Inventory-2(d) by athletes in anxious and excited scenarios. *Psychology of Sport and Exercise, 5,* 201–212.

Jones, R. T. (2002) Golden moment as Lynch storms to glory. *Irish Independent* (Sport), 23 September, p. *15.*

Jones, S. (1997) Seigne's only song: Je ne regrette rien. *Sunday Times* (Sport), 5 October, p. 14.

Jordet, G. (2009) When superstars flop: Public status and choking under pressure in international soccer penalty shootouts. *Journal of Applied Sport Psychology, 21,* 125–130.

Jordet, G., and Hartman, E. (2008) Avoidance motivation and choking under pressure in soccer penalty shootouts. *Journal of Sport and Exercise Psychology, 30,* 452–459.

Jordet, G., Elferink-Gemser, M. T., Lemmink, K. A. P. M., and Visscher, C. (2006) The "Russian roulette" of soccer? Perceived control and anxiety in a major tournament penalty shootout. *International Journal of Sport Psychology, 37,* 281–298.

Jordet, G., Hartman, E., Visscher, C., and Lemmink, K. A. P. M. (2007) Kicks from the penalty mark in soccer: The role of stress, skill, and fatigue for kick outcomes. *Journal of Sports Sciences, 25,* 121–129.

Junge, A., and Dvorak, J. (2000) Influence of definition and data collection on the incidence of injuries in football. *American Journal of Sports Medicine, 28,* 540–546.

Junge, A., Engebretsen, L., Mountjoy, M. L., Alonso, J., Renström, P. A. F. H., Aubry, M. J., and Dvorak, J. (2009) Sports injuries during the Summer Olympic Games 2008. *American Journal of Sports Medicine, 37,* 2165–2172.

Kabat-Zinn, J. (2005) *Coming to our senses: Healing ourselves and the world through mindfulness.* New York: Hyperion.

Kahneman, D. (1973) *Attention and effort.* New York: Prentice-Hall.

Karageorghis, C. I. (2008) The scientific application of music in sport and exercise. In A. M. Lane (ed.) *Sport and exercise psychology: Topics in applied psychology* (pp. 109–137). London: Hodder Education.

Karageorghis, C. I., Mouzourides, D. A., Priest, D. L., Sasso, T. A., Morrish, D. J., and Walley, C. L. (2009) Psychophysical and ergogenic effects of synchronous music during treadmill walking. *Journal of Sport and Exercise Psychology, 31,* 18–36.

Karageorghis, C. I., Priest, D. L., Williams, L. S., Hirani, R. M., Lannon, K. M., and Bates, B. J. (2010) Ergogenic and psychological effects of synchronous music during circuit-type exercises. *Psychology of Sport and Exercises, 11,* 551–559.

Kavussanu, M. (2008) Moral behaviour in sport: A critical review of the literature. *International Review of Sport and Exercise Psychology, 1,* 124–138.

Kavussanu, M., and Boardley, I. D. (2009) The Prosocial and Antisocial Behaviour in Sport Scale. *Journal of Sport and Exercise Psychology, 31,* 97–117.

Keane, R., with E. Dunphy (2002) *Keane: The autobiography.* London: Michael Joseph.

Keats, M. R., and Culos-Reed, N. (2009) A theory-driven approach to encourage physical activity in paediatric cancer survivors: A pilot study. *Journal of Sport and Exercise Psychology, 31,* 267–283.

Keefe, R. (2003) *On the sweet spot: Stalking the effortless present.* New York: Simon & Schuster.

Keh, A. (2010) A few things to think about when lining up that kick. *New York Times,* 30 May. Retrieved from www.nytimes.com/2010/05/31/sports/soccer/31penaltykicks.html on 29 September 2010.

Kelly, G. A. (1955) *The psychology of personal constructs*, Vol. 1. New York: Norton.

Kelly, L. (1998) Walton's new mountain. *Irish Independent*, 26 October, p. 9.

Kelly, L. (2010) Louis kept his head by seeing red. *Irish Independent* (Sport), 21 July, p. 7.

Kerr, G. A., and Miller, P. S. (2001) Coping strategies. In J. Crossman (ed.) *Coping with sports injuries: Psychological strategies for rehabilitation* (pp. 83–102). Oxford: Oxford University Press.

Kerr, J. H. (1997) *Motivation and emotion in sport: Reversal theory*. Hove, East Sussex: Psychology Press.

Kerr, J. H., Lindner, K. J., and Blaydon, M. (2007) *Exercise dependence*. London: Routledge.

Kervin, A. (2001) The power and the glory. *The Times* (Sport), 7 August, p. S6.

Kervin, A. (2005) From zero at Twickenham to World Cup heroes in Sydney. *The Times*, 3 October, pp. 72–73.

Kim, K. A., and Duda, J. L. (2003) The coping process: Cognitive appraisals of stress, coping strategies, and coping effectiveness. *Sport Psychologist*, *17*, 406–425.

Kimmage, P. (1998) I could almost tell the ball where to go. *Sunday Independent*, 24 May, p. 29L.

King, D., and Ridley, I. (2006) Arsenal lucky says Nedved as Wegner turns to shrinks to help young stars cope with bullies in Premiership. *Ireland on Sunday*, 2 April, pp. 82–83.

Kingston, K. M., and Hardy, L. (1997) Effects of different types of goals on processes that support performance. *Sport Psychologist*, *11*, 277–293.

Kingston, K. M., and Wilson, K. M. (2009) The application of goal setting in sport. In S. D. Mellalieu and S. Hanton (eds) *Advances in applied sport psychology: A review* (pp. 75–123). Abingdon, Oxfordshire: Routledge.

Kirkby, R. (1995) Psychological factors in sport injuries. In T. Morris and J. Summers (eds) *Sport psychology: Theory, applications and issues* (pp. 456–473). Brisbane: Wiley.

Kirkendall, D. T., and Garrett, W. E. (2001) Heading in soccer: Integral skill or grounds for cognitive dysfunction? *Journal of Athletic Training*, special issue: Concussion in athletes, *36*, 328–333.

Kirkendall, D. T., Jordan, S. E., and Garrett, W. E. (2001) Heading and head injuries in soccer. *Sports Medicine*, *31*, 369–386.

Kishi, Y., Robinson, R. G., and Forrester, A. W. (1994) Prospective longitudinal study of depression following spinal cord injury. *Journal of Neuropsychiatry and Clinical Neuroscience*, *6*, 237–244.

Klavora, P. (1978) An attempt to derive inverted-U curves based on the relationship between anxiety and athletic performance. In D. M. Landers and R. W. Christina (eds) *Psychology of motor behaviour and sport* (pp. 369–377). Champaign, IL: Human Kinetics.

Klein, C., DiazGranados, D., Salas, E., Le, H., Burke, C. S., Lyons, R., and Goodwin, G. F. (2009) Does team-building work? *Small Group Research*, *40*, 180–222.

Klein, M., and Christiansen, G. (1969) Group composition, group structure and group effectiveness of basketball teams. In J. W. Loy and G. S. Kenyon (eds) *Sport, culture, and society* (pp. 397–408). London: Macmillan.

Knowles, E. (ed.) (1999) *The Oxford dictionary of quotations* (5th edn). Oxford: Oxford University Press.

Kobasa, S. C. (1979) Stressful life events, personality, and health: An inquiry into hardiness. *Journal of Personality and Social Psychology*, *37*, 1–11.

Kohl, R. M., and Roenker, D. L. (1980) Bilateral transfer as a function of mental imagery. *Journal of Motor Behaviour*, *12*, 197–206.

Kohl, R. M., and Roenker, D. L. (1983) Mechanism involvement during skill imagery. *Journal of Motor Behaviour*, *15*, 179–190.

Kolata, P. (2007) "I'm not really running, I'm not really running …". *New York Times*, 6 December. Retrieved from www.nytimes.com/2007/12/06/health/nutrition/06Best. html on 8 April 2011.

Kolb, B., and Whishaw, I. Q. (2009) *Fundamentals of human neuropsychology* (6th edn). New York: Worth.

Kontos, A. P., and Feltz, D. L (2008) The nature of sport psychology. In T. Horn (ed.) *Advances in sport psychology* (3rd edn, pp. 3–14, 423–425). Champaign, IL: Human Kinetics.

Kornspan, A. (2007) The early years of sport psychology: The work and influence of Pierre De Coubertin. *Journal of Sport Behaviour*, 30, 77–93.

Kornspan, A. (2011) A history of sport psychology. In S. M. Murphy (ed.) *Handbook of sport and performance psychology*. Oxford: Oxford University Press.

Kosslyn, S. M. (1994) *Image and brain: The resolution of the imagery debate*. Cambridge, MA: MIT Press.

Kosslyn, S. M., Seger, C., Pani, J. R., and Hillger, L. A. (1990) When is imagery used in everyday life? A diary study. *Journal of Mental Imagery*, 14, 131 152.

Kosslyn, S. M., Ganis, G., and Thompson, W. L. (2001) Neural foundations of imagery. *Nature Reviews: Neuroscience*, 2, 635–642.

Kosslyn, S. M., Thompson, W. L., and Ganis, G. (2006) *The case for mental imagery*. Oxford: Oxford University Press.

Koutures, C. G., Gregory, A. J. M., and the Council on Sports Medicine and Fitness (2010) Clinical report – injuries in youth soccer. *Pediatrics*, 125, 410–414.

Kowler, E. (1999) Eye movements and visual attention. In R. A. Wilson and F. C. Keil (eds) *The MIT encyclopedia of the cognitive sciences* (pp. 306–309). Cambridge, MA: MIT Press.

Kramer, A. F., and Erickson, K. I. (2007) Capitalizing on cortical plasticity: Influence of physical activity on cognition and brain function. *Trends in Cognitive Sciences*, 11, 342–348.

Krane, V. (1994) The Mental Readiness Form as a measure of competitive state anxiety. *Sport Psychologist*, 8, 189–202.

Kratochwill, T. R., and Levin, J. R. (2010) Enhancing the scientific credibility of single-case intervention research: Randomization to the rescue. *Psychological Methods*, 15, 124–144.

Kremer, J., and Busby, G. (1998) Modelling participant *Motivation in sport and exercise*: An integrative approach. *Irish Journal of Psychology*, 19, 447–463.

Kremer, J., and Moran, A. (2008a) *Pure sport: Practical sport psychology*. Hove, East Sussex: Routledge.

Kremer, J., and Moran, A. (2008b) Swifter, higher, stronger: The history of sport psychology. *The Psychologist*, 21, 740–742.

Kremer, J., and Scully, D. (1994) *Psychology in sport*. London: Taylor & Francis.

Kremer, J., and Scully, D. (1998) What applied sport psychologists often don't do: On empowerment and independence. In H. Steinberg, I. Cockerill and A. Dewey (eds) *What sport psychologists do* (pp. 21–27). Leicester: British Psychological Society (Sport and Exercise Psychology Section).

Kremer, J., and Scully, D. (2002) The team just hasn't gelled. In I. Cockerill (ed.) *Solutions in sport psychology* (pp. 3–15). London: *Thomson*.

Kremer, J., Sheehy, N., Reilly, J., Trew, K., and Muldoon, O. (2003) *Applying social psychology*. Basingstoke, Hampshire: Palgrave Macmillan.

Kremer, J., Moran, A., Walker, G., and Craig, C. (2012) *Key concepts in sport psychology*. London: Sage.

Kress, J. L., and Statler, T. (2007) A naturalistic investigation for former Olympic cyclists' cognitive strategies for coping with exertion pain during performance. *Journal of Sport Behavior*, 30, 428–452.

REFERENCES

Kruger, J., Ham, S. A., and Kohl, H. W., III (2005) Trends in leisure-time physical inactivity by age, sex, and race/ethnicity – United States, 1994–2004. *Morbidity and Mortality Weekly Review*, *54*, 991–994.

Kübler-Ross, E. (1969) *On death and dying*. New York: Macmillan.

Kujala, U. M. (2002) Injury prevention. In D. L. Mostofsky and L. D. Zaichowsky (eds) *Medical and psychological aspects of sport and exercise* (pp. 33–40). Morgantown, WV: Fitness Information Technology.

Kyllo, L. B., and Landers, D. M. (1995) Goal-setting in sport and exercise: A research synthesis to resolve the controversy. *Journal of Sport and Exercise Psychology*, *17*, 117–137.

Land, M. F., and McLeod, P. (2000) From eye movements to actions: How batsmen hit the ball. *Nature Neuroscience*, *3*, 1340–1345.

Landers, D. M., and Arent, S. M. (2007) Physical activity and mental health. In G. Tenenbaum and R. C. Eklund (eds) *Handbook of sport psychology* (3rd edn, pp. 469–491). New York: Wiley.

Landers, D. M., and Arent, S. M. (2010) Arousal-performance relationships. In J. M. Williams (ed.) *Applied sport psychology: Personal growth to peak performance* (6th edn, pp. 221–246). New York: McGraw-Hill.

Landers, D. M., and Luschen, G. (1974) Team performance outcome and cohesiveness of competitive coacting groups. *International Review of Sport Sociology*, *9*, 57–71.

Landin, D., and Herbert, E. P. (1999) The influence of self-talk on the performance of skilled female tennis players. *Journal of Applied Sport Psychology*, *11*, 263–282.

Lane, A. M., Sewell, D. F., Terry, P. C., Bartram, D., and Nesti, M. S. (1999) Confirmatory factor analysis of the Competitive State Anxiety Inventory-2. *Journal of Sports Sciences*, *17*, 505–512.

Lane, A. M., Harwood, C., and Nevill, A. M. (2005) Confirmatory factor analysis of the Thought Occurrence Questionnaire for Sport (TOQS) among adolescent athletes. *Anxiety, Stress, and Coping*, *18*, 245–254.

Lang, P. J. (1977) Imagery in therapy: An information-processing analysis of fear. *Behaviour Therapy*, *8*, 862–886.

Lang, P. J. (1979) A bio-informational theory of emotional imagery. *Psychophysiology*, *17*, 495–512.

Lang, P. J., Kozak, M., Miller, G. A., Levin, D. N., and McLean, A. (1980) Emotional imagery: Conceptual structure and pattern of somato-visceral response. *Psychophysiology*, *17*, 179–192.

Lang, P. J., Greenwald, M. K., Bradley, M. M., and Hamm, O. (1993) Looking at pictures: Affective, facial, visceral and behavioural reactions. *Psychophysiology*, *30*, 261–273.

Larrick, R. P., Timmerman, T. A., Carton, A. M., and Abrevaya, J. (2011) Temper, temperature, and temptation: Heat-related retaliation in baseball. *Psychological Science*, *22*, 423–428.

Larson, G. A., Starkey, C., and Zaichkowsky, L. D. (1996) Psychological aspects of athletic injuries as perceived by athletic trainers. *Sport Psychologist*, *10*, 37–47.

Lashley, K. (1915) The acquisition of skill in archery. *Carnegie Institutions Publications*, *7*, 107–128.

Lau, R. R., and Russell, D. (1980) Attributions in the sports pages: A field test of some current hypotheses about attribution research. *Journal of Personality and Social Psychology*, *39*, 29–38.

Laurence, J. (1998) A saunter for champs. *Irish Independent*, 1 July, p. 23.

Lavallee, D., Grove, J. R., Gordon, S., and Ford, I. W. (1998) The experience of loss in sport. In J. H. Harvey (ed.) *Perspectives on loss: A sourcebook* (pp. 241–252). Philadelphia, PA: Brunner/Mazel.

Lavallee, D., Jennings, D., Anderson, A. G., and Martin, S. B. (2005) Irish athletes' attitudes toward seeking a sport psychology consultation. *Irish Journal of Psychology, 26,* 115–121.

Lavallee, D., Kremer, J., Moran, A., and Williams, M. (2012) *Sport psychology: Contemporary themes* (2nd edn). Basingstoke, Hampshire: Palgrave Macmillan.

Lawlor, D. A., and Hopker, S. W. (2001) The effectiveness of exercise as an intervention in the management of depression: Systematic review and meta-regression analysis of randomised controlled trials. *British Medical Journal, 322,* 1–8.

Lawrenson, M. (2008) String of poor signings indicated serious flaw. *The Irish Times,* 5 December, p. 19.

Lazarus, R. S. (1993) From psychological stress to the emotions: A history of changing outlooks. *Annual Review of Psychology, 44,* 1–21.

Lazarus, R. S., and Folkman, S. (1984) *Stress, appraisal, and coping.* New York: Springer.

Leddy, M. H., Lambert, M. J., and Ogles, B. M. (1994) Psychological consequences of athletic injury among high-level competitors. *Research Quarterly for Exercise and Sport, 65,* 347–354.

Lee, A. J., Garraway, W. M., Hepburn, W., and Laidlaw, R. (2001) Influence of rugby injuries on players' subsequent health and lifestyle: Beginning a long term follow up. *British Journal of Sports Medicine, 35,* 38–42.

Lee, M. J., Whitehead, J., and Ntoumanis, N. (2007) Development of the Attitudes to Moral Decision-Making in Youth Sport Questionnaire (AMDYSQ). *Psychology of Sport and Exercise, 8,* 369–392.

Leffingwell, T. R., Rider, S. P., and Williams, J. M. (2001) Application of the transtheoretical model to psychological skills training. *Sport Psychologist, 15,* 168–187.

Lehrer, J. (2010) How to raise a superstar. *The Frontal Cortex.* Retrieved from www.wired.com/wiredscience/2010/08/how-to-raise-a-superstar/ on 8 September 2010.

Lejeune, M., Decker, C., and Sanchez, X. (1994) Mental rehearsal in table tennis performance. *Perceptual and Motor Skills, 79,* 627–641.

Lemyre, P.-N., Roberts, G. C., and Ommundsen, Y. (2002) Achievement goal orientations, perceived ability, and sportspersonship in youth soccer. *Journal of Applied Sport Psychology, 14,* 120–136.

Lemyre, P.-N., Treasure, D. C., and Roberts, G. C. (2006) Influence of variability in motivation and affect on elite athlete burnout susceptibility. *Journal of Sport and Exercise Psychology, 28,* 32–48.

Lenk, H. (1969) Top performance despite internal conflict: An antithesis to a functionalist proposition. In J. W. Loy and G. S. Kenyon (eds) *Sport, culture, and society: A reader on the sociology of sport* (pp. 393–396). Toronto: Collier Macmillan.

Lenk, H. (1977) *Team dynamics.* Champaign, IL: Stipes.

Lepper, M. R., and Greene, D. (1975) Turning play into work: Effects of adult surveillance and extrinsic rewards on children's intrinsic motivation. *Journal of Personality and Social Psychology, 31,* 479–486.

Lequerica, A., Rapport, L., Axelrod, B. N., Telmet, K., and Whitman, R. D. (2002) Subjective and objective assessment methods of mental imagery control: Construct validation of self-report measures. *Journal of Clinical and Experimental Neuropsychology, 24,* 1103–1116.

LeUnes, A. (2008) *Sport psychology* (4th edn). New York: Taylor & Francis.

LeUnes, A., and Nation, J. R. (2002) *Sport psychology* (3rd edn). Pacific Grove, CA: Wadsworth.

Lewin, K. (1935) *A dynamic theory of personality.* New York: McGraw-Hill.

REFERENCES

Li, F., and Harmer, P. (1996) Confirmatory factor analysis of the Group Environment Questionnaire with an intercollegiate sample. *Journal of Sport and Exercise Psychology, 18*, 49–63.

Lidor, R., and Singer, R. N. (2003) Preperformance routines in self-paced tasks: Developmental and educational considerations. In R. Lidor and K. P. Henschen (eds) *The psychology of team sports* (pp. 69–98). Morgantown, WV: Fitness Information Technology.

Lilienfeld, S. O., Lynn, S. J., Namy, L. L., and Woolf, N. J. (2009) *Psychology: From inquiry to understanding.* Boston, MA: Pearson.

Livingstone, M. B. E., Robson, P. J., Wallace, M. W., and McKinley, M. C. (2003) How active are we? Levels of routine physical activity in children and adults. *Proceedings of the Nutrition Society, 62*, 681–701.

Locke, E. A. (1991) Problems with goal-setting research in sports – and their solution. *Journal of Sport and Exercise Psychology, 8*, 311–316.

Locke, E. A., and Latham, G. P. (1985) The application of goal setting to sports. *Journal of Sport Psychology, 7*, 205–222.

Locke, E. A., and Latham, G. P. (1990) *A theory of goal setting and task performance.* Englewood Cliffs, NJ: Prentice-Hall.

Locke, E. A., and Latham, G. P. (2002) Building a practically useful theory of goal setting and task motivation. *American Psychologist, 57*, 705–717.

Locke, E. A., and Latham, G. P. (2006) New directions in goal-setting theory. *Current Directions in Psychological Science, 15*, 265–278.

Locke, E. A., Shaw, K. N., Saari, L. M., and Latham, G. P. (1981) Goal setting and task performance: 1969–1980. *Psychological Bulletin, 90*, 125–152.

Loehr, J. E. (1982) *Athletic excellence: Mental toughness training for sports.* Denver, CO: Forum.

Logie, R. H. (1999) Working memory. *The Psychologist, 12*, 174–178.

Long, B. C., and van Stavel, R. (1995) Effects of exercise training on anxiety: A meta-analysis. *Journal of Applied Sport Psychology, 7*, 167–189.

Lonsdale, C., and Tam, J. T. M. (2008) On the temporal and behavioural consistency of pre-performance routines: An intra-individual analysis of elite basketball players' free throw shooting accuracy. *Journal of Sports Sciences, 26*, 259–266.

Lowe, S. (2011) I'm a romantic, says Xavi, heartbeat of Barcelona and Spain. *Guardian* (Sport), 11 February, pp. 6–7.

Lutz, R. S. (2003) Covert muscle excitation is outflow from the central generation of motor imagery. *Behavioural Brain Research, 140*, 149–163.

McAuley, E. (1985) Success and causality in sport: The influence of perception. *Journal of Sport Psychology, 7*, 13–22.

McAuley, E., and Blissmer, B. (2002) Self-efficacy and attributional processes in physical activity. In T. S. Horn (ed.) *Advances in sport psychology* (2nd edn, pp. 185–205). Champaign, IL: Human Kinetics.

McCann, S. (2008) At the Olympics, everything is a performance issue. *International Journal of Sport and Exercise Psychology, 6*, 267–276.

McCarthy, P., Jones, M. V., and Clark-Canter, D. (2008) Understanding enjoyment in youth sport: A developmental perspective. *Psychology of Sport and Exercise, 9*, 142–156.

McClelland, D. C., Atkinson, J. W., Clark, R. W., and Lowell, E. J. (1953) *The achievement motive.* New York: Appleton-Century-Crofts.

McErlane, M. (2002) Acting up. *Sunday Times* (Style), p. 3.

McEwan, S. E., Hujbregts, M. P. J., Ryan, J. D., and Polatajko, H. J. (2009) Cognitive strategy use to enhance motor skill acquisition post-stroke: A critical review. *Brain Injury, 23*, 263–277.

McGinley, M., Kremer, J., Trew, K., and Ogle, S. (1998) Socio-cultural identity and attitudes to sport in Northern Ireland. *Irish Journal of Psychology, 19*, 464–471.

McGinty, K. (2006) Kiwi finds his silver lining in clouds of Carton. *Irish Independent*, 18 May, p. 19.

McGrory, D. (2002) Heading footballs killed Jeff Astle, coroner says. *The Times*, 12 November, p. 3.

McHardy, A. J., Pollard, H. P., and Luo, K. (2007) Golf-related lower back injuries: An epidemiological survey. *Journal of Chiropractic Medicine, 6*, 20–26.

McIlveen, R. (1992) An investigation of attributional bias in a real-world setting. In R. McIlveen, L. Higgins, and A. Wadeley (eds) *BPS manual of psychology practicals* (pp. 78–92). Leicester: British Psychological Society.

McIntosh, M. (2002) Hate drives Lennon out. *Guardian*, 22 August, p. 34.

MacIntyre, T. (1996) *Imagery validation: How do we know that athletes are imaging during mental practice?* Unpublished MA thesis, Department of Psychology, University College, Dublin.

MacIntyre, T., and Moran, A. (2007a) A qualitative investigation of imagery use and meta-imagery processes among elite canoe-slalom competitors. *Journal of Imagery Research in Sport and Physical Activity, 2*, 1, Article 3.

MacIntyre, T., and Moran, A. (2007b) A qualitative investigation of meta-imagery processes and imagery direction among elite athletes. *Journal of Imagery Research in Sport and Physical Activity, 2*, 1, Article 4.

Mackay, G. J., and Neill, J. T. (2010) The effect of "green exercise" on state anxiety and the role of exercise duration, intensity, and greenness: A quasi-experimental study. *Psychology of Sport and Exercise, 11*, 238–245.

McKenzie, A. D., and Howe, B. L. (1991) The effect of imagery on tackling performance in rugby. *Journal of Human Movement Studies, 20*, 163–176.

McLean, N. (1995) Building and maintaining an effective team. In T. Morris and J. Summers (eds) *Sport psychology: Theory, applications and issues* (pp. 420–434). Brisbane: Wiley.

McNair, D. M., Lorr, M., and Droppleman, L. F. (1992) *Revised manual for the Profile of Mood States*. San Diego, CA: Educational and Industrial Testing Services.

MacPherson, A., Collins, D., and Morriss, C. (2008) Is what you think what you get? Optimizing mental focus for technical performance. *Sport Psychologist, 22*, 288–303.

McPherson, S. L. (2000) Expert-novice differences in planning strategies during collegiate singles tennis competition. *Journal of Sport and Exercise Psychology, 22*, 39–62.

McRae, D. (2008) Even great players can have tortured minds. *Guardian* (Sport), 15 July, 6–7.

MacRae, F. (2006) Sunday footballers at risk of brain damage: Heading the ball can lead to health problems. *Daily Mail*, 6 December. Retrieved from www.thefreelibrary.com/Sunday+footballers+at+risk+of+brain+damage%3B+Heading+the+ball+can+lead...-a0155581429 on 18 August 2010.

MacRury, D. (1997) *Golfers on golf*. London: Virgin.

Maehr, M. L., and Nicholls, J. G. (1980) Culture and achievement motivation: A second look. In N. Warren (ed.) *Studies in cross-cultural psychology* (pp. 221–267). New York: Academic Press.

Maguire, E. A., Gadian, D. G., Johnsrude, I. S., Good, C. D., Ashburner, J., Frackowiak, R. S. J., and Frith, C. D. (2000) Navigation-related structural change in the hippocampi of taxi drivers. *Proceedings of the National Academy of Sciences (USA), 97*, 4398–4403.

Mahoney, M. J., and Avener, M. (1977) Psychology of the elite athlete: An exploratory study. *Cognitive Therapy and Research, 1*, 135–141.

Mahoney, P. (2007) Swing doctors cash in as Baddeley joins quick-fix gospel's band of disciples. *Guardian* (Sport), 11 June, p. 5.

Mainwaring, L. M., Hutchison, M., Bisschop, S. M., Comper, P., and Richards, D. W. (2010) Emotional responses to sport concussion compared to ACL injury. *Brain Injury*, *24*, 589–597.

Mair, L. (2004) Faldo dismisses fear of failure in a heartbeat. *Daily Telegraph* (Sport), 15 July, pp. 2–3.

Mallett, C. J., and Hanrahan, S. J. (1997) Race modelling: An effective cognitive strategy for the 100 m sprinter? *Sport Psychologist*, *11*, 72–85.

Mallett, C. J., and Hanrahan, S. J. (2003) Elite athletes: Why does the "fire" burn so brightly? *Psychology of Sport and Exercise*, *5*, 183–200.

Mann, D. L., Ho, N. Y., De Souza, N. J., Watson, D. R., and Taylor, S. J. (2007) Is optimal vision required for the successful execution of an interceptive task? *Human Movement Science*, *27*, 343–356.

Marcotti, G. (2001) Made, not born. *Sunday Tribune* (Sport), 7 October, p. 9.

Marcus, B. H., and Forsyth, L. H. (2003) *Motivating people to be physically active*. Champaign, IL: Human Kinetics.

Marcus, B. H., and Simkin, L. R. (1993) The stages of exercise behaviour. *Journal of Sports Medicine and Physical Fitness*, *33*, 83–88.

Marcus, B. H., Bock, B. C., Pinto, B. M., Napolitano, M. A., and Clark, M. M. (2002) Exercise initiation, adoption, and maintenance in adults: Theoretical models and empirical support. In J. Van Raalte and B. W. Brewer (eds) *Exploring sport and exercise psychology* (2nd edn, pp. 185–208). Washington, DC: American Psychological Association.

Marshall, S. J., and Welk, G. J. (2008) Definitions and measurement. In A. L. Smith and S. J. H. Biddle (eds) *Youth physical activity and sedentary behaviors: Challenges and solutions* (pp. 3–31). Champaign, IL: Human Kinetics.

Martell, S. G., and Vickers, J. N. (2004) Gaze characteristics of elite and near-elite athletes in ice hockey defensive tactics. *Human Movement Science*, *22*, 689–712.

Martens, M. P., and Webber S. N. (2002) Psychometric properties of the Sport Motivation Scale: An evaluation with college varsity athletes from the US. *Journal of Sport and Exercise Psychology*, *24*, 254–270.

Martens, R. (1977) *Sport competition anxiety test*. Champaign, IL: Human Kinetics.

Martens, R., Landers, R. M., and Loy, J. W. (1972) *Sport cohesiveness questionnaire*. Unpublished manuscript, University of Illinois, Champaign, IL.

Martens, R., Burton, D., Vealey, R. S., Bump, L. A., and Smith, D. E. (1990) Development and validation of the Competitive State Anxiety Inventory-2 (CSAI-2). In R. Martens, R. S. Vealey, and D. Burton (eds) *Competitive anxiety in sport* (pp. 117–190). Champaign, IL: Human Kinetics.

Martin, A. (2007) More than words: Book of Serena the answer to Williams' prayers. *Guardian* (Sport), 3 July, p. 5.

Martin, A. J., and Jackson, S.A. (2008) Brief approaches to assessing task absorption and enhanced subjective experience: Examining "short" and "core" flow in diverse performance domains. *Motivation and Emotion*, *32*, 141–157.

Martin, J. J., and Gill, D. L. (1991) The relationships among competitive orientation, sport-confidence, self-efficacy, anxiety and performance. *Journal of Sport and Exercise Psychology*, *13*, 149–159.

Martin, K. A., Moritz, S. E., and Hall, C. (1999) Imagery use in sport: A literature review and applied model. *Sport Psychologist*, *13*, 245–268.

Martin, L. C., Carron, A. V., and Burke, S. M. (2009) Team building interventions in sport: A meta-analysis. *Sport and Exercise Psychology Review*, *5*, 3–18.

Martin, S. B., Kellmann, M., Lavallee, D., and Page, S. J. (2002) Development and psychometric evaluation of the Sport Psychology Attitudes – Revised Form: A multiple group investigation. *Sport Psychologist, 16*, 272–290.

Martindale, A., and Collins, D. (2011) Conclusion: Where next? Getting help in your pursuit of excellence. In D. Collins, A. Button and H. Richards (eds) *Performance psychology: A practitioner's guide* (pp. 393–401). Oxford: Elsevier.

Martinent, G., and Ferrand, C. (2007) A cluster analysis of precompetitive anxiety: Relationship with perfectionism and trait anxiety. *Personality and Individual Differences, 43*, 1676–1686.

Martinsen, E. W., and Morgan, W. P. (1997) Antidepressant effects of physical activity. In W. P. Morgan (ed.) *Physical activity and mental health* (pp. 93–106). Washington, DC: Taylor & Francis.

Massey, R. (2010) Sport radio "as risky as a drink if you're driving". *Daily Mail*, 2 July, p. 13.

Masters, K. S., and Ogles, B. M. (1998) Associative and dissociative cognitive strategies in exercise and running: 20 years later, what do we know? *Sport Psychologist, 12*, 253–270.

Masters, R. S. W. (1992) Knowledge, "knerves" and know-how: The role of explicit versus implicit knowledge in the breakdown of a complex motor skill under pressure. *British Journal of Psychology, 83*, 343–358.

Masters, R. S. W., and Maxwell, J. P. (2004) Implicit motor learning, reinvestment and movement disruption: What you don't know won't hurt you. In A. M. Williams and N. J. Hodges (eds) *Skill acquisition in sport: Research, theory and practice* (pp. 207–228). London: Routledge.

Masters, R. S. W., and Maxwell, J. P. (2008) The theory of reinvestment. *International Review of Sport and Exercise Psychology, 2*, 160–183.

Masters, R. S. W., Polman, R. C. J., and Hammond, N. V. (1993) "Reinvestment": A dimension of personality implicated in skill breakdown under pressure. *Personality and Individual Differences, 14*, 655–666.

Matheson, H., Mathes, S., and Murray, M. (1995) Group cohesion of female intercollegiate coacting and interacting teams across a competitive season. *International Journal of Sport Psychology, 27*, 37–49.

Mathieu, J., Maynard, M. T., Rapp, T., and Gilson, L. (2010) Team effectiveness 1997–2007: A review of recent advancements and a glimpse into the future. In J. A. Wagner and J. R. Hollenbeck (eds) *Readings in organisational behaviour* (pp. 321–380). New York: Routledge.

Matlin, M. W. (2009) *Cognition* (7th edn). New York: Wiley.

Matthews, J. (2009) *Increasing physical activity in adolescents: Exploring self-regulation in action*. Unpublished PhD thesis, School of Psychology, University College, Dublin.

Maynard, I. (1998) *Improving concentration*. Headingley, Leeds: National Coaching Foundation.

Mears, P., and Voehl, F. (1994) *Team building: A structured learning approach*. Delray Beach, FL: St Lucie Press.

Media Planet (2010) Mental strength key to Moody's successful career. *Media Planet 1* (supplement to *Guardian*), 16 September, pp. 4–5.

Medic, N. (2010) Masters athletes. In S. J. Hanrahan and M. B. Andersen (eds) *Routledge handbook of applied sport psychology* (pp. 387–395). Abingdon, Oxfordshire: Routledge.

Meister, I. G., Krings, T., Foltys, H., Boroojerdi, B., Müller, M., Töpper, R., and Thron, A. (2004) Playing piano in the mind – An fMRI study on music imagery and performance in pianists. *Cognitive Brain Research, 19*, 219–228.

REFERENCES

Mellalieu, S. D., Hanton, S., and Fletcher, D. (2006a) A competitive anxiety review: Recent directions in sport psychology. In S. Hanton and S. D. Mellalieu (eds) *Literature reviews in sport psychology* (pp. 1–45). Hauppauge, NY: Nova Science.

Mellalieu, S. D., Hanton, S., and O'Brien, M. (2006b) The effects of goal-setting on rugby performance. *Journal of Applied Behavior Analysis, 39*, 257–261.

Mellalieu, S. D., Hanton, S., and Thomas, O. (2009) The effects of a motivational general-arousal imagery intervention upon preperformance symptoms in male rugby union players. *Psychology of Sport and Exercise, 10*, 175–185.

Mellecker, R. R., and McManus, A. M. (2008) Energy expenditure and cardiovascular responses to seated and active gaming in children. *Archives of Pediatric Adolescent Medicine, 162*, 886–891.

Melnick, M. J., and Chemers, M. M. (1974) Effects of group structure on the success of basketball teams. *Research Quarterly for Exercise and Sport, 45*, 1–8.

Mental Health Foundation (2009) *Moving on up*. London: Mental Health Foundation.

Merikle, P. (2007) Preconscious processing. In M. Velmans and S. Schneider (eds) *The Blackwell companion to consciousness* (pp. 512–524). Oxford: Blackwell.

Mesagno, C., and Mullane-Grant, T. (2010) A comparison of different pre-performance routines as possible choking interventions. *Journal of Applied Sport Psychology, 22*, 343–360.

Meyers, A. W. (1997) Sport psychology services to the United States Olympic Festival: An experiential account. *Sport Psychologist, 11*, 454–468.

Mezulis, A. H., Abramson, L. Y., Hyde, J. S., and Hankin, B. L. (2004) Is there a universal positivity bias in attributions? A meta-analytic review of individual, developmental, and cultural differences in self-serving attributional bias. *Psychological Bulletin, 130*, 711–747.

Middleton, C. (1996) Losing out as the mind muscles in. *Sunday Telegraph* (Sport), 30 June, p. 15.

Miller, B. (1997) *Gold minds: The psychology of winning in sport*. Marlborough, Wiltshire: Crowood Press.

Milton, J., Solodkin, A., Hlustik, P., and Small, S. L. (2007) The mind of expert performance is cool and focused. *NeuroImage, 35*, 804–813.

Milton, J., Small, S. L., and Solodkin, A. (2008a) Imaging motor imagery: Methodological issues related to expertise. *Methods, 45*, 336–341.

Milton, J., Solodkin, A., and Small, S. L. (2008b) Why did Casey strike out? The neuroscience of hitting. In D. Gordon (ed.) *Your brain on Cubs: Inside the heads of players and fans* (pp. 43–57, 136–139). New York: Dana Press.

Miracle, A. W., and Rees, C. R. (1994) *Lessons of the locker-room: The myth of school sports*. Amherst, NJ: Prometheus.

Mitchell, K. (2010a) Hard regime in gym helps Murray find his feet on clay. *Guardian* (Sport), 29 April, p. 6.

Mitchell, K. (2010b) Nadal the humble conquistador has time on his side and the world in his hands. *Guardian* (Sport), 15 September, p. 7.

Moore, G. (2000) Sympathy but little satisfaction for Robson. *The Independent*, 4 December, p. 3.

Moran, A. P. (1993) Conceptual and methodological issues in the measurement of mental imagery skills in athletes. *Journal of Sport Behaviour, 16*, 156–170.

Moran, A. P. (1996) *The psychology of concentration in sport performers: A cognitive analysis*. Hove, East Sussex: Psychology Press.

Moran, A. P. (1998) *The pressure putt: Doing your best when it matters most in golf* (audiotape). Aldergrove, Co. Antrim, N. Ireland: Tutorial Services (UK).

Moran, A. P. (2000a) Improving sporting abilities: Training concentration skills. In J. Hartley and A. Branthwaite (eds) *The applied psychologist* (2nd edn, pp. 92–110). Buckingham: Open University Press.

Moran, A. P. (2000b) *Managing your own learning at university: A practical guide* (rev. edn, first published 1997). Dublin: UCD Press.

Moran, A. P. (2001) What makes a winner? The psychology of expertise in sport. *Studies, 90*, 266–275.

Moran, A. P. (2002a) In the mind's eye. *The Psychologist, 15*, 414–415.

Moran, A. P. (2002b) "Shrinking" or expanding? The role of sport psychology in professional football. *Insight – The FA Coaches Journal, 6*, 41–43.

Moran, A. P. (2003a) Improving concentration skills in team-sport performers: Focusing techniques for soccer players. In R. Lidor and K. P. Henschen (eds) *The psychology of team sports* (pp. 161–190). Morgantown, WV: Fitness Information Technology.

Moran, A. P. (2003b) The state of concentration skills training in applied sport psychology. In I. Greenless and A. P. Moran (eds) *Concentration skills training in sport* (pp. 7–19). Leicester: British Psychological Society (Division of Sport and Exercise Psychology).

Moran, A. P. (2004) *Sport and exercise psychology: A critical introduction.* London: Routledge.

Moran, A. P. (2009) Cognitive psychology in sport: Progress and prospects. *Psychology of Sport and Exercise, 10*, 420–426.

Moran, A. P., and MacIntyre, T. (1998) "There's more to an image than meets the eye": A qualitative study of kinaesthetic imagery among elite canoe-slalomists. *Irish Journal of Psychology, 19*, 406–423.

Moran, A. P., Byrne, A., and McGlade, N. (2002) The effects of anxiety and strategic planning on visual search behaviour. *Journal of Sports Sciences, 20*, 225–236.

Moran, A. P., Guillot, A., MacIntyre, T., and Collet, C. (in press) Re-imagining motor imagery: Building bridges between cognitive neuroscience and sport psychology. *British Journal of Psychology.*

Moran, G. (2005) "Oh dear, so near but yet so far away". *The Irish Times*, 12 July, p. 21.

Moran, S. (2001) The Gaelic Athletic Association and professionalism in Irish sport. *Studies, 90*, 276–282.

Morgan, W. P. (1977) Involvement in vigorous physical activity with special reference to adherence. In L. I. Gedvilas and M. W. Kneer (eds) *Proceedings of the National College Physical Education Association* (pp. 235–246). Chicago, IL: University of Illinois–Chicago Publication Service.

Morgan, W. P. (1979) Negative addiction in runners. *Physician and Sportsmedicine, 7*, 57–70.

Morgan, W. P. (1985) Affective beneficence of vigorous physical activity. *Medicine and Science in Sports and Exercise, 17*, 94–100.

Morgan, W. P. (1997) Mind games: The psychology of sport. In D. R. Lamb and R. Murray (eds) *Perspectives in exercise science and sports medicine: Optimizing sport performance* (Vol. 10, pp. 1–62). Carmel, IN: Cooper.

Morgan, W. P. (2000) Psychological factors associated with distance running and the marathon. In D. T. Pedloe (ed.) *Marathon medicine* (pp. 293–310). London: Royal Society of Medicine Press.

Morgan, W. P. (2001) Prescription of physical activity: A paradigm shift. *Quest, 53*, 366–382.

Morgan, W. P., and Dishman, R. K. (2001) Adherence to exercise and physical activity: Preface. *Quest, 53*, 277–278.

Morgan, W. P., and Goldston, S. E. (eds) (1987) *Exercise and mental health*. Washington, DC: Hemisphere.

Morgan, W. P., and Pollock, M. L. (1977) Psychologic characterization of the elite distance runner. *Annals of the New York Academy of Sciences, 301*, 382–403.

Morgan, W. P., Brown, D. R., Raglin, J. S., O'Connor, P. J., and Ellickson, K. A. (1987) Psychological monitoring of overtraining and staleness. *British Journal of Sports Medicine, 21*, 107–114.

Morris, K. (2006) The best players know the value of winning ugly. *Sunday Tribune*, 29 October, p. 24.

Morris, L., Davis, D., and Hutchings, C. (1981) Cognitive and emotional components of anxiety: Literary review and revised worry-emotionality scale. *Journal of Educational Psychology, 73*, 541–555.

Morris, P. E., Tweedy, M., and Gruneberg, M. M. (1985) Interest, knowledge and the memorizing of soccer scores. *British Journal of Psychology, 76*, 415–425.

Morris, T., Spittle, M., and Perry, C. (2004) Mental imagery in sport. In T. Morris and J. Summers (eds) *Sport psychology: Theory, applications and issues* (2nd edn, pp. 344–387). Brisbane: Wiley.

Morris, T., Spittle, M., and Watt, A. P. (2005) *Imagery in sport*. Champaign, IL: Human Kinetics.

Morrissey, E. (2009) Teenage screams make them so hard to beat. *Sunday Tribune* (Sport), 21 June, p. 16.

Mudrack, P. E. (1989a) Defining group cohesiveness: A legacy of confusion? *Small Group Behaviour, 20*, 37–49.

Mudrack, P. E. (1989b) Group cohesiveness and productivity: A closer look. *Human Relations, 42*, 771–785.

Mullen, B., and Copper, C. (1994) The relation between group cohesiveness and performance: An integration. *Psychological Bulletin, 115*, 210–227.

Müller, S., Abernethy, B., and Farrow, D. (2006) How do world-class cricket batsmen anticipate a bowlers' intention? *Quarterly Journal of Experimental Psychology, 59*, 2162–2186.

Müller, S., Abernethy, B., Reece, J., Rose, M., Eid, M., McBan, R., Hart, T., and Abreu, C. (2009) An in-situ examination of the timing of information pick-up for interception by cricket batsmen of different skill levels. *Psychology of Sport and Exercise, 10*, 644–652.

Munroe, K. J., Giaccobi, P. R., Jr, Hall, C. R., and Weinberg, R. S. (2000) The four W's of imagery use: Where, when, why, and what. *Sport Psychologist, 14*, 119–137.

Munroe-Chandler, K. J., Hall, C. R., and Weinberg, R. S. (2004) A qualitative analysis of the types of goals athletes set in training and competition. *Journal of Sport Behavior, 27*, 58–74.

Munsey, C. (2010) Coaching the coaches. *APA Monitor on Psychology, 41*, 58–61.

Murphy, C. (2010) Clean bill of health. *The Player* (in association with the *Irish Independent*), 25 August, pp. 24–25.

Murphy, Sam (2001) Back to nature. *Guardian* (Weekend), 22 September, p. 69. Retrieved from www.guardian.co.uk/theguardian/2001/sep/22/weekend7.weekend3 on 4 December 2011.

Murphy, Shane M. (1994) Imagery interventions in sport. *Medicine and Science in Sports and Exercise, 26*, 486–494.

Murphy, Shane M. (1999) *The cheers and the tears: A healthy alternative to the dark side of youth sports today*. San Francisco, CA: Jossey-Bass.

Murphy, Shane M., and Jowdy, D. P. (1992) Imagery and mental practice. In T. S Horn (ed.) *Advances in sport psychology* (pp. 221–250). Champaign, IL: Human Kinetics.

Murphy, Shane M., and Martin, K. A. (2002) The use of imagery in sport. In T. Horn (ed.) *Advances in sport psychology* (2nd edn, pp. 405–439). Champaign, IL: Human Kinetics.

Murphy, Shane M., Nordin, S., and Cumming, J. (2008) Imagery in sport, exercise, and dance. In T. S. Horn (ed.) *Advances in sport psychology* (3rd edn, pp. 297–324). Champaign, IL: Human Kinetics.

Muscat, J. (2007) Big hitting Roddick has to find his way forward. *The Times*, 26 June, p. 75.

Mutrie, N. (2001) The transtheoretical model of behaviour change: An examination of its applicability to exercise behaviour change. In B. Cripps, S. Drew, and S. Woolfson (eds) *Activity for life: Theoretical and practical issues for exercise psychologists* (pp. 27–34). Leicester: British Psychological Society.

Mutrie, N., Carney, C., Blamey, A., Crawford, C., Aitchison, T., and Whitelaw, A. (2002) "Walk in to work out": A randomised controlled trial of a self help intervention to promote active commuting. *Journal of Epidemiological Community Health, 56*, 407–412.

Myers, D., Abell, J., Kolstad, A., and Sani, F. (2010) *Social psychology* (European edn). Maidenhead, Berkshire: McGraw-Hill.

Nadel, L., and Piattelli-Palmarini, M. (2002) What is cognitive science? In L. Nadel (ed.) *Encyclopaedia of cognitive science* (Vol. 1, pp. xiii–xli). London: Nature Publishing Group.

Naish, J. (2009) Humankind on fast track to a standstill. *Irish Independent*, 18 August, p. 13.

Nakamura, J., and Csikszentmihalyi, M. (2002) The concept of flow. In C. R. Snyder and S. J. Lopez (eds) *Handbook of positive psychology* (pp. 89–105). New York: Oxford University Press.

Nakata, H., Yoshie, M., Miura, A., and Kudo, K. (2010) Characteristics of the athlete's brain: Evidence from neurophsyiology and neuroimaging. *Brain Research Reviews, 62*, 197–211.

National Coaching Foundation (1996) *Motivation and mental toughness.* Headingley, Leeds: National Coaching Foundation.

Navon, D., and Gopher, D. (1979) On the economy of the human information-processing system. *Psychological Review, 86*, 214–255.

Navratilova, M. (2009) Martina Navratilova: The grunting has to stop. *Sunday Times*, 7 June. Retrieved from www.timesonline.co.uk/tol/sport/tennis/article6446197.ccc on 17 March 2011.

Neiss, R. (1988) Reconceptualizing arousal: Psychobiological states in motor performance. *Psychological Bulletin, 103*, 345–366.

Nesti, M. (2010) *Psychology in football.* Abingdon, Oxfordshire: Routledge.

Newman, B. (1984) Expediency as benefactor: How team building saves time and gets the job done. *Training and Development Journal, 38*, 26–30.

Newman, P. (2010) The power and the glory. *Irish Independent* (Sport), 6 January, p. 12.

Nicholas, M. (2002) Control freak Faldo gives pointer to Hussain's men. *Daily Telegraph* (Sport), 9 December, p. S6.

Nicholls, A. R., and Polman, R. C. J. (2007) Coping in sport: A systematic review. *Journal of Sports Sciences, 25*, 11–31.

Nicholls, J. G. (1984) Achievement motivation: Conceptions of ability, subjective experience, task choice, and performance. *Psychological Review, 91*, 328–346.

Nicholls, J. G. (1989) *The competitive ethos and democratic education.* Cambridge, MA: Harvard University Press.

Nicholls, J. G. (1992) The general and the specific in the development and expression of achievement motivation. In G. Roberts (ed.) *Motivation in sport and exercise* (pp. 31–56). Champaign, IL: Human Kinetics.

Nichols, P. (2000) Ice-man Faulds keeps his cool. *Guardian* (Sport), 21 September, p. 7.

Nideffer, R. M. (1976) Test of Attentional and Interpersonal Style. *Journal of Personality and Social Psychology, 34*, 394–404.

REFERENCES

Nideffer, R. M., Sagal, M.-S., Lowry, M., and Bond, J. (2001) Identifying and developing world-class performers. In G. Tenenbaum (ed.) *The practice of sport psychology* (pp. 129–144). Morgantown, WV: Fitness Information Technology.

Nigg, C. R., Lippke, S., and Maddock, J. E. (2009) Factorial invariance of the theory of planned behaviour applied to physical activity across gender, age and ethnic groups. *Psychology of Sport and Exercise, 10*, 219–225.

Nigg, C. R., Basen-Engquist, K., and Atienza, A. A. (2011a) Introduction: Understanding the mechanism of physical activity behaviour change. Challenges and a call for action. *Psychology of Sport and Exercise, 12*, 1–6.

Nigg, C. R., Geller, K. S., Motl, R. W., Horwath, C. C., Wertin, K. K., and Dishman, R. K. (2011b) A research agenda to examine the efficacy and relevance of the Transtheoretical Model for physical activity behaviour. *Psychology of Sport and Exercise, 12*, 7–12.

Nisbett, R. E., and Wilson, T. D. (1977) Telling more than we can know: Verbal reports on mental processes. *Psychological Review, 84*, 231–259.

Nordin, S., and Cumming, J. (2008) Types and functions of athletes' imagery: Testing predictions from the applied model of imagery use by examining effectiveness. *International Journal of Sport and Exercise Psychology, 6*, 189–206.

Norrish, M. (2009) Andrei Arshavin's feat throws spotlight on ultimate case of monkey business. *Daily Telegraph*, 11 April. Retrieved from www.telegraph.co.uk/sport/football/teams/arsenal/5202158/Andrei-Arshavins-feat-throws-spotlight-on-ultimate-case-of-monkey-business.html on 10 September 2010.

Northcroft, J. (2009) They shall not pass. *Sunday Times* (Sport), 8 February, pp. 12–13.

Northcroft, J., and Walsh, D. (2010) England: The team that never was. *Sunday Times* (Sport), 4 July, pp. 6–7.

Noyes, F. R., Lindenfeld, T. N., and Marshall, M. T. (1988) What determines an athletic injury (definition)? Who determines an injury (occurrence)? *American Journal of Sports Medicine, 21*, 78–91.

Ntoumanis, N., Biddle, S., and Haddock, G. (1999) The mediating role of coping strategies on the relationship between achievement motivation and affect in sport. *Anxiety, Stress and Coping, 12*, 299–327.

O., J., and Munroe-Chandler, J. (2008) The effects of image speed on the performance of a soccer task. *Sport Psychologist, 22*, 1–17.

Oaten, M., and Cheng, K. (2006) Improved self-control: The benefits of a regular program of academic study. *Basic and Applied Social Psychology, 28*, 1–16.

O'Brien Cousins, S. (2003) Grounding theory in self-referent thinking: Conceptualizing motivation for older adult physical activity. *Psychology of Sport and Exercise, 4*, 81–100.

Observer (2004) The 10 lamest sporting excuses. *Observer Magazine*, 3 October. Retrieved from http://observer.guardian.co.uk/osm/story/0,,1315413,00.html on 30 December 2008.

O'Connor, P. J., Raglin, J. S., and Martinsen, E. W. (2000) Physical activity, anxiety and anxiety disorders. *International Journal of Sport Psychology, 31*, 136–155.

Ogden, J. (2000) *Health psychology*. Buckingham: Open University Press.

Ogden, J., Veale, D., and Summers, Z. (1997) The development and validation of the Exercise Dependence Questionnaire. *Addiction Research, 5*, 343–356.

Ogles, B. M., and Masters, K. S. (2003) A typology of marathon runners based on cluster analysis of motivations. *Journal of Sport Behaviour, 26*, 69–85.

O'Leary-Kelly, A. M., Martocchio, J. J., and Frink, D. D. (1994) A review of the influence of group goals on group performance. *Academy of Management Journal, 37*, 1285–1301.

Oliver, J. (2010) Ethical practice in sport psychology: Challenges in the real world. In S. J. Hanrahan and M. B. Andersen (eds) *Routledge handbook of applied sport psychology* (pp. 60–68). Abingdon, Oxfordshire: Routledge.

Olusoga, P., Butt, J., Maynard, I., and Hays, K. (2010) Stress and coping: A study of world-class coaches. *Journal of Applied Sport Psychology, 22,* 274–293.

Onions, C. T. (ed.) (1996) *The Oxford dictionary of English etymology.* Oxford: Clarendon.

Orbach, I., Singer, R., and Price, S. (1999) An attribution training programme and achievement in sport. *Sport Psychologist, 13,* 69–82.

Orchard, J., and Seward, H. (2002) Epidemiology of injuries in the Australian Football League, seasons 1997–2000. *British Journal of Sports Medicine, 36,* 39–45.

O'Riordan, I. (2010) "I just enjoy a battle: It's not that complicated". *The Irish Times* (Sport), 2 August, p. 7.

Orliaguet, J. P., and Coello, Y. (1998) Differences between actual and imagined putting movements in golf: A chronometric analysis. *International Journal of Sport Psychology, 29,* 157–169.

Orlick, T. (1986) *Psyching for sport: Mental training for athletes.* Champaign, IL: Human Kinetics.

Orlick, T. (1990) *In pursuit of excellence.* Champaign, IL: Leisure Press.

O'Sullivan, J. (2002a) Captain steers a steady ship. *The Irish Times,* 26 September, p. 19.

O'Sullivan, J. (2002b) Clark shows his strength as he leads from the front. *The Irish Times* (Sport), 30 September, p. 4.

O'Sullivan, J. (2010) "The Power" still has that driving force. *The Irish Times* (Sport), 15 September, p. 6.

Otten, M. (2009) Choking vs clutch performance: A study of sport performance under pressure. *Journal of Sport and Exercise Psychology, 31,* 583–601.

Oudejans, R. R. D., and Pijpers, J. R. (2010) Training with mild anxiety may prevent choking under higher levels of anxiety. *Psychology of Sport and Exercise, 11,* 44–50.

Owen, O. (2010) "I'd rather quit than be Ferrari's No. 2 driver" – Massa. *Guardian* (Sport), 30 July, p. 8.

Oxendine, J. B. (1984) *Psychology of motor learning.* Englewood Cliffs, NJ: Prentice-Hall.

Pain, M., and Harwood, C. (2009) Team building through mutual sharing and open discussion of team functioning. *Sport Psychologist, 23,* 523–542.

Paivio, A. (1985) Cognitive and motivational functions of imagery in human performance. *Canadian Journal of Applied Sport Science, 10,* 22–28.

Palmeri, T. J. (2002) Automaticity. In L. Nadel (ed.) *Encyclopaedia of cognitive science* (Vol. 1, pp. 290–301). London: Nature Publishing Group.

Papaxanthis, C., Pozzo, T., Kasprinski, R., and Berthoz, A. (2003) Comparison of actual and imagined execution of whole-body movements after a long exposure to microgravity. *Neuroscience Letters, 339,* 41–44.

Pashler, H. (ed.) (1998) *Attention.* Hove, East Sussex: Psychology Press.

Passer, M. P., Smith, R., Holt, N., Bremner, A., Sutherland, E., and Vliek, M. L. W. (2009) *Psychology: The science of mind and behaviour* (European edn). London: McGraw-Hill.

Pedersen, D. M. (1997) Perceptions of high risk sports. *Perceptual and Motor Skills, 85,* 756–758.

Pedersen, P. (1986) The grief response and injury: A special challenge for athletes and athletic trainers. *Athletic Training, 21,* 1–10.

Pelé (2006) Pelé, my story. *Guardian* (Sport), 13 May, p. 8.

Perry, H. M. (1939) The relative efficiency of actual and imaginary practice in five selected tasks. *Archives of Psychology, 34,* 5–75.

REFERENCES

Perry, J. (2007) *Rogues, rotters, rascals and cheats: The greatest sporting scandals*. London: John Blake.

Peterson, C., Semmel, A., Von Baeyer, C., Abramson, Y. L., Metalsky, G. I., and Seligman, M. E. P. (1982) The Attributional Style Questionnaire. *Cognitive Therapy and Research, 6*, 287–299.

Peterson, C., Buchanan, G. M., and Seligman, M. E. P. (1995) Explanatory style: History and evolution of the field. In G. M. Buchanan and M. E. P. Seligman (eds) *Explanatory style* (pp. 1–20). Hillsdale, NJ: Lawrence Erlbaum Associates.

Peterson, T. R., and Aldana, S. G. (1999) Improving exercise behaviour: An application of the stages of change model in a worksite setting. *American Journal of Health Promotion, 13*, 229–232.

Petitpas, A. J. (2002) Counselling interventions in applied sport psychology. In J. L. Van Raalte and B. W. Brewer (eds) *Exploring sport and exercise psychology* (2nd edn, pp. 253–268). Washington, DC: American Psychological Association.

Petrie, T. A., and Falkstein, D. L. (1998) Methodological, measurement, and statistical issues in research on sport injury prediction. *Journal of Applied Sport Psychology, 10*, 26–45.

Phelps, M. (2008a) Why pain and disorder led to an iron will to win. *Guardian* (Sport), 13 December, p. 10.

Phelps, M. (2008b) Perfect physique to rule the pool. *Guardian* (Sport), 13 December, p. 10.

Piet, S. (1987) What motivates stuntmen? *Motivation and Emotion, 11*, 195–213.

Pijpers, J. R., Oudejans, R. R. D., Holsheimer, F., and Bakker, F. C. (2003) Anxiety-performance relationships in climbing: A process-oriented approach. *Psychology of Sport and Exercise, 4*, 283–304.

Pitt, N. (1998a) Golden days beckon for Henman. *Sunday Times* (Sport), 29 September, p. 13.

Pitt, N. (1998b) Out of the Woods. *Sunday Times* (Sport), 19 July, p. 5.

Pleis, J. R., and Lucas, J. W. (2009) Summary statistics for US adults: National Health Interview Survey, 2007. *National Centre for Health Statistics, Vital and Health Sciences, 10* (240).

Podlog, L., and Eklund, R. C. (2009) High-level athletes' perceptions of success in returning to sport following injury. *Psychology of Sport and Exercise, 10*, 535–544.

Pope, H. G., Jr, Gruber, A. J., Choi, P., Olivardia, R., and Phillips, K. A. (1997) Muscle dysmorphia: An underrecognized form of body dysmorphic disorder. *Psychosomatics, 38*, 548–557.

Posner, M. I. (1980) Orienting of attention: The VIIth Sir Frederic Bartlett lecture. *Quarterly Journal of Experimental Psychology, 32A*, 3–25.

Posner, M. I., and Rothbart, M. K. (2007) Research on attention networks as a model for the integration of psychological science. *Annual Review of Psychology, 58*, 1–23.

Prapavessis, H., Carron, A. V., and Spink, K. S. (1996) Team building in sport. *International Journal of Sport Psychology, 27*, 269–285.

President's Council on Physical Fitness and Sports (2003) *Fitness fundamentals: Guidelines for personal exercise programs*, 9 August. Retrieved from www.fitness.gov/fitness.htm on 6 September 2011.

Pretty, J., Peacock, R., Hine, R., Sellens, M., South, N., and Griffen, M. (2007) Green exercise in the UK countryside effects on health and psychological well-being and implications for policy and planning. *Journal of Environmental Planning and Management, 50*, 211–231.

Prochaska, J. O., and DiClemente, C. C. (1983) Stages and processes of self-change in smoking. Towards an integrative model of change. *Journal of Consulting and Clinical Psychology, 51*, 390–395.

Prochaska, J. O., and DiClemente, C. C. (1984) Toward a comprehensive model of change. In W. E. Miller and N. Heather (eds) *Treating addictive behaviours* (pp. 3–27). London: Plenum.

Pylyshyn, Z. (1973) What the mind's eye tells the mind's brain. *Psychological Bulletin, 80,* 1–24.

Pylyshyn, Z. (1981) The imagery debate: Analogue media versus tacit knowledge. *Psychological Review, 88,* 16–45.

Quested, E., and Duda, J. L. (2010) Exploring the social-environmental determinants of well- and ill-being in dancers: A test of basic needs theory. *Journal of Sport and Exercise Psychology, 32,* 39–60.

Quinn, A. M., and Fallon, B. J. (1999) The changes in psychological characteristics and reactions of elite athletes from injury onset until full recovery. *Journal of Applied Sport Psychology, 11,* 210–229.

Radlo, S. J., Steinberg, G. M., Singer, R. N., Barba, D. A., and Melnikov, A. (2002) The influence of an attentional focus strategy on alpha brain wave activity, heart rate, and dart-throwing performance. *International Journal of Sport Psychology, 33,* 205–217.

Rahnama, N., Reilly, T., and Lees, A. (2002) Injury risk associated with playing actions during competitive soccer. *British Journal of Sports Medicine, 36,* 354–359.

Ramsey, R., Cumming, J., and Edwards, M. G. (2008) Exploring a modified conceptualisation of imagery direction and golf putting performance. *International Journal of Sport and Exercise Psychology, 6,* 207–223.

Ravizza, K. H. (2002) A philosophical construct: A framework for performance enhancement. *International Journal of Sport Psychology, 33,* 4–18.

Ray, C. (2003a) Steel wire tales land Straeuli in hot water. *The Irish Times* (Sport), 22 November, p. 8.

Ray, C. (2003b) Straeuli given one week to explain away Camp Barbed-Wire. *Guardian,* 28 November. Retrieved from www.guardian.co.uk/sport/2003/nov/28/rugbyworldcup 2003.rugbyunion on 10 September 2010.

Reed, C. L. (2002) Chronometric comparisons of imagery to action: Visualizing versus physically performing springboard dives. *Memory and Cognition, 30,* 1169–1178.

Rees, T., Ingledew, D. K., and Hardy, L. (2005) Attribution in sport psychology: Seeking congruence between theory, research and practice. *Psychology of Sport and Exercise, 6,* 189–204.

Reid, A. (2002) Subtle captaincy gave Europe edge. *Sunday Times* (Sport), 6 October, p. 22.

Reid, M., and Schneiker, K. (2008) Strength and conditioning in tennis: Current research and practice. *Journal of Science and Medicine in Sport, 11,* 248–256.

Rejeski, W. J., and Thompson, A. (1993) Historical and conceptual roots of exercise psychology. In P. Seragananian (ed.) *Exercise psychology: The influence of physical exercise on psychological processes* (pp. 3–38). New York: Wiley.

Rettew, D., and Reivich, K. (1995) Sports and explanatory style. In G. M. Buchanan and M. E. P. Seligman (eds) *Explanatory style* (pp. 73–185). Hillsdale, NJ: Lawrence Erlbaum Associates.

Richardson, A. (1967a) Mental practice: A review and discussion, Part I. *Research Quarterly, 38,* 95–107.

Richardson, A. (1967b) Mental practice: A review and discussion, Part II. *Research Quarterly, 38,* 263–273.

Richardson, J. T. E. (1999) *Imagery.* Hove, East Sussex: Psychology Press.

Ripoll, H., Kerlirzin, Y., Stein, J. F., and Reine, B. (1993) Decision making and visual strategies of boxers in a simulated problem solving situation. In G. d'Ydewalle and J. Van Rensbergen (eds) *Perception and cognition: Advances in eye movement research* (Studies in visual information processing, Vol. 4, pp. 141–147). Amsterdam: North-Holland/Elsevier.

Roberts, G. C. (2001) Understanding the dynamics of motivation in physical activity: The influence of achievement goals on motivational processes. In G. C. Roberts (ed.)

REFERENCES

Advances in motivation in sport and exercise (pp. 1–50). Champaign, IL: Human Kinetics.

Roberts, G. C., and Kristiansen, E. (2010) Motivation and goal-setting. In S. J. Hanrahan and M. B. Andersen (eds) *Routledge handbook of applied sport psychology* (pp. 490–499). Abingdon, Oxfordshire: Routledge.

Roberts, G. C., Treasure, D. C., and Balague, G. (1998) Achievement goals in sport: The development and validation of the Perceptions of Success Questionnaire. *Journal of Sports Sciences, 16,* 337–347.

Roberts, G. C., Spink, K. S., and Pemberton, C. L. (1999) *Learning experiences in sport psychology* (2nd edn). Champaign, IL: Human Kinetics.

Roberts, G. C., Treasure, D. C., and Conroy, D. (2007) Understanding the dynamics of motivation in sport: An achievement goal orientation. In G. Tenenbaum and R. C. Eklund (eds) *Handbook of sport psychology* (3rd edn, pp. 3–30). New York: Wiley.

Roberts, R., Callow, N., Hardy, L., Markland, D., and Bringer, J. (2008) Movement imagery ability: Development and assessment of a revised version of the Vividness of Movement Imagery Questionnaire. *Journal of Sport and Exercise Psychology, 30,* 200–221.

Robertson, I. (2002) *The mind's eye: An essential guide to boosting your mental power.* London: Bantam.

Robinson, D. W., and Howe, B. L. (1987) Causal attribution and mood state relationships of soccer players in a sport achievement setting. *Journal of Sport Behavior, 10,* 137–146.

Roland, P. E., and Friberg, L. (1985) Localization of cortical areas activated by thinking. *Journal of Neurophysiology, 53,* 1219–1243.

Ronay, B. (2008) Absolute Power. *Guardian,* 25 September. Retrieved from www.guardian.co.uk/sport/2008/sep/25/darts.sportinterviews on 4 September 2011.

Ronay, B. (2010) You only get one chance. *Guardian* (G2), 6 August, pp. 6–9.

Rooney, K. (2007) Rugby. *Irish Independent* (Sport), 13 January, p. 1.

Ross, P. E. (2006) The expert mind. *Scientific American, 295,* 64–71.

Rotella, B. (1985) The psychological care of the injured athlete. In L. K. Bunker, R. J. Rotella, and A. S. Reilly (eds) *Sport psychology: Psychological considerations in maximizing sort performance* (pp. 273–287). Ann Arbor, MI: Mouvement.

Rousseau, J.-J. (1953, originally published in 1781) *The confessions.* Harmondsworth, Middlesex: Penguin.

Rovio, E., Eskola, J., Kozub, S. A., Duda, J. L., and Lintunen, T. (2009) Can high group cohesion be harmful? A case study of a junior ice-hockey team. *Small Group Research, 40,* 421–435.

Rowe, R., Horswill, M. S., Kronvall-Parkinson, M., Poulter, D. R., and McKenna, F. (2009) The effect of disguise on novice and expert tennis players' anticipation ability. *Journal of Applied Sport Psychology, 21,* 178–185.

Rozelle, R. M., and Campbell, D. T. (1969) More plausible rival hypotheses in the cross-lagged panel correlation technique. *Psychological Bulletin, 71,* 74–80.

Ryan, R. M., and Deci, E. L. (2000) Self-determination theory and the facilitation of intrinsic motivation, social development and well-being. *American Psychologist, 55,* 68–78.

Ryan, R. M., and Deci, E. L. (2002) An overview of self-determination theory. In E. L. Deci and R. M. Ryan (eds) *Handbook of self-determination research* (pp. 3–33). Rochester, NY: University of Rochester Press.

Ryan, R. M., and Deci, E. L. (2007) Active human nature: Self-determination theory and the promotion and maintenance of sport, exercise, and health. In M. S. Hagger and N. L. D. Chatzisarantis (eds) *Intrinsic motivation and self-determination in exercise and sport* (pp. 1–19). Champaign, IL: Human Kinetics.

Sachs, M. L. (1981) Running therapy for the depressed client. *Topics in Clinical Nursing, 3*, 770–786.

Sack, A. T., Jacobs, C., De Martino, F., Staeren, N., Goebel, R., and Formisano, E. (2008) Dynamic premotor-to-parietal interactions during spatial imagery. *Journal of Neuroscience, 28*, 8417–8429.

Sackett, R. S. (1934) The influence of symbolic rehearsal upon the retention of a maze habit. *Journal of General Psychology, 10*, 376–395.

Sagar, S., Lavallee, D., and Spray, C. M. (2007) Why young athletes fear failure: Consequences of failure. *Journal of Sports Sciences, 25*, 1171–1184.

Sallis J. F., and Saelens B. E. (2000) Assessment of physical activity by self-report: Status, limitations, and future directions. *Research Quarterly for Exercise and Sport, 71*, S1–S14.

Salmon, P., Hanneman, S., and Harwood, B. (2010) Associative/dissociative cognitive strategies in sustained physical activity: Literature review and proposal for a mindfulness-based conceptual model. *Sport Psychologist, 24*, 127–156.

Samulski, D. M. (2008) Editor's note: Counselling Olympic athletes. *International Journal of Sport and Exercise Psychology, 6*, 251–253.

Sarkar, P. (2002) Olympic champion falls to earth and retires. *Guardian* (Sport), 23 November, p. 16.

Savelsbergh, G. J. P., van der Kamp, J., Williams, A. M., and Ward, P. (2005) Anticipation and visual search behaviour in expert soccer goalkeepers. *Ergonomics, 48*, 1686–1697.

Schippers, M. C., and Van Lange, P. A. (2006) The psychological benefits of superstitious rituals in top sport: A study among top sportspersons. *Journal of Applied Social Psychology, 36*, 2532–2553.

Schmid, A., and Peper, E. (1998) Strategies for training concentration. In J. M. Williams (ed.) *Applied sport psychology: Personal growth to peak performance* (3rd edn, pp. 316–328). Mountain View, CA: Mayfield.

Schmidt, R. A., and Lee, T. D. (1999) *Motor control and learning: A behavioural emphasis* (3rd edn). Champaign, IL: Human Kinetics.

Schmidt, U., McGuire, R., Humphrey, S., Williams, G., and Grawer, B. (2005) Team cohesion. In J. Taylor and G. S. Wilson (eds) *Applying sport psychology: Four perspectives* (pp. 171–184). Champaign, IL: Human Kinetics.

Schoenemann, T. J., and Curry, S. (1990) Attributions for successful and unsuccessful health behaviour change. *Basic and Applied Social Psychology, 11*, 421–431.

Schrader, M. P., and Wann, D. L. (1999) High-risk recreation: The relationship between participant characteristics and degree of involvement. *Journal of Sport Behaviour, 22*, 426–441.

Schuler, J., and Brunner, S. (2009) The rewarding effect of flow experience on performance in a marathon race. *Psychology of Sport and Exercise, 10*, 168–174.

Schuster, C., Hilfiker, R., Amft, O., Scheidhauer, A., Andrews, B., Butler, J., Kischka, U., and Etttlin, T. (2011) Best practice for motor imagery: A systematic literature review on motor imagery training elements in five different disciplines. *BMC Medicine, 9:75*, open access journal. Retrieved from www.biomedcentral.com/1741–7015/9/75 on 28 September 2011.

Schutz, R. W., Eom, H. J., Smoll, F. L., and Smith, R. E. (1994) Examination of the factorial validity of the Group Environment Questionnaire. *Research Quarterly for Exercise and Sport, 65*, 226–236.

Schwartz, D. (2008) Keeping athletes on track: Brains and brawn. *APA Monitor on Psychology, 39* (7), 54.

REFERENCES

Scully, D., and Hume, A. (1995) Sport psychology: Status, knowledge and use among elite level coaches and performers in Ireland. *Irish Journal of Psychology, 16*, 52–66.

Seligman, M. E. P. (1998) *Learned optimism: How to change your mind and your life* (2nd edn). New York: Pocket Books.

Seligman, M. E. P., Nolen-Hoeksema, S., Thornton, N., and Thornton, K. M. (1990) Explanatory style as a mechanism of disappointing athletic performance. *Psychological Science, 1*, 143–146.

Selvey, M. (1998) Getting up for the Ashes. *Guardian* (Sport), 20 November, p. 2.

Senko, C., Hulleman, C. S., and Harackiewicz, J. M. (2011) Achievement goal theory at the crossroads: Old controversies, current challenges and new directions. *Educational Psychology, 46*, 26–47.

Seppa, N. (1996) Psychologists making it to the big leagues. *American Psychological Association Monitor on Psychology, 27*, July, p. 28.

Shannon, K. (2008) How a champion uses mind control. *Mad About Sport* (*Sunday Tribune Sports Monthly*), March, p. 46.

Shapcott, K. M., and Carron, A. V. (2010) Development and validation of a Team Attributional Style Questionnaire. *Group Dynamics: Theory, Research, and Practice, 14*, 95–113.

Shaw, D. (2002) Confidence and the pre-shot routine in golf: A case-study. In I. Cockerill (ed.) *Solutions in sport psychology* (pp. 108–119). London: Thomson.

Shaw, W. A. (1938) The distribution of muscular action potentials during imaging. *Psychological Record, 2*, 195–216.

Sheard, M. (2010) *Mental toughness: The mindset behind sporting achievement.* London: Routledge.

Shephard, R. J. (2003) Limits to the measurement of habitual physical activity by questionnaires. *British Journal of Sports Medicine, 37*, 197–206.

Shields, D. L., and Bredemeier, B. L. (2001) Moral development and behaviour in sport. In R. N. Singer, H. A. Hausenblas, and C. M. Janelle (eds) *Handbook of sport psychology* (2nd edn, pp. 585–603). New York: Wiley.

Shields, D. L., and Bredemeier, B. L. (2007) Advances in sport morality research. In G. Tenenbaum and R. C. Eklund (eds) *Handbook of sport psychology* (3rd edn, pp. 662–684). New York: Wiley.

Shields, D. L., LaVoi, N. M., Bredemier, B. L., and Power, F. C. (2007) Predictors of poor sportspersonship in youth sports: Personal attitudes and social influences. *Journal of Sport and Exercise Psychology, 29*, 747–762.

Shontz, L. (1999) Area cyclists line up to share a ride with Spain's Indurain. Retrieved from www.post-gazette.com/sports_headlines/19990602cycle6.asp on 29 April 2003.

Short, S. E., Bruggerman, S. G., Engel, S. G., Marback, T. L., Wang, L. J., Willadsen, A., and Short, M. W. (2002) The effect of imagery function and imagery direction on self-efficacy and performance on a golf-putting task. *Sport Psychologist, 16*, 48–67.

Siebold, G. L. (2006) Military group cohesion. In T. W. Britt, C. A. Castro and A. B. Adler (eds) *Military life: The psychology of serving in peace and combat* (Vol. 1, pp. 185–201). Westport, CT: Praeger Security International.

Sime, W. (2002) Guidelines for clinical application of exercise therapy for mental health case studies. In J. Van Raalte and B. W. Brewer (eds) *Exploring sport and exercise psychology* (2nd edn, pp. 225–251). Washington, DC: American Psychological Association.

Simon, H. A., and Gilmartin, K. (1973) A simulation of memory for chess positions. *Cognitive Psychology, 5*, 29–46.

Simons, J. (1999) Concentration. In M. A. Thompson, R. A. Vernacchia, and W. E. More (eds) *Case studies in applied sport psychology: An educational approach* (pp. 89–114). Dubuque, IA: Kendall/Hunt.

Singer, R. N. (2002) Preperformance state, routines, and automaticity: What does it take to realize expertise in self-paced tasks? *Journal of Sport and Exercise Psychology, 24,* 359–375.

Singer, R. N., and Burke, K. L. (2002) Sport and exercise psychology: A positive force in the new millennium. In J. Van Raalte and B. W. Brewer (eds) *Exploring sport and exercise psychology* (2nd edn, pp. 525–529). Washington, DC: American Psychological Association.

Singer, R. N., Cauragh, J. H., Chen, D., Steinberg, G. M., and Frehlich, S. G. (1996) Visual search, anticipation, and reactive comparisons between highly-skilled and beginning tennis players. *Journal of Applied Sport Psychology, 8,* 9–26.

Sinnamon, S., Moran, A., and O'Connell, M. (2012) Flow among musicians: Measuring peak experiences of student performers. *Journal of Research in Music Education.*

Sinnett, S., and Kingstone, A. (2010) A preliminary investigation regarding the effect of tennis grunting: Does white noise during a tennis shot have a negative impact on shot perception? *PloS ONE, 5,* e13148 (doi 10.1371/journal.pone.0013148)

Sinnott, K., and Biddle, S. (1998) Changes in attributions, perceptions of success and intrinsic motivation after attributions in children's sport. *International Journal of Adolescence and Youth, 7,* 137–144.

Slade, J. M., Landers, D. M., and Martin, P. E. (2002) Muscular activity during real and imagined movements: A test of inflow explanations. *Journal of Sport and Exercise Psychology, 24,* 151–167.

Slaney, R. B., Rice, K. G., and Ashby, J. S. (2002) A programmatic approach in measuring perfectionism: The Almost Perfect Scales. In G. L. Flett and P. L. Hewitt (eds) *Perfectionism: Theory, research and treatment* (pp. 63–88). Washington, DC: American Psychological Association.

Slattery, P. (2010) *An empirical investigation of expertise and anticipation skills in martial arts and combat sports.* Unpublished doctoral dissertation, School of Psychology, University College, Dublin.

Smeeton, N., Williams, A. M., Hodges, N. J., and Ward, P. (2005) The relative effectiveness of various instructional approaches in developing anticipation skill in a "real-world" task. *Journal of Experimental Psychology: Applied, 11,* 98–110.

Smith, A. M., Hartman, A. D., and Detling, N. J. (2001) Assessment of the injured athlete. In J. Crossman (ed.) *Coping with sports injuries: Psychological strategies for rehabilitation* (pp. 20–50). Oxford: Oxford University Press.

Smith, A. M., Adler, C. H., Crews, D., Wharen, R. E., Laskowski, E. E., Barnes, K., Bell, C. V., Pelz, D., et al. (2003) The "yips" in golf: A continuum between a focal dystonia and choking. *Sports Medicine, 33,* 13–31.

Smith, B. (2010) Narrative inquiry: Ongoing conversations and questions for sport and exercise psychology research. *International Review of Sport and Exercise Psychology, 3,* 87–107.

Smith, B., and Sparkes, A. C. (2009) Narrative inquiry in sport and exercise psychology: What can it mean and why might we do it? *Psychology of Sport and Exercise, 1,* 1–11.

Smith, D., and Wright, C. (2008) Imagery and sport performance. In A. Lane (ed.) *Sport and exercise psychology: Topics in Applied Psychology* (pp. 139–149). London: Hodder Education.

Smith, D., Wright, C. J., Allsopp, A., and Westhead, H. (2007) It's all in the mind: PETTLEP-based imagery and sports performance. *Journal of Applied Sport Psychology, 19,* 80–92.

Smith, E. E., and Kosslyn, S. M. (2007) *Cognitive psychology: Mind and brain*. Upper Saddle River, NJ: Pearson.

Smith, E. E., Adams, N. E., and Schorr, D. (1978) Fact retrieval and the paradox of intelligence. *Cognitive Psychology, 10*, 438–464.

Smith, M. (2002) Practice makes perfect. *Daily Telegraph* (Sport), 15 February, p. S3.

Smith, M. (2003) Keepers focus on the spot. *Daily Telegraph* (Sport), 13 March, p. S3.

Smith, R. E. (2006) Understanding sport behaviour. *Journal of Applied Sport Psychology, 18*, 1–27.

Smith, R. E., and Smoll, F. L. (2002a) *Way to go, coach! A scientifically-proven approach to coaching effectiveness* (2nd edn). Portola Valley, CA: Warde.

Smith, R. E., and Smoll, F. L. (2002b) Youth sport interventions. In J. Van Raalte and B. Brewer (eds) *Exploring sport and exercise psychology* (2nd edn, pp. 341–371). Washington, DC: American Psychological Association.

Smith, R. E., Smoll, F. L., and Schutz, R. W. (1990) Measurement and correlates of sport-specific cognitive and somatic trait anxiety: The Sport Anxiety Scale. *Anxiety Research, 2*, 263–280.

Smith, R. E., Smoll, F. L., and Wiechman, S. A. (1998) Measurement of trait anxiety in sport. In J. L. Duda (ed.) *Advances in sport and exercise psychology measurement* (pp. 105–127). Morgantown, WV: Fitness Information Technology.

Smith, R. E., Smoll, F. L., Cumming, S. P., and Grossbard, J. R. (2006) Measurement of multidimensional sport performance anxiety in children and adults: The Sport Anxiety Scale-2. *Journal of Sport and Exercise Psychology, 28*, 479–501.

Smoll, F. L., and Smith, R. E. (2005) *Sports and your child: Developing champions in sport and life* (2nd edn). Palo Alto, CA: Warde.

Smoll, F. L., and Smith, R. E. (2010) Conducting psychologically oriented coach-training programs: A social-cognitive approach. In J. M. Williams (ed.) *Applied sport psychology: Personal growth to peak performance* (6th edn, pp. 392–416). Boston, MA: McGraw-Hill.

Smyth, C. (2009) How darts players can help children to aim higher in job market. *The Times*, 8 January, p. 15.

Solnit, R. (2001) *Wanderlust: A history of walking*. London: Verso.

Solodkin, A., Hlustik, P., Chen, E. E., and Small, S. I. (2004) Fine modulation in network activation during motor execution and motor imagery. *Cerebral Cortex, 14*, 1246–1255.

Souter, M. (2009) O'Gara gives heart to Ireland as they reach their pivotal moment. *The Times*, 23 March, p. 67.

Southgate, G. (2010) We are breeding players that are looking for excuses. *The Sunday Times* (Sport), 4 July p. 7.

Spence, J. C., and Lee, R. E. (2003) Toward a comprehensive model of physical activity. *Psychology of Sport and Exercise, 4*, 7–24.

Spielberger, C. S. (1966) Theory and research on anxiety. In C. S. Spielberger (ed.) *Anxiety and behavior* (pp. 3–20). New York: Academic Press.

Spink, K. S. (1990) Collective efficacy in the sport setting. *International Journal of Sport Psychology, 21*, 380–395.

Spink, K. S., Wilson., K. S., and Odnokon, P. (2010) Examining the relationship between cohesion and return to team in elite athletes. *Psychology of Sport and Exercise, 11*, 6–11.

Stadler, M. (2008) *The psychology of baseball: Inside the mind of the Major League player*. New York: Penguin.

Stapleton, A. B., Hankes, D. M., Hays, K. F., and Parham, W. D. (2010) Ethical dilemmas in sport psychology: A dialogue on the unique aspects impacting practice. *Professional Psychology: Research and Practice, 41*, 143–152.

Starkes, J. (2001) The road to expertise: Can we shorten the journey and lengthen the stay? In A. Papaionnaou, M. Goudas and Y. Theodorakis (eds) *Proceedings of International Society of Sport Psychology's 10th World Congress of Sport Psychology* (Vol. 3, pp. 198–205). Thessaloniki, Greece: Christodoulidi.

Starkes, J. L., and Ericsson, K. A. (eds) (2003) *Expert performance in sports: Advances in research on sport expertise.* Champaign, IL: Human Kinetics.

Starkes, J. L., Deakin, J. M., Allard, F. M., Hodges, N. J., and Hayes, A. (1996) Deliberate practice in sports: What is it anyway? In K. A. Ericsson (ed.) *The road to excellence: The acquisition of expert performance in the arts and sciences, sports and games* (pp. 81–106). Mahwah, NJ: Lawrence Erlbaum Associates.

Starkes, J. L., Helsen, W., and Jack, R. (2001) Expert performance in sport and dance. In R. N. Singer, H. A. Hausenblas, and C. M. Janelle (eds) *Handbook of sport psychology* (2nd edn, pp. 174–201). New York: Wiley.

Starmer-Smith, C. (2002) Stories behind the headlines. *Daily Telegraph* (Sport), 8 March, p. S5.

Statler, T. (2010) Developing a shared identity/vision: Benefits and pitfalls. In S. J. Hanrahan and M. B. Andersen (eds) *Routledge handbook of applied sport psychology* (pp. 325–334). Abingdon, Oxfordshire: Routledge.

Stavrou, N. A., Jackson, S. A., Zervas, Y., and Karteroliatis, K. (2007) Flow experiences and athletes' performance with reference to the orthogonal model of flow. *Sport Psychologist, 21,* 438–457.

Stoeber, J., and Stoeber, F. S. (2009) Domains of perfectionism: Prevalence and relationships with perfectionism gender, age, and satisfaction with life. *Personality and Individual Differences, 46,* 530–535.

Strachan, G. (2004) Winning the war before a ball has been kicked. *Guardian,* 22 October, p. 37.

Strahler, K., Ehrlenspiel, F., Heene, M., and Brand, R. (2010) Competitive anxiety and cortisol awakening response in the week leading up to a competition. *Psychology of Sport and Exercise, 11,* 148–154.

Straume-Naesheim, T. M., Andersen, T. E., Dvorak, J., and Bahr, R. (2005) Effects of heading exposure and previous concussions on neuropsychological performance among Norwegian elite footballers. *British Journal of Sports Medicine, 39,* Suppl. 1, 70–77.

Strauss, B. (2002) Social facilitation in motor tasks: A review of research and theory. *Psychology of Sport and Exercise, 3,* 237–256.

Suinn, R. M. (1994) Visualization in sports. In A. A. Sheikh and E. R. Korn (eds) *Imagery in sports and physical performance* (pp. 23–42). Amityville, NY: Baywood.

Summers, J. J. (1999) Skill acquisition: Current perspectives and future directions. In R. Lidor and M. Bar-Eli (eds) *Sport psychology: Linking theory and practice* (pp. 83–107). Morgantown, WV: Fitness Information Technology.

Summers, J. J., and Ford, S. K. (1990) The Test of Attentional and Interpersonal Style: An evaluation. *International Journal of Sport Psychology, 21,* 102–111.

Summers, J., and Moran, A. (2011) Attention. In T. Morris and P. Terry (eds) *The new sport and exercise psychology companion* (pp. 105–133). Morgantown, WV: Fitness Information Technology.

Sutcliffe, P. (1997) Out of tune with the rest of us. *Sunday Times,* (Supplement: Stress Manager, Part 4: Raising Your Game), 8 June, p. 6.

Swain, A. B. J., and Jones, G. (1995) Effects of goal setting interventions on selected basketball skills: A single-subject design. *Research Quarterly for Exercise and Sport, 66,* 51–63.

Swain, A. B. J., and Jones, G. (1996) Explaining performance variance: The relative contributions of intensity and direction dimensions of competitive state anxiety. *Anxiety, Stress and Coping, 9,* 1–18.

REFERENCES

Swift, E. J. (1910) Relearning a skilful act: An experimental study of neuromuscular memory. *Psychological Bulletin, 7*, 17–19.

Syed, M. (2010) *Bounce: How champions are made*. London: Fourth Estate (a division of HarperCollins).

Syer, J. (1986) *Team spirit*. London: Sportspages.

Szabo, A. (2000) Physical activity as a source of psychological dysfunction. In S. J. H. Biddle, K. R. Fox and S. H. Boutcher (eds) *Physical activity and psychological well-being* (pp. 130–153). London: Routledge.

Szczepanik, N. (2005) Focused Cech puts records low on his list of priorities. *The Times*, 30 April, p. 100.

Taranis, L., and Meyer, C. (2011) Associations between specific components of compulsive exercise and eating-disordered cognitions and behaviours among young women. *International Journal of Eating Disorders, 44*, 452–458.

Taylor, D. (2003) Warnock's walks on the wild side keep Blades on edge. *Guardian* (Sport), 12 April, p. 2.

Taylor, F. W. (1967) *The principles of scientific management*. New York: Norton (originally published in 1911).

Taylor, G. (2002) There is still a reluctance to recognise the part that psychology can play. *Daily Telegraph* (Sport), 1 June, p. S3.

Teigen, K. H. (1994) Yerkes-Dodson: A law for all seasons. *Theory and Psychology, 4*, 525–547.

Tenenbaum, G., and Eklund, R. C. (eds) (2007) *Handbook of sport psychology* (3rd edn). New York: Wiley.

Tenenbaum, G., Sar-El, T., and Bar-Eli, M. (2000) Anticipation of ball location in low- and high-skill performers: A developmental perspective. *Psychology of Sport and Exercise, 1*, 117–128.

Tenenbaum, G., Jones, C. M., Kitsantas, A., Sacks, D. N., and Berwick, J. P. (2003) Failure adaptation: An investigation of the stress response process in sport. *International Journal of Sport Psychology, 34*, 27–62.

Thacker, S. B., Gilchrist, J., Stroup, D. F., and Kimsey, C. D., Jr (2004) The impact of stretching on sports injury risk: A systematic review of the literature. *Medicine and Science in Sports and Exercise, 36*, 371–378.

Thatcher, J. (2005) Stress, challenge, and impression management among sports officials. *Sport and Exercise Psychology Review, 1*, 26–35.

Thatcher, J., Jones, M. V., and Lavallee, D. (eds) (2011) *Coping and emotion in sport* (2nd edn). Abingdon, Oxfordshire: Routledge.

Thelwell, R. (2008) Applied sport psychology: Enhancing performance using psychological skills training. In A. Lane (ed.) *Sport and exercise psychology* (pp. 1–15). London: Hodder Education.

Thelwell, R. (2009) Team goal setting in professional football. In B. Hemmings and T. Holder (eds) *Applied sport psychology: A case-based approach* (pp. 161–180). Oxford: Wiley-Blackwell.

Thelwell, R., Weston, N., and Greenlees, I. (2005) Defining and understanding mental toughness within soccer. *Journal of Applied Sport Psychology, 17*, 326–332.

Thomas, O., Maynard, I., and Hanton, S. (2007) Intervening with athletes in the time leading up to competition: Theory to practice II. *Journal of Applied Sport Psychology, 19*, 398–418.

Thomas, O., Mellalieu, S. D., and Hanton, S. (2009) Stress management in applied sport psychology. In S. D. Mellalieu and S. Hanton (eds) *Advances in applied sport psychology: A review* (pp. 124–161). Abingdon, Oxfordshire: Routledge.

Thomson, R. H. S, Garry, M. I., and Summers, J. J. (2008) Attentional influences on short-interval intracortica inhibition. *Clinical Neurophysiology, 119,* 52–62.

Thornley, G. (1993) Graf profits as Novotna loses her nerve. *The Irish Times,* 5 July, p. 6.

Thornley, G. (1997) Irish call in two psychologists. *The Irish Times,* 16 October, p. 20.

Thorp, M. (1998) Ferdinand has the faith not to falter at the final hurdle. *Guardian* (Sport), 22 May, p. 5.

Thorp, M. (1999) Sheringham praises Ferguson's pep talk. *Guardian,* 28 May, p. 34.

Times, The (2002) The Premiership today: Bergkamp faces FA probe, Royle lines up raid on Maine Road and Taylor calls in the shrinks. *The Times,* 30 October, p. 43.

Times, The (2008) Jonny Wilkinson: Injury factfile. *The Times.* Retrieved from www.time sonline.co.uk/tol/sport/rugby_union/article4859503.ece on 21 August 2010.

Title, The (1998) Daly is still fighting off the shakes. *The Title,* 29 November, p. 8.

Tod, D., and Lavallee, D. (2010) Towards a conceptual understanding of muscle dysmorphia development and sustainment. *International Review of Sport and Exercise Psychology, 3,* 111–131.

Tolman, E. E. (1932) *Purposive behavior in animals and men.* New York: Appleton-Century-Crofts.

Toner, J., and Moran, A. (2011) The effects of conscious processing on golf putting proficiency and kinematics. *Journal of Sports Sciences, 29,* 673–683.

Torstveit, M. K., Rosenvinge, J. H., and Sundgot-Borgen, J. (2008) Prevalence of eating disorders and the predictive power of risk models in elite athletes: A controlled study. *Scandinavian Journal of Medicine and Science in Sports, 18,* 108–118.

Triplett, N. (1898) The dynamogenic factors in pacemaking and competition. *American Journal of Psychology, 9,* 507–533.

Tripp, D. A., Stanish, W., Ebel-Lam, A., Brewer, B. W., and Birchard, J. (2007) Fear of reinjury, negative affect, and catastrophizing predicting return to sport in recreational athletes with anteriorcruciate ligament injuries at 1 year postsurgery. *Rehabilitation Psychology, 52,* 74–81.

Troiano, R. P., Berrigan, D., Dodd, K. W., Masse, L. C., Tilert, T., and McDowell, M. (2008) Physical activity in the United States measured by accelerometer. *Medicine and Science in Sports and Exercise, 40,* 181–188.

Trost, S. G., Pate, R. R., Sallis, J. F., Freedson, P. S., Taylor, W. C., Dowda, M., and Sirad, J. (2002) Age and gender differences in objectively measured physical activity in youth. *Medicine and Science in Sports and Exercise, 34,* 350–355.

Tuckman, B. W. (1965) Developmental sequence in small groups. *Psychological Bulletin, 63,* 384–399.

Turman, P. D. (2003) Coaches and cohesion: The impact of coaching techniques on team cohesion in the small group sport setting. *Journal of Sport Behaviour, 26,* 86–104.

Turner, E. E., Rejeski, W. J., and Brawley, L. R. (1997) Psychological benefits of physical activity are influenced by the social environment. *Journal of Sport and Exercise Psychology, 19,* 119–130.

Udry, E. (1997) Coping and social support among injured athletes following surgery. *Journal of Sport and Exercise Psychology, 19,* 71–90.

Udry, E. (1999) The paradox of injuries: Unexpected positive consequences. In D. Pargman (ed.) *Psychological bases of sport injuries* (2nd edn, pp. 79–88). Morgantown, WV: Fitness Information Technology.

Udry, E., and Andersen, M. B. (2008) Athletic injury and sport behaviour. In T. S. Horn (ed.) *Advances in sport psychology* (3rd edn, pp. 401–422). Champaign, IL: Human Kinetics.

Uhlig, R. (2001) Thinking about exercise "can beef up biceps". *Daily Telegraph,* 22 November, p. 3.

Uitenbroek, D. G. (1996) Sports, exercise, and other causes of injuries: Results of a population survey. *Research Quarterly for Exercise and Sport, 67*, 380–385.

Ungerleider, R. S., and Golding, J. M. (1991) Mental practice among Olympic athletes. *Perceptual and Motor Skills, 72*, 1007–1017.

Uphill, M. (2008) Anxiety in sport: Should we be worried or excited? In A. Lane (ed.) *Sport and exercise psychology: Topics in Applied Psychology* (pp. 35–51). London: Hodder Education.

Uphill, M., and Jones, M. V. (2004) Coping with emotions in sport: A cognitive motivational relational theory perspective. In D. Lavallee, J. Thatcher, and M. V. Jones (eds) *Coping and emotion in sport* (pp. 75–89). New York: Nova Science.

US Department of Health and Human Services (1996) *Physical activity and health: A report of the Surgeon General.* Atlanta, GA: US Department of Health and Human Services, Centers for Disease Control and Prevention, National Center for Chronic Disease Prevention and Health Promotion.

US Department of Health and Human Services (2010) *The Surgeon General's vision for a healthy and fit nation.* Rockville, MD: US Department of Health and Human Services, Office of the Surgeon General.

Uziell, L. (2007) Individual differences in the social facilitation effect: A review and meta-analysis. *Journal of Research in Personality, 41*, 579–601.

Vallerand, R. J. (2007) Intrinsic and extrinsic motivation in sport and physical activity: A review and a look at the future. In G. Tenenbaum and R. C. Eklund (eds) *Handbook of sport psychology* (3rd edn, pp. 59–83). New York: Wiley

Vallerand, R. J., and Fortier, M. S. (1998) Measures of intrinsic and extrinsic motivation in sport and physical activity: A review and critique. In J. L. Duda (ed.) *Advances in sport and exercise psychology measurement* (pp. 81–101). Morgantown, WV: Fitness Information Technology.

Vallerand, R. J., and Rousseau, F. L. (2001) Intrinsic and extrinsic motivation in sport and exercise. In R. N. Singer, H. A. Hausenblas, and C. M. Janelle (eds) *Handbook of sport psychology* (2nd edn, pp. 389–416). New York: Wiley.

Vallerand, R. J., Brière, N. M., Blanchard, C., and Provencher, P. (1997) Development and validation of the Multidimensional Sportspersonship Orientations Scale. *Journal of Sport and Exercise Psychology, 19*, 197–206.

Vandenberg, S., and Kuse, A. R. (1978) Mental rotations: A group test of three-dimensional spatial visualization. *Perceptual and Motor Skills, 47*, 599–604.

Van Meer, J. P., and Theunissen, N. C. M. (2009) Prospective educational applications of mental simulation: A review. *Educational Psychology Review, 21*, 93–112.

Veach, T. L., and May, J. R. (2005) Teamwork: For the good of the whole. In S. Murphy (ed.) *The sport psych handbook* (pp. 171–189). Champaign, IL: Human Kinetics.

Vealey, R. S. (1994) Current status and prominent issues in sport psychology interventions. *Medicine and Science in Sports and Exercise, 26*, 495–502.

Vealey, R. S. (2009) Confidence in sport. In B. W. Brewer (ed.) *Sport psychology: Handbook of sports medicine* (pp. 43–52). Oxford: Wiley-Blackwell.

Vealey, R. S., and Chase, M. A. (2008) Self-confidence in sport. In T. S. Horn (ed.) *Advances in sport psychology* (3rd edn, pp. 65–97, 430–435). Champaign, IL: Human Kinetics.

Vealey, R. S., and Greenleaf, C. A. (2010) Seeing is believing: Understanding and using imagery in sport. In J. M. Williams (ed.) *Applied sport psychology: Personal growth to peak performance* (6th edn, pp. 267–304). Boston, MA: McGraw-Hill.

Vealey, R. S., and Vernau, D. (2010) Confidence. In S. J. Hanrahan and M. B. Andersen (eds) *Routledge handbook of applied sport psychology* (pp. 518–527). Abingdon, Oxfordshire: Routledge.

Vealey, R. S., and Walter, S. M. (1994) On target with mental skills: An interview with Darrell Pace. *The Sport Psychologist, 8*, 428–441.

Vealey, R. S., Hayashi, S. W., Garner-Holman, M., and Giaccobi, P. (1998) Sources of sport-confidence: Conceptualization and instrument development. *Journal of Sport and Exercise Psychology, 20*, 54–80.

Vickers, J. N. (1992) Gaze control in putting. *Perception, 21*, 117–132.

Vickers, J. N. (1996) Control of visual attention during the basketball free throw. *American Journal of Sports Medicine, 24*, S93–S97.

Vickers, J. N., and Williams, A. M. (2007) Performing under pressure: The effects of physiological arousal, cognitive anxiety and gaze control in biathlon. *Journal of Motor Behaviour, 39*, 381–394.

Vidal, J. (2001) Call of the wild. *Guardian* (G2), 9 June, p. 2.

Villella, C., Martinotti, G., Di Nicola, M., Cassano, M., La Torre, G., Gliubizzi, M. D., Messeri, I., Petruccelli, F., Bria, P., Janiri, L., and Conte, G. (2011) Behavioural addictions in adolescents and young adults: Results from a prevalence study. *Journal of Gambling Studies, 27*, 203–214.

Viner, B. (2011) Beyond choke: What became of the sporting imploder? *Evening Herald*, 12 April, pp. 26–27.

Vyse, S. (1997) *Believing in magic: The psychology of superstition*. New York: Oxford University Press.

Wada, Y., Iwasaki, S., and Kato, T. (2003) Validity of attentional-style subscales for the Japanese version of the Test of Attentional and Interpersonal Style (TAIS). *Japanese Journal of Psychology, 74*, 263–269.

Wallace, S. (2007) Benitez vows to act over Bellamy "golf club attack". *The Independent on Sunday*, 19 February. Retrieved from www.independent.co.uk/sport/football/premier-league/benitez-vows-to-act-over-bellamy-golf-club-attack-436972.html on 5 September 2010.

Walling, M. D., Duda, J. L., and Chi, L. (1993) The Perceived Motivational Climate in Sport Questionnaire: Construct and predictive validity. *Journal of Sport and Exercise Psychology, 15*, 172–183.

Walsh, D. (2009) "You get only one shot at this – you can't play the game again". *Sunday Times* (Sport), 29 March, p. 9.

Walter, D. D., Sutton, J. R., McIntosh, J. M., and Connolly, C. (1985) The aetiology of sports injuries: A review of methodologies. *Sports Medicine, 2*, 47–58.

Wang, C. K. J., Biddle, S. J. H., and Elliott, A. J. (2007) The 2×2 achievement goal framework in a physical education context. *Psychology of Sport and Exercise, 8*, 147–168.

Wang, J., Marchant, D., Morris, T., and Gibbs, P. (2004) Self-consciousness and trait anxiety as predictors of choking in sport. *Journal of Science and Medicine in Sport, 7*, 174–185.

Warburton, D. E. R., Nicol, C. W., and Bredin, S. S. (2006) Health benefits of physical activity: The evidence. *Canadian Medical Association Journal, 174*, 801–809.

Ward, J. (2010) *The student's guide to cognitive neuroscience* (2nd edn). Hove, East Sussex: Psychology Press.

Ward, P., and Williams, A. M. (2003) Perceptual and cognitive skill development in soccer: The multidimensional nature of expert performance. *Journal of Sport and Exercise Psychology, 25*, 93–111.

Ward, P., Williams, A. M., and Hancock, P. A. (2006) Simulation for performance and training. In Ericsson, K. A., Charness, N., Feltovich, P. J., and Hoffman, R. R. (eds) *The Cambridge handbook of expertise and expert performance* (pp. 243–262). New York: Cambridge University Press.

REFERENCES

Warren, J. M., Ekelund, U., Besson, H., Mezzani, A., Geladas, N., and Vanhees, L. (2010) Assessment of physical activity – a review of methodologies with reference to epidemiological research: A report of the exercise physiology section of the European Association of Cardiovascular Prevention and Rehabilitation. *European Journal of Cardiovascular Prevention and Rehabilitation, 17,* 127–139.

Washburn, M. F. (1916) *Movement and mental imagery.* Boston, MA: Houghton Mifflin.

Waters, A. (2007) The use of imagery in sports rehabilitation: A literature review. *Sport and Exercise Psychology Review, 3,* 4–13.

Watson, J. B. (1913) Psychology as the behaviourist views it. *Psychological Review, 20,* 158–177.

Webbe, F., and Salinas, C. M. (2011) When science and politics meet: The case of soccer heading in adults and children. In F. M. Webbe (ed.) *The handbook of sport neuropsychology* (pp. 279–294). New York: Springer.

Webster, R. (1984) *Winning ways.* Sydney: Fontana.

Wegner, D. M. (1994) Ironic processes of mental control. *Psychological Review, 101,* 34–52.

Wegner, D. M. (2002) Thought suppression and mental control. In L. Nadel (ed.) *Encyclopaedia of cognitive science* (vol. 4, pp. 395–397). London: Nature Publishing Group.

Wei, G., and Luo, J. (2010) Sport expert's motor imagery: Functional imaging of professional motor skills and simple motor skills. *Brain Research, 1341,* 52–62.

Weinberg, R. S. (1988) *The mental ADvantage: Developing your mental skills in tennis.* Champaign, IL: Human Kinetics.

Weinberg, R. S. (2002) Goal setting in sport and exercise: Research to practice. In J. Van Raalte and B. Brewer (eds) *Exploring sport and exercise psychology* (2nd edn, pp. 25–48). Washington, DC: American Psychological Association.

Weinberg, R. S. (2008) Does imagery work? Effects on performance and mental skills. *Journal of Imagery Research in Sport and Physical Activity, 3,* article 1, 1–21.

Weinberg, R. S. (2009) Motivation. In B. W. Brewer. (ed.) *Sport psychology: Handbook of sports medicine* (pp. 7–17). Oxford: Wiley-Blackwell.

Weinberg, R. S., and Comar, W. (1994) The effectiveness of psychological interventions in competitive sports. *Sports Medicine Journal, 18,* 406–418.

Weinberg, R. S., and Gould, D. (2007) *Foundations of sport and exercise psychology* (4th edn). Champaign, IL: Human Kinetics.

Weinberg, R. S., and Weigand, D. A. (1996) Let the discussions continue: A reaction to Locke's comments on Weinberg and Weigand. *Journal of Sport and Exercise Psychology, 18,* 89–93.

Weinberg, R. S., Bruya, L. D., and Jackson, A. (1985) The effects of goal proximity and goal specificity on endurance performance. *Journal of Sport Psychology, 7,* 296–305.

Weinberg, R. S., Bruya, L. D., Garland, H., and Jackson, A. (1990) Effect of goal difficulty and positive reinforcement on endurance performance. *Journal of Sport and Exercise Psychology, 12,* 144–156.

Weinberg, R. S., Stitcher, T., and Richardson, P. (1994) Effects of seasonal goal setting on lacrosse performance. *Sport Psychologist, 8,* 166–175.

Weiner, B. (1985) An attributional theory of achievement motivation and emotion. *Psychological Review, 92,* 548–573.

Weiss, M. R., and Amorose, A. J. (2008) Motivational orientations and sport behaviour. In T. S. Horn (ed.) *Advances in sport psychology* (3rd edn, pp. 115–155). Champaign, IL: Human Kinetics.

Weiss, M. R., and Ferrer-Caja, E. (2002) Motivational orientations and sport behaviour. In T. S. Horn (ed.) *Advances in sport psychology* (2nd edn, pp. 101–183). Champaign, IL: Human Kinetics.

Weiss, M. R., Smith, A. L., and Stuntz, C. P. (2008) Moral development in sport and physical activity. In T. S. Horn (ed.) *Advances in sport psychology* (3rd edn, pp. 187–210). Champaign, IL: Human Kinetics.

Werner, S., and Thies, B. (2000) Is "change blindness" attenuated by domain-specific expertise? An expert-novice comparison of change detection in football images. *Visual Cognition, 7,* 163–173.

Westerterp, K. R. (2001) Pattern and intensity of physical activity. *Nature, 410,* 539.

Weston, N. J. V., Thelwell, R. C., Bond, S., and Hutchings, N. V. (2009) Stress and coping in single-handed, round-the-world ocean sailing. *Journal of Applied Sport Psychology, 21,* 468–474.

Weston, P. (2002) How to use exercise to aid diabetes. *The Irish Times,* 21 November, p. 15.

Whelan, J. P., Epkins, C., and Meyers, A. W. (1990) Arousal interventions for athletic performance: Influence of mental preparation and competitive experience. *Anxiety Research, 2,* 293–307.

Whitaker, D. (1999) *The spirit of teams.* Marlborough, Wiltshire: Crowood Press.

White, J. (1999) Ferguson assumes full control in title campaign. *Guardian,* 17 February, p. 26.

White, J. (2001) Interview: Stephen Hendry. *Guardian* (Sport), 15 October, pp. 18–19.

White, J. (2002a) Interview: Garry Sobers. *Guardian* (Sport), 10 June, pp. 20–21.

White, J. (2002b) Interview: Ian Woosnam. *Guardian* (Sport), 15 July, pp. 22–23.

White, J. (2002c) A potter's tale: any colour but the blues. *Guardian* (Sport), 20 April, pp. 10–11.

White, J. (2003) Interview: Peter Ebdon. *Guardian* (Sport), pp. 20–21.

Whitworth, D. (2008) On the waterfront. *The Times* (Magazine), 13 September, pp. 20–25.

Widmeyer, W. N., Brawley, L. R., and Carron, A. V. (1985) *Measurement of cohesion in sport teams: The Group Environment Questionnaire.* London, Ontario: Sports Dynamics.

Widmeyer, W. N., Carron, A. V., and Brawley, L. R. (1993) Group cohesion in sport and exercise. In R. N. Singer, M. Murphey, and L. K. Tennant (eds) *Handbook of research on sport psychology* (pp. 672–694). New York: Macmillan.

Widmeyer, W. N., Brawley, L. R., and Carron, A. V. (2002) Group dynamics in sport. In T. S. Horn (ed.) *Advances in sport psychology* (2nd edn, pp. 285–308). Champaign, IL: Human Kinetics.

Wiese-Bjornstal, D. M., Smith, A. M., Shaffer, S. M., and Morrey, M. A. (1998) An integrated model of response to sport injury: Psychological and sociological dynamics. *Journal of Applied Sport Psychology, 10,* 46–69.

Wilde, S. (1998) Freudian slips get new meaning with mind games catching on. *The Times* (Sport), May 18, p. 33.

Wildman, R. (2003) South Africans probe brutal camp. *Daily Telegraph,* 26 November. Retrieved from www.telegraph.co.uk/sport/rugbyunion/international/southafrica/2425836/South-Africans-probe-brutal-camp.html on 10 September 2010.

Wilkinson, J. (2006) *My world.* London: Headline.

Williams, A. M. (2002a) Visual search behaviour in sport. *Journal of Sports Sciences, 20,* 169–170.

Williams, A. M. (2002b) Perceptual and cognitive expertise in sport. *The Psychologist, 15,* 416–417.

Williams, A. M. (2003) Developing selective attention skill in fast ball sports. In I. Greenlees and A. P. Moran (eds) *Concentration skills training in sport* (pp. 20–32). Leicester: British Psychological Society (Division of Sport and Exercise Psychology).

Williams, A. M., and Burwitz, L. (1993) Advance cue utilization in soccer. In T. Reilly, J. Clarys, and A. Stibbe (eds) *Science and football II* (pp. 239–243). London: E. & F. N. Spon.

Williams, A. M., and Davids, K. (1998) Perceptual expertise in sport: Research, theory and practice. In H. Steinberg, I. Cockerill, and A. Dewey (eds) *What sport psychologists do* (pp. 48–57). Leicester: British Psychological Society.

REFERENCES

Williams, A. M., and Ericsson, K. A. (2008) From the guest editors: How do experts learn? *Journal of Sport and Exercise Psychology, 30*, 653–662.

Williams, A. M., and Ford, P. R. (2008) Expertise and expert performance in sport. *International Review of Sport and Exercise Psychology, 1*, 4–18.

Williams, A. M., and Ward, P. (2007) Anticipation and decision-making: Exploring new horizons. In G. Tenenbaum and R. C. Eklund (eds) *Handbook of sport psychology* (3rd edn, pp. 203–223). New York: Wiley.

Williams, A. M., Davids, K., and Williams, J. G. (1999) *Visual perception and action in sport*. London: E. & F. N. Spon.

Williams, A. M., Janelle, C. M., Davids, K. (2004) Constraints on the search for visual information in sport. *International Journal of Sport and Exercise Psychology, 2*, 301–318.

Williams, A. M., Ericsson, K. A., Ward, P., and Eccles, D. W. (2008a) Research on expertise in sport: Implications for the military. *Military Psychology, 20*, S123–S145.

Williams, A. M., Hardy, L., and Mutrie, N. (2008b) Twenty-five years of psychology in the *Journal of Sports Sciences*: A historical overview. *Journal of Sports Sciences, 26*, 401–412.

Williams, J. M. (2001) Psychology of injury risk and prevention. In R. N. Singer, H. A. Hausenblas, and C. M. Janelle (eds) *Handbook of sport psychology* (2nd edn, pp. 766–786). New York: Macmillan.

Williams, J. M. (2010) Relaxation and energizing techniques for regulation of arousal. In J. Williams (ed.) *Applied sport psychology: Personal growth to peak performance* (6th edn, pp. 247–266). New York: McGraw-Hill.

Williams, J. M., and Andersen, M B. (2007) Psychosocial antecedents of sport injury and interventions for risk reduction. In G. Tenenbaum and R. C. Eklund (eds) *Handbook of sport psychology* (3rd edn, pp. 404–424). New York: Wiley.

Williams, J. M., and Hacker, C. M. (1982) Causal relationships among cohesion, satisfaction, and performance in women's intercollegiate field hockey teams. *Journal of Sport and Exercise Psychology, 4*, 324–337.

Williams, J. M., and Leffingwell, T. R. (2002) Cognitive strategies in sport and exercise psychology. In J. Van Raalte and B. W. Brewer (eds) *Exploring sport and exercise psychology* (2nd edn, pp. 75–98). Washington, DC: American Psychological Association.

Williams, J. M., and Roepke, N. (1993) Psychology of injury and injury rehabilitation. In R. N. Singer, M. Murphey and L. K. Tennant (eds) *Handbook of research on sport psychology* (pp. 815–839). New York: Macmillan.

Williams, J. M., and Scherzer, C. B. (2010) Injury risk and rehabilitation: Psychological considerations. In J. M. Williams (ed.) *Applied sport psychology: Personal growth to peak performance* (6th edn, pp. 512–541). Boston, MA: McGraw-Hill.

Williams, J. M., Rotella, R. J., and Heyman, S. R. (1998) Stress, injury, and the psychological rehabilitation of athletes. In J. M. Williams (ed.) *Applied sport psychology* (3rd edn, pp. 409–428). Mountain View, CA: Mayfield.

Williams, J. M., Nideffer, R. M., Wilson. V. E., Sagal, M. S., and Peper, E. (2010) Concentration and strategies for controlling it. In J. M. Williams (ed.) *Applied sport psychology: Personal growth to peak performance* (6th edn, pp. 336–358). Boston, MA: McGraw-Hill.

Williams, R. (2002a) Captains split on the million dollar question. *Guardian*, 24 September, p. 28.

Williams, R. (2002b) Sublime Serena celebrates the crucial difference. *Guardian* (Sport), 8 July, p. 6.

Williams, R. (2002c) Torrance masters the fine art of creating an unbreakable bond. *Guardian*, 2 October, p. 30.

Williams, R. (2009) Alberto Contador makes decisive move and Lance Armstrong has no reply. *Guardian* (Sport), 19 July, p. 7. Also retrieved from www.guardian.co.uk/sport/2009/jul/19/france-alberto-contador-lance-armstrong on 23 September 2011.

Wilson, M. (2008) From processing efficiency to attentional control: A mechanistic account of the anxiety-performance relationship. *International Review of Sport and Exercise Psychology*, *1*, 184–201.

Wilson, M., Chattington, M., Marple-Horvat, D. E., and Smith, N. C. (2007a) A comparison of self-focus versus attentional explanations of choking. *Journal of Sport and Exercise Psychology*, *29*, 439–456.

Wilson, M., Smith, N. C., and Holmes, P. S. (2007b) The role of effort in influencing the effect of anxiety on performance: Testing the conflicting predictions of processing efficiency theory and the conscious processing hypothesis. *British Journal of Psychology*, *98*, 411–428.

Wilson, M., Wood, G., and Vine, S. J. (2009) Anxiety, attentional control and performance impairment in penalty kicks. *Journal of Sport and Exercise Psychology*, *31*, 761–775.

Wilson, P. M., and Rodgers, R. M. (2007) Human nature. In M. S. Hagger and N. L. Chatzisarantis (eds) *Intrinsic motivation and self-determination in exercise and sport* (pp. 101–112). Champaign, IL: Human Kinetics.

Wilson, V., Ainsworth, M., and Bird, E. (1985) Assessment of attentional abilities in male volleyball players. *International Journal of Sport Psychology*, *16*, 296–306.

Winter, G., and Martin, C. (1991) *Sport "psych" for tennis*. Adelaide: South Australian Sports Institute.

Winter, H. (2002) Coaches try to win mind games. *Daily Telegraph* (Sport), 8 November, p. S3.

Witol, A. D., and Webbe, F. M. (2003) Soccer heading frequency predicts neuropsychological deficits. *Archives of Clinical Neuropsychology*, *18*, 397–417.

Woll, S. (2002) *Everyday thinking: Memory, reasoning and judgment in the real world*. Hillsdale, NJ: Lawrence Erlbaum Associates.

Wollaston, S. (2010) TV review: The men who jump off buildings and Californication. *Guardian*, 29 July. Retrieved from www.guardian.co.uk/tv-and-radio/2010/jul/29/men-who-jump-off-buildings on 9 August 2010.

Wood, B. (2002) Morariu on mettle. *Daily Telegraph* (Sport), 28 August, p. S5.

Wood, G., and Wilson, M. R. (2010) A moving goalkeeper distracts penalty takers and impairs shooting accuracy. *Journal of Sports Sciences*, *28*, 937–946.

Woodman, T., and Davis, P. A. (2008) The role of repression in the incidence of ironic errors. *Sport Psychologist*, *22*, 183–196.

Woodman, T., and Hardy, L. (2003) The relative impact of cognitive anxiety and self-confidence upon sport performance: A meta-analysis. *Journal of Sports Sciences*, *21*, 443–457.

Woodman, T., Hardy, L., Barlow, M., and Le Scanff, C. (2010) Motives for participation in prolonged engagement in high-risk sports: An agentic emotion regulation perspective. *Psychology of Sport and Exercise*, *11*, 345–352.

Woods, Caroline, Hawkins, R., Hulse, M., and Hodson, A. (2002) The Football Association Medical Research Programme: An audit of injuries in professional football – analysis of preseason injuries. *British Journal of Sports Medicine*, *36*, 436–44.

Woods, Catherine B., Mutrie, N., and Scott, M. (2002) Physical activity intervention: A Transtheoretical Model-based intervention designed to help sedentary young adults become active. *Health Education Research*, *17*, 451–460.

Wraga, M., and Kosslyn, S. (2002) Imagery. In L. Nadel (ed.) *Encyclopaedia of cognitive science* (Vol. 2, pp. 466–470). London: Nature Group.

REFERENCES

Wulf, G. (2007) Attentional focus and motor learning: A review of 10 years of research. *Bewegung und Training, 1*, 4–14.

Yarrow, K., Brown, P., and Krakauer, J. W. (2009) Inside the brain of an elite athlete: The neural processes that support high achievement in sports. *Nature Reviews: Neuroscience, 10*, 585–596.

Yates, P. (2007) Ronnie O'Sullivan finds rhythm on the dot. *The Times*. Retrieved from www.timesonline.co.uk/tol/sport/more_sport/article3060192.ece 17 December 2007.

Yerkes, R. M., and Dodson, J. D. (1908) The relationship of strength of stimulus to rapidity of habit formation. *Journal of Comparative Neurology and Psychology, 18*, 459–482.

Young, B. W., and Salmela, J. H. (2002) Perceptions of training and deliberate practice of middle distance runners. *International Journal of Sport Psychology, 33*, 167–181.

Yue, G., and Cole, K. J. (1992) Strength increases from the motor program – comparison of training with maximal voluntary and imagined muscle contractions. *Journal of Neurophysiology, 67*, 1114–1123.

Yukelson, D. (1997) Principles of effective team building interventions in sport: A direct services approach at Penn State University. *Journal of Applied Sport Psychology, 9*, 73–96.

Yukelson, D., Weinberg, R., and Jackson, A. (1984) A multidimensional group cohesion instrument for intercollegiate basketball teams. *Journal of Sport Psychology, 6*, 103–117.

Zervas, Y., Stavrou, N. A., and Psychountaki, M. (2007) Development and validation of the Self-Talk Questionnaire (S-TQ) for Sports. *Journal of Applied Sport Psychology, 19*, 142–159.

Zinsser, N., Bunker, L., and Williams, J. M. (2010) Cognitive techniques for building confidence and enhancing performance. In J. M. Williams (ed.) *Applied sport psychology* (pp. 305–335). New York: McGraw-Hill.

Zorpette, G. (1999) Extreme sports, sensation seeking and the brain. *Scientific American* (Work, Home and Play section), *10*, 57–59.

Zuckerman, M. V. (1979) *Sensation seeking: Beyond optimal levels of arousal*. Hillsdale, NJ: Lawrence Erlbaum Associates.

Zuckerman, M. V. (1984) Experience and desire: A new format for sensation seeking scales. *Journal of Behavioural Assessment, 6*, 101–114.

Zuckerman, M. V. (1994) *Behavioural expressions and biosocial bases of sensation seeking*. Cambridge: Cambridge University Press.

Zuckerman, M. V. (2007) *Sensation seeking and risky behaviour*. Washington, DC: American Psychological Association.

Author index

Note: References to multi-author texts are listed as given in the text; however, references with four or more authors are listed only under the first name cited along with the year of publication. The method of alphabetization used is word-by-word. Names commencing with 'Mac' and 'Mc' are listed together.

Abernethy, B., and Russell, D. G., 210
Abernethy, B., Baker, J., and Côté, J., 218
Abernethy, B., et al. (2007), 139
Abernethy, B., Neal, R. J., and Koning, P., 224
Abma, C. L., et al. (2002), 192, 196
Adams, J., 297
Agassi, A., 316, 327
Aglioti, S. M., et al. (2008), 143
Aherne, C., Moran, A., and Lonsdale, C., 139
Ahronson, A., and Cameron, J. E., 253
Aidman, E. V., and Woollard, S., 298, 300
Ainsworth, B. E., 283, 284
Aitken, M., 5
Ajzen, I., 302, 303
Ajzen, I., and Fishbein, M., 302
Alderfer, C. P., 246
Allen, M. S., Jones, M. V., and
 Sheffield, D., 60
Allen, R., 251
American College of Sports Medicine, 283
Ames, C., 55
Andersen, J. L., Schjerling, P., and Saltin, B.,
 214
Anderson, A., 30
Anderson, A., and Lavallee, D., 303
Anshel, M., 92, 102, 123
Aronoff, S. R. and Spilka, B., 329

Aronson, E., Wilson, T. D., and Akert, R. M.,
 258
Arora, S., et al., 166
Arvinen-Barrow, M., et al. (2010), 321, 343
Ashcraft, M., 132
Associated Press, 148
Augé, W. K., and Augé, S. M., 24
Azar, B., 115, 291

Bakeman, R., and Helmreich, R., 260
Baker, J., and Horton, S., 203
Baker, J., Cobely, S., and Fraser-Thomas, J.,
 235
Baker, L. D., et al. (2010), 292
Baker, R. K., and White, K. M., 313
Bakker, F. C., Boschker, M. S. J., and Chung,
 T., 184, 185
Bandura, A., 10, 71, 259, 289, 291
Barker, J., et al. (2011), 23, 124, 181, 270
Barnes, S., 15
Baron, R. A., and Kalsher, M. J., 312
Bauman, A. E., 287
Bauman, J., 25
Baumeister, R. F., 112, 114, 115, 116, 147
Baumeister, R. F., and Showers, C. J., 112
BBC, 17
BBC Sport, 18, 316

Subject index